The WPA Guide to 1930s Iowa

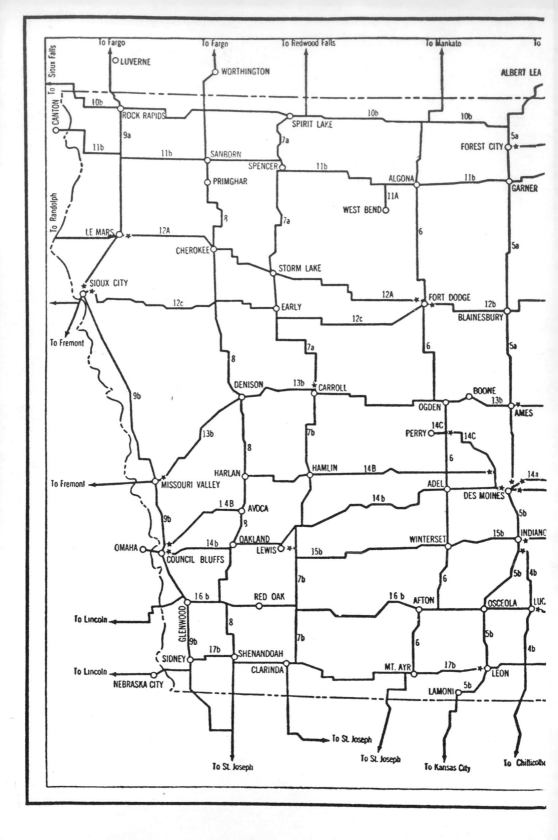

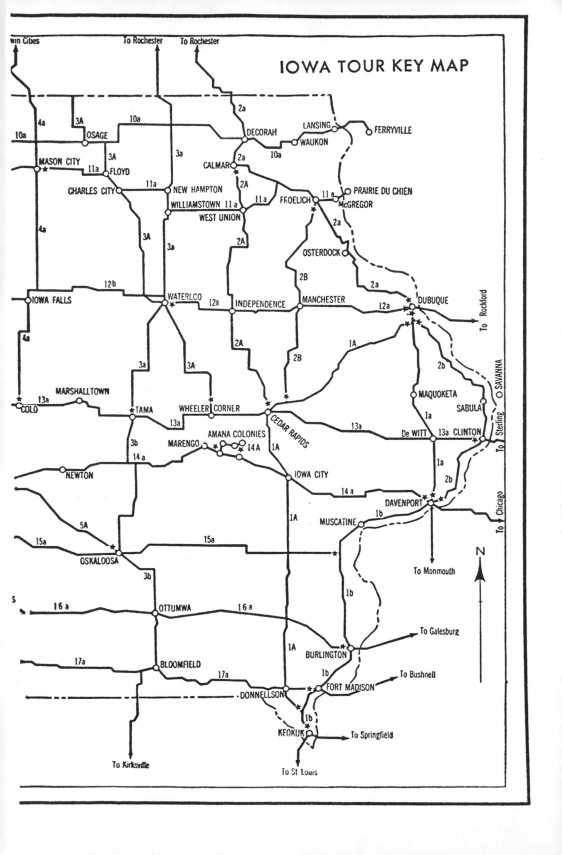

The WPA Guide to 1930s
IOWA

✴

*Compiled and Written by the Federal Writers' Project of the
Works Progress Administration for the State of Iowa*

INTRODUCTION BY JOSEPH FRAZIER WALL

THE IOWA STATE UNIVERSITY PRESS • AMES

1 9 8 6

First paperback edition, with an introduction, published in 1986
Originally published by Viking Press in 1938 under the title
Iowa: A Guide to the Hawkeye State

This reprint edition is from a copy provided
by the Parks Library, Iowa State University

Printed by the Iowa State University Press,
Ames, Iowa 50010

Library of Congress Cataloging-in-Publication Data

Iowa, a guide to the Hawkeye state.
  The WPA guide to 1930s Iowa.

    Reprint. Originally published: Iowa, a guide to the Hawkeye state. New York: Viking Press, 1938.
    Bibliography: p.
    Includes index.
    1. Iowa—Description and travel—1846–1950—Guide-books.   I. Federal Writers' Project.   II. Title.
F619.3.I68   1986   917.77′0432   85–23267
ISBN 0-8138-0997-5

Contents

Part I. Iowa: Past and Present

Part II. Cities and Towns

Part III. Tours

Part IV. Appendices

Introduction

by JOSEPH FRAZIER WALL

THE Federal Writers Project, established in the summer of 1935 under the auspices of the WPA, was like its companion federal projects in art and the theatre, an unprecedented venture by the federal government into the subsidization of the arts to provide emergency relief for professional artists, actors, dancers, musicians, and writers in the desperate days of the Great Depression. Like prohibition, these projects were hailed as a noble experiment, but unlike prohibition, these were noble experiments that actually succeeded beyond the hopes of their designers. Within the brief period of their existence, these projects brought a new strength, a maturity and full independence to American culture. Their products remain as tangible and lasting monuments to the best idealism of the New Deal.

As it was organized and developed, however, the Federal Writers Project was not at all what the beleaguered professional writers of America had envisioned or wanted. The writers had hoped that the national government would be a true patron in the Renaissance de Medici style, providing through individual grants the basic necessities of life so that creative writers could do their own work, could write those sonnets, novels, histories, and short stories that their personal muses dictated and yet at the same time know from where their next meal was coming. For too long in the 1930s the romantic fantasy of the starving genius in the garret had been a grim reality which now had no glamour at all.

But the hungry writers who applied for this patronage were quickly disabused of their false hopes. The newly appointed director of the Writers Project, Henry Alsberg, informed them that they were not to be communing with the Muses on Mount Helicon, but rather laboring on a designated project as determined by the bureaucrats in Washington. The project was to be an American Guide Series. The writers in each state were expected to produce a guide that would be a vast mirror in which each hamlet, town and city, each ethnic, religious and occupational group in America could see its own reflection. The purpose of this Guide Series, Harry L. Hopkins, the national administrator of the WPA, informed the public, was "to present to the American people a portrait of America—its history, folklore, scenery,

JOSEPH FRAZIER WALL is Professor of History, Grinnell College, and is author of *Iowa: A Bicentennial History* (1978) and *Andrew Carnegie* (1970).

cultural backgrounds, social and economic trends, and racial factors."[1] No small ambition here. And to the disgruntled creative writers, the project director, Alsberg, waxed even more lyrical. He conceded that the "tour form is a difficult form; it is like a sonnet; but, if you learn it, you can be more interesting in the description of a tour than in any novel. I have told that to our writers—that there is no reason why they cannot use their creative abilities even on those guidebooks."[2]

Many writers preferred not to learn. They would rather starve than compromise their talents. But hundreds of writers did grudgingly accept this assignment, partially consoled by the thought that they were limited by law to working only thirty hours a week on the project for which they would receive the then princely sum of $73 a month. This monthly wage would support them and still leave time for their own work. And to the surprise of many of these writers, they discovered that Alsberg had been right. The tour guides did provide an opportunity for creativity, and the research into local history and community folklore did furnish rich, hitherto untapped material for their own writing. Many a novel, short story, and biographical essay were to be by-products of what had initially seemed to be a most mundane assignment.

Iowa was one of the first states to take up the project. It was, after all, Harry Hopkins's native state, and it was expected to be one of the bellwethers in the production of state guides. Moreover, Iowa was looking forward to celebrating the centenary of its separate territorial status in 1938. There could be no more appropriate memorial for that centennial observance than the publication of *Iowa: A Guide to the Hawkeye State*. Speed was therefore an essential consideration.

Even so, the project got off to a rather rocky start. The national office had appointed as state director for the Iowa project an exceedingly able man, Jay DuVon. The only difficulty was that DuVon proved to be too able. Within a year, he was reassigned to be regional director for the Washington staff. Iowa was left without a director.

The man whom DuVon had chosen as editor of the project, Raymond Kresensky, was hastily promoted to the position of state director. It appeared to be a curious appointment. Kresensky, at the time of his initial appointment as editor, had been a Presbyterian minister in Algona, Iowa. But he was also a poet of some local recognition and was the president of the Iowa Poetry Day Association, which gave him a claim to being a writer. In later years, Katherine Kelloch, national field supervisor of the project and the person who had first proposed the American Guide Series, claimed that of all the various kinds of writers employed on the project—and they ranged from distinguished novelists to recent college graduates whose only experience was that of writing for their school paper—the best of the lot had been the poets, for they appreciated both the beauty of words and the necessity for economy in their usage. Kelloch might also have added that poets made good state directors, for although Kresensky was the only poet to serve in that capacity, he proved to be an able director. The combination of his poetic talent with his ministerial role was felicitous. Having contacts with Presbyterian ministers throughout the state as well as with local poets, Kresensky was able to utilize his two networks to find writers and researchers in many towns. These contacts proved invaluable, for unlike New York, Massachusetts, and Pennsylvania, professional writers and trained researchers in Iowa were in short supply.

Each state project, although working directly under the Washington central office, was expected to find its own state sponsor. Again, Kresensky chose wisely. Unlike many states where the sponsor was the state relief agency, the governor, or a special legislative committee, the Iowa director persuaded the legislature to make the State Historical Society of Iowa its sponsor, and thus as far as was possible, he divorced the project from state political pressure.

The major role of the sponsor was to enter into contractual relations with a commercial publisher for the publication of the state guide. The national office had very early decided that the state guides should be published not by the U.S. Government Printing Office but by a large trade publishing house which would have nationwide distribution and advertising facilities. But what role the sponsor would play in the supervision of the actual textual material was never made clear. State directors were informed that as soon as a particular section was completed in the state office, the copy was to go directly to the Washington staff for editing, and the editorial decision of the Washington office would be final. Any relationship between the state office and its state sponsor in regard to editorial content was left to the state director's discretion.

From the beginning, as the first copy was prepared, Kresensky made an effort to consult with the staff of the State Historical Society. Copy was sent to Superintendent of the Historical Society, Benjamin F. Shambaugh, and to his assistant, Ruth Gallaher, for comments on accuracy of the facts and for suggestions as to what should be added and what deleted. This procedure was carefully followed in respect to some of the general introductory essays on the history and the geography of the state. But as more and more material poured in to the state office from the tour researchers and as the pressure from Washington increased to expedite the material and get it into the central office, Kresensky found it difficult to maintain a working editorial association with the State Historical Society.

As a result, the relationship between the state director in Des Moines and the State Historical Society in Iowa City became at best tenuous, and at worst, strained. Shambaugh and Gallaher were never sure of their role in this production. They could not demand that copy come to them before it went to Washington, and even if they had been able to assert this kind of control, they were not sure they wanted to accept such an onerous task in addition to their regular duties. Yet they were also acutely conscious that as sponsor, the Society would be held accountable by the public for the accuracy of the data and for the interpretation made of that material by Kresensky's corps of anonymous writers. The Federal Writers Project WPA files in the archives of the State Historical Society contain many anxious letters from Shambaugh asking when the society would see the entire manuscript, and letters from Ruth Gallaher pointing out minor errors in those pages of text which had been sent to Iowa City, but also complaining that she simply did not have the time to give the material the careful check that it deserved.

Shambaugh as head of an organization that was dependent upon state legislative appropriations was particularly sensitive to public opinion and to delicate political nuances—concerns which Kresensky could safely ignore. Shambaugh worried about the book's being published by a New York (Viking) press. He knew he would have to face legislative grilling as to why he had not used an Iowa publisher, and Alsberg's assurance that all of the state guides were being published by eastern presses did little to quiet his fears.

Most of all, Shambaugh was concerned about what was being written on each town, each religious sect or racial group throughout the state. He kept pleading with Kresensky to see the entire manuscript before it went to Washington for final approval, but that was impossible under the procedures established by the Federal Writers Project. It was not until March 1938, after Washington had approved of the entire first section that Shambaugh saw the full text of the introductory essays. He sent off an agitated telegram to Alsberg:

> Do you want us to eliminate such obviously objectionable statements as Iowa "even has indications of culture," that Iowa farmers "distrust outsiders," that the Iowan is "commonly thought of as a great boaster," and that "his boasting is largely in self-defense, impelled by a sense of cultural inferiority," that "many of the people were not proud of being in the center of the hog belt," that "the farmer, conscious of his own deficiences, is willing to pay high taxes for the maintenance of educational insititutions"?[3]

The answer from Alsberg was no. The text would stay as written. Shambaugh would have to ride out the storm alone. It is hardly surprising that

Shambaugh in his prefactory letter which appeared on the opening page of the *Iowa Guide* tried to establish a *mea non culpa* for himself and his Society:

> The *Iowa Guide* is sponsored by the State Historical Society of Iowa in accordance with the provisions of an act which was placed upon the statute books of Iowa by the Forty-seventh General Assembly . . .
>
> While the Historical Society is pleased to carry out the will of the General Assembly, it cannot claim any of the credit that belongs to the project which has found fulfillment in the publication of this book.[4]

With this statement, Shambaugh was, of course, actually denying any claim to the discredit which he was sure would follow the publication of the guide.

Ruth Gallaher, who had read several of the introductory essays, was even more explicit in her letter to Kresensky in disavowing any personal responsibility for the text. "I hope," she wrote, "that no personal statement will appear in the final printed form which will suggest that I have approved the statements made in the various essays. I have not checked them sufficiently to be listed as approving them, and the changes I have suggested were merely those which occurred to me on a hasty reading." Kresensky gently reassured her that no mention would be made of her editorial role in producing the guide. He told her that it would be their private little secret.[5]

Iowa: A Guide to the Hawkeye State appeared in mid-August 1938 just in time for the Iowa State Fair, which had as its theme that year the Territorial Centennial, thus meeting the deadline they had all been aiming for. It was the fourth of the state guides to make its appearance, and the fears that Shambaugh and Gallaher had had of a negative response from the state were quickly allayed. Almost every major newspaper in the state gave it rave reviews not only on their book page but also in their editorials. Only the *Sioux City Tribune* sneered at it with the comment, "We hope that the physical efforts of the WPA will prove of more value to the state."[6] This showed a lack of appreciation for the chapter on Sioux City, which was one of the finest of the city essays, but then the Sioux City press never did like anything that bore the New Deal label.

Even the small towns liked the book, and the Iowa people seemed to relish the somewhat derogatory comments on Iowa culture which Shambaugh had found so distressing as to warrant deletion. Iowa's two major writers of the day were ecstatic in their praise. Ruth Suckow in her review in the *Des Moines Sunday Register* called it "a splendid piece of work," and Phil Stong hailed it as "one of the most engaging collections of anecdotes and one of the best descriptions of an American people in an American place that I have ever seen—or you either."[7]

The Iowa Guide scrupulously follows the format as laid down by the Washington office, which each of the states were expected to observe. Part One consists of the general essays on the state as a whole, covering such topics as: Natural Setting; Iowans: The Social Patterns; First Americans; History; Agriculture; Racial Elements; Transportation, Industry and Labor; Religion; Education; Literature and the Arts. These essays are of uneven quality. The section on Iowa History is quite adequate in its coverage, but uninspired in style. The best of these essays is that on Agriculture. We see in this section Iowa on the eve of a tremendous agricultural revolution which was to be accomplished in the following two decades. In 1938, oats still ranked along with corn as one of the two major cash grain crops, but there are hints of the revolution that is to come. There is a passing reference to the development of hybrid seed corn, which then made up only 13 percent of the Iowa corn crop. Soybeans get only a mention. They are seen as a valuable legume to restore the soil's fertility, but even so, they run a poor third to alfalfa and sweet clover. The full potential of soybeans as a cash crop second only to corn had not yet been realized. Most of the farmers were still using horses as a source of power in the fields, and the horse population in Iowa was nearly a third as large as the human population.

Omnipresent throughout this essay and many of the others, especially the chapters on Social Welfare and Industry and Labor, is the theme of the Great Depression. It is not railed against, but rather accepted as a continuing fact of life, like drought, disease, and death. Notice is given of the efforts of the New Deal to alleviate the economic crisis in the cities and on the farms, but the Guide can in no way be charged with being a propaganda tract for the Roosevelt administration. Kresensky and his corps of writers had used considerable discretion and care in sailing through rough political waters.

In her review for the *Des Moines Register,* Ruth Suckow found fault only with the essay on Literature, and she was quite right in her criticism. It is perhaps the weakest of the introductory essays—a rather curious failing for a Writers Project production. The essay is much too negative in tone, and dwells gloomily on the theme that all of the state's best writers made a point of leaving the state at a young age. It even assigns Suckow to exile, a banishment which she vigorously protested inasmuch as she had written all of her major novels while living in Iowa.

Part Two of the Guide deals in some detail with the seventeen cities in Iowa having the largest population. These essays also lack uniformity of quality. Sioux City, Dubuque, and Fort Dodge come off the best in both content and style, while the essay on Ames, exclusive of the section on Iowa State College, is not only the briefest but also the most pedestrian in style.

It is the third section on Tours, however, that is the true heart and soul of the book. Here the reader is taken on seventeen tours, following the major national and state highways as they crisscross the state from Larchwood in the far northwest corner to Keokuk where the Des Moines River joins the Mississippi in the southeast corner. Unlike the second section on Cities, where the selection was made solely upon the basis of population, here the emphasis is upon the anecdotal, upon communities of particular social and historic interest quite unrelated to demographic size or to economic significance. Some of the smaller towns such as LeMars (population 4,778) with its interesting colony of British nobility in the late nineteenth century, or Anita (population 1,256) with its annual Homecoming Day, get quite lengthy treatment, while other towns which had obviously not provided the writers with any material receive only a mention: "KLEMME, 41 m. (1,227 alt., 463 pop.) has a cooperative creamery; GOODELL, 47 m. (1,236 alt., 210 pop.) lies near the west bank of the Iowa River." And then there is the sad case of Whiting in Monona County. The reader is hurried along Highway 75 on Tour 9 B from Sloan to Onawa without even a passing nod at poor Whiting. This is unfortunate for the town is located in the center of Iowa's famous Western Loess Hills, which are unique in this country, and the town itself has an interesting history.

Often the reader is asked to pause in his travels for a general commentary on the Iowa scene, which has no particular relationship to the immediate locality in which he finds himself. There is, for instance, the lovely pastoral essay on Iowa farm architecture which we are given just outside Early, or the threshing scene which we come across on the road between Dallas Center and Panora and which compares well with a Grant Wood painting.

Some of the very best parts of the tours are where we turn off the main highway on to side paths. Here the road surface becomes dirt, or possibly mud, and the printed text in the Guide becomes very small. It is down one of these bypaths that we find the little community of Littleton, a village totally populated by a German pietistic sect whose inhabitants are known locally as the "Hook and Eye Dutch," because, along with automobiles, tractors, and electricity, they also forego the use of buttons and zippers on their clothes—only hooks and eyes are permitted. Here is a delightful bit of Americana that produces in words a Grandma Moses primitive painting. Or we turn off the Grand Army of the Republic Highway 6 at West Liberty to take State Road 1 to the village of Rochester, which all of the local inhabitants believe was the true birthplace of Sarah Bernhardt. And in the country graveyard at the edge of town, after some search through the weeds, we can find the grave of Mary King, the Divine Sarah's real mother, just as they say Bernhardt herself came back to visit the grave in the 1890s when she was on one of her many tours of the United States. One cannot find this historic landmark in Paris. Who dare say Iowa has not produced great artistic talent?

So with guidebook in hand, we travel the roads of Iowa, never knowing what surprise awaits us over the next hill or down the next side road on the left. It is an odyssey rich and varied where seldom either the anonymous Homers who compiled the saga or the readers of that saga ever nod.

Henry Alsberg said after the completion of the last state guidebook, that of Oklahoma in 1942, that it was a miracle, given the circumstances under which they were written, that a single guidebook ever got published. Yet all forty-eight states and four territories did produce books of surprisingly high quality, books that have kept their integrity and value over the years. Of course they are dated in some details. In Iowa some of the small towns, which the Guide in 1938 tells us are "nearly ghost towns," by 1985 are entirely gone. Even the ghosts have fled, leaving behind only a few stone foundations covered with weeds. But Clive, which in 1938 was only a country freight stop on a rail branch line, not worthy even of a mention, is now a rapidly growing suburb of Des Moines, and West Des Moines, which in 1937 had changed its name from Valley Junction, is now larger than several of the cities that merited in 1938 their own chapters.

The land, however, has remained, and so have the people with their folkways, values, and individual community histories. The Iowa Guide continues to meet the two critera which Katherine Kellock, the originator of the idea of an American Guide, sought to establish for all of the state guides: "The tours should be adjusted to the exigencies of the automobile, and the text should be interpretive rather than descriptive."[8] The American Guide Series, although often called the American version of the Baedekers, was meant to be quite different from those famous European guides which were designed for railroad travel and carefully avoided any interpretive editorial comment. These state guides sought to tell Americans where they were and who they were. The multivolumed series was, indeed, a vast Georges Seurat pointillist painting of the United States. If one stands close enough, the individual dots spring out in their own bright dabs of color, but if the viewer steps back, the entire canvas becomes a vast panorama with a unity of classic proportions.

The Iowa Guide, after nearly fifty years, still fulfills the grand design as envisioned by Hopkins, Alsberg, and Kellock. It deserves a new audience. *Wallace's Farmer and Iowa Homestead* in its review of the book in 1938 counselled, "When an Iowa family starts its next trip to the County Seat or the State Capitol or to Uncle Ebenezer's up in Jackson County, a copy of *Iowa: A Guide to the Hawkeye State* should go in the car alongside of the road map."[9] That is still good advice in 1985. To coin a phrase, "Don't leave home without it.".

NOTES

1. Hopkins quoted in Eleanor Touhey, "The American Baedekers," *Library Journal* 66(15 April 1941):339.

2. Testimony given by Henry Alsberg before the Sirovich Committee of the House of Representatives, February 1938, as quoted in William F. McDonald, *Federal Relief Administration and the Arts* (Columbus: Ohio State University Press, 1969), 694.

3. B. F. Shambaugh, telegram to Henry Alsberg, 7 March 1939, Federal Writers Project WPA files, State Historical Society of Iowa archives (hereafter referred to as FWP files, SHSI).

4. *Iowa: A Guide to the Hawkeye State* (New York: Viking Press, 1938).

5. Ruth Gallaher to Raymond Kresensky, 1 April 1937; Kresensky to Gallaher, 4 April 1937, FWP files, SHSI.

6. Quoted in the *Des Moines Sunday Register,* 18 September 1938.

7. Ibid.; Quoted in Touhey, "American Baedekers," 340.

8. Quoted in McDonald, *Federal Relief Administration and the Arts,* 668

9. Quoted in a pamphlet, *The Federal Writers Project of the Works Progress Administration of Iowa* (n.p., n.d.), FWP files, SHSI.

THE STATE HISTORICAL SOCIETY OF IOWA
IOWA CITY, IOWA
OFFICE OF THE SUPERINTENDENT
BENJ. F. SHAMBAUGH

This *Iowa Guide* is sponsored by The State Historical Society of Iowa in accordance with the provisions of an act which was placed upon the statute books of Iowa by the Forty-seventh General Assembly during its regular session in 1937.

While the Historical Society is pleased to carry out the will of the General Assembly, it can not claim any of the credit that belongs to the project which has found fulfillment in the publication of this book.

Indeed, whatever merit there is in these pages belongs to the many Iowans who took part in their compilation. Likewise, the credit for the selection of subject matter and the responsibility for the arrangement and editing of materials go to those persons who have faithfully directed the activities of the Federal Writers' Project for Iowa.

THE STATE HISTORICAL SOCIETY OF IOWA

BENJ. F. SHAMBAUGH

Superintendent

Iowa City, Iowa
July 1, 1938

WORKS PROGRESS ADMINISTRATION

HARRY L. HOPKINS, *Administrator*

ELLEN S. WOODWARD, *Assistant Administrator*

HENRY G. ALSBERG, *Director of the Federal Writers' Project*

◄◄◄◄◄◄◄◄◄◄◄◄◄◄◄◄◄◄◄◄◄◄☼►►►►►►►►►►►►►►►►►►►►►►►

Preface

IOWA: *A Guide to the Hawkeye State* may be considered the result of community effort rather than the achievement of any person or group of persons. This book, primarily a guide for sightseers from other States, will have another purpose, unsuspected when the work of making it began— to acquaint Iowans with Iowa. When the Federal Writers' Project got under way, with the purpose of presenting Iowa in a guide book, it became apparent that Iowa people generally had yet to know their own State, to define its history, to appraise their commonwealth's real values.

Iowans may appear indifferent to the natural beauty of their State and to its amazing power as a producer of foodstuffs, but when asked to help with the production of an Iowa guide book, they responded generously. Soon, from one border to the other, the book-in-the-making came to be regarded as a State enterprise, a job to be done with patriotic devotion. Those who were close to the task soon knew the thrill of working together for the good of their State, and from every county and city came evidence of the same feeling. Because of this book, Iowans have become better acquainted not only with Iowa, but with each other.

Out of the wealth of facts derived from manifold sources of information, the manuscript came finally to completion. Postmasters, librarians, ministers, teachers, historians, old settlers, newspaper men, and others supplied material; project workers and expert consultants in all branches of research contributed to the book's interest and factual exactitude.

The guide book workers are thankful for assistance from the State Historical Society of Iowa, the Iowa State Planning Board, the State Conservation Commission, State officers and members of their staff; the librarians in the State and city libraries in Des Moines and throughout the State. Others who have the gratitude of the Iowa Writers' Project are Adrian Dornbush, A. L. Case, Edgar R. Harlan, Prof. Ada Hayden, Prof. George Hendrickson, Harvey Ingham, Prof. George F. Kay, Prof. Charles Reuben Keyes, Edward A. Kimball, Charles F. Pye, Prof. Frank Luther Mott, Ira D. Nelson, Charles D. Reed, Miss Julia A. Robinson, Mrs. L. B. Schmidt, Prof. Ray Wakeley, and Jay du Von.

RAYMOND KRESENSKY, *State Director*

xxiii

List of Illustrations

List of Maps

Notations on the Use of Book

IOWA: *Past and Present* is designed to give a reasonably comprehensive survey of the State in its various aspects. Frequently persons, places, and events mentioned in the essays, are discussed at length in the city and tour descriptions. A classified bibliography is included.

Cities and *Tours:* Descriptions of seventeen cities have been removed from tours because of their length. At the end of each is a list of important nearby points of interest, with reference to the tours on which these places are described.

Maps are provided for ten of the cities. Points of interest are numbered in the descriptions, to correspond with numbers on the maps.

Conditions of admission to points of interest vary from time to time; those given in this book are for February 1938.

Most tours cover a highway bearing a single State or Federal number; they contain mile by mile descriptions of towns, points of interest, and the countryside on or near the route.

The inter-State routes are described from boundary to boundary of the State, but the tour headings bear in parentheses the names of the nearest out-of-State cities of importance, as an aid in identifying the routes.

Descriptions of minor routes branching from the main ones are printed in smaller type.

All main route descriptions are written from North to South and East to West, but can be followed quite easily in the reverse direction. The names of railroads paralleling highways are noted in the tour headings; the tour descriptions are useful to rail travelers as well as to motorists.

Mileages are cumulative, beginning at the northernmost or easternmost point on the main highways. Where long routes have been divided into sections, mileages have been started afresh at the beginning of each section. Mileages on side routes are counted from the junctions with the main routes. All mileages are necessarily relative; minor re-routings of highways, tire pressure, and individual driving habits, will produce variations between the listed mileages and those shown on speedometers.

Cities on the tour routes, but described in the Cities Section, are indicated by cross-references. Cities and towns at junctions of two tours are described on only one tour. The other tour gives a cross-reference to the one bearing the description.

Points of interest in cities, towns, and villages are indexed under the name of the particular point of interest, rather than under that of the community, because many persons know the name of a point of interest, but are uncertain as to the name of the community.

Great effort has been expended to make this book as accurate as possible, but it is realized that no volume covering such a wide range of material, some of it inadequately documented, can be free from mistakes. If those who find errors in fact will report them to the Federal Writers' Project in Washington, corrections will gladly be made in future editions.

General Information

(State map showing highways and points of interest, and transportation map showing railroad, air, bus, and water transport routes, in pocket inside back cover. For scenic map, published each year, write Iowa State Highway Commission, Ames, Iowa.)

Railroads: The 13 railroads are marked on the transportation map; they are given in connection with State Tours, and are listed in information section of cities.

Interstate Bus Lines: Burlington Transportation Co., Chicago, Milwaukee, St. Paul & Pacific R.R.; Interstate Transit Lines; Jefferson Transportation Co.; Black & White Transfer Co.; Missouri Transit Co.; Northland-Greyhound Lines, and Foster Bus Lines. Interurban bus lines are listed in information section of cities.

Air Lines: United Air Lines and American Airways. Private planes for hire at many of the 35 registered airports (1938) (*see cities concerned*). Ten airports and 13 landing fields equipped with lighting facilities for night flying. Aeronautics Division of the U. S. Dept. of Commerce maintains three lighted air routes across Iowa with radio station at Iowa City.

Highways: Iowa has a total of 102,533 miles of highways, of which 5,455 miles are paved, and 2,839 are graveled. Seven of the east-west roads and four of the north-south highways are surfaced throughout. U. S. highways 6, 30, 34, 52, 61, 161, 218, and 275 and State highway 7 west of Des Moines are entirely paved. All State laws concerning highway traffic, motor vehicles, and drivers are enforced by State Highway Safety Patrol of 103 men and by other peace officers.

Traffic Regulations: Speed limits for motor vehicles in Iowa are fixed by State law—20 miles per hour in business and school districts, 25 miles per hour in residence districts, and "prudent" speed in suburban and country districts. Motor vehicles drawing other vehicles are limited to 35 miles per hour. Local authorities and the State Highway Commission are authorized to make minor variations in the speed limits, but these are indicated by signs. Metal tires must not be used on motor vehicles or trailers. Lights must be dimmed when a car approaching is within 500 feet. Reckless driving and passing vehicles on hills and curves are prohibited, and may be punished by fine or imprisonment. Driving a car while intoxicated is punishable, on the first conviction, by fine of from $300 to $1,000; or by imprisonment in the county jail not to exceed one year; or by both fine and imprisonment. Any accident resulting in the death or injury of any person, or property damage estimated at $25 or more, must be reported to nearest peace officer or to sheriff or county attorney of county, or, in cities of the first class, to chief of police. Any driver involved in an accident must stop, give aid required by the circumstances, and give his name and address and the registration number of his car to the other party or, if that is impossible, to a responsible bystander. Failure to comply with these requirements may be punished by a fine of not more than $100 or imprisonment for not more than 30 days in case of property damage; and by a fine of from $100 to $5,000, or by imprisonment for from 30 days to one year, or by both fine and imprisonment if a person is killed or injured. The owner of a car is responsible for damages caused by his car if he is driving it or if it is driven by another person with his consent and permission. A non-resident may be served with notice of a damage suit by the serving of notice on the commissioner of the motor vehicle department of this State.

Parking: Parking time in cities and towns and in parks is prescribed by local authorities. Parking on the highways, especially on paved and hard-surfaced roads, is prohibited by State law. Parks usually charge from $1.00 to $3.00 per month for parking space, light, and water. Parking of cars or trailers in State parks is limited by law to two weeks and may be more restricted by the custodians.

Licenses for Cars: All cars owned in Iowa must be licensed and car license from one car may not be used on any other. License plates must be displayed on front and back of car and kept clean. The first part of Iowa license number—numbers from 1 to 99—designates county where license is issued (by county treasurer); counties are numbered in the order of alphabetical list of their names. Remaining digits are the registration number. Cars properly licensed in other States may be operated in Iowa for varying periods, depending on period of free operation granted Iowa cars in that State. All non-Iowa cars operated in State for as long as ten days must be registered with county treasurer, who will grant permit. Special permits may be issued to students.

Licenses for Drivers: Iowa resident must have driver's license to operate car. Provision is made for preliminary license for those learning. Drivers' licenses are issued by State Motor Vehicle Department, State House, Des Moines (fee 50 cts.) to persons 16 years of age or over found capable of driving a car. Examinations are given in county seat towns. For information as to dates, consult sheriff's office. Children between 14 and 16 may be given licenses to drive to and from school. A non-resident over 16 years of age with license from State of his residence may drive car properly licensed there (not an Iowa licensed car) for a period of 90 days or less. Persons over 18 years of age from States or countries which do not require drivers' licenses may drive cars in Iowa for the same period and on the same conditions. Drivers' licenses must be carried on the person, and the registration certificate designating ownership of car must be kept in view, either on the steering arm or dashboard, at all times. A non-resident driving in Iowa for longer than 90 days should procure Iowa driver's licence. Car owner is forbidden to permit another person to operate his car unless that person is legally authorized to drive in Iowa. A non-resident chauffeur, with license from place of residence, may drive or chauffeur car in Iowa, but must secure an Iowa license if he accepts employment from resident. Chauffeurs must be eighteen years of age or over. Persons operating vehicles in service of United States Army, Navy, or Marine Corps, and those operating certain types of farm or road machinery, do not require licenses.

Trailers: Trailer coaches must be equipped with adequate brakes which may be applied by driver of towing car. After January 1, 1939, trailers must be equipped also with automatic brakes. Maximum dimensions of trailers are: 8 feet in width, 12 feet in height, and 33 feet in length. Length of car and trailer must not exceed 45 feet and drawbar or connection must not exceed 15 feet. Trailer homes are subject to the same sanitation regulations as permanent homes.

Accommodations: Hotels are available in most towns and in all cities. Rates usually vary from $1.00 to $3.50 per day. Cabin tourist camps are frequent, with rates from 75¢ to $1.50 per day. Many of these have bathing and cooking facilities, with grocery stores and gas stations nearby. Gas stations are maintained at convenient places; barbecue stands and restaurants are available at many points. Fruit, vegetables, and milk may be purchased at farm homes or from stands along the roadside.

Liquor Regulations: Beer is sold at specially licensed establishments but intoxicating liquors such as wine, spirits, and alcohol are sold only in State liquor stores. Permit costing $1.00 is required for individual purchaser; special permit costing $3.00 for professional, laboratory, or scientific use.

Permits are obtainable at liquor stores. They may be revoked for drunkenness, desertion of dependents, or commission of felonies and misdemeanors in which alcoholic liquor was contributing factor. The sale or giving of liquors to minors except by parents or guardians or for medicinal purposes is prohibited. Liquor stores are closed on Sundays, election days, and legal holidays. Liquor may not be consumed in the State liquor stores, in other public places, or on streets or highways.

Fish and Game Regulations: Game fish—all bass, trout, pike, pickerel, perch, catfish, bluegills, sunfish, sturgeon, and so on. Non-resident fishing license, $1 for 6 days or $3 for year. Hunting license, $15 (for migratory waterfowl, $1 Federal stamp in addition); trapping license, $25. Complete regulations from State Conservation Commission, 10th and Mulberry Sts., Des Moines. Licenses are issued by county recorders, who will furnish necessary information. *Open Fishing Season (1938):* Trout between 5 a.m. April 1, and 9 p.m. Sept. 1. Inland waters where open— northern, sand, sauger, and wall-eyed pike, sheepshead, yellow perch, striped, yellow, and silver bass, minnows, May 15–Nov. 30; large- and small-mouth bass and warmouth bass, crappies, rock bass, sunfish, bluegills, June 15–Nov. 30; rock and sand sturgeon, paddlefish, Aug. 1–Nov. 30; rough fish continuous. Mississippi and Missouri Rivers—crappie, perch, yellow and silver bass, sunfish, bluegills, rock and warmouth bass, wall-eyed pike, minnows, May 15–Nov. 30; large- and small-mouthed bass, June 15–Nov. 30; rock and sand sturgeons, paddlefish, Aug. 1– Nov. 30; rough fish continuous. All streams not always open for fishing. Information from State Conservation Commission, Des Moines. Streams and lakes restocked from State fish hatcheries and nurseries. Artificial lakes closed to all fishing and minnow removal (1938): Upper Pine Lake, Lake Macbride, Lake Ahquabi, Springbrook Lake, Beed's Lake, Lake Keomah, Echo Valley Lake, Lake of Three Fires, Farmington Lake, Afton Reservoir, Greenfield City Reservoir, Lake Keosauqua, Swan Lake, and Red Haw Lake. *Catch and Size Limits:* Not more than 25 game fish daily including bullheads, redhorse, dace, chubs, shiners, or suckers, of which not more than 15 in the aggregate may be black bass, silver bass, rock bass, sand pike, wall-eyed pike, great northern pike, pickerel, salmon, crappie, catfish, perch, sunfish, bluegills; and not more than five of the 15 may be black bass, rock bass, silver bass, trout, sand pike, wall-eyed pike, or great northern pike. No more than the legal catch of two days may be in possession. No pike or pickerel less than 13 in.; no catfish less than 12 in.; no black bass less than 10 in.; no rock or silver bass, trout, crappie, or perch less than 7 in.; no sunfish less than 5 in. *Prohibited:* No use of drugs, lime, explosives, or electricity to kill or affect fish. No trolling from any gasoline, oil, or electric launch, or steamboat. No erecting or using shelter or artificial heat while fishing through the ice. No throwlines or trotlines in any stocked lake, or within 300 ft. of any dam or spillway, or within posted areas. No shipping beyond boundaries of State of frogs taken from State waters. Specific restrictions concerning use of spears, minnow seines, and tackle, and buying and selling fish. *Open Game Season:* Small game such as quail, pheasant, raccoon, fox, rabbit, and squirrel available in certain open areas each year, but open areas vary. Limited open season frequently declared on migratory and upland birds. Notice of season published in newspapers of district, 2 wks. prior to opening of season. In counties where there is an open season (1938) dates on quail are Nov. 1–Dec. 1, except in Lee Co., Nov. 15–Dec. 15; on pheasants and partridges, Nov. 12-14; on coots, jacksnipes, duck, geese, and squirrel, Sept. 15–Nov. 30; on rabbits, Aug. 1–Mar. 1; on deer, no open season. *Bag Limits:* Daily—squirrels, not more than 10; rabbits, not more than 10; pheasants, not more than 3, only one of which may be a hen; quail, not more than 8; ducks, not more than 10; geese and brant, not more than 4 in the aggregate; coots, not more than 15; Wilson's snipe or jacksnipe, not more than 15. Usually possession limit is daily bag limit; but allowed squirrel bag is 12, rabbit 20. *Prohibited:* No trapping, snaring, or netting game birds except under direction of State Conservation Commission; no use of poison or medicated food or any other substance in taking or killing game birds and animals. No more than 15 game birds or animals can be taken from State. *General Regulations:* Non-game birds are protected, and scientific collections can be made only with permission of conservation commission. The "take" must go to place of residence indicated on license, or must be carried so it can be inspected readily. License must be shown on request. General regulations govern hunting on game refuges, carrying guns on highways, and type of gun which may be used for shooting. *Evidences of Violations:* Evidences of violation are not to have license on person or to refuse to show it on request; to have in one's possession (1) any fish, game, furs, birds, birds' nests, eggs, or plumage, or animals unlawfully caught or killed; (2) fish or game when, or in place where, unlawful to kill (except in first 10 days of closed season following open season); and (3) implements, devices, equipment, and so on, for taking fish and game where possession and use are prohibited.

Operating Boats on Iowa's Lakes and Streams: Secure rules and regulations from State Conservation Commission, 10th and Mulberry Sts., Des Moines. General regulations: (1) Between ½ hr. after sunset and the hour of sunrise, motorboats cannot exceed 15 m.p.h.; (2) boats 20 ft. or under must carry lantern aft showing a white light at all times between sunset and sunrise; (3) boats larger than 20 ft. must show green light on starboard side (R) and redlight on port side (L) each light visible for ½ m.; (4) exhausts must be muffled; (5) boats operated for hire must be licensed and inspected. Fire extinguishers, and air tanks with sufficient capacity to sustain boat afloat when full of water and carrying crew and passengers are required.

Climate: Late spring and early fall are attractive seasons to tour Iowa. Topcoats necessary throughout cool weather of May and, sometimes, June. Fall days usually warm, nights cool. Indian summer pleasant time to tour; usually comes during last weeks of October. Hot days and nights mark months of July, August, and September. Winters not pleasant for traveling. Temperatures frequently below zero in northern half of State, zero weather general. Heavy snowfall temporarily blocks roads, but main highways kept open all winter. When roads glazed with ice, travel extremely hazardous; radio bulletins warn motorists.

General: Hundreds of miles of nature trails in State parks, woodland paths, and country roads for hiking. Along roads hiker must go L. against traffic. Poisonous snakes not common, though there are timber and prairie rattlers in southern and northeastern Iowa. Timber (banded or diamond) rattler encountered in rocky places or timber, and prairie rattler frequents marsh and slough lowlands. Extension of cultivated area has greatly reduced number of these snakes. Poison-ivy in parts of State parks, woodland areas, pasture lands, tourist camps, and roadsides. Poison-sumac found in lower swamplike areas. Jiggers and woodticks mainly in southern Iowa. Water in Iowa creeks and streams not usually safe for drinking. Tourist camps or farm wells provide safe water. Streams have little dangerous quicksand, but depths often deceiving. Wade or swim at public beaches. Most farmers have telephones which can be used when car troubles occur in open country.

Calendar of Events

(nfd means no fixed date; locations subject to change have been left blank.)

Mar. 5	Fort Des Moines	Regimental Day, Army Post
nfd	Des Moines	Boys' High School Basketball Tournament, Drake University Stadium
nfd	Des Moines	Girls' High School Basketball Tournament, Drake University Stadium
nfd	Iowa City	Play Festival (amateur players' competition)
Apr. 3d week	State-wide	Iowa History Week
nfd	Des Moines	Drake Relays, Drake University Stadium (national contest)
nfd	Des Moines	State Spelling Bee
May 1st Sun. suitable	Altoona	Blossom Time, Cyrus Harvey Fruit Farm
2nd week	Pella	Tulip Festival (Dutch celebration)
nfd		Annual Meeting, Iowa Ornithologists' Association
nfd	Iowa City	Governor's Day, State University (Governor reviews student regiments)
nfd	Mount Vernon	Music Festival, Cornell College
nfd	Ames	Veishea, Iowa State College (celebration with shows, dances, etc.)
nfd	Iowa City	Festival of High School Music Association
June 2d week	Dallas Center	Love Feast of Old Order of River Brethren
nfd	Ames	Girls' 4-H Club Annual Convention, Iowa State College
nfd	Grinnell	Institute of International Relations, Grinnell College
nfd	Fort Dodge	Band Day, biennial odd year (bands from all over State)
nfd		State Farm Bureau Picnic

July	first week		Men's State Golf Tournament
	last week		Women's State Golf Tournament
	beginning	Cedar Falls	Conference on Religion and Life
	last Sun.		(eight-day Bible conference)
Aug.	2d week	Burlington	Tri-State Fair
	3d week	Sidney	Championship Rodeo
	beginning	Des Moines	State Fair
	last week		
	nfd	Tama	Sac and Fox Indian Powwow (Indian dances in connection with fair)
	nfd	Davenport	Mississippi Valley Fair and Exposition
	middle		
Aug.	nfd	Britt	Hobo Day (national hobo convention)
	nfd	McGregor	American School of Wildlife (national nature-study camp)
Sept.	2d week	Fort Dodge	Beef Cattle Show
	nfd	Marshalltown	Central Iowa Fair
	nfd	Spencer	Clay County Fair (largest county fair)
	nfd	Ackley	Sauer Kraut Day (German celebration)
	nfd	Bluff Creek T., Monroe Co.	Reunion on Site of Buxton (Negro celebration)
	nfd	Harlan	Annual Picnic of Farm Holiday Assn.
Oct.	first week	Waterloo	Dairy Cattle Congress, Belgian Horse Show, and American Poultry Congress, Exposition Grounds
	nfd		Iowa Librarians' Association Meeting
Nov.	12-14	Ames	Little Midwest Horticultural Exposition, Iowa State College (competition open to Midwestern States)
Nov.	Sun. before Thanksgiving	State-wide	Harvest Sunday
	nfd	Des Moines	Iowa State Teachers' Convention
	nfd	Iowa City	University Homecoming
Dec.	Christmas Season	Ames	Handel's *Messiah*, Iowa State College Music Organizations
	nfd	Ames	Boys' 4-H Annual Convention, Iowa State College

PART I
Iowa: Past and Present

Natural Setting

A NORTH Central State wholly within the prairie region, Iowa stretches approximately 310 miles from the Mississippi River on the east to the Missouri and Big Sioux Rivers on the west; and from Minnesota on the north, the prairies extend approximately 200 miles southward to the Missouri Line. The total area of 56,147 miles (of which only 561 square miles are water surface) is one-fifth larger than that of New York and just one-fifth as large as that of Texas. Across the Mississippi River are the States of Illinois and Wisconsin, and on the west are Nebraska and South Dakota. The prolongation of the southern and eastern boundaries, to include the entire channel of the Des Moines River, gives Iowa a shape somewhat similar to that of the United States.

From Keokuk at the mouth of the Des Moines River, the southernmost point in the State, where the elevation is the lowest (477 feet above sea level), the land rises in gentle swells northward and westward until the highest point is reached (1,670 feet) near Sibley in Osceola County at the northern border. The rivers, following this natural drainage, flow eastward into the Mississippi and westward into the Missouri from a broad waterparting that runs almost directly north and south. The Upper Iowa, Turkey, Maquoketa, Wapsipinicon, Cedar, Iowa, Skunk, and Des Moines Rivers, which drain the eastern two-thirds of the State, flow slowly over long winding courses. The longest, the Des Moines, with its source in the far northwest, rises and lowers with the rains—in midsummer a shallow muddy stream, in spring a swift river over-flowing its banks and bringing southward a burden of broken branches, driftwood, and rich earth. In the north its valley is low and broad but, as the river moves on, high wooded hills and bluffs rise on both sides. The northern rivers in this eastern system cut through rock courses. Both the Iowa and Cedar River Valleys are hill and bluff sections, sometimes marked by limestone cliffs. In the western system the shorter courses of the Big Sioux, Floyd, Little Sioux, Boyer, and Nishnabotna Rivers tend to make the current rapid. The rivers here flow between steep grassy banks.

The greater part of the Iowa country is level land, a region of subtly

MISSISSIPPI RIVER, NEAR BURLINGTON

varying contours, where yellow light spreads over the great expanses and plays through the luxurious vegetation. Fields of corn and other grains are planted in even squares and rectangles, with straight roads following the section lines and defining more squares. Groves of trees shelter the farm buildings. Large herds of stock feed in the knolly pasture lands. Sudden breaks in this level country are the low river valleys, from one to ten miles wide and covered by natural woodlands that rise to irregular lines of hills or bluffs at the valley's edge.

The most marked differences are found only in the northeast and southwest. In the northeastern section cliffs rise abruptly from the banks of the Mississippi River sometimes to a height of 300 to 400 feet, with tree-covered hills extending westward. Here the tributaries of the Mississippi wind through rocky ravines and wooded valleys. In the west, south of the mouth of the Big Sioux River, a line of mound-like bluffs sweeps up from the flood plain of the Missouri to heights ranging from 100 to 300 feet.

Lakes of varying size are scattered throughout the northwestern area, extending about 50 miles from the Minnesota Line. Lake Okoboji, Spirit

Lake, and the many smaller lakes in Dickinson County constitute the principal region. Storm Lake, lying to the south of this region, and Clear Lake, to the east, are other important lakes. Some of the Iowa lakes, called "wall lakes," have rock-walled beaches, where the ice has forced the glacial rocks from the lake's bottom to the shore.

Wet springs, warm summers, long growing seasons, and favorable winds make the State admirably suited to agriculture. Temperatures range from 25° below zero in winter to 100° in the summer. The lowest temperature ever observed was 47° below zero, on January 12, 1912, at Washta in Cherokee County. The average for winter, however, is 21.6°. The highest temperature on record for summer is 118°, registered in the suburbs of Keokuk, July 20, 1934. Unusual extremes sometimes occur during a single season and the temperature may vary 50 degrees in a day. A wintry morning will be followed by a warm afternoon, or two days will be like spring and the next two like winter. An exceptional variation occurred in 1930 in Webster City; the temperature rose from 34° below zero on February 15 to 72° on February 24, a difference of 106 degrees in nine days.

Hailstorms sometimes occur during the hot summer months, but data for the 13 years preceding 1935 show that only 1.12 percent of the crops were hail-damaged. The greatest damage was suffered in the northwest and the least in the south-central counties. Crop-destroying droughts seldom cover the entire State, although twice since 1930 crops in the western and southern part have been so damaged that much of the corn was unfit even for fodder. In 1934 the southern and western sections felt the drought most severely, but in 1936 it was more widespread, with the southern counties again the most severe sufferers. According to Charles D. Reed, director of the weather division of the State Department of Agriculture, "It is not the drought but heat that causes most of the damage to crops in Iowa."

During the winters the snowfall is frequently heavy enough to store moisture in the ground for spring planting and growing. The average annual snowfall over a 50-year period at Des Moines was 31.8 inches. The greatest snowfall in a day was in December 1888, at which time 17 inches of snow fell. In the days before the State was thickly settled, blizzards roared unhindered across open country, but protecting groves of trees around the many farmhouses, and the presence of towns and cities, render such storms less devastating.

Most of the rain, coming on the south winds, falls in the growing season when the chief crops, corn and other grains, need it most. The average of 85 rainy days a year gives an average annual rainfall of about 26 inches in the extreme northwest and about 36 inches in the southeast. Annual precipitation—averaged for 63 years—is 31.62 inches. The rainfall is an important factor in the consistent fertility of the State. The long growing season ranges from 140 days in the northwest to 170 days in the southeast, or from the last killing frost in the spring (April 20 to May 3) to the first killing frost in the fall (September 25 to October 15). Sunshine is present on an average of 215 days in the year.

Resources and Their Conservation

In 1933 the *Report on the Iowa Twenty-Five Year Conservation Plan* was published for the Iowa Board of Conservation and the Iowa Fish and Game Commission. Although this report was in the nature of a research study outlining the State's recreational facilities in State parks, and its fish, game, and waterfowl refuges, it became the beginning of the State's program for the conservation of its land resources in general. Today the State Planning Board, appointed in part by the Governor, supervises such fact-finding projects dealing with land use and land waste as the making of soil surveys, studies of forests and streams in their relation to land waste, and investigations of methods of preserving soil fertility.

Very little land in the State is unsuitable for agriculture. The National Resources Board (1935) reported that 25 percent of all the grade-one land in the United States is in Iowa, and that this rich soil is the State's most important natural resource. The entire north-central section is part of the Wisconsin drift area, with some of the richest soils in the world. However, this great natural fertility is in danger of being depleted, by erosion in some sections and by intensive farming throughout the State.

The dark and heavy soil is not likely to blow away in "dust storms" in drought years, but erosion is a serious problem. Along the hillsides the soil is being gullied constantly, but this type of erosion does not cause so much land waste as does that known as "sheet erosion." The latter, although not so apparent as gully erosion, proceeds rapidly. In extreme cases as much as 50 tons of soil to an acre have been carried away in one rain. To regulate the flow of water and to check the washing away of land, the State is planting trees, building artificial lakes, and damming streams. Farmers, to guard against excessive losses, have developed plans of plowing, the furrows being laid transverse on the slopes.

From the earliest times in Iowa, farmers practiced rotation of crops, mainly wheat, oats, and barley against corn. Application of the Agricultural Adjustment Act made a more varied plan profitable. Pasture crops and such legumes as alfalfa and soybeans alternated with the regular crops and some of the land was left idle to "rest." Much of this is in the nature of experimentation, but it is checking the loss of the soil's fertility.

Extensive field experiments made during the past ten or 15 years show that approximately 75 percent of the soils are acid—in need of phosphate. However, they are benefited by applications of crushed limestone. Aside from this the soils are so well supplied with organic matter, nitrogen, and potassium, that it is comparatively easy to maintain their productivity.

An abundant surface-water supply is insured by the two large boundary rivers, and the many interior streams, lakes, and marshes. Rivers and watercourses carry off the wastes of industries and communities, and drain the farmyards. Lakes and numerous marshes, valuable for recreation and as havens for wildlife, are also a means for regulating stream flow.

The potential water power of the Iowa rivers is relatively slight. Power is generated by 64 hydroelectric plants including the one at Keokuk, among the greatest in the world, which generates power for this and surrounding States. The dam, nearly a mile long, holds back the waters of the Mississippi River, and 200,000 horse power is generated in the plant.

The urban centers of the northern part of the State depend mainly on the underground water supply. The public water supply of 500 municipalities comes from subsurface waters; few areas of equal size have so many communities thus dependent. Some of these lower water veins, tapped by larger communities, furnish as much as 4,000,000 gallons a day. However, in the southern part where the water-bearing strata are very deep, communities often find it more practical to use the surface waters.

The underground waters flow through the sandstones that lie fairly near the surface in northeast Iowa—at depths of 1,000 to 3,000 feet. In Wisconsin and Minnesota these strata come near enough to the surface to absorb the direct rainfall and percolation, but it is said that the movement of this absorbed water is so slow that it reaches the surface in Iowa wells many years after it has fallen as rain.

Shallow wells, developed in areas where there are glacial deposits of gravel, sand, or clay, are limited in yield. The glacial drift and the wind-deposited loess retain part of the rainfall and snowfall, carrying it underground to the lakes and streams. Tapping these top strata, drift wells (usually less than 100 feet deep) furnish the individual domestic supply as well as that of some of the smaller municipalities. Although the supply of water borne by these strata is usually limited, an exception occurs in the gravel deposit adjacent to and underlying the Raccoon River, which furnishes as much as 20,000,000 gallons a day—enough for the entire city of Des Moines.

As with the land, the State is faced with a problem of water conservation. Freeflowing wells once were left uncapped when not in use; marshes were drained, to the detriment of the surrounding country; communities too close together tapped the same water-bearing strata. Frequently industrial and community wastes pollute the streams.

Before setting up a definite program for the conservation of its valuable water supply the State is collecting accurate basic data; surveying the extent of river pollution, the availability of better public water supplies, and the possibilities of flood control and reforestation.

No metallic minerals are mined in Iowa, but sand, gravel, and limestone in the underlying and surface strata constitute an important resource. Almost all of the counties have clay deposits. Some types, suitable for the manufacture of common grades of clay products, are easily accessible; others, valuable in the composition of high-grade products, are more difficult to reach.

Limestones and shales necessary for making Portland cement are found, but this industry did not develop as quickly as the clay industry because the combination of the particular kinds of rock necessary, each conforming closely to a standard composition, is not readily available. The materials are near enough, however, for advantageous use and are utilized commercially at Davenport, Mason City, Des Moines, West Des Moines, and Gilmore City. The Mason City plants have both the required limestone and shale nearby.

Limestone, from a relatively small area in east-central Iowa, is used for building purposes, while limestones suitable for road surfacing, lime, and fertilizer are found in quantity throughout the entire eastern portion. The deposits of sand and gravel in the northern half of the State are largely used for road building. In 1935 there were 49 plants producing sand and gravel for road construction and building purposes.

An important deposit of gypsum at Fort Dodge makes possible a State production ranking second in the United States in quantity and value. In 1936 there were 344,221 tons mined. The deposits at Fort Dodge, in an area of more than 30 square miles, are made available largely through stripping and sluicing operations.

Beds of coal underlie approximately 20,000 square miles in 20 counties. One broad belt extends on both sides of the Des Moines River from Webster County to the Missouri State Line. It has been estimated that, according to present needs and rate of consumption, there is enough coal to

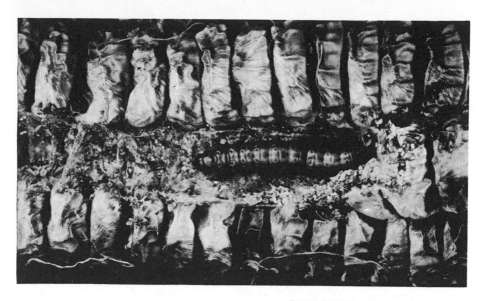

CORN BORER AT WORK

supply the State for more than 4,000 years. The bituminous coals lie comparatively close to the surface with the deepest shaft at only 387 feet. The deposits in most places are only 18 to 30 inches thick, and are easily mined as they stretch evenly between the series of bedrock. In most of southern Iowa the beds, though seldom deep, are usually continuous enough to make commercial development profitable. In 1935 the mines yielded 3,650,000 tons of coal.

Fauna

The open farming country with its grassy nesting grounds, the rush-grown sloughs, the low brush-land, the lake regions, and the wooded bluffs and hills along Iowa's streams are havens for birds of many species. Ornithologists have pointed out that this territory along the Mississippi and Missouri Rivers forms a natural channel (flyway) for the passage of migratory birds. Two feathered travelers that make the longest annual journey along this route are the bobolink and the purple martin. Both make trips of approximately 5,000 miles from the northern United States to South America, crossing by way of the Canal Zone and Central America. In the autumn, wood warblers pass through by the hundreds. The birds going north to nest or south to escape the cold weather often stop in the parks and refuges in passing.

In the counties along the Missouri River the species of birds differ somewhat from those to the east. Here, more characteristically western species, such as the lark-bunting, Lewis woodpecker, and red-shafted flicker, are found. Also, in northern Iowa around Clear Lake and Mud Lake, yellow-headed blackbirds are seen in large numbers, though they are seldom found elsewhere in the State.

Although there are hundreds of species and sub-species of birds in Iowa, the commonest are limited to relatively few species. The brown creeper, tree-sparrow, slate-colored junco, and northwestern shrike, here in the winter, migrate north in the spring to nest. The cardinal (red bird), blue jay, eastern goldfinch, crow, white-breasted nut-hatch, black-capped chickadee, English-sparrow, downy woodpecker, tufted titmouse, and starling remain throughout the year. The eastern goldfinch which, in the summer, is often seen feeding on the seeds of dandelions and thistle, was designated the State bird in 1933.

The meadow larks (eastern and western), bobolink, and red-winged blackbird, birds of the open meadows, and the bronzed grackle, fox sparrow, song sparrow, bluebird, robin, mourning dove, and rusty blackbird arrive early in the spring. Perhaps the loveliest singers among the spring birds are the white-throated sparrow and the prairie horned lark.

Migrating here in the late spring and summer are scarlet tanager, indigo bunting, red-headed woodpecker, wood peewee, crested fly-catcher, ruby-throated humming bird, northern yellow throat and yellow warbler, dick-cissel (considered the characteristic Iowa bird), rose-breasted grosbeak, Baltimore and orchard orioles, kingbird, kingfisher, cuckoos (rain crow), cowbird, brown thrasher, woodthrush, hermit thrush, olive and gray-cheeked thrushes, catbird, purple martin, migrant (loggerhead) shrike, whippoorwill, and several species of swallows. The night hawk, in appearance similar to the whippoorwill, and one of the summer birds, is well known to city dwellers.

Among the birds of prey, the bald eagle migrates along the longer rivers and the turkey vulture nests only in the southern half of the State. There are at least ten kinds of hawks, two of which are Cooper's and the sharp-shinned, both migrants in the fall and spring, although the Cooper's hawk is sometimes a resident. The marsh sparrow hawk and the red-tailed hawk remain through the summer months, less frequently in the winter. Several species of the owl family are found in the winter, among them the screech, barred, great-horned, long-eared, and short-eared; several species remain throughout the year. The snowy owl occasionally visits from December to March.

The American bittern, often called "shite poke" or "slough pump," was one of the most conspicuous of prairie birds to early settlers, but now is decreasing in numbers. American coots (mud hens), common throughout the area, nest here, though other water birds, such as rails and gallinules, are far less plentiful. Of the shore birds, most of them migratory—plover, woodcock, sandpiper, curlew, and snipe—the snipe (Wilson's snipe or jacksnipe) is the most common game species. The killdeer, a favorite with his melody, "kill-dee, kill-dee," lives in the marshy regions while the upland plover hunts out the higher grassy lands. Mallard duck and blue-winged teal nest in the marshes of northwestern Iowa and the Canada goose stops here during its migration. This northwestern lake region annually becomes one of the greatest concentration points for migrating wildlife in the Midwest.

Of game birds, the wild turkey, once common, is almost extinct, except for a small number introduced in the State parks. The quail (eastern bob-white), although it is not numerous, is found throughout the State. Prairie chicken (pinnated grouse), here in large numbers in the early days of settlement when conditions were favorable for its development, decreased rapidly until, in 1933, the highest estimate made of their numbers did not exceed 2,000, and few if any nested here. At one time there were many sharptail grouse, but now only a few winter migrants are seen; and the ruffed grouse, found in northeastern Iowa, is now limited in number.

Settlement naturally destroyed parts of the original habitats for the birds, but, realizing this, the State began early to introduce birds to fit the new environment. Ringnecked pheasants, easily adaptable to the locale, now are numerous enough in the northern area to permit open seasons. The European partridge (Hungarian), imported in 1902, also replaces some of the original supply of birds. The farmlands, the meadows, and the cultivated areas of Iowa now are as plentiful with bird life as the grasslands of pioneer days.

Game animals are rare in this region, except for white-tailed deer. Today there are an estimated 500 to 600 of them, mostly escaped from private herds. More than 50 can be seen around the Ledges State park near Boone, where 15 are confined within the park and the others roam at liberty. Herds roam near the town of Avoca and in the northern part of Washington County, and all are protected by law.

Of the smaller game and fur-bearing animals, beavers (protected by closed season) are still rare, although they are beginning to return to western Iowa along the Little Sioux River and some of its tributaries. The mink, muskrat, raccoon (coon), skunk, and opossum are not over-plentiful but the opossum, considered a southern animal, is increasing in numbers as this animal migrates northward through the country. The civet-cat and badger are not plentiful, nor is the gray fox, but the red fox, in spite of the vigor with which hunters track him down, is not in danger of extinction.

The jack rabbit is common in the northwestern area, while the smaller cottontail is found throughout the entire State. The jack rabbit can be seen bounding about the open prairie and fields but the cottontail prefers to be in or near low brush, thickets, and willow clumps. The fox squirrel is the most common of the squirrels, with the gray squirrel next; the red squirrel abundant only in a few places. Other rodents, such as the chipmunk and gopher, are fairly common everywhere. The groundhog (woodchuck), around which the legend of the spring's early or late arrival centers, can often be seen along the highways.

There are 25 species of reptiles here, of which only three are poisonous —the massasauga rattler, the prairie rattler, and the banded or timber rattler. The poisonous snakes are distinguished by their three-cornered heads. Other snakes are the bull-snake, fox-snake, milk-snake, king-snake, and blue racer, the food of which often consists of rats, mice, ground squirrels, and pocket gophers.

Although 131 species of fish have been described, only 26 are common. The streams in the northeastern region are usually cold and clear—good trout streams—where rainbow, brook (native), and brown trout are found; but the streams in southern Iowa, flowing to the east and west into the two great boundary rivers, have few fish except catfish and bullheads (a small catfish). The small-mouthed bass is one of the better game fish found in the northern lakes and some of the streams. Catfish—especially the little bullhead, crappie, bluegill (sunfish), carp, and sucker (redhorse) are the common river fish. The white sucker and buffalo are plentiful. The common pike (pickerel) is one of the best game fish of the rivers and streams, while wall-eyed pike (found in Lake Okoboji and Clear Lake) and yellow perch (found in great numbers in Spirit Lake) are also good game fish.

In the Twenty-five Year Conservation Plan it is pointed out that every element of conservation bears directly upon the restoration and preservation of wildlife. Under the plan, sanctuaries for upland game and bird refuges are set aside. Efforts are made to clear the streams and lakes, and to check pollution. Artificial lakes are built and natural lakes dredged and improved. Besides State-owned parks, there are some State-owned or State-leased lands designated as game and refuge areas, mostly around the northern lakes, that are recognized by the conservation commission as wildlife refuges.

Along the Mississippi are the Federal areas, closed to shooting. Three of these are in Allamakee County and one in Jackson County—all units of the Upper Mississippi Wild Life Refuge.

Flora

Before the Iowa country was cultivated, the prairie grass, growing as high as the wheels of the oncoming prairie schooners, covered the entire area. To the first settler the expanse of prairie seemed illimitable; deep within the coarse grasses, hundreds of varieties of flowers grew in profusion.

In early spring the knolls were blue with pasqueflowers. Clumps of grasslike sedge appeared. False dandelion, cream-flowered paintbrush, and mats of groundplum-vetch splashed the hilltops. Then followed the bird-foot violet, white-flowered larkspur, yellow lousewort, and lemon- and orange-colored gromwell. Along the shallow streams blossomed the marsh-marigold, small white moccasin-flower, purple heart-leaved violet, white cress, and yellow stargrass. White and yellow crowfoot floated on the ponds.

Summer brought a different color tone, with red phlox and yellow indigo side by side, silver-leaved psoraleas, prairie lilies with orange cups, porcupine grass, side-oats, New Jersey tea, spiderwort, and countless roses. Red-purple vetch, yellow parsley, golden alexander, and Canadian anemone blended their colors on the ever-changing prairie.

In midsummer, the golden coreopsis, silver-leaved leadplant, red and white prairie clovers, compassplant, stiff-bush clover, crepe-petalled primrose, and yellow toad flax mingled with spiked mesquite grass, tick trefoil, Indian grass, Eryngium, and Indian plantain. The prairie's flowers in the fall were the goldenrod, gentian, blazing-stars of many patterns, sunflower, coneflower, and blue, white, and purple prairie asters.

Even after years of careless tillage this grassland cover has not been entirely obliterated. Today it may be seen in a few patches—strips by the railroad rights-of-way, by country roads, and in rough lands not claimed for tillage or for pasture. In State parks and occasional privately owned properties, small fragments of the natural garden are preserved.

The wild flowers vary in sections—not to be clearly defined—as diverse geologic, topographic, and climatic conditions have favored certain plant forms, many of which have migrated into the State. In the northwestern region, where the Kansan glacial drift has been covered somewhat with

WILD ROSE: THE STATE FLOWER

loess soil, and southward along the loess-covered mounds of the Missouri Valley, plants from the western and southwestern plains of the United States appear—the golden-aster, large-flowered beard-tongue, narrow-leaved collomia, prairie trefoil, and the locoweed, well known as a poisonous plant. Hidden in the grass are prairie roses, blue, white, and purple asters, the orange-butterfly milkweed, red and white prairie clovers, and the deep-blue downy gentian. With the bluestems, common throughout the State, are the wire grass, three mesquite grasses, buffalo grass, and other southwestern species. The wind-blown loess supports many characteristically western plants such as the Spanish-bayonet (soaproot), Indian breadroot *(pomme de prairie)*, the red locoweed, and the pink dalea.

Honeysuckles here are represented by the western buckbrush (one of the snowberries), and primroses by the scarlet gauras. One of the spurges known as snow-on-the-mountain grows so profusely that often the hills are tinted by its pale green, white-edged leaves. The silverberry is a decorative plant with woolly gray leaves and oval silver fruit. Besides the common annual sunflower there are the rough-leaved, artichoke, and others; Maximilian's, a slender gray-leaved perennial, flourishes across the northern part of the State. Woolly mullen is found in the pastures. Blue-flowered lettuce contrasts with brilliant patches of the dotted blazing-star, and the plant known as bundle-of-switches clings to the flat-faced loess cliffs, opening its delicate pink flowers to the morning sun. In a few lakes of this region the American lotus blooms.

In the southern third of the State, although the majority of the plants are common to other sections, there are some native to the Ozark and Alleghenian centers and points as far south as Texas. Among these are the gamagrass, a member of the corn family, and the Ruellia, related to the classic acanthus. The trumpetflower, which kills many trees in its twining embrace, often displays its brick-red flowers from some porch trellis. The wild potato vine may be recognized by patches of moonflower-like bloom. Silky-leaved Virginia plantain, the rare diminutive bluet, and the long-bracted bur-marigold—all found on the Texas plains—are now naturalized Iowa flora.

In the central-northeastern section, where the boulder-strewn land is drained by the Cedar and Wapsipinicon Rivers, the prairie meadows abound with pink and white shootingstars, golden ragwort, and long-plumed purple avens (prairie smoke). Throughout the State there are many honeysuckles, including the coralberry (red-berried buckbrush), the black-fruited and black haw nannyberry, and the twining trumpet-honeysuckles.

Many conspicuous plants grow on the sands of river bottoms, on dune-like banks of lakes, in sand pits, and on ancient lake beds. Some of the rarest of these sand plants are found in the bed of extinct Lake Calvin. Sand-binding calamovilfa grass (whose roots aid in forming sod by checking the blowing of loose sand), fragrant spotted horsemint, the smart-weed-leaved spurge, green-flowered croton, the trailing wild bean, poisonous rattlebox, and goatsrue, all flourish in the sands. White-flowered woolly Froelichia appears like a ghost among plants of a generally greener hue; and, of the plants that successfully live on the barest sands, there are the spider-flower, blue phlox, and large-flowered beard-tongue.

The distinctive flora in the ponds and lakes represent three successive stages of development—submerged, floating, and emergent. In some of the bodies of water in northwest-central Iowa each of these stages can be traced. Among the plants living in diffused light under water are pond-weed, coontail, and bladderwort. When the duckweeds, like myriads of floating cushions, and the leaves of water-lilies begin to shade the submerged plants from the sun, the latter die and the decaying vegetation sinks to the bottom of the pond. From the accumulating soil, cattails, rushes, and sedges emerge above the water, raising their leaves to the light above the floaters and in turn shading them. As these latest emergent plants rise from the water into the light and accumulate earth about their roots, they are able to maintain themselves for a time. Then, as they too die and enrich the soil, the earth is able to support such plants as the arrowhead, the flag—making the marsh blue with its flowers—and colonies of rose-flowered water smartweed that cast a glow over the waters. The tall joe-pye-weed and the fluffy-leaved lobelias, with their spikes of dazzling blue, appear along the banks of meadow streams where the slowly accumulating soil rises almost out of the water.

In the tall-grass prairie, near the sources of the Des Moines River in northern Iowa, where springs bubble forth on hilltops in the poorly drained sections, colonies of bog flowers occasionally show themselves. One of these colonies observed in early autumn revealed a cluster of cattails, marsh-dock, and traces of marshmarigolds on the wet top of a knoll, and, just below the crest of the elevation, asters with blue-fringed swamp-gentián. Here the shining cup-flowered grass of Parnassus mingled with the yellow swamp betony and the slender pink foxglove. Outside the circle was a miniature sod plain of nut rush, deep blue lobelia of the marshes, white and rose boneset, arrow grasses, and hosts of asters inside a huge sunflower hedge. Plain asters, swamp asters, and western asters—blue, white, and purple—mingled with patches of slender-leaved goldenrod. Refugee plants of seacoast marshes, of tropical, boreal, and temperate regions, had all been able to maintain themselves in the bog.

The woodlands along the rivers and streams shelter many wild flowers —snow trillium, blood root, hepaticas (white, rose, and lavender), and white lamb's tongue. As the leafing trees shade the earth, anemones (true, false, and rue) spring forth among crowfoot, dutchmans-breeches, spring beauties, mayapple (mandrake), wild ginger, Solomonseal (true and false), and the yellow violet. On the rocky hillsides scarlet and red trumpeted columbines cling, bushy meadow rue and cranesbill color the open spaces, and jack-in-the-pulpit, with yellow or pink moccasin flowers, grow in the deeper shade of wood or hollow.

WILD CAT DEN STATE PARK, NEAR MUSCATINE

In localized areas on the Mississippi River and its tributaries where bell-worts and blueberries are found, grow many rare flowers—wild lily-of-the-valley, wintergreen, dwarf Canadian primrose, the twin-flower, the panicled bluebell, wild snowball, shrubby cinquefoil, and the sweet vernal grass used in basket making.

On the rocky cliffs along the rivers green or black mosses and matlike lichens cover the crevices. Clubmoss and rockmosses surround the bright pink fameflowers that hold tightly to the rocks in northwestern Iowa. In the natural rock gardens of eastern Iowa, a soft green undertone is given the countryside by the many ferns—the walking fern, the purple cliff-brake, the bulblet fern, and the rusty cliffbrake. Polypody fern, beechfern, brittlefern, maidenhair fern, and blunt-lobed woodsia often grow side by side with the blue harebell and white rockcress in sandstone crevices.

While the displacement of indigenous flora has been going on all over the State, other much less desirable plants have been introduced that compete with the native plant life for possession of the soil. After nearly 100 years of settlement by the white man it is estimated that immigrant flora constitute approximately 18 percent of the known Iowa flora. Records show that some of these plants are of Asiatic and European origin, introduced as impurities in garden and agricultural seeds and in straw for packing purposes. Although some plants have been introduced as ornamentals (flower-of-an-hour, butter-and-eggs, cypress spurge, snow-on-the-mountain, and Queen Anne's lace), in many cases the origin is accidental and unknown. One of these "imported" weeds is the blue vervain (verbena, sometimes called Venus's torch) that colors many farmyards and pastures with its purple and blue masses. The common white-flowered, pungent dogfennel also grows abundantly in barnyards.

Many noxious alien weeds have become so widespread that the State has attempted to control them through legislation. Among these are quackgrass, Canada thistle, European morning glory, Russian knapweed, Indian mustard, and many others that were unknown to the first settlers.

Iowa still possesses 2,500,000 acres of woodland (including woodlots) of its original 5,000,000 acres; of these, 23,400 acres are State-owned. These timberlands are chiefly along the streams in the eastern and southeastern part. Very little of the original timber is still standing, and practically all is second and third growth.

Along the main valleys grow hardwood forests represented by birches, maples, hickories, oaks, elms, and basswood. This bluff woodland gives way, along stream or lake borders, to elm, bur-oak, green ash, and cottonwood, which are able to stand the severe climate of the open prairie. The green ash of open spaces assumes a hardy prairie form in the midst of the grassland where the most common tree is the willow. Occasionally cottonwoods grow in the sandy ground remote from streams. In southeastern Iowa the hardwood forests contain the oaks—post, swamp, swamp post, swamp white, yellow chestnut, shrubby chestnut, black jack, and shingle— and the hickories, including pecan, king nut, and pig nut. Representatives of the southern broad-leaved forest occur among these, except near the middle of the State. Yellow and paper birches grow in northeastern Iowa among the conifers such as white pine, balsam fir, and Canadian yew— probably relics of a postglacial forest.

With its trees and shrubs, Iowa presents a colorful seasonal panorama from the opening of the maple buds in February to the last witch hazel blossoms in November. Along the creeks the greening pussy willows push forth furry catkins in the spring, and poplars and cottonwoods follow them with colorful, pendent flower clusters. Among the brushy treetops on the banks and cliffs the feathery whiteness of the shad-bush stands out in April. Thorny brown-plum thickets whiten and, over the southern half of the State, redbud and dogwood color the river woodlands in May. Persimmon and papaw are occasionally seen along the southern border, while snowy hawthorn and rose-flowered crab-apples in spring border the woodlands throughout the State. Elderberries blossom in early summer. In the autumn sumac colors the hillsides, the wild grape displays its purple clusters, and the hazel brush is brown with drying nuts. In winter the rare bittersweet contrasts with the drifts of snow.

One half of the small area of Iowa's original timberland is already destroyed and the State is beginning to develop plans for preserving the few trees it has and for reforesting the neglected areas. Besides its value for lumber, posts, and cordwood, the State realizes the value of its forests in the utilization of waste land, recreation facilities for its people, and the regulation of the flow of water in its streams. State-owned recreational parks, waterfowl and wildlife refuges (four of them Federal areas in eastern Iowa), and State-owned lakes, although not definitely set aside as forest preserves, are the nucleus of a large-scale plan for the preservation of the trees.

Geology

Geological surveys, beginning as early as the first quarter of the nineteenth century, have revealed several systems of sedimentary rock (indurated) formations that could have been deposited only in oceans as they advanced and retreated over the surface of this region hundreds of millions of years ago. The geological ages represented in these formations are: the Proterozoic, the Paleozoic, and the Mesozoic. The indurated rocks are covered for the most part with sands, gravels, and clay laid down by glaciers coming from the north in times recent in comparison to the ages of the indurated rocks. The record of this glacial period (the Pleistocene of the Cenozoic age), which lasted probably 1,000,000 years, is clearly shown.

The indurated rock formations that form the bedrock were originally loose soft layers of sediment spread out on the bottom of prehistoric seas. As the seas gradually receded, belts of rock were left exposed at the surface. The various layers of rock—each of which formed a sea bottom for a long period of geologic time—bent down under each new layer. In general the rock formations dip gently toward the southwest in the eastern half of the State, south in the north-central and central parts, and southeast in the northwestern section. All deposited essentially horizontally, they have been deformed to make a syncline. Numerous unconformities indicate that they were not all deposited in the same sea.

Many of the formations are visible at highway and railroad cuts throughout the State, where they will be found underlying the surface soil. Frequently they may be viewed along the banks of rivers and in various surface exposures, particularly in the northeast corner of the State.

The oldest and hardest of these rock formations is the Sioux quartzite (Pre-Cambrian), found as surface rock only in the far northwestern section. In a small area of Allamakee and Clayton Counties are found the second oldest rocks—sandstone, dolomite, and siltstone formations—in the St. Croixan series of the Cambrian system.

The Ordovician rocks, constituting the third oldest in Iowa, extend in a rapidly narrowing belt along the Mississippi River from Winneshiek County on the north into Clinton County on the south. Caves and grottoes are found in the many fissured layers of Galena limestone of this system. At Decorah, in Winneshiek County, a famous ice cave presents the phenomenon of warm temperature in late autumn and winter followed by temperatures that form layers of ice in spring and summer (see Tour 2). The Silurian strata (next youngest to the Ordovician) with its hard Niagaran dolomite, extends from the southern half of Fayette County southeastward nearly to Davenport in Scott County, making a belt about 35 to 50 miles wide and over 100 miles long.

Limestones, shales, and dolomites of Devonian age (next younger than Silurian) lie in an even broader strip from Worth, Mitchell, and Howard

Counties in northern Iowa to Muscatine and Scott Counties in the south-east. West of the Devonian rocks a great belt of shales and limestones be-longing to the Mississippian system (sixth oldest) reaches from Keokuk in the southeastern corner of the State to Algona in Kossuth County.

Because of its stores of coal and shales, the Des Moines series of the Pennsylvanian system (next youngest to the Mississippian) is probably the most economically important rock strata. Included in the system are the Missouri and the Virgil series, in southwestern Iowa, and the Des Moines series, underlying a large region in southern and central Iowa.

A rich though limited bed of red sandy shale and gypsum filled a deep valley in the neighborhood of Fort Dodge to a depth of 80 feet during Permian time, following the Pennsylvanian age. The formation of gypsum differs somewhat from the formation of most rocks, resulting as it does from the rapid evaporation of inland bodies of water. This bed is in the old valleys of the Des Moines strata (Pennsylvanian) and the Mississip-pian system.

Underlying the surface soil of west-central and northwestern Iowa, and cropping out in many localities of the lake region, are the youngest of the indurated rock strata of Iowa (the ninth in order numbering from the oldest to the most recent). Sandstones of the Dakota formation were formed here—comparatively recently—during the Cretaceous period. The area covered by Cretaceous rock extends from its southern tip in Monona and Crawford Counties, in a gradually widening belt, to the Missouri River on the west and the Minnesota boundary on the north, and lies next to the Pennsylvanian and Mississippian strata on the east. Indurated rocks of the Cretaceous system (the last of the systems deposited by oceans) at-tain a thickness of 250 feet.

Iowa owes its soils, sands, gravels, silts and clay—the non-indurated or mantle rocks—chiefly to the four great glaciers that covered all or part of the area during the Pleistocene period. It is a safe estimate that the last of these glaciers retreated only 25,000 years ago. The time involved in the ad-vance and retreat of each glacier and in the succeeding interglacial age constitutes a cycle. A striking fact is the great length of the interglacial ages in contrast to the duration of the glacial ages themselves, estimated at a minimum of 30,000 years for each.

As each glacier traveled into the region, at the estimated rate of one mile in ten years, it carried along with it the coarse and fine rock mate-rials picked up and scraped from the ground over which it passed. When the glacier reached as far south as the region including what is now Iowa, where the climate was warmer, it began to melt, or retreat, as slowly as it had come, leaving till (boulders of all sizes and fine clay) spread out be-hind it. During this time, streams that flowed out from beneath the melting glaciers carried immense quantities of sands and gravels, depositing them in valleys or on top of the till. The till, sands, and gravels together are known as drift. During the interglacial periods the drift was subject to weathering by air, wind, and water, and also underwent a certain amount of leaching and oxidation.

Drift of the first glacier, the Nebraskan, covered the entire region, even the area commonly called the "driftless area" in Allamakee County in northeastern Iowa. The drift of later glaciers did not cover this section and the early deposits have been almost entirely eroded away. Deep-cutting streams, valleys, and rugged bluffs characterize this section.

Perhaps 500,000 years ago (minimum estimate) the Kansan Glacier fringed the western edge of the old Nebraskan drift and covered all of the region except a small area in the northeast. About 300,000 years later a portion of the continental Illinoian Glacier invaded the southeastern part from what is now Scott County along the river to Fort Madison, but ex-tended no more than 30 miles inland. The widespread gumbotil, and re-lated materials that have undergone a chemical weathering, developed during the first three glacial periods.

Geologists have discovered that during the third glacial age, the Illinoian, the now long extinct Lake Calvin was formed, covering large areas in what is now Johnson, Cedar, Muscatine, Washington, and Louisa Counties. As the Illinoian Glacier crept westward, the Mississippi River, and the water therein, became blocked at the mouth of the Wapsipinicon River and was forced to a new channel about 25 miles west of the original. As the waters reached the vicinity of what is now Columbus Junction, the Illinoian Glacier again dammed the way on the southeast, and drift of the Kansan blocked passage on the southwest. From Columbus Junction the waters backed up into what is now the Iowa River Valley beyond Iowa City, and up the Cedar River Valley to West Liberty and Moscow, to form a large body of water of great depth—perhaps more than 80 feet—over parts of the present Iowa City, and deeper in other localities. Lake Calvin probably remained for 130,000 years, or until the approach of the fourth great ice sheet, the Iowan lobe of the Wisconsin.

More than 50,000 years ago the Iowan lobe of the fourth glacier, the Wisconsin, crept down through the central northeast from what is now Worth, Mitchell, and Howard Counties on the north to Linn County on the south, and by way of a slender strip to Clinton County on the east. This Wisconsin Glacier retreated to the north for a time. Many years later, the second lobe of the last ice sheet to invade Iowa entered from the northern part, along a path from Osceola County on the west to Worth County on the east and continued as far south as Polk and Dallas Counties. So recently did this second lobe (called the Mankato) melt away that the streams in that region are still shallow and meandering with ill-defined courses and loosely packed banks. Many lakes, shallows, and marshes are in this area. Pilot Knob State Park in Hancock County embraces many odd-shaped morainal deposits (mounds at the edge of the glacier when it rapidly melted) characteristic of this lake region.

The Iowan and Mankato drift areas contain some of the richest soils in the world. Following both of these glaciers the usual drift was deposited; but the chemical weathering of the drift into gumbotil and related materials did not follow, and a widespread black soil was formed. The alluvial soils, composed of what has been washed down from other soils plus decayed vegetable matter, may be found along the streams and river bottoms. The loess soils (deposits of wind-blown silt), covering approximately three-fourths of the State, are browner and thinner than the northern soils.

Iowa may be divided into five principal soil areas: the Mississippi loess area covering a strip of land in east-central Iowa; the Iowan drift area covering approximately the territory over which the Iowan lobe passed in north-central Iowa; the southern Iowa loess area extending over most of the southern part of the State; the Mankato drift area approximately identical with the land covered by the Mankato lobe of the Wisconsin Glacier; and the Missouri loess area extending along a wide belt on the western border, from Missouri on the south to Sioux City on the north.

Because of the opportunities for analyzing indurated and non-indurated rock strata, and because of the four distinct glacial ages represented in this region, Iowa has distinctive geologic importance. It was among the first States in the New World to be examined geologically. Thomas Nuttall, from England, studied the banks of the Missouri early in the nineteenth century. About 1870 an excellent cut was made in Capitol Hill at Des Moines, exposing many layers of rocks and soils and enabling geologists to verify their theories and hypotheses. At this point the Mankato drift, youngest in Iowa, was found resting on soil of the Kansan drift. A bridge today over the Court Avenue speedway on Capitol Hill connects the southern tip of the Mankato lobe on one side with the edge of the Kansan drift on the other, joining in a single arch non-indurated soils separated in geological time by nearly a million years. Samuel Calvin, appointed State geologist in 1892, was perhaps the first to study Iowa geology extensively and scientifically.

CRINOID, B. H. BEANE COLLECTION

Paleontologists have found an abundance of fossil remains imbedded in the successive rock strata of almost every part of the State. Fossils of one-celled animals, water-dwelling plants, and invertebrates have been discovered in the Paleozoic rocks. Large collections of shells and early forms of marine life have been taken from the layers of Burlington limestone in the vicinity of Keokuk, Fort Madison, and Burlington. Crinoids were found in this region in such abundance that Charles Wachsmuth and Frank Springer made a collection recognized as one of the most complete in the

United States *(see BURLINGTON)*, now in the Smithsonian Institution at Washington.

In the limestone quarries at Le Grand, Marshall County, finely preserved starfishes and crinoids (stone lilies) are found *(see Tour 13)*. The abundance of these fossils and their state of preservation have made the limestones of the Mississippian age here of international importance. Specimens have been sent to Paris and other foreign cities. The collection made by B. H. Beane, of Le Grand, is on display in the State Historical building in Des Moines.

Besides the many crinoids discovered, coal plants have been unearthed in Marion County, and single-celled animal fossils found near Winterset in Madison County. Fossils from shale were plentiful at Hackberry Clay Banks a few miles east of Mason City in Cerro Gordo County and near Rockford in Floyd County. Bones and teeth of ancient fishes and corals are found near Iowa City, and there are hornshaped corals near Monticello. Sponges and clam-like and snail-like fossils may be seen at Dubuque. Fossils of the trilobites and brachiopods are also imbedded in the sandstone of the steep slopes at Lansing in Allamakee County.

In the sand and gravel beneath the glacial drifts, fossils of the great Ice Age have been unearthed. Bones and teeth show that hairy elephants (mammoth and mastodon), camels, musk-ox, sloths, and giant beavers once roamed over Iowa. The skull of one of these beavers found near Avoca indicated the living beaver must have been more than nine feet long. The Cox gravel pit, southeast of Missouri Valley, and several places between Hamburg and Logan, along the Missouri River bluffs, have given up remains of prehistoric animals.

Iowans:
The Social Pattern

AN IOWAN is as likely to be found in any other of the forty-eight States as in his native one, if the term be taken simply to mean a person who was born in Iowa. By 1930, according to a survey made for the National Resources Board in 1935, more than one-third of all the children of Iowa were living elsewhere—1,084,000 persons. In that same year the State's population was 2,470,939. Between 1920 and 1930, nearly 160,000 emigrated from Iowa, and during the same period many thousands left their cornfields to find a richer living—or merely a living—in the larger industrial centers within the State.

The Iowan who remains at home has a choice of physical environments similar to those he would find beyond the State's boundaries. The beautiful lake region of northwest Iowa is not very different in natural setting or social customs from parts of Minnesota and Wisconsin; the western edge is like Nebraska; and the large towns, Sioux City and Council Bluffs, have characteristics that are definitely western; the southernmost tier of counties is indistinguishable from adjacent Missouri; and along the Mississippi the population looks to Chicago and the East. In Davenport, Dubuque, and the smaller river cities the economic, political, and artistic standards of eastern United States are quickly reflected.

But the real Iowa to the majority of Americans is the great central region, with Des Moines as its focal point: an expanse of fertile farmland, originally prairie, across which the State's own river flows. Here are the corn and wheat fields, the characteristic white houses, big red barns and tall silos; and, at regular intervals, grain elevators and church spires dominating the little towns. It is from this area largely that the State's agricultural prestige is derived.

With a larger total acreage of grade-one agricultural land than any other State—possibly twenty-five percent of the country's total—Iowa is unquestionably rich. It has excellent educational institutions, kindly citizens, and

Richard Haines

AGRICULTURE, MURAL IN POST OFFICE, CRESCO

considerable natural beauty. How then explain the phenomenal emigration of its people, especially of the young and middle-aged? That question the State itself is undertaking to answer.

Setting about making surveys and long-term plans is a tradition in Iowa, one of the earliest States to experiment with extension service from the colleges and the university to the farm. But there is evident now a new perspective and a new emphasis. In the past the test of any economic doctrine or political program was its possible effect upon agriculture. The Grange movement was a direct result of the people's insistence that the railroads should conform to agricultural needs—incredible as it may seem, there is no place in the State farther than twelve miles from a railroad. The innumerable small towns grew up in the center of farming populations, near a grist mill or a railroad station. The railroad often determined the town site on the prairie, loaded a tiny depot on a flat car and brought it to the spot. Next came the freight house for supplies and a stock pen for loading cattle; then a tiny grain elevator, a general store; a doctor, a lawyer, and a newspaper—a new town in Iowa.

The long struggle against spending money for highway improvement was due largely to rural opposition, and was ended when the farmer saw its value in terms of the farm. The size of the larger cities, scattered fairly evenly throughout the State, may be traced directly to the number of grain processing, meat packing, farm implement and tractor manufacturing plants; and their prosperity depends largely on the prosperity of the farmer. With the coming of the Nation-wide depression in the 1930's the Iowan was slow to realize that anything could affect for long the value of the farm or nullify the results of the farmer's labor, for generations, as unquestioned realities as the hot sun and the abundant corn.

But at length he realized that he was no longer independent as once he had been. On his neatly fenced farm of 80 to 200 acres the Iowan was accustomed to being his own manager, a business man as well as a tiller of the soil. In the World War period, he followed a national trend and speculated heavily in land. Farms sold at high prices and mortgages were common, one farm frequently being mortgaged to purchase another. Beginning in 1929 many of these mortgages were foreclosed and much of the land turned over to banks and insurance companies. The farmer today faces the fact that tenancy is common in this great farming State, and that more than half of the farms are rented properties. Unrest and dissatisfaction brought the farmers to organize, to strike, to declare farm holidays— co-operating as in pioneer days to maintain the established pattern of their lives.

In addition to the strictly agricultural problems, the Iowan faces, with the rest of America, the increasing pressure of modern industrialism. From the time that the State reached its peak in farm production, about the beginning of the present century, industry began to develop on a large scale. The small town began to feel the competition of the big manufacturing center. Potential farmers and farmwives began to work in office, store, and factory. With the depression, unemployment and social unrest became realities to a hitherto more or less self-confident people.

Owing to its fertile soil and the hardworking farmer and farmhand, per capita income in Iowa had been for many years greater than that in the country as a whole. But a gradual decline in farm income has reduced the State's per capita income until it is (1938) approximately equal to that of the Nation. Industrial income, however, is growing proportionately larger and has shown greater stability, on the whole, than that of the United States.

With the development of industry and dissatisfaction with farm life began the unusual flow of rural people to urban centers within the State; and this movement from the farm to the manufacturing towns was—and continues to be—but a step in the exodus to the great industrial and commercial cities of the rest of the country. It is this problem that the contemporary Iowan is attempting to solve—how to make Iowa a place where Iowans may live securely and happily.

No longer is the value of a plan or a development tested only by its value to the farm. How, the Iowan asks, can this State give a full and satisfying life to its people? In a sense this is not a new perspective; it is more a picking up of an early tradition simply lost sight of for a while, neglected because of the needs of the farm, often indeed from strict necessity.

With the first settlers education was a primary interest. In the early 40's, 50's and 60's, the New England tradition—of culture, religion, self-government—was brought directly or by way of New York, Pennsylvania, Illinois, Indiana, Virginia, and Kentucky. Small colleges, some of the earliest west of the Mississippi, were built before the railroads were. Iowa's stately Old Capitol, the cornerstone of which was laid in 1840 (two years after the first session of the Territorial assembly), has something of symbolic value today as administrative headquarters of the University of Iowa.

The early settlers brought also a tradition of tolerance, intensified in the new land by the common dependence on the soil. Later immigrants came from adjacent States, from Canada, and from many countries of Europe— Germans, Scandinavians, Hollanders, Bohemians, English, Irish, Russians, Italians—bringing new and vital elements of culture. All of these adjusted themselves to the prevalent agricultural pattern, but the desire for cultural development remained a pronounced characteristic.

The farmer was willing to pay high taxes for the maintenance of educational institutions and to go into debt to send his children to college. But this was not enough. The younger generation showed a definite reaction from farm life, and many of those who left Iowa did so to find a more congenial field for artistic expression and what they believed could be a richer human life. But memory of the prairie soil and skyline was reflected in their work, and the lives of the rural people furnished the theme for novel, poem, and picture.

Those who remained at home began to appraise critically the culture of which they were a part; literary, art, and music societies were organized; little magazines were established; and discussion groups stimulated thought in political, economic, and social fields. The depression years brought to many a more sensitive consciousness of the pattern of their society and of national conditions that were beginning to affect it. A few citizens "on the county" had always been accepted as inescapable, but the presence of many farmless farmers and great numbers of unemployed men and women in the cities required a new analysis of the State's economic conditions. The interrelationship between farming and industry had to be realized before any deliberate modification of the earlier pattern might be tried.

All these forces may have combined to bring about the centripetal movement now apparent among Iowans. The reverse swing of the pendulum seems to have begun and the general tendency among the college-trained is to remain and work in Iowa. Higher education is adjusting itself to meet modern necessities and, while the State College at Ames maintains its high rank as an agricultural school, emphasis is being laid more and more upon science, engineering, economics, and the professions. The State university sponsors schools of music, art, and drama. At the same time there is a distinctive development in the cities in the field of art. The Grandview Music Pavilion at Sioux City (the design for which was made by Henry Kamphoefner, Iowa architect, and submitted for the Paris prize of the Society of Beaux Arts), and the Davenport, Sioux City, and Cedar Rapids Art Galleries are evidences of the new direction.

The humanistic emphasis, so clearly to be seen in cultural activities, is present also in the State's approach to its economic problems. The increase of farm tenancy, particularly in the badly eroded southern counties, is being met with soil conservation programs, the forestation of land unsuited to agriculture, and other scientific measures; but not without provision for the future of the present tenants in some more prosperous area. Long-term leases are encouraged in order not only that the renter may have time to plan his crops and conserve the fertility of the soil but also that he may develop a sense of ownership and eventually become a farmer on his own property.

Careful study is being given to the development of industry and the planning for life in urban centers. Mechanization of the workers' lives, congested traffic, and slum districts are no longer unknown in the larger cities. Investigation of the possibilities of part-time farming, the provision for State and county parks within reach of everyone, traffic surveys, and the work of business bureaus indicate recognition of the problems, and something of the means by which they are being met.

A successful experiment in living, based on the fusion of agricultural and industrial forces, may possibly be carried out here, in this fertile middle-ground between the congested districts of the East and the more sparsely settled West. Iowa has the opportunity—rich land, remarkably uniform diffusion of the population, traditions of culture and tolerance.

It may be that a new spirit of humility is abroad in America and that

Iowans reflect a national attitude. At least they have passed beyond the self-conscious and boastful stage, once so commonly attributed to them. Aware that, in any economic pattern, their State is part of the "bread-basket of the world," they are trying to make their own adjustment to the new order—to accept the inevitable industrialization but to preserve the serenity and stability of a farm community.

First Americans

Mound Builders

FAR in the past, what is believed to have been a race of slant-eyed, copper-skinned men slowly and painfully piled stone upon stone, and heaped basket after basket of earth, day after day for many years, leaving as monuments to their dead the thousands of mounds scattered throughout Iowa. The homes of these people were of such insecure construction that scarcely any have been preserved, but the mounds they built reveal to archeologists something of their customs and culture. Some of these mounds were fortifications, or the foundations of religious structures; the great majority were built for burial purposes.

At the base of the burial mound was a shallow grave or low platform upon which the remains of the dead were deposited, along with offerings of personal or tribal possessions—meal, tobacco, weapons, or perhaps ornaments. Sometimes this platform was inclosed by a structure of wood or stone. Earth was heaped over this crude vault, and finally an outer covering of sand and gravel.

More than 10,000 mounds have been found in Iowa, and although years of work remain to be done in exploring and excavating them, archeologists in the past 50 years have arrived at several confident conclusions concerning the origin and lives of the mound builders.

There is little doubt that these people were the ancestors of the American Indian tribes found by the first explorers. But the diversity of cultures included within the term "mound builders" and the greater diversity of Indian customs at the historic level make it practically impossible to trace the culture of any specific tribe to a particular mound builder culture. However, on the basis of a limited number of characteristics, some archeologists believe that the Oneota culture provided the basis for the Siouan of historic times, and the Woodland the basis for the Algonkian.

The mound builders of Iowa have been divided into five groups—

Woodland, Hopewellian, Oneota, Mill Creek, and Glenwood—according to the materials found.

The time sequence of these cultures has not been definitely established, but in northeastern Iowa the Woodland culture is known to have preceded the Oneota. In Allamakee County, however, the remains of the Oneota have been found superimposed on those of the Woodland culture.

The Woodland is the most widespread mound builder culture identified by archeologists in Iowa, and may be found in almost every county in the State. Numerous village remains have been discovered in oak groves of the lake district of northwestern Iowa, and more than 60 rock shelters have been located in east-central Iowa. Most of the village sites are small, generally of two acres or less.

The Woodland people were master artisans in stone and flint, and left behind them more than 100 known types of chipped flint implements. They were also responsible for an individual type of pottery, the material of which was mixed with coarsely crushed granite. Woodland pottery objects are generally formed on a base in the shape of a rounded-off cone. The rims and sides are decorated with fabric impressions, and are embellished with punched, stamped, and incised designs.

Effigy mounds in the shape of birds and animals are found in Allamakee, Clayton, and Dubuque Counties. The famous "Woman Mound," on the Turkey River in Clayton, was built in the shape of a gigantic female with arms akimbo. It measures 70 feet between the out-thrust elbows and is 135 feet in length. There are also linear mounds in this quarter of the State and in the middle of the Des Moines River Valley. The conical mounds are numerous in nearly all sections.

The Hopewellian culture is found along the eastern border of Iowa upon the banks of the Mississippi River in Jackson, Scott, Muscatine, and Louisa Counties, from Dubuque south to the mouth of the Iowa River. An isolated group of Hopewellian mounds is farther north, in the Turkey River Valley in Clayton County. These latter mounds average three to 10 feet in height and 30 to 90 feet in diameter. The interiors are rectangular crypts of logs which served for burial congregations and sacrificial altars. The largest specimen of the Hopewellian culture in Iowa is on a bluff near Toolesboro at the junction of the Iowa and Mississippi Rivers.

The earthworks and large village sites of the Oneota culture are widespread over Iowa. The most extensive site, called Blood Run, covers more than 100 acres in Lyon County, overlooking the Big Sioux River. Originally there were 143 mounds here and an earthen enclosure of 15 acres.

Other examples of the Oneota appear along the Little Sioux River in Clay, Dickinson, and Woodbury Counties. Still others are adjacent to the Hopewellian culture at Toolesboro and along the Upper Iowa River in Allamakee County. The mounds of the Blood Run site best show the distinctive characteristics of this culture, the majority being conical, two and three feet high and 25 to 70 feet in diameter. Numerous boulder circles are often found with the Oneota remains, and these occur invariably on high bluffs or terraces overlooking rivers or streams.

Ancient remains of the Mill Creek culture have been traced along the Little Sioux River in northwestern Iowa from Linn Grove in Buena Vista County, across the southeastern corner of O'Brien County, and southwestward through Cherokee County to its southern border. Fourteen village sites of one or two acres are left. Two of these still show a broad moat encompassing 12 to 20 earth lodge sites. Approximately 100 mounds, two to four feet high, are in the Mill Creek areas. No cemeteries have yet been discovered. A single village site of the Mill Creek group is on Broken Kettle Creek (a tributary of the Big Sioux) in Plymouth County.

The pottery of this culture is dark, and like the Woodland has crushed granite in its composition. Most of the specimens are globular, decorated with cross-hatched rims, rounded indentations, diagonal and horizontal incised lines, and molded heads of birds and animals.

Glenwood is the temporary name of a culture of pre-historic peoples who lived in semi-subterranean lodges scattered along the Missouri flood plain in southwestern Iowa from about the center of Monona County to the Missouri State Line. The lodges here were large—from 20 to 60 feet in diameter. Today they appear as circular depressions from one to four feet deep, standing singly or in groups of two or three. A somewhat attenuated line of seven lodge sites, two miles west of Glenwood, is an unusual concentration. The pottery found here is quite different from that of the other Iowa cultures, and the other artifacts are also more or less differentiated. The bodies of many vessels, and sometimes the outer rims, show impressions of a coarse fabric or matting which has been partially smoothed. Tool remains indicate that the people used numerous knives made of chipped stone, roughly diamond-shaped.

Invariably the mounds and earthworks of the mound builders are found along the bluffs and terraces of rivers and smaller streams, or on lake shores, almost never on the wider, more open prairie areas. Village and camp sites are frequently discovered in connection with burial mounds. A series of 30 or more along the Little Sioux River constitutes what was once probably one of the more thickly settled areas in the State, and, in eastern

Iowa, caves and rock shelters in the cliffs bordering the tributaries of the Mississippi indicate another such center.

Cemetery burial apparently was almost as common as mound interment. In some cases, collected bones were removed from trees or scaffolds and buried in mass "ossuaries." Sometimes the bones of a single skeleton were tied and interred in a "bundle" burial. Many cemeteries containing such burials have been found in the Upper Iowa River Valley in northeast Iowa, and numbers of great ossuaries have been discovered in the cave region of east-central Iowa. Cremated remains have been unearthed in recent times, and burials in stone-covered graves were not infrequent. Some bodies are found to have been interred lying on the back, others in a squatting position or on the side with knees drawn up to the chin.

It is evident that agricultural activity was not uncommon among the mound builder peoples, and garden crops were raised in large quantities. Another important industry was the quarrying and working of stone. This is not surprising since there was an inexhaustible supply of glacial boulders and deposits of flint and hematite. Several of the stone quarries used by these men of antiquity have been exactly located, and stone mauls and axes have been found scattered over the hills from Burlington to Fort Madison, as well as in other places.

One of the most unusual and impressive structures built by Neolithic man in Iowa is the large stone dam across the Iowa River at Amana *(see Tour 14A)*, but the nearest approach to actual masonry among the mound builders is found in the numerous rows of stones sometimes forming irregular inclosures within many of the mounds.

The most widespread art was that of flint chipping. Ceremonial blades, daggers, and knives were skillfully chipped from flint rock. Catlinite was used for pipes and ornaments; copper was hammered into useful and decorative articles; and wood, worked by fire and cutting, was fashioned into bows, arrows, spears, and other necessary articles.

Artifacts uncovered in Iowa have included fetishes, ceremonial weapons, and sacred articles probably belonging to the priests and medicine men. Pottery-making was apparently a late development.

There are over 600 private and public archeological museums and collections in the State. Outstanding are those of the State Historical Society of Iowa *(see IOWA CITY)*, collected for the most part by Charles R. Keyes, Mount Vernon, and Ellison Orr, Waukon; the Historical, Memorial, and Art Department *(see DES MOINES)*; the Frank E. Ellis Museum at Maquoketa *(see TOUR 1)*; the Herrmann Museum *(see DUBUQUE)*; and the Davenport Museum *(see DAVENPORT)*.

Indians

Although no mounds were constructed by the historic Indian, his burials were as elaborate and often as complex as those of the mound builder; and it is evident that he had as great an awe of the supernatural and as intense a belief in an after-life as did his primitive forefathers.

The Iowa (Ioway), from whom the State takes its name, are Siouan and came here from the Great Lakes region, adopting to some extent the Algonkian culture. The Iowa roamed in all quarters of the Iowa country, but settled (mainly) in the central part along the Des Moines River Valley. French explorers, hearing the Sioux speak of these people, added their own terminals, forming the words "Ay-u-vois" (I-u-wa) and "Ay-u-ou-ez" (I-u-oo-ay), thus influencing the two different spellings of the word— Iowa and Ioway. The meaning of the word in the Sioux dialect is "dusty-faces," or "dust-in-the-faces"; but other interpretations, such as "drowsy ones," "here is the place," or "beautiful land," have been accepted.

The Omaha, Oto, and Missouri tribes lived in the western and southwestern part of the region, where they were in continual fear of warring bands of Sioux. Along with the Iowa Indians, the Oto and Missouri belonged to the Chiwere group of the Siouan stock, while the Omaha were allied to another division, the Thegiha.

The Sac (Sauk) and Fox, originally two distinct tribes of Algonkian stock, joined in defense against common enemies, and were forced by this warfare westward through the southern part of the Iowa country. The hostile Sioux, of the Dakota branch, hunted and fought and trailed their skin tepees all over the northern third of the area. The Winnebago, also Siouan, transferred here by the Government, built their villages in what is now northeastern Iowa. The Pottawattamie (Algonkian) were given homes in the far southwestern corner; the Mascoutin settled on the Mississippi River, giving to the present county and city of Muscatine their name. Generally, the tribes of Algonkian stock came down upon the area from regions east and north, the tribes of the Siouan stock entering from the north and west.

The Iowa region was a battle and hunting ground for all these tribes. Before white men settled in the country the various tribes warred with one another to possess the rich hunting ground, one driving out another, then each in turn either drifting on or being driven out. The history of Indians in Iowa centers around the Sac and Fox, and their leaders—Chiefs Black Hawk, Keokuk, and Wapello—and the ultimate purchase of their lands by the whites.

Events of the spring of 1804 led to confusion and bitterness among the Sac and Fox and laid the foundations for conflict between Black Hawk and the white settlers. An Indian killed a white man and out of the confusion came a treaty (1804) which Black Hawk considered unjust, since the makers did not properly represent the Indians and had arranged the treaty while the Indians were drunk.

It had been the practice of the British traders to let the Indians buy their supplies on credit, paying for them in the spring after the hunting season was over. This the American trader refused to do. His action, coupled with Indian resentment aroused by the trickery used to acquire a claim to the Indian lands, brought about an alliance, during the War of 1812, between Black Hawk and his followers and the British. A battle fought at Credit Island (see DAVENPORT) forced the Americans to retreat.

When the war ended, Black Hawk signed a treaty (1816) ratifying the treaty of 1804. Of this he writes in his autobiography, "Here, for the first time, I touched the goose quill to the treaty not knowing, however, that, by that act, I consented to give away my village."

In making these treaties, frequently negotiated with the aid of whisky, the whites persuaded the Indians to sign documents they did not understand; this led to confusion that was not lessened by the failure of the whites to carry out their own treaty obligations. Because of a provision in the treaty of 1804 providing that "as long as the lands which are now ceded to the United States remain their property, the Indians belonging to the said tribes shall enjoy the privilege of living and hunting upon them," Black Hawk felt that he and his people had a right to live in the Illinois village of Saukenuk, at the mouth of the Rock River, until the land was sold. The Government, ignoring this clause, sanctioned (1831) the action of squatters who invaded the Indian villages. The squatters tore down the red man's lodges, plowed up his cornfields, and beat those who protested —even Black Hawk himself.

Angered by the actions of the whites, who had not even permitted the Indian women to harvest the corn they had planted, Black Hawk, in the spring of 1832, tried to incite his tribesmen in Illinois to battle against the whites. Chief Keokuk was more conservative. Whether motivated by the realization of the hopelessness of struggle, or by the thought of gain he might secure for himself, he bowed to the will of the white man. He and Wapello persuaded many of the Sac and Fox to follow them across the river into Iowa. Black Hawk crossed to the west side also, but his stay there was short.

Early in April, Black Hawk, with about 1,000 braves, women, and children, recrossed the Mississippi River and set out for the north country of Illinois to visit the Winnebago among whom he hoped to find allies. Failing in this, he sent scouts to the whites to admit his defeat, and to say that he was ready at last to go across the Mississippi River. His emissaries were captured, and one of them was murdered. Convinced that his band would ultimately be destroyed, and enraged at the treachery and injustice of the whites, Black Hawk and a few of his braves made a surprise attack and routed a strong army of white men. Then the Indian chief with his people moved slowly northward in a great arc, up the Rock River, across the site of what is now Madison, Wisconsin, down to the mouth of the Bad Axe River. Black Hawk had hoped to cross before being overtaken, but the reorganized pursuers caught up with the little band just as they reached the river. Black Hawk raised the white flag of surrender. But the enemy paid no heed, firing on the Indian women and children as they struggled to cross. Most of those who reached the opposite bank were killed by the Sioux Indians who had been summoned for that purpose by the whites.

Black Hawk gave himself up to a band of Winnebago who turned him over to his conquerors. He was kept prisoner for a time and then released through the intervention of Chief Keokuk. The chief's last home was on the Des Moines River in the northeast corner of Davis County. Here Black Hawk died in 1838.

It is estimated that 8,000 Indians were in the Iowa country during the first decade of the nineteenth century. Traders, trappers, and soldiers had intermarried with them and the half-breed children began to make claims for a share in the Indian land. In 1824, as a provision for these half-breeds, the Sac and Fox Indians made their first cession of land in the Iowa region. A small triangle between the Mississippi and Des Moines Rivers in the southeastern corner was turned over to the half-breeds and became known as the Half-Breed Tract.

In 1825, at a conference of Indians at Prairie du Chien, Wisconsin, a neutral line was established to divide the territories of the warring Sioux from that of the Sac and Fox. In 1830 the Sac and Fox ceded a strip 20 miles wide south of this line and the Sioux made an equal cession north of this line. Later the Winnebago were transferred to this neutral strip. In 1832 the Sac and Fox, after the Black Hawk War, were compelled to move farther westward. The Black Hawk Purchase, effected by the United States Government in 1832, pushed the Indians beyond a line 50 miles west of the Mississippi River. A strip of 400 square miles around Chief

Keokuk's village was reserved for the chief, but in 1836 this also was ceded to the whites.

Antoine Le Claire, great-grandson of a Potawatami chief, and interpreter for the Indians, was one of their best friends during the days the Indians were being driven from the Iowa country. Joseph M. Street, appointed Indian agent in 1827, was another friend. He was stationed first at Prairie du Chien in Wisconsin and then at Fort Armstrong in Illinois prior to 1838, when he was transferred to an agency (later to become a town called Agency) in the Iowa country. Street manifested a kindly interest in the Indians and their problems that was unusual for those times. Understanding that, as the game supply became scarce, it would be increasingly hard for them to gain a livelihood by hunting, he advised the Government to teach them farming. It was said of Street that he was "an Indian agent whom the spoils of office could not buy."

Within 20 years after the Black Hawk Purchase, all the country that had been occupied by Indians was ceded to the whites. In 1837 a million and a quarter acres of land had been given up by the Sac and Fox, and in 1842 these Indians signed a treaty at Agency promising to be out of the State by 1845. The Potawatami Indians, who had been living in southwestern Iowa, were moved out in 1846, and the Winnebago, in northeastern Iowa, moved to Minnesota in 1848. The warlike Sioux alone remained in Iowa up to 1851, when they, too, were forced to give up their lands.

Wapello, friend of the white man, died in 1842 at Rock Creek, in Keokuk County. He is buried at Agency, where a monument has been erected to his memory. Keokuk lived until 1848, dying on a Kansas reservation. In 1883 his remains were moved to the city of Keokuk.

The Spirit Lake massacre of 1857 (see Tour 7, Arnold's Park), in which 42 whites were killed, was perpetrated by a renegade Sioux Indian and his band who wanted to avenge the killing of a relative by a white trader. The massacre was the last outbreak of Indian warfare in Iowa.

After 1845 small groups of Sac and Fox kept moving back into Iowa from Kansas to rejoin the remnants of their tribes. In time there were 80 of these Indians in the State. In 1856 the State passed a law permitting them to remain. The Governor was instructed to urge the National Government to pay the Indians their share of annuities. This the Government refused to do until 1867, when the Sac and Fox had been joined by more influential brothers from Kansas who had saved money from annuities for the purchase of land.

In July 1857, with Gov. James W. Grimes acting as trustee, the

Indians secured their first 80 acres in Tama County. Later this group, which had grown to 265, received $5,500 from the Federal Government. They used $2,000 of it to buy 80 more acres. Since then their holdings have increased and the Sac and Fox Indian lands *(see Tour 3, Tama)* in Tama County harbor the only remaining group of Indians in Iowa.

The cultural background of the Sac and Fox Indians fitted them in many respects for the life they live today on their own farms in Iowa. The Sac, although they were described as the most savage people Father Allouez had met (1667), were an agricultural group. In the fall they left their bark or reed houses to go into the woods to hunt game, but usually returned to their houses in the spring when planting time came. The women raised crops of pumpkins, corn, beans, potatoes, and melons. About 1780, after the Fox tribe had been almost annihilated by the French in Wisconsin, they joined the Sac. Described as a warlike, quarrelsome, but courageous group, their culture, like that of the Sac, was of the eastern wooded area.

Though the two tribes hold to some of their old customs, they live in close contact with white farmers and are gradually losing all touch with the past. They still enjoy hunting and dancing, the pastimes of their ancestors, but they carry on agricultural pursuits and are interested in raising good crops, just as their white neighbors.

History

The First White Men

LATE in June 1673, Pere Jacques Marquette noted in his journal: "To the right is a Chain of very high mountains, and to the left are beautiful lands . . ." He and his companions, Louis Joliet, French-Canadian trapper, and the five voyageurs, from their canoes in the quiet waters of the upper Mississippi, looked upon the steep bluffs just south of the present city of McGregor. Chosen by the Governor of New France to explore the great river about which they had heard much from the Indians, Marquette and Joliet had set out from St. Ignace (Michigan) on the long route across Lake Michigan, through Green Bay, and up the Fox River to the portage where they embarked on the Wisconsin River. They entered the Mississippi in late spring when the wilderness was in truth a beautiful land.

The party landed on June 25 on the west bank of the river, probably at some point near the mouth of the Iowa. It must have been with great joy they marked the signs of human feet on the prairie trail. "We silently followed the narrow path," wrote Marquette, "and, after walking about two leagues, we discovered a village on the bank of a river . . . Then we heartily commended ourselves to God . . . and approached so near that we could hear the savages talking . . . and I therefore spoke to them first, and asked them who they were. They replied that they were Illinois; and, as a token of peace, they offered us their pipes to smoke." The chief thanked the white men for making the earth bright with their visit. The explorers rested for two days in the Indian village.

In 1680, from Fort Crevecoeur at the mouth of the Illinois River, Robert de La Salle sent Michel Accault (Aco) to explore the upper Mississippi. Accault's expedition, including the Belgian missionary, Louis Hennepin, and Antoine Aguel, passed along the shore of what was later to be known as Iowa. La Salle, proceeding southward, reached the mouth of the

WESTWARD, MURAL IN STATE CAPITOL, DES MOINES

Mississippi in 1682, and claimed the whole of the great fan-shaped valley for France, naming the country Louisiana in honor of King Louis XIV.

By the terms of the secret Treaty of Fontainebleau in 1762, France transferred control of all the country west of the Mississippi to Spain, but the actual transfer was not completed until 1769. The upper Mississippi region remained a wilderness where Sac and Fox Indians hunted and warred at will, visited at infrequent intervals by white fur traders, missionaries, and army detachments. It is believed that Jean Marie Cardinal, who came to Prairie du Chien some time previous to 1763 to establish a trading post, visited the Iowa country from time to time. He may have known of, and possibly even worked, some of the lead mines there; although credit for the discovery of lead in what is now Iowa is commonly given to the wife of Peosta, a Fox warrior.

Toward the close of the eighteenth century, American, Spanish, French, and English interests in trade on the Mississippi began seriously to conflict. Napoleon Bonaparte, then First Consul of France, demanded from Spain the return of Louisiana. By a treaty made in 1800, and a second signed in 1801, the Louisiana country was retroceded to France but remained under Spanish administration. Napoleon, realizing that the territory was a political burden, sold it to the United States in 1803, scarcely a month after French control had been formally established.

The northern part of the Louisiana Purchase was organized as the Louisiana District and was attached for a short time to the Territory of Indiana. By a treaty at St. Louis (ratified by Black Hawk in 1816) with the Fox and Sac Indians, who controlled much of what is now eastern Iowa, land on the east side of the Mississippi River was ceded to the United States on November 3, 1804. Earlier in that same year Captains Meriwether Lewis and William Clark had started out on their two-and-one-half-year trip through the Northwest, traveling up the Missouri River along the Iowa shore. A member of the expedition, Sergeant Charles Floyd, died on August 20, 1804, and was "buried on a high bluff overlooking the [Missouri] River." This was the first recorded burial of a white man in Iowa soil.

On March 5, 1805, the United States Government created from the Louisiana District the Territory of Louisiana, and a few months later sent the second Government expedition to explore the region of which the Iowa country was a part. The expedition, in charge of Lieutenant Zebulon M. Pike, went up the Mississippi River, stopped at a village of Sac and Fox Indians, and visited Julien Dubuque's settlement (1788). A site on the heights near the present city of McGregor was designated as a possible location for a fort. However, the first fortification in Iowa was not built until 1808, on the site of the present Fort Madison.

During the War of 1812 one battle with the Indians under Black Hawk was fought at Credit Island, near what is now Davenport, and another around Fort Madison. In 1813, after several Indian attacks, the guards set fire to the fort and abandoned it.

Meanwhile, trappers and traders had entered the wilderness, and a few adventurous individuals even had attempted settlements in the Iowa country. During the period of Spanish rule, Julien Dubuque, the first white man to establish a home in Iowa, arrived at the west bank of the Mississippi. French voyageur and adventurer, Dubuque was attracted by the commercial possibilities of the lead mines near the site of the city which now bears his name, and in 1788 received permission, in a document signed by the Fox chiefs, to work the mines and to occupy a certain tract of land. Spanish title was given to his grant in 1796. The claim, which Dubuque deferentially named *Les Mines d'Espagne,* extended for twenty-one miles along the Mississippi from the Little Maquoketa to the Tetes des Morts River. Dubuque, as miner, farmer, and trader, was held in high regard by the Indians. At his death, in 1810, the members of his party disbanded and the Indians resumed control of the mines.

Another settlement had been made in 1799 by Louis Honore Tesson, in what is now Lee County. Riding upon a mule, Tesson brought from St. Charles, Missouri, a hundred seedling apple trees to plant in Iowa's first orchard. A rail fence enclosed his orchard, potato patch, and cornfield. A year later the Frenchman, Basil Giard, obtained from the Spanish Governor a grant of 5,680 acres in the present Clayton County, title to which was confirmed in 1803 by a patent issued by the United States Government.

The Des Moines and Mississippi Rivers and the regions nearby, rich in fur-bearing animals, were profitable territory for trappers and hunters,

The first trading posts were erected on the east side of the Mississippi, and here the Indians exchanged skins and pelts for firearms, blankets, ornaments, and whisky. The American Fur Company at St. Louis was influential in founding a number of posts in Iowa that later developed into towns: among these were Council Bluffs, Sioux City, Eddyville, Muscatine, and Keokuk. Later the Des Moines River region became the center for the Iowa fur trade, which in 1809 was valued at $60,000.

One of the best known fur traders was George Davenport, who came west with the United States soldiers as early as 1816. He traded with the Indians at Rock Island, south of the present city of Davenport, until 1845, winning their confidence and friendship. Maurice Blondeau, another well known pioneer in the industry, opened a trading post on the Des Moines River, under the auspices of John Jacob Astor.

Many of the trappers and some of the soldiers intermarried with the Indians, and in 1824 a small area in the extreme southeastern corner of the Iowa country was turned over to the children of these men. White settlement really began in this Half-Breed Tract. In 1820 Dr. Samuel C. Muir, a former Army surgeon who had married an Indian girl, built his home within the limits of the present city of Keokuk. Moses Stillwell also came to this district and his daughter Margaret was the first white child born in Iowa (November 22, 1829). Isaac Galland organized the first school, which opened on October 4, 1830, in a crude log structure near the town that now bears his name.

Noted men who crossed the Iowa country during the first decades of the nineteenth century were George Catlin, painter and student of Indian life; the Italian traveler, G. C. Beltrami; and John J. Audubon, the great naturalist. Captain Stephen W. Kearny and a body of United States dragoons crossed the region in 1820 in an attempt to establish a route from Camp Missouri (Omaha, Nebraska) to Camp Coldwater (Fort Snelling, Minnesota). According to Kearny, who kept a record of his observations along the way, this was the first exploration made of this route by white men.

Territory of Iowa

Although the Iowa country was included in the Territory of Missouri in 1812, when Missouri was admitted to the Union in 1821 this part was left unorganized. Hunters, traders, and trappers moved across the area at will. Some cabins were built and trading centers established, but settlement could not legally begin until matters were adjusted with the Indians. However, settlement began along the Mississippi River long before the legal entry dates. Whites rushed in to take the lead mines near the present city of Dubuque in 1830, after warring Sioux had almost annihilated a band of Sac and Fox who had been in possession. United States troops under Lieutenant Jefferson Davis immediately drove the usurpers out. But settlers continued to advance. Finally, a treaty with the Sac and Fox Indians was signed in 1832 at Rock Island, Illinois, under the terms of which the Indians ceded a part of eastern Iowa to the whites. This territory, called the Black Hawk Purchase, became part of the public domain on June 1, 1833. Federal laws prohibited settlement in such regions, but as the Government was lax in enforcement, settlers began to move into the Iowa country in large numbers. They were permitted to establish homes, and many laid out claims and built log cabins.

A group of miners took the first step toward establishing law and order. They met in Dubuque on June 17, 1830, for the purpose of drafting a compact, by which they might govern themselves. Settlers upon the public lands, too, found it necessary to establish rules and regulations for taking and holding claims. Claim associations were organized to limit the number of acres in any one claim and to fix the value of improvements required to make a claim valid. By this time the nuclei of future towns were beginning to take form. Dubuque was founded in 1833, and in 1836 Antoine Le Claire and others laid out the city of Davenport. John King established the first newspaper, the *Du Buque Visitor*, which appeared on May 11, 1836.

Meanwhile, a legal problem arose that drew the attention of the Federal Government to the need for some kind of established control in the new country. A group of men in Dubuque, organized as a vigilante "court," tried and sentenced to death Patrick O'Connor, a lead miner, for murdering his partner. O'Connor challenged the court: "Ye have no laws in the country and cannot try me." The case was appealed to the Governor of Missouri and to President Andrew Jackson, but both refused to grant a pardon because, they said, they lacked proper authority. O'Connor was hanged in June 1834, a month after the murder.

To remedy this embarrassing situation, the Iowa country was promptly made a part of the Territory of Michigan (1834) and the first two counties were formed—De Moine and Du Buque. A fort, the first of three to be named Des Moines, was established about the same time near the present site of Montrose (abandoned in 1837). Since the land had not been surveyed, claims officially could not be made; but the country was now under the jurisdiction of lawfully established courts. In June 1832, not more than fifty persons lived within the Iowa country, but during the next eight years more than 43,000 settled there, most of them coming from the eastern and southern States. Slavery was barred from the territory by the terms of the Ordinance of 1787 and the Missouri Compromise. The census of 1840 enumerated only 188 Negroes.

In the years 1836 and 1837 the roads following the watersheds and Indian trails were lined with wagons from the eastern States, usually in groups of two to five. The farmer came with his yoke of oxen, his cows, and his pigs. Along the way wild birds and game were plentiful. Captain Benjamin Clark, operating the first interstate ferry across the Mississippi at Buffalo—the transriver crossing from Illinois into Iowa—was kept busy night and day. Each family was numbered, and crossed in its turn; wagons were driven on to a flatboat, and every able-bodied man assisted in the rowing.

With the exception of farmers, it is said that there were more millers and millwrights in those early years than all other tradesmen combined. It was common for travelers to be hailed with the question, "Is the mill a-runnin'?" Quite often the response was, "Crick too high," "Crick too low," or "Froze up." A variation of three feet in the water might clog the mill wheel or leave it dry; and since it was usually a long trip to the mill, it meant much to the farmer to know before he set out whether the mill was operating or not.

The prairie sod was tough to break and six or seven yoke of oxen were required to plow it. Except for a few necessities such as salt and tobacco the pioneer was self-sufficient. He hunted and fished for food; raised his own sheep and sheared them. His wife carded and spun the wool. She also raised food for the household in her garden, and gathered berries, greens, and roots in the woods and on the prairie.

In 1836 the Iowa area was included in the newly formed Territory of Wisconsin. However, by this time the idea of the formation of a separate Territory was growing in favor, and the name Iowa began to be associated definitely with the region. Lieutenant Albert M. Lea, writing in 1836 of his travels with a party of United States dragoons through the Iowa country in 1835, referred to it as the Iowa District. Previously the name Iowa had been used for one of the local rivers; but Lea's little book effectively christened the territory.

In an issue of the *Patriot,* an early newspaper, first published in Illinois and later at Fort Madison, James G. Edwards, the editor, wrote concerning the creation of a new territory west of the Mississippi, "If a division of the territory is effected, we propose that the Iowans take the cognomen of

George H. Yewell

ROBERT LUCAS, FIRST GOVERNOR OF IOWA TERRITORY

Hawk-eyes. Our etymology can then be more definitely traced than can that of the Wolverines, Suckers, and Gophers, etc., and we shall rescue from oblivion a memento, at least, of the name of the old chief."

Madison was selected as the site of the capital of the Territory of Wisconsin, but men from the Iowa counties prevailed upon the lawmaking body to meet for the second session in Burlington. In 1838 a bill was introduced in Congress to subdivide the Territory. Senator John C. Calhoun of South Carolina, fearing the creation of another abolition State, opposed the bill, while George Wallace Jones, delegate from the Territory of Wisconsin, lobbied in favor of the division. Finally, on June 12, 1838, the Territory of Wisconsin was divided to create the Territory of Iowa. Laws passed by the Territorial legislature had to be approved by Congress; and the President of the United States appointed the principal officers, including the Governor and the three judges of the highest court.

On August 15, 1838, Robert Lucas was welcomed as the first Governor. The first Territorial legislature met on November 12 in a Methodist church building in the temporary capital at Burlington. Governor Lucas believed in his executive right "to veto what he did not like," and tried to retain personal control of all expenditures. The legislature, considering this attitude opposed to the idea of democracy, requested President Martin Van Buren for the "immediate and unconditional release" of Governor Lucas because of his "unfitness and stubbornness." The request was refused.

Government surveys were made of the new Territory; land offices were opened; a fixed price of $1.25 an acre was set. Meeting at Burlington from 1838 to 1841, the legislature provided for the building of roads, protection of settlers' claims against speculators, and the establishment of schools. After some debate a committee appointed by the legislature selected a site in Johnson County for the permanent capital, which was to be called Iowa City. The cornerstone of the Capitol was laid on July 4, 1840, but the first legislature to meet there in 1841 had to find other quarters. The Capitol, constructed of stone quarried in the vicinity, was first occupied in the fall of 1842.

The establishment of a capital city at this point shows the speed with which the Iowa country was changed from a wilderness to a settled area. In less than ten years the frontier line moved inland 80 or 90 miles from the west bank of the Mississippi River. Fort Des Moines, the second fort of that name, was erected at the fork of the Raccoon and Des Moines Rivers, on the western line of settlement. (This fort was abandoned in 1846, when the Indians under its control were moved to Kansas.) Other forts following the frontier as it moved westward were Camp Kearny

(1838–1840), near the present site of Council Bluffs; Fort Atkinson (1840), on the site of the Iowa town of that name; Fort Croghan (1842), at what is now Council Bluffs; and Fort Sanford (1842), on the Des Moines River near Ottumwa.

A notable decision was handed down by Chief Justice Charles Mason, of the Territorial judiciary, in the case of Ralph, a Negro. Ralph had worked in the lead mines of Dubuque for five years trying to accumulate the price of his freedom plus the interest agreed upon with his master in Missouri. The master, tired of waiting, attempted to force Ralph to return to Missouri and to slavery. The Negro's friends took the case to court. The Supreme Court of the Territory, which sat on Ralph's case in 1839, decided that, since he was not a fugitive slave, his master could not force him to return to Missouri. (The Kansas-Nebraska Act of 1854 and the Dred Scott Decision of the United States Supreme Court of 1857 both nullified this Iowa decision.)

A dispute over the Missouri boundary line occasioned the Honey War in 1839. An early Government survey (1816) had fixed the Sullivan Line, or the northern boundary of Missouri, with reference to "the rapids of the River Des Moines." The Iowans claimed that this clause described the rapids of that name in the Mississippi River, just above the mouth of the Des Moines. But in 1837, by order of the Missouri State Legislature, a line was run westward from the rapids in the Des Moines River, just above the present site of Keosauqua, thus reducing by some 2,000 square miles the area that was to become Iowa Territory.

Although tempers were boiling on both sides when Missouri undertook to extend its jurisdiction officially by collecting taxes in the disputed area, the destruction of bee trees in 1839 was the overt act that nearly brought about a civil war. Both Governor Robert Lucas of Iowa and Governor L. W. Boggs of Missouri, in December 1839, authorized the calling out of volunteer militias. The Iowa militia from Burlington, Bloomington, Davenport, and Dubuque assembled at Farmington. The forces were still being mustered on both sides when the Honey War came to an abrupt close with an agreement to leave the decision to the United States Government. (The Supreme Court decided the case in Iowa's favor in 1851.)

Statehood

As early as 1839 Governor Lucas had proposed that steps be taken toward statehood, but the voters were not ready. Under the Territorial regime the United States Government paid the salaries of the majority of

DAVENPORT IN 1844

the officials, but, with statehood, responsibility for these salaries would greatly increase taxation, a burden which the people did not wish to assume. Despite the rich farm land the pioneer was not wealthy; with hard work and few farm implements he was able to produce abundant crops, but it was not easy to market them.

Not until 1844 did the people vote in favor of a constitutional convention. The convention, meeting at Iowa City in that year, drew up a constitution, the crux of which was the settlement of the boundaries of the proposed State. When Congress had established the Territory of Iowa (1838) it had included all the area north of the State of Missouri, west of the Mississippi River, and east of the Missouri. The constitution fixed the boundaries of the new State as they are today, except for the northern line, but Congress rejected these limits. Had Iowa accepted the suggestions of Congress, the western boundary would have been only 40 miles west of the city of Des Moines, and the northern boundary would have been 30 miles beyond the present Minnesota line. These changes were twice rejected by vote of the people, who preferred to remain under Territorial government rather than give up the Missouri River as the western boundary. The present boundaries were agreed upon at a second constitutional convention meeting in May 1846, and later were approved by Congress. The second constitution was approved by the voters of the Territory on

August 3, 1846, and Iowa was admitted into the Union that year, the bill being signed on December 28 by President James K. Polk.

The debate preceding the admission of Iowa was of more than local interest, since the extension of slavery had become a vital national question. Florida had been earnestly seeking admission as a slave State ever since 1838; so, when Iowa applied for admission, it was paired with Florida to maintain a balance of power between the North and the South.

The first Iowa legislatures were evenly divided between Whigs and Democrats. In 1848 the Democrats elected the first United States Senators, Augustus Caesar Dodge and George Wallace Jones.

Many of the provisions of the second constitution were the same as those in the one rejected; the one important change was the prohibition of banks of issue. The frontier needed money, and much of the paper currency then in circulation was of doubtful value or entirely worthless. The one legally chartered bank in the Territory, the Miners' Bank at Dubuque, incorporated by an act of the legislature of the original Territory of Wisconsin, was in disrepute. Times were hard on the frontier. Corn and oats sold for 10¢ a bushel, and wheat for 20¢. The framers of the constitution of 1846 attributed much of this financial trouble to the "wild cat" bank notes, and decided to authorize no such banks. Ansel Briggs, later the State's first Governor, expressed popular sentiment when he said, "No banks but earth, and they well tilled."

Farmers had already discovered that here the corn grew "taller than any other place in the world," and many early inland towns grew up around mills started for the purpose of grinding the grist. Keokuk was the "gate city," and one of the liveliest points on the Mississippi above St. Louis, in this hey-day of the river town. Burlington, Davenport, and Muscatine grew rapidly. (William F. Cody, later known as "Buffalo Bill," was born in 1846 at Le Claire, one of the smaller river towns.) Council Bluffs, on the Missouri River, was an outfitting point for those on their way to California in 1849. Here, and at other such places, sometimes as many as a thousand teams were gathered together at one time, preparing for the westward trek. Returning prospectors brought a flow of gold into the State.

Beginning in the 1840's many Europeans, who had emigrated to escape poverty, famine, religious persecution, or political oppression in their native country, were attracted by the undeveloped lands of the rich prairie. Particularly, many Irish, Scots, Swedes, Germans, and Hollanders came. Racial groups sometimes settled in communities; and some, like the French Fourierites, carried away by visions of Utopia, planned socialized colonies.

In May 1846 the United States declared war against Mexico. An outstanding soldier from the Territory of Iowa was Lieutenant Benjamin S. Roberts of Fort Madison, who led the advance into the capital of Mexico and pulled down the Mexican flag. Later he was made a lieutenant colonel, and the Iowa Legislature voted him a sword. Many Iowa counties and cities, organized during this period, took their name from military leaders and battlefields. Among battalions that served with distinction was one formed by the Mormons, who had come to Iowa early in the spring of 1846.

Owing to the influx of immigrants, the population of Iowa had increased to 192,214 by 1850. The pioneers joined together to establish schools and churches, and in their farming and business activities. Annual fairs where farmers and merchants exhibited their commodities were great diversions. Hunting parties, sleigh rides, quilting and husking bees, church picnics, school parties, and celebrations of all kinds expressed the cooperative spirit and hospitality of the early pioneer.

Three of the State's important schools had their beginnings in the decade of intense development that ended with 1850. Iowa Wesleyan College at Mount Pleasant traces a continuous history from 1844, when the school was incorporated under the name of Mount Pleasant Collegiate Institute. Iowa College at Davenport, opened to students in 1848, was founded by three pioneer settlers and the "Iowa Band," a group of twelve young men, graduates of Andover Theological Seminary, who had come to the West as missionaries in 1843. The college was moved in 1859 to Grinnell, where it has continued as Grinnell College. Both town and college were named in honor of Josiah Bushnell Grinnell, one of the founders of the town and trustee of the college for thirty years (see TOUR 14). The State University at Iowa City, established in 1847 by an act of the First General Assembly, did not begin instruction until 1855. Anticipating the transfer of the capital to a more nearly central location, the First General Assembly turned over to the new seat of learning the old Capitol Building and grounds.

Fort Clarke, later Fort Dodge, the most northerly fort in Iowa, was built early in the 1850's; its abandonment in 1853 meant the passing of the military frontier. Later when Sioux Indians massacred white settlers around Spirit Lake in 1857, volunteer border brigades were organized; and, after the Sioux outbreak of 1862 in Minnesota, temporary stockades were erected. One of these, Fort Defiance, built on the site of Estherville, was occupied by soldiers for a short time, but after this uprising the Indians ceased to play any important part in Iowa history.

During the 1850's the population more than tripled, with the westward movement this time directed to northern Iowa. A caravan of 50 ox teams carrying immigrants arrived in Mitchell County in 1852. In the late 1850's the first Czechs settled in Johnson and Linn Counties, and French Icarians established a communistic colony in Adams County. The Danes made permanent settlement in Benton County in 1854. A German religious communistic colony, the Amana Society, built homes on the Iowa River in Iowa County, there establishing the village of Amana in 1855. By 1861 five more villages had been laid out within a short radius of Amana, and the town of Homestead had been purchased.

In 1856 about 1,300 Mormons arrived in Iowa City by railroad and camped near Coralville (just outside of the city) while arrangements for their trip to Utah were being completed. This second hegira was called the Handcart Expedition, for the new converts were obliged to load their supplies on carts and pull them to the new city.

Upper Iowa University at Fayette began instruction of students in 1857, although it did not receive its charter until 1862. People interested in the farming possibilities of the State began to plan a school that would teach farming scientifically, with the result that in 1858 the Iowa State College of Agriculture and Mechanic Arts was established by law at Ames. The school was ready for students in 1868.

The constitution of 1846 had scarcely been ratified when the people of Iowa began to take steps toward revision of the fundamental law. As long, however, as the Democrats controlled the General Assembly the Whigs refused to allow revision, even though the prohibition of banks and corporations brought serious problems. Many Iowa Democrats grew dissatisfied with their party. Because of the strong Quaker element and the New England ancestry of many of the people, both Whigs and Democrats joined the new Republican Party—organized in Iowa in 1856—which was becoming an anti-slavery party. This new party elected James W. Grimes, Governor, and immediately set about to make changes in the Iowa government. One of the results of the political upheaval was a new constitution for the State, ratified August 3, 1857, providing for the removal of the seat of government from Iowa City to Des Moines, and authorizing the incorporation of banks, including a State bank. The first Capitol Building in Des Moines was ready for occupancy in 1857.

The development of railroads began with the passing of the frontier to the inland settlements. Ground was broken for the Mississippi and Missouri Railroad at Davenport on September 1, 1853, and the first locomotive in Iowa was ferried across the Mississippi to Davenport in 1854. The

Mississippi and Missouri Railroad (now the Chicago, Rock Island, and Pacific) had completed its road to Iowa City by January 1856.

From 1850 to 1870 construction reached its height, with communities and individuals donating land and money, and with townships, towns, and counties levying taxes and issuing bonds for the benefit of the railroads. An early State assembly had asked Congress to grant land to the railroad companies, and paid lobbyists had worked successfully to that end. Every alternate section for six sections on each side of the proposed railroad, a total of more than 4,000,000 acres, was granted. The railroad companies dictated what Iowa's future should be. Towns were platted where they chose to plat them, and money from the sale of lots was used for building more roads. Freight rates were set as the railroads desired and, consequently, the farmer suffered. The constitution of 1857 limited the assistance that any community or organization might furnish the railroads.

In the agitation for the emancipation of slaves, Iowa played an important part. Many Quakers lived in the State, and the Underground Railroad frequently carried an escaping Negro through the Quaker towns to freedom. John Brown, abolitionist, with headquarters established at Tabor and Springdale, made Iowa the middle ground for three years for his band of followers.

When the call for troops was issued by Abraham Lincoln in 1861, and Governor Samuel J. Kirkwood asked that one regiment be formed in Iowa, ten times that many men offered themselves for enlistment. The State, in all, furnished President Lincoln with 48 regiments of infantry, nine regiments of cavalry, and four batteries of artillery. Nearly 80,000 men were enlisted. Among the battles and campaigns in which Iowa troops figured prominently were those of Wilson's Creek, under General Nathaniel Lyon; Fort Donelson, Shiloh, Vicksburg, and Chattanooga, under General Ulysses S. Grant; and Atlanta, under General William Tecumseh Sherman. While in a prison camp in Carolina, Adjutant S. H. M. Byers, an Iowan, composed the marching song, *Sherman Marched Down to the Sea*. Among Iowans with the rank of major general were Samuel R. Curtis, Grenville M. Dodge, Frederick Steele, and Francis J. Herron. Mrs. Annie Turner Wittenmyer, of Keokuk, was prominent for her work in installing diet kitchens in the military hospitals.

During the bitter debate over reconstruction, culminating in the impeachment of President Andrew Johnson, Senator James W. Grimes of Iowa, stricken with paralysis, was assisted to his feet in the Senate Chamber to vote "not guilty." In 1868 the State Constitution of Iowa, which

GREAT RAILROAD CELEBRATION, WASHINGTON

previously had granted suffrage only to white male citizens over 21, was amended to give the Negro the franchise and the right to hold office.

After the Civil War, a period of inflated prices was followed by a panic causing hard times and unemployment. The dissatisfaction of farmers with existing conditions gave rise to many suggestions for change. The Patrons of Husbandry was organized in 1868 at Newton, and for a number of years had more than 500 granges.

The North Western Railroad reached Council Bluffs in 1867 and the Chicago, Rock Island and Pacific Railway completed a trans-State railroad from Davenport to Council Bluffs in 1869. Later the Rock Island joined with the Union Pacific, forming part of a continuous line from New York to San Francisco. At the same time the Burlington Lines were laid across the State and by 1870 the Illinois Central reached Sioux City, giving Iowa four east and west trunk lines with a total mileage of 3,000. Des Moines, Cedar Rapids, Fort Dodge, and Waterloo grew into active railroad centers. Funds were appropriated for a new Capitol Building at Des Moines to replace the old one, which had become inadequate, and the cornerstone was laid November 22, 1871 (dedicated in 1884).

By 1870 the State's population had risen to 1,194,020. The mining of coal, development of factories, centralized marketing of farm products, and widespread advertising had their beginnings in these years. Iowa already ranked high in the production of corn and hogs. The so-called "herd law," an act passed in 1870, represented another step forward in agricultural development. Before this, most of the country had been unfenced; often the farmer's fields were damaged or entirely destroyed by a herd of carelessly tended cattle. By the act of 1870, owners were held responsible for all damage done by their stock.

The depression of 1873 aroused general discontent with the economic structure. The struggle for railroad extension merged into a conflict for control of the companies, the farmers charging the existing management with discrimination and extortion. In the fall of 1873 the Anti-Monopoly Party, with a program for State control of railroads, elected 50 of the 100 representatives chosen. (At that time the Grange had 1,800 subordinate granges and a membership of nearly 160,000.) The abundant crops and consequent low prices of 1874 so intensified the unrest that, in the Fifteenth and Sixteenth General Assemblies, the Anti-Monopoly Party, backed again by the Grange, enacted the so-called Granger Laws. Railroads were classified according to earnings, with a detailed schedule of rates for passengers and freight; classes were also established for the various shipments. In 1877, under pressure from the railroad companies, the Granger Laws were repealed. A commission was appointed to act as mediator between people and railroads, but was given little authority. Peter A. Dey, member of the commission from 1878 to 1895, was an outstanding figure in the development of the State's transportation system.

Although railroad traffic was gradually supplanting river traffic, a canal was completed in 1877, to take care of the lightering service around the rapids of the Mississippi River north of Keokuk. Here much of the freight had been carried over tracks.

The last settlement of any size made in Iowa by any racial group occurred in the late 1870's, with emigration from England promoted by press agents. These English people established large farms in northwestern Iowa, particularly around Le Mars (1876) in Plymouth County.

In 1880 the population of 1,624,615 represented a growth of almost half a million in one decade. The Iowa Normal School, now the State Teachers College, had been opened in 1876. Drake University was founded in Des Moines in 1881.

The 1880's were a stormy period in politics. Besides the railroad question, which was still before the people, prohibition was becoming an important issue. The movement had grown gradually from the time the first temperance society was organized in 1838 at Fort Madison. Robert Lucas, the first Governor, had advocated temperance. A State-wide prohibitory law, adopted by popular vote in 1855, was amended in 1857 to provide a license system; and a form of county local option followed in 1870. All this culminated in a constitutional prohibitory amendment adopted in 1882 but declared invalid by the State Supreme Court in 1883. However, on July 4, 1884, the State became dry by statutory prohibition.

In spite of the fact that the Grange had instituted a successful purchasing plan for the benefit of farmers, obtained railroad regulation, and managed factories for making its own machinery, the organization began to decline after 1885. Inner strife was responsible. When the question of railroad regulation came up during the administration of William Larrabee (1886–1890), and the Governor called upon the railroad companies to revise their freight rates, he found them as defiant and arrogant as ever. Proponents of railroad control coined the slogan, the "freight rate is the skeleton that lurks in every farmer's corn crib." During this period Judge N. M. Hubbard, representing the Chicago and North Western Railway, became almost a legendary figure in Iowa politics, the power behind the scenes of all political conventions. In Governor Larrabee's administration, the commission that had been established in 1877 was given authority (1888) to formulate the schedule for railroad rates based on distance traveled.

The Federal census of 1890 did not report a population growth for the decade comparable with that of the preceding ones, but its numbering of 1,912,297 showed an increase over 1880.

In the decade between 1880 and 1890 industry was beginning to take a definite place in the State, and, with the advance of industrialization, the farmer became increasingly interested in politics. There were many followers of the Greenback Party; and, though the State had been Republican since 1856, it had registered its discontent by electing Democratic Governor Horace Boies in 1889 and re-electing him in 1891. In 1892 General James Baird Weaver of Iowa was the People's Party candidate for President of the United States. In the gubernatorial campaign in 1893, Governor Boies was defeated by the Republican, Frank D. Jackson, whose program called for retention of the prohibition law but permitted the sale of liquor in municipalities which met the required conditions. This led to the adoption of the Mulct Law of 1894.

In 1893, a depression year, an army of unemployed, whose march brought into the open the political sentiments of Iowans, started moving across the country. Charles Kelly's army, arriving in Omaha in April 1894 on a Union Pacific train it had seized, was hustled across the Missouri River into Iowa. Worried by the presence of this formidable army, State officials persuaded Governor Jackson to call out the National Guard to stop an invasion of Iowa and to protect railroad property. Three hundred soldiers assembled at Council Bluffs. Kelly, an experienced soldier in the Salvation Army, ordered his men to their knees. Singing gospel hymns and waving flags, Kelly's marching army was cheered across the State of Iowa—the railroad companies refused transportation—and Jackson's army was jeered until the Governor withdrew the troops. General Weaver and the People's Party Political Club welcomed the men in Des Moines.

In the free-silver campaign of 1896, William Jennings Bryan came to Des Moines, and crowds of his supporters milled about the building of the old State *Register* (which adhered to the gold standard) shouting, "Down with the *Register*." Later, when William McKinley came to Des Moines as a Presidential candidate upholding the gold standard, the cries changed to "Gold! Gold! Gold!" The sentiment in Iowa was strong for annexation of the Philippine Islands, and McKinley is said to have based his campaign in this State on that sentiment.

In the war with Spain in 1898, Iowa furnished four regiments of infantry, two batteries of artillery, a signal unit, and one company of Negro soldiers.

The period from 1900 (when the population had grown to 2,231,853) to the World War in 1914 was one of increased general prosperity in Iowa. Six great crops—corn, wheat, barley, hay, oats, potatoes—brought top prices in the markets. Bank statements indicated the wealth of many citizens. Good roads and the introduction of the automobile added strength to the back-to-the-farm movement which offset, in part, the migration of Iowans to California and the Northwest.

In the first decade of the twentieth century the idea of the Farm Bureau Federation began to grow. District agents were appointed by the Government in 1900 to teach farmers by actual demonstration how to farm with profit and success. The first farm bureau was organized in Black Hawk County at Cedar Falls in September 1912, and a State federation was organized in 1918 at Marshalltown. About the same time, a group of farmers organized a branch of the Farmers' Union in Monona County (1915), which received a State charter in 1917. The purpose of the union was to discourage the credit and mortgage system, to develop co-operative buying and selling among farmers, and to secure cost of production plus a reasonable profit, eliminating at the same time speculation in farm products.

The word "male" is still in the section of the State constitution relating to suffrage but is nullified by the Nineteenth Amendment to the Constitution of the United States. A proposed amendment to the constitution granting women the right to vote was defeated in 1916, but the Federal suffrage amendment was ratified by the Iowa General Assembly in 1919 and went into effect in 1920. This, however, did not give women the right to seats in the General Assembly, and a special amendment (1926) to the State constitution was required to admit women to the legislature.

In 1915 Iowa without benefit of woman suffrage, but probably largely through the influence of women, returned to State-wide prohibition, and in 1919 ratified the Eighteenth Amendment to the Federal Constitution. By amendment to the State law in 1933 sale of malt beverages with not more than 3.2 percent alcoholic content was permitted; and, in the same year, a popularly elected convention ratified the repeal of the Eighteenth Amendment to the Federal Constitution. Provision was made in 1934 for State-owned liquor stores under a State Liquor Control Commission.

During the World War Iowa contributed 113,000 men to the Army, Navy, and Marine Corps. The third fort in Iowa to be named Fort Des Moines (established just outside that city in 1901) was used for a time as a training camp for Negro reserve officers. Camp Dodge, a cantonment of nearly 2,000 buildings, was erected also near Des Moines. The Third Iowa National Guard Regiment, part of the Rainbow Division (42nd), reached France in December 1917, and served until the Armistice. One of the first three Americans to die in the war was Private Merle Hay of Glidden. In all, there were more than 2,000 casualities among Iowa soldiers and sailors.

During the World War period, and the years immediately following, land in Iowa sold at boom prices. As early as 1920, however, farms were mortgaged heavily, and the land itself was being worked by an increasingly large percentage of tenants rather than by independent farmers. From 1920 on, farm debts increased as farm assets declined. By the time the depression was acknowledged formally in 1929, a rapidly increasing number of farmers were losing their land through mortgage foreclosures. In the national election of 1932, conditions had grown so bad that Iowa, although Republican since 1856 except for a short interlude, swung over to the Democrats.

The Farm Holiday Association, a militant group of farmers drawing its main strength from the Farmers' Union, was organized in 1931. Loosely organized and without any set program, its main purpose was to prevent farm foreclosures and to fight against prevailing low prices. At the first meeting, in May 1932, the members decided to inaugurate a Farm Holiday; they would buy nothing and sell nothing. To save the farms for impoverished owners, the association members used persuasion, and at times intimidation, against "outsiders" present at the foreclosure sales as prospective bidders. The "penny sale" became well known in this period. Mortgaged personal property was bought up at the auctions for several dollars, sometimes for less than a dollar, and turned back, free of burden, to the farmers who had just lost it. By 1933 the association was organizing picket lines and strikes, while clashes with the local officials were common.

Out of this and similar movements elsewhere came a focusing of State and national attention on the needs of the farmers. State moratorium acts were passed, but two years of drought (1934 and 1936) produced the most serious crop shortage on record in the southern and western counties, and left the farmer still in a precarious position. Farm mortgages continued to be foreclosed, until more than half of the farm land was operated by tenant farmers. Land that had once been homesteaded, or tilled by farmers who owned their own land, was turned over to absentee owners. Although the problem of farm tenancy remained, Federal subsidies and loans gave the farmers as a group a breathing spell, and saved them from immediate economic ruin. In 1936, when farms were being operated again without loss, farmers began to recognize the need of having a solution to their problems come through action of their own groups. The Farm Holiday Association was no longer a factor, having been largely absorbed by the Farmers' Union. A number of farmers' co-operatives on a State-wide scale developed, particularly in northwest Iowa. The movement is gaining strength as the farmer finds it more and more difficult to survive on the old independent basis as an owner of land.

The future development of Iowa will be influenced inevitably by this realization on the part of the farmers of their own particular problems, but as related to national and world affairs. It is probable that the opinion of the farmer will be, as it has been, a dominant factor in the history of a State primarily agricultural.

Government

In the present system of government under the constitution of 1857, as in that of the National Government, there are three branches—the executive, the legislative, and the judicial. Legislative power is vested in the General Assembly, composed of a senate and a house of representatives, which meets regularly once in two years at the seat of government, on the second Monday of January of each odd-numbered year. The executive department, with its supreme power vested in the Governor, is charged with the enforcement of all laws enacted by the General Assembly. The Supreme Court is the "cap sheaf of the judiciary." Beneath it are district courts, and inferior courts provided for by the General Assembly.

The Governor, whose term of office is for two years, conducts all official business, makes recommendations to the General Assembly, and has the power of veto over legislation. He is authorized to appoint the members of most of the many boards and commissions, and to grant reprieves or pardons for all offenses except treason and impeachment. In cases of necessity, he may convene the General Assembly by proclamation before the regular time of meeting. The Governor is commander-in-chief of the military forces of the State.

Other elected executive officers are: Lieutenant Governor, Secretary of State, Auditor of State, Treasurer of State, Attorney General, Secretary of Agriculture, all having two-year terms; and a Superintendent of Public Instruction, who has a four-year term. In the event of the death, resignation, or disability of the Governor, he is succeeded by the Lieutenant Governor.

The commerce commission, consisting of three members, is elected, but the Governor appoints the members of the other commissions and boards. Among them are the board of control of State institutions, the board of assessment and review, the board of parole, the board of education, the conservation commission, the board of social welfare, the unemployment compensation commission, and the highway commission. Among other officers appointed by the Governor are the comptroller, the superintendent of the department of banking, the adjutant general, the commissioner of insurance, the commissioner of public health, the commissioner of labor, the industrial commissioner, and the fire marshal.

General Assemblies are designated by number, the one meeting in 1937 having been the Forty-seventh. The senate has 50 members, elected for four-year terms. The Lieutenant Governor is the presiding officer of the senate, but the speaker of the house is elected by the representatives. The assembly passes all laws, creates all commissions, and can pass legislation over the Governor's veto by a two-thirds vote.

The Supreme Court has "appellate jurisdiction over all judgments and decisions of all courts of record, except as otherwise provided by law." The nine judges, elected by the people, serve for six years, three being elected every two years. The position of chief justice passes from judge to judge, each one holding the position in turn for six months. The oldest in term of service is the first chief justice. Presiding over the 21 judicial

OLD CAPITOL, IOWA CITY

districts in the State are 70 judges, each selected for four years. Each district has from two to six judges, the number being determined by statute. Below these courts are the municipal, superior, police, and mayors' courts (in municipalities without special courts).

Important in the history of the Iowa Supreme Court are the names of George G. Wright (1855–1870), John F. Dillon (1864–1870), Horace E. Deemer (1894–1917), and C. C. Cole. Judge Dillon won recognition when he upheld the right of the State to regulate railroads.

One of the important governmental powers is that of taxation. The system includes property, sales, income, and corporation taxes. In addition to these, inheritance, license, gasoline, motor vehicle, cigarette, beer, and chain store taxes provide a considerable portion of the total tax revenue. Homesteads are exempt from taxation up to a valuation of $2,500. Special privilege licenses, such as for hunting and fishing, add to the maintenance of their respective departments.

The county, divided into several townships, is the State's unit of local government. Each of the 99 counties has its own administrative set-up, including a board of supervisors which decides most of the policies of county administration. Other officials who aid in carrying on the county government are the auditor, the clerk of court, the treasurer, the recorder, the sheriff, the coroner, the attorney, and, in some counties, the engineer. The county superintendent of schools is elected for three years at a convention of the presidents of school boards throughout the county. The civil township—so important in the New England district from which so many of Iowa's first residents came—is not important here. Assessors are the only important township officers; in many cases, trustees or justices of the peace are not even elected.

Each city and town provides itself with one of three types of government: commission, manager, or mayor-council form. Unless the city votes for either of the other two, the mayor-council type is provided. There are four special-charter cities—Muscatine, Camanche, Wapello, and Davenport—whose government dates back to pioneer days, when the form of government was granted either by the Territorial legislature or the General Assembly of the State. The constitution of 1857 prohibits the granting of special charters, but these four are still held legal.

Any citizen of the United States, 21 years old or more, who has lived in Iowa six months and in the county 60 days, is entitled to vote. A foreigner must complete the process of naturalization before he may vote at any election.

Many native Iowans, from early pioneer days to the present, have been outstanding in the National Government. Notable contemporaries are Henry A. Wallace, Secretary of Agriculture; Harry L. Hopkins, Works Progress Administrator; and Herbert Hoover, Secretary of Commerce 1921–29, and President of the United States 1929–33.

Among those who have held Cabinet offices are Secretary of the Treasury Leslie M. Shaw, appointed February 1, 1902; Secretaries of War William W. Belknap, appointed October 25, 1869; George W. McCrary, March 12, 1877, and James W. Good, March 4, 1929; Postmaster General Frank Hatton, appointed October 14, 1884; Secretaries of the Interior James Harlan, appointed May 15, 1865, and Samuel J. Kirkwood (Iowa's Civil War Governor), March 5, 1881; and Secretaries of Agriculture James ("Tama Jim") Wilson, appointed March 5, 1897, who served under three Presidents up to 1913, Edwin T. Meredith, February 1, 1920, Henry C. Wallace, March 4, 1921, and Henry A. Wallace, March 4, 1933. The brothers Ray Lyman Wilbur and Curtis Dwight Wilbur, who served respectively as Secretary of the Interior and Secretary of the Navy, are native Iowans.

In the United States Senate, William B. Allison represented his State from 1873 to 1908, Jonathan P. Dolliver from 1900 to 1910, Albert B. Cummins from 1908 to 1926, and William S. Kenyon from 1911 to 1922. Samuel Freeman Miller was Associate Justice of the United States Supreme Court from 1862 to 1890. David Brenner Henderson, elected Speaker of the House of Representatives in 1899, and William Peters Hepburn, United States Representative for more than twenty years, were prominent in national affairs. Born in Scotland, Henderson served Iowa for many years in military and governmental posts. John Adams Kasson (1822–1910), active in the Post Office Department and in diplomacy, was born in Vermont but became an active force in the growth of the Republican Party in Iowa. George Windle Read, formerly Major General, United States Army, an officer of distinction, was born in Indianola, Iowa.

Agriculture and
Farm Life

AGRICULTURE and the activities related to it make up Iowa's basic industry. The population of 31 of the 99 counties is entirely rural and in only 14 counties do the urban groups (people living in cities of over 2,500 population) exceed the rural. The reports of the State Comptroller's office term all counties but three "agricultural." With the largest proportion of arable land of all States, the number of farms is estimated at 221,986 with a combined acreage of 34,359,000 acres (1935). Farm land may be roughly divided, according to types of farming, into the cash grain area, the dairy area, the western and eastern meat-producing area, and the southern pasture area. Farming produces from one fourth to one third of the State's total income, and an average of 6.9 percent of the entire country's gross farm income; it employs more than one third of the State's gainful workers. These figures, taken in part from *Agricultural Statistics, 1937* (U. S. Department of Agriculture) and from *Iowa Income: 1909–1934* (University of Iowa), give some indication of the place of farming in the general economy of the State.

Everywhere the land is tillable and, even in the coal county where it is underlaid with mines, the same crops are raised as elsewhere in the State. The panorama is of corn, growing in great square and rectangular fields, of grain ripening in the prairie winds; of grazing cattle, red barns, tall silos, white farmhouses; and of towns bordering the highway at regular intervals and dominated by grain elevators and church spires. The bird's-eye view shows a land of independent farmers of rich soil, and prosperity. Closer examination, however, reveals another aspect.

The Report of the President's Committee on Farm Tenancy, prepared under the auspices of the National Resources Board, found that the percentage of farms occupied by tenants has risen throughout the country from 25 percent in 1880 to 42 percent in 1935. In Iowa tenancy has risen steadily from 23.8 percent in 1880 to 49.6 percent in 1935. The percentage of land under lease to "cash renters" has also increased in

YOUNG CORN FARMER

Iowa, and farm owners are overburdened with heavy mortgages. Stated in other terms, 71 percent of the value of Iowa farm real estate did not belong to the immediate farm operator in 1930, as compared to 58 percent for the entire United States. Insecure tenure, whether of tenant or owner, is good neither for the farmer nor for the land. The insecure family moves frequently, the children suffer from lack of continuity in their schooling, and the family is deprived of normal social contacts. The land also suffers. The farmer is forced to engage in enterprises he can get into quickly and get out of quickly. This means that too high a percentage of land is used for cash crops such as corn and wheat, which take the most fertility out of the soil and are the most likely to cause erosion. A direct relation exists between length of farm occupancy and the amount of erosion.

February is moving time for the tenant farmers who must be ready for spring planting on their new farms by March. Trucks and wagons crowded with furniture rumble over the frozen roads and tired herds of cattle and sheep trudge in their wake. Load after load jolt past the farm houses, stretching out like a gypsy caravan going on to camp elsewhere for a brief time . . . hoping that the new farm will be a little better than the last one. Here is a tragic epitome of the problem of farm tenancy which is increasing so rapidly that there is real cause for alarm.

Tenancy and other forms of insecure tenure have many causes, a powerful one being that the market value of farm land has usually been higher than was warranted by returns to be had from that land. Prices for farm products went down in the 1920's and early 1930's, while interest rates, the price of farm equipment and land, and general living expenses remained high. The Iowa farmer, usually a peaceable person taking the middle way between conservatism and radicalism, was caught in a vise. The situation demanded drastic readjustments and in some cases called out his latent individualistic tendencies. National attention was focused on the State and the farmer's economic difficulties in the so-called Tipton Cattle War of 1931, when the State militia had to be called out to quell a riot of farmers opposing the State law on the testing of cattle for tuberculosis and the killing of infected stock. Of wider significance were the activities of the Farm Holiday Association with its "penny sales" (see HISTORY) and the milk strike of 1933 outside of Sioux City.

The plight of farmers in the country at large forced action on a national scale in 1933. The Agricultural Adjustment Administration aimed first to increase and stabilize farm income and later to conserve the soil; the Farm Credit Administration sought to increase security of ownership; and the Resettlement Administration (now the Farm Security Administration of

STOCK FARM, BENTON COUNTY

the Department of Agriculture) attacked the problem of special distress brought on by the drought years 1934 and 1936. Crop prices, soil conservation, and insecure land tenure are interrelated and are now being dealt with as a whole.

Several projects were begun in 1936 in which the AAA is co-operating with State experiment stations, the United States Bureau of Agricultural Economics, and the Farm Security Administration. The Iowa project, carried on in co-operation with the State Agricultural Conservation Committee and 28 county agricultural conservation committees, has already borne fruit in a number of concrete suggestions for increasing security of farm tenure. The bulletin *Farm Tenure in Iowa,* published by the Iowa State College of Agriculture, summarizes the findings of the study and includes data on the cost of a shifting tenantry—the wear and tear on machinery and household equipment, losses of feed and livestock, deterioration of land and improvements, community stagnation in economic, social, and cultural developments; it also includes data on the causes of frequent moving; types of leases that handicap the tenant in conserving the soil; and suggestions for changes in leasing arrangements looking towards rectifying these adverse conditions.

The modern Iowa farmer is more than a simple tiller of the soil. Under proper conditions, he is also a business man and a student of the science of farming. Nearly every farmhouse has a radio. It is one of the farmer's most valued allies, bringing him daily reports on markets, not only throughout the State, but from the important shipping centers of Kansas City, St. Louis, and Chicago. The conception of a "hay-seed" is being replaced by a truer picture—that of a progressive, business-like producer who sells almost 90 percent of his product and studies politics, weather reports, improved methods of production and marketing, crop control and soil conservation.

An integrated structure has been built to aid him and further his interests. The Iowa State Department of Agriculture and the office of secretary of agriculture were created by the Fortieth General Assembly in 1923. The work of the department is subdivided as follows: the animal industry division, which is responsible for the control of diseases of livestock, supervises the movement of livestock, and enforces laws in the field; the dairy and food division, which enforces laws dealing with sanitation, labeling, weights, and measures in connection with foods and their commercial usages; the State chemist, who makes laboratory tests of samples; the State entomologist, who is in charge of the inspection of nursery stock, the issuing of quarantine regulations, and the general control of crop pests; the weather and crop bureau, which collaborates with the Federal Government in gathering and disseminating information about livestock, crop, and weather conditions; and miscellaneous divisions directly under the assistant secretary of agriculture, who supervises the agricultural warehouse section, stallion registration, farmers' institutes, short courses of instruction, and poultry shows. Five associations are affiliated with the department —the State Dairy Association, Horticultural Society, Horse and Mule Breeders' Association, Beef Producers' Association, and Corn and Small Grain Growers' Association.

Closely co-operating with the State departments of education and agriculture is the State College of Agriculture and Mechanic Arts at Ames. The extension service at the college works with the United States Department of Agriculture, from which it receives part of its financial support. The information and other benefits provided by the experiment station, also connected with the college, are available to all. The research projects reported for the year ending June 30, 1936, included work in such major fields as: agricultural economics, agricultural engineering, animal husbandry, animal breeding, animal production, dairy husbandry, meats and poultry husbandry, bacteriology, botany and plant pathology, chemistry

FARMERS' COOPERATIVE GRAIN ELEVATOR

(animal chemistry and nutrition, and plant chemistry), dairy industry entomology, forestry, farm crops and soils, genetics, and horticulture.

There is a county farm bureau in every county in the State. Organized in 1918, the membership of the State Farm Bureau Federation in 1938 was estimated at 50,000 families, each one of which pays $10 in annual dues. The 4-H Clubs for boys and girls, associated with the farm bureaus, carry on educational work. County extension agents, employed by the county farm bureau groups with salaries set by them, direct the work of extending agricultural information. The United States Department of Agriculture and the extension service add contributions to the county appropriations and the farm bureau funds for this purpose. A close-knit organization has been developed, starting with the county agents, and widening out through the farm bureau groups, the State extension service, the college at Ames, to the United States Department of Agriculture. Some opposition to this benevolent hierarchy has found expression in the Farmer's Union (Farmers' Educational and Cooperative Union) and the Farm Holiday Association, the most important independent farm organizations in Iowa.

For more than a quarter of a century the agricultural publishing center of the United States has been in Des Moines. The names of Henry Wallace, Dante Pierce, and Edwin T. Meredith have been household words, and whatever they said has been accepted as farm gospel. They wrote with vision and courage, and discussed crop rotation, seed selection, better farming methods, and everything bearing on farming in their papers, *The Iowa Homestead, Wallace's Farmer,* and *Successful Farming.* Meredith was appointed United States Secretary of Agriculture, February 1, 1920. Wallace was the father of one Secretary and the grandfather of another—Henry C. Wallace, appointed in 1921, and Henry A. Wallace, 1933. Another Secretary of Agriculture from Iowa was James ("Tama Jim") Wilson, who was appointed March 5, 1897, and served under three Presidents.

Every winter a State agricultural convention is held at the Capitol Building to make arrangements for the annual State Fair. This fair, which is held each August at Des Moines, is conducted by a State fair board, a separate and distinct department of the government. The livestock shows, the 4-H Club exhibits by the farm youths, the agricultural displays, and the educational features make this an outstanding event and the climax of the agricultural year. The farmer brings his entire family, and a tent city springs up within the fairgrounds as if by magic. The entertainment furnished by concessionaires on the midway is rivaled by the display of hogs, corn and grain, horses, cows, and cackling chickens on display in the exhibition buildings. There are also 78 annual county fairs.

Principal Crops

When Iowa was first settled wheat was the most widely grown grain in the United States, so the pioneers naturally turned to growing of this crop. As the wheat belt moved westward, Iowa took her place among the leading wheat-producing States, and raised enough wheat by 1870 to stand second in rank. But the wheat belt moved still farther to the west, and by 1879 Iowa had fallen to sixth place. Today a comparatively unimportant winter wheat region lies in the southern half of the State and in the counties bordering on the Missouri and Mississippi Rivers, and there is a spring wheat region in the central-western and central-eastern sections. In 1937 Iowa produced 15,976,000 bushels of wheat.

Corn grew prolifically in the rich soil and, with the passing of the wheat belt to the more sparsely settled areas, Iowans turned toward the growing of this crop which fitted well into their system of crop rotation and intensified farming.

The Indian had every basic variety of corn grown today and a number no longer in production; through selective breeding, the white man has improved on these and developed mixed varieties. Most of the present Iowa corn (503,505,000 bushels produced in 1937) is derived from seed that came from the East from 1840 to 1910. The oldest variety originated in a cross made accidentally in 1847 in Tazewell County, Illinois, by Robert Reid. Reid had planted a crop of late-maturing, large-eared corn, which was probably of the shoe-peg variety. When this seed failed to produce a good stand, he replanted his field with an early small yellow flint corn. The resulting cross gave a great diversity of type, and Reid (and after him his son, James L. Reid) took care to pick out ears almost as large as the shoe-peg variety, but with smoother kernels, larger germs, and a greater proportion of starch. Most of the selection was done in the years between 1870 and 1890, but Reid's greatest triumph came in 1893 when he won a prize at the Chicago World's Fair. By that time the Reid Yellow Dent corn was being grown extensively by Iowa farmers. Today it is produced in larger quantities than all other varieties together. The most popular white corn, grown on a large scale in the northern part of the State, is the Silver King variety. For this, and for a yellow strain called Pride of the North, credit is given to J. Goddard of Fort Atkinson, who worked more than 30 years to find high-yielding, early corn, both white and yellow.

What may be described as "corn consciousness" overtook the farmers of the State from 1893 to 1910, when shows were held at various places, establishing the standards by which Iowa corn was judged. After the World War, the influence of these shows declined. By 1920, H. D. Hughes, professor at Iowa State College, had introduced the Iowa corn yield test—the first scientific approach to the problem of corn selection. Since 1925, a cross-fertilized variety known as hybrid corn, involving one or more inbred lines, has produced a large yield. Henry A. Wallace and Simon Casady of Des Moines, in 1922, were the first men to develop it. They had a contract with a seed company to produce one acre, but the inbreds were used unsuccessfully. After a few trials a successful hybrid corn technique was developed. The State agricultural experiment station at Ames has been growing it on an extensive scale, and in 1937 there was enough hybrid corn to plant 13 percent of the entire corn acreage.

Next to corn, oats is the most important grain both in acreage and in total value. As with corn, the farmer learned early in Iowa history that the growing of oats fitted well into his plan of crop rotation. A significant relation exists between corn acreage and the relative yield of oats. Where oats cannot be raised profitably, corn is given a larger place than in sections in which the relatively high oat yields make this crop fairly profit-able. The greatest production is found in the northern area; throughout the northwestern region the percentage of land in oats nearly reaches the percentage of land in corn. The average yearly total oats production in bushels from 1924 to 1933 was 208,467,000, with an estimated value of $65,805,000. The 1937 production was 258,975,000 bushels. Oats are not so important a cash crop as corn or wheat. Included in the corn-belt agricultural region because of their value as a crop intermediate between corn and grass, oats are used as a feed grain for farm animals—horses, dairy cows, and young stock. The balanced nutritive value of oats for building animal bone and muscle is not equalled by that of any other grain. However, not all the oats grown are fed to animals. The largest cereal factory in the world, at Cedar Rapids, uses much of Iowa's oat crop.

Legumes play a vital part in agriculture, for not only are they necessary for feeding livestock, but they are also valuable as fertilizer. The char-acteristics of legumes are varied, individual kinds serving different require-ments. Many years are needed, sometimes a century, to acclimate a crop to a different farm area. The early farmer had to be his own seedsman as well as his own experiment station. The State agricultural experiment station, when it came into existence, found that imported clover lacked winter hardiness if a stand were secured the first year; the plant was likely to be entirely dead the next spring. To mark the distinction between foreign and native seed the State law required that all imported seed be stained so that it could be identified by dealer and farmer. Red clover is the only legume field crop grown here since agriculture began, and it is still one of the most popular of the hay crops. Because red clover seed was high-priced, many farmers were forced to adopt substitutes, such as timothy, for which Iowa is today the world center. Though not a legume, timothy assists in retain-ing soil fertility.

Sweet clover, once regarded as a weed, is now recognized as one of the most valuable of legumes. An Iowan, to whom goes most of the credit for the growth of interest in sweet clover, is Frank Coverdale, who first turned his attention to this particular crop in 1900 when he began using it for bee pasture. He discovered that it had other good qualities, such as improv-ing the soil, and that it was valuable as a hay crop. Despite Coverdale's work with sweet clover, it would never have attained its present popularity had not the State agricultural experiment station perfected the huller and scarifier, which scratches the hard seed coats of sweet clover, making it possible for the seed to absorb moisture and germinate quickly.

Two other legumes—alfalfa and the soybean—have come into use

HEREFORD STEERS

within the last 25 years. In 1910 alfalfa was grown on less than 25,000 acres, practically all of which were in the southwestern part of the State. Today the production is approximately 400,000 acres a year. Since the drought of 1934 more farmers have begun to raise alfalfa, having learned that it is a drought-resisting legume. But alfalfa often receives set-backs due to excessive winter kill. Both alfalfa and sweet clover require soils that are either naturally sweet or mixed with lime. In the southern half of the State where the soil is especially acid, alfalfa and sweet clover do not thrive, and here the soybean has proved a valuable legume. Soybeans can be seeded at any time throughout a period of several weeks, with the practical assurance of a return before frost of from one to two-and-a-half tons of hay per acre. In 1937, there were 762,000 acres of Iowa land planted with this crop. In addition to the hay there is a valuable by-product in the form of soybean oil, which is extracted at several mills in Iowa.

Besides the leading crops of corn and oats, many smaller crops are raised, of local rather than State-wide importance. The potato crop is not outstanding except in a few counties which grow more than enough for their home use. Near St. Ansgar and Davenport are centers for the raising of onions. Muscatine is famous for its production of melons, and northern Iowa raises many sugar beets. A national center for popcorn is at Odebodt. Fruit growing has been successfully developed in many parts because the soil and climate are adapted to orchard trees and small fruit bushes. Apples are grown mostly for home use but there are a few commercial regions, particularly in the southwestern section. Near Council Bluffs grapes are grown. Pears, plums, and cherries thrive anywhere in the region, but are grown only for local and home consumption; peaches are grown successfully in the southern half of the State.

Not only in corn and oats does Iowa take the lead, but also in the production of hogs, fattened almost exclusively on Iowa corn. The first hogs were of the "razorback" type but, when the Iowa country began to be developed, new breeds of hogs were brought in and the original "razorback" type disappeared. The newer types were fineboned and easily fattened varieties. The first highly developed type introduced was the Chester White, followed later by the Poland China and Duroc Jersey types. From the 1850's to the present, hogs have been the major source of income. It is said that during the depression of 1857 and after, pigs saved the State from bankruptcy and enabled the farmers to pay their taxes. They are still the chief market for Iowa corn, and farm income goes up or down with the quotations on hogs in Chicago. The total number of hogs on Iowa farms, January 1, 1937, was 6,525,000. In early days corn was cheap and lard was high; consequently hogs were fed to weights ranging from 300 to 600 pounds. Today they are marketed at seven or eight months at a weight around 200 to 220 pounds. They are kept on pasture for a long time so that they will yield less lard and more meat. The hogs are vaccinated against disease, and are fed a variety of supplementary protein feeds in addition to corn and minerals.

As in the case of other livestock, the pioneer farmer did not concern himself with good breeds of cattle. A cow was a cow and purebred ones brought no more on the market than the others. Because Shorthorns were both good beef and good milking cattle they were popular. Later such breeds as Brown Swiss and Jersey were brought in. In 1936 more than three-fifths of Iowa's dairy cattle were Holsteins. On January 1, 1937, there were 4,335,000 head of cattle on Iowa farms. In the northeastern quarter, in the dairy area, much of the State's output of creamery butter (218,821,673 pounds in 1935, second only to Minnesota) is produced.

Ranking first of all States in the production of horses—there were 867,000 on Iowa farms on January 1, 1937—Iowa has been concerned with the breeding of good horses. Many noted sires of the leading draft breeds in the country came from Iowa farms, for the State ranks high in the percentage of purebred stallions. The tendency is to breed for the larger type horse. Almost every town in the State has a good-sized sales ring which does brisk business, and the annual show of Belgian horses at Waterloo is a fair of worldwide importance. The State also produces many sheep and mules. On January 1, 1937, there were on the farms an estimated 1,576,000 sheep and approximately 67,000 mules.

In the year 1936 there were 184,500,000 pounds of poultry produced from Iowa farms. Hatcheries for the production of baby chicks account for an increasingly large part of the poultry industry in the last ten years. The farm wife who used to set her hens now drives to town in her automobile and brings home the little chicks ready for feeding. The raising of turkeys has become a specialized industry, centralized on a few farms. Approximately 1,500,000 turkeys were produced in 1937.

A great amount of Iowa's foodstuffs finds easy access to outside markets at Omaha, St. Louis, St. Joseph, and Chicago. Within the State, the livestock market at Sioux City is one of the 12 in the country officially recognized by the United States Department of Agriculture. State industry also makes use of Iowa agricultural products. Not only are hogs slaughtered and processed, but dairying, cereal processing, canning, and refining industries furnish an active home market.

Racial Elements and
Folkways

IOWA'S population (estimated at 2,534,000 in 1935) is a blending of many elements, American and European. The first settlers were from the States to the East, as far away as New England, and to a lesser degree from the South. Thousands of Europeans forced to emigrate because of political unrest and hard times, were drawn to the Midwest by persuasive advertising.

The Irish who were among the first to arrive, driven from home by the famines of the 1840's, have settled mainly in the larger towns. Scotch immigrants spread throughout the Territory, but moved in large numbers to the mining towns when coal was opened up in southern Iowa. Norwegians first settled at Sugar Creek, Lee County, in 1840. The colony did not thrive, chiefly because the Norwegians were not adapted to the warm climate at the southernmost end of the State. A colony of American Fourierites, French in origin, also made an unsuccessful attempt at settlement on 320 acres of land near the present site of Oskaloosa in Mahaska County in 1843. Both Norwegian and French elements took root, however, in the late 1850's. Scandinavians—Norwegians and Swedes—settled in the western and central parts of the State, and in Jefferson County; a French group, called Icarians, came from Nauvoo, Illinois, and established the community of Icaria in Adams County. A large host of Mormons had come from Nauvoo ten years earlier, in 1846, seeking new homes. Driven first from Missouri to Nauvoo and later to Salt Lake by the antagonism of their neighbors, they established camps in the southern part of the Territory. The most important of these was Kanesville, on the Missouri River, now Council Bluffs.

German immigrants arrived in great numbers after the European revolutions of 1848 and settled chiefly along the Mississippi River. A German religious communal group, the Amana Society, set up homes in Iowa County along the Iowa River, and founded the village of Amana in 1855.

Immigrants from other European countries found hospitable welcome, spreading from county to county and adapting the customs of their native lands to meet conditions in their new home. Hollanders, led by their minister Henry P. Scholte, took root in Marion County and founded the town of Pella in 1847. Hungarians, who like the Germans fled from the European revolutions of 1848, attempted unsuccessfully to found a co-operative colony called New Buda in Decatur County in 1850. Many Jews had reached Iowa as early as 1840 and established themselves in commercial and professional fields. German Jews outnumbered those from all other countries in the early days but by 1936 most of the State's twenty thousand or so Jewish families were Russian and Polish. They, too, have gained leading places in business and the professions. The greatest concentration of Jewish population is in Des Moines.

In 1854 a small party of Danes made permanent settlement near Lucerne and later at Elkhorn. The Czechs came to Johnson and Linn Counties at about the same time and founded Spillville, in Winneshiek County. Forty years later Anton Dvořák, the composer, spent a summer in Spillville and no doubt found material here for his *Symphony from a New World*.

The peak of immigration was reached by 1890 and declined steadily thereafter. According to the United States census figures of 1930, only six percent of the total population of the State is now foreign-born. Of this, the largest number—53,901—is German. The Scandinavian countries and Denmark come next, though with much smaller numbers: 16,810 Swedes, 14,698 Danes, and 12,932 Norwegians. Iowa's foreign-born groups also include Hollanders, English, Czechs, Irish, Canadians, Russians, and Italians—their numbers descending in the order named from 10,135 Hollanders to 3,834 Italians. More than a dozen other countries are listed in the census as the birthplaces of foreign-born Iowans. Approximately a third of the foreign-born population lives in the larger cities and groups of from five to ten thousand are concentrated in each of the three cities—Des Moines, Davenport, and Sioux City.

In general, racial lines are tending to grow less distinct as the population merges into a unified whole. Enriching the culture of Iowa, many groups have retained their identity and the customs they brought with them from the Old World.

Chief among these are the Germans. Throughout the State the small German communities are held together by the Lutheran and Evangelical Churches, and the German Catholics, though associated with other racial groups in their church, tend to have their own rural and small town centers. German food, festive wedding parties, and family reunions are the rule, and in some villages and country districts German is the prevailing language. Well-defined German communities are found in Clinton and Bremer Counties and in Davenport and Dubuque. In the cities and larger towns the Germans have their *Turn Vereine* (gymnastic clubs) and their musical societies. Members of the Amana Society, particularly the older people, still cling to the old forms of dress and to German as their home tongue.

The Scandinavians, like the Protestant Germans, remain close to their Lutheran churches, and in many small communities Swedish, Norwegian, and Danish customs are common. The clean white town buildings of Pella and the well-kept farms of this district are characteristic of the Hollanders, who keep to the traditions of their fathers in these and other ways. In the Bohemian (Czech) sections of Cedar Rapids and parts of Linn County, the customs and language of the old country have also endured. The Czechs have their own banks, newspapers, doctors, lawyers, and business institutions. In the rural sections surrounding Protivin, St. Ansgar, and Calmar the observance of old customs is promoted by the Bohemian societies which provide social halls for the young people and encourage Czech folk games and music.

The Welsh, who originally settled in the coal-mining camps and are now found chiefly in Mahaska County, remain a unique group clinging to their *eisteddfods* (singing schools) and *cymanfa* (church conventions). They are naturally musical people, and many of the musical instructors in the schools throughout the State are descendants of the early Welsh settlers. There are groups of Italians and Greeks in the larger cities. In Des Moines particularly, the Italians have their own community and preserve their Old World customs. The Mexicans—a new element coming into the State—are spread through Polk, Cerro Gordo, Lee, and Des Moines Counties, with concentrated groups in Fort Madison, Mason City, and Bettendorf. Many of them work in the sugar beet fields in the northern part of the State.

Some Negroes came to Iowa in the first years after the Civil War, but the main migration of Negroes was from the South at the turn of the century. Imported by the Consolidated Coal Company to break a miners' strike near the present site of Oskaloosa, they gradually developed into a complete Negro mining settlement—the largest and best coal-producing camp in Iowa. During the World War Negroes came from the East as well as the South in search of higher wages and for military training at Fort Des Moines and at Camp Dodge. Approximately one-third of

Iowa's 17,000 Negroes live in Des Moines, where they have their own churches, restaurants, amusement centers and religious associations, and publish their own newspaper, the *Iowa Bystander*. Both in Des Moines and Sioux City the Negroes have played a creditable part in civic development. Here and elsewhere in the State they are found not only in the labor field but in business and the professions. A. A. Alexander, of Des Moines, received the degree of civil engineer from the University of Iowa in 1925, and was granted one of the two William E. Harmon Awards for Distinguished Achievement in industry in 1926—the first year these awards were made. In many towns the Negroes maintain their own churches and hotels, and take active part in the educational, religious, and political activities of the community.

Many of the existing folkways had their beginning in the house-raising, husking, hog-killing, rag-sewing (for carpets), quilting, and wood-chopping bees, which filled a need for social intercourse while serving their primary purpose of co-operation in some of the undertakings of pioneer farm life. Other customs are outgrowths of the singing schools and "spell-downs" common to all rural pioneer communities.

Farmers in Iowa assemble for many gatherings—family picnics, community celebrations, fairs in their small-town centers, and Saturday afternoon shopping. Much of the social activity is centered in the churches, and church suppers, "aids," meetings, and sociables of all kinds are festive events in any small town. The 4-H Clubs, farm bureau groups, and similar organizations foster social life.

It is in the round of farming activities, in the co-operation among neighbors, that the real Iowa folkways appear. As in most agricultural States threshing is a celebration as well as a co-operative venture. While the men work together in the fields getting the oats, wheat, barley, or rye to the threshing machine, the women gather to cook the threshing dinner. The community is likely to rate its cooks on the basis of their threshing dinners.

Community corn-picking, silo-filling, and plowing have become well established through the friendly spirit of mutual help handed down from the past. Iowa makes much of its corn-husking contests held each fall. The State contest, a picturesque event in which the county winners participate, is started by the report of a gun fired by the Governor. Crowds estimated at 20,000 follow the wagons as the huskers, bare-headed and shirtless, work down the rows of corn and send the ears flying through the air to strike against the "bang-boards." Hog-calling has been developed into another annual contest. At the State Fair each year contenders for the State title take their turn at "whoee-ing" the hogs, and the one with the most "reach" and volume to his voice wins.

The spirit that prompted the pioneer get-togethers survives today in various annual celebrations. These generally commemorate some event or tradition characteristic of the racial heritage of the locality. Thus Germans fondly remember the past when they take part in the annual celebration of Sauer Kraut Day in Ackley. The festival was first established in the late 1890's, and in 1909 the Germans of Lisbon established a similar event. Sometimes as much as 300 gallons of kraut and 600 pounds of wieners are eaten at these celebrations. During the annual Tulip Festival at Pella each May the town is transformed into a bit of Holland. People wear their cherished Dutch costumes and clop down the streets in wooden shoes; they dance old folk dances, sing folk songs, and feast on native Dutch dishes. Everywhere in Pella bloom the thousands of tulips imported from Holland. Other local events that are racial in origin are: Orangeman's Day at Deep River, held on July 12 when the North Irish assemble; and the Bohemian Fall Festival at St. Ansgar in October where many of the activities are carried on in the native tongue.

Annually in September hundreds of Negroes meet on the site of the town of Buxton in Bluff Creek Township in Monroe County. In 1910 Buxton was one of the largest coal-mining towns west of the Mississippi with about 6,000 inhabitants, 5,500 of them being Negroes. It is now abandoned, and the sites of the town's stores, churches, and schoolhouses are marked only by stakes. The Negroes in Sioux City have developed the pleasant custom of the "poor man's party" to which all the Negroes in the neighborhood come. Before the festivities are over, the "poor man" who has wares to sell has received for them cash enough to pay his rent and other bills.

The Sac and Fox Indians hold carnival with a powwow at Tama in August each year. The wikiups, tents of skins and burlap, appear on the powwow grounds, but each year the gathering is becoming more like the white man's county fair. The Indian farmers exhibit their prize ears of corn, their largest squash, and their best handicraft.

An easterner traveling through Iowa might notice the over-prominent "yah" for "yes," and other words not pronounced as they are in the East, but for the most part the speech is similar to that in other regions. Slang expressions from the cities to the East, words in the Negro dialect, and words characteristically New England are heard. "Crick" for creek, "finicky" for fastidious, "catty-cornered' for cater-cornered, "nubbins" for the small deformed ears of corn, and "lickety-split" for fast are common here.

Before radios, automobiles, and paved roads brought the farmer in close contact with the city, his human newspaper was the traveler. In common with other rural regions much of the Iowa farm lore concerns the coming of company. When the rooster crows in the doorway, or the cat licks his fur, company is on the way. The farmer knows, if he does not believe, the weather lore; and some continue to plant their potatoes, or other root vegetables, in the "dark of the moon."

Most of the folktales dealing with the Indians are lurid and romantic. The story of the Indian lovers who were refused permission to wed and committed suicide is common to many places. Local residents point out cliffs where Indian maidens leaped to their death until it would seem that the first duty of all Indian girls was to jump off cliffs. Maquoketa, for whom the river is named, is supposed to have jumped to her death, though the cliff cannot be identified. A tale, with its setting near Onawa, deals with an Indian lover who would not accept the decision of his Indian sweetheart to marry a white man. Taking the girl in his arms he leaped into the river and each year, on the anniversary of their death, the screams of the girl are heard. In the legend of Wapsi and Pinicon, for whom the Wapsipinicon River is named, the two lovers were gliding down the river in their canoe under the eyes of a rival. When Wapsi put her fingers to Pinicon's lips, the jealous lover shot an arrow into Pinicon's heart. Wapsi, rising to help him, upset the canoe and both were drowned.

Some of the legends are history retold . . . with trimmings. The stories of the naming of the *Têtes des Morts* (Heads of the Dead) River Valley are many. According to one, a battle between Indians and traders left the river filled with severed heads. Another tells of a battle between two Indian tribes in which one was forced over the bow (head) of the cliff into the river. In this version of the story, the trouble began when a young Winnebago chief fell in love with Nita, daughter of a Fox chief. Finding her with a member of her own tribe, he spat in his competitor's face; the Fox tribe wiped out the entire Winnebago group in retaliation.

The yarns of the pioneers, handed down from father to son, are tall tales such as men have always made of the adventures of earlier days. One group centers around Old Man Schoonover, who told stories to his men as they gathered at the mine shafts in southern Iowa. But no one knows Schoonover's real history and the stories of his great prowess run into endless variations. In northeastern Iowa the hunting and fishing stories spun by Old Marsh Hatfield are still repeated.

Quite different in character is the story about Sarah Bernhardt. Ever since she played in Iowa City the tale has persisted that she was born in the nearby little town of Rochester, and that Mary King, buried in the local cemetery, was her mother. The divine Sarah came (so they say) in a curtained carriage to place flowers on her mother's grave.

Transportation and Communication

IN THE decade after the first cession of land by the Indians in 1832, thousands of settlers came from the East, by way of the Great Lakes and the Ohio and Mississippi Rivers, and then overland into the Iowa country—by ox-drawn wagon, on horseback, on foot, or by stagecoach. At the Mississippi River they waited their turn to be taken across on the large steam ferries. The only roads in the new land were trails following the Indian and buffalo paths along the hilltops and watersheds, and crossing the rivers and streams at designated fords.

Waterways were at first the great transportation arteries. Instead of simple keelboats propelled by poles, paddle-wheeled steamers carried passengers and freight along the great rivers during the period of settlement. Tons of freight were frequently hauled in wagons for 150 miles to and from the river ports. Local packets, known as mail boats, carried newspapers and mail, and the sound of their whistle was as regular and familiar as the striking of the town clocks along their route.

Traffic on the Mississippi was at its height between 1819 and 1870. Many landings were established along the shore, from Lansing to Keokuk, where wood from the nearby woodlands provided fuel for the boats. A busy lumber industry sprang up after the first lumber rafts were floated down the Mississippi in 1830, and as the immigrant tide pushed steadily westward. Hundreds of stern-wheeled steamboats brought lumber on great rafts to Lansing, Dubuque, Bellevue, Clinton, Muscatine, and Burlington, where it was planed in the mills for use in the construction of houses and other buildings, wagons, and boats. The lumbering industry decreased as the northern forests were gradually depleted, and the coming of the railroads destroyed much of the commerce on the Mississippi, but river traffic continued up to the close of the nineteenth century. At one time Iowans had hoped also to develop their inland rivers for traffic but they proved too shallow.

William Bunn

THE THIRD DUBUQUE, MURAL IN POST OFFICE, DUBUQUE

When Iowa was organized as a Territory in 1838, there were no roads, and travelers following the trails were often lost on the open prairies or wandered far out of their way. The Territorial legislature in 1839 authorized the laying out of a road from Dubuque through Iowa City to the Missouri State Line. The United States Government appropriated $20,000 for this road, to expedite the movement of soldiers in case of Indian uprisings or frontier difficulties. According to the story, Lyman Dillon, under the guidance of an engineer, plowed the longest furrow on record—the 100 miles from Dubuque to Iowa City—to guide the road-builders. Dillon started from Dubuque with a huge breaking plow drawn by five yoke of oxen, and a two-horse emigrant wagon carrying provisions, cooking utensils, and bedding for the journey. Day after day the patient oxen drew the plow through the tough prairie sod, marking the path of the new road.

From river to river across the prairies and river valleys of the southern part of the State runs the old Mormon Trail, beaten by the wagons and the feet of thousands of Mormons, who fled in 1846 from the wrath of their Illinois neighbors. Similar trails were made by the Forty-niners on their way to California, one passing through Des Moines to Council Bluffs. Thousands of emigrant wagons passed over this road. Council Bluffs, where wagon trains were provisioned for the long trip ahead, grew rapidly in the early days. Stagecoaches carried passengers over the rough dirt roads, miring to the hubs in the spring mud, and taverns provided food and cheer along the route.

Until the twentieth century the State had little control of bridges or highways; the building of roads and culverts was handled by the township officers (New England township system). Later the counties assumed charge of the more important roads. Plank "toll roads" were authorized by the State legislature in 1855, but only the one connecting Burlington with Mount Pleasant was even moderately successful. A locomobile run by steam and a Haynes gasoline car, exhibited at a fair in Linn County in 1899, were the first "horseless carriages" in the State. Little permanent road improvement took place before the introduction of the automobile, but as the number of automobiles increased, the demand for good roads kept pace.

In 1904 the State legislature designated Iowa State College to act as a highway commission. A "good roads investigation" appropriation provided for the part-time services of an engineer, Thomas H. MacDonald, later head of the United States Bureau of Public Roads. About 1910 automobile owners and associations began to participate in the barnstorming meetings held by this commission to gain public support for better roads.

As a result, roads soon linked county to county, forming the River-to-River, the White Pole, the Lincoln, and the Hawkeye through-State highways. After the State legislature in 1913 established a highway commission with wide authority, the ten miles between Clear Lake and Mason City, on US 18, were paved. Federal aid for roadbuilding and the passage of the primary road law of 1919, which provided for highway improvements, advanced the cause of good roads. Five years later a paving program was inaugurated, and in 1937 there were 5,455 miles of paved highways out of a total of 102,533 miles of roads. Iowa has at last "come out of the mud."

Not satisfied with hauling their produce to market over long distances, Iowa farmers were quick to encourage the development of the railroads. The Mississippi and Missouri, the first railroad in the State, was completed from Davenport to Muscatine in 1855. By January 1, 1856, this road was extended from Davenport to Iowa City, then the State capital, and the first train puffed between the two cities even before the first bridge had been built to connect the rails with Illinois across the Mississippi. The Illinois Central from Dubuque, the Chicago and North Western from Lyons, and the Chicago, Burlington and Quincy from the city of Burlington started building their lines westward in 1855, competing with each other and with the Mississippi and Missouri to be the first to reach the western edge of the State.

A number of abortive attempts had preceded the building of these roads. In 1854 grading was begun by the Lyons-Iowa Central, which planned to run a road from Clinton to the Missouri River. But work stopped abruptly in the middle of the summer when the company went bankrupt. Wages were paid in groceries as long as the supply lasted. Then the workers who were still empty-handed took possession of the warehouse in Clinton. The company had nothing left but yards and yards of calico, and with this commodity it paid off its debts. The story of the unusual settlement spread through the State until the abandoned project was called the "Calico Road."

After the Civil War the railway network was extended with feverish haste, and expansion was naturally westward as plans for transcontinental routes were made. Iowans had watched eagerly the development of the line from Chicago to Rock Island, Ill., and had already made plans for a connecting link with this system. By 1866 the Mississippi and Missouri had been built some miles beyond Iowa City but was then forced to sell out to the Chicago and Rock Island Line. This line had completed its road to Council Bluffs two years after the North Western had reached that point in 1867. The Burlington Line stretched to the Missouri River in 1869, and a year later the Illinois Central completed its road to Sioux City. There were almost 3,000 miles of railroads in 1870. In the more settled areas in the eastern part, routes were established between small towns, each one anticipating the growth of the connected centers. In 1885 the Great Western had laid its tracks southward into Iowa from Minnesota, and the longer lines were complete for the most part at the end of the 1880's.

A number of electric railways were added later to serve sections on the north and south axis. In the southern part of the State, coal companies built lines extending the tracks into many mining towns to facilitate the marketing of coal. Today no point in the State is more than twelve miles from a railroad. The railway system consists of thirteen class-1 roads, with a total trackage of 9,517 miles. Council Bluffs on the western boundary, where some of these lines meet, is an important transfer point for transcontinental mail.

The first telegraph line was laid in the State in 1848, and in that year the wire between Bloomington (now Muscatine) and Burlington carried the first message sent through Iowa. When the news was wired to Bloomington that Zachary Taylor had been elected President, a Democrat, skeptical of the validity of telegraph messages, called it a "Whig lie" and made a bet that Lewis Cass had won. In 1877 the first telephone line was built. Today there are more than 500,000 telephones in use.

Back in 1836 there were only two post offices for the distribution and collection of mail. One of these, at Augusta, is still in operation. In 1937 post offices were established in 1,148 towns, 65 percent of them with carrier delivery. Rural free delivery was begun in 1897, when the Government established it in 44 States. In 1937 there were approximately 1,600 rural routes operating out of 828 centers on six days of the week. The average route is 40 miles long, making the total State coverage more than 64,000 miles.

In the enthusiasm for aviation which followed the World War, many Iowa communities prepared for this new form of transportation. By 1931 there were 49 registered airports, but in later years the number decreased. Iowa offers definite advantages to fliers. Because of the low flat country, planes can maintain even elevations, and there is sufficient good flying weather to permit operation the year round. Two airports in the State, at Des Moines and Iowa City (lighted for night flying), are stops on the route of scheduled plane service. The direct route of the United Air Lines, with scheduled service from New York to San Francisco, is across the lower third of the State, and is marked by radio beams and beacon lights.

STREAMLINER

The Des Moines airport is advantageously located. Its high elevation (960 feet) makes it possible to take care of all-weather landings and to stay open longer in bad weather than other Midwestern airports. A Chicago to Kansas City regular line crosses the southeastern corner of Iowa and has an emergency stop at Burlington.

One of Iowa's first aviators was William C. Robinson, who made a non-stop flight from Des Moines to Chicago in 1914; Clarence Chamberlin, born in Iowa, made one of the earliest trans-Atlantic flights in 1927. Among the first newspapers to use planes for news gathering was the Des Moines *Register and Tribune,* which began this service in 1928.

Industry, Commerce and Labor

ASIDE from the fur trade, the first business enterprise in Iowa was lead mining, begun by Julien Dubuque in 1788. Later, when financial pressure in the older parts of the country became acute, and the Iowa region was opened to settlement, settlers rushed westward to the cheap land. The original settlers were mostly people in poor circumstances. Money, indeed, was so scarce that estimates fix $1.80 as the per capita currency in 1846. The Miners' Bank at Dubuque had been granted a charter by the Territory of Wisconsin in 1836, but after investigations by the Iowa Legislature this charter was later annulled. The experience of Iowans with banks and bankers caused them to insert a clause in the State constitution of 1846, prohibiting the issuance of paper money by banking corporations. Nonresidents, however, flooded the State with wild-cat money. Those residents with money to lend often charged as high as 40 percent interest.

The new constitution of 1857 authorized the incorporation of banks and provided for a State banking system. After the panic of that year, industry began to move forward. Mining, printing, and publishing (of farm papers), meat packing, lumbering, and manufacturing found the new regulations favorable. Interested individuals were encouraged to combine their resources and develop large enterprises. The national banks, created in 1863, succeeded the State bank system, which had been in effect only a few years. Commerce continued to increase, as much because of the parallel growth of the transportation and banking structures as of the abundant sources of raw materials and available markets.

Industries often developed first to supply the farmers' needs; later they were started in order to process farm products. In the early years of farming, for example, board fences to keep wandering livestock at home often cost more than all other farm improvements. In the 1860's barbwire was invented by an Iowan to solve his own problem. Later, when the demand for it became general, several factories were started. During the 1880's

AIRVIEW, DAIRY CATTLE CONGRESS GROUNDS, WATERLOO

an eastern syndicate tried to corner the barbwire market and raise prices, but the farmers formed a protective association, manufactured their own wire, and held the price down.

This incident is fairly typical of the Iowan's attitude during the seventies and eighties toward large-scale eastern finance, especially that represented by Wall Street. The type of industries developed have usually required but little outside capital and the agriculturalists generally are inclined to view the Nation's money center with distrust.

Between the 1880's and 1933, banks extended their operations to farm financing, and the control of banking passed from individuals to State-regulated banks. Upon the establishment of land bank refinancing by the Farm Credit Administration in 1933, the absorption of farms by capital interests became less frequent. Farmers were allowed to continue on their land under interest arrangements similar to those effective with any corporation or business that operates under banking direction.

Along with the development of the banking system has come the growth of the insurance business in life, casualty, fire, and other classifications. Des

Moines, the center of the insurance business in Iowa, is also one of the largest centers in the Midwest.

One-fifth of the State's population is supported by manufacturing. In the value of manufactured products Iowa ranks sixteenth among all the States, and fifth among those west of the Mississippi. Much of the manufacturing is closely related to agriculture. Iowa hogs fattened on Iowa corn are slaughtered in Iowa abattoirs. Meat packing is a leading industry, followed closely in importance by the processing of cereals and the manufacture of grain products.

In contrast to the older practice of centralizing industry in a few large cities, most of the 3,317 manufacturing plants are established in small communities where land values and taxes are low. Two hundred towns, because of their proximity to both raw materials and markets, are the homes of important industries. Because of this decentralization, employees tend to become home owners and settled conservative residents in communities where living costs are low and social conditions generally better than in the crowded cities. The scattering of manufacturing centers is made possible by excellent transportation facilities, and the Mississippi River on the eastern boundary contributes to this primary advantage. Sioux City ranks first among the cities in the total value of its manufactured products, with Cedar Rapids second.

Industries may be generally classified in three groups: those that process farm products, those that produce goods for sale directly to farm markets, and those concerned with the extraction of raw materials. In addition there is the usual group of miscellaneous industries, including local factories that naturally develop in population centers, and others, like washing-machine and cosmetic plants, that compete in the national market.

The principal industry is the processing of farm products. Since Iowa ranks first among the States in hog raising, beef production, and the value of its livestock, its packing plants are naturally of the first importance. Annually these plants slaughter approximately 4,500,000 hogs, or about 30 percent of all raised in Iowa. Pork packing began as an industry in 1840 when J. M. D. Burrows of Davenport bought hogs from the farmers and established a "pork house." He reported dressing 19,000 hogs during the winter of 1853–1854. In 1878 a packing plant was opened in Ottumwa, and about the same time other plants were started in Sioux City. The latter has become the center of the State's packing industry and is ranked second to Chicago. Following in rank, in the value of livestock marketed, are Ottumwa, Cedar Rapids, Waterloo, and Mason City.

Trucking in Iowa began soon after 1920, with an extensive road paving program. In 1937 more than 90,000 licensed trucks were operated in the State, many by farmers who customarily haul their own cattle, hogs, sheep, and produce to the marketing centers. Regular routes have also been established by trucking companies. The large packing plants in Sioux City and Ottumwa have made these cities principal trucking centers for the livestock trade.

The State supplies, in some years, more than one-third of the national requirements of dressed and packed poultry. Since every farmer's wife has her own flock of chickens, ducks, geese, or turkeys, a network of packing plants, generally 25 to 40 miles apart, has been built throughout the State, with buying stations in most of the small towns. Statisticians credit Iowa with the production of approximately 200,000,000 dozen eggs a year. Four cities to the east—New York, Chicago, Buffalo, and Philadelphia—consume more than one-half of Iowa's eggs.

As a result of the development of dairying during the past 50 years, Iowa has become third in importance as a dairy State. Since the first creamery was established at Spring Branch in 1872, Iowa's butter, cheese, and ice cream have reached second rank among the State's manufactured products.

Many plants have been established for canning sweet corn, tomatoes, cucumbers, and beans. The value of corn products exceeds $22,000,000 annually. Two of the world's largest corn products factories are at Cedar Rapids and Clinton, respectively producing corn sugar, corn oil, and glucose, and starch and sugar. An abundant source of raw material for industry may be found in agricultural waste—mainly cornstalks, corncobs, oat hulls, and straw. Among the many possible corncob and cornstalk products only one—an insulating board—is now being manufactured in the State. The plant, in Dubuque, has a capacity of 100,000 square feet per day. The cereal industry has developed from about 600 gristmills scattered throughout the State in the early days. The Quaker Oats Company, established at Cedar Rapids in 1873, has the largest cereal plant in the world, and buys annually more than $11,000,000 worth of corn and oats from Iowa farmers.

Among the conspicuous manufacturing centers for the farm market is Charles City; from here tractors are shipped daily to all parts of the United States and the world. The largest tractor plant in the State is located at Waterloo. Supplying another farm need are the stump pullers manufactured at Centerville.

Only New York exceeds Iowa in producing plaster, tile, plaster of paris, and cement. Five gypsum plants at Fort Dodge and one at Centerville have

CEMENT PLANT, MASON CITY

a total annual production of 553,598 tons. Mason City, sometimes called "the brick and tile capital of the world," has seven plants for manufacturing clayware. Shipments from these plants have amounted to 12,000 carloads a year.

Coal mining in the southern area is one of the State's greatest industries. Much of the prosperity enjoyed by southern counties in the early twentieth century depended on bituminous coal. At one time all Iowa railroads, except the Illinois Central, depended largely on Iowa coal for their supply, and many thousands of tons were sent to Nebraska, Kansas, and South Dakota. The number of mines in operation varies from season to season; in 1936–1938 there were from 450 to 600 active mines. Coal beds in Iowa are practically horizontal and thus present few engineering difficulties for development.

The State is widely known for the manufacture of buttons; it produces about 20 percent of the Nation's total. This industry is centered in Muscatine. Formerly the Mississippi River and its tributaries yielded the clamshells from which the buttons were made, but today large supplies are imported.

When William H. Voss invented a washing machine at Davenport in 1877, he contributed the basis of a famous Iowa industry. Of the washing-machine factories at Newton, one of the centers of the industry in the United States, one alone supplies a third of the national market. At Bettendorf the makers of railroad equipment—steel freight cars and various supplies—dominate the Davenport industrial area. One of the largest calendar factories in the world is located at Red Oak, which is also an important center for advertising novelties. At Iowa City an advertising company issues more than 2,000,000 calendars a year. The fountain pen industry of Iowa began in 1913 in a back-room workshop in Fort Madison. A cosmetic plant, opened in Des Moines in 1915, has grown to international proportions.

The woodworking industry in Iowa grew up around the sawmills in many of the river towns. When this business declined, the mills were put to work planing lumber for doors, window frames, molding, and other parts. Ready-cut lumber for houses is planed in Davenport and furniture, caskets, and baskets are manufactured in Burlington. The growth of such an industry in a State without extensive timberlands is unusual, but it has been justified by the necessity of keeping factories close to the market.

Men who have taken a leading part in Iowa commercial life include George W. Douglas and Robert Stuart, who in 1873 brought the Scotch process for making oatmeal to Cedar Rapids; John H. Morrell, founder (1878) of the packing company at Ottumwa which bears his name; Frederick M. Hubbell, prominent in the development of Des Moines; Fred L. Maytag, of Newton, who began to manufacture washing machines in 1900; and W. A. Sheaffer, of Fort Madison, who established his pen company in 1913.

The scattering of people in towns and small cities has exerted a significant influence on the organization of labor in Iowa. Except among the miners, who began to organize as soon as their industry developed, there has been little unionization among workers. The primary reason is the character of industry, which generally exists in small units throughout the State. It is true, also, that the farmers have wielded the largest single influence on economic and political life, and their individualistic philosophy is reflected in the opinions of many workers. Labor has been reluctant to organize, and, until after the World War, was largely out of contact with the labor movement.

In 1867, while the miners were laying plans for their first formal organization, the Des Moines Cigar Makers' Union was organized. The Typographical Union followed in 1868. By 1876 the Knights of Labor had penetrated Iowa, and five years later they were included in the Des Moines Labor Assembly. In 1885, when the Knights were achieving national importance, there was a membership of 25,000 in the State, mostly of miners. This group was responsible for the first effective mine regulation, which became the basis for all later legislation in that field. In the period after the Civil War, the Granges were organized (1868), and it was this group that forced passage of laws regulating railroads and conditions of railroad labor. The Knights supported this group and the Anti-Monopoly Party.

The rise of the conservative and efficiently managed craft unions coincided with the decline of the Knights of Labor. When the American Federation of Labor was formed in Iowa in the convention of 1893, the Knights became practically non-existent. The miners, always a highly organized group, entered the A. F. of L. Although the International Workers of the World never gained a foot-hold, in the winter of 1914–1915 great numbers of them came in from the wheat fields to the west and invaded Sioux City. "Big Bill" Haywood, speaking under the protection of the Mayor—and with two guns strapped to his legs—was not able to win any substantial following for his organization.

In 1937 the Committee for Industrial Organization became active in the State. It succeeded in organizing many unorganized groups of workers, mainly in the utilities, meat packing, and light industries. The State branch of the American Federation of Labor, with a membership of approximately 20,000 has pursued a general policy of friendship and co-operation with the C. I. O. This has been true especially among the rank and file.

As elsewhere in the Middle West, the organization of farm labor along union lines has made little progress. A start in this direction in the State is to be seen in the Bee Workers Union, organized under the American Federation of Labor.

The first labor legislation to concern Iowa people was the Mechanic's Lien Law of 1813, passed by the Territory of Michigan, of which Iowa was a part from 1834 to 1836. In 1838, a more inclusive act on the same subject was passed by the Territory of Iowa, becoming its first important labor legislation. Revised in 1876, these laws safeguarded the laborer who had no contract for the collection of his wages and placed a lien on the employer's property if the wages were not paid.

As early as 1872, before labor was effectively organized, the miners were able to obtain the passage of laws to regulate mines and mining. When the Knights of Labor came to power, more regulations of the kind were enacted, the most important of them in 1874 and 1884. Provisions were made governing safety exits, the use and storage of explosives, ventilation, illumination, timbering, and liens for wages; and forbidding the employment of women and children in mines. The Knights of Labor also worked for the establishment of the Iowa Bureau of Labor Statistics (1888).

Railroad legislation to protect lives and change working conditions came early. The great number of deaths and injuries caused by hand coupling induced the General Assembly in 1890 to require automatic couplers on the cars of all companies operating in Iowa. Deaths and injuries declined, and the Iowa law became a model for Congressional legislation three years later.

The American Federation of Labor's legislative committee successfully sponsored several important laws. These protected laborers in the collection of their wages, provided for the inspection of illuminants used in mining, and obliged the certification of mine foremen and hoisting engineers. In 1902 a State Factory Act was passed; two of its provisions forbade the employment of women and children in dangerous occupations, and forbade any female under 18 years of age, or anyone under 16 years, to clean machinery in motion. In 1907, when investigation showed that engineers on the railroads were often forced to work continuously for as many as 57 hours, a Federal law was passed making 16 hours the maximum straight shift, with at least 10 hours off duty before a return to work. Subsequent legislation in the early part of the twentieth century restricted convict labor, and provided employers' liability and workmen's compensation laws (1913), in which Iowa was a pioneer.

Legislation against child labor has progressed slowly. Children on the farm have always been considered a necessary supply of labor. Employers in an attempt to void a State law were found at one time to have made parents sign agreements waiving all compensation claims for injuries. In 1904 a bill was introduced in the legislature to curb the evils of child labor, but it was defeated. One potent argument held that children released from factory toil would indulge in idle pastimes, and the fight against child labor on humanitarian grounds thus lost itself in a maze of moral wrangling.

Some employers, however, found telling economic reasons that proved effective against the practice. In 1906, when another bill was presented, they testified that they didn't "want the babies. They don't watch their business. . . ." The law of 1906 prohibited children under 14 years from working in any mine, shop, factory, or slaughter house employing more than eight persons, thus making concessions to the farm family of laborers who might be of any age. No one under 18 was to be employed in any dangerous capacity. Along with this came compulsory education laws that materially lessened the problem.

As early as 1851 a general conspiracy law, aimed at the labor boycott, prohibited any act which might be held injurious to the person, character, or business of any citizen. But formal recognition of trade unions and their right to organize and function was made in 1886. In 1888 the practice of blacklisting was forbidden, and treble damage was allowed any employee who was dismissed or forced to quit on grounds of unfair discrimination. A loophole was left, however, by the provision that the employer could send a record of the employee's service to the next employer. In 1912 a board of arbitration was appointed to settle disputes and prevent strikes and has functioned successfully on the cases placed in its hands. The major strikes in the coal-mining, railroad, and packing industries in 1921–1922 brought little violence or destruction of property.

During the country-wide "red scare" in 1919, a criminal syndicalism bill was added to the section dealing with treason. It carried sentences up to 20 years for "any person who, by word of mouth or writing advocates . . . crime, sabotage, violence, in accomplishing industrial or political re-form . . ." Under its terms, two or more people constitute a meeting and the landlord or custodian letting premises for such purposes is held guilty of misdemeanor. This law remains on the statute books, but has not been invoked in recent years.

In the general section dealing with treason and incitement to violence, and with hostility or opposition against the Government of Iowa or the United States, similar penalties are provided. The display of a red flag, banner, pennant, or badge is construed as inciting to insurrection and an insult to the United States flag.

These laws were invoked and enforced against several members of the International Workers of the World, but in the past few years they have been disregarded, and have had little effect on the organization of unions.

Religion

ROMAN Catholic priests were the first missionaries in the Iowa country, preaching among the Indian tribes as far west as the Missouri River, years before a white settlement had been made. Notable among those of the pioneer days was the Italian Father Samuel C. Mazzuchelli, a Dominican, who visited Dubuque in 1835. The people asked that he be assigned to their territory. In that same year he built St. Raphael's church, the first Roman Catholic church in Iowa. Until the time of his death Father Mazzuchelli worked among the white settlers in the Mississippi River towns, establishing churches—often designing them himself—and carrying on the duties of a priest. In 1837 Pope Gregory XVI created the diocese of Dubuque in the Territory of Wisconsin and appointed Mathias Loras as bishop. The Belgian priest, Father Pierre Jean De Smet, went among the Indians in the western part of the Iowa region, and in 1838 founded the St. Joseph mission for the Pottawattamie Indians at the present Council Bluffs. From his mission he worked among all the western tribes. His *Letters and Sketches,* and other accounts of his travels, have been widely read both in Europe and America. The Indians, holding him in high esteem, showed their affection when they said, "He is a white man who does not have a forked tongue," meaning he never lied to them.

As early as 1833 Methodist missionaries had been sent to the settlements of Flint Hills (Burlington) and Dubuque. Barton Randle, a circuit rider, wrote in that year, "We crossed the Mississippi River at the northwest corner of Illinois, went into Dubuque, and in the same evening of the day preached in the tavern of Jesse Harrison." The following year the first church of any denomination in Iowa, a log cabin 20 feet wide and 36 feet long, was built by the Methodists at Dubuque with the help of Irish, French, Dutch, and Negro contributions, and all religious denominations were free to hold meetings in the building, which also housed several courts. Another early church, the site of which is now occupied by a theater, was Old Zion in Burlington, where the first Iowa Territorial Legislature met in the fall of 1838. Barton E. Cartwright, the first Methodist missionary in the southern area, divided his time between preaching and breaking the prairie sod to raise food for himself, since he took no collection and received no salary.

The Methodists, together with the Presbyterians and Baptists, gave to Iowa the revival and camp meetings which were so popular among the pioneers. Many people who attended the camp meetings, held in a grove or by a spring or creek, pitched their tents and stayed a week. They brought cooking utensils, food for themselves, and fodder for their horses. Exhortations were furious and arguments were often prolonged, but this period of relaxation from everyday drudgery was as much social as it was religious in spirit.

By means of the circuit rider and the revival, the Methodists were able to cover the entire settled area, and to acquire many new members. The Iowa Conference had grown to such an extent by 1856 that it was necessary to divide the territory. An imaginary line was drawn across the State from east to west, beginning at Davenport, thus forming the Upper Iowa Conference. In 1860, the Methodists, with 344 congregations, led the religious denominations in Iowa.

The Reverend David Lowry, a Presbyterian minister, appointed teacher of a Government school for the Winnebago Indians, traveled to the headquarters on the Yellow River in northeastern Iowa in the spring of 1834. In the fall of that year the Yellow River Mission was completed but, even before this, what is said to be the first communion service in Iowa was held. Later, in 1837, a church was established at West Point and, in 1843, one at Round Prairie (Kossuth Church). Though most of the townspeople at West Point were from Kentucky and not in sympathy with the "blue nosed" Presbyterians' ideas of temperance, they were anxious to sell their lots. A barbecue was promoted to help the sale. To the surprise of all, the Presbyterians collaborated, acquiring ground for a church and parsonage, which later was occupied by the Reverend Launcelot Bell. The Presbyterians founded several colleges, one of the first being Parsons, at Fairfield (1875).

Baptists arrived as early as 1834 and organized the Long Creek Church at Danville. The first Iowa Baptist convention met in this church four years later, with nine of the ten delegates sitting in a row on a log while the moderator stood before them. The Society of Friends (Quakers) has held an important place in Iowa history since 1835, when Aaron Street founded Salem, the first Quaker settlement. Fifteen years later there were thirteen similar settlements. These people, noted for their piety and pacifism, promoted the Underground Railroad for escaping slaves, and aided John Brown in his work. The house in which John Brown's men spent the winter of 1857–1858 is still standing at Springdale.

The Congregational denomination was established also largely under the direction of missionaries, usually young men graduates of eastern colleges and theological seminaries, who organized churches, held meetings, and promoted temperance and education. The Reverend Asa Turner was the leader in this work, coming to Iowa in 1836 and settling in the town of Denmark. In 1840 a convention met here and organized the association of Congregational ministers "in and for the Territory of Iowa."

Students of Andover Theological Seminary began to make inquiries about this Mississippi River Valley as early as 1842. In reply to a letter of inquiry, the Reverend Asa Turner answered for Iowa, "Lay aside all your dandy notions which boys learn in college and take a few lessons of old farmers or grandmothers. The people will not call you Reverend Mr. B. but simply A. B. and your wife Polly or Peggy, or whatever her name may be." The result of the interest of these students was the formation of the "Iowa Band," originally composed of 12 college men, of whom 11 came to Iowa to found churches, schools, and colleges. William Salter, who came with this group in 1843 and preached at Burlington for many years, was also one of the State's leading historians.

In 1836 the Disciples of Christ were organized in Lee County and built a church at Lost Creek just outside of Fort Madison. A second church, built on this site in 1849, is still standing, preserved in detail inside and out as it was in pioneer days. In Davenport, the Disciples of Christ met in a carpenter's shop for almost a year. Having outgrown these quarters, the congregation decided in 1839 to send representatives to confer with Antoine Le Claire, founder of the city. Le Claire, it is said, had the habit of wearing his hat in a low forward position when his temper was bad. The two delegates waited before calling on Le Claire until a time when his hat was perched jauntily on the back of his head; their request for a lot was quickly granted. On this lot, the Disciples erected a meeting house which cost about $300.

The Protestant Episcopalians, never a large group in Iowa, came as early as 1837, and held, as one of their first services, an outdoor meeting in Davenport. At their first convention, assembled in May 1854, the Reverend Henry Washington Lee was made first bishop, a man six feet tall and weighing more than 300 pounds. It is said he met with many mishaps in traveling about the diocese—breaking carriages on the road, and chairs and bedsteads in the houses where he was entertained. In those days no one dared call his church a "cathedral" since that suggested the papacy; so it was spoken of as the Bishop's Chapel.

In the 1830's the progress of the churches was slow. Itinerant work was retarded by the long stretches of prairie between the small settlements. There were rivers to ford, and often blizzards and snow-blocked roads impeded travel. The *Home Missionary* magazine, in August 1842, stated that there were not more than 2,133 professing Christians in a population of 60,000. By 1840, however, both Protestant and Roman Catholic churches were well established. An unorthodox group settled in Van Buren County near Farmington under the leadership of Abner Kneeland, a free-thinker, but this group dissolved after Kneeland's death in 1844.

Changes in church constituencies after 1840 were caused chiefly by the great influx of immigrants from Europe. One of the first groups to arrive was that of the Hollanders who came to Pella in 1847. Under the leadership of Henry P. Scholte they established their Dutch Reformed church in a sod house on the prairie. The following spring they built a log church and inscribed above its door *In Deo Spes Nostra et Refugium.*

With the great immigration from Germany during the last half of the nineteenth century, the Lutheran Church began to predominate. Although Germans had arrived here before this time, they were mainly absorbed by the established religious groups. In 1854 the German Iowa Synod began at St. Sebald, near Dubuque, under the leadership of emissaries from the church in Germany. The American Lutheran Synod in the same year established one of the outstanding theological seminaries in the United States— the Wartburg Theological Seminary at Dubuque. The Evangelical Lutheran Synod was founded the following year. When Danes, Swedes, and Norwegians began to arrive in Iowa in the period following the Civil War, the number of Lutherans again increased.

The churches were pioneers in building hospitals, some of the first having been erected by Catholic orders. The Iowa Christian Home, under the care of the Protestant Episcopal Church, was established in Davenport in 1864 as a hospital for the sick and needy, irrespective of religious belief. The Sisters of Mercy opened a hospital in the same city in 1869. In the next decade they opened a hospital at Dubuque. Methodists, Presbyterians, and Lutherans followed with the founding of more hospitals.

From the time of the first settlements the church has furnished the meeting place for many of the social affairs of town and country; the box and pie suppers, the bazaars, the ladies' aid society meetings, the potluck suppers, and the church party or social. In many communities the only outlet

PIONEER ROCK CHURCH, NEAR GUTTENBERG

for musical expression is in the church where choirs and orchestras are conducted. Many a talented farmer's daughter, or small-town girl, has first been heard at the organ or piano in the church. Dramatic talent, too, is developed through plays produced in the various departments.

The present (1938) church membership, numbering approximately one-half of the population, is led by those of the three largest denominations —the Catholic, the Methodist, and the Lutheran—with congregations in all counties. Almost one-fourth of the entire membership is Roman Catholic. Northeastern Iowa, as well as the towns along the Mississippi River, has a high percentage of members of this church body. The organization consists of three dioceses and one archdiocese, at Dubuque. The Methodists, with three conferences, remain the strongest Protestant group. All the counties in the northern half of the State are strongly Lutheran. Established by Germans, Danes, Swedes, and Norwegians, who predominate in this large farming area, the churches are for the most part in the small towns and rural districts.

The Presbyterian denomination numbering about one-eleventh of the total church membership, and the Baptist probably rank next in point of numbers. Congregationalists, Universalists and Unitarians are mainly urban groups, remaining close to the centers where the New England founders lived. Likewise the large Jewish congregations, both orthodox and reformed, are in the large cities, particularly Des Moines and Sioux City.

The two important denominations among the Negroes are the Baptist and the Methodist, although there are several Lutheran congregations under Negro pastors.

There is a marked tendency toward consolidation among the smaller church groups, and an indication of union among the larger ones. Especially in the rural areas, where more than half the churches are found, consolidation has been necessary. This consolidation is generally along interdenominational lines. From 1926 to 1934 the community church had its greatest growth. With the extension of improved roads, city churches also have drawn great numbers from rural congregations, thus hastening the decline of the isolated country church.

Education

"THAT the people do not feel that their efforts to establish an ideal educational system have been entirely successful is evidenced by the frequent legislative bills introduced to amend school laws." This comment, taken from the report of an investigation of rural child life made by the Iowa Child Welfare Research Station (1930), prefaces a description of the complex school system. But it is noted in the report also that Iowa "has tried to develop an educational policy to fit the peculiar needs of an inland agricultural people."

Free tax-supported schools were legally authorized in this area while it was still a part of the Territory of Michigan, and later of the Territory of Wisconsin. In 1840, after the formation of the Territory of Iowa, a law was passed that defined the means of establishing free schools. This Territorial law, which has affected all subsequent legislation, was copied almost word for word from the educational statutes of the State of Michigan.

Private schools, however, preceded the establishment of public institutions. A private school, credited as the first one in Iowa, was opened in 1830, in the Half-Breed Tract, now Lee County. Here in a log cabin provided by Isaac Galland, Berryman Jennings taught the settlers' children how to read and write. Another early school was taught by George Cubbage at Dubuque in 1833. When Iowa was made a Territory in 1838 more than 40 schools had been established. Almost a century later, the lowest percentage of illiteracy in the Nation—eight-tenths of one percent—was Iowa's.

The present educational system from elementary schools up to the State University of Iowa, is based upon a law passed by the State legislature in 1858. The imprint of the famous educator, Horace Mann, a member of the educational committee, is in this law, for many of his recommendations were incorporated. Supervision of the public schools has passed through various changes, but the present office of superintendent of public instruction, an elective State office which today supervises and controls all the public schools, has been in continuous existence since 1864. The examination for teacher-certification is controlled through a State board of educational examiners of which the State superintendent is chairman.

The first law making education compulsory was passed by the General Assembly in 1902; subsequent legislation has extended the period of school attendance to 24 consecutive weeks every year for children between the ages of seven and sixteen. Part time schools were provided for by law in 1919 for children between 14 and 16 years old who are employed.

The principal unit in the school system is the school district. This may be a school township, a rural independent district, a consolidated district, or an independent district of a town or city. Voters of these districts choose the members of the school board, or board of directors; rural districts choose three, districts in towns or villages and second-class cities and consolidated districts choose five, and districts in first class cities and in cities under special charter choose seven. Each board elects its own officers—except school treasurers, who are elected by the voters of the district—levies taxes, engages teachers, pays its own bills, and, in general, controls the operation of the schools. The county superintendent of schools, under whose direct supervision the schools are operated, is chosen for a three-year period by the presidents of the schools boards in his county.

Rural education, an important factor in the system, developed more slowly than education in the cities, though the State department is attempting to equalize advantages, and has laid much stress on the rural system. In 1937 there were 9,119 country schools. The plain white schoolhouses appear along the roadside at regular intervals, two to four miles apart. Ten to twenty farm boys and girls sit on the benches inside.

But the standards of instruction and curriculum are higher than those of the rural school of twenty years ago. In all the 99 counties the "superior school" movement, with standards for country schools to meet, has aroused community interest. The office of State superintendent awards scholarships to rural students; standards of teacher-certification have been raised; and health education has been encouraged among rural children. The buildings and equipment likewise have been improved, and many new buildings have been constructed with ample lighting, heating, and sanitary facilities. Teachers in these schools receive their normal training in one of the State colleges or in one of the 170 high schools carrying a teacher training course.

Another important movement is for the replacement of several one-teacher schools with one modern building. The consolidated school district is restricted to certain limits by law; it may include an incorporated town

CAMPUS, STATE UNIVERSITY OF IOWA

as well as country districts. Children in such districts, living outside an incorporated town, and more than one mile from the school, travel daily back and forth at public expense. Both the elementary and the secondary grades are usually taught. This kind of school with its larger number of pupils can offer better facilities for teaching and recreation. All the advantages of a city school are thus brought to the rural districts. There are more than 400 consolidated school districts in Iowa, including approximately one-fourth of the total area of the State. A high school education with free tuition is made available to boys and girls in all districts where there are no high schools by a law requiring the district to pay their high school tuition in a neighboring district.

The David W. Smouse Opportunity School in Des Moines was one of the first (1931) public schools of its kind in the United States, a special public school for children whose physical condition prevent them from attending the ordinary school. The stairways, the special ramps, and the elevators at the Opportunity School fit the needs of handicapped children. Activities in the corrective gymnasium, the physiotherapy room, and the hydrotherapy tank often so improve the students' physical condition that they are able to return to their own district's public school. State schools are provided to meet the needs of the deaf and the blind—the Iowa School for the Deaf at Council Bluffs, and the Iowa School for the Blind at Vinton.

In high school teaching, emphasis recently has been put on vocational guidance. Boys and girls are taught sewing, manual training, and trades. Associated with the office of the superintendent of public instruction is a board of vocational education, established (1917) to meet the requirements set down by the Federal Government in the Smith-Hughes Act. Agricultural, trade and industrial, and homemaking education offered to regular high school students, part-time high school students, and adults is supervised by this board.

During the last twenty years, supervision of the study of students has been considered as important as supervised class recitations. Development by means of visual education is sought through motion pictures, lantern slides, stereopticon views, newspapers, and visits to industrial plants and other points of educational interest. Pre-school development and adult education are receiving increased attention.

Since the first public junior college was established in Mason City in 1918, the number of two-year colleges, usually operating in the established high school buildings, has increased until Iowa in 1937 with 27 in operation ranked second only to California. For the year ending June 30, 1936, the total enrollment of pupils in the elementary schools, high schools, and public junior colleges was 538,003, with an average daily attendance for the year of 456,226. The number of teachers employed was 25,106.

The Iowa State Teachers Association first convened at Muscatine in 1854 at the call of D. Franklin Wells, who was then in charge of a school in the village. Wells, who served twice as president of the association was made head of the normal department at the State University in 1856, and later served as State Superintendent of Public Instruction. In November of each year this association meets in Des Moines with as many as 21,000 teachers enrolled. A comprehensive institute is conducted by national leaders foremost in their fields. The association's journal, *Midland Schools,* provides material for teachers for improving the curriculum and instruction.

So that the parents of school children may meet the teachers of their children and become acquainted with the work in the public schools, the Parent-Teachers Association has been formed. Parents and teachers meet— usually monthly—at the school where programs are provided for their instruction and entertainment. Through this group funds are raised for needy children and recommendations for better teaching offered.

Under the State board of education, distinct from the office of the superintendent of public instruction, are the State schools of higher learning, the School for the Blind and the School for the Deaf. Established in 1847, the State University at Iowa City began instruction in 1855. Today more than 50 buildings are grouped around Old Capitol, the first capitol building, which was turned over to the University when the seat of government was moved to Des Moines.

Iowa State College of Agriculture and Mechanic Arts at Ames was established by law in 1858 but was not ready for students until 1868. Today this is one of the outstanding agricultural and engineering schools in the Nation, with some 70 buildings and more than 1,900 acres of land. The extension service, offered through printed matter, radio broadcasts, and home demonstration agents in home economics, reaches all parts of the State.

Iowa was a pioneer among the States in this co-operative extension service between farm and college. In 1866, Seaman Asahel Knapp came from New York State to Iowa, and later, as professor of agriculture and president of the State College at Ames, advocated connecting the experiment station with the colleges. Iowa people were active in the movement which culminated in the passage of the Smith-Lever Cooperative Extension Act in 1914; this act, accepted by all the States, released Federal funds to land grant colleges for the establishment of extension departments and for carrying on work in connection with the United States Department of Agriculture. A regular extension department, provided for by the State legislature, had been established at Ames in 1906, with the same rank as other college departments. Professor G. B. Holden was made the first superintendent of extension.

In 1876 the Iowa State Teachers College was founded at Cedar Falls on the site of a home for the orphans of Civil War soldiers. Today the campus extends over an area of 127 acres, near the southern limits of the city. Homer H. Seerley, appointed in 1886, and president for more than 40 years, was a particularly important figure in the development of this school.

There are 198 public libraries under supervision of the library commission, which is made up of the State librarian, the superintendent of public instruction, the president of the State University, and four members appointed by the Governor. Miss Julia A. Robinson, secretary of the commission since 1913, edits (1938) the *Iowa Library Quarterly,* a journal devoted to news, selected book lists, and various aids to librarians. A State traveling library, from which books are lent to schools where libraries are not available, to communities without public libraries, to small libraries, to clubs, to organizations, and to individuals, sent out more than 115,647 books in 1935.

In Des Moines, experiments in adult education have been carried out successfully. John W. Studebaker, superintendent of the public schools, and later (1938) United States Commissioner of Education, organized evening neighborhood forums in 1936–1937. Financed by donations and by funds from the Carnegie Foundation, speakers were presented who talked on economic and social problems. Special night classes were arranged and youth forums were organized. Continued as a civic function, under a council representing all civic and educational agencies, this plan of adult education has been an example and inspiration for similar plans in other localities.

Before publicly owned educational institutions had been established, the churches maintained elementary and secondary schools and also founded several schools of higher education. Iowa Wesleyan College at Mount Pleasant is the oldest college in Iowa, having a continuous history from the time it was founded as Mount Pleasant Collegiate Institute in 1844. The college has always been under the control of the Methodist Episcopal Church, though it has allowed students of any denomination, or of none, to enter. It was at this college that seven girls organized the P. E. O. Sisterhood in 1869, the meaning of the initials always being kept a secret.

Grinnell, a Congregational college, was founded by the "Iowa Band" (a group of young ministers who came to Iowa as missionaries in 1843) as Iowa College at Davenport and opened to students in 1848. A few years later the college was moved to Grinnell. At Mount Vernon, home of Cornell College, there is a legend that a Methodist circuit rider, one day in 1851, arriving at the top of a hill, stopped his horse and viewed the landscape. Realizing what an ideal site the place would be for a college, he knelt in prayer and dedicated himself and the hill to the cause of education. The following year at a Fourth of July celebration, plans were made for the erection of a seminary, and in 1853 the school was opened. The Chicago Symphony Orchestra annually presents a musical program at the spring music festival here, in collaboration with the music department of Cornell College.

Other colleges were established by the Methodists: Upper Iowa University at Fayette, Simpson College at Indianola, and Morningside at Sioux City. The Roman Catholics founded Clarke and Columbia at Dubuque, and St. Ambrose at Davenport. The Presbyterians established Parsons at Fairfield, Coe at Cedar Rapids, the University of Dubuque at Dubuque, and Buena Vista at Storm Lake. Central College at Pella was established by the Reformed Church. Luther College at Decorah was founded under the auspices of the Norwegian Lutheran Church of America in 1861. The Luther College Band and Schola Cantorum have toured the United States; the former has twice played in Europe. Another feature of Luther College is the museum of Norwegian-American history. William Penn College, established by the Iowa Yearly Meeting of Friends (Quakers), opened its first term in 1873 in Oskaloosa, where there was a settlement of Quakers.

Graceland, at Lamoni, is under the control of the Reorganized Church of Jesus Christ of Latter Day Saints; Western Union, at Le Mars, of the Evangelical Church; and Wartburg College, at Waverly, of the American Lutheran Church. John Fletcher College, at University Park (Oskaloosa), interdenominational in character, offers studies in the Bible and training for religious workers. One of the large privately endowed colleges is Drake University, at Des Moines. Established in 1881, it was named for Francis M. Drake, a former Governor.

Social Welfare

THE picture of how Iowa cares for its children and its aged, its criminals and delinquents, those handicapped by physical or mental ill health or by economic disaster is a mingling of light and dark; no general rating of the State's work in social welfare is possible, for in many branches it excels and in some, unfortunately, it falls below the average.

The National Society of Penal Reformation, in its 1928 survey, gave Iowa high ranking in the treatment of criminals and in general prison reform. The hundred years of prison history which began with the establishment of a prison at Fort Madison in 1839 have been marked by steady advance in this field. The directors of the first prison were authorized by the legislature to place every person "now convicted or hereafter . . . in the confines of this place, and to cause to be employed in the erection of the penitentiary, all such persons sentenced to hard labor." When the public realized that prisoners were crowded into small quarters and that violent punishment was used to control the unruly, a committee was appointed by the Territorial legislature to investigate (1845) and a serious study of the prison situation was undertaken. But other evils soon appeared. The contract system, now generally condemned by prison authorities, prevailed in the State from 1854 to 1915. Furniture, clothing, shoes, and other commodities were manufactured by prison labor. The need for improvement in methods of handling criminals was recognized as early as 1869, however, when George Shedd was sent East to make a thorough study of prisons. The foundations of the present adequate penal system were laid with the establishment of a board of parole in 1907. The abolition of the contract system came next (1915) when the legislature substituted a program of State-use industries under which prison labor, on the farms and in the shops, was used to supply the needs of all State institutions.

The penitentiary at Fort Madison, frequently rebuilt and enlarged, is today modern both in its physical plant (which includes a hospital, library, school, power house and machine shop) and in its treatment of inmates. Other penal institutions in the State include a reformatory for men at

Anamosa, opened in 1873; the women's reformatory in Rockwell City, which conforms to the standards of modern penology and is managed without bars, walls, or guns; the Eldora training school for boys and a similar school for girls at Mitchellville, both of which emphasize education and rehabilitation rather than punishment.

Iowa's enviable record in the care of criminals and delinquents is not duplicated in the field of public health. The State department of health was created in 1880, "with supervisory power over public health activities and legislative authority to make and enforce rules concerning contagious disease, quarantine, and health."

The activities of the department fall into two main groupings: Public health work—consisting of venereal disease control, child health and health education, public health nursing, State hygienic laboratories, vital statistics, epidemiological investigations, and public health engineering; licenses—consisting of licensure (by examination and reciprocal State agreements) of physicians, dentists, osteopaths, nurses, embalmers, etc., registration and renewal of licenses, and law enforcement. A three-point criticism of public health work in Iowa has been made by recognized authorities. First, the licensing activities of the State department use too large a proportion of time which might better be employed to develop the inadequate nursing, vital statistics, and epidemiological divisions. Second, the present set-up, with 2,528 independent local government health units (918 cities and towns and 1,610 townships) does not permit well-knit and smooth functioning of health work in the State as a whole. Third and most important, Iowa's appropriations for public health work are far too meager. Dr. Walter L. Bierring, health commissioner, makes this clear in his *Report of State Department of Health,* for the biennial period ending June 30, 1934.

"Basic elements of a preventive health service," he writes, "can be obtained for the average Iowa community for an expenditure of 50 cents per capita, and for state public health administration 10 cents per capita is regarded as a minimum requirement. In Iowa at the present time the annual per capita appropriation for the work of the State health department is less than 3 cents, the lowest of any state in the Union; while that for local boards of health does not exceed 10 cents. This is one of the main reasons for the low fundamental basis on which public health work is carried on in Iowa." It should, however, be pointed out that these expenditures are for supervisory activities and do not represent all of Iowa's public health work. For example, many schools, cities, and counties provide nurses; medical and surgical care of indigent persons is given in State or other hospitals at the expense of the counties. Both the general death rate and the infant mortality rate in Iowa are below those of the United States as a whole.

The University of Iowa Hospitals at Iowa City, with general services established in 1898 and a children's hospital added in 1919, is the largest hospital in the State and is recognized as one of the country's great medical centers. The bacteriological laboratory, serving the State department of health, does diagnostic work of higher quality and greater volume (hence more useful) than that of most States. Included in the set-up of the hospital is one of the largest dental clinics in the world (180 chairs) where dental students give treatment to thousands of patients at fees covering only the cost of material.

Provisions for hospitalization in the State seem far above the average. The 181 hospitals have a combined bed capacity of 8 beds for every thousand population in contrast to the recognized standard for general hospitals of 4.6 beds for every thousand population. Only 61 percent of hospital beds were occupied in 1936—which may point to the need for more free care or to the wisdom of diverting funds now used for hospital maintenance to other health work.

The seven mental hospitals caring for the insane, feebleminded, and epileptics, present a different picture. Recent studies show that these are filled to capacity; in fact three report that they are from thirty to fifty percent overcrowded. The first hospital for the insane was established at Mount Pleasant in 1861. Within the next twenty-five years institutions were opened at Independence, Clarinda, and Glenwood, the last being for feebleminded children. There is also a hospital for the insane at Cherokee and a hospital for epileptics and school for feebleminded children at Woodward. The counties still take care of many of the less serious cases in the county homes (poor farms), a questionable procedure from the point of view of prevention and cure. Signs of more enlightened methods are to be found in the fact that persons whose insanity is caused by drugs or alcohol were sent to prison prior to 1902, but are now treated in hospitals for the insane; and in the establishment of the Psychopathic Hospital as part of the University of Iowa Hospital system in 1919.

In its work with children, Iowa has been progressive on all fronts. The first child labor law was passed in 1897, forbidding the employment of any child under fourteen years of age in coal mines. The law also prohibited children under twelve from even entering a coal mine. In 1906 the law was widened to prohibit the employment of children under fourteen in mines, factories, and similar establishments where eight or more persons were employed. No child under sixteen was to be employed at work dangerous to safety, health, or morals. These and additional laws have done much to eliminate child labor. Employers have helped by setting high educational standards for their workers. Boys and girls are required to have a grammar school, or in some instances a high school education, and are thus encouraged to remain in school.

Under the leadership of Cora Bussey Hillis, Iowa established the first child-welfare research station in the United States (1917) at Iowa City. As stated in the legislative act, its purpose was to investigate the best scientific methods of conserving and developing the normal child, to disseminate information, and to train students for work in such fields. Dr. Amy Louise Daniels, one of the country's leading dietitians, is in charge of the nutrition department, which undertakes special research and study in foods and nutrition, and trains nutrition specialists. The three State schools—the University, the College of Agriculture and Mechanic Arts, and the Teachers College—are co-ordinating centers for child study and parent education. Field laboratory work is carried on through the organization and guidance of groups of parents and workers with children. Radio broadcasts, bulletins, and pamphlets are used as media of information. The children's division of the University of Iowa Hospitals, already mentioned, does special work in orthopedics, particularly in bone diseases, under the direction of Dr. Arthur Steindler, noted orthopedist. Funds are provided by the State, counties, and various agencies for those unable to pay and ambulances bring patients from all parts of the State. Children were the first to be admitted to the university hospitals at public expense, but this provision was later extended to needy adults.

A home for orphans was established in Davenport soon after the Civil War and similar shelters were opened at Glenwood and Cedar Falls. The Davenport home still cares for orphan and neglected children and a second orphanage was established at Toledo in 1921.

In the field of recreation, a number of organizations provide camps for under-privileged children. Especially noteworthy is the Des Moines Salvation Army camp on the Des Moines River, where mothers and children from the city are given summer outings lasting one or two weeks. Many of the larger cities have Boy Scout, Girl Scout, and Camp Fire Girl camps subsidized in part by municipal community chests. In Des Moines, civic and fraternal organizations provide "campships" for boys and girls who cannot pay their own expenses. For the young men and women outside of the public schools' control, both the Young Men's Christian Association and Young Women's Christian Association offer residence and employment services, and opportunity for social, educational, and recreational

activities. For many years the indoor swimming pools owned by these organizations were the only ones available.

Since Territorial days and for some time thereafter, the granting of relief to the poor and, for the most part, to the aged was a function of
county government. Because the problem was not then acute, State-wide
plans were not considered necessary. Homes or county farms were opened,
some public financial help was given, and private citizens struggled along
with the problem of caring for their needy neighbors, raising funds by
collections. The first move in caring for those in need, along lines other
than purely local, was when the legislature provided money for the erection of the Old Soldiers' Home at Marshalltown (1887). All soldiers
legally resident in Iowa and honorably discharged from the Army are admitted, in some cases with their aged wives, if unable to support themselves.

But in the late 1920's hard times hit the Iowa farmer and the urban
people dependent on his prosperity. The bureau of social welfare of the
University of Iowa recognized that professional measures were needed and
pointed out that public welfare activities should be unified under the direction of one trained person. Some counties responded in part by employing social welfare workers and county nurses. In the fall of 1931 the
Governor recognized that an emergency existed and that an effort must be
made to co-ordinate welfare activities in the various counties, but the State
assumed no financial or legal responsibility at that time. Counties were
given flour, milled from grain surpluses purchased by the United States
Government in the summer of 1932, and provided emergency relief in the
form of food, clothing, rent, light, medical services, or cash. Red Cross
units also furnished clothing. By the end of 1932 half of the counties were
no longer able to meet the needs of their unemployed. Six months later
the Federal Government authorized the Reconstruction Finance Corporation to make loans to the States for financing their relief operations. The
Iowa Emergency Relief Administration began action under the direction
of the Federal Emergency Relief Administration in June 1933.

Today, in Iowa as in the rest of the country, the unemployed are cared
for by the Works Progress Administration and other work programs, by
general relief, and (for young men) by the Civilian Conservation Corps.
The special problems arising from farm tenancy and soil impoverishment
and how they are being solved is discussed in another section of the Guide
(see Agriculture and Farm Life).

Up to 1934 the problem of the aged had been met to some extent by
providing care in county poor farms. The first step towards a better solution was taken that year with the granting of old-age pensions to needy

persons over 65, not in public homes. One of the qualifications imposed by the law was that the applicant "has no child or other person responsible under the law of the State, and found by the board or by the commission able to support him." The next step was the State's law for old-age assistance as provided by the Social Security Act (1936). Figures issued by the Federal Social Security Board show that in January 1938 there were 45,440 Iowans over 65 years of age receiving old age pensions; this number represents 209 out of every thousand persons in this age group in the State.

A State board of social welfare was created in 1937, with similar boards co-operating in the counties, to administer the Federal funds made available to Iowa under the Social Security Act. In addition to old-age assistance, laws covering unemployment compensation, aid to the blind, and aid to dependent children have been enacted and approved.

Sports and Recreation

IN THE days before extensive settlement, sportsmen from the East came to the prairies in great numbers for the wild game and fowl that hid away in the tall grasses or frequented the lakes and sloughs. As the prairie sod was turned and settlement advanced, this great supply of wildlife decreased and many species disappeared altogether. Today the best hunting is in the autumn, when frequently an open season is declared for the colorful ring-necked pheasant, an introduced game bird that provides the best wild-fowl hunting in the State. The best hunting for ducks and geese is along the marshes of the boundary rivers. Rabbit hunting (either jack or cottontail) is good in the northwestern part, though the smaller rabbits can be hunted any place in Iowa.

Fishing grounds for select game fish are hard to find. In the streams throughout there is some fishing for catfish and carp; and there is trout fishing in northeastern Iowa, where the streams are clear and cool. In general, the northern lakes provide the best fishing.

Every year thousands of persons visit the lake region in the northwest. Lake Okoboji and Spirit Lake, the largest and most popular waters, offer a diversified program of recreation. A line of steamers operates on the lakes, making regular trips to all parts; and numerous launches are available for pleasure rides or trips. Swimming, boating, and fishing attract vacationists in the summer to the cottages along the water's edge. One town, Arnolds Park, is a city of cabins and summer homes, dance halls, concessions, and amusement features. With special sections set off by the State for game and natural preserves, the lake region offers every form of sport and recreation.

At many of the larger river towns along the Mississippi, at Davenport, Muscatine, Keokuk, and Dubuque, daytime or moonlight boat excursions are provided during summer months. The vacationist at McGregor will find opportunity for trips up the Mississippi River through scenic and historic country. Canoeing is popular on the rivers of eastern Iowa and tours of two and three days' length are often organized.

The building of the Davenport Dam on the Mississippi River has

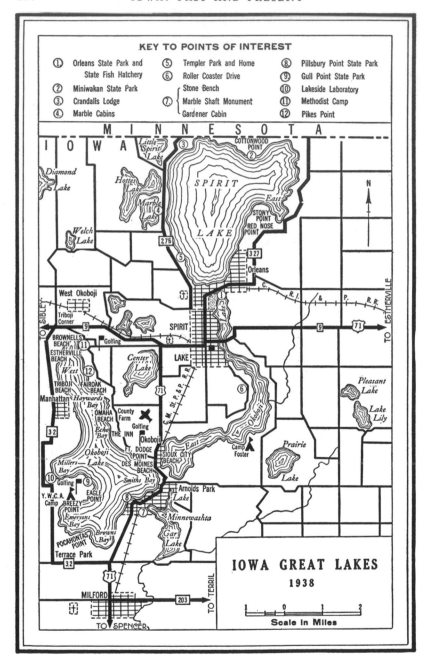

KEY TO POINTS OF INTEREST

① Orleans State Park and State Fish Hatchery
② Miniwakan State Park
③ Crandalls Lodge
④ Marble Cabins
⑤ Templer Park and Home
⑥ Roller Coaster Drive
⑦ Stone Bench / Marble Shaft Monument / Gardener Cabin
⑧ Pillsbury Point State Park
⑨ Gull Point State Park
⑩ Lakeside Laboratory
⑪ Methodist Camp
⑫ Pikes Point

IOWA GREAT LAKES
1938

Scale in Miles

created a lake of 6,000 acres. The Mississippi between Davenport and Le Claire was difficult to navigate because the river flowed over a series of limestone ledges. After the completion of the dam, these rocky reefs were deep beneath the waters of a lake, which forms one of the finest motorboat race courses in the country, and is a center of activity in winter as well as in summer. Back of the Keokuk Dam is a similar lake.

The northeastern region locally known as "Little Switzerland," the roughest part of the State, is one of outstanding natural beauty. Here the bluffs on the Mississippi River rise to a considerable elevation, and many are wooded with native timber. Hiking is popular from the time the willow unfolds its delicate green in the spring until the flaming red haw drops its fruit in the fall. A wildlife school is held during August on McGregor Heights.

Within the last 25 years the State has set aside some 18,500 acres for park areas and recreational grounds. Backbone, the oldest of the 72 State parks and preserves, covers more than 1,000 acres. Three have been named for men whose work in the establishment of these parks was of major importance: John F. Lacey, United States Representative from Iowa (1889–1907); Louis H. Pammel (1862–1931), professor at Iowa State College; and Thomas H. Macbride (1848–1934), of the State university. As in many other parks in Iowa that lack a natural water area, an artificial lake has been created at Macbride Park. Free camping grounds and facilities are available for tourists, and many natural trails for hikers. Some of the State parks enclose historic sites and features of geological or botanical interest.

Enjoyment of what is essentially Iowa is to be found along the side roads, taken in a quiet leisurely way. Here the wild grape and elderberry drop their fruit almost into the wagon tracks, and hawthorn with its red apples colors the scene in the autumn. On the less-frequented lanes the woodchuck and cottontail rabbit venture boldly along the ditches, and the timid yellow warblers and other attractive birds fly through the bushes. Here, too, is the best chance to view the farmer's cornfields and meadows, and to converse with him behind his horses.

Among athletic sports, baseball has been a popular game since its introduction after the Civil War. Today many towns have baseball teams, and hundreds of people play kittenball (soft ball) in the evenings in electrically lighted fields. Also from the informal Sunday afternoon baseball game in the back pasture there has come a highly commercialized sport. Charles W. Williams established the kite-shaped race track just outside of Independence.

TROTTING RACE, STATE FAIR

High schools, academies, colleges, universities, and social groups have teams of swimmers, wrestlers, baseball players, football players, basket ball players, and track and field men. Some colleges have introduced fencing, hockey, and rowing. There are State tennis tournaments, and some of the colleges have tennis teams. Golf receives State-wide attention; nearly every town has its country club that supports a golf course, and the State tournament held each summer is an important affair.

The Drake Relays, held annually in April at Des Moines, is the State's most popular athletic event and one of the most prominent track and field meets held in the United States. Founded by John L. Griffith, commissioner of athletics of the Big Ten Conference (1938), the first meet took place at the old Drake University Stadium in 1910. Since that time the "classic" has steadily grown in size and popularity. Two thousand five hundred athletes were entered in the meet in 1936. Covering a period of two days, the event is held in the stadium, which was built as a natural amphitheater to seat almost 20,000.

Many of Iowa's early settlers were Germans who brought their *Turn-*

vereins to the State. The Bohemians developed *sokol* clubs. Doubtless these influenced other Iowans to take up gymnastics, and almost every school and college has made physical training a compulsory course. In consolidated schools, girls and boys go through setting-up exercises; practice tumbling, trapeze work, and rope climbing; and train for basketball, even though they must go home at night and milk cows. In March of every year high school boys' and girls' basketball teams gather at Des Moines to compete in the annual State contests. Because the games represent the final achievements in winter sports and are participated in by teams from the smallest town to the largest city, they draw thousands of people.

Horseshoe contests are held in the smaller towns on holidays, and elimination contests for the State and Midwest championships run for days at the State Fair. Professionals make it their business to win, and old timers object to being matched with them; they want the $500 in prizes to go to amateurs only, who declare they play only for fun. Among Iowa's three world champions in this sport is "Putt" Mossman (1928), a Midwest barnstormer who gives exhibitions of his skill at small town celebrations, county fairs, and tournaments. He won the National at Minneapolis (1924), at St. Petersburg, Florida (1925), and at Chicago (1926). Motorcycle stuntriding is Mossman's sideline. Several Iowa players make their livelihood by exhibition and tournament play, appearing in the Midwest in the summer and in California in the winter.

Forty years ago the young people entertained themselves indoors with parlor games—post office, wink-on-the-sly, and spin the platter—but today they look for entertainment at the movies and band concerts; the dance hall, pool hall, and beer parlor also displace the home to some extent. Checkers, however, is still a popular game, and even the farmers have adopted bridge—once considered an evil pastime.

Press and Radio

Newspapers

THE *Du Buque Visitor,* published by John King at the Dubuque lead mines in what was then the Territory of Wisconsin, continuing from May 11, 1836, to June 3, 1837, was the first newspaper in Iowa. King brought a Smith hand press from Ohio for his paper. Later he sold his press, and the first newspapers of Minnesota and South Dakota are said to have been printed on it. In the State historical museums of both States is a small machine asserted to be the *Visitor* press.

The second newspaper, established by Dr. Isaac Galland (1837) at Montrose, called the *Western Adventurer,* lasted nine months; then the machinery was sold to James G. Edwards, who moved it to Fort Madison. He made his newspaper an organ of the Whig party, called it the Fort Madison *Patriot,* and in an early editorial proposed that Iowans take the name Hawk-eyes, a suggestion which won immediate favor. During the Territorial years, 24 newspapers were started, only ten of which were still in circulation when Iowa became a State in 1846. One of these, the *Territorial Gazette and Burlington Advertiser* (1837), is now the Burlington *Hawk-Eye Gazette* and the oldest paper in the State. In 1851 Daniel S. Curtis, writing his emigrant guide, *A description of Wisconsin, Illinois and Iowa with remarks on Minnesota and other territories,* listed more than 30 newspapers, mainly in the towns in the eastern and southeastern areas.

Early newspapers bristled with information about politics, business, improvements, religion, education, and social life in the hundreds of communities. Although news items appeared intermixed with advertisements, the editorial was the important feature. Early settlers freely criticized political and personal opinions that did not coincide with their own. The main purpose of publishing a newspaper was to support the policies of a political party. Denunciations directed against policies of legislators concerning such matters as contracts for legislative printing and the chartering of banks often led to fist fights. The duels of words continued long after the political issue was settled.

Typical was the verbal battle between two editors in Iowa City, when the capital was situated there—a battle not confined entirely to words, since the two once met in the capitol and caned each other soundly. Ver Planck Van Antwerp, known as the "General," called the rival paper of the young Whig, William Crum, a "Whiggery Humbug." Crum came back at the Democratic *Capitol Reporter* with the epithet "Loco-foco Rag," and declared Van Antwerp's "longwinded speeches are as frothy as beer and as empty as his head." "Contemptible slang-whanger of the 'Standard,' " was Van Antwerp's reply.

When pioneer editors were not casting verbal stones at each other, they praised nature, boasted about community progress, urged people to be honorable and temperate, and worried about their own finances. In winter the wind blew through the cracks of the frame buildings, filling type cases with snow and almost freezing the printers' fingers. Summer droughts, spring floods, and loss of credit delayed shipments of paper from St. Louis and Chicago. Publication days had to be postponed, and sometimes an issue was skipped. Subscribers were often "frozen assets," and early editors had to admonish them continually on the matter of unpaid bills or the practice of borrowing their neighbors' papers. Anything might be accepted in subscription payment, from grain to old clothes. An Iowa City newspaper in the 1840's listed wood, flour, tallow, lard, and honey as negotiable for the payment of subscriptions. "It is the height of folly," declared one printer, "to tell an editor to keep cool when he has to burn exchange papers to keep warm." Often the editor gathered up his meager equipment, moved to another town, and began again.

Advertising in the papers of the 1840's offered a buggy for hire at a dollar a day, "invariably cash in advance." A husband proclaimed himself not responsible for his wife's debts, and a society of women asked for quilts for the needy. One "master" offered a dollar reward for "George . . . a boy about 18 years, small size and spare made, and supposed to be lurking about Iowa City." The boy was an indentured apprentice and people were cautioned not "to harbor or trust . . . on my account."

The busy period of settlement and development (1836–1860) was a time of mushroom newspaper growth, but 118 of the 222 newspapers established were discontinued after a brief existence. By the time of the Civil War the press had grown in power. Editors were appointed postmasters for their political efforts. Equipment was being improved; steam presses replaced the old hand press. The traveling printer with his "shirt tail full of type" became more settled in his ways and more permanent in his residence.

In 1856 the Free Soil *Iowa Citizen* was established in Des Moines and, on January 9, 1860, it became the *Iowa State Register,* under the editorship of Coker F. Clarkson. James S. Clarkson, his son, became editor after 1870, and the Republican editorial page of his paper became a force in the State's political history. Clarkson's editorial style was partisan and personal. No retreats were ever sounded. The election of William B. Allison as Senator in 1873 was a victory for Clarkson. It is said to have made him the undisputed leader, and the *Register* the recognized organ of the local Republican Party. Loyalty to James G. Blaine was one of his obsessions, and, in 1884, Clarkson was so reluctant to concede victory to Grover Cleveland that mobs threatened to burn his building.

John P. Irish, who assumed the management of the Iowa City *Press* in 1864, worked to reform the partisan character of school boards and secured additional endowment funds for the State university through editorials in his paper. In Sioux City, George D. Perkins established the *Journal,* a paper which did much to mold public thought in northwestern Iowa.

The number of newspapers increased with the population, until in 1907, the hightide year, there were 934 newspapers, or one to every 2,366 persons. The Des Moines *Register* was still the chief political force. James S. Clarkson's paper supported—in some cases discovered—many men who later won prestige and power in national affairs. In the first years of the twentieth century his protégés, Senators William B. Allison (1873–1908) and Jonathan P. Dolliver (1900–1910), Secretary of Agriculture James ("Tama Jim") Wilson (1897–1913), and Secretary of Treasury Leslie M. Shaw (1902–1903), were powerful in Washington. At that time Iowans presided over five important Congressional committees. It became a popular saying of those times that a man who had Iowa on his side could get whatever he wanted in Washington. Clarkson suffered his first major defeat on the issue of railroad rates, when he favored the railroads and fought reforms. He wrote in his paper that "the attempt to confiscate railroad property and to disregard the rights of absentee holders retired the strong men of Iowa to the rear, and brought to the front smaller men than I had supposed Iowa could produce."

Joke-loving editors of the first years of the twentieth century perpetrated several of Iowa's most notorious hoaxes. Lurid tales described a monster, seven feet tall and eighty feet long, that could be killed only by a cannonade with kegs of railroad spikes. Stories were published about it in the Oskaloosa *Herald* and widely circulated before the hoax was exposed. Editor Bailey, of Britt, staged another hoax in 1900 that brought reporters from all over the United States. He announced a Hobo Convention, with glowing tales of the "Knights of the Road." When the reporters were unable to find any hoboes at the convention, they passed the hoax on to the public, writing fanciful accounts that were widely printed as the truth. The publicity actually established an annual convention of hoboes, who meet each year at Britt and elect a king.

Today the most attractive features of the weekly newspaper are the columns of social news and the so-called "personals." Income is derived to a great extent from the publication of official notices of local governmental bodies. Cooking schools, newspaper weddings, and special editions are established methods of increasing circulation. The old personalized treatment of news, characteristic of early country journalism, has almost disappeared. Many of the editorial pages are written in a matter-of-fact style— often syndicated material that is the same in all papers.

Editors of the new generation concern themselves more with the promotion of community activities than with the making of virulent personal attacks, so common in early newspapers. Occasionally, however, editorials are directed against conditions which the editor believes to be contrary to the public welfare. In 1936, for example, Verne Marshall, editor of the Cedar Rapids *Gazette,* was awarded the Pulitzer Prize for service in promoting law enforcement in the State.

The Traer *Star-Clipper* was voted the best weekly newspaper in the United States by the National Editorial Association at its 1927 convention in Omaha. The association, meeting at Los Angeles in 1932, made the same award to the Storm Lake *Pilot-Tribune.* In 1930 and 1933 the *Pilot-Tribune* received the Best Front Page award. The Spencer *News Herald* won first prize in 1935 for general excellence among weeklies. The Guthrie Center *Guthrian* in 1936 won first prize for community service rendered by a weekly. The Sheldon *Mail* received first award for the best use of illustrative material in 1937. E. P. Chase (1879–   ), of the Atlantic *News Telegraph* (daily), won the Pulitzer award in 1933 for the best editorial of the year.

The Des Moines *Register and Tribune* convenes its carrier-salesmen annually. This paper was one of the first in the Midwest to introduce a carrier system that required boys to promote circulation as well as to distribute papers. Jobs depend on the ability of the boys to meet circulation quotas.

The Iowa Press Association, founded in 1915, maintaining headquarters in Des Moines, and the Iowa Daily Press Association, founded in 1921, keep members informed as to the latest journalistic ideas and trends. In 1936 approximately 2,500,000 Iowans were served by 568 newspapers. Of these 47 were dailies, 13 semiweeklies, 508 weeklies, one semimonthly, and six monthlies. Three foreign language papers are published weekly: the Davenport *Iowa Reform,* in German; the Cedar Rapids *Listy,* in Bohemian; the Decorah *Posten,* in Norwegian. One semiforeign paper, the Schleswig *Leader,* has one page in German. There are 13 labor papers published, most of them representative of single editorial viewpoints rather than organizational policies. More than 20 newspapers and magazines are published by religious institutions to serve the needs of their special denominations.

Radio

Radio station WSUI, at the State university, began its regular broadcasts in 1919 as one of the first in the United States to broadcast educational programs. The second commercial broadcasting station licensed in the United States, and the first west of the Mississippi River, was WOC of Davenport (1921).

Today (1938) there are 11 commercial and four educational stations, ranging from one of 50,000 watts (WHO) to the small 500-watt station, as well as police and aviation broadcasting stations. WHO, Des Moines, went on the air in 1924; but with the mushroom growth of countless stations throughout the country, reallocations had to be made in 1928 which resulted in pairing WHO with WOC. This grouping continued until 1930, when the two stations were synchronized and operated under one owner, B. J. Palmer of Davenport. For years radio broadcasting in Iowa was led by these two stations. In March 1933, however, they were separated again and WHO has now the only clear channel in the State.

In 1924, Henry Field of Shenandoah began putting on the air, over KFNF, his old-time fiddlers, choir singers, and evangelists until today he sells everything from "prunes to silk stockings" through radio sales and advertising. In some years this commercial station has done a business of $500,000. So popular did this station manager become that, in 1932, he was nominated for the office of United States Senator, reviving the old-time torch-light parade as part of his campaign.

Norman Baker of Muscatine began broadcasting from his radio station KTNT a reputed cancer cure, which the American Medical Association did not accept. On June 5, 1931, after a long siege in the courts, the Baker station was ordered by the Federal Radio Commission to cease broadcasting.

When lack of school funds brought about a public school holiday in Des Moines during January 1933, the commercial radio station KSO in the city co-operated with the city board of education and the teachers to broadcast daily lessons to the school children. For one week, or until the classes in the schools were resumed, children in grades ranging from kindergarten through the last year of high school received their lessons by air.

At the Iowa State College of Agriculture (Ames) WOI broadcasts weather and market reports received over a wire directly from Washington. It also provides short courses and lectures on phases of agriculture for the benefit of the farmer. The university station at Iowa City, WSUI, has a television studio where interesting broadcasts are given. This university was the first in the United States to offer a regular course in radio broadcasting.

Literature

WITHIN the last twenty-five to fifty years young men and women, seeking fame and freedom from the commonplace, have retraced the footsteps of the pioneers; leaving behind them the peace of country living, they have dared the sophistication and metropolitan indifference of New York, some stopping first in Chicago and others detouring through London and Paris. As courageous as their forefathers, many left the security of a job on a Cedar Rapids, Davenport, or Des Moines newspaper and sought the wide—if not too open—spaces of the literary and artistic world. They took with them vitality, knowledge of their own country ("regionalism"), perspective, and sometimes wisdom.

That the West and the Middle West furnished to the already crowded East an unbidden company of would-be writers is not in itself important. More significant are the traces to be found in their work of day by day companionship with "the sky so high and the horizon so low . . . the tender plants and the shining flowers" (Hamlin Garland). But the real contribution lies in their preoccupation with immediate problems and everyday living, particularly that of farm and small town people, in these United States—a preoccupation actuated by desire for wider spiritual horizons than those of their early environment. Like the writers from the South—Wolfe, Faulkner, Caldwell, and others—they may be said to have given a new groundwork to American writing; they have helped to release it from dependence on European patterns, and to build instead an indigenous literature.

Iowa has high rank as the birthplace or early home of recent and contemporary writers, although many have traveled so far afield it is possible that few readers think of them as Iowans—Thomas Beer, Ellis Parker Butler, Marquis Childs, George Cram Cook, Paul Engle, Arthur Davison Ficke, John T. Frederick, Susan Glaspell, James Norman Hall, Harry Hansen, Josephine Herbst, Emerson Hough, MacKinlay Kantor, Honoré Willsie Morrow, Ross Santee, James Stevens, Phil Stong, Ruth Suckow, Carl Van Vechten, Margaret Wilson. Others not native to Iowa but associated with the State through their life or their work came there from neighboring, and similar, States—Nebraska, Illinois, Wisconsin, Ohio, Missouri—thus sharing somewhat the same physical and mental environment. In this sense Hamlin Garland, Alice French (Octave Thanet), Herbert Quick, Floyd Dell, Albert Shaw, and Edwin Ford Piper are important figures in Iowa literature.

Often the titles chosen by Iowa writers directly or subtly refer to their home country: *Main Traveled Roads* (Garland), *Country People* (Suckow), *Farmer in the Dell* (Stong), *Barbed Wire and Wayfarers* (Piper), *Frontier Life* (Hough), *Black Soil* (Donovan), *State Fair* (Stong), *Iowa Interiors* (Suckow).

In imagery and metaphor as definitely as in subject matter and title they reveal deep consciousness of country living. This is the more striking when found in unexpected places. The anthology, *New Oxford Poetry 1936*, reprints two excerpts from *Break the Heart's Anger*, written by Paul Engle, the young Iowa poet (then in residence at Oxford, England). It is unfair to quote so briefly from this fine poem but a few lines will show Engle's irremovable memory of the farm:

> It is better now
> For all to wander
> From auto and plough
> Through clay or sand or
> Loam where are
> No men, and eyes
> Need not bother
> To watch the paid
> Hands of a man
> Betray another
> Or be betrayed.

Sensitive love of the land marked one of the earliest authentic pieces of Iowa literature, the autobiography of the Indian chief Black Hawk, which was dictated in 1833 and turned into English by the interpreter Antoine Le Claire, an Iowan of French and Indian blood. "My reason teaches me," said Black Hawk, "that land cannot be sold. The Great Spirit gave it to his children to live upon, and cultivate, as far as it is necessary for their subsistence; and so long as they occupy and cultivate it, they have the right to the soil. . . . Nothing can be sold but such things as can be carried away."

During the period of settlement, 1833–1883, source material for literature was being stored up in the form of notes, diaries, letters, amateur histories, and reports of pioneer meetings; and long before the treeless prairie and the early settlers themselves were gone, the work of preserving these documents had begun. The State Historical Society of Iowa, since its establishment at Iowa City in 1857, has collected and published the annals of the State, both in its quarterly and monthly magazines and in numerous bound volumes and pamphlets. Many other books valuable as history and often as literature have been published by the Society *(see Bibliography)*.

Frequently these are reminiscences or accounts of picturesque periods such as Cyrenus Cole's *I Remember, I Remember* (1936) and William J. Petersen's *Steamboating on the Upper Mississippi* (1937).

The first comprehensive history of Iowa was presented in four volumes in 1903 by Benjamin F. Gue, at one time editor and publisher of the *Iowa Homestead*. Two years later (1905) William Salter published his little volume, *Iowa: The First Free State in the Louisiana Purchase*.

Not until the last decade of the nineteenth century, when the pioneer period was slipping out of memory, when industry and agriculture were well established and many towns had grown up, did Iowa writers begin to produce work that was to have important effect upon national literature. Davenport, a large river town, became a center because it offered the stimulus of a remarkably cosmopolitan outlook and, perhaps most of all, because it happened to be the birthplace or home of many talented men and women.

Alice French (Octave Thanet) wrote of the Davenport of that time in *Stories of a Western Town* (1893). Born in Andover, Massachusetts, in 1850, Miss French spent most of her life in Davenport, and her work reflects the lively intellectual atmosphere of the town. A characteristic that was to mark most of Iowa literature was evident in her first sympathetic stories of village and small-town life in the Middle West. A long novel, *Expiation,* was published in 1890, and *The Missionary Sheriff* in 1897. Concern with the common people brought her, in her later novels, to serious treatment of the problems of capital and labor, and in the use of this material in the form of fiction she was a pioneer. *The Man of the Hour* (1905) is a notable example.

Hamlin Garland began in this same period his realistic re-creation of the development of Iowa and the Middle West—"the first actual farmer in American fiction." He was born in Wisconsin in 1860 but moved with his family from Minnesota to Iowa in 1868 and graduated in 1881 from Cedar Valley Seminary at Osage. *Boy Life on the Prairies* (1907) is a sincere and vivid account of his experiences as a farm boy "on the middle border." In 1884 Garland abandoned a claim in Dakota and went East to write, but in 1893 the West called him back. His early stories gave a bitterly honest account of the hardships of life in the Midwest (*Main Traveled Roads,* 1890) and set a new standard of realism in the treatment of American farm life on the frontier. Though the lash and sting of his earlier work is largely lacking from his best-known book, *A Son of the Middle Border* (1917), it contains some of his finest writing and depicts without bias the period following the Civil War.

Perhaps the best interpretation of pioneer life in Iowa before the Civil War, when the plow had just begun to break the ground, is in Herbert Quick's novel, *Vandemark's Folly* (1922), the first of a trilogy dealing with Iowa life through the early 1890's. Born in Missouri in 1861, Quick —like Garland—began life as a farm boy, but his native interests led him to law and literature. In Iowa he taught school and practiced law. He helped edit *LaFollette's Weekly* for a time, and then became editor of *Farm and Fireside.* He saw groves of trees, plowed fields, and towns replace the prairies, "once a land of unbroken sky line with no object in sight taller than the yellow blossoms of the compass plant." His trilogy tells the story. *The Hawkeye* (1923) followed *Vandemark's Folly* with a dramatic description of Iowa life between 1857 and 1885. In the third book, *The Invisible Woman* (1924), Quick gives a realistic picture of rapid development, with its attendant political corruption, in northwest Iowa during the boom days of the 1880's and early 1890's. *One Man's Life* (1925), an autobiography, in a measure rounds out the story of pioneer Iowa.

The Covered Wagon (1922), an epic of the Oregon Trail of 1848, gave Emerson Hough (1857–1923) an enormous audience. While faithful in historical detail, Hough idealized the pioneer and "the gaunt and sad-faced woman sitting in the front seat of the wagon . . . her head hidden in the same ragged sunbonnet which has crossed the Appalachians." The *Story of the Cowboy* (1897), *54–40 or Fight* (1909), and *North of 36* (1923), as well as *The Covered Wagon,* set a pattern for many imitators.

Meanwhile several of the outstanding members of the Davenport group were in New York, taking part in the restless experimental movement sometimes called the "renascence of American literature."

In 1915 a little theater began in Provincetown, Massachusetts, which was to have profound significance for American drama and literature in general, and which was to discover one of the foremost modern playwrights—Eugene O'Neill. The moving spirit of the Provincetown Players was George Cram Cook (1873–1924), "whose devotion to the playwright remained one of the guiding principles. . . . The old timers do not agree on Jig Cook's qualities as a thinker or an artist, but all remember him as the unifying force of those early days" (*The Provincetown,* by Helen Deutsch and Stella Hanau, 1931). Cook wanted to present plays by American playwrights, and to give free play to the creative and experimental spirit. Above all he had the rare gift of inspiring others. Susan Glaspell (1882–   ), his wife, with O'Neill, were the two leading playwrights. The Provincetown presented plays by Floyd Dell, who had been part of the Davenport group, and a guest performance of *Mr. Faust,* by Arthur Davison Ficke, another Davenport writer.

Cook found his ideal in the early Greek, but, with all his wide knowledge of the world literature, he was rooted in Iowa and dreamed of returning to "make Davenport another Athens." In Iowa he had been a professor at the State University, a market farmer, and a writer; he had gone to Chicago as literary editor of the Chicago *Evening Post,* and from there to New York. In 1922 he went with Susan Glaspell to his beloved Greece to spend the last two years of his life among the peasants of Delphi, and there he is buried beside the Temple of Apollo.

It is difficult to discuss the work of Cook apart from that of his wife, as he did his best writing in collaboration with her. Two of their most popular plays are the one-act *Trifles* and *Suppressed Desires.* His own favorite was *The Spring,* a full-length play of great originality on the theme of reincarnation with its setting in Iowa. *The Athenian Woman* is an original treatment of the Lysistrata story. Perhaps his best-known novel is *The Chasm* (1911).

After the death of her husband, Susan Glaspell returned to Provincetown and wrote *The Road to the Temple* (1926), the story of Cook's life and, in part, of her own. She wrote several novels before beginning her important work as a playwright, notably *The Glory of the Conquered* (1909); and, in later life, *Brook Evans* (1928), a poignant recollection of her early background, and *Fugitive's Return* (1929). *The Inheritors,* a full-length play indicting the war spirit and set in a Mississippi river town, was given by the Provincetown Players in 1921; and *The Verge,* an experimental play on the theme of insanity, in the same year. In 1930 Miss Glaspell won the Pulitzer Drama Prize with *Alison's House,* based on the life of Emily Dickinson.

The Provincetown group produced several of Floyd Dell's plays (1916–1918): *King Arthur's Socks, A Long Time Ago,* and *Sweet and Twenty.* Born in Barry, Illinois, Dell worked for a Davenport newspaper for a time, going from that to the position of literary editor for the Chicago *Evening Post,* and then to New York as managing editor of *The Masses.* *Moon-Calf* (1920), a partly autobiographical novel, is the story of a schoolboy, factory hand, poet, and cub reporter in the river towns of the Middle West; the city of Port Royal is Davenport. His *Little Accident* was one of the popular plays of 1928. A valuable contribution to literature is his all-English text of Burton's *Anatomy of Melancholy,* edited with Paul Jordan Smith (1927).

The realist tradition was carried on by many of the Iowa exiles, particularly Ruth Suckow, Josephine Herbst, and Phil Stong. To many who have never known the prairies, Miss Suckow's *The Folks* (1934) has given an explicit and detailed picture—the corn fields, the spare rooms and the parlors, the churches, and—with deep understanding—the folks of Iowa. The strong and stoic quality of farm life, and the younger generation's revolt against it, are clear in this honest and memorable novel, as in most of Miss Suckow's work—*Iowa Interiors* (1926), *Country People* (1924), *The Odyssey of a Nice Girl* (1925), *The Bonney Family* (1928), *Cora* (1929), *Children and Older People* (1931).

Josephine Herbst, who was born in Sioux City, is a realist of a somewhat different order, looking farther back into the past and more widely around the world. In 1937 and 1938 she reported conditions in Germany, Cuba, and Spain for the New York *Evening Post* and *The Nation.* Her earlier short stories and novels—*Nothing Is Sacred* (1928) and *Money for Love* (1929)—deal with the frustrated ambitions and difficult lives of middle-class people, especially the young who seek a more satisfactory world. The trilogy which will be completed with *Rope of Gold* (to be published in 1938) is considered her most important work as a novelist. The earlier volumes, *Pity Is Not Enough* (1933) and *The Executioner Waits,* are concerned with the economic pattern of everyday life, and are marked by irony and bitter truth.

Phil Stong, formerly a columnist for the New York *World* and now living in Connecticut, draws on Iowa life for his masterly farmer portraits. *State Fair* (1932) brought him to the attention of critics who found in his robust, straightforward story of his own people a good example of native literature. He writes without affectation or moralizing about a way of life that he knows. In *Buckskin Breeches* (1937) Stong returned to the pioneer theme.

MacKinlay Kantor, known in the State as "a born story teller" and one of its most accomplished writers, uses historical material, but not alone that of the early West. *Long Remember* (1934), a history of the Battle of Gettysburg, is an attempt to recapture the events that Lincoln believed would outlive in man's memory his own great address on the battlefield. The novel was one of the three books by American writers submitted for the *Prix Femina* American Award. A briefer story, *The Voice of Bugle Ann* (1935), was extraordinarily well received.

The romantic historical tradition was continued by Honoré Willsie Morrow, former editor of *Delineator* and a native of Iowa, in many popular novels: *Still Jim* (1915), *We Must March* (1925), *Forever Free* (1927), *Argonaut* (1933), a story of the gold rush days, and *Yonder Sails the Mayflower* (1934).

A good modern treatment of the pioneer theme is Margaret Wilson's *The Able McLaughlins,* which was awarded the Pulitzer Prize in 1923— a narrative of the life of a Scotch immigrant family who made their homes on the prairie. The women especially are sympathetically shown, carrying for many miles slips of plants and flower seeds for their gardens, and protecting their chickens from quick-rising storms and low-hovering hawks.

Grandmother Brown's Hundred Years, by Harriet Connor Brown, which won the Atlantic Monthly Prize for the most interesting biography of 1928, is an epic tale of American life in the Middle West. "Grandmother Brown," who was born in Ohio, came to Iowa as a young wife and spent most of her hundred years in the State. *Black Soil,* by Josephine Donovan, won the prize offered in 1930 by *Extension Magazine* and the Stratford Company for the best Catholic novel; the story is set in northwestern Iowa among immigrant farmers of many nationalities. Walter Muilenberg in *The Prairie* writes of much the same kind of life. Bess Streeter Aldrich, author of *A Lantern in Her Hand* (1928) returns to early Iowa and Nebraska.

James Norman Hall went farther afield perhaps than any other Iowan, choosing Tahiti for his home and for the subject matter of his popular short stories and novels, many of them written in collaboration with Charles Nordhoff. *Mutiny on the Bounty* (1933, with Nordhoff) brought him celebrity, but many readers already knew the pleasantly romantic *Faery Lands of the South Seas* (1921).

The explorer tradition and the historical meet in *The Great Commodore* (1935), a biography of Matthew Galbraith Perry, who opened Japan to Western trade, written by Edward M. Barrows. Mr. Barrows, whose early home was Iowa, is the son of Allen C. Barrows who taught at the State College at Ames, and brother of Frank E. Barrows, founder of Simpson College School of Music.

In contrast to these writers, Thomas Duncan, Karlton Kelm, Eleanor Saltzman, Ruth Stewart, Elmer T. Peterson, and Winnifred Mayne Van Etten (whose novel *I Am the Fox* won the Atlantic Monthly Prize in 1936) live in Iowa and draw on the Middle West for literary material.

Griffith Beems returns to Iowa for his short stories; and Paul Corey, author of "Bushel of Wheat, Bushel of Barley" (short story), chose to live on a farm in the East.

William Wister Haines, whose birthplace is Des Moines, created the character of *Slim* (1914), well liked in the novel and in the motion picture of the same name. Richard Sherman, novelist and short story writer, lived occasionally in the State. His novel, *To Mary With Love*, was made into a popular motion picture. Cornelia Meigs, formerly of Keokuk, Marion Hurd McNeely, and Olivia McCabe of Des Moines are well known for their stories for children.

Ross Santee, State director of the Federal Writers' Project in Arizona, is a native Iowan, as was the late Dick Wick Hall of Salome, Arizona. Salome is in desert country, and Hall in vivid humorous sketches for his typed journal, the Salome *Sun*, described life in the arid West. Later, national periodicals reprinted the sketches. Santee, in *Cowboy* and his other stories, is known both as author and artist for his authentic pictures of the open range.

Besides Josephine Herbst and Honoré Willsie Morrow, many Iowa editors and newspapermen have found place in metropolitan journalism, notably Albert Shaw, founder of the *Review of Reviews* and its editor for forty-five years; Harry Hansen, literary editor of the New York *World-Telegram;* Marquis W. Childs, Washington correspondent for the St. Louis *Post-Dispatch;* and Beatrice Blackmar Gould and Bruce Gould, co-editors of the *Ladies' Home Journal.*

Harry Hansen includes in *Midwest Portraits* (1923) studies of the writers of Davenport, his own town. His *Carl Sandburg: The Man and His Poetry,* published as one of the Little Blue Books (E. Haldeman-Julius, 1924) was given important place in metropolitan literary reviews. Marquis Childs, who was born in Clinton, has gained a wide audience through magazine articles on political problems. His *Sweden: The Middle Way* (1936) was important because it attracted attention to the co-operative movement as a possible development in America. Mr. Childs has written many short stories with Iowa as the background and a novel, *Washington Calling* (1937), with its setting in the national capital.

Henry Wallace, grandfather of Henry A. Wallace (Secretary of Agriculture under President Franklin D. Roosevelt), established *Wallace's Farmer* in Des Moines in 1895. Secretary Wallace is himself the author of several important books on agriculture and economics: *Agricultural Prices* (1920), *Corn and Corn Growing* (1923), *New Frontiers* (1934).

The financially frail "little" magazine is a characteristic expression of the experimental spirit, and Iowa's writers have been true to form in this respect. The first literary magazine, *The Midland Monthly,* was founded in 1894 by Johnson Brigham (State Librarian for more than thirty years) "to encourage the creative spirit in the Middle West." Ellis Parker Butler was its humorist and Emerson Hough's first published story appeared in its pages.

John T. Frederick, who established *The Midland* at Iowa City in 1915, deserves high rank among editors for his "modest attempt to encourage the making of literature in the Middle West"; an attempt that was continued for eighteen years, during which the little magazine published poems and stories of young writers from all parts of the country. Mr. Frederick, now State director of the Federal Writers' Project in Illinois, is the author of two successful novels, *Druida* (1923) and *Green Bush* (1925), and was for many years a member of the English department of the State University of Iowa. Frank Luther Mott, professor of journalism in the university, was assistant editor of *The Midland*. *A History of American Magazines, 1741–1850,* published in 1930, is his most important work. An earlier study, *The Literature of Pioneer Life in Iowa* (1923), and his story of "The Man with the Good Face" are also well known.

The Left, published at Davenport in 1930 and 1931, and *The New Quarterly* (in nearby Illinois, 1932) encouraged experimental writing and free expression of thought. After *The Midland* was discontinued in 1933 various "regional" magazines sprang up: *The Hub* and *The Dubuque Dial* (edited by Karlton Kelm) in 1934, and *Hinterland* from 1936 to the present (1938). A promising adventure is *American Prefaces,* begun at Iowa City in 1935 and published under the supervision of Norman Foerster of the University of Iowa, author of *Humanism in America* (1930). At Cornell College in Mount Vernon, *The Husk,* edited by Clyde Tull, has published some of the younger poets, including Jewell Bothwell Tull and Edward Weissmiller, winner of the Yale Series of Younger Poets' Prize in 1936 with his *The Deer Come Down.*

In these courageous little magazines short story writers and poets may express their sense of the beauty and tragedy of farm life—of all life— in whatever pattern or technique they wish to try. The poets perhaps have benefited most of all from this opportunity. Jay G. Sigmund (1885–1937), whose poems and short stories derive from his native Waubeek, had some of his earlier work published first in *The Midland*. Contemporary poets of ability found encouragement in these reviews: Edwin

Ford Piper, James Hearst, Raymond Kresensky, Mildred Fowler Field, Don Farran, Marion Louise Bliss, and many others.

Arthur Davison Ficke, Edwin Ford Piper, and Paul Engle, because of the volume and quality of their work, are the ranking Iowa poets. Piper, born in Auburn, Nebraska, has been connected with the State university as teacher of English, and of poetry especially, for more than thirty years. His first book, *Barbed Wire and Other Poems,* appeared in 1917. *Barbed Wire and Wayfarers* followed in 1923, *Paintrock Road* in 1927, and *Canterbury Pilgrims* in 1935. Virtually all Piper's poetry—narrative or lyric—deals with pioneer life. *The Land of the Aiouwas,* a masque conceived with vigor and beauty, was performed at the Diamond Jubilee of the University of Iowa in 1922.

Arthur Davison Ficke's poetry is excellently designed, reflecting an interest in Oriental art. His first volume, *From the Isles,* was published in 1907, and the second, *Chats on Japanese Prints,* in 1915. Ficke's love poetry is well known, especially in *Sonnets of a Portrait Painter* (1922) and *An April Elegy* (1917). One of his more recent poems, "Nocturne in a Library" is a powerful presentation of the tragic state of the modern world. Beauty of form and sincere conviction mark many of the poems in Mr. Ficke's later collections—*Selected Poems* (1926), *Mountain Against Mountain* (1929), and *The Secret* (1936).

Paul Engle, youngest of the three, began by rejecting the attitude of futility and cynicism common to many recent poets, and taking as his theme the beauty of America and the pageantry of its history. *American Song,* a long narrative poem describing the development of the United States, won the World Century of Progress Prize in 1933. Engle's work today shows great technical development and maturity of emotion and thought. *Break the Heart's Anger* is in the major tradition of poetry for, though it is a bitter protest against cruelty and confusion, it expresses grief of so high an order that it becomes affirmation.

The Arts

Graphic and Plastic Arts

THE homely richness of the Iowa scene—its tiled silos, the geometric patterns of its corn fields, the barns and cattle and sturdy farm houses—has long sustained the pride and patriotism of the State. It is only during the last twenty years, however, and more particularly during the 1930's, that the well-known and well-loved homeland has been used as subject matter for the paintings and murals of contemporary artists. But what has been hailed as "regional art" may well be found, upon examination of the many factors which led to its birth, to be part of a wider and perhaps far more significant movement. The fine arts in Iowa should be viewed in relation to the cultural development of the entire country.

The first art was, of course, that of the mound builders and Indians, but it is a thing apart and has had little or no influence. George Catlin, who was one of the first artists of note to paint the Indians, spent some months in the early 1830's living among them and studying their life. Three of his works, a bear dance of the Sioux Indians and two portraits of Chief Keokuk, are in the National Museum at Washington.

There was little time for artistic expression in the hard life of the early settlers, except in those products which served a useful as well as an æsthetic purpose. The quilt that provided warmth also gave opportunity for skill and beauty in its making. Designs for quilts and coverlets were passed from neighbor to neighbor, and quilting bees were popular. Gay colors went into the knitted mufflers and mittens; lace of intricate pattern trimmed petticoats and pillowcases; and samplers carried in cross-stitch such mottoes as "God Bless Our Home." The pioneers followed the general Colonial tradition in the native arts with interesting variations. These were chiefly in the nature of a new sturdiness and simplicity, imposed by the rigorous demands of pioneer life and the restricted supply of materials and tools.

Interest in handicraft was acceptable, but anyone who had a talent and love for painting worked alone and as secretly as possible. He found no place in the methodical and hard-driving farm life, and more often than not was considered "a bit queer" or "a lazy good-for-nothing."

But two unrelated events in the 1860's brought about a change of attitude, and in a general way influenced developments in the field of art. George Henry Yewell, whose childhood had been spent in Iowa, won recognition abroad with his *Children of the Seashore, Normandy,* painted in 1861; and the Davenport Academy of Sciences arranged a series of lectures and an exhibition of paintings in 1867. (Several of Yewell's portraits of Iowa Governors are still preserved in the State Historical Building in Des Moines.) For the next half century Iowa imported its art and exported its potential artists, or at least estimated them by the yardstick of the recognition they received elsewhere—preferably abroad. The artists themselves played a passive part in the growing interest in art, since in general they left the State for their training, never to return, or to return only (as did Yewell) to paint the portrait of the Governor or of some other dignitary. The story of this period, in contrast to that of the present time, is one not of artists but of institutions and personalities that fostered an appreciation of art.

Their activities upheld the efforts of the more sophisticated East to "civilize the backwoods," and were welcomed rather than resisted by the Iowans, who were adventurous and eager to keep abreast of the times. The eastern and academic standards thus imposed, together with the influx of manufactured goods and the vulgarization of taste which followed the Civil War, destroyed the pioneer arts before they had time to take root.

One unique exception is the Amana Society, a German religious sect which founded seven villages in Iowa County during the 1850's (*see Tour 14A*). The handicraft tradition was part of the Amanite pattern of economic self-sufficiency, and the Society developed skillful craftsmen and some interesting indigenous crafts derived from the original German. Today it produces furniture, rugs, textiles, and a number of functional and ornamental objects in wrought iron, and carries on a successful business enterprise in wools and blankets. In recent years, through the encouragement of outsiders, the Amana Society has established a museum in one of its little communities which houses some of the best examples of craft culture in the State.

In the generation before the World War the two most influential personalities in the State's art development were Charles F. Cummings and Lorado Taft. Although the lesser of the two in scope and quality of leadership, Cummings was the more important locally since he worked

VETERINARY MEDICINE   *FARM CROPS*

MURALS IN LIBRARY OF

from within the State while Taft made his headquarters in Chicago. On a number of other points, however, their influence was similar. Though today their position seems academic and they wasted their last years in a futile battle against modernism, both contributed measurably to the orien-

Grant Wood

ANIMAL HUSBANDRY

IOWA STATE COLLEGE

tation toward the fine arts in the Midwest. This they did chiefly by translating the esoteric art jargon into terms the Midwesterner could understand.
Cummings established the Cummings School of Art in Des Moines in
1895, and fifteen years later became the head of the newly formed depart-

ment of graphic and plastic arts at the State university, serving in this capacity until 1927. He made Iowa familiar with the works of his fellow academicians in the East, particularly Edward W. Redfield, Gardner Simons, and Elmer Schofield; and exerted an influence on J. S. Carpenter, a construction engineer, who built up the first private collection in the State and encouraged others to follow suit. (A memorial collection of nineteen portraits by Cummings hangs in the Iowa Historical Library at Des Moines.) Taft is known both as a sculptor and as the author of authoritative books in this field, notable among which is his exhaustive work *History of American Sculpture*. He taught and lectured for many years at the Art Institute in Chicago and at the University of Chicago.

It is perhaps due to his influence that Iowan sculptors won recognition sooner than did the painters. Sherry Edmundson Fry, who was born in Creston in 1879, modeled his first pieces in Iowa clay. He left the State to work under Lorado Taft in Chicago, but later returned to study Indian life. While in Paris, he modeled his prize-winning statue of *Chief Mahaska,* which was cast in bronze and now stands in the city square at Oskaloosa. Another native-born sculptor, Nellie Verne Walker (1874–) executed the statue of *Chief Keokuk* (1913) and the panels at Iowa State College (1924). She worked first in the shop of her father, who was a marble cutter, and she too studied under Taft. *Her Son,* an idealized mother and son group, is in the collection of the Art Institute in Chicago. Although David Edstrom (1873–) was born in Sweden and returned there, he spent his boyhood in Ottumwa, and designed the Civil War Soldiers monument (1918) which stands in the central park. Harriet A. Ketcham of Mount Pleasant executed the monument to Iowa soldiers and sailors (1890) on the capitol grounds in Des Moines. Harry Stinson, whose Lewis and Clark monument was erected in 1935 at the city limits of Council Bluffs, teaches sculpture at the State university. Another of his works is the figure of Black Hawk (1934) in Lake View. Christian Peterson, a Danish immigrant, executed the terra cotta murals of the dairy building, the gymnasium, and the veterinary quadrangle at Iowa State College. *The Girl on Roller Skates* and other figures in the Metropolitan Museum in New York, and *Little Mother* in the Art Institute in Chicago, are by Abastenia St. Leger Eberle (1878–), who was born in Webster City. The bronze bust of Lorado Taft by Alice L. Siems, the portrait heads by the farmer Clifton Adams, and the statue of the Indian girl *Sacajawea* in Washington Park, Portland, Oregon, by Alice Cooper Hubbard are additional examples of Iowa's contribution in the field of sculpture. Though not born in the State, Vinnie Ream Hoxie (1847–1914), famous for her statue of Lincoln, spent her summers in Iowa in the late 1880's, working on life-size figures of Governor Samuel J. Kirkwood and Senator James Harlan. These are now in Statuary Hall, Washington, D.C.

The influence of Cummings and Carpenter brought paintings from the East (particularly from the National Academy and the Grand Central Galleries, New York) to the galleries of Des Moines, Iowa City, and Cedar Rapids, and made Iowa familiar with what may be termed accepted works of art. But the wave of nationalism which accompanied the post World War boom gave rise in the East to a reaction against European dominance in the arts, and this reaction was reflected in the Midwest by a growing awareness of American and especially of local talent.

Thus the 1920's saw an acceleration of public interest in painting. Art associations in various towns, started chiefly in the 1890's, opened their galleries to the public with traveling exhibitions of paintings routed by the American Federation of Arts, the College Art Association, the National Galleries, and similar exhibition agencies. The Des Moines Association of Fine Arts, organized in 1918, began to bring exhibits to the city and promote study clubs. The association today owns paintings by Redfield, Miller, Symons, Tanner, Schofield, Brangwyn, Henri, and Kroll, on display in the city library. The Davenport Municipal Art Gallery was founded in 1925, and now records as many as 25,000 visitors each year. The Blanden Memorial Gallery at Fort Dodge was established some years later. At Cedar Rapids, the Little Gallery was opened by the American Federation of Arts in 1928, with funds subscribed by the Carnegie Foundation. The sponsors' hopes of making it an influence and an example for similar galleries were amply fulfilled under the dynamic leadership of its director, Edward B. Rowan.

Colleges, women's clubs, and finally the artists themselves responded to the general awakening of interest. The Iowa State Fair admitted painting and sculpture to its exhibits. Women's clubs set up art departments and study groups, and popular lecturers on the arts, such as Dudley Crafts Watson of Chicago, were always assured of large and enthusiastic audiences. The State Teachers College now gives normal courses in both creative art and art appreciation; Cornell, Grinnell, and Coe Colleges, and Drake University have excellent art departments, and special work in the silicate industries—tile, terra cotta, and pottery—are offered at the State College. The University of Iowa, with its art department housed in its own building on the bank of the Iowa River, exerts a major influence. Its permanent collection includes a number of paintings by academic American artists and a representative collection of sculpture.

With the American art world seeking a cultural pole in the heart of America rather than in Europe or on the eastern seaboard, with Iowa developing an art consciousness and an awareness of its own potentialities— the soil was prepared for the flowering of the genius of Grant Wood, who today ranks as the outstanding artist of the State and among the distinguished painters of America. Born on a farm near Anamosa, the son of a Quaker farmer, he shows many of the good qualities as well as the limitations of his former neighbors. He is conservative, deliberate, obstinate, and honest; and his pioneer background is evident in the patient, meticulous, and somewhat rigid craftsmanship shown in his work. Wood was first a worker in metal and homemade jewelry, and (after his return to Iowa from the World War) a teacher of art in the public schools of Cedar Rapids. In 1920 he took a short leave of absence for study in Paris and thereafter began to paint seriously and develop his own technique. He first attracted attention with the portrait *John B. Turner, Pioneer,* followed by the portrait of his mother, *Woman with Plants,* now owned by the Cedar Rapids Art Association. Unexpected and wide acclaim greeted *American Gothic* (1930), which shows a farmer and his wife standing before a farmhouse, the lines and mood of the picture suggesting a firm but barren sense of devotion to duty. *American Gothic* is now in the Art Institute, Chicago, and Wood's well-known *Dinner for Threshers* is in the Whitney Museum, New York.

A group of younger artists, heartened by Wood's success, and inspired by his use of Iowa subject matter flocked to his standard. Together with Rowan and Adrian Dornbush, Wood founded the Stone City artists' colony in 1932. (*See Tour 1A.*) Here for two summers a number of artists and students painted the rolling prairie, the barns, corn fields, and scenes of farm life typical of southeastern Iowa.

Three among the younger artists share Wood's rural background: Robert Tabor of Creston, whose *Country Auction,* painted in 1934 under the Public Works of Art program, was hailed as an Iowa primitive; Karl Flick, a former grocery clerk and member of the Amana Society, who won notice with his *Amana Interior;* and the farmer Tom Savage, a young painter of promise from the vicinity of Fort Dodge.

Many other influences have contributed to the present lively and vigorous art movement. Among the annual exhibitions are the State Fair Salon and the Iowa Artists' Art Fair, both in Des Moines; the exhibit of the Iowa Artists' Club; the Tri-city exhibition at Davenport; the Dubuque artists' exhibit; and the traveling exhibition of the Iowa Art Guild. The strong and racy work of Jay Darling (Ding), cartoonist on the Des

Moines *Register and Tribune,* has had a prolonged and vital influence in the State and, through syndication, in the entire country. Cartooning is still generally linked with so-called commercial art, and Darling himself would be the first to disclaim position as an artist. Nevertheless cartooning can be ranked with certain forms of illustration as one of the most forceful art expressions in the American vernacular, and it is as such that Darling's work should be given recognition. The *Register and Tribune,* under the editorship of the younger Cowles—the sons of the founder—has persistently fostered not only the enjoyment of the arts but, more important, given space and encouragement to local artists. Two murals by Russell Cowles, on the walls of the business offices of the Register and Tribune Building, represent the *Functions of the Newspaper* and *Freedom of Speech.*

Among the leaders of the younger group of artists are Francis Robert White, State Director of the Federal Art Project of the Works Progress Administration, Chris Glazell, Lowell Houser, and Dan Rhodes. Grace French Evans, Evelyn Blunt Fiche, Louise Garst McBroom, and Edith Bell are also active in the younger group. Kate Keith Van Duzee, of Dubuque, has long been a leader of art in her own community, as well as an artist who has caught the quaint flavor of that river town. Some artists of talent —such as David McCosh, of Cedar Rapids, William Palmer, of Des Moines, and Carl Free, of Davenport—have followed the traditional practice of leaving the State for their final training.

The Federal Government, in granting funds to artists, is undoubtedly a major factor in the Iowa art situation today. The Procurement Division of the Treasury Department, the Federal Art Project of the Works Progress Administration, and (formerly) the Public Works of Art Projects have given Iowa artists the opportunity of developing their talent at home and thus of enriching both themselves and the State.

Nine murals depicting phases of agriculture were designed by Grant Wood for the foyer of the library of the Iowa State College, and developed and executed by assistants under his direction. White (mentioned above) has been appointed to design the murals for the Federal building in Cedar Rapids. Assisting him are Harry Jones, who is also directing the fresco work (1938) on the walls of the children's room in the Des Moines city library, Everett Jeffery, and Don Glassell, who came to America from Denmark when he was seventeen and is now on the staff of the Sioux City Art Center. Richard Haines, of Cresco, is designing the mural for his home city post office, and has also received the regional award for the execution of the post office mural in Wichita, Kansas. Murals for the post

EVOLUTION OF CORN, MURAL IN POST OFFICE, AMES

offices at Osceola (1936) and Pella (1937) are being executed by Byron Ben Boyd, of Des Moines, and the commission for the post office mural at Ames was awarded in 1935 to Lowell Houser of that city, known for his wood blocks, black and white drawings, and oils made from his Central American sketches. Other Iowa artists to receive commissions include Richard Gates, Mildred Pelzer, Bertrand Adams, William Bunn, Arnold Pyle, and Savage, Glazell, Rhodes, and Tabor (mentioned above).

Lawrence Stewart's *Symphony in Smoke,* a Des Moines riverfront scene, painted in 1934 under the Public Works of Art Projects, was among the works exhibited at the Corcoran Gallery in Washington. The Federal Art Project exhibition, "New Horizons in American Art," held at the Museum of Modern Art in New York in October 1936, and later sent throughout the country, included paintings by Arnold Pyle and George Chamberlain.

A Federal Art Project undertaking of deep significance for Iowa is the Community Art Center of Sioux City, sponsored by the Project and the Sioux City Society of Fine Arts, and launched·with the co-operation of the entire city. Individuals, business firms, and organizations donated time, money, material, and labor. The two local newspapers outdid themselves in supporting the Center; volunteer workers, some with funds so meager that they lacked even streetcar fare, came daily to help; electricians and carpenters on the Works Progress Administration payroll voluntarily contributed additional hours on the job; young men from the National Youth

Lowell Houser

Administration and the public school manual training department built equipment; and members of the Plumbers and Steamfitters Union, Local 18, donated their labor. More than two thousand people came to see their art center on the opening day, February 20, 1938, and three hundred registered for courses. Here, indeed, is a new horizon in American Art.

The Theater

In 1838, a few years after the first settlers reached Iowa, The Iowa Thespian Association advertised a performance of "the much admired play, *The Glory of Columbia,* by William Dunlap, Esq., to conclude with a variety of Songs Duets, and Trios." Snow boats were tying up at the wharfs of the Mississippi River towns by the mid-century, bringing Carl Wagner's Minstrels, Duprez and Benedict's Minstrels, and J. A. Wallace's Great Palace Circus. Strolling mimics, singers, and acrobats were performing in the dining rooms, taverns and market places of Dubuque, Burlington, and Davenport, and a complete Shakespearean repertoire was presented at the Julien Theater in Dubuque in 1860.

Iowa's early interest in the theater was stimulated by the arrival of German immigrants, who brought with them a love for the drama and in some instances professional training. They put on German productions of the plays of Schiller, Goethe, and Molière.

Road companies soon found a hearty welcome in the larger towns, where elaborate opera houses received them. Burlington in particular was a popular theater town from its earliest show-boat days, and a favorite stand for New York road shows. These played at the old Grimes Opera House and at the Grand Opera House, built in 1881. The latter was known in the theatrical world as "that theater way out west where they always play to a packed house," and was the first theater in the State to use uniformed ushers and an orchestra.

The so-called professional theater today centers in Des Moines, Cedar Rapids, Davenport, and Iowa City. The Shrine Temple in Des Moines, built in 1927, can seat an audience of five thousand. But when stars such as Katharine Cornell, Ina Claire, and Leslie Howard play there the famous SRO (standing room only) sign, so dear to all theatrical managers, is hung out for many a performance.

The Chautauquas supplemented the early road shows and brought to large sections of the population their only experience with spoken drama. People from surrounding towns and farms often pitched tent cities on the Chautauqua grounds and stayed for the entire ten-day meeting.

The movies, in Iowa as elsewhere, largely displaced both road shows and Chautauquas, though the latter were still popular in the early nineteen hundreds. By 1936 road shows stopped in only the larger cities, and the number of Chautauquas in the State had been reduced to one.

But interest in the theater persisted in another and perhaps more satisfactory form. Burlington, carrying on its tradition as a show town, gave the first Little Theater performance in Iowa in 1915. A Little Theater group was formed in Waterloo the following year, and a similar group was soon organized in Sioux City.

In Des Moines the idea of using home talent instead of depending entirely on road shows had first been put into practice at the Princess Theater which opened in 1909. Here a stock company gave training to inexperienced actors, half a dozen of whom later became famous on Broadway and in Hollywood. Among these are Conrad Nagel, Fay Bainter, and Ralph Bellamy. Ten years later, the city's Little Theater society was organized, fol-

lowing the enthusiastic reception of three plays written and produced by
Des Moines citizens and sponsored by the Iowa Press and Authors' Club.
This group, later widening its activities to become the Des Moines Community Drama Association, has presented plays by O'Neill, Shaw, Strind-
berg, Ibsen, Capek, Lula Vollmer, and other modern dramatists. In 1931
the association launched the Sylvan Theatre in Greenwood Park. A notable musical performance with a cast of two hundred was given before an
audience of more than eight thousand in 1937—a high light in the history
of the Sylvan Theatre.

The Little Theater, or community theater, movement has developed steadily and become State-wide in scope and significance. Interest in giving
plays and requests for advice led Iowa State College to set up the Little
Country Theater at the State Fair in 1922. As a result, and with the help
of the college extension service, members of 4-H clubs and other rural
community groups began to produce plays. Each winter during Farm and
Home Week college students and rural organizations give performances
at the Theater Work Shop at Iowa State College. From seven to eight hundred plays have been presented at fairs and cattle congresses, and before
local audiences. In 1935 these widely scattered groups combined to give a
successful performance of *The Bohemian Girl* at Ames, although the entire cast was able to hold only a few rehearsals. The following figures give
some indication of the vitality of the rural community theater movement:
in 1936 drama committees were functioning in 288 townships, and 38
drama schools, county-wide in scope, were helping them with their productions.

Meanwhile, the State University at Iowa City was fostering interest in
the theater on a different front. An experimental theater was organized
in 1921 and produced more than 150 plays during the following 15 years.
In addition to plays representing various trends and periods in dramatic
history, new playwrights—some of them students—first tried out their
work here. Virgil Geddes, E. P. Conkle, and Richard Maibaum, later to
win recognition in New York and elsewhere, saw the first productions of
many of their plays at the Experimental Theater. Geddes, one of the original directors of the Federal Theater Project in New York, is well known
for his plays *The Earth Between, In the Tradition,* and *Native Ground.*
In 1935 a new university theater was built with modern equipment including a revolving stage.

Another activity which is developing a State-wide interest in the theater
is the play festival, held for four days each spring at Iowa City. A thousand or more high school and junior college students present eighty to

ninety plays in a play competition; winners receive university scholarships entitling them to training in playwriting and production.

The Iowa Federation of Women's Clubs cooperates with the State University Division of Drama in encouraging production of plays, the observance of Drama Week and the fostering of local talent. In these and other ways the federation is aiding the growth of interest in regional plays and in local community drama throughout the State.

George Cram Cook and Susan Glaspell, two writers whose work has had a far reaching effect on the theater of the entire country, were born in Iowa. They guided the fortunes of the Provincetown Players, the group which gave first productions of Eugene O'Neill's early plays and developed other notable playwrights as well as actors. Cook and Glaspell also wrote plays which were especially suitable for Little Theater production and thus gave impetus to the Little Theater movement.

Music

The first known music of the Iowa country was that of the Indian tribes, chiefly the Sac and Fox. Other tribes invaded the territory to hunt or fight, and the Potawatamie and Winnebago—the last to leave Iowa—moved through the country as the Government drove them northward. Partly because these tribes occupied adjacent or overlapping territories, their music was similar and the songs of one tribe were often found in the language of another; some of the sacred songs of the Iowa, for example, were in the language of the Winnebago.

Percussion and wind instruments were used by the historic Indians: drums, rattles, various kinds of whistles, and the red cedar flute. The drum, like the smaller tambourines, consisted of a skin stretched over a wooden framework or a section of hollowed wood. The chants of the Winnebago medicine ceremony were accompanied by drum and rattle. Tribal chants in general had a wider range than the five to six note limit of the flute, which was used for love and courtship music. The love song played by a young man on his flute identified him at long distance.

Caleb Atwater, Indian Commissioner, in his *Memoirs on the Sauks and Foxes* noted that "the tunes of most of the Indians . . . are dull and monotonous, because with only from three to five musical notes they must be so . . . yet even such tunes sung by some soft, clear, melodious voices, both of males and especially females, the music in them is quite agreeable and enchanting."

Many of the Indian songs had no definite words, only vocables to carry the music. When words were used they indicated the many aspects of social life into which music entered. There were songs for many special occasions: religious ceremonies, war, dancing, mourning, courting, and hunting.

Music played a greater part in the lives of early Iowans than did any of the other arts. As successive waves of settlers—native and European—moved west from the Mississippi River to the Des Moines River Valley, they brought with them their own music—songs, dances, and musical "play-party games." Even before German, Czech, and Welsh immigrants formed their bands and choral groups, music had developed with the coming of the "singing professor" and Thursday night "singing school." Starting in the fall after cornhusking, these schools continued until February, drawing young people from miles around to learn notes and scales, simple tunes, part reading, and group singing.

Iowa is outstanding among Middle Western States for its American traditional folk music. Carl Van Vechten has written of a leisurely but fruitless jaunt in the vicinity of Cedar Rapids (his birthplace) in search of folk music, but competent collectors in the State believe that they have only begun to explore the neglected folk music field. No authoritative collection has been made, but the songs and dances of the miners, farmers, railroad men, and other working people are there waiting to be written down.

The barn dance, originally held to celebrate the building of houses and barns, became a definite part of the social life of farming communities. It continued as a custom independent of any special occasion, the locale changing from seasonally emptied haymows to farmhouses, schoolhouses, grange halls, opera houses, and lodge halls. In 1936 one of the State's largest radio stations was sponsoring a synthetic Saturday night barn dance program.

The martial drum and fife bands of the military organizations supported by early settlers were used at celebrations of all sorts. They were the forerunners of the brass bands which, in later years, contributed to the development of the modern dance band. In 1841 the first Territorial

Whig Convention in Davenport met at the LeClaire House and marched with a band consisting of one bugle and a clarinet. Circus and tent show bands stimulated interest in music and, before the railroads came and the river towns had built their first opera houses, showboats advertised "A First Rate Band of Music Will Be Aboard."

Sacred music held an important place in the lives of the settlers and, as early as the 1850's, Iowa was distinguished for its composers of hymns. William S. Pitts, visiting at Bradford in 1857, wrote *The Little Brown Church in the Vale*. A simple frame church, built by village people in 1864, was named for the song. The background of "singing school" helped to further music in the churches, whose choirs in turn developed both talented individuals and groups.

European immigrants—especially those from Germany, Sweden, Bohemia (Czechoslovakia), and Wales—brought with them the highly developed music of their own lands, and tried to adapt it for use in the new country. Forty years later, Anton Dvořák came to spend a quiet summer in the small village of Spillville, where he went for walks along the Turkey River, played the village church organ, and perhaps composed some of the music of his *New World Symphony*. In the period before the Civil War professional musicians began to arrive from the larger cities to the south and east, and by 1860 more sophisticated music was heard in Iowa. Reed organs from the East were regularly part of church equipment and, with a few pianos, they found place in the parlors of the well-to-do— possession of either organ or piano being a high social distinction. The first piano, a rosewood belonging to a Mr. Evans, was brought down the Ohio by barge in the 1830's, then overland and by ferry to Montrose and Keokuk.

Long before 1890 exponents of European music had widened the breach already existing between old time folk and more formal music. Resident teachers gave music lessons to young people whose parents could afford instruction and instruments; talented students went to conservatories in Chicago, the East, and Europe for advanced study. One of the foremost European-trained grand opera stars of the 1890's was Alice Ettinger of Waterloo, whose stage name was Madame Ettinger Braun. Clarence Eugene Whitehill, baritone of the Metropolitan Opera Company of New York, was born in Marengo in 1871.

By the beginning of the twentieth century, the music of the early Iowans—folk songs and dance music, Civil War songs, hymns, and the classic and folk music brought from Europe—was submerged in a flood of "rag time" and "coon" music which reached the Midwest by way of the first World's Fair of Chicago. Although musical leaders opposed rag time, *Ta Rah Rah Rah Boom de Ay* (considered sinful in many homes) replaced *Turkey in The Straw,* and the rag time crazes of the 1890's, *Elisha Green's Cake Walk* and *Ben Hur's Chariot Race,* were sung oftener than *The Little Brown Church in the Vale* and *Only a Pansy Blossom.*

Today, instrumental and band music instruction is given in many public schools, and military organizations, colleges, cities, and towns have uniformed bands. They are the life of parades and political rallies, football games, and celebrations, a fixture in hundreds of communities where band concerts divert farmers and townspeople as they "trade." Many of these bands compete at the biennial Band Day, established by Karl King in Fort Dodge. The *Iowa Corn Song*—"That's where the tall corn grows"—is blared forth by bands on most occasions. The melody was adapted from *Travelling,* a tune popular at the end of the nineteenth century, and the words were written in 1912 by two Des Moines Shriners as a series of verses in honor of the various cities they visited.

In the churches, hearty congregational singing is being replaced by classical music performed by trained choirs, soloists, and instrumentalists. Except in small isolated communities, or among the various "fundamentalist" groups, such spirited singing as that encouraged and exemplified by Billy Sunday, the Iowa evangelist, is passing. However, the tradition of hymn writing persists. Adelaide A. Pollard, born near Bloomfield and now living in London, England, wrote the words of the popular church hymn, *Have Thine Own Way, Lord,* and is the author of more than 100 hymn lyrics. Hungarian-born Elias Blum, who has taught at Grinnell College for many years, has written numerous fine anthems and religious compositions, including *Bow Down Thine Ear* and *How Lovely Are Thy Dwellings.* Another Iowa composer of religious music is Sumner Salter, son of William Salter of the Iowa Band, and nationally known director, organist, and author.

Among the Iowans who have written popular songs are Egbert Van Alstyne of Mount Vernon, who composed *In the Shade of the Old Apple Tree,* and Mortimer Wilson of Chariton, whose score for the *Thief of Bagdad,* an early motion picture, was one of the first compositions for musical films. Thurlow Lieurance, who is known for his many Indian lyrics, notably *By the Waters of Minnetonka,* was born in Oskaloosa. Frederic Knight Logan, composer of *Pale Moon,* the famous *Missouri Waltz,* and other popular waltzes, was also of Oskaloosa. Louise Crawford, pianist and composer at the Coe College School of Music, Cedar Rapids, is regarded by some critics as Iowa's foremost woman composer. Leon

("Bix") Beiderbecke, who was born in Davenport in 1903 and died in New York City in 1931, was eminent in the field of popular music both as a composer and performer. In addition to writing *In a Mist, Candlelight, In the Dark,* and other pieces which caught the public fancy, Beiderbecke was a brilliant exponent of improvisation, a feature of jazz which has its roots in folk music, particularly that of the Negro. He began playing the trumpet on showboats while still in his teens and was among the first band musicians to use the Negro style of playing. Later Beiderbecke developed into a cornetist of high originality. His playing, and particularly his unique talent for improvisation, influenced musicians in both the jazz and more scholarly fields.

Iowa has cultivated music in its rural districts to an extent equalled by few other States. C. A. Fullerton of the Teachers College at Cedar Falls is known nationally for his pioneer work in music training for children in rural schools. His methods as outlined in the text book, *A One-Book Course in Elementary Music and Selected Songs for Schools* (1925), were instrumental in the development of the Iowa Choir, whose State-wide programs finished its first five-year cycle in 1934. Inaugurated for the musical development of rural children, the choir is made up of children who have passed an actual singing test in a selected group of songs and are entitled to State certificates. The success of the program was demonstrated when a massed choir sang at the State Fair in 1930 and in 1934. It is estimated that 50,000 rural school children know the fifty songs in the repertoire of this choir. The annual high school music contest and festival at Iowa City owes its origin, in part, to G. T. Bennett of Rockford, who conducted a State-wide contest in 1921. Training in singing, theory, harmony, orchestra and band playing, and music appreciation is given in the public schools. The music contest has grown to such an extent that in 1937 about 5,000 high school students from 516 schools, representing at least 50,000 pupils having some degree of competence, gathered at Iowa City.

During the past three decades the State's institutions of higher education have developed and enlarged their music departments, their graduates mainly finding place in the public schools. The first Music Supervisors' National Council was held in Keokuk in 1907, and from this meeting grew a national organization with a membership of 7,500. These teachers have developed choirs, symphony orchestras, and musical clubs, presenting such oratorios as *Elijah,* annually. The Sinfonia Trio, an outstanding chamber music group, is composed of the directors of three music departments at Drake University, Des Moines. Most of the colleges have small symphony orchestras. The Chicago Symphony Orchestra plays each June at the Cornell Music Festival, first held in 1899 at Mount Vernon. At the State University the music department under Professor Philip G. Clapp has done much for the advancement of music in the State. Of wider importance is the psychological laboratory of Dean Carl Seashore where tests for musical talent, recognized as standards in schools, have been developed. The work of Seashore and his colleagues is known throughout the world and, though it has been subject to extensive controversy, it stands an important contribution in the fields of music and psychology. It has also thrown light on how musical ability is inherited and has thus rendered basic service to the science of heredity. Seashore's text books, *The Psychology of Musical Talent* and *Psychology of Music* (1937), are the most comprehensive of their kind.

An active and influential group cooperating with educational institutions is the Iowa Federation of Music Clubs, organized in Davenport in 1916 with 13 charter members. The federation, which had 94 affiliated clubs in 1930, sponsors young artists' and composers' contests, and has raised thousands of dollars to provide scholarships for students and guest artists for the music loving public.

Architecture

The first types of houses in what is now Iowa were permanent dwellings of the prehistoric Indians—large round earth-covered lodges—and the tepees and wigwams of later tribes. These influenced the later architecture only by suggesting to the white men the use of such materials at hand as logs, sod, clay, bark, and mats.

During warm weather the pioneer camped in his wagon till his cabin was built. Sometimes he constructed a "lean-to" of saplings under which to sleep until his home was finished.

During the construction of these early buildings there was no sound of the hammering of nails nor the rasping of saws; only the dull thud of the pioneer's ax was heard. Instead of nails, screws, bolts, bars, or iron of any description, the pioneer used wooden pegs hewn from logs. The corners

OLDEST HOUSE, DUBUQUE

of the cabin were "planted" in the earth, and logs were lifted one upon the other until a height of seven or eight feet was reached. At first rough logs were used, but later the pioneers smoothed off the bark and squared the logs so that the inside and outside of the cabin presented flat surfaces. The two gables sometimes were formed by using progressively shorter logs until the peak at each end of the building was reached, pinning each log to the one below. A more common practice in this part of the country was to frame the gable end with a vertical stud wall of lighter timbers, and then to face this with shingles or horizontal siding. When the sheltering roof was complete, the small cracks between the logs were chinked with split wood, and daubed inside and out with mortar of clay and straw.

The door was made by leaving an aperture of the required size in one side of the room. A blanket or skin might be hung across this opening until a wooden door could be made. In most cases the chimney was made of split wood and clay mortar, with the back and sides built of stone. Some flues were constructed of squares of sod, laid out as a mason lays a wall of brick, and plastered on the inside with clay. The clay floor was often overlaid with a puncheon floor made of slabs hewn from logs.

The log cabins of the pioneer, most of them built in the 1830's and 1840's, have all but disappeared. Sometimes a vacant cabin stands among the trees along the river, or on the open slope of some prairie hill. Occasionally old log houses, now used as summer kitchens or workshops, are still seen among the newer farm buildings. One well preserved cabin, built in the 1840's on the Beacon Road west of Oskaloosa *(see Tour 15)*, is kept as a memorial. A log cabin of the "dog-trot" or double type (two cabins with one roof extending over a passageway between them), built sometime before 1834, stands in Eagle Point Park in Dubuque.

In the northern and western parts of the State, where wood was scarce and unbroken soil plentiful, the sod house was easy to build, partly above and partly below the surface of the ground. An excavation was made a few feet in depth, and blocks of tough prairie sod were piled up to make the upper portion of the walls. Roofs consisted of poles covered with grass, and chimneys were constructed of sod blocks. Few wall openings relieved the somber exterior. The excavation was so made that a seat of earth was left around the room.

As settlement moved westward and northward, the log cabin was replaced by buildings of lumber, brick, and stone. Brick was early used in the towns along the Mississippi. Brick houses were erected in Burlington and Dubuque in 1836. All of these early buildings were plain structures with gable roofs and a chimney at each end.

The earliest forts were made of logs in the blockhouse style, but the fort erected in 1840 at Fort Atkinson was built of gray limestone quarried nearby. Homes and taverns were constructed (1840–1860) of this same stone throughout eastern Iowa. Those still standing, like the Butterworth Home (1852) *(see Tour 1, Andrew)*, present a mellow romantic appearance.

Partly owing to the religious beliefs of a people who shun ostentation, the architecture of the Amana colonies, in Iowa County, is a stern and elementary example of early housing. The seven villages have an oddly colorless aspect, owing to the predominance of unpainted weather-stained buildings, all in the same style—one might almost say, absence of style—of architecture. These houses, built between 1855 and 1870, are plain rectangular structures of frame, brick, or a peculiar brown sandstone that is found in the vicinity. Happily the severe outline is softened somewhat by the low-pitched roofs and, in summertime, by a singularly charming arrangement of vines. Trained over a framework or trellis, built a few inches from the building to prevent injury to the walls and at the same time afford an adequate support, the vines run high up the walls of house, church, school, and hotel, covering them almost to the eaves.

In Pella, a town settled by the Dutch in 1847, many of the houses are plain one-story frame and brick cottages, some with green and yellow shutters, modeled after the cottages of Holland. In the central, and oldest, section of the town, severe brick houses, closely grouped, stand at a uniform distance from the street.

Along the Mississippi River, in such towns as Lansing, McGregor, Guttenberg, Dubuque, and Bellevue, are found tall old buildings of native limestone, built by the German settlers in this region in the late 1840's and early 1850's. With little space on the terraces (which extend back to the bluffs usually less than a quarter of a mile) the buildings crowd together along one or two narrow streets. Though they fit perfectly their environment, these rows of stone houses, sometimes three and four stories high, with deep-casemented windows and doors, suggest the atmosphere of the Old World. At St. Donatus the settlers from Luxembourg, in the 1850's, practically reproduced one of their native villages. Here two-story houses without eaves, built of stone quarried in the vicinity, stand close together; in some instances with the stable under the same roof.

A name associated with the building of early Iowa churches is that of Father Samuel C. Mazzuchelli, a pioneer priest. This versatile and brilliant churchman, educated in Italy, came to Dubuque in 1835. He included architecture in the scope of his activities, and was responsible for the design of numerous churches in eastern Iowa.

John Francis Rague was the architect of the first capitol building, at Iowa City. This edifice, almost 100 years old, is an example of the Greek Revival style. With its tall porticos, Corinthian columns (in the dome), Doric detail, and hanging staircase, the structure is perhaps the most interesting architectural work in Iowa. The old courthouse at Lansing, built in the 1850's and now abandoned, is another notable example of the same period. At the time of the building (1840–1842) of the Old Capitol, Rague had risen to such prominence in his field that many commissions came his way, including those for the county jail and city hall in Dubuque.

The first churches, fashioned of brick, stone, or wood, were simply designed and unornamented, following the pioneers' idea of practicality. Most of them were long, narrow structures with Gothic windows and a steeple. An outstanding church done in this severe manner, reminiscent of New England Puritanism, is the Little Brown Church in the Vale near Nashua, made famous by Dr. William Pitts' song of the same name *(see Tour 3A, Bradford)*. In his schoolhouses the first builder also held to

AMANA VILLAGE

functional lines. But in his courthouses he indulged himself. These structures, set in the city squares, combine the good and bad features of various styles of architecture; but most of them are large square buildings topped with a tower.

More ornamental still, the opera houses illustrate the general taste of the people during the latter half of the nineteenth century. Many of the larger cities in Iowa erected new opera houses in the 1880's, and each was pointed to with pride as the most pretentious building of its kind west of the Mississippi. These edifices were used for lectures, political speeches, dramatics, and, at rare intervals, for opera. They were very much alike throughout Iowa, following models of an earlier period of playhouse construction. On the main floor the parquet sloped back to an elevated "dress circle" which curved in horseshoe fashion. Iron posts in the ornate Corinthian style held up the enormous balcony and interfered with the view. Folding seats were upholstered in red or green plush. The walls were decorated by garish murals, and the faces of the boxes adorned with gilded ornament on a red or blue background. Many of these "wonder palaces" of the 1880's are still in use.

An interesting example of native architecture, and one illustrating the taste of the period, was the exposition palace, decorated with corn, grass, or coal. An excellent corn harvest in 1887 in the northwest part of the State, at a time when the rest of the country suffered from drought, called for a public expression of thanksgiving. Someone in Sioux City suggested a palace of corn. The suggestion was greeted with much enthusiasm, and experiments with grain as a building material reached such importance that the Sioux City Corn Palace Exposition Company was formed with a capital stock of $250,000.

The first of five giant corn palaces built in Sioux City was designed by E. W. Loft. Fantastically Moorish in appearance, it possessed, nevertheless, an architectural design peculiarly adapted to the use of corn and to the purpose for which it was intended. At each front door there was a square tower. Great arched entrances opened to the streets, and above each entrance was a panel wrought in colored corn. The towers were connected by the battlemented walls of the edifice, above which rose graceful pinnacles. Behind this cresting was the corn-thatched roof—a solid mass of green. Other "palaces," such as the Blue Grass Palace at Creston and the Ottumwa Coal Palace, were less pretentious. The design of these impermanent exposition buildings represented the architectural trend of their day, the 1880's and the 1890's, when showy palace-like buildings were the fashion. The use of circular windows, towers, and jigsaw decorations set

SPIRAL STAIRCASE, OLD CAPITOL

off the newer structures from the plain buildings of pioneer days, which had been planned for use alone.

There are notable examples of Victorian Gothic, and neo-classic styles. The New Melleray Abbey of the Trappist monks, near Dubuque, was founded in 1849 but most of the present buildings were constructed around 1875. The white stone walls, arched windows, buttresses, spires, and ornamental chimneys are reminiscent of medieval Gothic buildings. Planned in the manner of that period, four large structures with gabled wings enclose a rectangular court. Barlow Hall, near Sioux City, designed in the English style, is the only vestige of that epoch (1876–1885) when baronets and viscounts hunted foxes in Iowa meadows (see Tour 12).

The State Capitol at Des Moines, completed in 1884, was designed by A. Piquenard. The massive structure, with gilded central dome and four smaller domes at the corners, has an air of grace and lightness despite its ponderous size. The campus of the University of Iowa, including about 50 buildings, is centered in Old Capitol, Iowa's first capitol building. In general the buildings on the east side of the Iowa River are designed in the Italian Renaissance style, while those on the west side are of a modified early English type. The Iowa State College buildings at Ames are an impressive group. In the center of the campus is a campanile in the style of the Gothic Revival, surrounded by 70 buildings of Georgian Colonial and Classic Revival design.

The first farm homes were necessarily roomy, for the farmer had numerous children and farm hands. Additions built to accommodate the increasing family resulted in the rambling homesteads found throughout the Iowa countryside. Most of the farmhouses erected in the period from 1910 through the 1920's are large box-like, two-story structures on high foundations. Standing out on the low prairie knolls, these houses—generally painted white, and grouped with modern red farm buildings, tall silos, and sheltering groves of trees—present a characteristic Iowa picture, although they do not follow the low horizontal lines of a style of architecture possibly better suited to the prairie.

More recent construction shows a variety of influences: the New England Colonial, the Dutch Colonial, the Southern Colonial, American Georgian, Classic Revival, French Provincial, Norman, Italian, Spanish, and "modern." Occasionally a structure in the "prairie style," built by a native architect perhaps, shows the influence of Louis Sullivan or Frank Lloyd Wright, two outstanding architects whose practice was chiefly confined to Chicago and the Middle West. In the larger cities there is a trend toward functional design, not completely modern in character but with a

DETAIL, WOODBURY COUNTY COURTHOUSE, SIOUX CITY

leaning toward the Classic. The towered Woodbury County Courthouse, designed by W. L. Steele, in its bold mass and line and concentration of rich ornament, is reminiscent of the style developed by Sullivan and Wright.

Sullivan's theory of functionalism is expressed in the five buildings he designed in Iowa between 1911 and 1914. Of one of these (now the office of the Druggist Mutual Insurance Company) in Algona, Hugh Morrison said, in his biography of Sullivan, "Few buildings of that period . . . match it in quality." It is a simple rectangular mass, ornamented with unusual restraint. The Peoples Savings Bank in Cedar Rapids and the Merchants' National Bank in Grinnell are also excellent examples of Sullivan's work. The Grinnell bank is representative of his lyrical tendency with intricate foliated forms against a structure geometrically exact. The design for St. Paul's Methodist Church in Cedar Rapids, a circular building constructed in 1913–1915, is also Sullivan's; a local architect made a few minor changes but the fundamental conception is there. Sullivan also designed the Van Allen drygoods store in Clinton (1913–1915).

Frank Lloyd Wright's influence is not so marked as Sullivan's. However, the Stockham house and the Park Inn (hotel) in Mason City were designed by him in the "prairie style," which is so well adapted to the Iowa country. The home is much as Wright designed it, but the hotel, with a bank adjoining, has been changed—the hotel but slightly, the bank beyond recognition.

Widespread interest in architecture is reflected in the factories as well as in the homes and the public buildings. The Quaker Oats Company built one of the largest cereal mills in the world at Cedar Rapids in 1905. Its seven gigantic elevators, with a combined capacity of 9,500,000 bushels of grain, rise upward and dominate the structure. The packing plant at Waterloo, all new buildings constructed in the last ten years, and the one at Ottumwa, are examples of the purely utilitarian in architectural design.

Farm buildings, too, constitute an indigenous type that is essentially modern. Cylindrical silos, usually of red brick, tile, or cement (sometimes of wooden staves) ; barns, in which the predominant note is the utilization of all available space, often with hipped roofs to give more room for hay; grain elevators, in every town and at the little roadside stations—all these vertical, tall structures are expressions of functional design.

PART II
Cities and Towns

Ames

Railroad Station: Main St. bet. Grand and Clark Sts., for Chicago & North Western Ry.
Bus Station: Sheldon Munn Hotel, Main and Kellogg Sts., for Jefferson Lines and Interstate Transit Lines.
Street Buses: Circling the downtown district and making regular 20-minute trips to the college campus, 7¢.
Taxis: First zone, 25¢, second zone, 50¢.

Accommodations: Hotels, two downtown, one at campus; restaurants and rooming houses in both parts of town; Memorial Union, Iowa State College campus.

Information Service: City Hall, 5th and Kellogg Sts.

Radio Station: WOI (640 kc.)
Motion Picture Houses: Three.
Swimming: Carr's Pool, end of Duff St., NE. city limits.
Golf: Overland, 9 holes, 2 m. S. on US 65, 50¢; Homewood, 9 holes, NE. edge of city, 50¢.
Tennis: College courts.
Ice Skating: Lake LaVerne, college campus.
Band Concerts: City Park, downtown, at music pavilion once a week during summer.

Annual Events: Veishea, college celebration, annually in May; Girls' 4-H Club Convention, June; Horticulture Exposition, Nov.; Boys' 4-H Convention, Dec.; *Messiah* Concert, Dec.

AMES (926 alt., 10,261 pop.), a college town, lies on rolling prairie, near the geographic center of Iowa. Squaw Creek bisects the town, the northeastern corner of which touches Skunk River. From a distance the town appears to be a dense grove extending between the water towers and smokestacks at the eastern and western ends of the town. To the casual observer, Ames is two adjacent towns, since the college farmlands separate the original town from the section that clusters thickly about the college —Iowa State College of Agriculture and Mechanic Arts. Each section has its own business center. Modern buildings line the wide streets of the downtown section; and shops, catering to student trade, border the southern edge of the campus.

Near the college are two of the newer residential districts—Ridgewood and College Park. Here the streets wind about between modern homes. Squaw Creek flows along the eastern boundary of the meadows that intervene between the residence sections. At the east side of the campus stately dormitories stand out boldly against the heavy foliage of trees.

With the large number of students from all over the State and Nation and various parts of the world, the town assumes a metropolitan character and coloring. Students spend an average of $4,000,000 a year in this city.

CAMPANILE, IOWA STATE COLLEGE, AMES

The State Highway Commission, with its office workers and road crews centered here, likewise attracts a great many people. With its well-kept homes and wide shaded streets the town wears an air of cleanliness and charm. The city prides itself on its schools and churches. The health work of the public schools was recognized as the best in the country by the National Tuberculosis Association for the three years ending in 1933, thus giving them permanent possession of the association's silver cup.

The site of Ames, slough and marshland, was not the kind early settlers usually chose for a town. When Mrs. Cynthia Duff bought the farmland occupying the future town site in 1864, no one knew she was buying it for John I. Blair who planned to build a depot for the Cedar Rapids and Missouri Railroad (later the North Western) on the land. Although Blair had been offered 20 acres of free land south of College Farm, located at this point in 1859, he built the station and laid out the town on the land acquired by Mrs. Duff. Blair named the new town site for Oakes Ames, one of the proprietors of the railroad. Noah Webster (not the compiler of the dictionary) built the first home in the town in 1864. Until January 1866, Ames bore the post office name of College Farm because it was adjacent to the land purchased for the State Agricultural College and the Model Farm.

With the development of the railroad and the drainage of the land, more settlers began to come in, until at the end of 1865 there were 300 living here. Special laws were passed by the State legislature to safeguard the students of College Farm, including one prohibiting the sale of any kind of alcoholic beverages.

The town was incorporated in 1870; four years later the Narrow Gauge line (now the North Western) from Des Moines to Ames, helped to complete what the college had already started—the making of a brisk small town from what had been little more than a flag station. Always an important railroad center, Ames, for a time, was also the terminal of the Cedar Rapids and Missouri, making it a place of "considerable railroad stir." By 1886 the local time tables boasted that "there were 20 chances to leave Ames every 24 hours."

In 1887 fire destroyed the greater part of the business section, but it was rebuilt by 1891. "The dinky," a railroad built from Ames to the college in 1891, made it more convenient for students to visit the town; and in 1893 Ames qualified as a second class city when it extended its corporate limits to include the college. It had a city waterworks in 1891; a library association in 1893; and a municipal lighting system in 1896.

The fire at the college in 1900 intensified local interest in the school. When the trustees of the college announced that the dormitories would not be rebuilt, townspeople at once began to construct large rooming houses. This was the beginning of the residence section surrounding Iowa State College.

In 1900 the college was reorganized. A public library was built in 1903 and in 1910, when most Iowa towns were still struggling with dirt streets, the first Ames paving was laid. The city manager plan of government was adopted in 1920, at the beginning of the decade in which Ames made its greatest growth (6,270 to 10,261 in 1930). Industries in the town today include a canning factory, a pottery, a hatchery, a garden tools factory, and a factory making supplies for fraternities.

Campus Tour—*1.2m*

Iowa State College campus extends from Beech to Sheldon Avenues on Lincoln Way, which passes the southern edge of the campus, bordering Lake LaVerne. Scheduled summer tours are conducted by the Extension Service for county Farm Bureau groups and others; see Superintendent of Tours, Morrill Hall.

Unless otherwise indicated, buildings, with the exception of classrooms in use, are open to the public during school hours. Those interested in agriculture and the experimental farm should apply for information at Agricultural Hall.

The campus has a broad sweep of lawn and trees broken here and there by imposing buildings, arranged by department groups. An outstanding feature is the natural grouping of trees and shrubbery, almost as they might appear in the original Iowa landscape. The paths across the campus and along College Creek, the hills, the bird shelters, the clusters of trees and hedges are native Iowa at its best.

A legislative act of 1858 provided for the establishment of a State Agricultural College and Model Farm "for the purpose of giving academic instruction to the industrial classes." It also provided $10,000 for the purchase of a farm to be used for agricultural experiments and for the erection of the college buildings. After the people of Story County had voted bonds of $10,000 and given enough more in land and money to bring the total contribution to about $21,000, that county was selected for the farm site on June 21, 1859, and a farm of 648 acres, including the present campus, was purchased. Daniel McCarthy drove the first stake on the college farm in 1860 and donated $75 to have the land surveyed.

The Iowa General Assembly at a special session in September 1862 accepted the conditions of the Morrill College Land Grant Bill, passed by Congress the same year, and received a grant of 204,000 acres of land. The college opened to students in the fall of 1868.

A number of United States Secretaries of Agriculture have received training at Iowa State College, including James (Tama Jim) Wilson who served during the administrations of William McKinley, Theodore Roosevelt, and William Howard Taft. Henry C. Wallace, Secretary of Agriculture under President Warren G. Harding, and Henry A. Wallace, under Franklin D. Roosevelt, were graduates of the school.

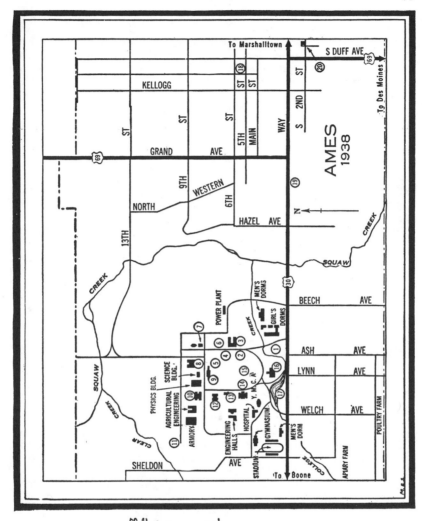

AMES 1938

KEY TO POINTS
OF INTEREST

AMES

1. The Knoll
2. Agricultural Hall
3. Dairy Industry Building
4. Historic Old Farmhouse
5. Horticultural Buildings
6. Landscape Architecture
   Studio
7. Meats Laboratory
8. Veterinary Quadrangle
9. Home Economics Build-
   ing
10. Chemistry Hall
11. College Cemetery
12. College Library
13. Morrill Hall
14. Central Building
15. Campanile
16. Memorial Union
17. Lake Laverne
18. Site of Noah Webster
    House
19. Iowa State Highway
    Commission Bldg.
20. Octagonal House

Other well known persons associated with the college included W. T. Hornaday, zoologist, and L. H. Pammel, botanist. Dr. Hornaday, at various times director of the New York Zoological Park (1896–1926), had been a collecting naturalist for the American Museum, chief taxidermist for the United States National Museum (1882–1888), and the winner of many medals from various countries for his work. He is author of *Our Vanishing Wild Life* and *Thirty Years War for Wild Life* (1931). L. H. Pammel, first associated with Iowa State College in 1889, became widely known in Iowa as an advocate of conservation and State Parks.

The college with its campus and experimental farms occupies 1,998 acres. The 70 buildings are ranged on a campus of 250 acres. The planned new buildings of the inner zone fringing the lawn of the main campus, are to be built of stone and those in the outer zone of brick. The total expenditures of the college, the physical plant of which is valued at $11,-450,000, was in the fiscal year ending 1937, $3,490,000. More than 97 percent of this sum went for education and research. The enrollment of 5,966 students in 1936–37, included students from 23 foreign countries. Divisions of the college include Agriculture, Engineering, Home Economics, Industrial Science, Veterinary Medicine, and the Graduate College. Through its experimental farms and well-equipped laboratories, the college has aided agricultural and industrial development in every section of the State.

The Extension Service in agriculture and home economics is financed jointly by the State and the United States Department of Agriculture. The Engineering Division offers industrial short courses, extension classes and correspondence study in Industrial Teachers' Training courses. Jointly with the Agricultural Extension Service the Engineering Division gives a visual instruction service in motion pictures, slides, and charts. Radio station WOI provides educational programs.

N. from Lincoln Way, on Campus Rd.

1. THE KNOLL *(private)*, Campus Rd. (L), is the home of the president of the college. On the right is that part of the campus set aside for the Women's Dormitories, Georgian in architectural style, which furnish homes for approximately 900 women.

2. AGRICULTURAL HALL, Campus Rd. across College Creek (L), top of hill, erected in 1907, is a four-story structure of gray Bedford stone, built in Italian Renaissance style. Part of the inner circle of buildings, it faces the central campus and houses nine laboratories that provide modern equipment for studying soil fertility, soil management, soil survey, and soil bacteriology. The *Iowa State Student,* tri-weekly student newspaper, the *Green Gander,* humor magazine, and other departmental periodicals are published by the Collegiate Press, Inc., in the basement.

Directly on the right is Agricultural Hall Annex.

3. DAIRY INDUSTRY BUILDING, Campus Rd. (R) beyond Agricultural Hall Annex, has TERRA COTTA PANELS on the north and south walls of the main entrance, created by Christian Petersen. They are historical in theme and show butter-making in two eras. TERRA COTTA PAN-

ORAMA in the central open court symbolizes the dairy industry in Iowa. In the center are four terra cotta cows, so arranged that they seem to be drinking from a real fountain of water. Laboratories, classrooms, and the general office are in the main building. In the wings are rooms where butter, cheese, ice cream, and condensed and powdered milk are prepared. The college is one of the few places in the United States where Roquefort cheese is made, and its output finds a ready market.

4. HISTORIC OLD FARMHOUSE *(private)*, Campus Rd. (L) N. of the Dairy Industry Building, occupied by one of the college deans, was once a stagecoach stop and inn. Robert E. Lee stayed here about 1860 when he was surveying in this part of the country. A tablet, giving the history, is in the front yard.

5. HORTICULTURAL BUILDINGS, Campus Rd. (L), have two groups of laboratories, adapted classic in style, two ranges of greenhouses, and various farm buildings. In the principal range of 14 greenhouses adjoining the new building are rare plants and conservatory and garden plants. North of the greenhouses are the formal and trial gardens, and west, the Botany Building.

6. LANDSCAPE ARCHITECTURE STUDIO, Campus Rd. (R) across from greenhouses, Georgian in style, was once a college stable, now remodeled to house classrooms, a lecture hall, and offices for the faculty and students in landscape architecture. It is said that President A. S. Welch gave the first lecture course in the United States on landscape architecture.

7. MEATS LABORATORY, NE. cor. Campus Rd. and North Drive, N. of Landscape Architecture Studio, is fully equipped for the killing of cattle, sheep, and hogs, for the handling of carcasses, cuts, and byproducts, and for the curing of meats. This structure, adapted Gothic in style, has the appearance of a church. Judging pavilions and barns, north of the Meats Laboratory, house livestock. Many of the draft horses kept here have taken first prizes at leading livestock shows in the country.

L. from Campus Rd. on North Dr.

8. VETERINARY QUADRANGLE, North Dr. (R), has half a dozen structures of brick and terra cotta built in an adapted Gothic style. They center around an open court that is entered through an attractive brick archway. The VETERINARY HOSPITAL has hospital stalls, kennels, operating and clinic rooms.

9. HOME ECONOMICS BUILDING, North Dr. (L), a three-story building of Bedford stone, classic in style, facing the inner zone, houses laboratories, classrooms, the Catherine McKay Auditorium with a seating capacity of 700, and a tea room. Across the drive north of the Home Economics building about a block, are the Nursery School Annex and four Home Management Houses.

10. CHEMISTRY HALL, North Dr. (R), third building W. of Veterinary Quadrangle, has a MUSEUM OF GEOLOGY, second floor, containing a collection of 7,000 minerals, rocks, and paleontological specimens.

11. COLLEGE CEMETERY, W. end of North Dr., NW. of Armory (R), is one of the few college cemeteries in the world. A distinctive memorial marks the graves of the first president, A. S. Welch, and wife, Mary

TERRA COTTA DETAIL, DAIRY INDUSTRY BUILDING, AMES

Beaumond Welch, who was the founder of the Division of Home Economics at Iowa State College. Kung Fan Chi, a Chinese youth who died reputedly as "the seventieth direct lineal descendant of Confucius," is buried here. The body of L. H. Pammel, eminent botanist and conservationist, occupies another of the graves. On the east edge of the cemetery is a marker indicating the SITE OF THE FIRST PICNIC held on the Fourth of July (1859) to celebrate the inception of the college.
L. from North Dr. on Inner Campus Rd.

12. COLLEGE LIBRARY *(open 8-12 weekdays)*, Inner Campus Rd. (R), one of the stone buildings of the inner zone, an adaptation of the Italian Renaissance in style, houses the valuable Schneider Music Library of Orchestrations. MURALS on the walls, painted by Grant Wood and his assistants under the Civil Works Administration, illustrate Daniel Webster's text, "When tillage begins other arts follow." They present first a pioneer plowing scene, followed by panels showing associated useful arts such as veterinary medicine, chemical and mechanical engineering, and home economics.

13. MORRILL HALL, Inner Campus Rd. (R), S. of Library, is one of

the oldest buildings on the campus. Romanesque in style, it was named in honor of Justin S. Morrill, the originator of the "land grant" for colleges of agriculture and mechanic arts. The offices of the agricultural extension service and the bulletin shipping rooms are here.

14. CENTRAL BUILDING, Campus Rd. (R), Italian Renaissance in style, facing Agricultural Hall across inner campus, contains the executive offices. The tall columns and the wide steps at the main entrance are notable features of its architecture.

15. CAMPANILE, center of main campus (L), houses the college carillon. Constructed of yellow brick in modified Gothic design, this 110-foot tower was donated by Dr. Edgar W. Stanton as a memorial to his wife, Margaret McDonald Stanton, the first Dean of Women, who died in 1899. After Dr. Stanton died (1920), the Campanile was made a memorial to both. Twenty-six bells were added to the original 10, making the chime a carillon. The largest bell weighs 3,584 pounds. The carillon is heard best at least 500 feet away where there is no confusion of overtones.

16. MEMORIAL UNION *(open—cafeteria and dining rooms)*, S. of Campanile, built on the hillside at the Lynn Ave. entrance, is designed in a modified Italian and Spanish Renaissance style of architecture. The social life of the campus is centered in this building. One of its features is GOLD STAR HALL, the main entrance to the building. The high vaulted stone ceiling is supported on a row of columns at each side of the room. Between the columns on the stone walls are carved the names of the 118 alumni who gave their lives in the World War. Pledges from alumni, faculty, and students provided funds for the building.

17. LAKE LAVERNE, below Memorial Union, a beautiful, artificial body of water, covering four and one-half acres, was named in honor of its alumnus donor, La Verne Noyes. Swans glide in its waters in the summer. In the winter it is a favorite skating rink.

R. from Inner Campus Rd. at Lake LaVerne; continuing to Lincoln Way

Scattered over this section are general college and engineering department buildings. On the hilltop as the road curves west appear the Music Hall, the Alumni Hall, and the Hospital. ENGINEERING HALL, N. of the hospital, a four-story structure of Bedford stone built in modified German Renaissance style, is the largest of the cluster of engineering buildings. Crop and market reports are received daily for broadcasting over the COLLEGE RADIO STATION WOI *(open)*, top floor of the south wing of the Engineering Annex. In the CHEMICAL LABORATORIES and INDUSTRIAL ARTS BUILDING are laboratories where research is carried on to determine how agricultural waste products, such as cornstalks, can be utilized. Already this research has resulted in patents for the State on a process of manufacturing synthetic wallboard and two types of compounds similar to bakelite. A product somewhat like gunpowder can be made from cornstalks and research is in progress on the manufacture of paper from cornstalks and straw. The LOCOMOTIVE, south of Engineering Annex, set on a narrow gauge track and first used by the "Burlington" in eastern Iowa in 1855, has been on the Iowa State campus since 1905. Some authorities claim it was the first locomotive to cross Iowa.

South and west of campus

Numerous experimental farms are scattered throughout the area south and west of the campus. These farms, ranging in size from 30 to 200 acres, are used for carrying out farming experiments. At the Apiary Farm, the availability of nectar and pollen for bees is studied in test plots. Students have their own segregated apiaries where they can study the different races of bees. The Poultry Farm breeds most of the leading varieties of domestics fowls on its 36-acre tract. The many types of poultry houses, the laboratory buildings, the varying kinds and sizes of incubators, the feeding batteries, and the brooders all provide an excellent opportunity for carrying on tests. The Agronomy Farm and Experimental Fields provide 170 acres which are used entirely for experiments with farm crops and soils. The Animal Husbandry Experimental Farm of 182 acres is used exclusively for feeding and breeding experiments with beef cattle, hogs, and sheep. The Dairy Husbandry Farm supplies much of the feed for the college dairy herd. Experimental work with pastures and other crops is carried on here.

OTHER POINTS OF INTEREST

18. SITE OF NOAH WEBSTER HOUSE, NE. corner 5th St. and Douglas Ave., the first house erected in the city, is marked with a boulder.

19. IOWA STATE HIGHWAY COMMISSION BUILDING, Lincoln Way between Grand and Elm Aves., houses the commission that has developed Iowa's network of good roads. Five commissioners, appointed by the Governor for four-year terms, have charge of the construction and maintenance of primary roads, the general supervision of secondary roads, and the giving of engineering assistance to other State departments. The State authorized Iowa State College to act as the first highway commission in 1904. In 1913 the State Highway Commission was reorganized by legislative act and given real authority. A subsequent reorganization in 1927 increased the membership to five and designated that the construction and supervision of primary roads through the State be taken over by the commission. For many years the commission was housed at Iowa State College.

20. OCTAGONAL HOUSE, 129 Sumner Ave. *(private),* built about 1870 to satisfy an astronomical whim of Dr. Starr, the designer and first owner, is known in Ames as the "old round house." Dr. Starr, a student of astronomy, used the large octagonal-shaped cupola that originally formed the fourth floor as an observatory. Because the cupola portion of the octagonal house was in bad condition, it was removed by the present owner shortly after he bought the house. A rectangular addition has been built at the rear of the building, covering two sides of the octagon, but the original shape is still evident.

POINTS OF INTEREST IN ENVIRONS

William (Billy) Sunday's Birthplace—4 *m. (see Tour 5);* William Sunday's Home, Nevada—7 *m. (see Tour 13, sec. b).*

‹‹‹‹‹‹‹‹‹‹‹‹‹‹‹‹‹‹‹‹ ☼ ›››››››››››››››››››

Burlington

Railroad Station: Union Depot, 300 S. Main St., for Chicago, Burlington & Quincy R.R. and Chicago, Rock Island & Pacific Ry.
Bus Station: Union Bus Depot, 315 Valley St., for Burlington Trailways, M. Foster Lines, Illinois Transit Lines.
Airport: Municipal, city limits SW. on Summer St. S. (US 61), taxi fare not over 50¢, Braniff Air Lines to Kansas City.
Dock and Warehouse: Municipal, Inland Waterways and Federal Barge Lines at river end of Columbia and Washington Sts.
Interurban Station: NW. cor. Main and Jefferson Sts. for bus to W. Burlington.
Street Buses: Fare 10¢, three tokens 20¢.
Taxis: Rate 25¢ first mile; 10¢ each additional .5 mile.

Accommodations: Five hotels, three tourist camps.

Information Service: American Automobile Association and Chamber of Commerce, Hotel Burlington, NE. cor. 3rd and Valley Sts.

Theaters and Motion Picture Houses: Four motion picture houses, one legitimate theater, one Little Theater.
Tennis: Crapo Park, Burlington High School Stadium Courts.
Swimming: Kiwanis Pool, S. end Main St., near Crapo Park.
Ice Skating: Crapo Park.
Golf: Crystal Springs, public, 2600 Bluff Road (State 99), 9 holes, weekdays, 25¢; holidays and Sun., 40¢.
Excursion Boats: Dock, River Front Park, J. S. Streckfus lines.

Annual Events: Tri-State Fair, 2nd week in Aug.; Corn Show or Fall Festival, 1st Thurs., Fri. and Sat. in Oct.; Wallaneeh, Halloween Festival, Oct. 31.

BURLINGTON (532 alt., 26,755 pop.) is scattered over four hills along the Mississippi River. The commercial section lies in the Valley where Hawk Eye Creek, now scarcely discernible, bisects the city southeast to northwest. Front Street, the old thoroughfare stretching along the Mississippi River, is noisy with the rattle and clatter of trucks and the air is redolent with the odor of fruits in season, for the wholesale dealers whose buildings dominate the south end of the street are always loading and unloading—perhaps cantaloupe today, apples tomorrow. Barges tie up at the municipal dock, motor boats race by, or an occasional excursion boat pulls out with its paddle wheels splashing. Bridges bound the street at either end. Autos stream over the MacArthur Bridge, and frequently the draw of the railroad bridge swings open to allow a large steamboat to pass.

In the bottoms north along the river lies a commercial district that surrounds the Willow Patch, a settlement started previous to the Civil War. Then the greater part of the land was under water, making it a convenient harbor for houseboats of fishermen and towmen. Today the Willow Patch is known for the fine woven nets and seines that the people make. Life here is simple and somewhat primitive. In West Burlington are the shops of the Chicago, Burlington and Quincy Railroad where more than 500 men are employed.

Burlington has a substantial appearance, owing perhaps to the many old stone homes and churches. Early settlers quarried the stone in or near the city to erect buildings and to pave many of the streets and alleys now worn smooth. The streets that climb the hills from the business and commercial districts do not run in straight lines for any distance. The steepness makes them angle off out of sight to skirt a bluff or disappear over a hill. This irregularity of topography presents homes with 70 or 80 steps leading to them.

Descendants of the early German, Irish, and Swedish settlers still predominate in the population and the settlements that clustered about the pioneer industries are still distinguishable. Living in many of the smaller box-like cottages of Dutchtown, known as Germania and Lincolnville, are older Germans who cling to Old World customs. Along these streets German housewives wear breakfast caps until the morning tasks are over. A few families annually celebrate October 6, the day German colonists established themselves in America.

On West Hill, the Swedish district is traceable in the neat and well landscaped grounds surrounding the homes, in many of which *lutefisk* (dried stockfish), imported from Sweden, is a favorite dish from November to March each year. In the section known as Hibernia old houses still stand on the sides of the hills and slopes first chosen by Irish immigrants. With characteristic vigor the Irish organized the West End Improvement Club, believed to be one of the first community center organizations in the United States.

The site of Burlington, called Sho-ko-kon (Flint Hills), was valued by the Indians for the flint found there. Lieut. Zebulon Pike referred to it when he wrote the story of his expedition (1805) to explore the Mississippi River from St. Louis to its source, to find strategic locations for forts, and to make friends with the Indians.

Tai-mah (Tama) set up his Indian village (Shokokon) on the site of Burlington in 1820 but later moved his band to Tama Town Prairie, nine miles north. Simpson S. White, Morton McCarver, and Amasa Doolittle were the first permanent settlers. After the Black Hawk treaty was signed in Sept. 1832, throwing open the territory on the west side of the river to white settlers, effective June 1833, some 10 or 12 families, too impatient to wait longer on the east side of the river, crossed over. Complaints of the Indians, however, forced the soldiers at Fort Armstrong to send them back. They re-occupied their claims in 1833, and in August of that year Dr. William R. Ross opened the first store.

John Gray, a native of Vermont, arrived in Flint Hills in March 1834, and was allowed, upon purchasing a lot, to name the settlement Burlington, after his home town. The Reverend Peter Cartwright, presiding elder of a large part of Illinois and all of the Iowa country, organized a Methodist class at Dr. Ross's cabin in April and about the same time 16 children

attended the first school, taught by Zadock C. Inghram. By the close of the
year, Burlington was the chief settlement in Demoine County.

The second legislature of the Territory of Wisconsin convened at Burlington on the first Monday in November 1837 in the temporary capitol erected
to serve until the capitol at Madison was completed. In 1837 the town was
incorporated.

When the Territory of Iowa was created in 1838, the first Legislative
Assembly convened that fall at Burlington, the temporary capital, and
appointed a commission to select the permanent capital.

Drums rattled, fifes whistled; and bugles blew in Burlington when the
first Iowa militia assembled there to settle the Iowa-Missouri boundary
dispute, soon after the first assembly met. Roistering groups of would-be
soldiers surged through the streets. Dropping plow handles and axes in
the field, they came wearing make-shift uniforms and carrying an odd
assortment of weapons. They jostled shoulders in the taverns and hunted
excitement along the riverfront. Boisterous hilarity and drunken brawls
marked their brief sojourn. Many companies were still en route to Burlington when settlement of the question was delegated to the United States
Supreme Court.

On July 3, 1839, the body of Black Hawk, Indian chief, disappeared
from its grave on James Jordan's farm near Iowaville. Burlington was
aroused from a mid-summer doze when Nasheakusk, Black Hawk's son,
with about 50 other Indians marched through the streets to inform Governor Robert Lucas of what had happened. A year later the bones were
recovered from a dentist in Quincy, Illinois, who had received them from
St. Louis. Black Hawk's widow left the bones in the care of the "good
old man," Governor Lucas. Later they were placed in the museum of the
Burlington Geological and Historical Society and lost when the building
was burned in 1855.

The murder of John Miller and the subsequent public hanging of
William and Stephen Hodges, the convicted murderers, was an event in
1845. Thousands jammed the streets to see the condemned men paraded
from the jail to the execution hill near the edge of town. Four companies
of riflemen, marching to the dirge of a brass band, preceded the convey-
ance in which the condemned men, shrouded and in chains, sat astraddle
their coffins.

In 1855, Dick, the first fugitive slave caught near Burlington, was tried
in Marion Hall before a crowd determined upon seeing him freed. Iowa
had just elected its first anti-slavery Senator, hence, joyous shouts greeted
Judge Rorer's dismissal of the case.

The continual stream of immigrants that entered Iowa at Burlington
reached its peak in August 1856 when 20,000 people crossed the Mississippi on the ferry. Then the bustling town had three pork packing plants
important enough to give Burlington the name, "Porkopolis of Iowa."
Hundreds of steamers docked to discharge freight that the prairie schooners
were to carry inland, or to load pork, lard, and farm produce.

Railroads eventually changed Burlington from a lively river town to a
bustling railroad center. A jubilant excursion from Chicago to a point op-

posite Burlington celebrated the completion of the second continuous railroad from Chicago to the Mississippi in 1855. The next year the Burlington & Missouri River Railroad, organized in 1851, began operations in Iowa, following the Hawk-Eye Creek valley. Temporarily Burlington streets were crowded with the rough and hardy railroad workers, but they moved westward as the railroad approached the Missouri.

Marion Hall was crowded with men registering for service at the time of the Civil War, adding other companies to the Rifles, the Blues, the Irish Volunteers, the Washington Guards, and an artillery company already in existence. Camp Warren was established at the Fair Grounds.

During the war, railroad freight had to be rafted across the river but a bridge was built in August 1868. The next year the Chicago, Burlington & Quincy absorbed the Burlington & Missouri River Railroad which then extended to the Missouri. From that time river traffic gradually slackened. In the 1870's, when livestock had become an increasingly important shipment from Omaha to Chicago, extensive stockyards grew up on the east side of the Mississippi, opposite Burlington. Here the bawling, restless cattle were unloaded, bedded, watered, and fed.

The year 1871 marked the peak of prosperity for the lumber industry. Burlington, a lumber shipping point, exported as much as 57,000,000 feet of lumber in a year. Raftsmen bringing the logs down the river from Wisconsin to the mills added, for a time, a lusty note to the growing town. In 1873 a disastrous fire, destroying five solid blocks of the business section, temporarily held back the town's development. In 1874, after the city had been rebuilt, horse-drawn cars were inaugurated. The horses pulled the cars up the many hills, and then rested on the rear platform of the cars while they traveled down-grade.

In 1875 the city's special charter was abandoned when the municipality was organized under council form. In the period from the end of the Civil War to 1885 Burlington experienced its largest industrial, commercial, and cultural growth.

The next few decades were not without their events. By 1890 the old-fashioned horse-drawn cars were supplanted by electric cars. Pleasure boats began to increase on the river about 1900 and regattas for speed boats became popular celebrations. In 1909 the city adopted the commission form of government. The last raft of lumber from the north, towed by the steamer *Ottumwa Bell* with Capt. Walter Hunter in charge, passed the city in 1915. In May 1922 a cloudburst brought the waters from the hills nearby down into the city's center, but the losses suffered were soon replaced. In the last decades of the nineteenth and the first of the twentieth centuries, Burlington developed its manufacturing and jobbing—furniture, baskets, coffins, and monuments—until in 1925 the factory output reached a high peak, valued at over $12,000,000.

Robert Jones Burdette (1844–1914) brought attention to the city through his humorous sketches in the *Hawk-Eye* when he first began to publish them in the 1880's. Two other men associated with the city who received international fame are Charles Wachsmuth and Frank Springer, whose common interest—collecting fossils—drew them together. In 1897

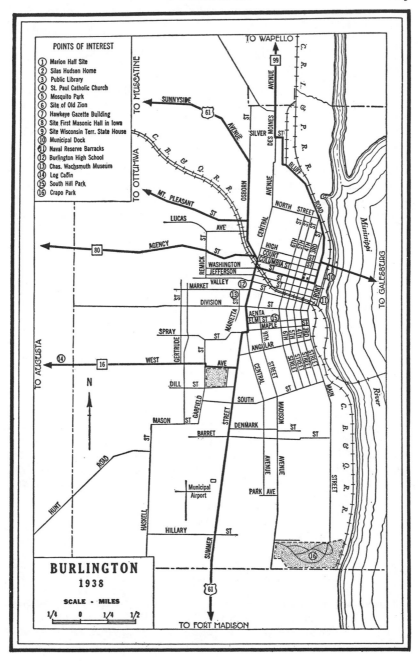

POINTS OF INTEREST

1. Marion Hall Site
2. Silas Hudson Home
3. Public Library
4. St. Paul Catholic Church
5. Mosquito Park
6. Site of Old Zion
7. Hawkeye Gazette Building
8. Site First Masonic Hall in Iowa
9. Site Wisconsin Terr. State House
10. Municipal Dock
11. Naval Reserve Barracks
12. Burlington High School
13. Chas. Wachsmuth Museum
14. Log Cabin
15. South Hill Park
16. Crapo Park

BURLINGTON
1938

SCALE · MILES

1/4   0   1/4   1/2

the two scientists published the results of their study of crinoids in a monumental book.

POINTS OF INTEREST

1. SITE OF MARION HALL, NE. corner 4th and Washington Sts., is now a park. In 1855 the Dick Slave Trial, was held here. Dr. Edwin James, whose home just outside Burlington was a station on the underground railroad, was forced by several Missourians to return from Illinois with Dick, a fugitive slave. Burlington authorities arrested the slave when the Missourians claimed they were the agents of Thomas Rutherford to whom Dick belonged. At the trial before a courtroom crowded with Dick's sympathizers, Rutherford's son testified that the slave before him did not belong to his father. Judge David Rorer dismissed the fugitive, who later went to Canada.

SNAKE ALLEY, 6th St. between Washington and Columbia Sts., is the local name for this steep block of 6th Street that makes five sharp curves in ascending the steep grade, thus acquiring its name.

2. SILAS HUDSON HOME (private), NW. corner Columbia and 5th Sts., erected in 1844, is where Abraham Lincoln stayed when he visited Burlington in 1858. Through the influence of his boyhood friend, Silas Hudson, Lincoln delivered a speech in the GRIMES OPERA HOUSE (site NE. corner Valley and Main Sts.) on October 9, 1858, in his campaign against Stephen A. Douglas for Senator from Illinois.

3. PUBLIC LIBRARY (open 9-9 weekdays; June 1 to Sept. 1, 9-5), SW. corner Columbia and 4th Sts., entrance 501 N. 4th St., has among its exhibits a small model of the Old Zion Church and the Philip M. Crapo collection of 320 shells and specimens from oceans around the world. Its files of the Iowa Patriot, Burlington Hawk-Eye, and Wisconsin Territorial Gazette, and Telegraph, dating from 1837, and valued at more than $25,000, are kept in well-bound volumes.

4. ST. PAUL ROMAN CATHOLIC CHURCH, NE. corner 4th and Columbia Sts., English Gothic in style, was built in 1892. It contains the old pulpit, hand carved by Father Samuel Mazzuchelli, and a bell (one of the first in the State) from the first church, designed by Father Mazzuchelli, pioneer priest, in which the council of the second Territorial legislature met in 1839.

5. MOSQUITO PARK, corner Franklin and 3rd Sts., high on North Hill Bluff, affords a view of the Willow Patch with its fisherman's cabins and boats, the Mississippi River's rugged shore line and wooded islands, and the rolling Illinois prairies.

6. SITE OF OLD ZION, first Iowa Territorial Capitol, W. side of 3rd St. between Columbia and Washington Sts., is now occupied by the RIALTO THEATER, known as the Old Grand Opera House in the days of Lillian Russell, Edmund Booth, John Drew, and the Barrymores. A bronze PLAQUE on the theater building marks the site. Old Zion served as assembly hall, courthouse, and public meeting place. Here three Territorial assemblies met (1838–1841) to settle Indian controversies and boundary

disputes. Judge Charles Mason sentenced the Hodges brothers to death from Old Zion pulpit in 1845. By 1851 the church needed repairs. When J. S. McKenney, editor of the *Daily Telegraph,* printed posters, "Old Zion wants a new roof," he named the church. Old Zion bell still swings from the square Gothic belfry of the present FIRST METHODIST CHURCH, 5th and Washington Sts.

7. HAWK-EYE GAZETTE BUILDING, 311 Washington St., houses Burlington's only daily newspaper (1937), the consolidation of two pioneer newspapers, the Burlington *Hawk-Eye* and the Burlington *Gazette.* The building, Renaissance in style, has a terra cotta front. *The Hawk-Eye Gazette,* the State's oldest newspaper in continuous publication, is the only Iowa newspaper with files running back to 1837 (available at public library). The *Gazette,* established in 1836 by James Clarke, later Governor of the Territory of Iowa, was first known as the *Wisconsin Territorial Gazette and Burlington Advertiser.* James G. Edwards, a New York reporter who had purchased the *Western Adventurer* and published it in Fort Madison as the Fort Madison *Patriot,* moved his paper to Burlington in 1838. The paper had a succession of names—Burlington *Patriot, Iowa Patriot, Hawk-Eye and Iowa Patriot*—before Edwards finally called it the *Hawk-Eye* on June 1, 1843, at the suggestion of his wife. Edwards, later called "Old Hawk," had suggested the nickname, Hawk-Eyes, for the people of the Iowa country.

8. SITE OF FIRST MASONIC HALL IN IOWA, SE. corner Main and Columbia Sts. is marked by a bronze TABLET attached to the north side of the Mid-West Print Shop. The House of Representatives of the Wisconsin Territorial Assembly met in rooms over the store of Remey and Webber, grocers, which originally stood on this site.

9. SITE OF WISCONSIN TERRITORIAL STATE HOUSE, on Front St. just N. of Columbia St., is covered by the back portion of the Mississippi Pearl Button Company's office building. The Assembly Hall, built in 1837 by Jeremiah Smith, Jr., one of the Iowa District's representatives, was used by the second Wisconsin Territorial Assembly until fire destroyed the building on December 13, only a few months after it was built. This was the first legislative assembly to meet in Iowa.

10. BURLINGTON MUNICIPAL DOCK, Front St. between Washington and Columbia Sts., dedicated in October 1928, has ample trackage for loading and unloading 10 railroad cars on a single track. By the use of switch lines, 40 cars can be unloaded. Two escalators operate in the warehouse. The dock and warehouse are leased to Inland Waterways Corporation.

11. UNITED STATES NAVAL RESERVE BARRACKS, Front St. at ft. of Valley St., has a drill floor equipped to represent a battleship. The building, originally of the Swiss cottage type, was once a boat house. The members of the Burlington unit, the 42nd Fleet Division of the Ninth Naval District, have drilled here since 1927. RIVERFRONT PARK begins at the north end of the barracks.

12. BURLINGTON HIGH SCHOOL, W. end University Place, houses the senior high school and BURLINGTON JUNIOR COLLEGE, the second

oldest junior college in the State, and noted for its vested choir. A PUBLIC MUSEUM *(open 9-4 on school days)* in the high school basement, has part of the Charles Buettner collection, originally willed to the public library, and historic, geologic, and natural history specimens.

13. CHARLES WACHSMUTH MUSEUM *(private)*, 111½ Marietta St., a small brick building which once housed the internationally known collection of crinoidea camerata fossils, now in the Smithsonian Institution, Washington, D. C., has been remodeled into a residence. The frail health of Charles Wachsmuth of Hanover, Germany, and the deep interest of Frank Springer, a young lawyer, were responsible for Burlington's reputation in this field. These flower-like fossils of crinoids (star lilies), related to starfish or sea urchins, but attached by long stems to the sea bottom, were found near Burlington in great abundance in early days. Wachsmuth began to collect fossils when he was ordered to spend as much time as possible outdoors; while Frank Springer decided to settle in Burlington after he heard Prof. Louis Agassiz of Harvard University lecture on crinoids at the University of Iowa. Later Wachsmuth and Springer, who became warm friends, built and supervised the Wachsmuth museum. They compiled and published *The North American Crinoidea Camerata* as Vols. X and XI of the *Memoirs of the Museum of Comparative Zoology*, Harvard College, Cambridge, Mass. (1897).

14. LOG CABIN *(private)*, at the Hay homestead, 2700 West Ave., cabin of Jeremiah Smith, Jr., erected in August 1833, now covered with weather boarding, is believed to be the oldest house in Des Moines County. The chinking of white plaster made the three-room cabin a white landmark for pioneers following dim trails. Chief Black Hawk brought his Indians to sit about its fireplace. It was a pioneer center for distinguished guests, trappers, and families on the way West.

15. SOUTH HILL PARK, corner 6th and Elm Sts., has the BOULDER MONUMENT, NW. corner of park, marking the only point in the world where the solar eclipse of August 7, 1869, was seen. Many well known scientists gathered in Burlington at that time.

16. CRAPO PARK, S. end of Main St. on a high bluff overlooking the Mississippi, has PIKE MEMORIAL, a boulder monument, near the flag pole and cannons, placed by the D.A.R. in 1905 to locate the spot where Zebulon M. Pike is believed to have landed on August 23, 1805, and unfurled the American flag to designate his choice of a fort site. Other authorities believe Lieutenant Pike landed at North Hill Bluff. BLACK HAWK SPRING, named for the Indian chief, flows from a rock cavern below the top of the bluffs and tumbles to the Mississippi a short distance away. A BRONZE PLAQUE commemorates the spring to Black Hawk, who is said to have used the spring while hunting here.

POINTS OF INTEREST IN ENVIRONS

Flint Hills State Park—*3.5 m.*, Starr's Cave—*5 m.* Our Lady of Grace Grotto, W. Burlington—*4 m.*, Jimtown, historic stagecoach stop—*16 m. (see Tour 1, sec. b).*

Cedar Rapids

Railroad Stations: Union Station, 4th St. bet. 3rd and 5th Aves. SE., for Chicago & North Western Ry. and Chicago, Rock Island & Pacific Ry.; Milwaukee Depot, 4th St. and 1st Ave. SE., for Illinois Central R.R. and Chicago, Milwaukee, St. Paul & Pacific R.R.

Interurban Station: 328 2nd St. SE. for Cedar Rapids & Iowa City Ry. and Waterloo, Cedar Falls & Northern Ry.

Bus Station: Union Bus Depot (Interurban Station), for Interstate Transit Lines (Northwestern Ry. and Union Pacific R.R.), M. C. Foster Lines, Jefferson Transportation Co., Cedar Rapids & Ottumwa Line, and Waterloo, Cedar Falls & Northern Motor Coaches.

Street Buses: Cedar Rapids City Lines, fare 5¢; service between towns of Marion and Cedar Rapids, 10¢.

Taxis: First 2 m. or less, 25¢; 10¢ for each additional passenger.

Traffic Regulations: No U-turns in business district, no double parking in "loop." Free parking at 5th St. and 5th Ave. SE.

Street Order and Numbering: 1st Ave., N. & S. dividing line, Cedar River E. and W. line. City divided into quarters designated as NE., NW., SE., and SW., Sts. and aves. numbered; N. of 1st Ave. listed alphabetically.

Accommodations: Six hotels in business center, smaller ones nearby.

Information Service: American Automobile Association, 223 3rd Ave. SE.; Chamber of Commerce, Memorial Bldg., Municipal Island.

Radio Station: WMT (600 kc.).

Motion Picture Houses: Six.

Athletics: Hill Park (Three I League), E Ave. and 13th St., NW.

Swimming: Ellis Park bathing beach, Ellis Blvd. NW.; American Legion Pool, Thomas Park, at town of Marion, NE. of city; YMCA, NE. cor. 1st Ave. and 5th St., open to both sexes.

Tennis: Bever Park, at Bever Ave. or Grand Ave. and Memorial Drive SE.; Daniels Park, Oakland and H Aves. NE.; Ellis Park; Riverside Park, C St. and 11th Ave. SW.; also B Ave. and 20th St. NE.

Golf: Ellis Park, 9 holes, green fees 26¢ wk. days, 36¢ Sun.; Kenmore Golf Course (commercial), Oakland Rd. and 35th and 42nd Sts., 9 holes, green fees 31¢ Mon.-Fri. only, 18 holes, green fees 41¢ wk. days, 45¢ Sat. and Sun.

Boating and Canoeing: Cedar River at Ellis Park.

Annual Events: Boat Races, Ellis Park, Aug.; All-Iowa Livestock Exposition, Hawkeye Downs, Sept.; Silver Skates Tournament, municipal skating rink, Dec.; Golden Gloves matches, Memorial Coliseum, Feb.

CEDAR RAPIDS (733 alt., 56,097 pop.), named for the swift rapids in the river at this point, is the county seat of Linn County and principal industrial center of east-central Iowa, in the midst of a rich agricultural area. The Cedar River, flowing southeast, divides the city neatly into the East and West Sides. The business district lies in a wide flat valley. North and south on the flatlands are the larger manufacturing plants, the railroad yards and shops, and other industries. On First Street at the east side of

MEMORIAL BUILDING, CEDAR RAPIDS

the river most of the shops are low structures of two or three stories, erected at the turn of the 19th century. They present an old-time atmosphere, difficult to reconcile with the briskness of the city and the many tall office buildings and modern hotels nearby.

The proximity of the giant Quaker Oats plant to the downtown district and the four railroads that traverse the main business section along Fourth Street, plus the fact that the Cedar River, and an island in it, are incorporated into the city plan rather than isolated from it, contributes to the sense of commercial and civic unity.

Cedar Rapids is noted for its residential districts that extend back into rolling hills on both sides of the river. So rapidly have these sections grown that the sites now occupied by modern homes were but a few short years ago pasture and woodland.

Cedar Rapids gives the impression of being uncrowded; there are no slum areas; residences are set far back from the streets and staunch old trees line the broad avenues, their branches meeting overhead to form archways of green. In the newer residential districts the streets curve and turn as they follow the contour of hill and valley.

Czechs, commonly known as Bohemians, constitute the major foreign population of Cedar Rapids, there being about 18,000 in the city (1938). The majority live in a bilingual district in the southwest end of the city, in the vicinity of Sixteenth Avenue, known as "Little Bohemia." Here they have their own shopping district where *kolaches* (a tart filled with cottage cheese, fruit, or poppy seeds) and other native foods can be obtained. The Czechs first came to Linn County in 1852 to work in the T. M. Sinclair packing plants and as the settlement grew they established churches, schools, and social organizations. One of their social clubs, the Reading Society, formed in 1869, later developed into a Little Theatre movement that presents plays in the native language. The Czech weekly newspaper, the Cedar Rapids *Listy,* was established in 1906 and in 1933 the Czech Fine Arts Society was organized to further Czech culture among the English-speaking younger generation.

The race has long been prominent in the political and civil life of the city and county. A Czech alderman was elected in 1877 and Karel Jonas, later to become Lieutenant Governor of Wisconsin, came to Cedar Rapids in 1858, along with Vojtech Naprstek, Czech patriot and Joseph Sosel, said to be the first Czech lawyer in the United States. Sosel, who was noted for his revolutionary activities in his native country, was smuggled out of Austria in a barrel, and because of his ability to speak the English language soon became legal and business adviser to the local Czech colony.

Sac and Fox Indians hunted and trapped in this region before 1838, the year Osgood Shepherd built his shack on the east side of the river at what is now First Avenue and First Street. The first survey of the city was made in 1841 by N. B. Brown, George Greene, and others who purchased squatter rights held by Shepherd. These men gave the name of Rapids City to the newly formed town.

Early in the 1840's a dam was constructed across the Cedar River, which furnished power for the grist and sawmills, already becoming lively industries. Robert Ellis, who settled on the west side of the river, built three flatboats about the same time and loaded them with 4,000 bushels of wheat for New Orleans, the first outlet for the community's farm products. The first newspaper was established in 1851 and the next year David W. King laid out the town of Kingston on the west side of the river. At this time the old ferry across the river was replaced by a toll bridge. In 1858 the citizens of Cedar Rapids launched *The Cedar Rapids,* a steamer built for them at Beaver, Pa. It made several trips between St. Louis and Cedar Rapids, but a collision on the Mississippi River resulted in the loss of their investment. In June 1858 the railroad reached the city and river traffic was abandoned.

With the coming of the railroad, interest turned to manufacturing and marketing. In 1870, the town of Kingston was annexed to Cedar Rapids and during the next ten years the Douglas and Stuart oatmeal mills were established, gas for illumination was installed, streetcars drawn by horses began operations, and a boulevard was opened between Cedar Rapids and Marion, then the county seat. In that decade also Henry Ward Beecher spoke to a capacity audience at the Methodist Church and William H. Seward, Secretary of State under Abraham Lincoln, stopped in the city while on a trip around the world. The following description of the town is credited to him: "Of the towns which have sprung up on the plains, we notice Cedar Rapids. During ten minutes' stay there we saw suburban cottages, with pointed roofs of the Norwegian settlers, surrounded by dark-green meadows, covered with flocks of geese and eider-ducks. We heard airs from *Trovatore* on a Chickering piano, in a dwelling not yet painted or plastered. We saw a Mansard mansion of the speculator in the city lots . . . There seem to be all sorts of churches for all sects of Christians—one surmounted with a Catholic cross, and one with a dome and minaret borrowed from a Mohammedan mosque."

On December 27, 1880, Greene's Opera House was dedicated with a performance by the Emma Abbott Opera Company, and in the same year the Cedar Rapids Business College was established, with Austin Palmer, later noted for his Palmer Method of Penmanship, as one of the teachers.

In the 1890's churches and schools were rebuilt and enlarged; a new post office was constructed; electric cars were introduced and the Union Station built. With the advent of the 20th century Cedar Rapids was a prosperous city. In the span of 50 years it had come from Indians to automobiles.

Perhaps the most colorful of the city's characters were the Cherry sisters —Effie, Addie and Jessie—who went on the stage at the turn of the 19th century with an act that was so poor it was good. Because of their performance the Oscar Hammerstein Theatre in New York was able to pay off its mortgage and the audiences were "laid under the seats." It is said their act was at times presented behind nets to protect the sisters from vegetables, fruit, and other missiles hurled at them. The Cherry sisters, with the exception of their one season in New York, spent their entire lives in Cedar Rapids.

POINTS OF INTEREST

1. MUNICIPAL ISLAND, in the channel of the Cedar River reached by 1st, 2nd or 3rd Ave. bridges, between E. and W. business districts, is Cedar Rapids' civic center. The original island, supplemented by river walls, is landscaped. The place was the rendezvous of the Shepherd gang of squatters until 1851. The original purchase price was $7.50. Later, it was known as May's Island, and was bought by the city in the early 1900's for $105,000. MEMORIAL BUILDING *(open 8-5 Mon.-Fri.; 8-12 Sat.)*, N. end of the narrow island, between 1st and 2nd Ave. bridges, a limestone building of neo-classic design, was dedicated in 1928 to those who served their country in its wars. The main structure is seven stories high. Surmounting it is a colonnaded observation tower topped with a symbolic sarcophagus on a cenotaph base. There are two main entrances. The Second Avenue façade has Doric columns extending from the fifth to seventh floors, exclusively. The two doors are separated by a stained glass window, designed by Grant Wood, Iowa artist, and manufactured in Germany, under his supervision. The central figure is an allegorical symbol of Victory holding a laurel wreath in one hand and a palm branch in the other. Below are six uniformed soldiers representing each of the wars in which the United States has engaged. Insignia of the various branches of the United States Army and Navy form a border around the window. The visitor by day should enter the south entrance to see the outside light through the window. At night floodlights illuminate the window from the inside. The First Avenue entrance to the building is three stories high, recessed. The columns are Corinthian in style. Concerts of the Cedar Rapids Symphony orchestra, organ recitals, lectures, and other events of city-wide interest are presented in the auditorium, seating 4,000.

LINN COUNTY COURTHOUSE *(open 8-5 Mon.-Fri.; 8-12 Sat.)*, facing 3rd. Ave., is at the south end of the island. The building, completed in 1926, is constructed of Indiana limestone. The main entrance, facing the plaza, is enriched by Ionic columns. The area between the memorial and county buildings is a landscaped plaza, laid out in formal fashion with a circular mirror pool and a wall fountain.

2. FEDERAL BUILDING *(open Mon.-Fri. 8-5; Sat. 8-12)*, 1st St. between 1st and 2nd Aves. SE., houses the city's post office and the Federal offices. The murals and panels representing the theme, *Law and Culture* were executed under the sponsorship of the U. S. Treasury Art Project. A mural in the courtroom and panels in the first floor lobby are the work of four artists, Robert Francis White, Everett Jeffrey, Harry Jones, and Don Glasell. These paintings are executed in egg tempera (dry pigments mixed in egg yolk and applied to the walls). The technique is considered second to the fresco method in permanency. The building, completed in 1933, is classic in style with an Indiana limestone exterior. There are three main entrances to the post office lobby. Columns and cornice are Ionic in design. Windows of cast iron frames and mullions, and a tiled roof back of the balustrade parapet are other features.

3. MONTROSE HOTEL, SW. corner 3rd Ave. and 3rd St. SE., a six-

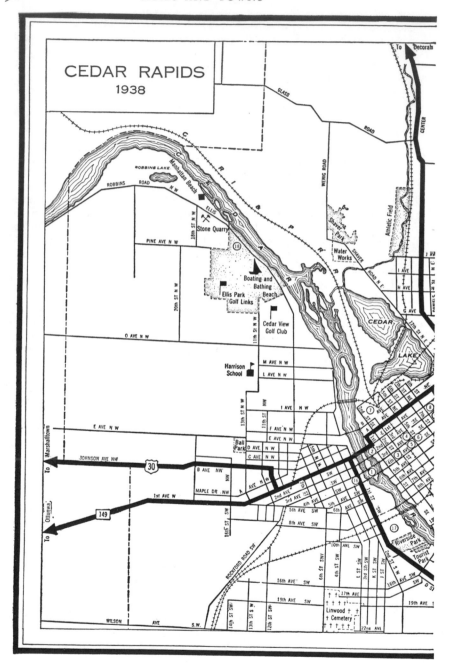

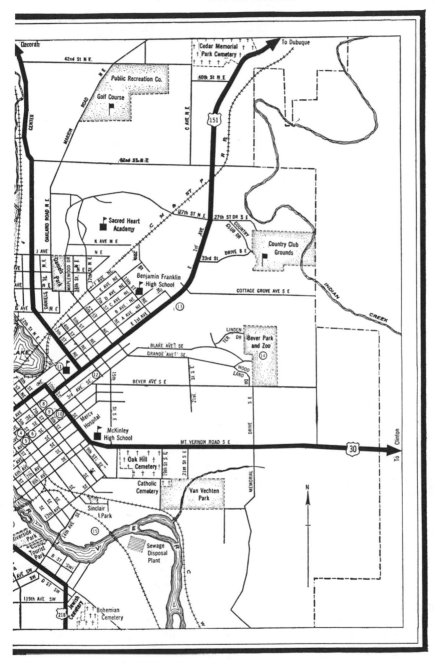

story, red brick structure, is noted for the murals of Iowa farm life painted by Grant Wood, Iowa artist, that decorate the dining room opening on to Third Avenue.

4. PUBLIC LIBRARY *(open weekdays 1-5; Sun. and holidays 2-6)*, 428 3rd Ave. SE., has a collection of books in the Czech language among its 76,000 volumes. The building, completed in 1906, is Italian Renaissance in general architectural style. The exterior is of Roman size pressed brick, gray in color, and Indiana limestone. CEDAR RAPIDS ART ASSOCIATION GALLERY *(open library hours)*, is located on the second floor. Here both permanent and traveling exhibits are presented. Included in the permanent collection is *Woman With Plants,* a first painting that launched Grant Wood to fame.

5. GREENE SQUARE, 3rd and 4th Aves., SE. between 4th and 5th Sts., is named for George Greene, one of the city's founders. The square is cut diagonally by a walk, passing through a stone shelter in the center of the park. Flower beds, stone markers and green lawns distinguish this restful downtown park.

6. FIRST PRESBYTERIAN CHURCH, SE. corner 3rd Ave. and 5th St. SE., of modified Gothic design, was completed in 1890. Built of Iowa limestone, the exterior walls are buttressed. There is a memorial window in the south transept section, the gift of the T. M. Sinclair family.

7. QUAKER OATS PLANT *(open Mon.-Fri. Tours 9 AM; 2:30 PM)*, N. end of 3rd St. NE., is the city's largest industry and one of the largest cereal mills in the world. The mill, founded in 1873 by Robert Stuart, began with a daily capacity of 200 barrels. It was totally destroyed by fire in 1905, and rebuilt. The buildings comprising the plant, erected as necessity demanded and strictly utilitarian in design, have been admired by artists and architects for their unified strength and beauty. Seven gigantic concrete elevators, cylindrical in construction, with a combined capacity of 9,500,000 bushels, are required to store the grain; and an average of from 90 to 160 carloads of grain products and other materials move over the railroad sidings daily. Output ranges from rolled oats and puffed grains to flour and feed. Oats are carried to the top floor of the 13-story building where they are weighed, sorted, and cleaned. The hulls are re-

---

KEY TO CEDAR RAPIDS MAP

1. Municipal Island
2. Federal Building
3. Montrose Hotel
4. Public Library
5. Greene Square
6. First Presbyterian Church
7. Quaker Oats Plant
8. Iowa Masonic Library
9. Turner Alley

10. Immaculate Conception Catholic Church
11. Coe College
12. St. Paul's Methodist Church
13. Douglas Estate
14. Bever Park
15. Wilson Packing Plant
16. Peoples' Savings Bank Building
17. Penick and Ford Plant
18. Shakespeare Garden

QUAKER OATS PLANT, CEDAR RAPIDS

moved, and the oats pass through steam chests to slow-turning rollers. They emerge as rolled oats. There are tables over which the groats (hulled and cracked oats) pass under ultra-violet rays. Afterward they move downward through the building on conveyors, emerging at the bottom in packages.

8. IOWA MASONIC LIBRARY *(open weekdays 8-12 and 1-5)*, 813 1st Ave. SE., contains one of the oldest and largest Masonic libraries in the United States. It was established in 1844 by Theodore S. Parvin, who remained Grand Secretary and Librarian from the time of its founding until his death in 1901. Parvin came to Iowa in 1838 as secretary to Robert Lucas, Iowa's first Territorial Governor. The library includes works bearing upon the secret societies of the Middle Ages, and books pertaining to the history of the Nestorians, Dervishes, Thugs, Druids, Rosicrucians, and the Guilds. The first section of the museum department is devoted to collections of Masonic interest. Other items include a collection of firearms, two complete suits of Japanese armor, Indian arrow and hammer heads, a mosaic table containing 37,473 pieces of wood gathered from every State in the Union and foreign countries, a collection of personal items once owned by Theodore S. Parvin, and the first telephone made in Iowa. The general offices for the library are located in an old residence built in the 1880's. The library proper, extending to the east, is of red brick, and was added to the building in 1909. The building stands on the SITE OF DOUGLAS PUBLIC SQUARE, named for Stephen A. Douglas, who gave a talk in a grove here shortly after his debate with Abraham Lincoln.

9. TURNER ALLEY *(private)*, 8th St. SE. between 1st and 2nd Aves., is the common name for the hayloft workshop at the rear of the Turner

property where Grant Wood, Iowa artist, created some of his paintings. In the reception room of the Turner mortuary are permanently hung a group of 30 of his early canvases. Wood is best known for his paintings, *Daughters of Revolution* and *American Gothic*.

10. IMMACULATE CONCEPTION CATHOLIC CHURCH, SW. corner 3rd Ave. and 10th St. SE., was designed by E. F. Masquera who planned the Catholic Cathedral in St. Paul, Minn. Of Romanesque design, the building is constructed of red brick, trimmed with Indiana limestone, and is surmounted by a Renaissance cupola of antique bronze. The interior is Italian Renaissance in style.

11. COE COLLEGE, 1st Ave. between 12th and 13th Sts. NE., and extending N. to E Ave., occupies eight city blocks. The college, a co-educational Presbyterian institution had its beginning in 1851 when the Rev. Williston Jones opened a school in his home for 16 Cedar Rapids young people. In 1866 it became Parsons Seminary and the first building, now a part of "Old Main," was built. But since February 2, 1881, the present name has been used. In 1919 Leander Clark College was absorbed.

The college buildings on the main campus center around the T. M. SINCLAIR MEMORIAL CHAPEL, a red brick building of Gothic design with a cruciform plan. The dormitory for girls, the gymnasium, and the four buildings for classes are connected by neat walks. Tall oaks and elms shade the area. OLD MAIN, housing offices and classrooms, the oldest structure on the campus, is a tall, narrow building of old brick, covered with ivy. The west half was completed in 1868 and the east in 1883. The BERT HEALD BAILEY MUSEUM, top floor of Science Hall *(open on application)*, is one of the largest in Iowa. Exhibits of vertebrates, invertebrates, geological formations, botanical collections, together with ethnological displays are found here. STEWART MEMORIAL LIBRARY, N. side B Ave. facing campus *(open weeksdays 9-9)*, is modified Georgian Colonial in design. It is of red brick and Indiana limestone. Windows and other trim are of wood, painted white. The MEN'S GYMNASIUM is off the main campus on C Avenue.

12. ST. PAUL'S METHODIST CHURCH, NW. corner 3rd Ave. and 14th St. SE., was originally designed by Louis Sullivan (1913) but altered by another architect. The design of the building is a radical departure from traditional ecclesiastical architecture. The structure is circular in plan and is lighted by three rows of square windows. The stairways are placed outside of the auditorium proper. The massive exterior is dominated by a square tower surmounted by an illuminated cross.

13. DOUGLAS ESTATE *(private)*, 1st Ave. and 20th St. SE., was established in 1872 by Mrs. T. M. Sinclair, wife of the founder of the Cedar Rapids meat packing industry. The home is a large two-story structure of red brick with a slate roof. The general architectural style is French Renaissance. The interior was completely remodeled in 1900 by Howard Shaw (Chicago). The main hall is paneled in butternut. The dining room, painted white, is French Renaissance. In 1908 Mrs. Douglas built a guest house in the early American style. Swimming pool, tennis court, and gar-

den are features of this estate that rises through a series of terraces from First Avenue.

14. BEVER PARK, Bever Ave. at Memorial Drive SE., a thickly wooded area, with picnic facilities, contains the JOHN VARDY HOUSE *(private)*, a plain, white one-story building, constructed in 1842 by one of the town's earliest settlers (John Vardy). It is said to be the first frame house in the city. Moved to its park location from 300 6th Ave. SE., the house is furnished in the style of the 1840's and preserved as a museum.

15. WILSON PACKING PLANT, S. end of 2nd, 3rd, and 4th Sts. SE., is in a curve on the E. side of the Cedar River *(open weekdays; tours 8:30, 9:45 a. m.; 12:30, 1:45 p. m.)*. During the early history of the city the company, which employs a large number of Bohemians, was known as the T. M. Sinclair Co.

16. PEOPLES' SAVINGS BANK BUILDING, West side 3rd Ave. and 1st St. SW., erected in 1911, was designed by Louis Sullivan and is typical of his smaller buildings. It is a buttressed edifice with square set-back towers. The grill-work in the towers and the terra cotta griffins on the upper part of the building, and at the entrance, are the only exterior decorations.

17. PENICK AND FORD PLANT *(open, tours 10-2, weekdays, adults only)*, 1st St. between 8th and 11th Aves. SW., manufactures corn sugar, glucose, starch and other similar products. At one time this plant was in the hands of the Douglas family, promoters of Douglas starch. An explosion in the plant in 1919 caused much property damage in the neighborhood and the loss of many lives.

18. SHAKESPEARE GARDEN, in Ellis Park, end of the Ellis Park car-line and Ellis Lane, is maintained by the Cedar Rapids Woman's Clubs and contains species of flowers grown in William Shakespeare's garden in England.

POINTS OF INTEREST IN ENVIRONS

Marion, first county seat—*6 m. (see Tour 1A, sec. a)*; Mount Vernon, site of Cornell College—*17 m.*, Palisades Kepler State Park—*27 m.* through Mount Vernon *(see Tour 13, sec. a)*.

Clinton

Railroad Stations: 11th Ave. S. and S. 4th St. for Chicago & North Western Ry.; Union Station, 12th Ave. S. and S. 3rd St., for Chicago, Milwaukee, St. Paul & Pacific R.R., Chicago, Rock Island & Pacific Ry., and Chicago, Burlington & Quincy R.R.
Interurban Station: 123 5th Ave. S. for Clinton, Davenport & Muscatine Ry.
Bus Station: Lafayette Hotel, SE. cor. 6th Ave. S. and S. 2nd St., and 123 5th Ave. S., for Scenic Stage Lines and Walrod Bus Line; Lafayette Hotel for Interstate Transit Lines (North Western Ry. and Union Pacific R.R.).
Street Buses: 10¢ or 3 for 25¢.
Taxis: Anywhere in the city, 25¢.
Parking Space: S. 1st St. bet. 4th and 6th Aves. S.
Business Districts: 5th Ave. S. from S. 2nd St. to S. 3rd St., and S. 2nd St. from 4th Ave. S. to 7th Ave. S. in the main town of Clinton; N. end of city in the old town of Lyons (still known as Lyons) W. from river, foot of US 30.

Accommodations: Seven hotels, numerous private homes open to tourists.

Information Service: Eastern Iowa Motor Clubs, Lafayette Hotel; Chamber of Commerce, 4th Ave. S. and S. 1st St.

Theaters and Motion Picture Houses: Public auditorium, 4th Ave. S. and S. 1st St.
Swimming and Tennis: River Front Park.
Golf: Kiwanis Golf Links, 9 holes, 12th Ave. N. and N. 3rd St., fee 25¢.

Annual Events: Gateway Classic, Middlewest High School Track Meet, in the spring.

CLINTON (593 alt., 25,726 pop.), an industrial and railroad center, stretches seven miles along the west bank of the Mississippi River at the foot of a ridge of bluffs to the north and of hills to the south.

A great many of the 6,000 elms planted in 1855 are still standing, their branches meeting above the streets to form vaulted archways block after block. Mansions of the late 19th century along Fifth Avenue South and on the bluffs to the west, stand as evidence of the time when Clinton claimed 17 millionaires—in the heyday of the lumber industry. Victorian in style, with embellishments such as diamond-leaded window panes, bays, oriels, gables and sloping roofs, most of these dwellings have been converted into rooming houses or turned over to public enterprises, such as the American Legion and the Young Women's Christian Association. It is these old houses, and the many trees, that give the city a comfortable, even sleepy, atmosphere that belies the industrial hum and activity of factories and railroad yards.

In the southern end of the city, and following a narrow strip along the river, are the railroad yards; numerous tracks converge at one point and turn out—east over the river, south and west across the open country, and northward, close to the river, through the city's waterfront park where a

FIFTH AVENUE, CLINTON

railroad line passes over the green grass of a lawn. Factory buildings in this area are white with powdered grain.

Elijah Buell, first settler in what is now Clinton, came to the Narrows at Fulton in 1835. He established a ferry across the Mississippi River to accommodate the many people on their way into the new West. Joseph M. Bartlett laid out a town in 1838 where the city now stands, naming it New York. In 1855 the Iowa Land Company, a promotion concern, made up of the officers of the Chicago, Iowa & Nebraska Railroad (now the Chicago & North Western) acquired the site and replatted it, naming it for DeWitt Clinton, one-time Governor of the State of New York.

A post office was established in 1856 and, in the same year, the Randall Hotel was built. A spacious brick building, with marble mantels and hot and cold water, it had a five-story brick outside toilet, accessible from all floors, a marvel of convenience in those early days. The hotel was dubbed Randall's Folly by the skeptical who had no faith in the city's growth. But where once had been swampland and slough—the present shopping center —a city came into being. On the banks of a slough, where the courthouse now stands, was a boat-building factory. The finished boats were floated through a canal, crossing the main thoroughfare, to the river. The slough extended westward to what was then the fairgrounds, where there was a brick plant that transformed the grayish-green Maquoketa shale, which is a part of Clinton's bluffs, into red brick.

Clinton was incorporated as a city in 1859. In 1864 striking railroad workers dumped the running gear of the freight cars into the Mississippi River, where they are said to remain. In those early days streetcars were drawn by mules. Many of the wooden sidewalks were built on stilts and frequently floated down the river during high water.

In 1878 the town of Ringwood was annexed to Clinton. The city's rapid growth followed the establishment of the sawmills, reaching the peak of production in the early 1880's, when Clinton was recognized as the largest lumber-producing city in the world, with five mills from Lyons on the north to Chancy on the south. In summer an average of 40 to 50 steamboats passed daily up and down the river and hundreds of log rafts were floated down from the north in the spring. Workers in the mills were mainly Irish who came here in the days of famine in Ireland.

One of the biggest problems the mills had was to dispose of sawdust. The entire north end of Lyons for two and a half blocks west from the river is still underlaid with sawdust to a depth of 20 feet or more. Sloughs and streams were filled in with it and large portions of the city were built on sawdust bottoms. If exposed to air, spontaneous combustion starts smouldering fires in the buried sawdust which it sometimes takes days to extinguish.

The city in these days grew so fast that new papers of incorporation were taken out in 1881. In the 1890's both Chancy and Lyons were annexed to the growing city. The interests of the lumber people were transferred to railroading with the last log raft arriving from the north in 1906 and from then on the city turned its attention to manufacturing, trading and retailing. Most of the present-day business structures were built in the first two decades of the twentieth century and public improvements were developed along with them. However, the city's development was not without labor troubles. In 1919 a strike in a local factory resulted in the death of one of the strikers and in 1922, strikes on the North Western Railroad led machinists and clerks to walk out for six weeks, when a satisfactory agreement was reached.

Lillian Russell, the girl who first made the beauty of American women internationally famous, was born in Clinton in 1861. Her home, the newspaper office where her father worked, and the Davis Opera House where she first made a stage appearance, have been torn down.

POINTS OF INTEREST

OLD CLINTON THEATER, 213-15 6th Ave. S. *(not open)*, of modified Romanesque design with a brick and red sandstone front, was built in 1882 and remodeled in 1936. Here Emma Calvé, Maude Adams, Nora Bayes, Alla Nazimova, John Drew, Otis Skinner, Margaret Anglin, and Lillian Russell once performed. Plush stage curtains, a carriage man in dark green uniform, a colored maid in charge of the ladies' retiring room, were metropolitan touches. C. E. Dixon spent each summer in New York booking the finest productions obtainable, and he still retains a valuable framed collection of pictures of over 200 stars who appeared on the Clinton stage.

SITE OF UNDERGROUND RAILROAD STATION, SE. corner 6th Ave. S. and S. 2nd St., is occupied by the Lafayette Hotel. On this site in the days immediately preceding the Civil War stood a small house that was a station on the underground railroad. Missouri slaves frequently escaped into Iowa where sympathizers helped them to escape, routing them along the underground railroad. Hidden under straw in wagon boxes, the slaves, referred to as "volumes bound in black," were brought to the western outskirts of Clinton where they found refuge in dugouts or root cellars in the hills and bluffs, until they could be handled through the local station.

RIVER FRONT PARK, between S. 1st St. and the river, stretches almost a mile from 9th Ave. N. to 6th Ave. S. The new STADIUM, built with WPA labor in 1936, is a feature of the park, which also contains the city's $90,000 SWIMMING POOL, tennis courts and baseball diamonds. The AL LUBBERS MEMORIAL FOUNTAIN, designed by Leo Hannaher, Clinton's Superintendent of Public Parks, another feature of the park, was built in 1934–5, in the form of a fountain and waterfall combined. At night it is illuminated with colored lights. At the entrance to the park is a MEMORIAL FLAG POLE designed by Lorado Taft and dedicated to the veterans of the Civil, the Spanish-American, and the World wars. The square base of the pole is adorned with military figures at each corner.

A PLAYHOUSE, 318 6th Ave. S., in the rear of the American Legion Home, was at one time the property of Frank Ellis, a lawyer. Built on the lawn for his young daughter, Jane, who expressed a wish to have a playhouse like the home of her parents, it was moved during the World War by the Red Cross to a spot near the railroad station and used as a canteen from which to serve soldiers passing through. At the end of the war it was returned to the Ellis lawn, and sold with the home to the American Legion. Today the playhouse is the headquarters for a Girl Scout troop sponsored by the Legion Auxiliary.

ST. JOHN'S EPISCOPAL CHURCH, 240 5th Ave. S., is designed in the manner of an English Gothic parish church, with open timbered roof. Back of the altar, covering the entire stone wall, is the BREWER MEMORIAL MOSAIC, one of the finest examples of that art in America. It is a faithful copy of the central group of figures in an Italian painting, *The Light of the World*. The memorial is the work of six Italian workmen under the direction of Lorenzo Zantatto. The figure of Christ with four angels, on a background of glass squares backed by goldleaf fused into the glass, produces the illusion that the figures are silhouetted against an immense golden window.

CLINTON COMPANY PLANT *(open Mon.-Fri. 8-4; Sat. 8-12; guides)*, 2415 Liberty Ave., started operations early in the twentieth century. It has equipment capable of grinding 30,000 bushels of corn a day and uses over 100,000 tons of coal a year. The company manufactures syrup and various other corn byproducts, large shipments of which go to England, the Philippines and the Orient.

OLD STONE HOUSE *(private)*, 850 S. Bluff Blvd., is a long, one-story building of native, hand-quarried stone, with a plain low-pitched gable roof. It was built in 1837, and is the oldest house in Clinton County. In 1934 the house was remodeled so skillfully that it lost none of its early charm. First a squatter's cabin, it was later a tavern, then a farmhouse. Built directly on the old Indian trail which paralleled the Mississippi River from lakes to gulf, travelers paid 25¢ for the privilege of sleeping on the hard earthen floor in front of the fireplace, furnishing their own blankets.

MOUNT ST. CLAIRE ACADEMY, Springdale Dr. between 4th and 5th Aves. N., a building of Romanesque architecture on a beautiful estate, is supervised by the Sisters of Saint Francis and has been in operation as a school for girls for more than 40 years. It provides college preparatory work, two years college credits in liberal and fine arts courses, secretarial work, and teacher's training for its 125 students. The MUSEUM *(open weekdays, 9-8)* houses a collection of original paintings. One large painting was found in a little back room of a church in Kentucky where it was neglected for so many years that the canvas had been snagged. Accumulated dust almost obscured the subject. It is believed to be more than 300 years old, an original by the Dutch master, Van Dyck (though this has not been substantiated). The painting is thought to have been owned in the early part of the 19th century by Louis Philippe (later King of France), who was exiled during the French Revolution and came to America, bringing with him many of his personal treasures. Fond of the Trappist monks, who came from France and founded Gethsemane Abbey, near Bardstown, Kentucky, Louis Philippe spent much of his time at their retreat. Before leaving, he presented the Trappists with some of his paintings.

ELIJAH BUELL HOUSE *(private)*, 2517 N. 3rd St., erected in 1857 on a high knoll by Clinton's first settler, has been occupied ever since. It is a large, square, 12-room house built of brick, hauled many miles overland by oxen, with a hip roof topped with a small flat deck and square lookout room.

EAGLE POINT PARK, end of N. 3rd St. on the Mississippi River bluffs, was once known as Joyce's Park, the land having been given to the city by David Joyce. On a limestone cliff is an enormous natural STONE FACE which, according to Indian legend, is an emissary of the Great Spirit, and guardian of fish and game. On a grassy knoll in the park is a 35-foot OBSERVATION TOWER *(open, daily)*, built of stone quarried on the premises. Construction is along lines similar to that of the old watch towers of the Norsemen.

POINTS OF INTEREST IN ENVIRONS

Camanche, early chartered town with pecan groves, *6 m. (see Tour 2 sec. b)*.

Council Bluffs

Railroad Stations: 1115 W. Broadway for Chicago & North Western Ry., Union Pacific R.R., and Wabash Ry.; 1216 W. Broadway for Illinois Central R.R.; 1201 S. Main St. for Chicago, Rock Island & Pacific Ry. and Chicago, Milwaukee, St. Paul & Pacific R.R.; 900 S. Main St. for Chicago, Great Western R.R.; 407 11th Ave. for Chicago, Burlington & Quincy R.R.

Bus Station: Union Bus Station, 33 Pearl St., for Interstate Transit (North Western Ry. and Union Pacific R.R.), P. R. Davis Lines, and Bert Cannon Lines; 101 Pearl St. for Burlington Bus Lines.

Streetcars: Between Omaha (Nebr.) and Council Bluffs every 15 minutes, every 5 minutes during rush hours, fare 10¢, city feeder lines 20-minute schedule, fare 10¢, 3 for 25¢.

Taxis: 15¢ first m. for one or more persons, 10¢ each additional m.

Accommodations: Six hotels, all centrally located.

Information Service: Chamber of Commerce, Chieftain Hotel, 38 Pearl St.

Motion Picture Houses: Three.

Swimming: Crystal Pool, 29th and 5th Ave.

Tennis: Fairmount Park, end of 9th Ave. on High St., and Dodge Park, end of Broadway on the river, municipal.

Golf: Dodge Park, municipal, 18 holes, fee 25¢.

Annual Events: Flower Show, May.

COUNCIL BLUFFS (984 alt., 42,048 pop.), seat of Pottawattamie County, is a railroad center and an important transfer point for transcontinental mail. The original town, built against the bluffs, is laid out irregularly but the new part along the Missouri River is platted in even blocks. Approached from the east, the city on the lowland is seen from hills that rise abruptly to a height of 100 to 300 feet. A natural point for east and west crossing, the city is one of the largest mail transfer points in the United States. Eight trunk lines converge here, and more than 100 freight trains and 68 passenger trains enter and leave the city daily. It is this railroad activity that gives to the city a marked liveliness. Close to the railroad yards, in the southern end of the city, are the many modest homes of the working people, stretching for block after block.

The city, suburban in character, is a place of quiet and peace away from the railroad tracks. One of the State's historic cities—the first on the western edge—tradition plays an important part in the lives of many of the people.

Indians first met along the river bluffs in this region to sell their furs to French traders, and the explorers, Lewis and Clark, camped near the site in 1804. Itinerant traders and trappers moving through the territory later designated the whole bluff territory along this part of the Missouri, the Council Bluffs. Council Bluffs was early known as Hart's Bluff, named for a white man of unknown origin, who, legend says, traded at this point before 1824. Francis Guittar settled at this point permanently in 1827 when he was appointed agent of the Hart's Bluff Post of the American Fur Company.

In 1837 the Potawatami Indians were moved into the region and Federal troops were established in a temporary camp to protect them from other tribes. Other than Davis Hardin, farming instructor provided by the Government in 1836, the Indians had no teacher until Father Pierre Jean DeSmet arrived in 1838. For the three years the mission was conducted, Father DeSmet used the camp block house as a church.

On June 14, 1846, the first Mormons arrived, and changed the name of the settlement, first to Miller's Hollow, and then to Kanesville for Thomas L. Kane, an Army officer who was friendly to them. Kanesville, an unorganized section of Indian country, was ruled by Orson Hyde, priest, writer, editor, lawyer, and chief of the church's quorum of 18 apostles. Everything was controlled by the church, which did not tolerate idleness and dissipation. Wishing to participate in the Congressional election of 1848, Hyde and a group of Mormons applied at Albia for a township government and an election precinct. The candidates for Representative, knowing that the Mormon vote would decide the election, showered Kanesville with gifts. Controversy over the Mormon vote, however, made a second election necessary.

During the California gold rush in 1849, Kanesville, directly in the line of travel, was a stopping place where travelers rested and prepared for the long trip to the west coast. Gamblers, traders, thieves, and desperadoes flocked to the town to prey on the gold-crazy throng. Vigilance committees, organized by the citizens, decided more than one trial by lynching.

In 1850 the number of Mormons in the vicinity reached 7,828, but in 1852 Brigham Young called all the faithful to join him in Utah. Selling farms, stores, and cabins, often at great sacrifice, most of the Mormons departed for Salt Lake City. After Orson Hyde and his high council left Kanesville in the spring of 1852, the town was without government. Later the 1,000 people remaining in the town reorganized, and renamed the community Council Bluffs. In 1853 the State legislature provided a government for the newly named town, and it was incorporated the same year.

In 1852 Grenville M. Dodge came to Council Bluffs and surveyed the Platte River Valley for a railroad that is now a part of the Rock Island system. In 1859, while Dodge was at the old Pacific House in Council Bluffs, he talked with a young lawyer, Abraham Lincoln, about railroads, telling him under a barrage of questions a good deal more than he had intended. It is said that Lincoln's visit to Council Bluffs and his chat with Dodge, influenced him, in 1863, as President of the United States, in selecting this city as the eastern terminus of the Union Pacific. General Dodge returned from the Civil War in 1866 and was appointed chief engineer of the Union Pacific Railroad. By 1870, five railroads made connections with the Union Pacific at Council Bluffs.

LEWIS AND CLARK MONUMENT, COUNCIL BLUFFS

Charles T. Kelly's army of the unemployed, on its way to Washington to petition for jobs, stopped here in 1894. An estimated 1,500 men were with Kelly when the Union Pacific train, commandeered in Ogden, Utah, arrived. Citizens of Omaha and Council Bluffs gave the men 1,000 pounds of beef and 1,000 pies.

During the World War (1917–18), Council Bluff's Unit K, Mobile Hospital No. 1, under Dr. Donald Macrea, Jr., won many medals, thus distinguishing the city. By 1920, the introduction of manufacturing and the development of the nearby farm markets, had brought more than 36,000 people to live in the city. In 1932 the city was the center of farm strikes, with the Farm Holiday Association picketing all roads into town.

Today manufacturing includes a wide range of articles—playground equipment, beekeepers' supplies, artificial limbs, candy, and railroad car wheels. The seven large grain elevators here have a total capacity of 10,000,000 bushels. Some of the largest vineyards in the Middle West surround Council Bluffs, introducing a pattern that varies from the miles of corn and grain fields. Many of the vineyards, almost within the city limits, spread along the river lowlands from three to ten miles in width, and others cover the nearby hills with acre after acre of blue Concord grapes.

POINTS OF INTEREST

1. PUBLIC LIBRARY *(open weekdays 10-9)*, SW. corner Willow Ave. and Pearl St., constructed of brick, trimmed with stone, was built in 1904. There are more than 55,500 volumes and valued collections including letters, articles, scrapbooks, and speeches of Grenville M. Dodge, his brother, Nathan Dodge, Dexter C. Bloomer and Mrs. Amelia Bloomer.

2. MORMON TRAIL MEMORIAL, center N. side Bayliss Park, 1st Ave. and Pearl St., is a huge boulder bearing two bronze tablets commemorating the passing of the Mormons through the city in the early days.

3. FATHER DeSMET MEMORIAL, E. Broadway and State St., is a bronze tablet on a granite boulder marking the site where Father Pierre Jean DeSmet, a Jesuit missionary, established a mission among the Pottawattamie Indians in May, 1838. Accompanying him were Father Verreydt and Brother Mazzelli. After two years, Father DeSmet was sent farther west to work among the Flathead Indians and other tribes in the Rocky Mountain region, there becoming known as the "Apostle of the Rockies."

4. BLOCKHOUSE SITE, E. Broadway and Union Sts., is marked by a large boulder and a bronze tablet. The troops of Capt. D. B. Moore built the blockhouse upon their arrival here in August 1837, and occupied it until November, at which time they were ordered to Fort Leavenworth.

5. J. F. WILCOX GREENHOUSES *(open)*, 1132 E. Pierce St., with more than 121,000 square feet under glass, are said to have two of the largest rose houses in the world. Built into the bluffs, the greenhouses rise in tiers above the street levels. Established in 1867, the company is the largest of its kind west of the Mississippi River. Usually there are 225,000 rose plants grown, and more than 640,000 other kinds of plants.

6. LAINSON GREENHOUSES *(open)*, 1300 Canning St., has 250,000 feet of glass covering, where flowers and tropical plants—a specialty of this company—and more than 3,500,000 roses a year are grown. Banana, date, fig, lemon, orange, grapefruit, and papaya trees, orchids, gardenias, and other rare flowers and plants are displayed here.

7. GRENVILLE M. DODGE RESIDENCE *(open by permission)*, 605 S. 3rd St., erected in 1870 at a cost of $35,000, is one of the city's historic houses. Situated on a high rock-walled terrace at the foot of a cliff overlooking the city, this three-story brick building has a mansard roof and large French windows. The interior is notable for its walnut woodwork, Italian marble fireplaces, valuable paintings, antique furniture, and relics of historic significance. A caretaker maintains it as it was at the time of General Dodge's death.

8. COOPERATIVE MARKET BUILDINGS of the Council Bluffs Grape Growers Association *(open by permission)*, 900 S. 7th St., most active during September and October, markets through private sales as many as 4,500,000 pounds of grapes grown in the community. About 25 percent of the grapes are made into wine—port, muscatel, and sherry—the bulk of which is sold through the Iowa State liquor stores. In 1937 there were 75,000 gallons of wine made for use in 1941, after the wine has aged. The association, formed in 1893 with 17 members, now has 262

farmer members. Prof. T. J. Maney, pomology expert at Iowa State College, says of the Council Bluffs area, "The character of the soil deposit and the topography of the land are comparable to those of the famous Rhine valley in Germany. This grape-growing region of the country enjoys freedom from the common diseases and insect pests."

9. MEMORIAL FOR GRENVILLE M. DODGE, 1512 S. Main St., on the Rock Island passenger station lawn, is a brown stone marker with a bronze tablet. It was placed here in 1922 to commemorate the 70th anniversary of the work Dodge did in 1852 in selecting the route of the Rock Island Railroad across Iowa.

10. UNION PACIFIC TRANSFER DEPOT, 10th and 21st Sts., a red brick U-shaped structure, built in 1878, once contained the popular transfer hotel, on its second floor. This depot houses the first terminal railway post office set up in the United States, an office that, on the basis of volume handled, was in 1937 the third largest in the country.

11. UNION PACIFIC BRIDGE, W. end of 12th Ave., bears a large bronze buffalo head, seven feet tall, placed on the east portal (1916) to welcome travelers to the land of the buffalo west of the Missouri River. This head, modeled by Capt. Edward Kenny of Perth Amboy, New Jersey, was cast in bronze by Etienne Favy, New York. General Dodge was chief engineer of the original Union Pacific bridge which was started in 1868 and opened to traffic in 1873. In 1887 the first bridge was replaced by a second one to take care of the increased traffic. In 1914 the present structure was begun. Erected just south of the old bridge, the new high bridge, extending 1,722 feet and weighing 5,750 tons, was moved into place with five hoisting machines after the old bridge had been shifted to temporary piers. The bridge shift delayed train service only four hours and 20 minutes. Now there is an average of one train across the bridge, every five minutes.

12. LINCOLN PARK, Military Ave. and Oakland Dr., a tiny triangle of land at the edge of Rohrer Park, is owned by the Pottawattamie County Historical Society. A Log Cabin *(open Sun. 1-8)* erected in 1934 at the curve of the drive, serves as a museum, housing Indian relics, gifts of historic value, and other interesting collections.

13. LINCOLN MONUMENT, Point Lookout, head of Oakland Dr. and Lafayette Ave., is a tall granite shaft, commemorating the visit of Abraham Lincoln to the city August 12-14, 1859. The memorial was erected by the Council Bluffs chapter of the D. A. R. in October 1911 at the point from which Lincoln looked over the valley of the Missouri River.

14. FAIRVIEW CEMETERY, E. end of Lafayette Ave., contains one of the outstanding memorials in the vicinity, the bronze Angel of Death that was erected in 1918 in memory of Anne B. Dodge (Mrs. Grenville M. Dodge) by her daughters. The inspiration for the monument came from a constantly recurring dream about which Mrs. Dodge told her children before her death. It is a fountain piece in which the Angel of Death stands on a barge and extends a bowl, brimming over with the water of eternal life. The water falls into the pool where the barge floats.

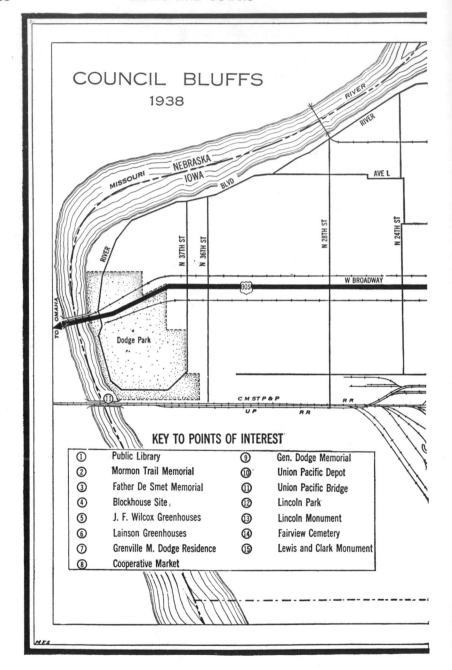

COUNCIL BLUFFS
1938

KEY TO POINTS OF INTEREST

①	Public Library	⑨	Gen. Dodge Memorial
②	Mormon Trail Memorial	⑩	Union Pacific Depot
③	Father De Smet Memorial	⑪	Union Pacific Bridge
④	Blockhouse Site	⑫	Lincoln Park
⑤	J. F. Wilcox Greenhouses	⑬	Lincoln Monument
⑥	Lainson Greenhouses	⑭	Fairview Cemetery
⑦	Grenville M. Dodge Residence	⑮	Lewis and Clark Monument
⑧	Cooperative Market		

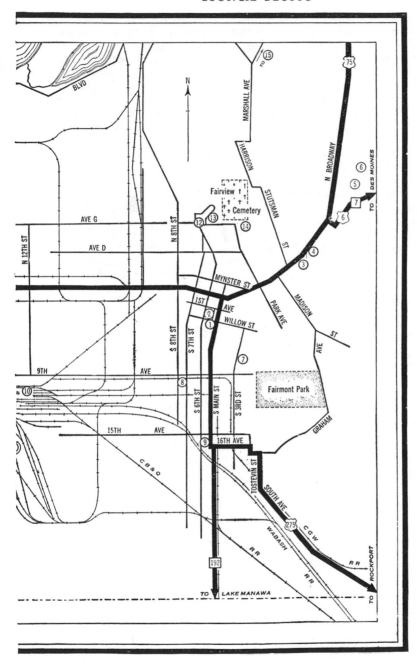

Daniel Chester French, American sculptor, executed the piece, which he considered his masterpiece, since the face and figure of the woman are unusually beautiful. The GRAVE OF AMELIA JENKS BLOOMER, also here, is visited by many interested in women's rights. Mrs. Bloomer.(born in New York, 1818; died in Council Bluffs, Dec. 30, 1894), a pioneer in the woman suffrage movement, was also an advocate of dress reforms, one of which the public dubbed "bloomers" for her. Moving to Council Bluffs in 1855, Mrs. Bloomer continued her work for woman suffrage and prohibition, and was chosen president of the Iowa Woman's Suffrage Association in October 1871.

15. LEWIS AND CLARK MONUMENT, four miles north of the business district on Scenic Rainbow Dr. was erected in 1935 to commemorate Lewis and Clark's council with the Oto and Winnebago Indians on their historic expedition up the Missouri River in 1804. Some historians place the council site at Fort Calhoun, Neb., although Lewis and Clark maps of 1814 designate it on the Iowa side. The shaft monument, built of native stone, was designed by Harry Stinson of the University of Iowa and erected in November 1935. Sculpturing on the south panel shows the Indians bringing melons and fruits to exchange with Lewis and Clark for medals and flags, while the north panel depicts the meeting of Lewis and Clark holding council with the Indian chiefs in full ceremonial regalia.

POINTS OF INTEREST IN ENVIRONS

Lake Manawa, State game reserve, *1.25 m.;* Iowa School for the Deaf, *5 m. (see Tour 9, sec. b).*

←←←←←←←←←←←←←←←←←←←※→→→→→→→→→→→→→→→→→→→

Davenport

Railroad Stations: 5th and Harrison Sts. for Chicago, Rock Island & Pacific Ry.; Union Depot, 1st and Harrison Sts., for Chicago, Milwaukee, St. Paul & Pacific R.R. and Chicago, Burlington & Quincy R.R.

Bus Stations: 418 Main St. for Burlington Trailways; 213 Perry St. for Clinton, Davenport and Muscatine R.R. Co. buses; 321-23 Perry St. for Interstate Transit Lines (North Western Ry. & Union Pacific R.R.), Illinois Transit Lines, Blackhawk Motor Coach Co., Scenic Stages, and Greyhound Lines.

City Buses: All city service, including Bettendorf, 10¢; service to Rock Island and Moline (Illinois), 15¢.

Streetcar: Bridge Line car to Rock Island, 10¢.

Taxis: 25¢ a trip for 1 to 5, fare by meter, or dime fare.

Ferry: Levee, ft. of Main St., to Rock Island (Illinois), 15-minute service, fare 5¢, no service Jan., Feb., Mar.

Bridges: Government, near business center, toll-free to Rock Island, Ill.; Bettendorf, Iowa-Illinois Memorial Bridge, US 6 to Moline, Ill., toll.

Airports: Cram Field, NW. cor. of city, on State 122, licensed repair shop, private plane service; Moline (Ill.), transcontinental service, United Air Lines, follow US 6 (city route) across Government Bridge through Rock Island to Moline and 3 m. S. on US 150; taxi, $1.50.

Traffic Regulations: No U turns; free parking, Municipal Levee, ft. Main St., one hour; visitor's parking card, obtained from merchants, allows longer than usual one hour parking in loop.

Accommodations: 13 hotels; many boarding and rooming houses.

Information Service: Chamber of Commerce, 402-406 Main St.; Eastern Iowa Motor Clubs, 418 Main St.

Radio Station: WOC (1370 kc).

Motion Picture Houses: Eight.

Steamboat Excursions: Intervals during summer and fall months; arranged by Streckfus Co., St. Louis, Mo.

Tennis: Credit Island, on US 61, turn at Schmidt Rd. off Rockingham Rd.; Lindsay Park, E. River Dr. and Mound St.

Swimming: Municipal Natatorium, 120 S. Main St., Y.M.C.A.; Main and 4th Sts.; Lend A Hand Club, ft. of Main St.

Golf: Credit Island, 18 holes, 31¢; Duck Creek Park, E. end of Locust St., 18 holes, 41¢; both courses municipal.

Baseball: Credit Island; Fejervary Park, entrance W. end 12th St.; Lafayette Sq., 4th St. and Gaines St.; Municipal Stadium, ft. of Gaines St. (Western League).

Ice Skating: Vander Veer Park, Lombard and Main Sts.; Credit Island.

Annual Events: Chrysanthemum Show, Vander Veer Park Conservatory, Thanksgiving time; Mississippi Valley Fair, W. Locust St., Aug.; Annual Tri-City Art Exhibit, Davenport Municipal Art Gallery, Spring.

DAVENPORT (559 alt., 60,751 pop.), seat of Scott County and the third largest city in Iowa stretches along the Mississippi River for nearly five miles, where the river widens to form Lake Davenport. The business district, five blocks wide at the center of the city, broadens to almost a

GOVERNMENT LOCKS AND DAMS, DAVENPORT

mile at the western end, while the residential section spreads over and beyond the bluffs rising to 160 feet above the level of the business district. From this lofty land one glimpses the cities across the river in Illinois—Rock Island and Moline, which, with Davenport, form the Tri-Cities group.

Directly on the bluffs stand the older homes, mansionlike in size and dignity, although many have been changed into apartment houses. Amid the winding roads to the northeast the newer homes of the McClelland Heights neighborhood grace the hills, while many other new and attractive homes border the tree-shadowed drives westward around the edge of the city. There are no slum areas and even though from its settlers of the 1850's the citizenry has been largely German and some Irish, the nationalities have never set themselves apart in foreign groups.

The city has many and varied industries, but is noted chiefly as a shopping and trading mart. Second and Third Street shops cater to the farming and small-town people on the Iowa side and also attract shoppers from the larger centers on the Illinois side, for the Tri-Cities constitute a closely-knit community with a large interchange of business. Any hour of the day a continual stream of traffic—some on a national highway—pours southward across the Government bridge and eastward to the Bettendorf bridge.

Several times a year millions of caddis flies, similar to dragon flies, invade the city from the Mississippi River for their one night of life. The next day they are shoveled up and dumped into the river by the truckload. Harmless, but very annoying, they take possession of the city during their unwelcome visit; people stay indoors and as many street lights as possible are turned out. These caddis invasions are common to all the eastern river towns.

The site of Davenport, important in the development of the territory beyond the Mississippi River, was a trading center of the American Fur Company, and a battleground of the War of 1812. Fort Armstrong, established on Rock Island in 1816, brought to the vicinity two men who were to influence the growth of the future city—Col. George Davenport, for whom the city was named, and Antoine LeClaire, one of its pioneer founders. Colonel Davenport, an Englishman who had served in the United States Army, came to Fort Armstrong with the first troops to conduct the Army store. Becoming interested in the rich fur trade, he established a post of his own. From this time the Davenport area was a trading center. Antoine LeClaire, a French halfbreed, reared around trading posts at Milwaukee and Peoria, and later educated, was highly valued because he spoke French, Spanish, and English, as well as several Indian dialects.

Gen. Winfield Scott (for whom the county was named) and John Reynolds, with Chiefs Keokuk and Wapello of the Sac and Fox tribes, negotiated a treaty here in 1832. LeClaire acted as interpreter. At the request of the tribes, the United States Government gave to LeClaire the section of land opposite Rock Island, and one section of land at the head of the first rapids above Rock Island, the site where the treaty was made. LeClaire's first Iowa home, built near this spot, was in fulfillment of his promise to Keokuk. LeClaire later acquired the land adjoining his reserve on the west and sold it, with the exception of an eighth interest, to Colonel Davenport and six other men. On this tract, Davenport was founded in 1836.

During the 1837–38 term of the Wisconsin Territorial Legislature, when Scott County was organized, there was a brisk fight between Davenport and Rockingham, now a part of Davenport, for county seat honors and three elections were held before the matter was finally settled in favor of Davenport. The city received its first charter in 1839 and a second in 1843.

From 1850 to 1860 the population rose from 1,848 to 11,267, owing in a large measure to German and other European immigrants who came to the United States to escape political difficulties abroad. The Germans organized their *turnvereins* and singing societies, one of the first in Davenport being a *maennerchor,* organized in 1851.

Davenport was the first city in Iowa to have railroad service, and it was at this point that the first train crossed the Mississippi in 1856. The Mississipi and Missouri Railroad Company began construction of the road from Davenport to Council Bluffs in 1853. On August 25, 1855, the first passenger train to leave the city was drawn by a locomotive that had been ferried across the Mississippi. This road, completed to Iowa City by January 1, 1856, was not extended farther for several years. Almost at once the city was aroused to the possibilities of a bridge to link the railroads on either side (later consolidated as the Chicago & Rock Island railway). The Mississippi River Bridge Company, organized in 1853 to build a bridge at Davenport, began work in 1854 but encountered opposition. Rivermen and steamboat owners considered the river "a navigable waterway consecrated by nature" for their use alone. The steamboat men carried their fight to court to prevent the bridge's construction, but it was rushed to completion in April 1856.

Events leading to the Civil War touched Davenport through two well-known characters—Dred Scott and John Brown. Dred Scott, Negro slave, based his famous fight for freedom upon his residence in Davenport with his master, Dr. John Emerson, for whom he occupied a preemption shack.

John Brown, the famed abolitionist, celebrated Fourth of July, 1857, in Davenport buying supplies for the trip to Kansas that preceded the Harper's Ferry episode, which culminated in his arrest. At another time he concealed a band of runaway slaves in a railroad boxcar as he took them through Davenport enroute to Chicago, then Canada and freedom.

During the Civil War there were several camps in the vicinity of Davenport. Among the more important was Camp McClellan where Sioux Indians, who took part in the massacre of 1862 in Minnesota, were imprisoned. Another was Camp Roberts, later Camp Kinsman, converted after the war into the Iowa Soldiers' Orphans' Home. Gov. Samuel J. Kirkwood and his military staff had their headquarters in the city, for telegraph facilities terminated in Davenport at the opening of the war, thus giving the town an important position in relaying the news.

The river traffic of the 1860's, 1870's and 1880's added romance and color to life in Davenport and gave it activities missing in inland towns. The city was an important port for boats plying between St. Paul and New Orleans.

During the 1880's excellent limestone quarries were developed, making possible the establishment of the cement business, now a leading industry. The principal plants fabricating steel and iron were also started about this time. In 1888 the city developed the second electric trolley (streetcar) in the United States. By the 1890's the immigration of Germans, which had been continuous for almost 40 years, came to a close. During the World War more than 18,000 individuals were employed in the Rock Island arsenal just opposite Davenport.

Manufacturing in the city ranges from pearl buttons to ready-made houses. Chiefly a sawmill town and exporter of raw foodstuffs in its earlier days, Davenport now manufactures cement, cigars, beer, foundry products, pumps, steel wheels, washing machines, men's clothing, wooden sole shoes, meat products, and wool products.

The third charter, adopted in 1851, and since amended, is still in use. This charter makes it possible for Davenport to secure indirectly special legislation to fit the particular needs of the city. Several times the charter privileges have facilitated such local civic actions as the levee improvement commission and the park board. No State law, concerning municipal government, affects Davenport unless it specifically mentions charter cities.

From the day Matthais Rholfs, who brought his piano with him from Germany in 1847, gave Davenport's first piano recital before a group of wide-eyed Indians, music has played a large part in the life of the city. The *Germania Saengerchor*, turner *Gesang-Sektion*, and *Vorwaerts* are maintained by the German population while the Davenport Music Students Club (one of the earliest formed in the State), the Davenport Philharmonic Society for the study of the oratorio and the opera, and the Concordia Society are other well-known organizations. The wide cultural interests of many of the early settlers resulted in the establishing of the Davenport Public Museum and the Municipal Art Gallery, largely through the efforts of William C. Putnam, who provided the Putnam Foundation, an endowment of nearly $500,000 for the Davenport Academy of Sciences, from which the Public Museum emerged.

Octave Thanet (Alice French) whose many novels and short stories drew a realistic picture of the Midwest in the 1890's, did much of her writing while a resident of Davenport. Charles Edward Russell, Arthur Davison Ficke, George Cram Cook, Harry Hansen, Susan Glaspell, all born in Davenport, and Floyd Dell, began to write and form early friendships in this cosmopolitan Mississippi river town. Charles Edward Russell, born September 25, 1860, journalist and author, learned the business end of journalism in his father's newspaper office, the Davenport *Gazette*. In 1927 his biography, *The American Orchestra and Theodore Thomas,* was awarded the Pulitzer prize. His son, John Russell, novelist and short story writer, was also born in Davenport. Susan Glaspell, born July 1, 1882, was awarded the Pulitzer prize in 1930 for her play, *Allison's House.*

POINTS OF INTEREST

1. ANTOINE LE CLAIRE PARK, ft. of Main St. at the river (R), has seven acres of scenic area made by filling in the low river shore to the Government dock line and planting it in trees and flowers. Near the center of the park is a duplicate of Capt. John Litch's LOG CABIN STORE *(private),* built in 1836. The old New Hampshire sea captain brought a whiskey still with him to supply one of the "necessities" he furnished to his customers. BLACK HAWK TREATY BOULDER, in the middle of the park, near the Harrison Street entrance, sent by a State geologist from northwestern Iowa, contains a bronze plaque, giving the history of the Black Hawk treaty. Through this treaty, negotiated September 21, 1832, the United States gained six million acres of land for the sum of 14 cents an acre. At the west end of the park is the PETERSON MEMORIAL MUSIC PAVILION from which concerts are presented. Back of this is the MUNICIPAL STADIUM, entrance at the foot of Gaines Street. This stadium, seating 5,000, is used by the Western League baseball team and serves as a center for many other community activities.

2. MUNICIPAL NATATORIUM *(open June to Sept.),* 120 S. Main St., is supplied by artesian water. In front of the natatorium is a MONUMENT, dedicated June 15, 1921, honoring Judge John F. Dillon (1831–1914), pioneer lawyer, president of the American Bar Association and author of numerous books on jurisprudence.

3. HINRICHSEN MURAL, in a building at 201 W. 2nd St., executed by Helen Johnson Hinrichsen, was presented to the city by Charles Wal-

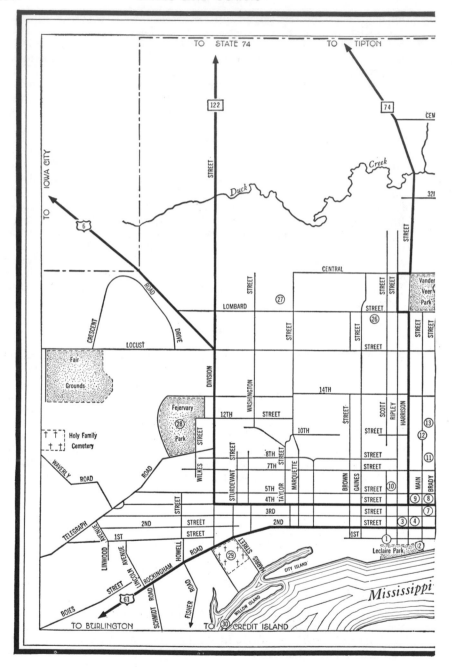

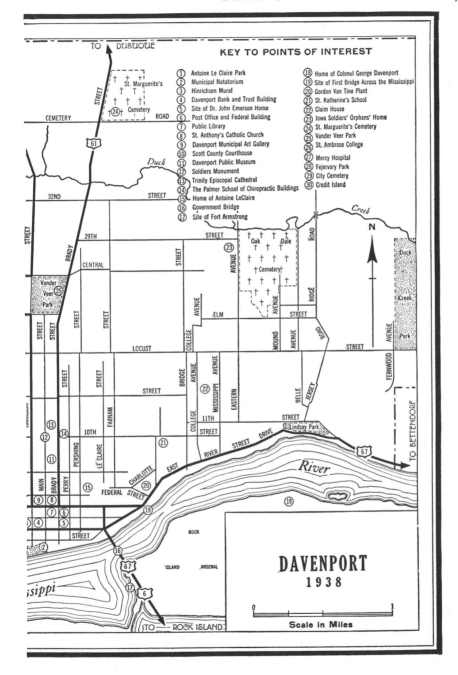

KEY TO POINTS OF INTEREST

1. Antoine Le Claire Park
2. Municipal Natatorium
3. Hinrichsen Mural
4. Davenport Bank and Trust Building
5. Site of Dr. John Emerson Home
6. Post Office and Federal Building
7. Public Library
8. St. Anthony's Catholic Church
9. Davenport Municipal Art Gallery
10. Scott County Courthouse
11. Davenport Public Museum
12. Soldiers Monument
13. Trinity Episcopal Cathedral
14. The Palmer School of Chiropractic Buildings
15. Home of Antoine LeClaire
16. Government Bridge
17. Site of Fort Armstrong

18. Home of Colonel George Davenport
19. Site of First Bridge Across the Mississippi
20. Gordon Van Tine Plant
21. St. Katherine's School
22. Claim House
23. Iowa Soldiers' Orphans' Home
24. St. Marguerite's Cemetery
25. Vander Veer Park
26. St. Ambrose College
27. Mercy Hospital
28. Fejervary Park
29. City Cemetery
30. Credit Island

DAVENPORT
1938

Scale in Miles

green. Depicting the first 100 years of Davenport's history, it is presented in three panels: Indians, pioneers, and builders. The mural was painted on a specially prepared board measuring 30 feet by eight feet, so that it can be moved.

4. DAVENPORT BANK AND TRUST BUILDING, SW. corner 3rd and Main Sts., the highest building in the city, has 19 stories, of which seven compose the CLOCK TOWER, with a beacon light that is visible for 20 miles. The structure is designed in a modified Classic style. On the south wall of the lobby is a MURAL, depicting the negotiating of the Black Hawk Purchase Treaty. Hiram Thompson, formerly of Davenport, painted the mural which was placed on the wall in 1928.

5. SITE OF DR. JOHN EMERSON HOME, 217 E. 2nd St., marked by a plaque, where the master of Dred Scott, Negro slave, planned his home, is now occupied by the Crane Company office and warehouse. Emerson died before the house was completed and Dred Scott lived with the family on other Emerson property. Davenport was alternately a part of the Michigan and Wisconsin free territories during the period Dred Scott lived here. In 1836, Emerson took Scott along with him when he accompanied the Fort Armstrong troops to Fort Snelling. Later they returned to Jefferson Barracks, Missouri. It was here that the action was begun in the circuit court at St. Louis to test the question of Scott's freedom. After the death of Doctor Emerson, Dred Scott was hired out by Mrs. Emerson to various persons, one of whom was Captain Bainbridge who took Scott with him to Corpus Christi during the Mexican War. Upon his return, Scott tried to purchase freedom for himself, his wife, and two daughters from Mrs. Emerson. She refused, so Scott brought suit for his emancipation, on the ground that residence on free soil released him from slavery. The case was tried at St. Louis, May 15, 1854. The court found that "Dred Scott, a Negro slave, was the lawful property of the defendant." The Supreme Court refused an appeal, announcing, March 6, 1857, that Scott's case could not be tried in court because as a slave he had no standing in the court. The decision did much to stir the already aroused feeling of anti-slavery advocates and hurried the crisis of the Civil War.

6. POST OFFICE AND FEDERAL BUILDING, SW. corner 4th and Perry Sts., Davenport's 13th post office building, was opened September 4, 1933. The three-story Minnesota granite and Mankato marble structure, of modern neo-classic design, is the work of Seth J. Temple, architect. During the first months of its history the city had a walking post office, Antoine LeClaire, the first postmaster, carrying the mail in his pocket and delivering it just as he chanced to meet those to whom it was addressed. Afterward, the post office had a dozen homes—a log house, then various brick and frame structures, often shared with other businesses—before it was established in the present Federal Building. On the second floor of the Federal Building is housed one of the six divisions in the Southern Iowa Federal Judicial District.

7. PUBLIC LIBRARY *(open weekdays 9-9)*, SE. corner 4th and Main Sts., is an adaptation of the Classic style, modified by the French Renaissance. Built of Bedford limestone and three stories high, the structure has

an imposing entrance, from the ramps and steps of which rise two Doric columns to the full height of the building. A domed ceiling, with penetrating arches forming lunettes, characterizes the interior. A six-story stack room, opening into the lobby, provides space for the more than 121,000 volumes the library circulates. In the collection of 113 books presented by the late C. A. Ficke in 1919 are some printed by hand or handwritten before 1500 A.D. Others are manuscripts from the Orient and specimens of the early presses and hand-illuminated books of the Middle Ages. The building was presented to the city by Andrew Carnegie in 1902.

8. ST. ANTHONY'S CATHOLIC CHURCH, NE. corner 4th and Main Sts., is a landmark in the city. The rough-cut stone building, built in 1853, is of modified Georgian architecture. The PARISH SCHOOL BUILDING, at the rear, was St. Anthony's—and Davenport's—first church. It was erected in 1837–38 with some of the first brick manufactured in Davenport. The Very Rev. Samuel Mazzuchelli is credited with the design of the building. Its architecture reflects the sturdiness of the pioneers who built it. Since 1853 the structure has been used exclusively as a school.

9. DAVENPORT MUNICIPAL ART GALLERY *(open weekdays except Mon., 10-5; Sun. 2-6)*, 120 W. 5th St., is housed in a remodeled armory. The gallery, opened in October 1925, was one of the first to be municipally owned in the United States. The collection, now valued at $500,000, began with the donation of 330 paintings from the private art group of C. A. Ficke. There are 671 original paintings and 2,700 reproductions in the collection. Among the artists represented are Andrea del Sarto, George Inness, and Sidney Dickinson.

The gallery is the center of Tri-Cities art activities with the Tri-Cities Art Exhibit an annual feature, when as many as 80 artists of Davenport, Rock Island, and Moline compete for the prizes offered. Meetings of art organizations are held here, nationally and internationally known artists lecture in the auditorium, and art shows of note are presented. The free school for children on Saturdays is sponsored and supported by the Friends of Art, an auxiliary institution.

10. SCOTT COUNTY COURTHOUSE, NW. corner 4th and Ripley Sts., was erected in 1888. At each corner of this structure, built of rough chipped stone, turreted towers rise above the roof of the central mass. The site was one of the original park squares (Lafayette) set aside when the city was platted. Decorations symbolizing pioneer times and life in the Mississippi Valley adorn the outside of the building. In the main entrance the marble tablets mounted on the walls bear the names of the pioneers who settled in Scott County before December 31, 1846. On the East side of the third floor is the JAMES GRANT LAW LIBRARY *(open weekdays 8–4)*, belonging to the Scott County Bar Association. There are more than 10,000 books. On the lawn before the courthouse is the COL. GEORGE DAVENPORT MEMORIAL, a boulder with bronze plaque giving the story of Davenport's life.

11. DAVENPORT PUBLIC MUSEUM, 704 Brady St. *(open Sat., 9-4; Sun. and holidays, 2-5; other days by appointment)*, was originally a two-story brick building, erected in 1877, but has been enlarged by two

ANTOINE LeCLAIRE HOUSE, DAVENPORT

additions, one, the old Presbyterian church, annexed in 1902, and the other, a concrete structure added in 1929. The museum contains an important mound builder collection, many items of which were gathered in the vicinity of Davenport, an area rich in remains of the Hopewell mound builder culture. There are Indian, Eskimo, Mexican, Peruvian, and Midwest pioneer collections, among which is a pioneer wagon brought to Iowa in 1840. Exhibits from Egypt (including a mummy), Greece, Rome, Babylon, Japan, and China fill most of the main floor of the annex. Geological specimens on the lower floor, from recent to the most ancient periods, tell the local geological story. In the museum's scientific library are many books that date back to the sixteenth, the seventeenth, and the eighteenth centuries. The collections represent gifts of more than 2,000 friends and members of the controlling corporation over a period of 70 years.

The Davenport Public Museum grew out of the Davenport Academy of Natural Sciences, founded December 14, 1867. The small group of organizers immediately began to build up collections and a library, and to promote local scientific interest. The eminence of its founders and early members, scientists such as Dr. C. C. Parry, botanist; Prof. D. S. Sheldon, conchologist; J. Duncan Putnam, entomologist; and Dr. W. H. Barris, geologist, gave a high standing to the academy. The publication and exchange of its proceedings carried the name of Davenport to all parts of the United States and foreign countries. The scope of the academy collections was soon extended from the natural sciences to include the art and culture of ancient and modern peoples from all parts of the world.

12. SOLDIER'S MONUMENT, middle of Main St. between 10th and

12th Sts., dedicated July 4, 1881, is a 50-foot solid English granite shaft carved with emblems of the various branches of the Civil War service and tributes of valor.

13. TRINITY EPISCOPAL CATHEDRAL, 1121 Main St., is an ivy-covered structure of English Gothic design, consecrated June 18, 1873. The church, the parish house, and the residence of the Bishop, the Vicar, and the Dean occupy the entire block. Spacious lawns dotted with black oaks surround the buildings.

14. THE PALMER SCHOOL OF CHIROPRACTIC BUILDINGS *(open weekdays 8-5)*, Brady St. between 11th and 8th Sts., are easily located by the tall steel tower of the radio station WOC (one of the oldest stations in America) that can be seen from almost any point in the city. The long rambling buildings, crowded together on two square blocks, are of no special architectural style.

The science of chiropractic was discovered by D. D. Palmer, who gave his first chiropractic adjustment in 1895. B. J. Palmer, son of the founder, developed the school and in the 1920's, there were as many as 3,000 students in attendance from all over the world. The school has 150 full-time employees, and has graduated over half of the practitioners of this profession in the country.

A LITTLE BIT O' HEAVEN, on the school grounds *(open weekdays 10-6; Sun. and holidays 10-8; May 15 to Labor Day, Tues. and Thurs. 7-9 p.m.)*, is a museum which grew from one of B. J. Palmer's hobbies. Among the curios are ancient idols from Siam; the Chapelle Petite, one of the smallest chapels in the world; and the Shrine of the Wishing Buddha. The *Birth of Venus*, in Carrara marble, was executed by Bruno, an Italian.

15. HOME OF ANTOINE LE CLAIRE *(open Memorial Day)*, 217 E. 5th St., on an embankment of the Rock Island Railroad, was also the first railroad station in Iowa. Antoine LeClaire, one of the founders of Davenport, built this house in 1833. Moving later to a larger home, he gave the first one to serve as the railroad station, from which the first train started west from Davenport in 1855. In 1923 the local chapter of the Daughters of the American Revolution induced the railroad company to move the building to the present location near its original site, now a part of the railroad yards. The chapter restored the log structure, covering it with clapboards. Each Memorial Day the cabin is furnished with pioneer antiques.

16. GOVERNMENT BRIDGE, 2nd St., ft. of LeClaire St., with its massive swinging draw, is one of the few toll-free bridges across the Mississippi. From the bridge one may view the front yard of the Tri-Cities. On either side of the bridge is a good view of the GOVERNMENT LOCKS and DAMS. This roller gate type of dam is the largest of eight in the United States. There are two parallel locks, one 600 feet in length. Both are 110 feet wide, about the same width as the Panama Canal locks. A sea wall begins about 136 feet below the first roller gate on the Iowa side and extends upstream 1.81 miles. Dam 15, part of the nine-foot channel project, raises the water level of the Mississippi River.

17. SITE OF FORT ARMSTRONG, near end of Government bridge (R), on Rock Island, is marked by a BLOCKHOUSE *(open)*, a duplicate of one of the three constituting the original fort. Fort Armstrong was built in 1816. Much of the activity of the Black Hawk War centered around this fort.

18. HOME OF COLONEL GEORGE DAVENPORT, end of bridge (L), on the Rock Island Arsenal grounds *(open by permission, Arsenal Commandant),* was recently restored. The plainness of this Colonial structure, built in 1833, is relieved by a portico, with four columns, Doric in detail. Davenport is named for this Englishman who served in the United States Army for 10 years before coming to the Fort Armstrong site with soldiers detailed to establish a fort here in 1816. Several years later he gave up his agency of supplying the Government troops with provisions, to enter the fur trade with the Indians. In 1833 he replaced his log cabin with the large two-story home that he occupied during the rest of his life. In this home, on February 23, 1836, six of the eight men interested met and executed the articles founding the city of Davenport. In this house on July 4, 1845, while his family was attending a celebration in Rock Island, Ill., Colonel Davenport was murdered by bandits, incited to the act by a former servant. After his death the house was neglected for many years, but with restoration by the Federal Government, it now appears (with the exception of two wings) as it did when Colonel Davenport lived there. Also on the arsenal grounds are a military museum, a Confederate cemetery, a national cemetery, and the arsenal buildings.

19. SITE OF FIRST BRIDGE ACROSS THE MISSISSIPPI, junction of 3rd and 4th Sts., is marked by a boulder indicating the north abutment of the bridge, which was finished in 1856. The rivermen attempted not only to prevent the erection of the bridge, but also to have it removed, once it was built.

The first case, Hurd et al *vs.* Railroad Bridge Company, grew out of the accident to the *Effie Afton,* which struck a pier of the bridge and caught fire. Abraham Lincoln, then a young attorney, represented the railroad company in the case, which was tried before the United States Circuit Court. Lincoln's argument that even in transportation the survival of the fittest exists, blocked the charge of the steamboat captain who called the bridge "a nuisance and an obstruction." He showed that the river was closed by ice four months each year while the bridge was always open, and that the railroad had carried 74,179 passengers and 12,586 freight cars over the bridge, proving its worth. This case ended in a jury disagreement and was dismissed, but the feeling between the rivermen and the railroad men continued to grow until the United States Congress instructed its Committee on Commerce to investigate the bridge situation (Jan. 4, 1858). The committee came to the conclusion that the bridge was an obstruction but that the United States courts possessed "full power to remedy the evil."

Not until 1862, in another case, was the long fought question of bridging navigable streams settled. Three years before, James Ward, steamboat captain of St. Louis, filed a bill asking the State of Iowa to remove its

COL. GEORGE DAVENPORT HOUSE, DAVENPORT

portion of the bridge. The court in this case ruled the bridge "a common nuisance" and ordered the three piers and superstructures in Iowa removed The Mississippi and Missouri Railway appealed to the Supreme Court on the basis that river commerce mainly used the Illinois channel, and the removal of the Iowa portion would leave this channel unchanged for the river traffic. The Supreme Court reversed the decision, thus giving the railroads the legal right to bridge any navigable river in their westward path.

20. GORDON VAN TINE PLANT *(tours weekdays 8-5)*, 702 Federal St., manufactures ready-cut houses. To the north and east of the plant is an Irish district, known in early times as the "Patch," a settlement almost wiped out by the fire of 1901. Some of the homes in the rehabilitated "Patch" are the ready-cut houses produced in the plant.

21. ST. KATHERINE'S SCHOOL (Episcopal), SE. corner 10th St. and Tremont Ave., has a campus of 10 acres of wooded bluffs overlooking the Mississippi. Opened in 1884, the school cares for 50 boarding and 100 day students from kindergarten through high school. Three of the seven buildings have square towers rising above the main part of the building as the central feature. ST. KATHERINE'S, a two-story, red brick house, is embellished with wide cornices, a modified mansard roof, and iron balustrades. The high narrow windows of ST. MARGARET'S distinguish this two-and-a-half-story stone structure. ST. MARY'S CHAPEL, of red brick and Bedford stone, is of modified Gothic design.

MASS MOUND, southwest of the main building, is a revered spot on a hill overlooking the Mississippi. Father Charles Van Quickenborne, a Jesuit ministering to the Indians before the country was settled, erected a crucifix carved from native walnut, and built an altar at this spot. When the crucifix fell under the wear of storms and winds, it was broken into pieces that were carried away by interested persons. John L. Davies, a pioneer lumberman, acquired the hill land and built a home here. During the Episcopate of the Right Reverend William Stevens Perry, the second bishop of Iowa, the Episcopal church came into possession of the property and St. Katherine's school was established in the Davies home. A crucifix was erected 1929. Two years later an altar of stone, marked with a bronze tablet that tells the story of Mass Mound, was erected before the crucifix.

The "little wedding pillow" of St. Katherine's has traveled far during the 40 years it has figured in the weddings of brides who attended the school. The custom originated when Fawn Hamilton, now Mrs. Robert Cook, made the pillow and covered it with satin from her wedding gown. Each succeeding bride who uses the pillow re-covers it, putting the layer of her wedding gown material on top of the one which preceded it. Mrs. Cook is custodian of the pillow, which has also been used by her daughter.

22. CLAIM HOUSE *(private)*, 1329 College Ave., built in 1832 or 1833, is said to be the oldest building in the city. Incorporated within the lines of the remodeled structure is the original house that was 18 feet by 18 feet. The present building includes a small addition on the north end, a lean-to kitchen, a dormer, and a front porch. A modern brick chimney replaces the original one of stone. George L. Davenport, first white child born in the community, is said to have built the house to protect his self-asserted rights to the land on which it stood, a tract east of Antoine Le-Claire's section. In 1867 the house was taken apart and moved to its present location.

23. IOWA SOLDIERS' ORPHANS' HOME, 2800 Eastern Ave., was originally organized to care for the orphans of Civil War soldiers. The first group of 150 children orphaned by the war, arrived in Davenport on November 16, 1865, by steamer. A staff of 63 people, including four doctors, now take care of 500 dependent or neglected children, among whom are about 100 who are orphans of World War soldiers. One of the buildings is named for Mrs. Annie Wittenmyer, who started and directed the movement for an orphans' home in fulfillment of promises made to many dying soldiers. There are 26 buildings which include a number of cottage-dormitories, barns, a silo, a hospital, and school buildings. The latter are utilitarian in style. At the immediate right of the entrance a cement marker indicates the SITE OF CAMP ROBERTS, later known as Camp Kinsman, a training camp for soldiers of the Civil War.

24. ST. MARGUERITE'S CEMETERY, Cemetery Rd. between Brady St. and Eastern Ave., is one of four cemeteries on the slopes overlooking Duck Creek in the distance. Here the GRAVE OF ANTOINE LeCLAIRE, well-known Indian interpreter, and one of the founders and promoters of Davenport, and the GRAVE OF LeCLAIRE'S WIFE, Marguerite, grand-daughter of an Indian chief, are marked by a tall obelisk, inscribed in both French and English.

25. VANDER VEER PARK, Lombard St. and Central Ave. between Harrison and Brady Sts., is attractively landscaped with an electric fountain, lagoons, beds of flowers, and a glass-enclosed conservatory that has beautiful and rare flowers in and out of season. A chrysanthemum show is an annual event at the floral conservatory at the north entrance of the park.

26. ST. AMBROSE COLLEGE *(open 8-4:30, weekdays)*, 518 W. Locust St., occupies four buildings in a wooded area of 15 acres. AMBROSE HALL, built of brick and sandstone in 1887, is a four-story building with two extending wings. The windows are rounded at the top and a mansard roof extends over the main portion and wings. LEWIS MEMORIAL SCIENCE HALL and DAVIS HALL are newer brick buildings, plain and rectangular in their modern utilitarian lines.

This endowed Roman Catholic institution, founded in 1882, is under the jurisdiction of the Bishop of Davenport and a board of trustees. Bachelor of Science and Bachelor of Arts degrees are granted. In addition to the regular courses there are Saturday and evening classes, and a summer session. Advanced courses are open to women students and there is an academy for students preparing for college courses.

27. MERCY HOSPITAL, NW. corner Lombard and Marquette Sts., is a five-story building of modern design. The large cross on top is visible day and night. The Sisters of Mercy control the hospital but people of all creeds helped in its establishment (1868). Judge Gilbert C. R. Mitchell, whose family was interested in charitable and civic affairs, donated the land for a girls' academy, which later became the first unit of the hospital. Two other hospitals, ST. JOHN's and ST. ELIZABETH's, are also on this property. The combined capacity of the four hospitals is 300 beds.

28. FEJERVARY PARK, W. end of 12th St., on wooded bluffs, is noted for its MONKEY ISLAND, where in summer a colony of monkeys romp and gambol as in a natural habitat. Within the park are buffalo, elk, deer, and ostriches. This area came into the park system indirectly through intrigues and strife among the nobility of Europe. In 1853, following the collapse of the insurrection in Hungary, Count Nicholas Fejervary, unhappy over the turn of events, came to Davenport. With his family, he entered into the activities of developing this community from a frontier settlement to the established city it was at the time of his death in 1895. After the death of her parents, the daughter, Celestine Fejervary, presented the old homestead, with 21 acres of wooded hills, to the city for park purposes, and returned to Hungary to claim the family estates.

29. CITY CEMETERY, corner Rockingham Rd. and Sturdevant-Harris St., is the oldest cemetery in the city. In it is the grave of Dr. John Emerson, owner of the Negro slave, Dred Scott. Different sections of the cemetery indicate, somewhat, the history of the city. In the southwest corner are graves which record the tragic cholera epidemic in the early 1870's when the victims were often buried in a common trench. Interred in the northeast corner are the remains of more than 200 Union soldiers who died at Camp Black Hawk, a cavalry training camp during the Civil

War. This section is preserved as an open space decorated with American flags.

30. CREDIT ISLAND, end of Schmidt Rd., once a battlefield, is an island park, acquired by the city in 1918. Near the entrance of the park is a large granite BOULDER inscribed with the story of the battle between the Americans and the British and their Indian allies in 1814 on this site. Three hundred thirty-four American soldiers under the command of Maj. Zachary Taylor, later President of the United States, arrived with eight unwieldy keelboats, which they had sailed and dragged by rope from St. Louis, to punish the Indians for their attack on Campbell Island, six weeks before. A force of about 30 to 60 British soldiers, aided by about 1,000 Sac, Fox, Sioux, and Winnebago Indian allies, defeated the Americans on September 5 but allowed them to return down the river since the British supply of ammunition was scanty.

POINTS OF INTEREST IN ENVIRONS

Birthplace of Buffalo Bill, *15 m. (Tour 2, sec. b)*.

Des Moines

Railroad Stations: 4th and Vine Sts. for Chicago, Rock Island & Pacific Ry., and Minneapolis & St. Louis R.R.; Union Station, 6th and Cherry Sts., for Chicago, Burlington & Quincy R.R., Chicago, Great Western R.R., Chicago, Milwaukee, St. Paul & Pacific R.R., and Wabash Ry.; E. 4th and Locust Sts. for Chicago & North Western Ry.
Interurban Station: 2nd St. and Grand Ave. for Des Moines & Central Iowa Ry., and Fort Dodge, Des Moines & Southern Ry.
Bus Stations: Union Depot, 5th and Grand Aves., for Interstate Transit Lines, Jefferson Lines and Des Moines-Winterset; 6th Ave. and Mulberry St. for Burlington Lines.
Airport: Municipal, SW. 21st St. and Army Post Rd., 4.5 m. SW. city, United Air Lines, transcontinental service; taxi fare from city, 75¢ if arranged through airlines.
Taxis: 35¢ first 2 m., 10¢ additional ½ m., no charge for extra passengers.
Streetcars: Fare 10¢; descriptive map available at Des Moines Railway Co., 2nd St. and Grand Ave.
Traffic Regulations: Loop district parking and no-parking areas designated on curbs. No R. turn permitted against red light.

Accommodations: Forty-seven hotels, 14 tourist camps.

Tourist Information Service: Chamber of Commerce, Savery Hotel, 4th and Locust Sts.; American Automobile Association, Motor Club of Iowa, Hotel Fort Des Moines, 10th and Walnut Sts.

Radio Stations: WHO (1,000 kc); KSO (1,430 kc); KRNT (1,320 kc).
Theaters and Motion Picture Houses: Three theaters; 22 motion picture houses.
Swimming: Camp Dodge, Merle Hay Rd.; Birdland Pool, 2345 6th Ave.; Ashworth Memorial Pool, via 45th St. and Greenwood Park, S. of Grand Ave.; Good Park Pool, 17th and University (Negroes).
Golf: Grand View Park, municipal, E. 29th St. and Arthur Ave., 18 holes, 25¢, week ends and holidays 50¢; Waveland Park, municipal, 48th and University, same fees.
Tennis: Descriptive list available at office of Park Dept., City Hall, E. 1st St., bet. Locust St. and Grand Ave.

Annual Events: Regimental Day, Fort Des Moines, Mar. 5; Drake Relays, April; Iowa State Fair, last week in Aug.

DES MOINES (800 alt., 142,559 pop.), capital of Iowa and Polk County seat, is an important commercial center lying in the midst of a leading agricultural area. The gently rolling land of central Iowa is broken here by the Des Moines River that flows south through the city, and the Raccoon that winds east to empty into the Des Moines. Brown and sluggish, both rivers rise and fall as their currents are affected by rains or drought at their sources. The four Milan arch bridges across the Des Moines River, which bisects the city at the Civic Center, where the gray stone municipal and Federal buildings are grouped, give an impression of orderly civic planning. Toward the east the East Side business center, a small city

THE CAPITOL, DES MOINES

in itself, pushes up to the foot of Capitol Hill, where the State buildings, culminating in the gold dome of the Capitol, tower above the metropolis. Beyond the park area of the Hill, business houses and homes spread out widely over level land, with a manufacturing center to the south and small acreages on the outskirts.

West of the Civic Center the skyscrapers of the main business district rise in an uneven line from the valley's floor, the tower of the Equitable Building dominating them all. To the northwest is Drake University and a residential area interspersed with small shopping centers, while to the west, a section of once fashionable residences reveals the transformation of a formerly aristocratic residential district. Mansions have been remodeled; apartments and gasoline stations are wedged among houses that still cling to their former prestige.

Far to the south and east is the Italian quarter; on the near north and west, the Negro district; while people of Swedish descent predominate on the East Side. On the southern limits is Fort Des Moines, an important Army post, and, to the north of the city, Camp Dodge, now used by the National Guard; these establishments make the city the focal point of military activity in Iowa. West Des Moines (once known as Valley Junction) is an incorporated village with Portland cement plants as its sole industry.

The city, covering a space of 66 square miles, is roomy. Residences, fronted by broad yards and wide streets, extensive park areas, small acreages, vacant lots, and undeveloped lands along the river spread away from the low valley. From the business section wooded horizons are visible, and from the manufacturing centers open prairie and green meadows give wide vistas. At evening as the moist air above the river cools, rising mists gather smoke and dust until the vicinity is obscured by a dense haze. In spite of its open country and apparent airiness, Des Moines is one of the Midwest's smokiest cities.

Des Moines, a prairie city, derives its support from the adjacent farming regions. Unlike the river towns to the east, and the western prairie towns, to the farmers and small-town people in the State it is not only their capital city but Iowa itself. During the numerous annual conventions that meet here, the "Iowa Corn Song" resounds through the meeting halls in salute to the capital city. John T. Beeston and George Hamilton of Des Moines wrote the verses, adapting them to the tune of "Travelling," a song popular at the turn of the nineteenth century.

The name Des Moines is probably traceable to the mound builders who long ago lived near the banks of the rivers. The Indians called the main stream *Moingona* (River of the Mounds). French voyageurs, who followed Marquette and Joliet into the Midwest, called it *La Riviere des Moines,* from the monks who once dwelt in huts beside the water. It was spelled phonetically *De Moin, De Moyen, Demoine,* and *Des Moines.* The term, *De Moyen,* translated as "middle," was understood to refer to the principal river between the Mississippi and the Missouri. Another variation in the meaning is "the less" or "the smaller," referring to a small tribe of Indians living on the river.

The Raccoon Fork of the Des Moines River received official mention in December 1834, when John Dougherty, Indian agent at Fort Leavenworth, wrote the War Department recommending a chain of military posts to protect the Indians as "untutored children." The territory was explored in the summer of 1835, when Col. Stephen W. Kearny with 150 men and officers, among them Lieut. Albert M. Lea, studied the advantages of the site as a possible garrison.

In July 1841 John C. Fremont was ordered west by the War Department to survey the Des Moines River, from the Raccoon Forks to its mouth, in order to complete Jean Nicholas Vicollel's map of the territory. He determined the astronomical position of Raccoon Forks, estimated the fall of the river, studied the flora of the valley, and returned to Washington in October.

The proposed military garrison was established in May 1843, when Capt. James Allen and his company of First Dragoons arrived by the steamer *Ione* from Fort Sanford with another company from Fort Crawford. Captain Allen proposed to name the site Fort Raccoon, but this was vetoed by the War Department as being "shocking; at least in very bad taste" and Captain Allen was directed to use the name Fort Des Moines until further notice. Wilson Alexander Scott, familiarly known as "Aleck," had preceded Captain Allen and his men by some months. When the fort was established, he obtained a permit to settle nearby and raise corn and hay for the garrison. At midnight October 11, 1845, after the Sac and Fox had relinquished their rights, the territory was thrown open to white settlers. When the cannon at the fort boomed out the zero hour, settlers rushed in to take the land, setting fire to the deserted Indian wigwams and staking out their claims. Captain Allen and his men occupied the fort until March 10, 1846, and in the same month "Aleck" Scott purchased 500 acres of land on the east side of the Des Moines River. During the next year he operated the first ferry, and later built the first bridge across the river at this point.

Fort Des Moines, after some dissension among rival settlements, was chosen to be the seat of Polk County. The first newspaper, *The Star,* appeared in the summer of 1849 under the editorship of Barlow Granger. The fort, situated on one of the main immigrant trails to California, was the stopping place of hundreds of gold seekers. Their contagious enthusiasm led many of the settlers to forsake their newly-acquired prairie homesteads and seek fortunes on the coast; but *The Star* of May 1, 1851, notes another side to the picture: "Most of those who come from the east this year, remain here, satisfied that they can find no better country by going farther west."

The word Fort was dropped with the adoption of a city charter in 1857. The city officially assumed its role as State capital in January 1858, after 10 yoke of oxen had hauled into town two bobsleds of archives from Iowa City. During the growth and development of the city, through the 1850's, the Des Moines River was a consequential, if precarious, waterway. One day in April 1859 five steamboats dropped anchor and loaded or discharged cargoes at the landing but, after the railroads entered, river traffic declined.

News of the outbreak of the Civil War aroused varied emotions in Des Moines. Stilson Hutchins, editor of the *State Journal,* Des Moines, wrote an editorial attacking the policy of coercion adopted by President Lincoln. At that time mails were slow and uncertain, for there were no railroads. The "pony express" carried newspapers (The Burlington *Hawkeye*) from Eddyville to Des Moines in eight hours; letters from Keokuk reached the capital in from three to five days. When letters arrived in the city bringing the news from Charleston, local patriots talked seriously of violence against the editor. Marcellus M. Crocker (later commended by General Grant as a leader "fit to command an independent army") presided at a mass-meeting when he asked for volunteers to accompany him to the front. One hundred responded immediately. May 4, 1861, the "Capital Guards" started for Keokuk to be mustered in. Other units were formed from time to time, and a recruiting station was maintained on Capital Square.

"Copperheads" (Southern sympathizers) contended fiercely for control of the Democratic Party in Iowa. Henry Clay Dean, a leader of this group, held secret meetings nightly at the Demoine House, plotting to put every possible obstacle in the way of both State and national governments. One winter day, a large crowd assembled at the Methodist church where Dean was scheduled to speak. The stovepipe functioned improperly and, as suf-

focating smoke thickened the air, the audience departed in a near panic.
Frank Palmer of the *Register* commented, "Carnal-minded people might
not regard this as a judgment, but we do."

Des Moines soldiers saw action at Fort Donelson, Pea Ridge, Shiloh,
and Corinth. Crocker was made a brigadier general for "the masterly handling" of his troops in the two latter battles. Early in June 1862 casualties
from the battle of Pittsburg Landing began to arrive in Des Moines.
Women of the city encouraged enlistments and patriotic activities. When,
in May 1864, Governor Stone called for 100-day recruits, 41 married
women signed a petition asking to take the places of business and working
men to enable them to go to the front. Then 46 unmarried women made
a similar offer, adding that the pay of the men should be continued. Recruits were found, however, without the aid of such stimulation.

Toward the end of the war local citizens labored to expedite the extension of the Des Moines Valley Railroad to Des Moines. The company
asked for stock subscriptions amounting to $100,000, and $33,000 was
promptly raised. The first cars of this line ran into Des Moines August
29, 1866.

Railroad passes were issued in 1870 to all Iowa veterans of the Civil
War, to enable them to attend the Grand Reunion in Des Moines August
31, of that year. Thirty thousand former soliders were present. Gen. William T. Sherman and Gen. W. W. Belknap, Secretary of War, were guests
of honor. The two generals again visited the city, September 9, 1875,
when President Grant appeared to address the Ninth Annual Reunion of
the Army of the Tennessee. Grant's speech before this gathering was considered epoch-making. He urged the Free School and "all needful guaran-
tees for the more perfect security of free thought, free speech, a free press,
pure morals, unfettered religious sentiment and of equal rights and privileges to all men irrespective of nationality, color or religion."

Late in April and early May 1894, "Kelly's Army" of nearly 1,000 unemployed men who were marching from Omaha to Washington to plead
their cause in Congress, descended upon the city. The citizens of the
community, anxious not to anger this formidable and determined throng,
received them hospitably, providing ample meals and lodging. Crowds
turned out to watch the parade, when Charles T. Kelly, "King of the
Commons," rode a dark bay horse through the streets at the head of his
men. But rain spoiled the reception and, continuing, tempted the visitors
to linger in their dry and comfortable quarters. They refused to move on
unless transportation was provided. Des Moines authorities feared the
army might remain indefinitely, and were wondering how to meet the situation, when their attention was attracted by the rapidly swelling river. "It
would float an army!" remarked someone. "Or a navy!" said another.

"General" Kelly and his men, invited to sail down the Des Moines
River toward Keokuk on the next lap of their journey, set to work under
the direction of the local carpenters' union and built 150 flatboats. Towns-
people willingly contributed money to buy lumber. The boats were finished
May 9, and the "industrial fleet" got under way and started downstream.
Each man was provided with a small American flag that he waved in salute

GRAND AVENUE, DES MOINES

and Des Moines' last sight of the adventurers was through a flurry of red, white, and blue as the boats slipped around the bend of the river. Among the "sailors" was the writer, Jack London, who some years later referred to his experiences in Des Moines.

During the war with Spain, 1898–99, the Fair Grounds, deeded to the State June 26, 1885, were pressed into service for mobilization of the National Guard. Four regiments, the 49th, 50th, 51st, and 52nd Infantries, gathered there at Camp McKinley. Many Des Moines men enlisted in the 51st Infantry, and altogether 5,859 Iowans were mustered in or trained at the camp.

The city again gained military significance November 13, 1903, when the cavalry post, Fort Des Moines, was dedicated. Urged by Congressman John A. T. Hull, the 56th Congress passed a bill appropriating $219,000 for the establishment of the post, after a group of citizens had subscribed $40,000 toward the purchase of a 400-acre site. Troops from six other forts—Omaha, Crooks, Riley, Russell, Meade and Crawford—joined Fort Des Moines soldiers in "The Great Tournament" in June 1909. Infantry, cavalry, artillery, and other branches of the service competed for medals and corps area honors. President William Howard Taft reviewed the various units as they paraded in the finale of the five-day event, and presented the awards.

After the United States entered the World War, in 1917, the National Guard mobilized at the Fair Grounds, and a regiment designated as the 168th Infantry was sent to France with the 42nd (Rainbow) Division. Fort Des Moines, abandoned for some time as a cavalry post, served as a training camp for Negro officers, and later was converted to a base hospital. The population reached a new peak when thousands of friends, relatives, and war workers took up residence in the city to be near soldiers who were being trained at Camp Dodge, 12 miles northwest of Des Moines. Forty thousand men passed through the camp in June 1918, thousands more were mustered in or out and quartered here between August 1917 and the summer of 1919.

Des Moines assumed national importance September 4, 1936, when President Franklin D. Roosevelt arrived at the State House to consult with various State and Government officials regarding the drought problem in the Midwest. Unusual interest was attached to the event because the Republican Presidential candidate, Gov. Alfred M. Landon of Kansas, participated.

The Des Moines Plan of city government provides for a municipal business administration by a city council made up of representatives of the city at large in place of individual wards. The mayor and four commissioners, each responsible for his own department, form the council. The departments are: accounts and finance, public safety, streets and public improvements, parks and public property. The 33rd General Assembly (1907) passed the plan as a law after a preliminary bill had been submitted by a committee.

The city is widely known as an insurance center. The Equitable Life Insurance Company, incorporated in 1867, was the first of its type to be or-

ganized west of the Mississippi. The Bankers' Life, begun in 1879, was operating in 35 States at the end of 1934. Forty-seven insurance companies maintain home offices in the city and give employment to more than 16,000 people.

Des Moines, partly because of the vast amount of printed matter used by the insurance companies, is one of the six largest publishing and printing centers in the United States. Fifty-seven journals, ranging from national farm and home magazines to fraternal and commercial papers, are published regularly here.

Other industries are varied. More than 400 factories manufacture clothing and hosiery, woolen goods, fur, leather, foundry, grain, dairy, clay and cement products. Several cosmetic companies make face powder, cold cream, hair tonic, and hand lotion. Much of Iowa's corn finds its way to market on the hoof in the several packing plants in southeast Des Moines. Twenty mines adjacent to the city or in nearby Polk County, the center of an extensive bituminous coal field, produce 500,000 tons annually and employ hundreds of miners.

The Des Moines Public Forum, a community civic plan of adult education financed by the Carnegie Corporation, has served as a model for several other cities. Its special feature is the evening neighborhood forum in which noted speakers from all parts of the world lead programs in designated schools and club rooms of the city. The leaders talk on political, economic, and social problems, and are then questioned by a panel of selected representative citizens. The audience is encouraged to join the discussion. John W. Studebaker, superintendent of the Des Moines schools, later United States Commissioner of Education, procured funds from the Carnegie Corporation to carry on a five-year experiment ending with the 1936–37 season. At that time the school board decided to continue the forums as a civic function, under an Adult Education Council representing all civic and educational agencies.

POINTS OF INTEREST

Civic Center

1. The PUBLIC LIBRARY *(open weekdays 9-9; Sun. 2-6)*, 1st St. between Walnut and Locust Sts. W. Riverbank, completed in 1904, is built of sandstone and marble weathered to a grayish-black. At the east entrance rows of steps lead to the riverbank; at the west a small marquee is supported by Corinthian columns. There are approximately 250,000 volumes in the library. Valuable items include the Cummins collection of Americana, a gift of the late Senator A. B. Cummins; the Otis collection of Shakespearean works; an extensive library on the death of Lincoln; and comprehensive libraries on music and art. DES MOINES ASSOCIATION OF FINE ARTS COLLECTION, second floor *(open weekdays 9-6, except Mon., 9-9)*, represents 25 contemporary artists, including Robert Henri, Frank Brangwyn, Eugene Speicher, Louis B. Rittmann, and Leon Kroll. Local exhibitions are held here.

2. The COLISEUM, between Locust St. and Grand Ave., W. River-

bank, is a buff brick edifice that has played an important part in the city's cultural and recreational life since its construction in 1910. With a seating capacity of 8,500, it has sheltered such varied attractions as a poultry show, the Russian Ballet, and a State teachers' convention. Here Nijinsky once danced in *Scheherazade;* President Woodrow Wilson addressed a mass-meeting; Paderewski and Kreisler thrilled crowds; *Faust* was sung by Lucian Muratore; and Earl Caddock wrestled "Strangler" Lewis for the heavyweight championship of the world.

3. A BOULDER, E. end Grand Ave. bridge, N. side of st., bears a bronze tablet commemorating the first ferry, at the junction of the Des Moines and Raccoon Rivers, operated in 1847; the first pontoon bridge, at Sycamore Street (now Grand Ave.), built in 1856; and the first toll bridge, at Court Avenue, built in 1856.

4. CITY HALL, E. Riverbank between E. Locust St. and E. Grand Ave., completed in 1910, constructed of Bedford stone and Tennessee and Vermont marble, is neo-classic in style. On this site stood the first mill in the present city of Des Moines, erected and operated in the early 1850's.

5. NEW FEDERAL BUILDING (UNITED STATES COURT-HOUSE), E. Riverbank at E. Walnut St., was built in 1930. The main entrance of this Bedford stone structure, neo-classic in style, has eight large Corinthian columns set between rows of French windows. On the roof is an observation station of the United States Weather Bureau. One of the most important offices in the building is that of the Collector of Customs. Fine china, earthenware and glassware arrive here by the barrel, much of it shipped in from Czechoslovakia, to be sold in Des Moines and other Iowa cities. Tomatoes are imported from Mexico in the early spring, before local crops can mature; a variety of clover seed comes in from Poland and Russia; diacetyl, a flavoring used in the manufacture of butter, is ordered from Denmark by dairy operators. British woolens, Irish linens, olive oil and food delicacies from Italy, and scientific and technical books from Germany are items that regularly pass through this office.

6. SITE OF FORT DES MOINES, W. Riverbank at Elm St., has a marker to commemorate the spot where Captain Allen and his soldiers established their garrison. The granite monument is nearly lost to view in a jungle of warehouses and factories.

7. THE CITY MARKET HOUSE, NW. corner 2nd and Locust Sts., is a two-story building, originally built in 1912 and remodeled in 1936 when the section of outdoor booths was enclosed by brick walls. Renters in this section can sell only products that they raise themselves, while those on the inside can sell both their own and commercial products. The market is under city supervision, directed by the Commissioner of Finance.

8. MARINE MUSEUM *(open),* Brown Hotel, NW. corner 4th St. and Keosauqua Way, displays many varieties of mounted fish and seafowls gathered in domestic and tropical waters by the late Ernest W. Brown. The collection originated with an 18-foot sawfish, 1,500 pounds in weight, caught by Mr. Brown near Port Arkansas, Texas.

9. EQUITABLE BUILDING *(open weekdays 8-6),* SW. corner 6th Ave. and Locust St., home office of the Equitable Life Insurance Com-

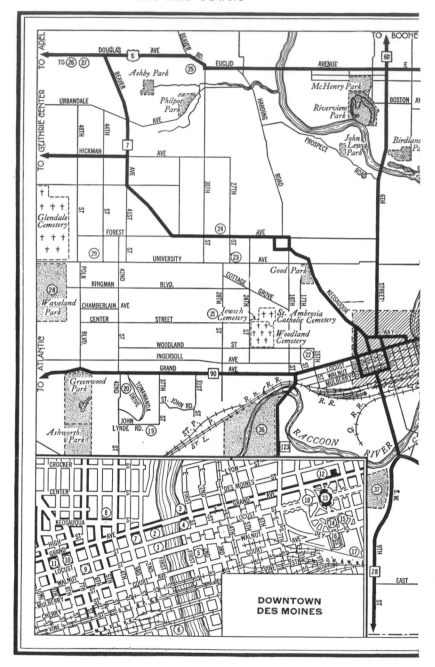

DOWNTOWN
DES MOINES

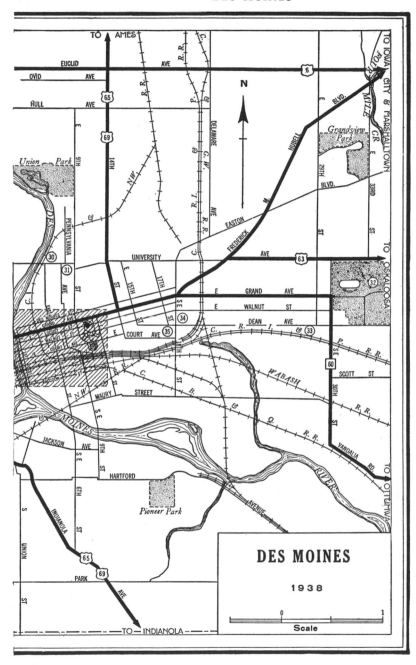

DES MOINES

1938

Scale

pany of Iowa, is said to be the tallest office building in the State—318 feet, 19 stories. Designed by Proudfoot, Bird and Rawson of Des Moines and completed in 1924, the red brick building, Gothic in style, is trimmed with Vermont granite and terra cotta.

10. REGISTER AND TRIBUNE BUILDING *(open, guides furnished 10 a.m. and 2:30 p.m. weekdays)*, 715 Locust St., is the home of the Des Moines *Register* and the Des Moines *Tribune*. A decorative feature of this 14-story gray stone building is the arrangement of columns. Two Doric columns extend from the second to the fourth floor, and four Corinthian columns from the 11th to the 13th floor. Two MURALS by Russell Cowles, on the walls of the business office, represent respectively the *Functions of the Newspaper* and *Freedom of Speech*. Also by the same artist are portraits of Gardner Cowles, publisher, and Harvey Ingham, editor.

11. SITE OF THE FIRST PUBLIC SCHOOL, NE. corner 9th and Locust Sts., is indicated by a plaque on the wall of a business building. The school was erected in 1858 and abandoned in 1869.

CAPITOL HILL

12. STATE HISTORICAL, MEMORIAL AND ART BUILDING *(open weekdays 8-5; Sun. and holidays 12-5)*, NW. corner E. 12th St. and

---

KEY TO DES MOINES MAP

1. Public Library
2. Coliseum
3. Boulder
4. City Hall
5. New Federal Building
6. Site of Fort Des Moines
7. City Market House
8. Marine Museum
9. Equitable Building
10. Register and Tribune Building
11. Site of the First Public School
   Capitol Hill
12. State Historical Memorial and
   Art Building
13. State Capitol
14. Soldiers and Sailors Monument
15. Allison Memorial
16. Stone Viaduct
17. Grave of Wilson Alexander
   Scott
18. The Pioneers
19. John M. Schlitz Home
20. Salisbury House
21. David W. Smouse Opportunity
   School
22. Hoyt Sherman Place
23. Drake University
24. Drake Stadium
25. United States Veterans' Administration Facility
26. Memorial to Merle Hay
27. St. Gabriel's Monastery
28. Drake University Municipal
   Observatory
29. Des Moines Seismological
   Station
30. Polk County War Memorial
31. Log Cabin
32. State Fair Grounds
33. Rollins Hosiery Mills
34. Redhead Park
35. House of the Seven Gables
36. Waterworks Park
37. Fort Des Moines
38. Macrae Park

Grand Ave., houses some of the State's most valuable collections. The Historical, Memorial and Art Department of Iowa was founded by Charles Aldrich, the first curator, who presented a collection of autographs to the trustees of the State library in 1884. The department was originally quartered in the State Capitol. Later, the 26th General Assembly arranged for the purchase of a site and the erection of a building and Governor Leslie M. Shaw laid the cornerstone May 17, 1899.

The edifice, completed in 1900, is constructed of stone from LeGrand Township in Marshall County. Four Ionic columns surmounted by an eagle with wings outspread adorn the entrance, which is Italian Renaissance in style. The central structure, topped with a stone dome, is flanked by east and west wings, their cornices bearing, respectively, the legends, "Library" and "Museum." The building is 260 feet by 110 feet, and 96 feet in height, including the dome.

After Aldrich's death, his assistant, Edgar Rubey Harlan of Keosauqua, was appointed curator (1908–1937).

In the Historical Department, left wing, main floor is the ALDRICH AUTOGRAPH COLLECTION, which includes a manuscript page from Darwin's *Origin of Species;* a chapter from Macaulay's *History of England;* and, among famous signatures, those of John Quincy Adams, Napoleon Bonaparte, Edgar Allan Poe, and John Greenleaf Whittier.

The HISTORICAL LIBRARY room, adjoining, contains about 38,000 volumes, including 3,513 works of Iowa authors, among them two novels dealing with phases of life in Des Moines—*State Fair* by Phil Stong and *Capital City* by Ruth Stewart. Among the valuable references are: *Annals of Iowa* collection; complete histories of each of the 99 counties; a section devoted to works on primitive tribes; and biographies of men associated with the State—John Brown, William F. Cody and others. *The North American Crinoidaea Camerata,* a monumental three-volume work by Charles Wachsmuth and Frank Springer, contains references to fossils found at Keokuk, Burlington, LeGrand, and Pleasant Grove, Iowa.

GRENVILLE M. DODGE MEMORIAL ROOM, west wing, main floor, contains papers and photographs that belonged to General Dodge, as well as maps and blue prints used in building the Union Pacific Railroad. Just beyond, at the extreme west, is the EMERSON HOUGH MEMORIAL ROOM, containing correspondence of the author and pages from original manuscripts.

Maps, manuscripts, and a large collection of bound newspapers are housed in the basement of the building. The oldest paper on file is an issue of the Boston *Chronicle,* dated January 4, 1768. A file of the Du Buque *Visitor,* the first newspaper published on Iowa soil, is also in the collection. An INDUSTRIAL EXHIBIT of carriages and automobiles in the basement represents early modes and methods of transportation. Pioneer implements of trade and manufacture in Iowa are likewise displayed.

The GENERAL DIVISION of the Iowa State Library, east wing of the main floor, mezzanine and second floors *(open weekdays 8-5; Sat. 8-12 in summer, 8-4 in winter),* includes all classes of books. There is a Medical Department, a large file of leading American publications, outstanding

English, Irish, and Scotch reviews, and also some in French, German, Italian, and Spanish. The Nourse collection of Oriental literature consists of texts and translations from Arabic, Persian, Chinese, and Sanskrit.

Portraits of 134 Iowa Territorial and State Governors, and of other prominent citizens hang in the second floor PORTRAIT GALLERY. In the MUSEUM opening from the portrait gallery, swords and pistols, canteens, flags and relics, recall Iowans who fought in the Civil War. Looms, wheels, frows, hoes, sickles, flails, and cradles perpetuate the memory of early settlers and there is also a varied collection of mounted animals. The third floor MUSEUM, a continuation of the Historical Department, is devoted to prehistoric and early Indian objects. A wikiup, or native hut, is an interesting item. Documentary material from the various State departments are in the ARCHIVES DIVISION, in the west wing of the third floor. The WORLD WAR ROOM, also on the third floor, has a collection of portraits, said to include the photograph of every Iowan who took part in the World War. Guns, helmets, posters, and autographs of statesmen and generals of the war period form the bulk of the display.

IOWA TRAVELING LIBRARY *(open weekdays 8-5; Sat. 8-4)*, managed by the Iowa Library Commission, has its offices in the east wing, ground floor, of the Historical Building.

The Capitol grounds, more than 93 landscaped acres, extend from East Grand Avenue to the railroad tracks, between East Ninth and East 13th Streets. The hilltop is landscaped with formal gardens, with sloping lawns broken here and there by patches of shrubbery, groups of trees, and paths and roadways extending west and south.

13. STATE CAPITOL *(open daily 8 a.m.-11:30 p.m.)*, E. 12th St., between Grand Ave., and E. Walnut St., looks down on the city from its park site on an eminence east of the Des Moines River. The gilded dome, its design suggested by that of the Hotel des Invalides in Paris, and visible for many miles, tops the rustic gray mass. The building covers 58,850 square feet; the height to the top of the finial above the dome is 275 feet. Stone of the main superstructure was taken from Carroll County, Iowa, and St. Genevieve, Missouri, quarries. The building, generally Italian Renaissance in design, combines features of various styles. The principal motifs are a central tower with gilded dome and four square towers capped with copper-hued domes on the corners of the two wings. At the main entrances on the four sides are Corinthian columns, supporting an ornamental pediment, six on the east and west and four on the north and south sides. The arcaded first story, forming a base of the superstructure, is of heavy rusticated stone. The main cornice around the entire building is topped with a balustraded parapet eight feet high. Above this is an attic story in each of the four towers. The high drum of the central dome, adorned with Corinthian pilasters, is set on a square base. The cap of the dome is heavily ribbed and paneled. The whole is surmounted by the lantern embellished with eight engaged columns and entablature and pierced with narrow windows.

A grand rotunda under the dome, 64 feet in diameter, extending from the basement to the attic story, is the principal feature of the interior.

Ionic columns on the principal floor and Corinthian on the second grace the rotunda. Adjoining corridors on each floor have pilasters and cornices corresponding in design to those of the rotunda. The interior is finished in fine marbles, granite, and various woods such as walnut, butternut, cherry, oak, and catalpa.

Battle flags of Iowa regiments are preserved in niches on the main floor. The twelve statues placed about the rotunda, representing History, Science, Law, and similar subjects were executed by S. Cottin. Kenyon Cox, American artist, painted the eight lunettes surrounding the rotunda. The mural *Westward,* work of Edwin H. Blashfield of New York, occupies the east wall over the main stairway. Six mosaics, designed by Frederick Dielman of New York, are set above the Blashfield mural. A bronze bas relief honoring pioneer Iowa suffragists, by Nellie Walker, was unveiled in the lobby in May 1936.

The law, economics and sociology division of the IOWA STATE LIBRARY *(open Mon.-Fri. 8-5, Sat. 8-12)* is on the second floor and contains two copies of the *Code of Hammurabi.*

The SENATE CHAMBER and the HOUSE OF REPRESENTATIVES ROOM, opposite one another on the second floor of the Capitol, adjoin the library on the west. Enclosed steps lead up to the dome.

The Capitol, begun in 1871 and completed in 1884, was designed by A. Piquenard, who also designed the Illinois Capitol. Born in France, he joined the advance guard of Icarian colonists under the French Socialist, Etienne Cabet, who left Havre for the United States February 3, 1848. Later he established himself in his profession in the Midwest.

The cornerstone, cut from granite obtained in Buchanan County, Iowa, originally bore the date, A.D. 1871 and the names of the commissioners and the architect were carved on the face of it. But soon afterward, some of the stone in the foundation proved to be defective, and it was necessary to remove the cornerstone. The next General Assembly directed that the inscriptions be removed and that only the word Iowa should appear upon it. A stonecutter, J. G. Waers, was engaged to make the change and also to alter the date to A. D. 1873, the year the alterations were completed. Waers played a practical joke on the State by faintly cutting his own name and initials into the letters of Iowa. They remained as he cut them.

14. SOLDIERS AND SAILORS MONUMENT, E. Walnut St. directly S. of the Capitol, was erected in 1897 in honor of veterans of the Civil War. The monument, designed by Harriet A. Ketcham of Mount Pleasant, has an heroic feminine figure symbolizing Iowa, four life-size horses and riders, and many other figures, reliefs, and medallions. At the top of the shaft is a figure representing the Wingless Victory, carrying the two palms of Peace and Victory.

15. ALLISON MEMORIAL, E. of Soldiers and Sailors Monument, erected in 1913 in honor of the late Senator William B. Allison of Dubuque, is the work of Evelyn B. Longman. A figure symbolic of the Republic, eight feet high, carved from Tennessee marble, surmounts a pedestal about which six erect figures in bronze form a guard of honor.

16. STONE VIADUCT, over Court Ave. speedway S. of Capitol,

marks the presence of GLACIAL DRIFT PHENOMENA. Two thick drift sheets, which cover the hill, were exposed by road cuttings about 1870, and have been identified as the Wisconsin drift, youngest in the State, and the Kansan drift, second oldest; a million years, geologically, separate the deposits on either side of the cut. The discovery of this evidence of successive ice ages aroused the attention of the scientific world, and when, years later a memorial bridge was constructed connecting the tips of the two drifts, the site attracted geologists and students.

17. GRAVE OF WILSON ALEXANDER SCOTT, SE. corner Capitol grounds, is marked with a tablet. Alexander "Aleck" Scott, born in Crawford County, Indiana, November 20, 1818, came to Des Moines in 1846. Overwhelmed in the financial crash of 1857, he died near Fort Kearney, Nebraska Territory, en route to Pike's Peak, June 23, 1859. By his expressed wish, his body was returned and interred in the earth which, as his homestead, had been exempted from seizure of his debts. Scott donated 10.2 acres of land in 1856 for the Capitol grounds.

18. THE PIONEERS, Finkbine Dr. on W. terrace before Capitol building, is an heroic bronze group designed and modeled (1893) by Carl Gerhardt, a close friend of Mark Twain. Several wide flights of steps lead past the bronze group to the front entrance of the Capitol. Guns placed about the grounds were captured in the Spanish-American War.

19. JOHN M. SCHILTZ HOME *(garden open at all times)*, 3724 John Lynde Road, has a private BIRD REFUGE at the rear, which shelters various kinds of fowls and some raccoons in its seven acres. In season 50,000 tulips bloom on the grounds.

20. SALISBURY HOUSE *(open by arrangement to artists, archeologists and students)*, 200 Tonawanda Dr., was patterned after a 16th century English manor (Kings House, Salisbury) and incorporates in its structure many antique materials brought from abroad. This Tudor mansion, constructed of old paving bricks, is entered through a Gothic archway. Mullioned windows, and a large front window two stories in height and leaded with oddly shaped pieces, add to the ancient appearance. Within are art treasures, books and manuscripts collected by Mr. and Mrs. Carl Weeks, who presented the property to Drake University for a School of Fine Arts. The art collection includes examples of Van Dyck, Corot, and Raeburn. In the library are the Alexander Brune annotated copy of Ben Johnson, first folio; the extra illustrated (Alexander) copy of Forster's *Life of Dickens;* and the letter from the consignees of the shipment of tea in the Boston harbor to John Hancock, Esq., moderator of the town meeting assembled at Faneuil Hall on the night of the Boston Tea Party, refusing to assume the British tax on the tea. The result was the "Boston Tea Party."

21. DAVID W. SMOUSE OPPORTUNITY SCHOOL, SW. cor. 28th and Center Sts., was presented to the city by Dr. and Mrs. Smouse in 1931 for the benefit of physically-handicapped children. It is built of brick and stone on a 10-acre wooded tract and finished within in soft harmonious colors and with furniture that can be adjusted to the individual needs of each child.

22. HOYT SHERMAN PLACE *(open, 9-5, weekdays)*, Woodland Ave. at 15th St., was built in 1877 by Maj. Hoyt Sherman, brother of Gen. William Tecumseh Sherman. Major Sherman served in the Civil War as a paymaster, appointed by President Abraham Lincoln. President and Mrs. Ulysses S. Grant and Maj. William McKinley visited the house, a social center of the city at the time. The City Park Commission purchased the home in 1907 and shortly afterward leased it to the Des Moines Women's Club for a period of 49 years (later changed to a 99 year lease), providing that the club build an art gallery, open to the public at least three days a week. An addition to the original house is the large auditorium building, three stories high and Romanesque in design. In this addition are recreational and library rooms, and the auditorium seating 4,000. The art gallery houses a collection of pictures by notable artists; also a collection of paintings, statuary, and hand-carved furniture presented by Maj. S. H. M. Byers.

23. DRAKE UNIVERSITY (open during school hours), University Ave. between 25th and 28th Sts., established in 1881, was named for one of its founders, Gen. Francis Marion Drake. The brick buildings are grouped about a shady campus covering three city blocks.

This co-educational school is under the auspices of the Disciples of Christ. Daniel Walter Morehouse, who assumed the presidency in 1923, was awarded the Donahue Comet Medal in 1908 for the discovery of the comet which bears his name. More than 2,200 students are enrolled in the colleges of Education, of Fine Arts, of Commerce and Finance, of Bible, and of Liberal Arts, and the Law School. Each college offers the bachelor's as well as the master's degree in Arts, in Science and in Education, and the Doctor of Philosophy degree.

The ADMINISTRATION BUILDING, constructed in 1882, is of modified Gothic design, the red sandstone of the walls considerably weathered. Administration offices as well as offices of the Department of Journalism that supervises the publication of the *Quax* and the *Drake Times-Delphic*, student publications, are located here. SAGE HALL, better known as Science Hall, is a four-story structure of Bedford stone and buff brick. COLE HALL, neo-classic in design, was erected in 1903. On the second floor is the university law library containing 17,000 volumes. HOWARD HALL, erected the same year, houses the College of Fine Arts. MEMORIAL BUILDING, built for the college of Bible in 1905, is neo-classic in design, with two Doric columns at the entrance. CRAIG HOUSE, residence of the president, the LIBRARY, with 71,000 volumes, and the WOMEN'S DORMITORY, at the extreme west end of the grounds, are other buildings on the campus. Classes in religious education are held in the UNIVERSITY CHURCH OF CHRIST, on the southwest corner of 25th Street and University Avenue.

CHANCELLOR'S ELM, at the southeast corner of the Administration Building, was responsible for the location of the University at that site. George J. Carpenter, the Reverend D. R. Lucas, and others visited the wooded tract where, among native elms, oaks, and hickories, one elm stood out majestically above the rest. Mr. Carpenter climbed toward the top of the tree, and looking down over the wooded landscape and rivers of the city, decided to build the University there. Carpenter was the first chancellor, as the president was then known.

24. DRAKE STADIUM, Forest Ave. between 27th and 28th Sts., with the FIELD HOUSE at the east end, has a seating capacity of 17,000. Among its athletic events are the Drake Relays, held here every April.

25. UNITED STATES VETERANS' ADMINISTRATION FACILITY *(open daily 1-4 p.m.; Wed. and Sun. 7-8:30 p.m.)*, SW. corner 30th St. and Euclid Ave., covers a 48-acre site at the top of a hill thickly wooded with oak. The main structures are the hospital of 300 beds for general medical and surgical cases, clinical, pathological laboratories, and other essential units; a dietetics building, a nurses' home, and residences for the staff, all constructed of brick in Georgian Colonial style. In addition to professional treatment, a recreational program of therapeutic value is carried out.

26. MEMORIAL TO MERLE HAY, highest point on Merle Hay Road, .6 miles north of the junction with Douglas Ave., is a plaque and boulder placed in honor of Merle Hay, one of the first three American casualties of the World War. A flag staff, 50 feet high, stands at the base of the boulder.

27. ST. GABRIEL'S MONASTERY, NW. corner Merle Hay Rd. and Douglas Ave., belongs to the Passionist Order. The priests of this order, founded by St. Paul of the Cross in Italy in 1720, live a life of rigid discipline. Their major duty is to conduct missions in the Catholic churches in their area. The monastery, built of brick and cement in 1922, is Gothic in design, with a cruciform plan. The front section contains the chapels and the rear section is given over to kitchen, dining room, library and recreation rooms. The upper floors of the building, as well as the two side wings, comprise the cloisters; a public chapel is in one of the wings.

28. DRAKE UNIVERSITY MUNICIPAL OBSERVATORY *(open Mon., Wed. and Fri. 7:30-10 p.m.)*, Waveland Park, 48th St. and University Ave., has an 8.25-inch photographic lens and a 5-inch photographic doublet; also measuring machines, a thermo-electric photometer and a blink comparator.

29. DES MOINES SEISMOLOGICAL STATION *(open by arrangement)*, 1224 44th St., is privately owned and operated by Mrs. Vernon Seeburger in her home. Equipped with two instruments for recording earthquake shocks, the station belongs to the network reporting to the United States Coast Geodetic Survey.

30. POLK COUNTY WORLD WAR MEMORIAL, E. University Ave., at E. 6th St., erected in 1926, is a monument in Balfour pink granite, bearing a bronze group in high relief designed by Charles Niehaus. The Recording Angel is represented as writing the names of the warrior dead on the Book of Necrology, while a youth places his father's implements of war at the foot of the Nation's altar. The monument is dedicated to the memory of all Polk County soldiers who lost their lives in the war.

31. LOG CABIN *(private)*, 800 E. University Ave., was used as a powder house for the United States Dragoons on the riverbank in the 1840's. Built of hewn logs chinked with yellow clay, the 10 by 12-foot

structure possesses its original doors. When moved to its present site in 1865 it served as a home. It is now a tool house.

32. STATE FAIR GROUNDS, E. 30th St. between E. University and Dean Aves., E. edge of city, is the setting during the last week in August of the Iowa agricultural and industrial show. The phrase, "Million Dollar Stock Parade," coined some years ago to describe the procession of curried and beribboned animals which passes in front of the grandstand just before the close of the fair, is considered an inadequate valuation of the farm "bluebloods" representing two or three times that amount. Four-H Club (farm boys and girls) activities are a feature of the fair.

Popular attractions are the State Conservation Commission exhibit, left of main entrance, where hundreds of live fish, game birds and animals native to the State are on view in aquariums, cages, and pens respectively; the Iowa Art Salon, underneath the grandstand, where Iowa painters display their work; and the Varied Industries building, right of main entrance, where the latest mechanical devices and home and farm equipment are displayed.

Besides the stock displays there are poultry, garden, dairy, cooking, canning, and other exhibits dealing with the farm and farm home.

Some scenes for the motion picture *State Fair,* adapted from Phil Stong's novel, were filmed at the fair grounds in 1932.

33. ROLLINS HOSIERY MILLS *(open weekdays, tours at 9 and 2:30),* SW. corner E. 28th St. and Dean Ave., employ 800 workers, 65 percent of which are women. Founded by Henry M. Rollins in 1894, the firm was known as the Des Moines Hosiery Mill until 1922, when the present name was adopted. The average annual output exceeds 325,000 dozen pairs of full-fashioned stockings.

34. REDHEAD PARK, Dean Ave. to Logan Ave. between E. 17th and E. 18th Sts., was presented to the city by Wesley Redhead. A marker placed by the Grenville M. Dodge Camp, Sons of Volunteers, commemorates Camp Burnside (1862) where Civil War volunteers camped.

35. HOUSE OF THE SEVEN GABLES *(private),* 1757 Dean Ave., home of the Herbert S. Redhead family, a red brick structure devoid of extraneous ornament, was built in 1867 from plans drawn by William Foster, pioneer architect. Three of the seven gables are on the front façade, the remaining four on the sides, the long lines of the roof adding grace to the old building.

36. WATERWORKS PARK, on SW. 21st St. extending S. to Valley Drive and Park Ave. and W. to city limits, was developed by the Des Moines Water Board. Fifteen hundred acres constitute a bird sanctuary, with bird shelters and feeding grounds, known as one of the two best quail areas in Iowa. Twenty-six miles of roadway wind through grounds kept in a natural state. There are horseback and hiking trails. The greenhouses, fountains, and a lagoon near the entrance lend a tropical appearance during warm weather.

37. FORT DES MOINES, SE. corner Army Post Rd. and SW. 9th St., third Army post in Iowa to bear the name, is now the regimental headquarters of the 14th Cavalry. Stationed here are also the Third Battalion

of the 80th Field Artillery, a detachment from the supply unit, and quartermaster, signal, and medical corps. Although technically a cavalry post, the Artillery Battalion is one of the most modern motorized units in the United States and is often sent to surrounding States for demonstration reviews. The battalion is capable of covering approximately 200 miles a day under ordinary circumstances, and many additional miles on a forced march. A horse show is held annually on March 5, Regimental Day in the RIDING HALL. Polo games are played every Sunday afternoon throughout the summer, and the Post Band presents outdoor concerts several evenings each week.

38. MACRAE PARK, SW. 9th St. extending N. from Davis Ave. to banks of Raccoon River, named for Donald MacRae, Des Moines man killed in France with the 168th Infantry, is a natural wooded area with two ponds and picnic facilities.

The ITALIAN QUARTER, extending N. and E. from Clifton Ave. and Indianola Ave., primarily in the S. Union St. area, was, in the early days of the city, a Dutch and German settlement, with a sprinkling of Irish. The neighborhood was originally known as Sebastopol—the name of a brewery built there in 1857. The town was incorporated in 1875 and formally designated Sevastopol, the "v" substituted for the "b" by the town council. The first Italian to come to Des Moines (1879), a cheesemaker by trade, was attracted by the brewery, and within a few years had gathered many of his countrymen about him. Gradually the Dutch, Germans and Irish were pushed back toward the river, and "Little Italy" reigned in Sevastopol, which supports a community house and church, an Italian post of the American Legion, and a newspaper, *The American Citizen,* published every Friday. THE BOTTOMS, east along the river, almost to the city limits, suffer from floods and high water. Transients from the railroad tracks, and other homeless persons, often camp here in rude huts and makeshift cabins. There are, however, many small, comfortable homes in these areas, with gardens flourishing in the rich alluvial soil.

POINTS OF INTEREST IN ENVIRONS

Walnut Woods State Park—*9 m. (see Tour 14, sec. a)* ; Camp Dodge—*12 m. (see Tour 14C).*

Dubuque

Railroad Stations: Foot of 3rd St. for Chicago, Burlington & Quincy R.R. (bus to E. Dubuque trains across the river); 8th Ave. and Elm St. for Chicago, Great Western R.R.; 3rd and White Sts. for Chicago, Milwaukee, St. Paul & Pacific R.R.; Jones and Iowa Sts. for Illinois Central R.R.
Bus Stations: Union Bus Depot, 876 Locust St., for Northland-Greyhound Line, Inc., Jefferson Transportation Co., Interstate Transit Lines, Black & White Transportation Co., Orange Line, River Trails Transportation Co., and Winneshiek Lines.
City Buses: To all parts of the city; 8th Ave. and Main St. for buses to E. Dubuque every 30 minutes; 10¢, three tickets for 25¢.
Taxis: 25¢ anywhere in the city, group rate 50¢ from two to five persons with one destination, more than five, 10¢ each additional passenger.
Bridges: S. end of city, to E. Dubuque (Ill.), 25¢ car and 5¢ additional passenger round trip; N. end of city, Wisconsin bridge, 35¢ and 5¢ additional passenger round trip; both bridges over Mississippi River.

Accommodations: Four hotels, all near Main St. bet. 2nd and 4th Sts.

Information Service: American Automobile Association, Union Bus Depot.

Motion Picture Houses: Six.
Swimming: Municipal Pool. NE. city limits, near the end of Rhomberg Ave.
Tennis: Eagle Point Park, NE. city limits, end of Shiras Ave. off Rhomberg Ave.; Grandview Park, S. end of city on Dubuque-Cascade Rd.; Comiskey Field, 24th and Jackson Sts.
Steamboat Excursions: Streckfus Lines of St. Louis in the summer, dates announced.
Fishing: Little Maquoketa River and islands in the Mississippi.
Canoeing: Boats, Schuster's Canoe Club, N. of Municipal Swimming Pool.

DUBUQUE (698 alt., 41,679 pop.) on the Mississippi River opposite the junction of the Wisconsin and Illinois State boundary lines, is one of the State's oldest cities. The business and industrial centers are crowded into a narrow strip of land close to the river's edge. Wide bottomlands, often flooded over, spread out to the north and south of this circumscribed area. High bluffs, some of them rock precipices, all but jut out over the business center where tall buildings reach to their height. Main Street, on the first natural rise above the river, forms the principal artery of business. Side streets reveal long rows of houses against the stone bluffs where streets come to a sudden stop.

Back on the hilly plateau is a residence section, extending from Mount Carmel Road on the south to Eagle Point Park on the north. Some homes stand at the cliff's edge overlooking the city like ancient citadels. Streets here wind around hills and up steep slopes where tall trees help to emphasize the isolation of the section which is never seen from the highways leading in and out of the city.

SHOT TOWER, DUBUQUE

Relative to other cities of the prairies, century-old Dubuque gives an impression of settled age and established tradition, to which the German and Irish have contributed in their own way.

The city, which adopted the city-manager form of government in 1920, draws much of its trade from the farmers of the rich agricultural region nearby, many of whom sell their products at the municipal market. Foremost among the city's varied industries are the sash and door mills. Metal working and plumbing plants are also important, as is the shipbuilding yard.

Julien Dubuque, a French Canadian, for whom the city is named, arrived in Prairie du Chien (Wis.) about 1785; three years later, he obtained permission to mine the lead ore in the river bluffs at Catfish Creek, near Kettle Chief's Indian village. The first white man to settle permanently in the Iowa region, Dubuque made his home just south of the present city. Later he certified his claim to the land doubly by naming it, "The Mines of Spain," and obtaining formal recognition from Baron de Carondelet, then Governor of Louisiana under the Spanish government.

"Little Night," as Dubuque was known to the Fox Indians, seemed to possess great power over them. There are several legends regarding this power, the most popular being associated with the refusal of the Fox to grant one of Dubuque's requests. Even Dubuque's threat to burn the entire Mississippi did not move the stubborn Indians. So, while one of his associates emptied a barrel of oil into the water above the bend of Catfish Creek, Dubuque called the Indians from their lodges for consultation around the big bonfire he had built on the bank. Seizing a firebrand, he threw it on the water, smooth with oil. The sheet of flame rising instantly so terrified the Indians that they conceded all Dubuque asked. Then, supposedly at the exercise of his will, the fire went out.

When Dubuque died, the Indians buried him with honors befitting a chief, competing with one another for the privilege of carrying his body to the grave. A tomb of wood and stone was erected and upon a cross was inscribed: "Julien Dubuque, Miner of the Mines of Spain; died March 24, 1810, age 45 years, six months."

For years after his death, the Fox did not allow others to mine the lead. White men tried to take possession of the district in June 1830, but since they had violated agreements with the Indians, the United States Government forced them to return to the east side of the river. On June 1, 1833, under terms of the treaty with Chief Black Hawk, the territory was thrown open to white settlers.

Before Dubuque was a year old stores, saloons, and cabins bordered both sides of the muddy main street. The first school, started in 1833, was taught by George Cubbage who, it is said, was captured by the Indians during the Black Hawk War. Later he was sold to a trader for a plug of tobacco because he was baldheaded and could not be scalped.

At this time there was no government in the Territory. Lawlessness prevailed. Patrick O'Connor, a miner, killed his partner, George O'Keaf, and readily admitted his crime, assuming that he could not be prosecuted since there were no laws. The settlers, however, took matters into their own hands, established a court, tried, sentenced, and hanged O'Connor in June 1834. Shortly after this, the Methodists erected a log church, the first church building in Iowa. In September 1834 when the Territory of Wisconsin created the two original counties in Iowa, Dubuque was made the seat of government of Dubuque County, which included all of the Black Hawk treaty land north of Rock Island.

Dubuque, lusty and ambitious, felt superior to other cities on the river. A boisterous mining town, it sheltered intellectuals side by side with illiterates. So great was the income from lead mining here that the Territorial Legislative Assembly of Wisconsin chartered the Miners' Bank of Dubuque, the first bank in Iowa, in 1836. In this year, too, the town boasted the first newspaper in what is now Iowa, the Du Buque *Visitor,* printed on the first press in the territory north of Missouri and west of the Mississippi.

The people of Dubuque expected their city to be made the capital of the Territory of Wisconsin. As one of its newspapers predicted: "A proud city shall be reared where at present stands our flourishing village . . . when the lofty spires of the State house and churches glitter in the rays of the sun and the glossy bosom of the fair Mississippi shall swell beneath the weight of commerce." However, when another city was chosen, Dubuque did not lose its belief in its importance as the Queen City of the Northwest.

The settlers in Dubuque voted for their first representatives to the Legislative Assembly of the Territory of Wisconsin in the fall of 1836, almost a year before a local government was established. The city was not formally organized until the next spring when the citizens met in the Methodist church building to elect a board of five trustees. In 1841 the town adopted the charter granted it by the Territory of Iowa.

During the 1840's and the 1850's Dubuque lost its place as the largest city in Iowa to Burlington. Three colleges were opened during this period; the University of Dubuque, 1852; Wartburg Seminary, 1854; and Clarke College, 1859. In 1855 the Illinois Central Railroad reached the shore opposite Dubuque. Cannons roared and bands blared as Dubuque people turned out in the sweltering heat to celebrate the event and to hear Senator Stephen A. Douglas toast the railroad as "the great work of the age." The Dubuque & Pacific Railroad Company, which built the fourth railroad to cross Iowa, was formed April 22, 1857, the people of the city and the county voting bonds for $600,000. Eleven years passed before the Mississippi was bridged at this point. In 1867 the two railroads were consolidated.

With the influx of many immigrants to the fertile prairies of northeastern Iowa, by 1860 Dubuque had again become Iowa's largest city. Lumbering had replaced mining as the important industry, and the mills were increasing their production daily. Huge log rafts were floated down from the north and converted into lumber and ties for the railroads that were opening new paths into Iowa. Another asset was the Dubuque-East Dubuque wagon bridge across the Mississippi, which opened in 1887, and brought in an external trade territory to the east.

Dubuque suffered four disasters from 1876 to 1919. Thirty lives were

FEDERAL BARGE LINE TERMINAL, DUBUQUE

lost in the Catfish Creek flood of 1876; in 1894 almost the entire lumbering district was wiped out by fire, and in 1911 a second conflagration destroyed practically the entire industry. The last disaster was the 1919 flood, which took seven lives and caused property damage in excess of $100,000.

The lumber industry came to a close in 1915, but out of it grew the large wood working factories that today constitute the city's leading industry.

The daily newspaper, the *Telegraph Herald and Times Journal,* traces its descent from the first paper in Iowa, the Du Buque *Visitor.* The *Catholic Daily Tribune,* printed here, is the only daily Catholic newspaper in the English language printed in the United States. George Wallace Jones (1804–1894), one of Iowa's first two United States Senators; William B. Allison (1829–1908), who was United States Senator from 1873 to the time of his death; and David B. Henderson (1840–1906), Speaker of the House of Representatives and outstanding legislator, made their home in the city. Among the city's authors are Marion Hurd McNeely, novelist and poet, accidentally killed in 1930. She is remembered for her children's stories and novels which include *Rusty Ruston, The Jumping Off Place,* and *The Way To Glory.* The Reverend M. M. Hoffmann of Columbia College has written *Antique Dubuque,* a history of the Dubuque territory before 1833.

POINTS OF INTEREST

1. CITY MARKET, Iowa St. and Central Ave. between 12th and 13th Sts., has been in existence for many years. Early in the morning farmers back their wagonloads of garden truck to the edge of this curbstone market where they display and sell their fruit and vegetables from packing cases and splint baskets piled high on a table. Everyday is market day,

FOURTH STREET ELEVATOR, DUBUQUE

but Saturday draws hundreds of farmers with their products from the surrounding country and the neighboring parts of Wisconsin and Illinois.

2. ST. LUKE'S METHODIST EPISCOPAL CHURCH, SW. corner W. 12th and Main Sts., Romanesque in style, has nine pictorial windows and 100 opalescent windows of Tiffany glass throughout the building. The chime in the tower has 11 bells, the largest of which weighs about 3,000 pounds.

3. CARNEGIE STOUT FREE PUBLIC LIBRARY *(open weekdays 9-9; in summer 9-8)*, SE. corner W. 11th and Bluff Sts., erected in 1901, is a Romanesque-Corinthian structure containing more than 64,000 volumes and the MARY E. LULL COLLECTION OF PAINTINGS. Among the canvases are *Victorian Survival* and *Appraisal* by Grant Wood, native Iowa artist.

4. RESIDENCE OF THE ARCHBISHOP OF DUBUQUE *(private)*, NE. corner W. 11th and Bluff Sts., built of red sandstone in the architectural style of the Victorian era, with its plate glass windows, bays, and elaborate ornamentation, was once the home of Frank D. Stout (1854–1927), prominent in the development of the lumbering industry in the city.

5. FEDERAL BUILDING, W. 6th St. between Bluff and Locust Sts., dedicated in 1934, presents an interesting picture with its simple and graceful modern lines. This three-story stone structure fronts the wooded Washington Park, and houses the post office and other Federal departments.

6. FOURTH STREET ELEVATOR *(fare five cents)*, W. 4th and Bluff Sts., is an inclined cable car that runs to the summit of a bluff that rises more than 300 feet above the business district. The platform at the summit is arranged to give an unobstructed view north to Eagle Point Park, south to Julien Dubuque's grave, and east across the river into Illinois and Wisconsin.

7. ST. RAPHAEL'S CATHEDRAL, W. 2nd and Bluff Sts., is Gothic in design with a 130-foot tower that is surmounted by four lofty pinnacles. In 1835 when Samuel Mazzuchelli, missionary priest and architect, reached Dubuque, he immediately set about building a church, the first Catholic church in Iowa. In 1839 the Reverend Mathias Loras, appointed first bishop of the new diocese of the West, came to Dubuque, the episcopal seat. The cornerstone of the present church was laid in 1857. In the crypt lies the body of Bishop Loras and, beneath one of the altars, the body of St. Cessianus, a Roman martyr of the second century whose bones constitute the Patronal Relic of the State of Iowa.

8. KELLY'S BLUFF, directly behind St. Raphael's Cathedral, S. end of Cardiff St., edge of the bluff, affords a clear view of the harbor and the southern part of the city. The bluff was named for Thomas Kelly, a parsimonious and eccentric miner and recluse who settled in Dubuque in 1832 to develop the rich lead mine on this hill. When he died on May 15, 1859, he left no chart to the whereabouts of his fortune, which he had buried in the ground. Sums of $10,000, $1,200, $1,800, and $500 have been found over a period of 70 years at various points on his property.

ST. RAPHAEL'S CEMETERY, on Kelly's Bluff, was the first Catholic burial ground in Iowa. Many of the ancient monuments, some of which date as far back as 1839, remain in the tangle of the underbrush on the bluff. Inscribed upon these are epitaphs, characteristic of a by-gone age, such as:

"Morris Kerby—1859

Weep not my friends,
Weep not for me,
(For) Where I am
You soon must be."

Near the cemetery may be seen the foundation of a Catholic seminary building never completed.

9. FEDERAL BARGE LINE TERMINAL AND HARBOR, Jones St. at river, completed in 1928, is equipped with modern loading and unloading facilities. Towboats and barges, making regular trips between St. Louis and Minneapolis and St. Paul stop at Dubuque, giving it direct connections by water with the East, South, and foreign countries. The river traffic season runs from late March to early November. Stern-wheel towboats, barges, and smaller craft winter in the harbor, immediately north of the terminal.

DUBUQUE BOAT & BOILER WORKS, N. bank of harbor, is one of the few inland shipbuilding yards in the United States. The company builds five or six large boats a year, including towboats for the Federal fleet of barges and boats for use on the Great Lakes. The torpedo boat, *Ericsson,* used in the Spanish-American War, was built in this yard.

10. SHOT TOWER, junction of River and Tower Sts., was erected in 1855, for molding lead shot. The lead was melted and dropped through a screen at the top of the tower, thus forming balls which cooled as they fell and solidified as they dropped into water at the base. It was afterward used by the Standard Lumber Company as a watch tower until it was gutted by a disastrous fire in 1911. Smoke from underground fires, caused by spontaneous combustion, often issues from the earth which covers the sawdust-filled marshes in the vicinity of the old tower.

SASH AND DOOR MILLS DISTRICT, between White and Elm Sts., extends from E. 6th to 11th Sts. These mills (not open to public), comprise one of the city's important industries. The Farley & Loetscher plant, NE. corner 7th and White Sts., is said to be the largest sash and door factory in the world. At the peak of production the mills employ more than 2,100 people.

11. WARTBURG THEOLOGICAL SEMINARY *(open school hours),* end of Wartburg Pl., maintained by the American Lutheran Church, is exclusively a theological school, only graduate students being admitted. The design of the three buildings of the seminary, of massive Romanesque style, is based upon that of Wartburg Castle in Germany, the tower of the main building being a copy of the Wartburg Castle tower. The buildings, constructed of yellow Galena limestone, excavated on the school

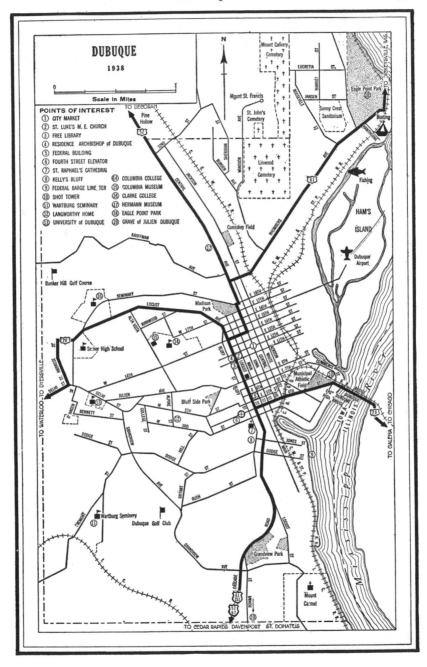

DUBUQUE

1938

Scale in Miles

POINTS OF INTEREST

1. CITY MARKET
2. ST. LUKE'S M. E. CHURCH
3. FREE LIBRARY
4. RESIDENCE ARCHBISHOP of DUBUQUE
5. FEDERAL BUILDING
6. FOURTH STREET ELEVATOR
7. ST. RAPHAEL'S CATHEDRAL
8. KELLY'S BLUFF
9. FEDERAL BARGE LINE, TER
10. SHOT TOWER
11. WARTBURG SEMINARY
12. LANGWORTHY HOME
13. UNIVERSITY of DUBUQUE
14. COLUMBIA COLLEGE
15. COLUMBIA MUSEUM
16. CLARKE COLLEGE
17. HERMANN MUSEUM
18. EAGLE POINT PARK
19. GRAVE of JULIEN DUBUQUE

grounds, were dedicated in 1916. In the court of the seminary grounds is a bronze STATUE OF MARTIN LUTHER, 12 feet high. This small seminary, founded in 1854 for the express purpose of training young men to serve as ministers in the central-western part of the United States, lists more than 700 graduates scattered over the United States and serving as missionaries in foreign lands. The HOGSKIN ROOM, administration building (R), has a special Reformation period collection of rare books and Lutheran irenics and polemics. The seminary also has an interesting display of ethnological specimens from New Guinea.

12. EDWARD LANGWORTHY HOME *(private)*, 1095 W. 3rd St., erected in 1847, was designed by John Francis Rague, who was also the architect for other buildings in the city and the Old Capitol at Iowa City. The house, octagonal in plan, with a wing extending to the rear of the kitchen and servants' quarters, is constructed of brick and white pine. An octagonal cupola with windows on four sides surmounts the structure. The large parlor with its high ceilings still contains the original hangings, furnishings, and ornate fixtures of the 1840's. Two marble fire places and two ceiling-high mirrors adorn the walls of the parlor.

13. UNIVERSITY OF DUBUQUE, 2050 Delhi St., founded in 1852, conducts a Presbyterian theological seminary in addition to its college of liberal arts. The school, organized by the Reverend Adrian Van Vliet to train ministers to follow the German immigrants pouring into the Mississippi Valley, was first known as the German Theological School of the Northwest, but, in 1870 was affiliated with the Presbyterian Church U. S. A. Women were first admitted to classes in 1912. The college enrollment in 1937–8 was 401. Buildings on the campus that are architecturally interesting include MAIN HALL, English Gothic in design, and PETERS COMMONS designed in modified Gothic style.

14. COLUMBIA COLLEGE, W. 14th St. between Alta Vista and Henion Sts., developed from St. Raphael's Seminary, which was founded in 1839. The school has been under the immediate supervision of the Archbishop of the Dubuque archdiocese, since that date. The enrollment, including the academy, was 1031 in 1936–37. Although the school is a man's college, sisters of religious orders are admitted to classes. The school has been renamed a number of times, the last change occurring in 1920 when the present name was adopted. ST. FRANCIS HALL has a mansard roof in the manner of the French Renaissance style, while the CHAPEL with its square tower is more typical of the Italian Renaissance. The school is housed in eight buildings spread out over the 50-acre hilltop campus. Work in the various departments leads to the degree of Bachelor of Arts. The LIBRARY *(basement)*, Loras Hall *(open weekdays 8-9:30; Sun. 10-12 and 7-9)*, one of the largest private collections in the State, has over 70,000 volumes. The rare bookroom contains nearly 1,000 valuable items, many of them from Bishop Mathias Loras' (the founder) personal library. Among the important volumes are Syllius Italicus Cum Commentariis Petri Marsi, published in 1492, and a first edition of *Laws of the Territory of Louisiana.*

15. COLUMBIA MUSEUM, Alta Vista St. between Kirkwood and W.

GRAVE OF JULIEN DUBUQUE

14th Sts. *(open Mon.–Fri. 9-5; Sat. 9-12; Wed. 7-9 p.m.; guides)*, housed in Science Hall, Columbia College, is sponsored by the Midwest Antiquarian Association as a memorial to the pioneers of the Midwest. Among more than 100,000 exhibits and 1,500 paintings on display are the Indian artifacts, the Hearn collection of ivory carvings, a collection of icons and religious carvings, the reproduction of the interior of a miner's cabin of 1840, and historical material. The art treasures include paintings by Homer, Inness, Remington and Sargent.

16. CLARKE COLLEGE, junction Seminary and W. Locust Sts., founded in 1844 as Mt. St. Joseph's Academy at St. Joseph's Prairie, eight miles southwest of Dubuque, was moved to Dubuque in 1859. The school, established on its present 60-acre site in 1889, added a college department in 1901. Degrees awarded are B.A., M.A., and B.S. The library has 13,000 volumes and more than 3,000 pamphlets. The school under the immediate supervision of officers appointed by the Mother-General of the Sisters of Charity was renamed Clarke College in 1928.

17. HERRMANN MUSEUM *(open by appointment)*, 2419 Central Ave., is the private museum of Richard Herrmann who for more than 60 years has collected weapons and implements, used by the Indian tribes of this part of the country, and fossils, minerals and zoological specimens.

There is also an extensive collection of Indian pipes, and charts and records dealing with the early history of Dubuque and vicinity.

18. EAGLE POINT PARK, end of Shiras Ave., NE. corner of city, covers an area of 133 acres. The north portion of the driveway overlooks the Mississippi, the towering bluffs and the surrounding country. Seven thousand tons of native stone were used in constructing a large LEDGE GARDEN 790 feet long that was built upon natural ledges of limestone. Near this garden at the edge of the bluff are three INDIAN COUNCIL RINGS which are reached along natural stone trails. A LOG CABIN, the oldest house in Dubuque and said to be the oldest in Iowa, stands in the center of the park. From the bluffs several hundred feet above the Mississippi, there is an unobstructed view of the GOVERNMENT LOCKS AND DAM (R. from end of Rhomberg Ave. on Lincoln Ave.). The locks and gates of Dam 11, one of the nine-foot channel series along the Mississippi River, were closed in September 1937 to form the huge lake almost 10,000 feet in width. The tree-covered hills and bluffs of Wisconsin and Illinois can be seen from the pavilion.

19. GRAVE OF JULIEN DUBUQUE, ½ m. walk from end of R. fork of Rowan St., is marked by a circular tower of Galena limestone, medieval in design, erected in 1897. Dubuque was buried by his Indian friends on this high bluff overlooking the Mississippi, the site of his long deserted "Mines of Spain."

POINTS OF INTEREST IN ENVIRONS

Crystal Lake Cave—7 *m.*, St. Donatus, Luxemburg settlement—*15 m. (see Tour 2, sec. b);* New Melleray, Trappist Abbey—7 *m. (see Tour 1A).*

Fort Dodge

Railroad Stations: Terminal station, 401 4th Ave. S., for Illinois Central R.R. and Minneapolis & St. Louis R.R.; Central Ave. and 12th St. for Chicago, Great Western R.R.; Terminal Bldg., Central Ave. and 11th St., for Ft. Dodge, Des Moines & Southern Ry. (electric).
Bus Station: Union Bus Depot, Wahkonsa Hotel, Central Ave. and 10th St., for Interstate Transit Lines (Northwestern Ry. and Union Pacific R.R.).
Street Buses: Ft. Dodge Transportation Co., 116 N. 7th St., buses to all part of the city.

Accommodations: Five hotels, two cabin camps.

Information Service: Chamber of Commerce, Armory Bldg., 710 1st Ave. N.

Theaters and Motion Picture Houses: One theater, concert hall at High School Auditorium, 1010 5th Ave. N.; five motion picture houses.
Swimming: Exposition Park, N. end 7th St.
Golf: Exposition Park, nine holes, 25¢ weekdays, 50¢ Sun.
Tennis: Oleson Park, 1200 S. 17th St., municipal.

Annual Events: Beef Cattle Show, Exposition Park, 2nd wk. in Sept.; Band Day, biennial in June of odd years.

FORT DODGE (1,115 alt., 21,895 pop.), seat of Webster County, is situated on both sides of the Des Moines River at the point where Fort Dodge once stood. The city lies chiefly on plateau land above the river flats, in the center of a productive agricultural and mining district, with one of the largest deposits of gypsum in the Nation at its southeastern edge. The civic and business center ends at City Park, once included in the old fort grounds. West of City Park, Central Avenue descends abruptly to the industrial section along the river and railroad tracks, but to the east the avenue climbs the slope that passes through the chief business district. Within the radius of a few blocks are all the important public buildings and the shopping district. The industries of the city—a packing plant, a tile factory, a serum company plant, hatcheries, and gypsum mills—are congregated about the three railroads that cut through the city on the east side.

Some of the largest industries are sandwiched in with the more dilapidated residential sections on the flat between the east side of the river and the Illinois Central tracks. The red brick city waterworks building and a 2,000,000 gallon reservoir surrounded by landscaped grounds loom up on Island Park.

Early settlers in the territory were harassed by Sidominadotah's *(Two Fingers)* band of 500 Sioux Indians, who had been exiled from the tribe. One of the settlers, Henry Lott, was accused by Two Fingers in 1846 of illegal possession of his land. Mrs. Lott died shortly after the trouble started and her 12-year old son also died while trying to follow the Des Moines River to the nearest settlement for help. Lott blamed Two Fingers for their deaths and in retaliation killed him and his family. This trouble is believed to have been partly responsible for the Spirit Lake Massacre (see Tour 7).

In 1850 the Federal Government established a fort, first called Fort Clarke as a courtesy to the commander of the Sixth Infantry, Brevet Maj. Newman S. Clarke. It was changed on June 25, 1851, to Fort Dodge for Henry Dodge, U. S. Senator from Wisconsin, who fought in the Black Hawk and other Indian Wars. Roving bands of Indians that continued to plunder the country east, west, and southeast of the fort caused the only trouble, and in 1853, the fort, no longer necessary, was abandoned. Maj. William Williams, sutler for the United States troops, purchased the barracks and fort site in 1854 and laid out the town of Fort Dodge.

John F. Duncombe, described in an old newspaper as "an engine in pants," arrived in Fort Dodge in 1855. Through his efforts Fort Dodge, then a tiny settlement, wrested the county seat from Homer, a thriving town. County histories only hint at the final chapter in the story by saying, "In April 1856, after a very exciting canvass, the citizens of the county decided by a large majority to move the county seat from Homer to Fort Dodge." The old and yellowed newspapers tell the story of the "exciting canvass" that ended in a wrestling match finally deciding the question. An election was first held and both factions stuffed the ballot boxes. When the tabulated votes gave the county seat to Fort Dodge, John D. Maxwell, who led the fight for Homer, exploded. A suggestion that Maxwell and Duncombe wrestle it out brought action. In Homer's public square with the whole town watching, the two wrestled for an hour. Whether it was a scissor-hold or a half-nelson that gave Duncombe the victory is conjecture; but Fort Dodge was county seat without further controversy.

In 1858 clay resources of the city were first used commercially by Henry A. Flatt, an early brick-maker. In the same year the first attempts to improve the wagon trails over the prairies were made by a horse drawn scraper cutting off the turf between the wagon wheel ruts. Many of these wagon trails, according to legend, were pointed out by Wahkonsa, a Sioux Indian who frequently mapped with sticks the most available route over the prairies for the settlers. Intelligent and friendly, he sometimes reported movements of hostile bands. Fort Dodge citizens, hoping to profit by river navigation, purchased the *Charles Rogers* which arrived in Fort Dodge on April 6, 1859, although lower Des Moines River pilots declared the boat would never make it. The entire population lined the river bank to welcome the boat, but soon learned the river was navigable for steamboats only at flood stage.

The visit to Fort Dodge in July 1868 of George Hull of Binghamton, N. Y., and H. B. Martin of Marshalltown, Iowa, resulted in the nationally famous Cardiff Giant hoax. The "prehistoric man" whose "discovery" caused a widespread stir of excitement during the last quarter of the 19th century, was cut for Hull and Martin by Michael Foley from a ledge of gypsum.

Freighted from Fort Dodge to Chicago, the slab was carved into a giant by two German stonecutters who pricked it with a leaden mallet faced with needles to give it a human-looking skin, then bathed the finished work in sulphuric acid to give the appearance of great age. The stone man, 10 feet long, two and one-half feet wide, and weighing 3,000 pounds, encased in a strong box, arrived in Union, N. Y., on October 12, 1858. A few weeks later it was buried near Cardiff, N. Y., by a Mr. Newell, brother-in-law of George Hull. A little later Newell "discovered" the giant while digging a well. Soon the Cardiff Giant was famous. Sculptors, geologists, and writers believed him to be a "prehistoric man." James Hall, New York State geologist, pronounced him "the most remarkable archeological discovery ever made in this country." Hiram Powers, sculptor of the Greek Slave, declared "No chisel could carve such a perfect man."

Among the skeptics who did not believe the Cardiff Giant was a "petrified man" was Oliver Wendell Holmes. He drilled through the giant's head to prove to his own satisfaction that the statue was an old image, probably several hundred years old. Interest was so widespread that magazines and papers everywhere carried stories about the giant, and up-to-date encyclopedias mentioned it. During the time the giant was part of P. T. Barnum's show, millions of people paid 50 cents to see him. Interest flamed to such a peak that the New York Central changed its train schedules to permit passengers to stop and see the wonder when it was shown at Syracuse. In 1901 the giant attracted more people than almost anything else at the Pan American Exhibit at Buffalo, and it was the talk of the day until Prof. Othniel C. Marsh of Yale exposed it as a fake. Afterward people forgot the Cardiff Giant for nearly a quarter of a century. He was then shown at Emmetsburg, Iowa, in July 1935, and featured in the Centennial Parade on August 17, 1935, at Fort Dodge. Shortly afterward he was an attraction at the Iowa State Fair. The giant is now in the private museum of Gardner Cowles, Jr., a Des Moines newspaper executive.

It was during the period of the Cardiff Giant episode that Fort Dodge developed its gypsum resources. In 1869 two quarries were opened, one in Gypsum Hollow and the other on Soldier Creek. The first mill for the manufacture of wall plaster, the old Iowa Mill, built about 1872, stood between the Illinois Central tracks and the Des Moines River. The soft white gypsum, exposed on all sides of the hills, made quarrying easy after the soil was stripped off. By 1890 there were four mills for producing about 21,000 tons a year. When the Cardiff Mill, named for the Cardiff Giant, sank a shaft in the open prairie to mine gypsum, a new era in the industry began. Most of it was marketed in the form of hard wall plaster, although some went into wall board, partition and roof tile, insulating material, and fertilizer.

The gypsum bed covers nearly 30 square miles. It is from 10 to 30 feet deep, extends in a northeast to southwest direction and is covered with clay, shale and sandstone. It is said that if 1,000,000 tons were used annually the supply would still last 150 years. Production has amounted approximately to 170,000 tons annually, although four times as much was produced in the peak year of 1927. Coal and clay supplement the gypsum deposits, much of the coal being used in the gypsum mills.

Along with the development of its gypsum resources the city expanded as a center for a large agricultural region. Besides its retail establishments, farm markets were developed. In 1892 Tobin College was founded, a school that served the north central part of Iowa up to 1929 when the building burned.

Two nationally known men lived in Fort Dodge. Jonathan P. Dolliver, who served as a Representative in Congress from 1888 to 1900, and as United States Senator to his death in 1910, and William S. Kenyon, who succeeded Dolliver as United States Senator and held that position up to 1922 when he was named judge of the United States Circuit Court for the Eighth Judicial District. Judge Kenyon wrote a decision on the Teapot Dome oil lease litigation (1923) that was a bitter denunciation of the transaction. He died in 1933.

POINTS OF INTEREST

WEBSTER COUNTY COURTHOUSE, SE. corner S. 7th and Central Ave., standing on the original plot of ground purchased by the county in 1858, was dedicated in 1902. Built of stone, the four-story structure with its clock tower and steeple dominates Central Avenue. Courtroom and offices of county officials and superintendent of schools are in the building. In the west end of the fourth floor is the county jail.

PUBLIC LIBRARY *(open daily 9-9)*, 605 1st Ave. N., lists 36,585 volumes. The library was started in 1883 by a private association but in 1895 it came under the supervision of the city. The present building was erected in 1902. The WEBSTER COUNTY HISTORICAL MUSEUM *(open 1-6 p.m., Sat.)* is in the basement. Among the items are the original plat of the city, a piece of walnut from the sill of the old fort, bows and arrows belonging to Wahkonsa, a buffalo skull from South Lizard Creek near the city, and a drum carried in the battle of Lundy's Lane (1812).

KING MUSIC HOUSE, 604 Snell Bldg., was established in 1920 by Karl King, a composer and director of band music. King conducts the municipal band, judges band concerts throughout the country, and gives concerts at celebrations. His musical compositions include more than 200 band pieces.

SITE OF OLD MILITARY POST, NW. corner 1st Ave. N. and N. 4th St., is marked with a five-foot boulder bearing a bronze tablet on which is inscribed the history of the fort. Wahkonsa school now stands on the site occupied by the old fort, and children play where the soldiers' barracks stood.

A TWO-STORY BRICK BUILDING *(private)*, 26 N. 4th St., directly across the street from Wahkonsa school, housed the first court session in the city, the first post office, and the first drug store. Dr. Pease, who erected the building for an office in 1857, had the brick hauled from Dubuque by ox team. The Webster County Historical Society marked the building.

BLANDEN ART GALLERY *(open 2-5 Sun. and special occasions)*, SE. corner 3rd Ave. S. and S. 10th St., has its main entrance on the south side. On both sides of the entrance hall are large galleries with lighting to display the pictures to advantage. A collection of pictures and art objects from the estate of the late Charles G. Blanden, donor of the gallery, is on permanent display. One of these, a sketch entitled *Butchering*, by Tom Savage of Fort Dodge, was selected by Mrs. Franklin D. Roosevelt for exhibition at the White House.

LITTLE ITALY GARDEN, 1100 12th Ave. SW. *(open)*, was started in 1915 by Rosi Marix, an immigrant, who came to Fort Dodge in 1904. The cinder dump behind the M. & St. L. roundhouse, which was a part of his own yard, did not please him, so he set to work beautifying it, hauling new dirt and planting many varieties of shrubs, trees, and flowers, some of them imported. He expressed his Italy in vivid flowers, a tiny canal, and a miniature depot with a train and track.

LOG CABIN *(open by permission)*, Oleson Park, 1200 S. Park Blvd., built about 1850, was originally the office of the Adjutant when the town was a fort. The cabin, moved to the park from the site of the old military post, was found when Wahkonsa school was purchased in 1912. At that time the siding was stripped from an old house standing there and under it was discovered a three-room log cabin. In the building are articles of historical interest.

TOBIN PACKING CO. PLANT *(open by permission)*, N. 1st St. at 7th Ave. N., occupies four acres of a 16-acre tract. The plant was built in 1934. Almost 7,000 animals are slaughtered each week, for which the company pays stock raisers more than $100,000.

FORT DODGE SERUM COMPANY PLANT *(open by permission)*, NW. city limits, manufactures anti-hog-cholera serum, its principal product, and a complete line of biological and pharmaceutical products used in veterinary medicine. The plant includes machine shops, rendering works, feed grinding mills, and modern laboratories. The company carries on experimental work when there is an outbreak of any disease and gives special study and diagnosis to the many pathological specimens it receives.

POINTS OF INTEREST IN ENVIRONS

Dolliver Memorial State Park, Woodman Hollow State Scenic Preserve, Wild Cat Cave—*17 m. (see Tour 6)*; Gypsum Mills—*8 m. (see Tour 12, sec. b)*.

Iowa City

Railroad Station: 115 Wright St. bet. Clinton and Dubuque Sts. for Chicago, Rock Island & Pacific Ry.
Interurban Station: Cor. Front and Burlington Sts. for Cedar Rapids & Iowa City. Ry.
Bus Station: 213 E. College St. for Burlington Lines, Interstate Transit (Northwestern Ry. and Union Pacific R.R.), C. M. Foster Lines, Jackson Lines.
Street Buses: Bus through business section to W. campus, stops S. side Old Capitol campus; fare 5¢, five lines with 18-hour service.
Taxis: Five lines, 25¢ one passenger and up to 75¢ for five persons.
Airport: Municipal Airport, US 218, ¾ m. from city, United Air Lines transcontinental service. Taxi from any part of the city, 50¢.

Accommodations: Five hotels, E. side of river; three tourist camps.

Information Service: Iowa City Auto Club, 204 S. Gilbert St.

Radio Station: WSUI (880 kc.).
Theaters and Motion Picture Houses: University Theater, Fine Arts Campus, W. river front, college plays; five motion picture houses.
Swimming: City Park, "Big Dipper," NW cor. of park, N. end of city.
Golf: Finkbine Field, University Golf Course, 1 m. W. center of city on US 6, moderate fees; Fairview Course, 2 blks. S. Jefferson Hotel and 3 m. E. on US 6, 9 holes, 25¢ weekdays and 35¢ Sun. and holidays.

Annual Events: University Homecoming and Dad's Day, fall; Governor's Day, spring, Governor reviews ROTC troops; State Music Festival, spring; State high school Brain Derby, summer.

IOWA CITY (685 alt., 15,340 pop.), the State's first capital, and Johnson County seat, is the home of the State University of Iowa. The city, lying along both sides of the Iowa River, extends from the river's bank over hills and bluffs. On the crest of the steep limestone bluffs on the west side is the medical unit of the university and a residential section that spreads along the gentle slopes of the hills as they move out to the prairies. On the east side, surrounded by university buildings, is the white porticoed Old Capitol, built of native rock, its columns and dome rising at the top of the high green banks of the river. The main business district touches the east campus area, yet the grey limestone and red brick buildings, surrounded by tall trees, remain aloof.

There are a number of small manufacturing plants and various businesses associated with farming, but Iowa City is primarily a college town. Restaurants and hotels hire student help, and, like the retail establishments, depend on the college trade.

At Homecoming each fall the city belongs to the enthusiastic swarms of students and alumni. On that day (set to coincide with an important football game) the town resembles a field of corn with every telephone and light pole decorated with painted ears of corn. Thousands of alumni arrive by train, bus, auto, and air to join the students in their celebration.

The university's medical center—general hospital, children's hospital, and hospital for the treatment of psychopathic cases—is one of the largest in the country. It is more than a local university institution as it serves people all over the State.

Iowa City was founded as the capital of the Territory of Iowa. The founding act, approved by the first Legislative Assembly in Burlington (January 21, 1839), provided that three appointed commissioners select the most suitable 640 acres in Johnson County, employ surveyors and laborers to lay out the town, and supervise the plans and erection of the capitol, stipulating that the commissioners meet not later than May 1. On March 3, Congress agreed to donate the section of land to be selected. Settlers flocked to Napoleon, Johnson County seat, May 1, 1839, to wait for the three commissioners, one from each judicial district, who were to meet there and select the capital site. Excitement ran high when noon came and only Chauncey Swan had arrived, as two commissioners had to be present to make action legal. Delay might lose the capital, since other counties coveted the honor. Commissioner Swan sent a volunteer, Philip Clark, to bring John Ronalds of Louisa County, nearest absent commissioner, to Napoleon before midnight. Ronalds lived only 35 miles away, but the distance was great in those days of prairie trails and bridgeless streams and few believed he could arrive in time, but at five minutes to 12, by Swan's watch, he was there. The justice of the peace swore the two men into office immediately so that the papers could be dated May 1. Observant persons noted, however, that the hours from midnight until sunrise were remarkably short. Swan and Ronalds selected a wild valley sloping up to one of the hilltops overlooking the Iowa River as the site and named it Iowa City.

Surveyors laid out wide city streets around the 12-acre capitol square before the first sale of town lots was held in August at Lean Back Hall, a rudely constructed rooming house and saloon. Funds from the land sale were used to start work on the capitol. Both the county seat and the post office at Napoleon were transferred to the new backwoods capital. Immigrants, the majority of them young men without families, began to arrive. Because travelers often lost the trail, the settlers hired Lyman Dillon in 1839 to plow a furrow from Iowa City to Dubuque. A road, well beaten by the wheels of the white-topped wagons of the incoming settlers, soon stretched beside the furrow, nearly 100 miles long. Later, Old Military Road followed this trail.

Log cabins and a few frame houses clustered about the site chosen for the capitol when its cornerstone was dedicated on July 4, 1840. Governor Lucas issued a proclamation designating Iowa City as the Territorial capital on April 30, 1841, and although the capitol was not finished, the Fourth Territorial Legislative Assembly convened in the city on December 6, 1841, in a frame building donated for temporary use by Walter Butler.

State constitutional conventions were held in the capitol during October 1844 and May 1846. Both the constitutions, adopted at these conventions,

UNIVERSITY HOSPITAL, IOWA CITY

provided that Iowa City "shall be the seat of State Government until removed by law." With settlement moving rapidly toward the Missouri River, the western boundary, Iowa City was no longer near the population center of the State, and in spite of Iowa City's vigorous protests, the assembly selected Monroe City as a new capital site in 1847, pacifying Iowa City by making it the seat of the State University. Public opinion, however, did not approve of Monroe City, so the capital remained at Iowa City until 1857, when Des Moines was selected. Iowa City had no municipal government until the General Assembly incorporated the town under a charter in 1853.

The episode of Hummer's Bell added spice to pioneer life in the late 1840's. Iowa City Presbyterians owed back salary to their pastor, the Reverend Michael Hummer, when he was excommunicated for his spiritual activities. In payment he claimed most of the movable church property. When he was ready to take the bell a crowd gathered to watch him climb the belfry and lower the bell to the ground. Just as it was lowered, several men removed the ladder, marooning the sputtering minister. The bell was loaded into a wagon, hauled to the mouth of Rapid Creek, and sunk in deep water. Hummer never recovered it. Later it was removed from the creek, taken to Utah, and sold to Brigham Young.

The first railroad company to lay tracks to the interior of Iowa, the Mississippi and Missouri, set the goal for reaching Iowa City before January 1, 1856. Tracks were still 1,000 feet from the station at nine o'clock the night before. Prominent citizens toiled side by side in zero weather with the railroad hands to complete the task. Great bonfires gave heat and light as each section of track was laid. Slowly the engine moved forward. At 11 o'clock, 200 feet from the station, the engine would not run. Undaunted, some of the men pushed the engine forward with crowbars while the others feverishly put down the remaining yards of steel. With only seconds to spare, the engine was crowbarred into the station, and the cheers echoed back from the hills. On January 3 the first train from Chicago entered the city.

For several years Iowa City was a railroad terminus, resulting in a large transient population from the East, the South, and Europe, most of them headed for the far West.

The Mormon handcart expedition of 1856 brought about 1,300 European converts to Iowa City in answer to the call of Brigham Young. When the converts arrived, they had to camp during the spring and summer just west of the city and construct their own handcarts from the material available. With the inadequate wooden-wheeled vehicles ready, the first party of 226 set out June 9 toward the goal that lay more than 1,000 miles away over river, plain, and mountain. There was one pushcart for each five persons, piled with the allotted 17 pounds apiece, and one oxen-drawn wagon to each 100 individuals. Four other groups left Iowa City during the summer, the last party leaving July 28.

The act establishing the State University of Iowa was approved February 25, 1847, but the school did not open until 1855 when 75 students assembled, in answer to an advertisement, for a short term of study under three professors. In 1857, when the capitol building was turned over to the university, there were 124 students. Lack of funds permitted only a normal department until 1860, when the university was reorganized.

In 1861 the old Johnson County fairgrounds, now part of the city airport, was used as Camp Fremont, the Civil War assembly ground for the 10th Iowa Infantry.

In the 1870's the town had one of the largest breweries in the State. The Iowa City grape sugar factory produced 12,000 cases yearly of grape sugar, glucose, and corn syrup products during the 1880's. In the last years of the 19th and the first of the 20th centuries a flint glass company and the Iowa City packing plant were important in the city's enterprise. Later a plant was started where hybrid corn, a new variety, is shelled, sorted, tested, dried, and sacked for shipping to both national and foreign markets. Iowa City also has a large advertising calendar plant that turns out more than 2,000,000 calendars a year.

The Child Welfare Research Department at the university, established in 1917, is widely known for its pre-school laboratory, its variety of pamphlets for parent education, its radio child study, and the reports of its surveys of child life. The department is the outgrowth of the work of Cora Bussey Hillis, who organized the Iowa Child Welfare Association in 1914.

THE STATE UNIVERSITY OF IOWA

The Iowa River cuts through the university grounds between stone-walled banks, dividing it into an east and west campus. Fifty buildings are scattered on the 386-acre area. Old Capitol, the focal point of east-side campus, is elbowed on the north and south by stately buildings of Bedford stone, primarily Italian Renaissance in style. Other buildings of this campus are placed along the streets that radiate from the square on which Old Capitol stands. To the west a grassy area sweeps down a slope to the Iowa River, about a block away, where bridges connect the east and west campuses. Across the bridge to the north is the landscaped fine arts section of the west campus. Above this, to the south, on the hill are the hospital buildings. Most of the structures on the west side are modified early English in style.

State appropriations and an income from Federal land grants support the university, which is under the direct control of the Iowa State Board of Education. The University has nine colleges—liberal arts, medicine, law, dentistry, pharmacy, engineering, education, commerce, and graduate. Associated with one or other of the colleges are the schools of journalism, nursing, religion, fine arts, and letters. About 8,000 students from the United States and all parts of the world register annually.

The executive who served the longest term as president of the university (1916–34) was Walter A. Jessup, who in 1934 was appointed president of the Carnegie Foundation for the Advancement of Teaching. During his administration the university doubled in enrollment and its physical value increased to approximately $11,000,000.

EAST-SIDE CAMPUS

Unless otherwise indicated, the college buildings are open during school hours, except those rooms where classes are in session.

1. The OLD CAPITOL, Clinton St. at Iowa Ave., center of Old Capitol Campus (Madison and Clinton Sts. bet. Washington and Jefferson Sts.), erected during Territorial days (1838–1846), is the State's most honored building, now used for the university's administration offices. John F. Rague, supervising architect, worked out the main details; historians believe the Reverend Samuel Mazzuchelli, Roman Catholic missionary during Territorial days, helped him with the design. The strength and grace of Old Capitol reveals itself in every detail from the balanced proportions of the thick foundation walls to the column-supported dome. Four Doric columns adorn the entrance portico on the east and west sides. The cupola, high above the entrance vestibule, has an octagonal base from which rise eight Corinthian columns supporting the dome. Inside, a hanging spiral staircase leads to the floors above. In 1924 the building was restored and fireproofed.

2. SCHAEFFER HALL, Washington St. at Capitol St., Old Capitol Campus, a four-story structure of Indiana limestone, Greek Period in style, was named to honor President Schaeffer, who was instrumental in its planning and completion. The LEIGH HUNT COLLECTION, housed in a room adjoining the basement exhibition room *(open by special permission)*, was collected by Luther Brewer of Cedar Rapids and acquired by the university in 1934. This collection of rare books and manuscripts, not replaceable, contains approximately 2,000 volumes associated with Leigh Hunt, an English poet and essayist of the early 19th century. The LIBRARY OF THE STATE HISTORICAL SOCIETY OF IOWA, third floor *(open weekdays 8-12; 1-5; 7-10)*, containing 86,366 volumes, has historical pictures, flags, and relics of early days. The society and library, which has always been maintained at Iowa City, had its beginning in 1857 when the Sixth General Assembly in session at the Old Capitol, voted a permanent annual appropriation of $250 to be used in organizing the society. Research and publication are prime considerations. Among its publications are the *Annals of Iowa* (first series), *Iowa Historical Record,* the *Palimpsest,* and the *Iowa Journal of History and Politics,* edited by Benjamin Franklin Shambaugh, political scientist, whose Campus Course brought wide attention to the university.

3. The PHYSICS BUILDING, Washington St. at Capitol St., Old Capitol Campus, has a duplicate of the Foucault Pendulum invented by Jean Foucault in 1850, hanging in an abandoned elevator shaft. The original is in the Pantheon in Paris. The instrument consists of a pendulum hung from the roof above a circular base in the basement, clock-faced in form, that shows the earth's hourly movement. The university's duplicate was procured in 1925 by Prof. John Adams Eldridge.

4. The HALL OF ENGINEERING, SE. corner Washington and Capitol Sts., houses WSUI, the university radio station (on the top floor) and the Time and Motion Laboratories. Here Carl Emil Seashore, pioneer psy-

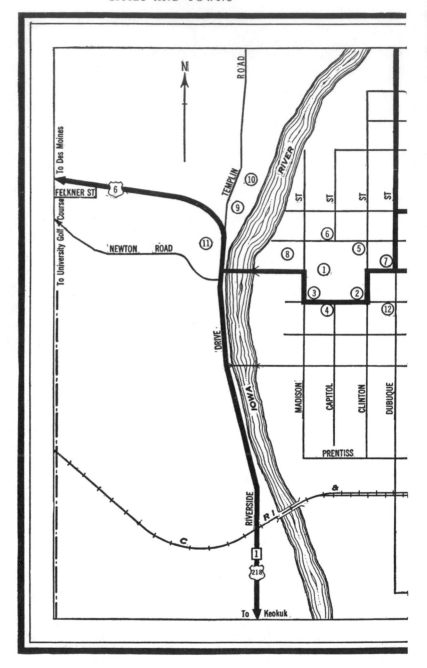

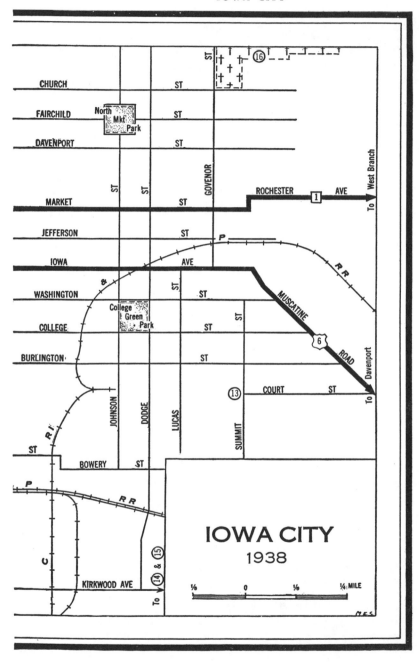

IOWA CITY
1938

⅛   0   ⅛   ¼ MILE

chologist and inventor of the laboratory method of photographing the human voice, carries on his experiments.

5. MACBRIDE HALL, Jefferson St. at Capitol St., Old Capitol Campus, harmonizing in style and proportions with Schaeffer Hall, is named for Thomas Macbride (1848–1934), president and president emeritus of the university who founded the Lakeside Laboratory of Scientific Research at Lake Okoboji *(see Tour 10)* and was first president of the Iowa Park and Forestry Association, organized in 1901. In the building are the General Library and an auditorium seating 1,000. The MUSEUM OF NATURAL HISTORY, third floor, *(open weekdays 8-5; Sun. 1-5)*, has a MAMMAL HALL and a BIRD HALL separated by the balcony of the auditorium. The outstanding feature of the Bird Hall is the LAYSAN ISLAND CYCLORAMA, housed in an adjoining room. The cyclorama of this Pacific coral island bird refuge shows the geological formation, and the rare sea birds that breed there. Prof. Homer R. Dill, designer and executor of the reproduction, lived on the island for a time in 1911, studying and collecting the necessary material.

6. The GEOLOGY BUILDING, NW. corner Capitol and Jefferson Sts., first used as the Museum of Natural History, houses a GEOLOGICAL MUSEUM with an extensive collection of fossils, building rocks, and soils of the State, and specimens of the Amana meteor.

7. The JOURNALISM BUILDING, corner Dubuque St. and Iowa Ave., houses the printing plant of the eight-page *Daily Iowan,* the college newspaper. Local headquarters of the Associated Press are on the second floor.

8. MEMORIAL UNION, SW. corner Market and Madison Sts., the student social center, is dedicated to the university men and women who died in the World War. The broadcasting studio of Station WSUI adjoins the lounge.

KEY TO IOWA CITY MAP

THE STATE UNIVERSITY OF IOWA

EAST-SIDE CAMPUS

1. Old Capitol
2. Schaeffer Hall
3. Physics Building
4. Hall of Engineering

5. MacBride Hall
6. Geology Building
7. Journalism Building
8. Memorial Union

WEST-SIDE CAMPUS

9. Fine Arts Building
10. Dramatic Art Building

11. University Hospital

OTHER POINTS OF INTEREST

12. Jefferson Hotel
13. Shaft
14. Robert Lucas Home

15. Home of Samuel J. Kirkwood
16. Oakland Cemetery

WEST-SIDE CAMPUS

9. The FINE ARTS BUILDING *(open 8-5 Mon.-Fri.)*, Templin Rd. at Market St. footbridge, stands in landscaped grounds with green bluffs in the background and the river in the foreground. Among the private studios is one used by Grant Wood, Iowa artist. Exhibits include gift collections of medieval paintings, Renaissance carvings, plaster casts, bronze statuary, portrait sketches, and a collection of paintings by American artists.

10. The DRAMATIC ART BUILDING *(private)*, Templin Rd. at River St., has a revolving stage. The University Theater, a leader in the western theater movement, presents two types of plays—Broadway and London successes and regional material.

11. The UNIVERSITY HOSPITAL, Newton Rd. between Templin Rd. and Woolf St., opened in November 1928, is an E-shaped brick structure, modified early English Gothic in style, in which the 145-foot white stone tower forms the center wing. There are private, cost, and indigent patients, with a majority of the latter. The hospitals care for about 800 bed patients a day, and treat approximately 22,000 individual patients a year. In 1915 the General Assembly provided that children under 16, financially unable to obtain surgical or medical treatment, might be sent to the university hospitals at public expense, and in 1919 made the same provision for adults. Many children are sent to the hospital to obtain the services of Dr. Arthur Steindler who has distinguished himself with orthopedic treatments. Eighteen ambulances travel about 5,500 miles a day over the State to transport the incoming and outgoing patients. Since 1932, when the service was established, approximately 80,000 patients have been carried over 5,500,000 miles with only one serious accident to mar the safety record.

OTHER POINTS OF INTEREST

12. The JEFFERSON HOTEL, SW. corner Washington and Dubuque Sts., is on the site where a group of men gathered in pre-Civil War days to lynch John Brown, but a friendly warning enabled Brown to escape. The series of eight murals in the hotel lobby, executed by Mildred Pelzer in 1934, portrays the settlement, growth and development of Iowa City.

13. A SHAFT, corner Summit and Court Sts., of native weather-beaten limestone, erected to mark the southeast corner of Section 10 on which Old Capitol stands, is the probable point where the first stake marking the site of Iowa City was driven in 1839. The shaft was marked with bronze tablets May 4, 1935, because the reading on the shaft had become dim and worn.

14. The ROBERT LUCAS HOME *(private)*, 727 Switzer Ave., was built in 1844 by the first Governor of the Territory of Iowa. The large brick house, originally surrounded by a plum thicket and known as Plum Grove Farm, is now a three-family dwelling. As the town grew the Lucas home was incorporated within the south city limits.

15. The HOME OF SAMUEL J. KIRKWOOD *(private)*, 1028 Kirkwood Ave., was originally a small frame structure, since remodeled. Kirkwood was Iowa's Civil War Governor and held an interest in the Coral Flour Mills at Coralville just outside Iowa City. It is said that he burst into Iowa politics when he went to a convention, dressed in his working clothes, and "bepowdered" from head to foot with flour.

16. The OAKLAND CEMETERY, corner Governor and Brown Sts., is the burial place of Governors Lucas and Kirkwood. It also contains the *Black Angel*, a monument in bronze on the grave of William Dolezal, designed by Mario Korbel. A short time after the monument was erected it turned black, a fact that has been the foundation for a number of sinister stories.

POINTS OF INTEREST IN ENVIRONS

Site of Mormon Camp, Coralville—*2 m.;* State Tubercular Sanatorium, Oakdale—*5 m.;* Herbert Hoover's Birthplace, West Branch—*10 m. (see Tour 14, sec. a).*

‹‹‹‹‹‹‹‹‹‹‹‹‹‹‹‹‹‹‹‹‹⚓›››››››››››››››››››››

Keokuk

Railroad Station: Union Station, Exchange and Water Sts., for Wabash Ry., Chicago, Rock Island & Pacific Ry., and Chicago, Burlington & Quincy R.R.
Bus Station: Union Station, 13 N. 4th St., for Illinois Transit Lines, Burlington Trans. Co., M. C. Foster Lines, Jackson Motor Bus Lines, Kirksville Bus Co., and Wendt Motor Bus Lines.
City Buses: Fare 10¢, Sat. 5¢.
Taxis: Rates uniform, 25¢ any part of the city.
Bridges: Keokuk-Hamilton (Ill.), toll bridge, pedestrians 5¢, vehicles, 25¢; Keokuk-Alexandria (Mo.), free bridge.
Traffic Regulations: One-hour limit on Main St. for parking.

Accommodations: Three hotels; numerous cabin camps and private homes cater to tourists.

Information Service: American Automobile Association, Hotel Iowa, 4th and Main Sts.

Motion Picture Houses: Two.
Athletics: Joyce Park, 3201 Main St.
Swimming: Manhattan and Glaser Beaches, 1½ m. on River Blvd.
Golf: Fairview Golf Club, Old Fair Grounds, W. of city limits, 9 holes, non-resident fee $1.00.
Steamboat Excursion Pier: Foot of Main St. for Streckfus Steamer Co., in season.

Annual Events: Memorial Service, National Cemetery, May.

KEOKUK (478 alt., 15,106 pop.), a city rich in historical associations, is also noted for the great dam that stretches across the Mississippi River before it, and the power house close to the Iowa shore. The city's long main street runs at right angles with the river, following the gentle hills on the plateau and dropping abruptly to the water's edge. The residence district lies to the north of this street and the business and industrial section, south. Many old buildings—some of them erected before the Civil War—lend an occasional touch of age to the otherwise modern city. Besides the usual business of marketing and trading, incidental to a farming region, and some manufacturing, the area has an unfailing natural resource in its supply of commercial fish. Hundreds of tons are boxed and barreled each year for shipment to St. Louis, Chicago, and other markets.

In the early days the Indians called this place Puck-e-she-tuck, meaning "where the water runs shallow" or "at the foot of the rapids." *Voyageurs* and fur traders designated it The Point. The first white man to make a permanent settlement within the present limits of the city was Dr. Samuel C. Muir (1785–1832)—a former surgeon in the United States Army —who erected a log cabin here in 1820 for his Indian wife and family. Moses Stillwell and Mark Aldrich opened a trading post in 1829 for the American Fur Company and that same year, at the July 4 celebration, it

KEOKUK DAM ACROSS THE MISSISSIPPI

was proposed and adopted that the settlement be named for Chief Keokuk of the Sac tribe.

Chief Keokuk was three-quarters Indian. His father was a full-blooded and his mother a half-breed Sac. Keokuk was born in 1780 at the village of Saukenuk, not far from the present site of Rock Island, Illinois. Known as an orator of extraordinary eloquence, Keokuk culled his figures of speech from nature and based his arguments on skillful logic. After Black Hawk's defeat in the war of 1832, the Federal Government recognized Keokuk as the principal chief of the Sac and Fox Indians in this vicinity.

In 1831 the American Fur Company constructed a row of five hewn-log buildings, the first building boom here; later these cabins were known as Rat Row. The first fully recorded religious services in Iowa took place from October 6 to 9, 1832. During that period Father Van Quickenborne conferred the Sacrament of Baptism and performed five marriages. The first schoolmaster in Keokuk was Jesse Creighton, a shoemaker, who in 1834 had a class of eight pupils.

In the spring of 1837 the city was platted by Isaac Galland (1790–1858), an agent of the New York Land Company. Itinerant preachers of various faiths began about this time to hold religious services in the town's auditorium (one of the Rat Row buildings), a long log building running along the levee near what is now the foot of Main Street.

Beginning with the 1840's Keokuk was the manufacturing and jobbing headquarters for the pioneer Middle West. In the early days before the railroads, when rivers constituted the main means of transportation, it was known as the Gate City, not only for Iowa but for the North and West as well, because of its position at the foot of the Des Moines rapids on the Mississippi. Steamboats were unable to go beyond this point. All passengers and freight had to be unloaded here and lightered over the rapids or continue the journey on land. Up to this time the Half Breed Tract was involved in many disputes between Indians, white men, and half breeds as to title to individual holdings. Francis Scott Key, who wrote *The Star Spangled Banner,* national anthem, had a part in settling the litigation involved here. An attorney for the New York Land Company in 1841, he drew up the decree of partition of the lands. The plat established then is the basis for all titles today. The city of Keokuk was incorporated under a special charter in 1847.

A medical college that became the first medical department of the University of Iowa was established here in 1850, and moved to Iowa City in the 1860's. From a scientific standpoint the geological formation of the Keokuk area early proved interesting, the surrounding sections becoming classic in the annals of geology. Keokuk was the starting point for the classification of the Lower Carboniferous limestones throughout the entire Mississippi basin, being defined and described according to modern geological methods in 1858. Nearly the entire county is underlaid with this limestone, every variety of which affords a good grade of stone, easily quarried and readily dressed.

During the Civil War, Keokuk served as the port of embarkation of practically every Iowa regiment (except cavalry) and for those of several neighboring States. During this period more than 200 Keokuk citizens were commisioned officers, many serving in the higher commands. Six war hospitals were established here to care for the wounded, later resulting in the creating of a National Cemetery, the only one in Iowa.

A railroad line was established in 1856 to haul freight from Keokuk to a point about 12 miles up the river, beyond the rapids, where the materials were loaded on boats again for points beyond. In 1870 this short line was taken over by the Chicago, Burlington & Quincy Railroad. The navigation problem of the five hazardous chains of rapids above Keokuk was finally solved when a canal, built by the Government at a cost of $7,500,000, was opened for river traffic on August 22, 1877. The canal, with three locks, was nine miles long and 250 feet wide, with a minimum low water depth of five feet. Keokuk's supremacy as a river port, along with that of other river towns, had gradually declined with the coming of the railroads, but from 1910, when work was started on the Keokuk dam, the city entered into an era of renewed activity.

Keokuk has many reminders of the colorful days of the nineteenth century when the State was being settled and the town gained its title of Gate City. Under the waters of Lake Keokuk and back of the great power dam of today lie the rocks that caused the early rapids in the river. The Mark Twain Zephyr, a streamlined train named for the great humorist, streaking into town, is a reminder that Mark Twain (Samuel Clemens, 1835–1910) once lived and worked here.

Mrs. Annie Wittenmyer (1827–1900), who organized the Army diet kitchens during the Civil War, made her home in this city. Two Secretaries of War were among other Keokuk people to call the city home—W. W. Belknap, appointed in 1869, and George W. McCrary, in 1877. John W. Noble of this city took office as Secretary of the Interior under President Benjamin Harrison in 1889. Mary Timberman (1863–1899), actress, was born here and received her early dramatic training under a talented mother. Miss Timberman acted with Robert Keene, and in supporting roles with Richard Mansfield, Robert Mantell, and others. Cornelia Meigs, who was awarded the Newberry Medal for 1933–34 for *Invincible Louisa,* her biography of Louisa M. Alcott, received her education in the Keokuk schools, where Rupert Hughes, another writer of repute, was also educated.

POINTS OF INTEREST ASSOCIATED WITH MARK TWAIN

PUBLIC LIBRARY, SE. corner 3rd and Main Sts. *(open weekdays, except holidays; 9-6, June 1-Sept. 30; 10-9, Oct. 1-May 31),* a two-story building of modified Romanesque design, built in 1881, houses a collection of curios and an extensive selection of State and national historical and governmental publications, in addition to the customary library collections. A copy of the city's FIRST DIRECTORY, published in 1856, is a model of the printer's art of that day. Most of it was set by Mark Twain when he was working in the Keokuk job-printing shop of his brother, Orion Clemens. In it, as in almost everything else he touched during his long career, Mark Twain left the mark of his humor. Although then a printer by trade, he listed himself in this early directory as an antiquarian. When he was asked the reason for this he replied that he always thought every town should have at least one antiquarian, and since none appeared for the post, he volunteered. A copy of the beautiful old MENU FOR NEW YEAR'S OF 1856, printed on white silk for the Ivins House, entirely Twain's handiwork, is among the curios.

OLD IVINS HOUSE (now Hawkeye Hotel), NW. corner 1st and Johnson Sts., a two-story brick structure built in 1850, is a landmark intimately associated with Mark Twain. This hotel was not only the regular boarding house of Twain but was also the scene of his first after-dinner speech.

IOWA STATE INSURANCE BUILDING, SW. corner 2nd and Main Sts., is a plain office structure, built in 1855 and remodeled in 1925. In remodeling the building, the MARK TWAIN MEMORIAL ROOM *(open by permission),* on the third floor, was preserved with its original walls and floors. In this room, where Mark Twain did his job printing, are his old print shop pictures, type cases, and chairs.

REES PARK, S. 7th St. at city limits, contains the old REES HOMESTEAD and several adjacent lots presented to the city in 1921 by Thomas Rees. The house is an enlarged log cabin covered with weather boarding. Rees printed Mark Twain's first paid articles, the "Three Snodgrass Letters," in the Keokuk *Saturday Post*. From the bluffs comprising the park it is possible to see three States—Iowa, Illinois, and Missouri—also the monument on the site of old Fort Edwards at Warsaw, Illinois.

OTHER POINTS OF INTEREST

DAILY GATE CITY PLANT, 18 N. 6th St., houses a newspaper which was established by Robert B. and John W. Ogden as a weekly May 15, 1847, called the Keokuk *Register* and later the *Des Moines Valley Whig and Keokuk Register,* commonly known as "The Whig." On the first of March 1854, James B. Howell, the then owner, suddenly decided to beat the Keokuk *Dispatch,* a rival paper, in issuing a daily and the next morning, March 2, 1854, the Keokuk *Daily Whig* appeared—one of the first daily newspapers in the State of Iowa. It continued under this name until after the decline of the Whig Party in 1855. On March 2 of that year was printed the first issue under its present name, the *Daily Gate City.* Among the paper's outstanding editors was Samuel Mercer Clark (1842–1900), whose editorials were widely read. His versatility and ability won for him the title, "Master Stylist of the Iowa Press."

FEDERAL BUILDING, 7th and Blondeau Sts., erected in 1889, is an ornamental structure of modified Romanesque architecture. It is constructed of brick, stone, and terra cotta. A four-dial town clock is built into the large square tower surmounting the building. The clockworks are in a room on the third floor, 40 feet below the dials, with a connecting steel rod mechanism. The building houses the post office, United States Circuit and District Courts, various Federal offices, United States Signal Service Department, and the Weather Bureau.

A method of foretelling weather facts on a scientific basis and making them available to the public was developed here in 1866 by Dr. H. A. Kinnaman, then a train dispatcher for the Des Moines Valley Railroad. Kinnaman's method was primarily responsible for the act of Congress, authorizing weather observations at military stations and other points in the interior.

KEOKUK DAM, foot of Orleans and Franklin Sts., was built in 1910–13. Stretching across the Mississippi to Hamilton, Illinois, the dam is nearly a mile long. Hugh L. Cooper was the designer and engineer. Built into the hard limestone rock on the river bed, this gravity type dam is so designed that it can withstand all pressure by reason of its bulk, without braces or additional provisions for stresses and strains. The dam contains approximately the same amount of masonry as one of the great pyramids of Egypt. The GOVERNMENT DRYDOCK, and the GOVERNMENT LOCK, near the Iowa shore, are among the largest ever constructed. The Mississippi River Power Company built the dock and lock for the Government in return for the privilege of building and operating the HYDROELECTRIC PLANT, farther out in the stream *(open daily; conducted trips hourly, 9-11, 1-3).* Two hundred thousand horse power are generated in the plant and the turbines are four times the size of the largest previously built. Generation of power from the Des Moines Rapids of the Mississippi was conceived in 1837 when Robert E. Lee, then a lieutenant in the Army, made a report on the water power that could be obtained.

Special OBSERVATION PLATFORMS have been erected at various points for visitors—2nd and Fulton Sts., head of 6th St., and head of 9th St. Excellent views of the project can also be obtained from the highway and bridge between Keokuk and Hamilton, Illinois.

LAKE KEOKUK (sometimes called Lake Cooper, and designated by the War Department as Pool 19), extending in the Mississippi River from the Keokuk Dam to Burlington, was formed when the dam was built across the river. It comprises an area of 100 square miles and extends nearly 65 miles northward, varying in width from three quarters of a mile to three miles.

On north and south flights ducks and geese by the thousands seek the lake sanctuary for a restful half-way stopping place between the Gulf and the northern breeding grounds. Federal game laws prohibit the shooting of game birds from water craft of any kind and the birds seem aware of this protection. The Federal Government and the States of Iowa and Illinois have stocked the lake with black bass. In season, catfish, crappie, sunfish, perch, salmon, pike, carp, shad, and other fish may be caught—perhaps the largest variety of fish in all of Iowa.

NATIONAL CEMETERY, W. end of Cedar St., is one of 83 in the United States and the only one in Iowa. Established by the Government in 1861, over 750 soldiers were buried here before the end of the Civil War, eight of whom were Confederate prisoners. The dead of four other wars lie in the three acres which comprise the cemetery—the Mexican War, the Indian Wars, the Spanish-American War, and the World War. A monument erected in memory of the UNKNOWN SOLDIER stands in the central park.

CORNERSTONE OF THE OLD ESTES HOUSE, main entrance to cemetery (R), is all that remains of the house built in 1857. The building was a pretentious hotel for that time and place, containing 200 rooms and costing in the neighborhood of $60,000. Early in 1862 it was transformed into a hospital.

RAND PARK, NE. corner of city, main entrance at 15th St. and Grand Ave., bordering the Mississippi River, contains the GRAVE OF CHIEF KEOKUK and the monument erected to him. The monument, facing the river, consists of a statue and pedestal, designed by Nellie Walker, a native of Iowa. The statue, regarded as a remarkable likeness of the famous chief, is more than 10 feet high, and rests on a brownstone pedestal 20 feet in height. Chief Keokuk died and was buried in Kansas in 1848, but his body was later returned to Keokuk, together with the marble slab erected over his Kansas grave. This slab is fitted into the present monument.

POINTS OF INTEREST IN ENVIRONS

Galland, site of first schoolhouse in Iowa—7 *m.*, Montrose, site of early settlement, Tesson's Orchard, and first Fort Des Moines—*12 m. (see Tour 1, sec. b).*

Marshalltown

Railroad Stations: E. Nevada St. bet. S. 3rd and S. 4th Aves. for Chicago, Great Western R.R.; SW. cor. E. Madison St. at S. 3rd Ave. for Chicago & North Western Ry. and Minneapolis & St. Louis R.R.

Bus Station: Pilgrim Hotel, NE. cor. 3rd Ave. and E. Main St., for Interstate Transit Lines.

Street Buses: Regular service; 5¢.

Accommodations: Seven hotels; three tourist camps.

Information Service: Chamber of Commerce, Hotel Tall Corn, 2nd Ave. and E. Main St.

Radio Station: KFJB (1200 kc).

Motion Picture Houses: Four.

Swimming: Riverview Park (City Park), end N. 3rd Ave.

Golf: Rolling Hills, 3 m. W. of city on US 30, 18 holes, 35¢ weekdays, 50¢ Sun. and holidays.

Annual Events: Church and Bible School Pageant, June; Central Iowa Fair, fairgrounds, E. Main St., early autumn; Tall Corn Exposition, Memorial Coliseum, early Oct.

MARSHALLTOWN (863 alt., 17,373 pop.), industrial center and seat of Marshall County, is a city on the prairie, stencilled with railroad tracks and hard-surfaced highways and bordered on the north by the Iowa River. It is built around the courthouse, as is traditional with county seat towns in Iowa. The friendly dials of the clock tower, luminous above a fringe of green trees on Main Street, command the entire community. Farmers in "Sunday best" or everyday overalls, drive in from the country to transact business here and, lingering in the square, discuss the latest prices at the canning factory which contracts with them for sweet corn. Their wives and daughters, strolling along Main or Center Streets, window-gaze or purchase items on their shopping lists. A constant ebb and flow of foot and automobile traffic suggests the many brisk activities of the neighborhood.

From the courthouse, the residence district spreads fanwise toward the west and north. Most factories are in the southeast. Thousands of trees shade the wide boulevards; in the summer the city appears to be covered with arbors of green from which emerge smokestacks, the courthouse, and the tower of the Iowa Soldiers' Home in the northwest environs. Beyond Marshalltown's borders is the corn country—flat, almost timberless prairie extending for miles.

Marshalltown's population is 91 percent native white; its factory and other workers being largely recruited from neighboring rural sections.

The city was named for Marshall, Mich., by the first permanent settler, Henry Anson, who emigrated from the East by covered wagon in the spring of 1851. The suffix "town" was added later to distinguish it from another town in the State. The first court of Marshall County (created in 1846) was held by Judge Williams in the fall of 1851 in John Ralls' cabin in a grove north of Anson's home, and in the same year Marietta was chosen as the county seat. Henry Anson was furious. He roused his neighbors to action, insisting that their town should be chosen. The Marietta residents jeered at "Anson's Potato Patch." A bitter seven-year wrangle followed, drawn out by personal and political disputes and legal sparring. The Supreme Court of Iowa finally decided in favor of Marshalltown in December 1859.

On June 11, 1859, a group of Marshalltown business men, headed by Greenleaf M. Woodbury, formed the Cedar Rapids & Missouri River Railroad Company in order to build a line west from Cedar Rapids to the Missouri River. The Government issued the company a land grant March 24, 1860, stipulating that the first 40 miles of the new road should be finished by January 1, 1862. A subscription list was started; those who could not spare money volunteered to work, give free board and room to other workers, or lend teams of horses. As the time limit approached, crews worked day and night to finish the required section of the road. The last spike was driven at midnight, December 31, 1861. A year later, January 1863, the line was completed to Marshalltown.

Many men from Marshalltown and the surrounding country fought with the Union forces in the Civil War. A local unit, the Bowen Guard, was mustered into service July 1861 as Company D, 5th Iowa Infantry. W. P. Hepburn, Marshall County prosecuting attorney, organized a company of the Second Cavalry, serving as its captain. Marshalltown, incorporated in 1863, was one of several cities that held sanitary fairs that year. A large amount of money was raised and sent to the front to improve first aid and hospital work.

Industrially the city's development began in the first years after the Civil War with the establishment of flannel, blanket, woolen goods, wagon and carriage factories and an iron foundry. Repair shops and terminal property of the Central Railroad of Iowa (Minneapolis & St. Louis) were located in Marshalltown when the railroad was built through in 1869.

Twice during the 1870's flames threatened to destroy commercial Marshalltown. The first fire, May 2, 1872, spread rapidly, owing to a high wind, sweeping over an area of 15 acres and causing damages in excess of $200,000. The town was little more than rebuilt when, April 6, 1876, another blaze burned $30,000 worth of elevators, warehouses, and lumberyards.

When hospitalization of Civil War veterans became a matter for State consideration, Marshalltown offered to donate 28 acres of ground for a home. The city also raised $12,000, later increasing the amount to $30,000 and adding to the acreage. The General Assembly in 1887 accepted the offer, appropriating $100,000 for the erection and maintenance of an institution.

When Henry Anson died November 30, 1905, at the age of 79, the city he founded and fostered was an important shopping and manufacturing center. Since that time, Marshalltown has quietly expanded its manufactures in keeping with changing times. In 1935 a local company made spot and taillight gaskets for more than 80 percent of American automobiles. A furnace manufacturing company brought out domestic air-conditioning equipment. Trowels, governors, and steam specialties are among the other products manufactured. Altogether 56 factories are in business, giving work to hundreds of local people and paying wages of $300,000 annually.

POINTS OF INTEREST

MEMORIAL COLISEUM, 22-28 W. State St., completed in February 1929 "In Memory of Those Who Offered Their Lives for Our Country," has an auditorium that seats 2,500 people. The two-story stone, brick and concrete structure is modern in design, its severity relieved by the columned entrance of Italian Renaissance inspiration. The stones of the front elevation, Ohio sandstone brick, are hand-cut. Stage and dressing rooms, dining room and kitchen facilitate the scheduling of many types of events in the building, chief among which are the Tall Corn Festival and political gatherings.

PUBLIC LIBRARY *(open, weekdays 9-9 Sept.-May; Mon.-Fri., 9-6, June-Aug.)*, SW. corner State and N. Center Sts., was built in 1903, after Andrew Carnegie had contributed $30,000 toward its construction. The two-story sandstone edifice in modified Classic style, is distinguished by the four half-buried Roman columns on the entrance, facing on the street corner. Circulation and reference rooms occupy the first floor. The library has 27,628 volumes. On the second floor is a children's room, also a MUSEUM housing historic and geologic collections.

SITE OF FIRST HOUSE, 112 W. Main St., is marked by a boulder indicating the birthplace of the first white child in Marshalltown, Adrian C. (Pop) Anson (1852–1922). After finishing school Anson became a professional baseball player and in 1883 was manager of the Chicago White Stockings (now known as the Cubs).

EVANGELICAL DEACONESS HOME AND HOSPITAL *(open daily 10-11, 1-4, and 7-9)*, 3rd Ave. and Main St., is sponsored by the Evangelical and Reformed Church in America. The three-story brick building is modified Classic in style. Since 1913, when the hospital was built, two wings have been added. The Nurses' Training School and Sisters' Home are south of the main edifice. A 132-acre farm outside the city supplies milk, vegetables, and meat for the hospital.

IOWA SOLDIERS' HOME *(open daily 1-4)*, Summit St. between N. 9th and N. 15th Sts., NW. edge of the city, is a residence for disabled Iowa veterans. Curving driveways sweep back from the street under vaulted rows of elms to the central two-story red brick building trimmed with white stone. The style is English Romanesque. Brick arches are over the windows; a square tower juts up above the white frame portico. The hospital, like the four other main buildings, is of harmonizing design with porches and balconies finished with iron and wooden railings and window-lets. The Commandant's home, assembly hall, cottages, and maintenance shops are grouped on the grounds that comprise 156 acres on the south bank of the Iowa River. Natural timber—predominantly oaks and elms—shades half the park-like area. The residents include veterans of the Indian, Civil, Spanish-American, and World Wars. JOHNNY GREENE MEMORIAL, NE. of the Commandant's House, is a stone shaft, erected in June 1918, honoring Johnny Green—Che-Me-Use (1795–1868), Pottawattamie Indian chief believed buried there. During his lifetime this chieftain formed a deep and lasting friendship with the Marshall County pioneers.

RIVERVIEW PARK, end of N. 3rd Ave., bordering the Iowa River, is a favorite 40-acre recreation center. The Marshall County Historical Society erected a LOG CABIN MEMORIAL here in 1936 to commemorate the arrival of early settlers. Descendants of pioneers financed and sponsored the cabin. Stones brought from the farms of the county form the foundation and fireplace. Logs of native timber, oak, elm and hickory, were cut by an old sawmill especially set up for the purpose. Each of 195 logs is dedicated to a pioneer and is marked with a brass plate bearing the name and date of settlement. The first logs placed in position were for the families of Thomas Hauser and William Arney, who settled in the county in 1849.

POINTS OF INTEREST IN ENVIRONS

LeGrand, stone quarries and fossil exhibits—*9 m.*, Mormon Ridge, route of Mormon exodus through Iowa—*10 m. (see Tour 13, sec. a).*

Mason City

Railroad Stations: 600 2nd St. NW. for Chicago, Great Western R.R. and Chicago, Rock Island & Pacific Ry.; 900 S. Pennsylvania Ave. for Chicago, Milwaukee, St. Paul & Pacific R.R.; 600 1st St. SW. for Chicago & North Western Ry.; 428 3rd St. NE. for Minneapolis & St. Louis R.R.
Bus Station: 16 1st St. SW. for Jefferson Trans. Co.
Interurban Line: Mason City & Clear Lake (resort), regular bus service, 22 2nd St. NW.
Street Buses: Fare 10¢, four tokens for 25¢.

Accommodations: Four hotels; four cabin camps.

Information Service: Chamber of Commerce, Globe Gazette Bldg., 121½ E. State St.; Public Library, 208 E. State St.

Radio Station: KGLO (1210 kc).
Motion Picture Houses: Four.
Golf: American Legion Municipal Course, N. end of N. Rhode Island Ave., 9 holes, 50¢.
Tennis: East Park, 8 blks. E. from square on E. State St.; Roosevelt School, 1221 4th St. SE.

MASON CITY (1,130 alt., 23,304 pop.), seat of Cerro Gordo County, is a railroad and manufacturing town in north central Iowa. The city, rising from rolling prairies, is the center of a fertile agricultural region. There are few large towns in this part of the State, making this city the trading mart for an area extending 40 miles north, 50 miles east, and 60 or 70 miles west and northwest. Mason City is also a focal point for a large system of bus and truck transportation. Although the city has the friendly, intimate feeling of a small town, it is a prominent industrial center. Smoke stacks pour forth black clouds over fields of corn and oats, and factories are separated from farms only by a barbwire fence.

Most of the pioneers in the territory were of the Masonic order and the first settlement was named Shibboleth. Mason City was originally known as Masonic Grove, but when the town was platted in 1854 the name was changed. The county (Cerro Gordo) was organized in 1851 and named for a battlefield of the Mexican War.

John B. Long and John L. McMillan, said to have been Mason City's first settlers, arrived in 1853 and made extensive claims along Lime Creek. An Indian uprising (Grindstone War at Clear Lake) on July 4, 1854, stampeded most of the settlers to the older towns on the Cedar River, leaving the county practically depopulated. Gradually the settlers returned and secured claims at a land auction, which opened on September 4, 1854. Cabins were built, sod was turned, and seed planted. The first mill was erected in 1855 on Lime Creek by Elisha Randall, who at the same time built a lime kiln. In 1872 he invented and patented what was known as

Randall's Perpetual Lime Kiln, which proved so successful that it was adopted in many parts of the country.

Until 1855, Mason City was without local government, as Cerro Gordo County had been attached to Floyd County for administrative purposes. In August the citizens voted again for the organization of Cerro Gordo as an independent county and three commissioners were appointed to determine the county seat. Mason City and Clear Lake were the chief competitors and Mason City, as the point nearest the geographical center of the county, was chosen. However, the Sixth General Assembly, in December 1856, designated Clear Lake, under the name of Livonia, as the seat, but at a county election held in April 1858 Mason City was again selected.

As early as 1869, Mason City gave promise of becoming a railroad center, the Milwaukee railroad laying its track to the city in that year and, in 1870, completing it northward to Austin, Minnesota. In 1870 the Iowa Central railroad finished its line into the city and 16 years later the Great Western arrived, followed by the Chicago & North Western in 1889. The last line laid to the city was the St. Paul & Des Moines short line (now Rock Island), which came in 1909. An interest in air transportation was evident here as early as 1915 when two local men, Kenneth Jay and Charles Hathorn, constructed home-made planes. An airport was established in 1927, and in the same year Mason City adopted the city-manager form of city government.

The development of the clay tile industry began here in the 1880's, when much of northern Iowa had to be drained and tile was in demand. Until about 1934 Iowa used more drain tile than any other area of equal size in the world, and Mason City was the center of this manufacture. It is said that enough tile was made here every year to reach half-way around the world.

Today Mason City employs in its factories more than 2,500 people. A packing plant processes 800,000 hogs and 100,000 cattle annually, and the American Beet Sugar Refining Company, just north of the city, handles more than 100,000 tons of beets a year. However, it is in the manufacture of brick, tile, and Portland cement that the city is outstanding. From the outskirts of the city the burning kilns and smoking stacks are visible in the distance. The combined annual capacity of the brick and tile plants is more than 200,000 tons of manufactured clay ware. The two cement plants in the northern part of the city produce five percent of the entire output of the United States, and are valued at $5,000,000. They have a daily capacity of 12,000 barrels or about 25,000 carloads annually.

The first public junior college in the State was established here, March 19, 1918, and in 1934 high school musicians won the national championship in both band and orchestra competition.

POINTS OF INTEREST

FIRST NATIONAL BANK, NE. corner Federal Ave. and State St., was the scene in 1933 of a hold-up said to have been led by John Dillinger. At 2:45 on a weekday afternoon, seven men entered the building and held up the customers and management. In a short space of time a great crowd gathered on the streets outside to watch the bandits, who went about their business calmly and efficiently, and escaped with $52,000.

PARK INN, 15 W. State St., was designed by Frank Lloyd Wright, distinguished American architect who introduced radical innovations in architectural treatments, particularly in his "prairie style." Later architectural changes have been numerous in the hotel, but have not destroyed the general character of the structure. The low squat building, with horizontal lines paralleling the natural prairie lines, is still recognizable as Wright's special contribution.

PUBLIC LIBRARY *(open weekdays 9-9, Sun. 3-6)*, 208 E. State St., built in 1903 of Bedford limestone, is classical in design. On each side of the entrance, at the top of the wide granite steps and scotiae extending outward bordering the steps, are two Doric columns rising to the flat roof. The interior is finished in terrazzo and various kinds of hardwood with floors of floral terrazzo; green glass in conventional design adds to the appearance of warmth in the interior. The library began with a reading room where free coffee and doughnuts were served on Saturday nights. In 1902, Andrew Carnegie donated $20,000 toward the construction of the present building and, in 1905, the city with a population of only 8,660, managed to raise $10,000 more.

ROCK GLEN, E. State St. just W. of Willow Creek bridge, comprises a group of homes, again showing Frank Lloyd Wright's influence. Emphasis here, as in most of the Wright buildings, is placed on the horizontal line. Walter Burleigh Griffith, disciple of Wright, was one of the architects who designed this group of homes. The houses, placed near the street on a higher level, have a small private park at the rear on the banks of Willow Creek. The gray stone of the houses fits naturally into the environment of limestone bluffs and stream.

HERBERT QUICK HOUSE *(private)*, 219 6th St. NE., was the home of the Iowa novelist. The small gray house with its ell stands on a secluded spot off the paved streets. Herbert Quick (1861–1925), a local school teacher, was admitted to the bar in 1890, after which he moved to Sioux City to practice. Quick is noted for his stories of pioneer Iowa—*Vandemark's Folly* and *The Hawkeye.*

MASON CITY BRICK AND TILE PLANT DISTRICT *(plants open by permission)*, is in the southwest part of the city, between 7th and 19th Sts. The hut-shaped kilns, clustered around the tall plant buildings, add picturesqueness to the surrounding farming lands. In this area are seven plants, all in a radius of one square mile.

NORTHWESTERN STATES PORTLAND CEMENT PLANT *(open by permission)*, 2100 N. Federal Ave., is one of the largest producers of Portland cement in the world. Boilers in the mills are run with waste heat from the rotary kilns, thus eliminating stokers, firemen, and the coal formerly used in the furnaces. These mills, with their mammoth buildings, are an impressive sight.

DECKER MEAT PACKING PLANT *(open weekdays, 9-2; guides)*, 320 15th St. NE., houses Mason City's largest industry. Twelve hundred men and women are employed and the annual payroll is in the neighborhood of $1,800,000.

POINTS OF INTEREST IN ENVIRONS

Clear Lake, resort and State Park—*10 m. (see Tour 11, sec. b)*.

Muscatine

Railroad Station: SE. cor. Iowa Ave. and Front St. for Chicago, Rock Island & Pacific Ry. and Chicago, Milwaukee, St. Paul & Pacific R.R.
Interurban Station: 109 Iowa Ave. for Clinton, Davenport & Muscatine Ry.
Bus Station: C. D. & M. Station for Burlington Trailways, C. D. & M. Motor Coach Line, and Foster's Bus Line.
Street Buses: 2nd St. and Iowa Ave., 20-min. schedule, fare 10¢.
Taxis: 15¢ per passenger any part of the city.

Accommodations: Four hotels.

Information Service: Chamber of Commerce, City Hall, SE. cor. 3rd and Sycamore Sts.

Motion Picture Houses: Three.
Swimming: Weed Park, E. part of city on N. side US 61.
Baseball: League Ball Park, end of Bleeker St., S. Muscatine.
Golf: Mad Creek Golf Course, 2100 Mulberry Ave., 9 holes, 25¢.
Tennis and Ice Skating: Musser Park, S. part of city.
Steamboat Excursions: Foot of Iowa Ave. at irregular intervals, advertised in advance.

Annual Events: Halloween parade, downtown sts., Oct.

MUSCATINE (552 alt., 16,778 pop.), seat of Muscatine County, is about 30 miles farther west on the Mississippi River than its neighbor city of Davenport. The business district, cupped in a bowl between East Hill on one side, West Hill on the other, the river to the south, and a gradual rise of the rolling prairie to the north, is built mainly along two streets. Many old brick buildings line the narrow brick-paved streets that slope away from the river, dipping between the hills. Other streets are unpaved, the natural gravel of the land forming a good material for the roads. Residence districts spread out over the hills, with the shacks of factory workers in South Muscatine. Beyond this the Mississippi River swings away from the bluffs forming a tract of bottom land known as Muscatine Island, famous for its watermelons, muskmelons, and fine vegetables.

Although predominately a manufacturing center, the city is a trading point for a large rural population. There are many Germans and Hollanders and the German language is frequently heard. On Friday nights the Germans celebrate with fried fish and beer suppers in the taverns, or with a dance at the Kraut House.

The river has become of less importance as the clam beds have been worked out. Only where the banks and bluffs have been reclaimed by parks does the atmosphere of a river city still prevail. Close to the water are the many squatters' shanty boats.

The name Muscatine is of Indian origin, derived from the Mascoutins, a tribe whose camping grounds were in a grove of oak trees on the river, four miles from the present city. In their language they referred to the site as "Burning Island" because of the underbrush and prairie fires that blazed every fall, and they themselves became identified as "People of the Place of Fire."

Muscatine first came into existence as a trading post in the summer of 1833, when Col. George Davenport of Rock Island, Ill., operator of a string of such posts, sent a Mr. Farnham into the territory to set up a store. James W. Casey staked a claim near the present Broadway Street and the river in 1835, and began the cutting of timber for fueling the steamboats that stopped, thus giving the place its early title of Casey's "Woodpile" or Landing. John Vanatta, prospector and adventurer, and Capt. Benjamin Clark paid $200 for quit-claim deeds from Colonel Davenport for the land where Farnham had held his trading post, later disposing of the land to new settlers.

During May of 1836 the site of the town was surveyed and called Bloomington, probably for Bloomington, Ind., John Vanatta's birthplace, but in 1849 the name was changed to Muscatine. On August 22, 1837, the boiler of the steamer *Dubuque* exploded and 22 lives were lost. The steamer *Adventure* towed the disabled vessel to Muscatine where 17 of the dead were buried in one grave. A post office was established in 1837, and new settlers, including many Germans, arrived daily, encouraged by tales of the rich farm lands in the Iowa country.

Muscatine became an important river stopping place. In 1839 records report 399 steamboats docked at the wharf. Ferryboats for many years formed an integral link in the transportation system. The first of these was the *Polly Keith,* a flat-boat put into service in 1839, followed by a steam ferryboat, the *Iowa,* in 1842. The first sawmill in Muscatine was erected in 1843 at the foot of what is now Sycamore Street. It was built by Cornelius Cadle, who came to the Iowa country from New York. In those days, when logs were floated down the river in huge rafts, the town assumed importance as a lumbering center, maintaining this activity for years. Pork packing, another important industry, was introduced by Isett and Blaydes in 1844.

In 1853 the Mississippi & Missouri Railway Company was incorporated in Iowa, the first company to operate a train (1855) to Muscatine. During the Civil War Muscatine was a military post with Camp Strong, on the island, a concentration point.

From the early sixties to the late nineties Muscatine maintained an important position both as a lumber and as a river town. The packet boat *Muscatine* made its appearance April 1, 1864. This 600-ton boat was 201 feet long with 34-foot breadth of beam. It accommodated 200 persons. In 1870 a single order of 400,000 feet of lumber, lath, shingles, and pickets was shipped to a firm in Omaha, Neb. A sash and door factory, still in existence, was opened in 1872. In 1891, when the High Bridge was finished, the last of the ferryboats, the *Ida May,* owned by Captain Eaton, was discontinued.

About 1891 the manufacturing of pearl buttons began to supplant other river industries. A swimmer's mishap is said to have turned the attention of J. F. Beopple, a German immigrant, to the fresh-water mussels abundant in the Mississippi and its tributaries. Beopple cut his foot on a sharp object that turned out to be a mussel. Investigating further, he discovered that mussel shells grew in beds along the bottoms of fresh-water streams in the vicinity of Muscatine. When he attempted to get money for manufacturing buttons, he was laughed at, but he persisted and in 1891 constructed a machine somewhat like a turning lathe and operated by foot power. Continuing his experiments, Beopple jealously guarded his secrets, purchasing watch dogs, and even sleeping in his shop so the process could not be stolen. Beopple opened the first button-making factory in the city; others soon followed and Muscatine became the center of this industry. About 1910, when the industry was at its height, the annual output was more than 17,000,000 gross.

In 1911 a strike by the workers for better wages and working conditions resulted in a lockout, during which the manufacturers farmed out the cutting of buttons to workers in their homes (a practice that is still largely followed). The strike and lockout came at a time when the supply of fresh-water mussels was decreasing, with the result that most of the companies moved out of the State. The 50 firms still in Muscatine provide employment for about 4,000 men, women, and children.

Other important factories make steel split pulleys, button-making machinery, and sash, door and other millwork products. A company still turns out saddles and harness on the same site where it began business as a tannery in 1845. Four food-preserving companies, two of them owned locally, assure farmers regular markets for tomatoes, pumpkins, cucumbers, asparagus, and cabbages. During the peak of the busy season in average years, 2,000 persons are employed in the canning industry.

Muscatine, granted its original charter by the First Territorial Legislative Assembly in 1838, and a revised form in 1852, is one of the four cities in Iowa operating under this form of government.

Samuel Clemens (Mark Twain) made his home in Muscatine at one time, and found here some of the material he used in his writings. He once said of this city, "I remember Muscatine for its summer sunsets. I have never seen any on either side of the ocean which equaled them."

POINTS OF INTEREST

COURTHOUSE, between 3rd and 4th Sts. extending from Mulberry to Walnut Sts., is the third county building on this site. The first, completed in 1841, burned in 1864; the second building was replaced by the present structure in 1909. The building is three stories high with a dome supported by stone pillars. The walls of the second and third stories are plain and smooth while those of the first floor, forming a heavy base to the superstructure, are rough Bedford stone. The austerity of the rectangular structure is relieved by the graceful line of the arched doorways.

CIVIL WAR VETERANS' MEMORIAL, on the southwest corner of the Courthouse Square, was first dedicated in 1875 and rededicated in 1925.

On a fluted column 30 feet high is the figure of a Civil War soldier in full field equipment, standing at "parade rest."

SITE OF COLONEL ISETT'S GOTHIC STABLES, 2nd St. between Walnut St. and Mulberry Ave., now occupied by a business building, has a local legend connected with it. Across the street is the old stone Trinity Episcopal Church. The colonel's wife is said to have contributed generously when this church was built in 1856; the colonel, not a church-going man, objected in vain. In reprisal he is said to have erected the stables directly across from the church, following the architecture of that house of worship, even to spires, steeples, and stained glass windows.

HIGH BRIDGE, Walnut St. between Front and 2nd Sts. *(car and driver, 15¢; passenger toll, 5¢ each)*, connects Iowa and Illinois. High enough to allow the largest steamboat to pass underneath, 112 feet above the river at the main span, it has no draw span, and is 3,101 feet long. Construction was begun in July 1889. The bridge is a favorite look-out spot for views up or down the stream.

MARK TWAIN HOUSE *(private)*, 109 Walnut St., alley at end of bridge (R), is a small, one-story building, home of Mark Twain (1835–1910) for a brief time during 1853–54 when he lived with his widowed mother and brothers, Henry and Orion, the latter part owner of the Muscatine *Journal*.

PUBLIC LIBRARY *(open weekdays, 9-9)*, 304 Iowa Ave., was given to the city by P. M. Musser, lumberman and philanthropist. Designed in the English Tudor style, the brownstone building is set about 25 feet back from the street on a landscaped lawn. There are about 30,000 volumes in the library, including the Iowa Collection of history, descriptions of city and county, and fiction with Muscatine background. Books by Ellis Parker Butler, Irving B. Richman, and George Meason Whicher, writers born in the city, and a collection of more than 800 pictures of the city's pioneers are other features.

SITE OF FIRST HOUSE, Front St. at Iowa Ave., is indicated by a Stone Marker set in the pavement. The house was built in 1833 by a Mr. Farnham, associated with Col. George Davenport in operating the trading post near this spot.

OLD FIRST ST. MATHIAS CHURCH, 211 W. 8th St., stands on the grounds of the present Mathias Church. This was the first Catholic church in Muscatine, erected on Cedar Street in 1842 by the Reverend Samuel Mazzuchelli, and used until 1856. The building was moved to this site in 1931 to be preserved as a memorial. It is a shed-like structure of wood, with overhanging cornices and windows of plain glass. There is no tower, but a small wooden cross, not more than 30 inches tall, tops the ridge pole. Although only the sagging clapboards have been replaced and none of the interior yet restored, the building is typical of the plain, useful structures designed by the first priests in this territory. Constructed at Prairie du Chien, Wis., it was rafted down the Mississippi and joined together in Muscatine. It is the only structure of early days left standing in the city.

The BUTTON FACTORIES *(not open to public)* occupy an area

from 2nd St. between Mulberry Ave. and Orange St., to 6th St. on the North. The McKee Button Co., 1000 Hersey Ave., and The Iowa Button Co., 315 W. Front St., are two of the largest concerns. In the beginning, the secrets of the various processes were closely guarded, and even now visitors are not welcomed. After the mollusks are killed by boiling and the meat is removed, the shells go through four main operations in their evolution into buttons: First they are cut by a machine, similar to an ordinary turning lathe, into disks known as "blanks"; then the bark-like substance that covers them is removed by grinding; in the third operation the holes are drilled and the edges are trimmed at the same time; and, lastly, the blanks are submerged in acid, washed, dried with sawdust, and sorted according to the final polishing.

HOME OF ELLIS PARKER BUTLER, 607 W. 3rd St., stands on the back part of the original Butler lot. Ellis Parker Butler (1869–1937), author of *Pigs is Pigs,* was born in Muscatine and graduated from the local high school. The building was once labeled ICE—to recall one of Butler's stories. He related that when he returned to his home town he wandered about looking for some sign that he was remembered there. Finally he saw a large sign "ICE" and came to the conclusion that it must mean "In Commemoration of Ellis."

WEED PARK, Washington St. just off River Rd., extreme NE. part of city, lies on a bluff overlooking the river, the Government lock and dam, and the Illinois shore. Here the land slopes from the river to form a natural amphitheater, and basin for two artificial lakes. This recreation center has a WILD FLOWER PRESERVE supervised by the Muscatine Garden Club. Growing in the preserve, which has two pools and a rustic bridge, are 150 marked varieties of wild flowers. The club also has marked 18 varieties of trees found in the park.

POINTS OF INTEREST IN ENVIRONS

Muscatine Island—*1 m.,* Fairport, U. S. fish hatcheries—*8 m.,* Montpelier, Wild Cat Den State Park and Old Mill—*11 m. (see Tour 1, sec. b).*

‹‹‹‹‹‹‹‹‹‹‹‹‹‹‹‹‹‹‹‹❀›››››››››››››››››››››

Ottumwa

Railroad Stations: Foot of Washington St. at river for Chicago, Burlington & Quincy R.R. and Chicago, Rock Island & Pacific Ry.; Jefferson and Mill Sts. for Chicago, Milwaukee, St. Paul & Pacific R.R. and Wabash Ry.; or Sherman St. station for Chicago, Milwaukee, St. Paul & Pacific R.R.
Bus Stations: 219 E. Main St. for Burlington Lines; 125 E. 2nd St. for Missouri Transit, Interstate Transit Lines (North Western Ry. and Union Pacific R.R.) and Ottumwa & Cedar Rapids bus line.
Taxis: 25¢ up to 10 blks.; 10¢ each additional ⅓ m.
Street Buses: Fare 7¢.

Accommodations: Three hotels, three tourist camps.

Information Service: Motor Club of Iowa, 535 E. Main St.; Chamber of Commerce, 111 E. 2nd St.

Motion Picture Houses: Four.
Baseball: West End Park, 1400 blk. on W. 2nd St.; Pickwick Ball Park, cor. Milner and Mary Sts.
Tennis: Riverside Park, S. end Market St. bridge, four courts.
Swimming: Municipal pool, Keota and Milner Sts.
Golf: Municipal course, 18 holes, US 63, 3 m. N. of courthouse, 35¢ and 45¢.

Annual Events: Morrell Packing Plant employees' picnic, Wildwood Park, Aug.

OTTUMWA (649 alt., 28,075 pop.), divided into two sections, North and South Ottumwa, by the Des Moines River, spreads over bottomlands and rises on a series of terraces northward to the city limits. Areas of homes and industrial centers crowd into the river bottoms, east, south, and west, while the main business center is crowded into a narrow strip of land on the north shore of the shallow river.

The two sections are like two distinct cities. North Ottumwa, the hill section, with its many fine homes, churches, public buildings and schools, appears to be removed geographically and socially from the industrial scene below. The rumble of truck loads of cattle or hogs along the highway, the stock trains, or the rattle of gondolas loaded with coal from the rich bituminous beds nearby, hardly disturb its citizens. Winding through the northeast residential section, roads seek lower levels, passing through, in the vicinity of Court Street, an immense gateway suggested by the towers of the courthouse and St. Mary's Church. From the business section acres of marshland—some of it reclaimed for community gardens—are visible across the river to the south.

The economic life of the city depends on the processing of pork. If work in the plant slackens, business in general is correspondingly low. As much a part of the region as the plants, the mines, and the farms, thousands of workers merge into a mass of many diverse characteristics, thronging the streets during work days and pay nights.

PACKING PLANT, OTTUMWA

The name Ottumwa is the white man's interpretation of the Indian word meaning "rippling waters." On May 1, 1843, the territory was opened to settlement by the whites. For days men with their families camped on the outskirts waiting for the signal and at midnight of April 30, hundreds of pioneers in their covered wagons, buckboards, and other vehicles dashed across the open country to stake out claims. Flaring torches lighted the night. For miles around the sound of axes resounded. In the morning it was found that many claims overlapped and some of the land had been forgotten. It is said that Wapello County received 2,000 men, women, and children in the few days of the land rush, and that the city of Ottumwa literally sprang up over night.

The Appanoose Rapids and Milling Company (organized in 1842) claimed much of the land in what is now Ottumwa. It promoted the town, and donated lots to the county providing Ottumwa was made the seat of government. In 1844 the city was named Louisville, but the present name was adopted the next year. The first hotel was built in 1844 and by 1848 the place was a thriving village. Ottumwa was incorporated in 1851 and chartered as a city in 1857.

One of the first bridges to span the Des Moines River, was constructed at Ottumwa in 1860 for two day's service. During the Lincoln-Douglas campaign there was a mass meeting in Ottumwa. The meeting was held on the south side of the river and since there were no bridges across the shallow stream, the farmers placed their wagons in two rows, end to end. End boards were removed so the people could pass easily from one wagon to the next. This unusual bridge, 800 feet in length, was built at the foot of Green Street. At the same spot 10 years later a wooden toll bridge was constructed, but was later swept away in a flood.

From 1860 to 1880 the city developed slowly, little affected by the turbulent days of the Civil War, but gradually developing in the general expansion of the middlewest that followed the struggle. In 1888, with the establishment of the John Morrell and Company packing plant, the city began definitely to turn its interest to industry, added impetus being given by the development of the deep beds of bituminous coal beneath the farms. In 1890 the city of Ottumwa built a "Coal Palace" to advertise the town. It was 230 feet long and a central tower with high battlement walls rose to a height of 200 feet. The edifice had numerous turrets, and the tall narrow windows made it appear almost medieval, this effect being intensified by the glittering jet of the coal which veneered the walls. Underneath the palace was a reproduction of a coal mine. A Mardi Gras and fair were held, and visitors were attracted by the thousands. Among these visitors were President Benjamin Harrison in 1890 and William McKinley in 1891. The palace was torn down in 1892.

In 1894 the courthouse was completed and, in 1902, the public library, thus beginning the cluster of public buildings about the public square. Following the decline of the coal mining industry, Ottumwa became the center of the packing industry.

Honoré Willsie Morrow (Honoré McCue), the novelist, was born in Ottumwa and Edna Ferber, author of *So Big, Show Boat,* and many other novels, lived here during her early childhood and began her education in the city's schools.

POINTS OF INTEREST

CENTRAL PARK, Court St. between 3rd and 4th Sts., is Ottumwa's civic center. For years after the plot was donated to the city, it was surrounded by hitching posts where farmers, shopping or celebrating, tied their teams. At the north end of the park is the CIVIL WAR VETERAN'S MEMORIAL, a tall column topped with a bronze eagle, designed by David Edstrom in 1918, and financed by the savings of school children. Edstrom, at seven an immigrant from Sweden, once worked in the Morrell packing plant.

COUNTY COURTHOUSE, NW. corner 4th and Court Sts., stands out boldly when approached through Central Park's shady paths. The exterior construction is rough-cut sandstone. The outstanding feature of this structure, dedicated in 1894, is the STATUE OF CHIEF WAPELLO, the Fox Indian for whom the county is named. This statue stands directly over the Fourth Street entrance in the apex of the courthouse, in the center of the façade. At the corner of the building is a high square tower housing a four-dialed clock, illuminated at night. The floors of the interior corridor are of inlaid tile. A single flight of steps leads from the first floor to the sheriff's office on the landing, which is connected with the next-door county jail by a safety tunnel.

ST. MARY'S CATHOLIC CHURCH, NE. corner 4th and Court Sts., of English Gothic design, is constructed of stone with tall spires, and stands on a site where the Indians once cultivated maize. The first plans for the church, with its stained glass windows imported from Germany, were laid by Dean Frederick W. Hossman, but the structure was erected in 1930 by his successor, Msgr. John M. Walsh, who came to Ottumwa in 1924. The building, cruciform in plan, is constructed of rough-faced Bedford limestone. The design of the tower is similar to that of the courthouse.

OTTUMWA PUBLIC LIBRARY (open weekdays 9-9), 129 N. Court St., is a Carnegie institution of Italian Renaissance design built in 1902. The first story is of stone and the second of brick trimmed with terra cotta. The main entrance is approached by a broad flight of stone steps that lead to a large portico, on either side of which are stone columns. The lobby with the four wall panels painted by Johannes Scheiwe portray History, Science, Poetry and Art. In the dome of the building is a mural by the same German painter, representing an Italian garden scene. The library has a collection of Babylonian tablets, one of the oldest dating as far back as 2350 B.C.

ARMORY-COLISEUM BUILDING, riverfront between S. ends Market and Jefferson St. Bridges, set in landscaped grounds overlooking the Des Moines River, is a massive structure of brick and concrete that houses the various local units of the Iowa National Guard. The SITE OF FIRST FERRY LANDING, west side of the south end of Market Street Bridge, and a large COTTONWOOD TREE, east side, under whose branches Chief Wapello once smoked the pipe of peace with Joseph M. Street, Indian agent, are interesting historical points along the riverfront.

HIGH SCHOOL, NE. corner College and 2nd Sts., erected at a cost of $1,000,000, stands on the site of an early private school known as "The College." This modern school contains a model home, a greenhouse, a printing plant, a library, a cafeteria, and other equipment. On the rear lawn in a brick and concrete bell cote is the VICTORY BELL. This bell hung in the city's first schoolhouse in 1869. It was removed to its present site in 1936 and is used to announce the school's athletic victories.

JOHN MORRELL & COMPANY PLANT (open 9, 10:30 and 1:30 weekdays; guides), end of Hayne St. between Iowa and Walnut Aves., founded in 1878, is the center of the city's packing industry. The plant, covering 100 acres and occupying 102 buildings, employs 2,200 workers, the largest independent pork processing business in the world. Upon their arrival at the plant, hogs are unloaded, graded, weighed, and comfortably penned in the "hog hotel" where they have constant access to fresh water. Government inspectors carefully check them for external signs of disease, after which they are driven to the sprinkling pens for shower baths, and then into shackling pens. Here they lose their identity as "hog" and assume the status of "pork." From the time they are shackled until they are ham, bacon, spare ribs, or sausage, they are constantly on the move. Endless chains permit the dressing of livestock at controlled rates of speed. By means of a revolving wheel, the hogs are hoisted from the shackling pen to an overhead rail from which they are suspended by one hind leg. They are then conveyed to the butcher who severs the jugular vein with a skillful thrust of a knife. The hogs lose consciousness within a few seconds and are then dropped into a hot water vat (136° F.), and by means of a mechanical "ducker" are propelled along to the dehairing machine. The carcasses emerge from this machine scraped and spotlessly clean. Again suspended on an overhead rail, rapid transformations take place. As the chain moves along, each worker performs his individual task and shortly the dressing process is completed. During transit the carcass goes through several shower baths and many careful inspections by Government employees. At the end of the line it is scrupulously clean and ready for the stamp of approval. The weekly carloadings average 170 cars or 5,000,000 pounds —bacon, dressed meat, smoked foods, lard, and canned foods.

POINTS OF INTEREST IN ENVIRONS

Agency, graves of Chief Wapello and General Street, Garrison Rock, Monkey Mountain, 5 m. (see Tour 16, sec. a).

Sioux City

Railroad Stations: Burlington Station, 3rd and Douglas Sts., for Chicago, Burlington & Quincy R.R. and Great Northern Ry.; 2nd and Pierce Sts. for Chicago, Milwaukee, St. Paul & Pacific R.R.; North Western Station, 2nd and Nebraska Sts., for Chicago, St. Paul, Minneapolis & Omaha Ry., Chicago & North Western Ry., and Illinois Central R.R.

Bus Stations: Union Bus Depot, 5th & Douglas, for Arrow Stages, Inter-City, Interstate (North Western Ry. and Union Pacific R.R.), Northland Greyhound, Inc., and White Star. Also Jackson Hotel, 5th and Jackson Sts., for Arrow Stages.

Streetcars: Fare 10¢, 3 for 25¢.

Taxis: First m. four passengers or less 25¢, 10¢ for each additional half m., each passenger over four, 25¢.

Accommodations: Six hotels.

Information Service: Sioux City Automobile Club, Hotel Martin, 4th and Pierce Sts.; Chamber of Commerce, 4th floor, Commerce Bldg., 520 Nebraska St.

Radio Stations: KSCJ (1330 kc), KTRI (1420 kc).

Motion Picture Houses: Eleven.

Golf: Floyd Park, 2101 S. Rustin St., 9 holes, municipal, 25¢; Meadow Grove Links, 9 holes, 37th St. and US 75, 25¢; Sunset Heights Club, 3119 Dearborn St., 9 holes, 30¢; Happy Hollow, Stone Ave. and S. St. Aubin St. (Morningside), 9 holes 15¢; Twin Valley, 1800 W. 26th St., 9 holes, 15¢.

Baseball: Stockyards Ball Park, 300 S. Steuben St., games nightly in season, Western League.

Boxing and Wrestling: Summer months, Uptown Arena, W. 7th and Bluff Sts., Mon. and Wed.; winter cards, Auditorium, 7th and Douglas Sts.

Swimming: Riverside Park, Lewis Park, Carlin Park.

Ice Skating: Hubbard Park and Gilman Park.

Riding: Stone Park Stables, 3609 Rebecca St.

Annual Events: State Shorthorn Breeder's Association Exhibition, Sioux City Stockyards, Mar.; Monahan Post Band Concert Season, nine events at Grandview Park beginning in June; Swedish Midsummer Festival at Riverside Park in June.

SIOUX CITY (1,135 alt., 79,183 pop.), lying along the Big Sioux and Floyd Rivers at the point where they empty into the Missouri, spreads over bluffs and river valley at the western boundary line where Iowa meets Nebraska and South Dakota. A seemingly endless series of bluffs enclose the smokestacks and tall buildings of the commercial district on the flats along the rivers. Homes on the bluff are almost hidden among the trees. Differing from the usual pattern of industrial towns, Sioux City does not crowd its people into tenements or apartments that elbow their neighbors beneath the shadows of smokestacks and factory buildings. Instead, there are small homes surrounded by yards where children can play, suburbs that are towns in themselves, and many attractive undeveloped spaces within the city that give the town the appearance of newness as well as of having enough room to grow.

The U-shaped area along the Floyd and Perry Creek valleys is occupied by the industrial and business section, with the business and civic center at the base. Spreading fan-wise from this industrial heart are the residence suburbs lining the contours of the tree-covered hills, where some of the residents can see three States from their lawns. As Pearl (Grandview Blvd. above 8th St.), Douglas, Nebraska, and Pierce Streets push north from the river, the architectural history of the town can be traced in almost chronological sequence—simple frame houses, ornate structures with towers and cupolas, bungalows, and Colonial and English type homes. In the business district the straight lines of the newer buildings contrast sharply with the elaborate towers and turrets of the old.

The river-town heritage, the stockyards and the packing plants do much to give the town a Western atmosphere. The citizens are proud of the town's democratic spirit. Almost everyone here realizes that the prosperity of his town depends on crops and litters, since the industrial life is closely allied with the surrounding farms, and Saturdays are "slow" when the farmers are planting or harvesting.

The interest of the community for miles around centers in the livestock market and packing companies in southeastern Sioux City. Late on Sunday nights and early on Monday mornings the highways leading into the city are filled with trucks of livestock for the week's opening market. The trade territory reaches as far as Montana and includes portions of Wyoming, Colorado, North Dakota, South Dakota, Nebraska, and Minnesota. Hundreds of trucks rumble along the streets of Sioux City at all hours of the day. Truck drivers loiter about the taverns and dance halls during the evenings. Like the boat hands of the old days, they add color to night life.

According to one story, stock-trucking commenced in the early 1900's when a farmer near Sioux City loaded a cow, a calf, and four or five lusty shoats into his old farm truck and drove to the stockyards. Although the attendants joked about it, the idea caught on. Other farmers brought stock to market in their own trucks, taking back loads of feed or other merchandise on the return trip.

The growth of trucking, however, was sporadic until Iowa started to hard-surface and gravel its roads. Then double-decker stock trucks were introduced and the stockyard company established its own motor truck division.

Sioux City has dairy farms, poultry farms, livestock feeding lots, and hay and grain fields within its corporate limits. These urban farms are worked by tenants who value them highly because of their proximity to creameries, produce houses, and stockyards.

The 1930 Federal census reported 1,064 Negroes in the city. The majority today are employed as unskilled labor with the packing houses utilizing the services of most of them. The largest Negro section is on the West Side, extending west from the business part of the city on West Sixth, Seventh and Eighth Streets to Panoah Street.

The junction of the Missouri, the Big Sioux, and the Floyd Rivers was important both to Indians and animals long before the invasion of the white man. Military Road, the main traffic artery northwest into South

STOCKYARDS, SIOUX CITY

Dakota, was originally an old buffalo trail that traversed the entire length of what is now Sioux City and extended southward to Sergeant Bluff. Omaha, Oto, and Sioux Indians beat a trail along the buffalo's path, and French traders, penetrating into the region, followed.

The explorers, Lewis and Clark, on their expedition up the Missouri River passed through this region in 1804. George Catlin, early painter of Indian life, described the site of Sioux City in enthusiastic terms on his return from a trip up the river in 1832. J. N. Nicollet, a geographer and scientist, also commented on the spot in 1839. The great naturalist, John James Audubon, who journeyed to Fort Union in 1843, remembered the region because he saw so many dead buffalo that had drowned while attempting to cross the thin ice above the mouth of the Big Sioux River.

In September 1848, William Thompson came from Illinois and platted the town of Thompsonville, now within the southeastern limits of Sioux City. Theophile Bruguier, a French-Canadian trader, arrived in May 1849, with his wives, their father, Chief War Eagle, and other Sioux Indians to settle along the banks of the Big Sioux at a site he said he had seen in a dream. Later in the same year Robert Perry established himself near the present Ninth Street on the creek that bears his name.

Bruguier's relationship to War Eagle and his tribe kept the Indians from seriously harassing the pioneer settlement. War Eagle indicated his attitude when he left the Santee Sioux tribe in the region of St. Paul, Minnesota, after it showed its hostility to white settlers. He joined the Yankton Sioux and was made their chief. War Eagle's friendship for the whites was so sincere that President Martin Van Buren called him to Washington in 1837 and presented him with a medal. Thus to the founders of Sioux City the Algonkian meaning of the word Sioux, "the snake-like one," or "enemies," had little significance.

Joe Leonais, a trapper, in 1852 paid Bruguier $100 for his claim, 160 acres running from the Missouri River north to the present Seventh Street and lying betwen Perry Creek and the present Jones Street. Leonais' widowed sister, Mary Ann Lapore, the first white woman to settle in Sioux City, came from Canada to join him in 1854. Leonais had raised three crops of corn on his farm when, in 1855, he sold it to Dr. John K. Cook for $3,000. The latter platted it as Sioux City, East Addition.

Political favor seems to have played a large part in the development of the town. Through the political connections of Dr. Cook, a land office and post office were opened in 1855, and for the next 20 years the land office served the territory covered by 12 counties. Dr. S. P. Yeomans, the first registrar of the land office, described the location thus: "The appearance at that time was very unpromising. There were but two cabins and the town site was pretty much covered by a large encampment of Indians. In the treetops at the mouth of Perry Creek were lashed a number of dead Indians, while upon scaffolds on the summits of the bluffs west of the town were more 'sleeping the long sleep.'"

Woodbury County was first called Wahkaw, but was changed to Woodbury in 1853, apparently for Judge Levi Woodbury, a former United States Senator from New Hampshire, as the Sioux City *Eagle,* in its first issue in 1857, stated there were more residents in Sioux City from New Hampshire than from any other State. In May 1856, by popular vote, the county seat was established at Sioux City, which had 90 buildings and about 400 people. The town was incorporated in 1857.

Although the Missouri River was a canoe route for early fur traders, it was not until 1856 that the steamboat *Omaha,* arrived with a $70,000 cargo of provisions and lumber from St. Louis, for which the consignee, James A. Jackson, son-in-law of Dr. Cook, paid a freight bill of $24,000 It included a sawmill, lumber, drygoods, hardware, and other commodities. Later Jackson had a frame store constructed in St. Louis and sent to Sioux City in sections.

This was the beginning of a regular freight service between St. Louis and Sioux City, and during the 1860's there were usually four or five boats tied up at the levee discharging freight.

When settlers first poured into the Northwest, the Missouri was one of the important arteries of travel, and both overland and river travelers made Sioux City their supply base for the long trip ahead of them.

The first Negroes came to Sioux City in the sixties as boat hands, and many remained. One of them, Henry Riding, a Civil War veteran, made a success of his hotel business and purchased other property. His subsequent actions provided table talk for the townspeople. When the railroad was put across his property without his consent, he seized a shotgun and drove the track layers away. Later, the railroad company paid him $21,000 for

CORN PALACE (1890), SIOUX CITY

the privilege of crossing his land. He again startled the residents by having his tombstone erected when he was in prime health.

One of the popular Negroes of the late 1860's was Aunty Wooden. Her opossum dinners were so famous that business and professional men bid to get an invitation. Pearl Street, the city's first principal thoroughfare, was named for a Negro woman, a cook on one of the boats that docked at the foot of this street.

The Pacific Railroad was extended from Missouri Valley to Sioux City in 1868. The arrival of the Illinois Central, 1870, built directly across the State, made Sioux City an important shipping point. In these years it was also the shipping center for the Army in its activity on the upper river.

By 1886, the floating population of traders, miners, adventurers, steamboat crews, and river travelers, had given the town of 20,000 a nationally unsavory reputation. When the Rev. George Channing Haddock came to Sioux City in October of 1885, he became the leader in the fight against licensed brothels, gambling houses, and saloons. Because no Sioux City lawyers would take the cases, Haddock hired an outside legal firm to work with him. When he was in the midst of his legal fight, he was murdered by his enemies. The public reaction after Haddock's assassination forced the proprietors of the saloons and kindred enterprises to leave the city.

An accident started the meat-packing industry that changed Sioux City from a village to an industrial city. When a boatload of wheat sank in the Missouri River opposite the city, James E. Booge recovered and purchased the grain. Finding the water-soaked grain was good for nothing but feeding hogs, he started in that business. There was no market for live hogs, so Booge slaughtered them and sold the meat. He built a small plant and hired packing house butchers from St. Louis. Others soon began to traffic in livestock, furnishing feeders to a limited territory and giving farmers an opportunity to utilize their surplus corn and fodder by supplying stock to the packers. Out of this activity came the Live Stock Exchange, organized in 1887, and the Live Stock Exchange Building, erected in 1892.

In 1887, the citizens of Sioux City promoted a festival, the principal attraction being the world's first Corn Palace. It was designed by E. W. Loft, a local architect, and erected at Fifth and Jackson Streets. Over a skeleton of wood, volunteer workmen placed sheaves of grain and red, yellow, white, and vari-colored corn in diverse patterns. Circling the dome was an allegorical picture of Mondamin, the Indian god of corn, showering the products of the region from a horn of plenty, in company with the deities, Ceres and Demeter. An agricultural display and pictures designed in corn and other grain, notably a reproduction of Millet's *Angelus,* were inside. Four other Corn Palaces followed, all at Sixth and Pierce Streets. Colored reproductions of the last one are curiously suggestive of the Church of St. Basil at Moscow. In the spring of 1889 a Corn Palace train toured the East, stopping at Washington for the inauguration of President Benjamin Harrison.

In 1889 a steam railroad line, one and a half miles of which was elevated to solve the problem of dangerous railroad tracks and to avoid the often flooded lowlands, was opened between Third and Jones Streets and Morningside. Built at a cost of $586,000, it was electrified in 1893, and is now part of the transit system.

In the fall of 1914, the Industrial Workers of the World, otherwise known as the wobblies, made their first official appearance in Sioux City. By the middle of March 1915, speakers for this organization were haranguing crowds night after night. For 30 days the agitation went on. By April 17 the jails were overcrowded and the city imported granite rocks for the prisoners to work on, attempting to force out the great number of transients that had come into town on the wave of enthusiasm for labor. A local minister, Wallace M. Short, made an issue of the persecution of I.W.W. organizers and transient workers in his political campaign for mayor, and with Sioux City's laborers supporting him, won the election. Strikes in the packing plants in 1921 and 1922 also brought the labor problem to the city's attention. The next serious strike, however, was brought about by conditions in the farming area.

During the early 1930's low prices, drought, and grasshoppers combined to create hard times for the farmers, out of which conditions came the militant Farmers' Holiday Association and the farm strikes of 1932 and 1933. The first strike in which nearly 1,000 farmers and sympathizers participated, was called by the newly formed association in August 1932 and virtually closed the Sioux City market to truckers for more than a month. Roads leading into the city were blocked by strikers. Vehicles carrying farm produce were stopped at the entrance and their contents placed beside the road. Drivers were given the choice of proceeding into the city without their produce, or of returning home with it. If the driver protested too much, his produce was "dumped" before his eyes, or distributed among the needy in the vicinity. Eighty-seven farmers were arrested in this strike.

Some farm produce came into the city by rail, and in the strike of 1933, one train of the Great Northern attempting to run into the city, was halted near the town of James by a burning bridge, for which the strikers were blamed although they were not responsible. The Illinois Central was also stopped by a burning bridge in Cherokee County.

The Monahan Post Band, outstanding among American Legion bands, gives weekly concerts during the summer months. The *a Cappella* choir of Morningside College, which makes annual tours of eastern and southern cities, is also rated high by critics. During the winter the local symphony orchestra, under the direction of Leo Kucinski, presents a series of concerts featuring guest artists of international reputation. The Civic Art Center, sponsored by the Sioux City Society of Fine Arts, was organized in 1937. Free classes for adults and children are conducted in the graphic arts, design, drawing, oil and water color, modeling, and ceramics. George D. Perkins who, with a brother, established the Sioux City *Journal* in 1870, was a prominent Iowa editor. Some local writers are nationally known. Herbert Quick, once mayor, and author of *Vandemark's Folly,* and Josephine Herbst, author of *The Executioner Waits,* both used local material and background in their novels.

POINTS OF INTEREST

1. The WOODBURY COUNTY COURTHOUSE, SE. corner 7th and Douglas Sts., was designed by W. L. Steele and built in 1918. Constructed of light brown Roman brick with terra cotta trim, a six-story setback tower rises above the main structure, two stories high and covering a quarter of a block. Pilasters add interest to the long stretches of wall. The frieze of heroic-sized figures above the Douglas Street entrance, two figures above the Seventh Street entrance by Alfonso Ianelli, and a sculptured eagle on the tower are distinctive decorations. The rotunda, 75 feet square, with murals by John W. Norton of Chicago, was intended for public meetings, but was so used on only one occasion—a public reception room for the Vatican Choir in 1919. However, during the Farm Holiday disturbances in 1932 and 1933 it was often host to crowds of belligerent farmers.

2. The OLD FEDERAL BUILDING, NE. corner 6th and Douglas Sts., was constructed under the supervision of the United States Treasury Department in 1896–97 (William Martin Aiken, supervising architect) and

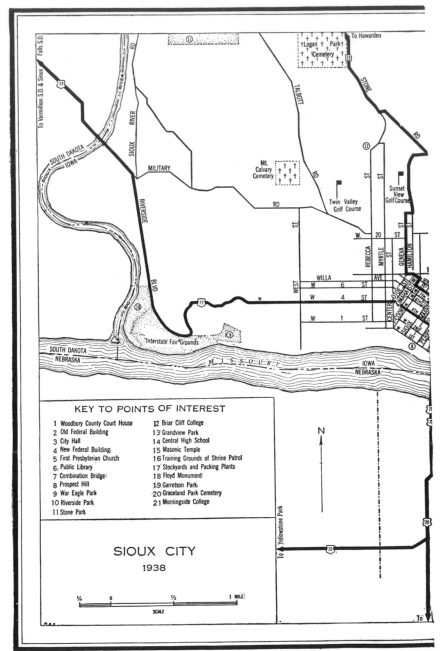

KEY TO POINTS OF INTEREST

1 Woodbury County Court House	12 Briar Cliff College
2 Old Federal Building	13 Grandview Park
3 City Hall	14 Central High School
4 New Federal Building	15 Masonic Temple
5 First Presbyterian Church	16 Training Grounds of Shrine Patrol
6 Public Library	17 Stockyards and Packing Plants
7 Combination Bridge	18 Floyd Monument
8 Prospect Hill	19 Garretson Park
9 War Eagle Park	20 Graceland Park Cemetery
10 Riverside Park	21 Morningside College
11 Stone Park	

SIOUX CITY

1938

¼   0   ½   1 MILE

SCALE

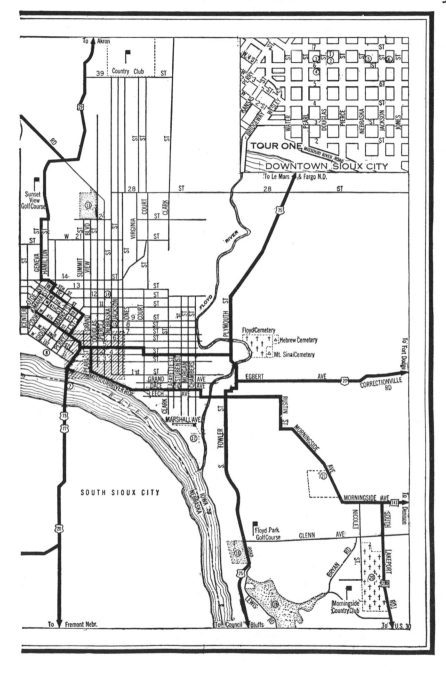

was occupied by the post office until late in 1933. The rough sandstone structure, three stories high, covering almost a quarter of a block, was designed in the Florentine style. The tower, 148 feet from base to peak, houses "Old Ben," Sioux City's town clock. In 1935 this building was given over to Federal and county offices of emergency relief agencies.

3. The CITY HALL, NW. corner 6th and Douglas Sts., built in 1891, is one of Sioux City's oldest office buildings. This sandstone block structure, in a mixture of architectural styles—Romanesque predominating—was built and originally owned by the Citizen's Library and Building Association. The entire building is now occupied by city offices.

4. The NEW FEDERAL BUILDING (Post Office), SW. corner 6th and Douglas Sts., completed in 1933, is constructed of white Indiana limestone. Of straight modern lines, the three-story building, covering one-half block, was built at a cost of $900,000. A penthouse is used by the Weather Bureau and a Naval radio station. The Federal courtroom on the third floor is paneled in solid walnut, with the coffered ceiling in bright colors and gold leaf.

5. The FIRST PRESBYTERIAN CHURCH, NE. corner 6th and Nebraska Sts., was built in 1907, of smooth sandstone, in adapted Gothic style. The first of the three carillons in the city is housed here. It includes two octaves of the chromatic scale, and is operated in conjunction with the church pipe organ. Both organ and chimes are attached to an electrically operated amplifying system. The bell in the tower was salvaged from a sunken steamboat and has been used in various edifices of the Presbyterian organization since 1857.

6. The PUBLIC LIBRARY *(open weekdays 9-9)*, NE. corner 6th and Jackson Sts., is the center of the city's library system. The two-story rectangular brick building, with overhanging red tile eaves and a flat roof, was completed in 1913. Rooms on the second floor house a MUSEUM, sponsored by the Academy of Science, and a small collection of pictures, including an Inness and two paintings by Stillman, belonging to the Sioux City Society of Fine Arts. The museum collection includes extensive groups of bird specimens, the smaller native animals, Indian relics, and miscellaneous items—among them, a plaster cast of the skull of Sgt. Charles Floyd, first white man buried in Iowa, made before his reinterment in 1895.

7. The COMBINATION BRIDGE, foot of Wesley Way, is the largest and oldest pivot-span bridge in service in the vicinity. Begun in 1891, the four steel spans measuring 1,940 feet were completed in 1896, joining the city with South Sioux City.

The bridge received its name because it was built originally for the use of the Pacific Short Line Railroad as well as for vehicles and pedestrians. This railroad used the bridge for about nine months. Shifting sandbars that diverted the current made it necessary to sink the piers to bedrock and ramp the approaches to prevent erosion. The end spans open to allow the passage of boats and barges. There are two traffic lanes and two pedestrian walks. The cost of the bridge was about $1,000,000.

8. PROSPECT HILL, Bluff and W. 1st Sts., on the bank of the Mis-

souri River, overlooking Nebraska, affords the most complete view of the
city. Early settlers saw Indian burial scoffolds atop this bluff. Joe Leonais
(one of the earliest pioneers) records there were also bear dens. A legend
relates that he drove his horse over the bluff when returning from a celebration of the sale of his land to Dr. Cook. The horse drowned in the
river, then flowing directly at the foot of the bluff, but Leonais was res-
cued by Indians from the place he had lodged, part way down the slope.

The gray granite MONUMENT in the form of a shaft on an elongated
base, 15 feet high, was erected by the Presbyterian Church in the U. S. A.
in 1913 to memorialize a prayer meeting held here by three ministers in
April 1869. Among them was Sheldon Jackson, one of the greatest of
Presbyterian missionaries. Jackson was meeting with the Presbytery of Missouri in Sioux City. When he reached the top of Prospect Hill with his two
friends and saw hill after hill rolling to the west, north and south, he
dropped to his knees and prayed for wisdom and strength, rededicating
himself to the evangelizing of the country west of the Missouri.

9. WAR EAGLE PARK, end of War Eagle Drive, on a high bluff
below which the Big Sioux joins the Missouri River, contains WAR
EAGLE'S GRAVE, marked with a cast concrete block, three by five feet and
set with two bronze plaques, erected in 1922 by the War Eagle Memorial
Association. There is a view of South Dakota and Nebraska, marked by the
winding channel of the Missouri River as it meanders through the bottom
lands past Sioux City. From this lookout Chief War Eagle watched the
approach of friends or enemies. Some authorities claimed the chief was
buried according to Indian custom, astride his horse. However, this was
disproved in 1922 when excavations were made for the construction of the
monument. Mrs. Conger, a granddaughter of War Eagle, who attended the
dedicatory ceremonies and who also witnessed War Eagle's burial in 1851,
said the chief was buried in a reclining position.

10. RIVERSIDE PARK, 400-700 Riverside Blvd., an area of 42 acres,
is the city's oldest recreation park. It was a favorite camp site of the Indians.
COUNCIL OAK TREE, standing on the Sioux City Boat Club grounds in
this park, is associated with a legend to the effect that Indians assembled
here beneath the wide-flung branches to hold war councils. The legend
has been proved a fiction manufactured for publicity purposes by the
promoters of the park in 1888, but it is still related as a fact. BRUGUIER'S
CABIN (private), south of Council Oak Tree, used for the "Girls of '68"
cabin, was lost for many years. It was not until 1934, during the razing of
a vacant house, that it was discovered. The house had been built around
the cabin, the outside walls sided, and the interior plastered over. The
cabin, built of square hewn cottonwood logs, about 20 feet by 32 feet, was
the second dwelling within the boundaries of Sioux City. Bruguier homesteaded the land on which the cabin now stands, but it originally stood on
land he technically purchased from Joseph Juette, November 1, 1856.

11. STONE PARK, Sioux River Rd. (R) at outskirts of city, a State
park, has 801 acres, including precipitous bluffs and thickly wooded valleys along the east bank of the Big Sioux River. Among the many high
peaks in the park, the most conspicuous is Mt. Lucia, named for Lucia

GRANDVIEW MUSIC PAVILION, SIOUX CITY

Stone, donor of the park. A scenic drive comes to an end on top of this peak, 1,410 feet above sea level. From this point the great plains of South Dakota can be seen stretching into the distance. Winding drives, picnic areas, Boy Scout, Girl Scout, and Salvation Army camps, and a public camping area are within the park.

JUNIOR BOYS OF '68 LODGE, near W. entrance (L), one of the first frame structures in the city, was made in sections and shipped from St. Louis about 1859. The original building was 16 by 30 feet at the base. It served as an office for G.W.F. Sherwood, a surveyor, banker and real estate agent. During the 1860's it was used as a Congregational church and later as a schoolhouse.

12. BRIAR CLIFF COLLEGE, 32nd and Rebecca Sts., a woman's college conducted by the Sisters of St. Francis, stands on a rolling bluff which overlooks the Perry Creek Valley. Four-story Heelan Hall, the first unit of a proposed group of buildings, built in modern style with traces of the Tudor, is of tan brick with Kasota stone trim. George B. Hilgers was the architect and the building was opened in 1930. The land was donated to the sisters in 1929 by the Right Reverend Edmond Heelan, Bishop of Sioux City. The campus of 60 acres includes tennis courts, athletic field and golf links.

13. GRANDVIEW PARK, Stone Park Blvd., and 24th St. between Summit and Douglas Sts., a 32-acre plot, is the only major non-rustic park

in the city. There are numerous paved drives, elaborate flower beds and a municipal rose garden. Shrubs and trees adorn the well-tended terraces. A BAND SHELL, designed with remarkable acoustics by Henry Kamphoefner, a local architect, was built in 1934 under FERA and CWA auspices. The natural amphitheater has a seating capacity of 6,000. Band concerts are given each Sunday evening from June 1 to September 1 by the Monahan Post, American Legion Band. A music festival is held in May. The loftiest point in the park is crowned with two huge municipal water reservoirs, having a combined capacity of 8,000,000 gallons. At the south exit stands a bronze STATUE OF ABRAHAM LINCOLN, erected August 31, 1924 and designed by Granville Hastings.

14. The CENTRAL HIGH SCHOOL, 12th, 13th, and Nebraska Sts. (main entrance on 12th St.), is the older of Sioux City's two high schools. The rough red sandstone building is called the "Castle on the Hill," because of its feudal architec e, marked by towers, parapets and buttresses. The student body aggregat 2,000.

15. The MASONIC TEMPLE (private), SE. corner 9th and Nebraska Sts., a light buff-faced brick building covering a quarter of a block, has a striking Moorish motif in brilliant colored tile and fresco panels at the main Ninth Street entrance. This motif is carried out in the lobby that opens into the auditorium seating 2,000 people. The three-story building was completed in 1921.

16. The TRAINING GROUNDS OF SHRINE MOUNTED PATROL (hours Tues. and Fri. 6:30-8:30 p.m. during summer), NW. corner Dace Ave. and S. Steuben St., is the drill grounds for 30 pure-white Arabian horses of the patrol. The horses are owned and maintained by individual members of the Shrine.

17. The STOCKYARDS AND PACKING PLANTS (open weekdays 8-5), ft. of Chambers St. on a fork of land bet. the Floyd and Missouri Rivers, owned by the Sioux City Stockyards Company, have facilities for handling 45,000 hogs, 25,000 cattle, 25,000 sheep, and 1,000 horses and mules. The property includes 100 acres, of which 86 acres are used for yardage where reinforced concrete structures with modern feeding, water, and cleaning facilities are provided. The Terminal Railroad Company, also owned by the stockyards company, operates 15 miles of tracks in the stockyards. The trainload or truckload of stock is unloaded on a continuous reinforced concrete platform about ¼ mile long, equipped with 50 chutes or runways. From the runways the stock is taken to open pens, such as the two-story hog house that has 14 acres of floor space. The stockyard operates its own grain elevator, and uses from 15 to 20 carloads of hay and alfalfa a day. The largest packing companies have runways from the stockyards pens to their own pens. One of the packing plants has a capacity of 750 cattle, 1,600 sheep, and 2,000 hogs daily.

LIVE STOCK EXCHANGE BUILDING, 800 S. Chambers St., is a three-story structure owned by the stockyards company. It houses the company's administrative offices, the Live Stock National Bank, railroad and telegraph offices, a restaurant, the Department of Agriculture office from which livestock reports are broadcast daily over KSCJ, and the offices of many livestock buyers, traders, and commission firms. The traders buy cattle, sort them according to age, size, and condition, then resell them to packers or farm feeders.

18. FLOYD MONUMENT, SW. corner Lewis Rd. and Glenn Ave., at summit of Floyd's Bluff, an obelisk of white sandstone rising 100 feet high, marks the place where Sgt. Charles Floyd is buried. The shaft was dedicated in 1901. A member of the Lewis and Clark expedition, Floyd died (1804) a short distance below Sioux City but his body was taken a little farther up the river and buried with military honors on this bluff. A half century afterward his grave was disturbed by the eastward movement of the river current, necessitating the reburial of his bones somewhat higher on the same bluff. The monument and its one-acre plot were deeded in 1913 to Sioux City by the Floyd Park Memorial Association.

19. GARRETSON PARK (South Ravine), SE. corner Ravine Park Drive and Lewis Rd., the second largest of Sioux City's parks, is a thickly wooded area consisting of 120 acres of precipitous hills and deep ravines. Because it is within the city and yet secluded, it is a popular place for outings. Rustic footbridges span the ravines and several of the steep inclines have stairs built of small logs and short timbers. Adjacent to the main thoroughfare in the park is a BOULDER MONUMENT TO HERBERT QUICK, the novelist. He practiced law in Sioux City for 19 years and served as mayor from 1898 to 1900. His earlier fiction successes were written here.

20. The GRACELAND PARK CEMETERY, 2701 S. Lakeport St., contains the BISHOP LEWIS MONUMENT, NW. part of cemetery, a granite shaft flanked by granite urns, erected in memory of the bishop, who was president of Morningside College. Afterward he was a missionary bishop in China for 13 years. The SPANISH-AMERICAN WAR VETERANS' MEMORIAL, standing on a grassy knoll overlooking the burial section of the organization, was placed there in memory of local men who served in that war. The memorial, 10 feet tall, is in the form of a bronze figure of an infantryman.

21. MORNINGSIDE COLLEGE, 1601 Morningside Ave., has five modern buildings and an athletic field on its 23-acre campus. The Methodist Episcopal Church founded the school by merging the University of the Northwest (Sioux City) and the Charles City College in 1894. The college, co-educational and non-sectarian, awards the degrees of Bachelor of Arts, Bachelor of Science, and Bachelor of Music.

POINTS OF INTEREST IN ENVIRONS

Moville, farmers' strike center in 1933—*18 m. (see Tour 12 sec. c)*.

Waterloo

Railroad Stations: Union Station, Bluff St. bet. W. 4th and W. 5th Sts., for Chicago, Great Western R.R. and Chicago, Rock Island & Pacific Ry.; E. Side Station, 7th St. bet. Sycamore and Lafayette Sts., for Chicago, Great Western R.R.; Water St. bet. 3rd St. and E. Park Ave. for Illinois Central R.R.

Interurban Station: Terminal Bldg. (bus station), 325 E. 4th St., for Waterloo, Cedar Falls & Northern Ry. (also S. to Cedar Rapids, bus traffic routed to Cedar Rapids over this line).

Bus Station: Terminal Bldg. for Waterloo, Cedar Falls & Northern (buses), Black & White Trans. Co., Jefferson Trans. Co. and Interstate Transit Lines.

Street Buses: Fare, 10¢; four tokens 25¢.

Accommodations: Fourteen hotels; tourist park, City Camp, Park Rd., Fullerton St., Willard and Bryant Aves. on US 218.

Information Service: Motor Club of Iowa and Chamber of Commerce, Russell-Lamson Hotel, W. 5th and Commercial Sts.

Motion Picture Houses and Theaters: Six motion picture houses.

Swimming: Cedar River Bathing Beach, Cedar River Park.

Golf: Byrnes Park, W. section of city (municipal), weekdays 35¢, Sun. 50¢.

Skating: Exposition Grounds, NW. part of city, Rainbow Dr., American Legion skating rink.

Baseball: Waterloo Baseball Park, Rainbow Dr. cor. Whitney Rd.

Annual Events: Dairy Cattle Congress (includes Horse, Poultry, Waterfowl, and Industrial Shows), Exposition Grounds, late Sept. and early Oct.

WATERLOO (856 alt., 46,191 pop.), seat of Black Hawk County, derives its support mainly from the packing and farm machinery industries. The Cedar River, wide and clear, flows through the city in a southeasterly direction. At the business center the stores and public buildings of East and West Waterloo crowd close to the stream and the stone-walled river fronts are terraced and landscaped into parks. To the south the grounds of a packing plant and, to the north, those of the farm machinery manufacturing plants cover the low lands. Buildings in the business centers were mostly erected in the 1920's and 1930's.

Waterloo's situation in a rich agricultural region and its transportation facilities have led to its development as a marketing point and manufacturing center. One-fifth of all farm-type gasoline engines manufactured in America are made here. Other important industries are meat packing (handling more than a million head of hogs annually), tractor, cream separator, and cement mixer manufacturing, and the marketing of farm implements by mail order.

Waterloo is a workingman's town with business largely dependent on the weekly pay checks. Although there are many small homes there are no slum areas. With work in the plants partly seasonal, many transient work-

HORSE SHOW, DAIRY CATTLE CONGRESS GROUNDS, WATERLOO

ers are employed during the busy seasons and then living quarters are scarce. With the introduction of trailers large numbers of transient workers made camps nearby the city, until the township trustees passed regulations governing them.

In 1845 George W. Hanna established a home on the west bank of Cedar River and by 1848 there were settlers on both sides of the stream. The place was first known as Prairie Rapids, the name given to it by the Hanna family. In 1851 the seven signers of the petition asking for a post office left the name blank when Charles Mullan took the document to Cedar Falls to obtain the signature of the postmaster there. While he was leafing through the post office directory, Mullan happened to see Waterloo listed. It had the "right ring to it," so it was inserted in the petition.

With eastern papers booming the attractive possibilities in Iowa, Waterloo and the surrounding settlements were crowded with incoming settlers. In 1858 the Cedar River rose to one of the highest points recorded in local history. Two hundred feet of the Dubuque and Pacific railway embankment were washed away. The flood waters poured in torrents through two ravines on the west side of the city, inundating the lowest portion. Settlers rowed boats through the streets and post office officials had to build a raised platform from which the mail sacks were delivered by boat. The high waters made it possible for the *Black Hawk,* a small steamboat, to come up the river from Cedar Rapids, and, for a while, the people thought

the Cedar a navigable stream, but the steamboat trips in this flood year
were the only successful ones.

By 1860 Waterloo had 1,800 inhabitants. In the following decade the
Illinois Central arrived, wheat elevators were built, the first park areas
were planned, a brick schoolhouse was erected, and a new dam across the
river replaced the old log one, and by 1870 the city had a population of
5,000. Beginning about 1875 and lasting until 1895 the city was known
for its horse races, some noted trotting and racing contenders being bred
here in those years.

Free carrier mail delivery was started on July 1, 1887, and improved
streets had their inception in 1891 when East Fourth Street was paved
from the river to Franklin Street. In 1892, after John Froelich, of Elkader,
Iowa, had successfully harvested a crop of grain with his newly invented
gasoline engine, the Waterloo Gasoline Traction Engine Company was
organized. From then on the history of the city is closely paralleled by the
history of the tractor industry. The city's population increased from 12,580
in 1900 to 46,191 in 1930.

The Waterloo *Daily Courier,* the city's one newspaper, was founded in
1858. Sinclair Lewis, novelist, author of *Main Street,* was a reporter on the
Courier in 1908–1909. In 1889, Horace Boies, then a resident of Waterloo, was elected the first Democratic Governor of Iowa since 1854. Theodore Vail, who taught school in Black Hawk County in the 1880's, and
was later nationally prominent as a promoter of the telephone industry,
claimed Waterloo as his home.

POINTS OF INTEREST

1. BLACK HAWK COUNTY COURTHOUSE, NE. corner Sycamore
St. and E. Park Ave., is French Renaissance in style. The squarish building, with tower rising from the center of the gabled roof, that replaced
the original courthouse, built in 1856, is built of Bedford limestone and
granite and was completed in 1902. There are two large copper statues,
high above the front doorway. One represents *Agriculture* (with grain
and plows), the other *Law, Liberty* and *Justice.*

2. BOULDER CHURCH, 500 Mulberry St., is so named because it is
constructed from the broken rock of a gigantic granite boulder that was
found on a farm near the city. The granite mass, 30 feet in length, 20
feet in width and 27 feet in height, weighing over 5,000,000 pounds, was
broken up to furnish rocks for the church structure. The building, dedicated on September 13, 1891, was the former home of the First Presbyterian Church congregation, but is now used by the Salvation Army.

3. FIRST PRESBYTERIAN CHURCH, SE. corner Franklin St. and
E. Park Ave., is designed in the English Gothic style of architecture.
The building, completed in 1922, has massive oak beams ornamenting the
vaulted roof of the nave and transepts. The ceiling decorations are of an
unusual tessellated design in panels. A tower, 80 feet high and 20 feet
square, rises above the rest of the building, housing the chime and a modern clock device for striking the hour and Westminster chimes at the

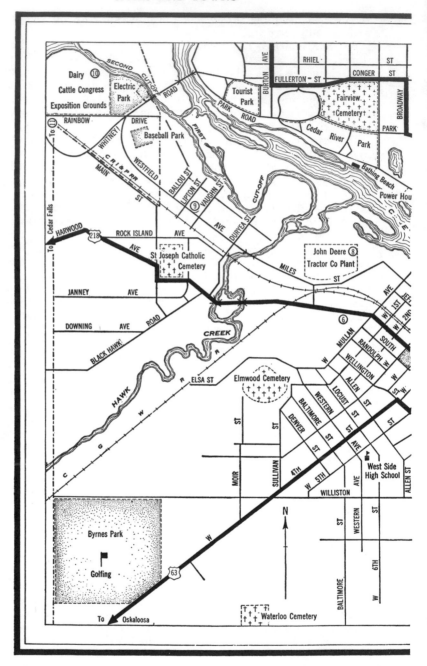

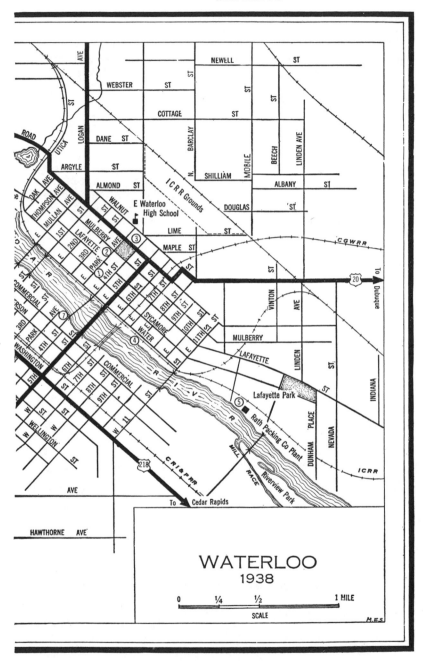

WATERLOO
1938

0   ¼   ½   1 MILE

SCALE

M.E.S.

quarter hours. The church group, organized August 27, 1854, was the first in the city.

4. PIONEER PARK, E. bank of the river between 5th and 11th Sts. (so named because it contains reproductions of pioneer buildings), was dedicated in 1935. Landscaped with rock-walled pools and flower beds, the park extends along the bank for a half mile. Among the buildings reproduced (all made from limestone found along the river) are a cyclone cellar, a cabin, and a fort. There is also a log shelter house and a reproduction of an old German fort.

5. RATH PACKING PLANT *(open weekdays; tours 9, 10, 11, and 1)*, Sycamore and Elm Sts., is composed of five main brick buildings, all adjoining each other. Constructed from 1927 to 1937, they are entirely plain except for a narrow design of white bricks at the top. South of the main buildings extend the sheds, barns, and pens where cattle and hogs are kept for butchering. More than 1,500,000 animals are handled here annually. The approximate number of men and women employed is 3,400.

6. SITE OF FIRST CABIN, 166 Falls Ave., is indicated by a marker. The builder, Charles Mullan, named the city and was its first postmaster.

7. THE HENRY W. GROUT EXHIBIT *(open by permission)* is in the Y. M. C. A. BUILDING, 152 W. 4th St. This Iowa collection made by Grout covers the following four groups: minerals and crystals of ancient formation; fossil animals, both vertebrate and invertebrate; Indian arrow heads, clothing and items; books, coins, and domestic articles of pioneer days.

8. JOHN DEERE TRACTOR PLANT *(open by appointment)*, Miles St. at the junction of Black Hawk Creek and Cedar River, covers more than 90 acres of ground, and gives employment to 5,000 skilled workmen. The company manufactures 13 types of tractors for every kind of field and orchard operation, as well as stationary and portable engines ranging in size from two to 42 horsepower. The many buildings, foundries, assembly rooms, warehouses, and offices join each other and appear as one to the passerby. The John Deere Company is the successor to the original Waterloo Gasoline Tractor Engine Company that in 1905 put on the market a gasoline engine known as the "Waterloo Boy" familiar to many farmers throughout the West.

9. GALLOWAY PLANT *(open by appointment)*, Westfield Ave. between Lipton and Vaughn Sts., W. side of river, houses the large agricultural machinery mail order house that had part in the development of

---

KEY TO WATERLOO MAP

1. Black Hawk County Courthouse
2. Boulder Church
3. First Presbyterian Church
4. Pioneer Park
5. Rath Packing Plant
6. Site of First Cabin
7. The Henry W. Grout Exhibit
8. John Deere Tractor Plant
9. Galloway Plant
10. Dairy Cattle Congress Exposition Grounds
11. Home of Clyde S. Mill's Rodeo

farm machinery in Iowa. At one time manufacturing plows, it now makes many kinds of farm machinery which it markets through its mail order department. The stone buildings follow the bizarre design of the early 1900's. The plant structure is representative of factory development just before the modern period. Connected with the plant is a subsidiary company manufacturing oil from soybeans for commercial purposes.

10. DAIRY CATTLE CONGRESS EXPOSITION GROUNDS *(open daily)*, Rainbow Dr. NW. part of city, is the home of the Dairy Cattle Congress and Allied Exposition, a permanently situated dairy cattle show of national scope, founded in 1910. On the 60-acre tract of land are the 21 buildings housing the exhibit and associated shows, the largest of which is the steel and concrete Hippodrome, 300 feet long and 214 feet wide, with a seating capacity of 8,200.

Associated with the Congress is the National Belgian Horse Show (held during the exposition). In 1936 the aggregate attendance was 185,000. Although it is national in scope, the exposition is financed entirely by Waterloo capital and the board of directors of this non-profit agricultural corporation are residents of the city.

11. HOME OF CLYDE S. MILL'S RODEO *(open daily)*, Rainbow Dr., NW., city limits, is headquarters for the show that travels through midwestern towns every summer, from May to October. Here the famous bucking broncos are kept; many of them cannot be broken to saddle. Thirty-five riding horses, all of them fine, pedigreed, American, five-gaited saddlers; and the Brahma steers, difficult to ride, are kept here during the months they are not in transit from one town to another.

POINTS OF INTEREST IN ENVIRONS

State Teachers College, Cedar Falls—*8 m. (see Tour 12 sec. b).*

PART III
Tours

‹‹‹‹‹‹‹‹‹‹‹‹‹‹‹‹‹‹‹✿›››››››››››››››››››››

Tour 1

(La Crosse, Wis.)—Dubuque—Davenport—Burlington—Keokuk—(St. Louis, Mo.) ; US 61
Wisconsin Line to Missouri Line, 200 m.

C. M. St. P. & P. R. R. parallels this route between Maquoketa and Muscatine; M. B. & S. R. R., between Muscatine and Oakville; M. N. & S., between Oakville and Burlington; C. B. & Q., between Burlington and Keokuk.
Interstate Transit Bus Lines follow highway between Dubuque and Davenport, Burlington and Keokuk; a branch of the Jefferson Bus Line, between Muscatine and Keokuk.
Roadbed paved throughout.
Accommodations of all kinds available, chiefly in cities.

Section a. WISCONSIN LINE to DAVENPORT, 76 m.

US 61 crosses the Wisconsin Line, 0 *m.*, 128 miles S. of La Crosse, Wis., on the EAGLE POINT BRIDGE over the Mississippi River *(car and driver, 20¢; passengers, 5¢ each; trucks, 20¢ to 75¢).*
DUBUQUE, 1 *m.* (698 alt., 41,679 pop.) *(see DUBUQUE).*

Points of Interest: Shot Tower; Sash and Door Factories; University of Dubuque; Columbia Museum; Eagle Point Park; Grave of Julien Dubuque.

Dubuque is at the junction with US 151 *(see Tour 1A);* US 52-67 *(see Tour 2);* and US 20 *(see Tour 12).*
Between Dubuque and Davenport US 61 winds through the hills and valleys of eastern Iowa, except for a few miles S. of Dubuque, where it traverses an area marked by high rocky bluffs, and deep, narrow gorges.
ROCKDALE, 3.5 *m.* (619 alt.), a small suburb of Dubuque, L. of the highway, was settled in 1831, but is now almost non-existent. In 1833 a smelting furnace was built here, and in 1835 a gristmill, possibly the first in the State, was erected on Catfish Creek just above its entrance into the Mississippi. Grain could be transported up and down the river for long distances, and the inland patronage from other sections of Iowa increased the mill trade to enormous proportions during the 1850's. During a storm in 1876, Catfish Creek swelled to a depth of 20 feet and a width of 2,000 feet. Thirty persons were drowned in the flood, and every building in Rockdale was washed away except the mill, which remained unscathed. In 1878 the mill burned to the ground, but was soon rebuilt.
At 4 *m.* is the junction (L) with US 52-67 *(see Tour 2).*
KEY WEST, 4.5 *m.* (841 alt.), was founded by a group of Irish farmers in 1834; ST. JOSEPH'S CATHOLIC CHURCH was built here in 1875.
At 5 *m.* is the junction with US 151 *(see Tour 1A).*

COUNTRYSIDE, NORTHEASTERN IOWA

ZWINGLE, 17 *m.* (893 alt., 145 pop.), a small village on Otter Creek, is a center for dairy and other farms. It was named for Ulrich Zwingli, the Swiss Protestant reformer. South of Zwingle, many small streams flow under the road.

At 33 *m.* the highway crosses the South Fork of the Maquoketa River.

MAQUOKETA, 34 *m.* (688 alt., 3,595 pop.), has been the seat of Jackson County since 1873, when it was transferred from the town of Andrew *(see below)*.

The ELLIS MUSEUM OF ARCHEOLOGY AND ANTHROPOLOGY *(adm. 25¢),* a new brick building, built by Frank E. Ellis, contains an extensive collection of fossils and relics. Here also is a large grandfather's clock, long ago owned by Lt. Andrew McFarlane of County Tyrone, Ireland, who served first with the English during the Revolutionary War, was captured as a spy, and later served with the Americans. A tiny moon moves across a dial at the top of the clock, indicating the real moon's exact position on each day of the month.

Many of the archeological specimens are relics of the mound builders, and there are also skeletal fragments of animals such as the dinosaur and pterodactyl. A relic of ancient tree burials is a bone from an arm that was sawed from a large elm tree near Fulton, Iowa; the wood in which this bone is embedded indicates that the body had been placed in the crotch of the tree. It was the custom of some tribes of Indians in Iowa to place their dead thus in trees. After the body decayed the bones usually fell to the ground, and friends and relatives gathered them, wrapped them in animal hides, and interred them in the ground.

1. Left from Maquoketa on State 62, graveled, an old BRIDGE, 2 m., spans the Maquoketa River near the inland terminus of steamboat lines that operated when the river was open for navigation. The Maquoketa was formerly navigable from the bridge to the Mississippi River, about 25 or 30 miles E.

ANDREW, 8 m. (870 alt., 212 pop.), was the home of Ansel Briggs, first Governor of Iowa (1846–50). Briggs, who carried the mail along the old Military Road to Dubuque (1836–1846), lived in the BUTTERWORTH TAVERN, half a mile N. of the town. The tavern stands on the site of an old log tavern. Built in 1852, the present tavern is a long stone building; the entire second floor was formerly used as a dance hall, and a dance here was an important social event. A monument erected by the State of Iowa stands at the head of Briggs' grave in the cemetery; a stone marker in the center of the town indicates the large elm tree planted by him.

2. Right from Maquoketa on State 130 is the MAQUOKETA CAVES STATE SCIENTIFIC PRESERVE, 9 m., a wooded tract containing a number of geological curiosities. Several caves and rock shelters here are believed to have been the homes of prehistoric Indians. One cavern is approximately 75 feet high, 100 feet wide, and 60 feet deep. Also in the park is a NATURAL BRIDGE connecting two bluffs about 25 feet above the valley floor, and a BALANCED ROCK, weighing about 15 tons, resting on a base but 1 foot in diameter. The caves lining the walls of the cliffs were apparently carved by the torrential waters that once swept through this narrow canyon. There are picnic facilities and a number of nature trails, lined with many kinds of flowers, shrubs, and trees.

3. Right from Maquoketa on State 64, is LAKEHURST PARK, 1 m., a 33-acre wooded area bordering the rocky shores of LAKE HURST. (Fishing, bathing, and boating facilities; picnic areas; tourist cottages, bandstand, and dance pavilion.)

At 39.5 m. are (L) the SUNKEN GARDENS (open) on the Fenton farm. The house was destroyed by a fire in 1928. The owners, who could not afford to rebuild, turned the basement into a sunken rock garden in their spare time; they planted and cultivated many varieties of rock garden plants, shrubs, flowers, and vines about the grounds, making an unusually beautiful spot.

WELTON, 47 m. (701 alt., 80 pop.), dating back to 1850, was so named because of a fancied resemblance in the surroundings to Welton Dale in Hull, England.

DEWITT, 54 m. (710 alt., 2,041 pop.) (see Tour 13), is at the junction with US 30 (see Tour 13).

At 60.5 m. US 61 crosses the Wapsipinicon River, known locally as the Wapsie. On both sides of the highway for a considerable distance along this river are lowlands that were formerly an excellent duck-hunting region; wild ducks of many kinds fed here on the oily acorns, shrubs, wildrice, and the corn nubbins uncovered by melting snows. During the spring thaw the river overflows its low banks, spreading through the underbrush, around the trees, isolating sandbars, flooding fields and meadows, until it is miles wide. The mallard, "butterball" teal, brant, pintail, bluebill, redhead, canvasback, Canadian goose, and many other varieties visited here in great numbers. Now it is only on stormy fall days and during sleet storms that the ducks seek shelter up the Wapsie, coming inland to escape the rough water and weather on the Mississippi.

Hunters formerly used a scullboat, about 15 feet long and 5 feet wide. Large enough to carry a thousand pounds, including passengers and camping equipment, it also served as living quarters in bad weather or when no camping places were available above the flood.

At 67 *m.* is the junction with a graveled road.

Right on this road is LONG GROVE, 2 *m.* (782 alt., 134 pop.), named for SCHULTZ'S GROVE, a large tract of timber that was standing here when the town was settled. About 40 acres of the grove remain. In 1838 Alex and James Brownlie built cabins of logs and boards in the east end of the grove. They sawed lumber with a whipsaw, and sold it to pioneer families in the neighborhood. The stagecoaches on the Davenport-DeWitt line regularly stopped here.

DAVENPORT, 76 *m.* (559 alt., 60,751 pop.) *(see DAVENPORT)*.

Points of Interest: the Palmer School of Chiropractic; Antoine LeClaire Park; Credit Island; St. Ambrose College; Iowa Soldiers' Orphans' Home.

Davenport is at the junction with US 67 *(see Tour 2)* and with US 6 *(see Tour 14)*.

Section b. DAVENPORT *to* MISSOURI LINE, 124 m.

Between Davenport, 0 *m.*, and Muscatine the highway follows the bluffs along the west bank of the Mississippi, dropping occasionally to bottom-lands less than 100 yards from the river.

BUFFALO, 10 *m.* (559 alt., 547 pop.), is near the point where Clark's ferry brought many early settlers into the Iowa territory in the late 1830's. Pearl buttons are manufactured here from the shells of mussels, which were formerly found in great numbers in shallow lagoons and sloughs along the river. Many clam scows once dotted the streams, and barges delivered the shells to factories along the river; but so great a quantity has been removed and utilized in the manufacture of pearl buttons and by-products that most of the shells are now shipped to the factories from distant points.

From June to October the clam fishers are active along this part of the Mississippi. The fisherman's scow is a flatboat about 18 feet long and 4 feet wide, carrying on each side a pair of upright forked stakes supporting horizontal iron pipes, 12 to 15 feet long, parallel to the side of the boat. From these pipes, at intervals of several inches, dangle chains 2 or 3 feet long, to which are attached several wire grappling hooks with four flukes, each the size of a large fishhook, called "crow feet." One of the bars is lowered from the side of the scow, or John-boat, by a thick rope, and dragged slowly over the bottom. As the boat drifts along, the bar is raised from time to time—for when the "crow feet" come in contact with open mussels they immediately close. Then the fisherman pulls in his haul. When one drag has been restored to its place on the forked sticks and its load dumped aboard, the other is lowered.

This method of clamming is the one most commonly used, though long-handle tongs, rakes, and forks are more effective in shallow water. In the

OLD MILL, WILD CAT DEN STATE PARK, NEAR MUSCATINE

past, when clams were abundant in deep water, special power dredges were used to some extent, but they have been discarded for the simpler equipment. In the early days of the button industry—after clams were found in the vicinity of McGregor, Iowa, about 1890—steamers towed long trains of clam-laden barges, sometimes five in a row with combined loads of 500 tons, to various factory towns along the river.

The fisherman's haul usually contained a wide assortment of shells: the niggerhead, with its round, flat exterior and milk-white interior, which would produce many blanks able to bear a bright, lustrous polish, was the luckiest "draw" and commanded the highest price; others, all salable, were the warty black, yellow back, mucket, washboard, pocketbook, pig toe, maple leaf, and elephant's ear.

When the clam-fishing and pearl-button industry was at its height in this vicinity in 1916, the equipment was inexpensive, the catch certain and easy, and little experience was necessary. But it was not a particularly pleasant occupation, for after a long tedious day the sticky pile had yet to be rowed ashore and cleaned before it was ready for sale at an average price of $1.50 a load. After being brought ashore, the shells were cooked in long, flat tin boxes until the meat fell out. As there was no market for the meat, it was dumped on the shore to rot. Then the shells were sorted according to types and sold to the manufacturers.

Clam fishermen still drag the waters for what they will yield. A day's wages for a good catch is not large, but the fisherman gambles on the chance that his haul will produce baroques or slugs, which bring good prices; and he hopes, with some justification, that he will find an occasional pearl. Dead mussels—the sorted shells—are carefully examined for pearls. Occasionally, lucky fishermen found pearls that were large and fine and, forsaking their trade, often merely a sideline, indulged in travel or invested in business or a farm. As news of pearl discovery spread, a new trade developed in the clamming business—that of the "middleman." The pearl trader was rarely honest; his tricks and deceptions were numerous. His business was conducted in any river town where the "mussel muckers" brought their pearls. He purchased slugs or perhaps a "shiner," and his sales, made where the light was not too strong, often gave him a large, if not legitimate, profit.

MONTPELIER, 15 *m.* (566 alt., 100 pop.), was a station on the old stagecoach route between Muscatine and Davenport in the 1850's; it was named in 1834 by its first settler, Benjamin Nye, who built several large gristmills in southeastern Iowa, some of which are still standing in varying conditions.

At 18 *m.* is the junction with State 160, graveled.

Right on this road is WILD CAT DEN STATE PARK, 1.8 *m.* *(picnicking facilities)*, a scenic area of 291 acres. At 2 *m.* the park road crosses Pine Creek just below a large old MILL *(open Sun. 3:00-4:15 p. m.)* and DAM built by Benjamin Nye about 1848. Settlers from miles around brought their grain to this mill to have it ground; the mill also served as the first post office in Muscatine County. Through the years the mill and dam broke down in many places; both were reconstructed by C. C. C. workers. Picturesque nature trails wind through the park; among the hills and rocks bordering Pine Creek, Steamboat Rock and other unusual formations have been carved by the action of wind, rain, and snow. Much of the area is covered with a thick forest of white pine and oak trees, and wild plants grow in abundance. *(Danger: adjacent to picnic grounds quicksand forms the bed of Pine Creek from bank to bank.)*

FAIRPORT, 21 *m.* (567 alt., 250 pop.), a harbor town on the Mississippi, was first known as Wyoming. On the eastern edge of town is a large UNITED STATES FISH HATCHERY. For perhaps half a mile rows of fish-rearing ponds lie between the highway and the river.

For about 40 years Fairport was known as "Jug Town" because of its pottery works. John Feustel, a German immigrant, started making his pottery about 1869, beginning with stoneware and flower pots. Feustel often took carloads of his stoneware up the Mississippi on his own boat, sometimes traveling as far north as Red Wing, Minn. The boat was called *Fairport,* but was known all along the river and by steamboat men as *The Jug Boat.* Fifteen men were employed in Feustel's factory, and at one time there were five other potteries operating here. None remain.

Clay used for the stoneware was brought from Illinois, directly across the river. Feustel hired all the teams he could get in the winter to haul the clay across the river on the ice, and enough could be brought to Fairport to keep the factory going throughout the rest of the year. Feustel also owned a number of river islands, and each winter, cut several hundred cords of wood which were also carried across the ice for use in the pottery kilns. Stores and wholesale liquor houses were large buyers of Feustel's jugs and pottery ware.

MUSCATINE, 29 m. (552 alt., 16,778 pop.) *(see MUSCATINE).*

Points of Interest: Mark Twain House; button factories; home of Ellis Parker Butler.

South of Muscatine the high bluffs on the shore of the Mississippi swing away from the river, leaving a low, flat, sandy tract of more than 25,000 acres known as MUSCATINE ISLAND. This tract is enclosed by the Mississippi (L) and Muscatine Slough (R), a narrow, winding stream. The slough runs southwestward to LAKE KEOKUK, then southeastward, across US 61, through LAKE CLUM and MUSCATINE LAKE, into the Mississippi near the mouth of the Iowa River, about 18 miles S. of Muscatine. Formerly Muscatine Slough extended north through the city to the Mississippi, actually forming an island from the eastern ends of Muscatine and Louisa Counties, but that part of the slough within the city limits was filled in a number of years ago.

For more than 60 years Muscatine Island has been known in the markets throughout the Middle West and East for the watermelons, cantaloupes, and sweet potatoes grown here—particularly watermelons, the principal crop. Because of the exceptionally fine sandy soil, easily shifted by winds, the growers have sometimes found it necessary to sow oats or wheat in their melon fields to prevent the seeds from being uncovered. In August the ripe, green watermelons are hidden in broad fields of wheat extending from the highway to the river (L), and to the bluffs (R). In 1934 there were 153 farms in this area, with a total of 980 acres planted in watermelons.

For some time melon wilt—a disease that prevents melons from maturing—has been the bane of the farmers, affecting the soil so that even crop rotation is of little avail. But during the last few years horticulturists from the Iowa State Agriculture College at Ames have made many experiments with wilt-resisting melons, and have done much to improve the crop.

At 34 m. is the junction with a graveled road.

Left on this road is FRUITLAND, 1 m. (552 alt.), a small shipping center in the heart of the melon-growing district. Sweet potatoes, apples, pears and peaches are also raised in this region. The town was first known as Island, because of its location on Muscatine Island, but was renamed as a result of the rapid growth of the fruit industry in the vicinity.

At 38 m. is the junction with State 305, graveled.

Right on State 305 is the junction with County Rd. L., graveled, 2.5 m.

1. Left on this road 1 m. is LETTS (650 alt., 329 pop.), a small inland village originally known as Ononwa. As there was another Iowa town called Onawa, mail to the two towns was continually interchanged. About the time it was decided to change the name of Ononwa to end the confusion, the Methodist Church needed a bell and fixtures costing about $600. A townsman, Madison Letts, announced that he would donate $100 if the congregation would supply the rest. In gratitude, presumably, the residents voted to rename the town Lettsville; however, the Post Office Department and the C. R. I. & P. R. R. shortened the name to Letts.

2. Right 2.8 m. on County L to junction with another graveled road; L. crossing

the C. M. St. P. & R. R. tracks to CRANSTON, 3.8 *m.* (663 alt.). At 4 *m.* is a
junction with another road; R. on this road to 4.5 *m.;* L. to another junction at 5.2
m.; R. to OAK GROVE CHRISTIAN CHURCH, 5.8 *m.* (R). In the northwestern corner
of OAK GROVE CEMETERY (L) is a grayish weather-beaten obelisk, more than 3
feet high, which has been the subject of much controversy. The inscription reads as
follows:

JOHN F.
LINDENBERG
Born in Brunswick
King of Hanover
Germany
June 26, 1796
DIED
June 15, 1873
Blessed are the dead
that die in the Lord

Lindenberg's granddaughter and others maintain that Lindenberg was ruler of Hanover, who was removed from the throne in 1866, when the principalities of Germany were united under Prince William I, and forced to flee from the country. The
younger people in the community declare that the word "King" is an abbreviation
of the word "Kingdom," made necessary because of the limited space on the stone,
and that Lindenberg was just another emigrant from the Kingdom of Hanover.

At 44 *m.* is the junction with State 2 *(see Tour 15)*.

At 48 *m.* the highway crosses the Iowa River, a large river wholly
within Iowa.

WAPELLO, 51 *m.* (588 alt., 1,502 pop.), seat of Louisa County, is a
sleepy river town sprawled along the low south bank of the Iowa River.
It is one of the four specially chartered towns in Iowa, the State legislature having issued its charter in 1856. It was named for Chief Wapello,
and the county was named in 1837 for Louisa Massey, a pioneer heroine
who shot and wounded her brother's murderer.

In 1840 a brick courthouse was erected here, replacing an earlier structure of cottonwood logs. Two courthouse buildings have been erected here
in recent times, but the old brick one remains at the northwest corner of
the courthouse square.

Northwest of Wapello the Iowa River provides excellent fishing, and
an extensive wooded area along the river is used for camping. Crappie,
bass, sunfish, perch, channel cat, and pickerel are plentiful in this district,
and ducks and geese in season are found in great numbers on the numerous small lowland lakes between the Iowa and Mississippi Rivers.

Left from Wapello, State 99, graveled, cuts through the center of the low swampy
area between the Iowa and Mississippi Rivers, just above their confluence. TOOLES-
BORO, 9 *m.,* a hamlet overlooking the junction of the Iowa and Mississippi Rivers,
is the site of mounds left by the mound builders. The mounds curve around the
northern edge of Toolesboro in the shape of a crescent. They are from 3 to 10 feet
high and from 30 to 90 feet in diameter. Formerly there were about 100 mounds in
this group, but many have been obliterated or reduced by cultivation of the land.
Many skeletons have been found in them, often in rectangular crypts of logs. The
Davenport Academy of Sciences in the 1870's sent a party here for exploration, and
placed many of the specimens and relics in the Davenport Public Museum. In one
mound, copper, mica, and obsidian were found, and removed to the Museum of Natural History at Iowa City.

Left from Toolesboro on an unimproved dirt road about 1.5 *m.* is the SITE OF

BURRIS CITY, a deserted boom town that once flourished on the north bank of the Iowa River at its junction with the Mississippi. The largest single mound of the Hopewell people (mound builders) in Iowa is on a bluff in the angle made by the two rivers.

In the 1850's a railroad line through Iowa was planned—to cross the Mississippi a short distance above the mouth of the Iowa River, pass through Toolesboro and Wapello, and thence to Council Bluffs. About 1858 V. W. Burris platted a town at this strategic point between the two rivers. He erected sawmills, planing mills, and brickyards, with the help of eastern capitalists who were seeking profitable exploitation of the West at that time. Within 60 days, more than 100 buildings were constructed. Burris' agent, C. R. Dugdale, went East to advertise the new town, taking with him several maps and lithographs of Burris City—bird's-eye views of a "great metropolis", showing a wharf lined with steamboats; a part of the Air Line R. R.; street cars, churches, park, lakes, and drives. Lots sold rapidly at $1,000 each. A three-story brick hotel, with marble-floored billiard rooms and a saloon in the basement, was erected. But old settlers around Burris City knew that the land on which the town was built was subject to the ravages of a flooded Mississippi. Burris was aware of this also, but he planned to grade the site above the high-water mark, shipping dirt in during the winter before the spring floods. Unfortunately, fall rains in 1858 were heavy and continuous. Six to eight feet of water flowed through the streets of Burris City, and boats were used to save the residents from drowning. The hotel owner found 14 drowned victims in his billiard room—and his cook caught a 10-pound catfish in the oven of the kitchen range. The flood washed away embankments, filled wells and cisterns with sand, and generally demoralized the surviving residents, who left without delay. The few buildings that remained were soon torn down and carried to other locations. Burris once refused an offer of $30,-000 for his holdings in the city; but when he left they had become valueless.

State 99 turns R. in Toolesboro, running along the bank of the Iowa River, crossing it at 12 m. OAKVILLE, 18 m. (543 alt., 389 pop.), lies on the south shore. Between Oakville and Yellow Spring Creek the road crosses semi-swampy marshland of the river bottoms, about 3 or 4 miles west of the Mississippi River. In this marsh is the 100-acre ALLEN GREEN WATERFOWL REFUGE. Green came to Oakville in 1911 and bought many hundreds of acres of bottomland, most of it tillable. The marshland gave him a chance to study and photograph wildlife. Building a steel mesh fence around a 100-acre area he used it as a refuge, and wintered ducks there on corn from his farm. Then came financial reverses; bit by bit his farm lands had to be given up to satisfy mortgages. Finally only his refuge was left. Hunters offered him $5,000 for it, but as thousands of wild fowl found it a haven from hunters' guns in the surrounding region, and as this sale would permit their slaughter, he refused the offer. Later, the State of Iowa bought the area as a waterfowl refuge for $1,360. Green has a large collection of wildlife specimens and photographs here, to which students and wildlife lovers have access. In the marsh region are golden birch, willow, cottonwood, some giant pecan trees, and many ancient black walnut trees. In early spring several varieties of native iris color the swamps in shades of lavender to deep purple. Later, arrowhead, calamus, and cattails grow in great quantities, and in August the ponds are covered with American lotus (pond lily). In the fall lotus seed pods are food for migratory waterfowl.

KINGSTON, 17.5 m. (525 alt.), a small town, is in an area particularly interesting to archeologists. More than 100 mounds, many of them containing burials, are scattered along the sandy bluffs between Kingston and Burlington. In the lowlands below the bluffs are many village sites of the Siouan tribes, where numerous relics have been found. Occasionally, mounds have been found also on these sites, built high enough to keep them above the high-water line. Formerly the country south of Kingston consisted mostly of ponds, sloughs, and lakes, but many have been drained, and the danger of flood has been lessened by the installation of pumping stations and the building of long levees along the Mississippi.

At 22 m. the highway crosses Yellow Spring Creek; at 27 m. is the junction with an improved road; R. on this road 0.5 m. into FLINT HILLS STATE PARK (picnicking facilities, golf), a 110-acre tract on a high sandy plateau overlooking the

Flint River, 500 feet or more below. Wooded ravines and gullies surround the high central part of the park area. The Flint River stretches to the southwest where it empties into the Mississippi; from its mouth the slender line of a high arched bridge curves into the smoke hovering over the business district of Burlington. At 37 *m.* is BURLINGTON *(see below)*.

MEDIAPOLIS, 64 *m.* (774 alt., 793 pop.), is at the junction with an improved road.

Left on this road is KOSSUTH, 2 *m.,* once a thriving educational center, but now one of Iowa's many deserted towns. Nothing remains except a soldiers' memorial, an old church built in 1853, and a few other landmarks. In the little cemetery adjacent to the village is the grave of Frederick Ware, who served in the Revolutionary War, first as a private and later as a lieutenant in the York County Militia of Pennsylvania. In the cemetery is a monument erected in commemoration of soldiers who were killed in the Civil War.

At 75 *m.* is the junction with an improved road.

Left on this road is the junction with the Irish Ridge Road, 1.5 *m.*
Right on Irish Ridge Road, through dense timber and towering hills to the Flint River, 2.5 *m.;* on the north bank is STARR'S CAVE *(adm. 15¢)*, a huge rift in the rock. There are picnic grounds nearby.

At 75.5 *m.* US 61 crosses the Flint River.
BURLINGTON, 79 *m.* (532 alt., 26,755 pop.) *(see BURLINGTON)*.

Points of Interest: Site of Wisconsin Territorial Capitol; Municipal Docks; Charles Wachsmuth Museum.

Burlington is at the junction with State 99 *(see above)*, and with US 34 *(see Tour 16)*.

Right from Burlington on State 16 is the AVERY PLACE, 6 *m.,* on the Lower Augusta Road, the oldest farm in Des Moines County; it is still occupied by descendants of Robert Avery, who came here in 1836. The house, construction of which was started in 1837, is a two-story frame structure of 13 rooms; built of black walnut, with white oak lath, it has enormous sills and beams and five fireplaces. Avery was in the nursery business, once the largest in the State, with more than 500,000 fruit trees, 160,000 of which were apple. A large vineyard of 125 acres produced thousands of gallons of wine, which was stored in a limestone cave 60 feet long, 22 feet wide and 15 feet high. In the front yard stands a giant yellow ash tree, given to Henry Avery by Henry Clay.

At 87 *m.* US 61 crosses the Skunk River. In the fall of 1884 it was reported that a huge sea monster, 7 feet tall and 81 feet long, had made its way from the Mississippi up the Skunk River about 100 miles, almost to Oskaloosa, Iowa. The story of its discovery, pursuit, and killing with a cannon loaded with a keg of railroad spikes at a shoal in the river (after rifle and revolver shots had failed to penetrate its hide) appeared first in the Oskaloosa newspaper, signed by John Mead. The story was strengthened and apparently verified by reports in the Vicksburg *Chronicle* that such a monster had swallowed two Negro children; the Cairo, Mo., *Post* also reported that a monster, said to be 150 feet long, had attacked a ferry boat as it crossed the river. Hundreds of newspapers in the Middle West carried the story before they learned that it was a hoax, conceived by Dr.

Gorrell, a wag in Newton, Iowa, and initiated with the help of a few editors.

WEVER, 89 m. (540 alt., 200 pop.), was platted in 1891. It owes its existence to a branch line of the C. B. & Q. R. R.

JOLLYVILLE, 90 m., was founded in 1856, but when the railroad was built most of the residents moved to Wever.

At 90 m. the highway crosses JOLLYVILLE HILL, which overlooks approximately 15,000 acres of fertile land, known as GREEN BAY BOT-TOMS. Several public dirt roads branch from the highway into the bottoms between Jollyville and Wever. Fishing is permitted in Green Bay proper, but it is reached by crossing private property for which consent of the owners must be obtained.

At 92.5 m. lie the bottoms proper, consisting normally of about 8,800 acres, lying between the Skunk and Mississippi Rivers. Lost Creek, rising in the highlands of upper Lee County, flows into the bottoms near Jollyville; from this point in rainy seasons heavy waters from the uplands spread over a large area; the Skunk River also adds its heavy stream. The entire area, inundated periodically, consists of about 15,000 acres; it is about 12 miles in length and from 4 to 8 miles wide; the main channel through the bay is 20 feet deep. The bottoms developed as a result of water backed up by the dam (1913) at Keokuk. In 1915 the district was organized for drainage, and a levee was built around the tract; large pumps were installed, the cost amounting to $600,000. Farmers paid a maintenance tax to keep the pumps in operation. But with successive crop failures and low prices, the land owners were unable to pay the increased maintenance tax and the pumps were shut down in 1931. Water rising over and through the levees soon covered the greater part of the lowlands. The bottoms are well supplied with many kinds of game fish, and are often the feeding and resting place for migratory fowl.

FORT MADISON, 97. m. (522 alt., 13,799 pop.) (see Tour 17), is at the junction with State 3 (see Tour 17) and State 103, graveled.

Right on State 103 is LOST CREEK CHURCH, 5 m., built in 1849 by the group of pioneers who organized the first Church of Christ in Iowa in 1836. It is constructed of brick, and replaced the log cabin that first housed the congregation.

South of Fort Madison is (L) a 60-acre vineyard. On this farm also are produced large quantities of fruit of many varieties, including apples, peaches, pears, and plums.

At 100 m. is the junction with State 3 (see Tour 17).

At 109 m. is a small stone marking the grave of a daughter of a Sac Indian Chief; the girl, Kalawequois, died in August 1837, of tuberculosis, a disease previously unknown to the Indians. She was buried by moonlight by members of the tribe. For several years after the Sac left this vicinity, they returned annually to the grave, removing dead branches of trees that had accumulated, and standing in silence in a circle around the small, unlettered stone. Mrs. Lydia H. Sigourney of Hartford, Conn., read an account of this Indian Memorial Day in an issue of the Montrose *Western Adventurer*, published by Dr. Isaac Galland (see below), and was inspired to write a lengthy poem in memory of the Indian girl. The poem first appeared in Galland's newspaper, and is now included in A. R. Fulton's book, *The Red Men of Iowa*.

Near here, the Mormon exodus across the Iowa country began. Following the assassination of their prophet, Joseph Smith, and increasing expressions of mob violence, the Mormons fled from Nauvoo, Ill., where they had recently completed their temple. Brigham Young, the new leader, said they left "to get away from Christians" and expressed the determination to take his followers outside the jurisdiction of the United States to some place in the Far West—where, he did not know.

On Feb. 15, 1846, about 2,000 emigrants crossed the frozen Mississippi River with wagons, cattle, horses, mules, and sheep. Continuing nine miles inland, the Saints encamped along Sugar Creek to prepare for the long journey and wait for others to arrive. The thermometer registered —20°, and the people shivered in their temporary camp.

The group began its trek westward through the southern Iowa country. At a point on the Des Moines River, now Farmington, they turned north, following the east bank of the river.

The roads were muddy and only oxen could pull the heavy loads. Six miles was at times the longest distance traveled in a day. The people lived on wild turkey, prairie chicken, and deer. In one place a bevy of quail, settling near the hungry camp of Israel, caused the leaders to praise God for the miracle. During April the rain swept through the camps causing miserable delays. Sometimes the rain froze at night, fastening the mud-clogged wheels to the earth. Such wood as was obtained for fires was damp and could be lighted with difficulty; when fires were made, rains often beat them to earth. There was no fodder for the animals and travel was still more delayed by their weakness. A few of the travelers wanted to return home, but the majority kept on, cheered by Captain Pitt's brass band, whose members were English converts. In addition to encouraging the travelers, the band brought some money to the public coffers by entertaining the people of the countryside through which the emigrants journeyed.

At several places groups of Mormons remained to plant crops and establish temporary settlements to aid the many bands that were to follow. A group led by Elder Orson Pratt crossed the Fox River and, a few miles above Bloomfield, struck an old trail of 1838, following it to the banks of the Chariton River, which was forded somewhere north of the present Centerville. A flood detained them "in a heavy body of timber", but in late April they reached a place in Decatur County, called Garden Grove, where a group remained to establish a settlement.

On May 11, some of the leaders left Garden Grove to search out a route to the Missouri River. At Mt. Pisgah, they halted and established another camp *(see Tour 6)*.

The main body had continued across Iowa, reaching the Missouri River at what is now Council Bluffs in June of 1846 *(see COUNCIL BLUFFS)*. Here they were joined by the James Emmett party, which had left Nauvoo in 1844 and wandered as far north as the Dakotas *(see Tour 13, Mormon Ridge)* and then returned to Nauvoo.

MONTROSE, 110 *m.* (531 alt., 621 pop.), close to the Mississippi River, is the site of one of the first permanent settlements made by white men in Iowa. It was laid out in 1837 by D. W. Kilbourne, after the first Fort Des Moines, established there in 1834, had been abandoned in 1836. The settlement, at the time the fort was built, was known as Cut Nose, in honor of Indian Chief Cut Nose, who lived nearby. It was later called Mount of Roses, because of the many wild roses on the nearby hillsides. This was contracted to Montrose.

Louis Honore Tesson, a French-Canadian, established a trading post here in the summer of 1799 when this region was still a part of Spanish territory. He received a grant from the Spanish Government, and was instructed to plant trees, sow seeds, instruct the Indians in the science of agriculture, and to spread the tenets of the Catholic faith.

Tesson planted a grove of apple trees. The site of this orchard was later submerged by the waters of LAKE KEOKUK, backed up on the river by the Keokuk Dam *(see below)*, which reach their greatest width opposite Montrose. In 1930 a bronze tablet was placed on a boulder in the Montrose schoolyard, three blocks to the L. of US 61—"In Commemoration of The First Orchard in What is Now The State of Iowa." A pump marks the barracks used by the soldiers of Fort Des Moines, now less than a dozen feet from the river, and the site of the old fort is marked by a bronze plate on a small granite rock beside the railroad tracks, about a half block from the railroad station.

A steam ferry *(50¢ per car; 7-6 weekdays, 10:30-6 Sun.; no service Nov. 1—Apr. 20)* connects Montrose with Nauvoo.

Left from Montrose, Lake Shore Drive, unimproved, parallels the Mississippi, here backed up behind Keokuk Dam and called Lake Keokuk. The rugged terrain is a striking contrast to the comparatively smooth country N. of Montrose.

GALLAND, 3 *m.* (532 alt.), formerly Nashville, a little village long deserted, lies near the site of the first schoolhouse in Iowa. Dr. Isaac Galland, for whom the town was named, founded the settlement and opened a school in 1830. The benches were of puncheon, with sticks inserted in slanting auger holes for legs; books were few, and makeshift desks were fastened against the walls under the windows. The building stood in a clearing on the bank of the river at the head of the Des Moines Rapids, but the waters of Lake Keokuk submerged the site in 1913 when the Keokuk Dam was built. Berryman Jennings, a Kentuckian, was employed by Dr. Galland as the first teacher, and opened school on Oct. 4, 1830. A bronze tablet, erected in 1924 in commemoration of the school, stands several hundred yards from the original site.

SANDUSKY, 5.5 m. (532 alt.), also practically abandoned, was established as a trading post in 1820. During the building of the Des Moines Rapids Canal large warehouses and machinery shops were maintained here. Begun in 1866 and completed in 1877, the canal was cut through the rapids to facilitate navigation up the Mississippi, an engineering feat that attracted worldwide attention. However, Lake Keokuk now covers both the rapids and the canal. At 8 *m.* Lake Shore Drive enters the city of Keokuk *(see below)*.

South of Montrose US 61 turns from the Mississippi Valley into upland country, passing along the divide between the Mississippi and the Des Moines Rivers.

At 112 *m.* is the junction with US 218 *(see Tour 1A).*

SUMMITVILLE, 115 *m.* (674 alt.), is a small village serving a farming community.

At 116 *m.* is the LEE COUNTY HOME FOR THE POOR (R). The home has accommodations also for a limited number of patients suffering from mental ailments.

MOOAR, 117 *m.* (674 alt.), a rural hamlet, named for Judge D. Mooar who owned the land there, is at the junction with an improved road.

Left on this road is the E. I. DUPONT DE NEMOURS POWDER PLANT, 1.5 *m.,* producing black blasting powder *(visitors permitted on grounds, but not inside fence enclosing plant, except by special permission from supervisor).* In 1889 a tract of 1,100 acres was purchased here and $200,000 was spent improving the grounds. The plant, consisting of about 50 buildings, was built in 1890, and two company towns were established, accommodating about 200 or 300 workers in 45 homes. Rolling woodland surrounds the powder mills, and roads, scenic driveways, and footpaths have been constructed. The daily production at the plant during the World War averaged 6,400 kegs, and the daily quota since the war has averaged 3,600 kegs. Despite safety precautions, there have been three serious explosions here, with loss of life. The greatest tragedy occurred Mar. 14, 1903, when one mill blew up. Two men were killed, three horribly wounded, and the stone building, 50 by 100 feet, on the side of a ravine, was demolished. Six tons of powder were stored in the cellar of this building, but the cause of the explosion is still unknown. The shock of this explosion was felt for many miles. Keokuk suffered a considerable amount of property damage. Today workers are required to wear special shoes, with no metal in them, and specially made overalls. No smoking is allowed, and a daily search for matches is conducted before men are permitted to enter the working area.

KEOKUK, 122 *m.* (477 alt., 15,106 pop.) *(see KEOKUK).*

Points of Interest: Dam and Hydroelectric Plant, National Cemetery, Rand Park, Mark Twain Memorials.

At 124 *m.* US 61 crosses the Des Moines River, which at this point is the Missouri Line, 181 miles N. of St. Louis, Mo.

Tour 1A

Junction with US 61—Anamosa—Cedar Rapids—Iowa City—Mount Pleasant—Junction with US 61; US 161, US 218.
Junction with US 61 to Junction with US 61, 174 m.

The C. M. St. P. & P. R. R. parallels this route between Monticello and Cedar Rapids; the C. R. & I. C. Electric R. R. parallels it between Cedar Rapids and Iowa City.

COUNTRYSIDE NEAR NEW MELLERAY ABBEY

The Jefferson Bus Lines follow this route between Cedar Rapids and Iowa City;
Interstate Transit Bus Lines, between Dubuque and Iowa City.
Roadbed paved throughout.
Accommodations of all kinds available, chiefly in cities.

Section a. JUNCTION WITH US 61 *to* CEDAR RAPIDS; *66 m.,* US 161.

US 151 branches SW. from US 61, *5 m.* S. of Dubuque, and winds
through hills and valleys to Cedar Rapids, roughly paralleling part of the
route of the Old Military Road marked by Lyman Dillon's furrow, and
later extended southward to the Missouri border.

At 7 *m.* is the junction with an improved road.

Right on this road is a Trappist monastery, NEW MELLERAY ABBEY, 2 *m. (open
daily except Sun., only men admitted).* The road is marked to the abbey. In the
gray stone building, medieval Gothic in style, live 40 monks, under the same strict
rules of discipline that St. Benedict outlined for his followers about 500 A.D. Living a communal life, strictly apart from the outside world, the monks—aged 20 to
90—maintain almost complete silence, speaking only to their superiors. There are no
newspapers or radios; the monks abstain from eating meat; their heads are partly
shaved and they wear beards. Leaving the monastery only by permission of the
bishop, or for reception of honors from the church, these monks rise at 2 a.m. and
retire at 7 p.m. They devote 11 of the intervening hours to prayer, religious service,
and meditation. The remaining six hours are spent in manual labor. The Cistercian,
or Trappist, order is one of the few groups within the Catholic Church that follows
such strict rules. "Trappist" is derived from the monastery at La Trappe, France,

whence came the group that founded Mount Melleray Monastery in Ireland. In July 1848, the Abbot of Mount Melleray decided to found a new monastery in America because of overcrowded conditions in Ireland. Bishop Mathias Loras offered the tract of land southwest of Dubuque, and the foundations for New Melleray Abbey were laid in 1849. The institution soon became self-supporting, and its holdings were gradually increased to more than 3,200 acres. The monks have a herd of excellent dairy cattle, an immense chicken farm, and acres of corn, wheat, hay, and other products. Recently a guest house was erected on the grounds, to accommodate visitors and those who come to the week-end retreats.

FILLMORE, 14.5 *m.* (830 alt.), on White Water Creek, was settled in 1864 when gold was discovered along the creek. The town was originally called Hempstead, probably for Gov. Stephen Hempstead (1850–54).

At 15.5 *m.* is the junction with a graveled road.

Left on this road is WHITE WATER CANYON, 2 miles in length, along White Water Creek. The Dubuque Y. M. C. A. camp is here.

CASCADE, 21 *m.* (832 alt., 1,221 pop.), on the banks of the North Fork of the Maquoketa River, was named for the cascades in the river. This village was the home of Lyman Dillon *(see above).*

Early settlers of Cascade, predominantly of Irish ancestry—a few of their descendants here still speak Gaelic—migrated from the East and attempted to utilize the natural waterfall here as a source of power. Because the dam they built was small and railroad facilities were inadequate, the town did not become the industrial center its founders planned. The dam is almost beneath the bridge just before the highway enters the town from the east. Following 1849, the influx of Irish and German farmers, who developed the fertile valley into a rich agricultural region, shifted the interests of the community to agrarian rather than to industrial pursuits.

"Red" Faber (1888), of Cascade, was pitcher for the victorious Chicago White Sox baseball team in the World Series games with the New York Giants in 1917. Faber won three games—a record equalled but never broken.

MONTICELLO, 31 *m.* (839 alt., 2,259 pop.), is on the west bank of the Maquoketa River. On an autumn day, three years before the Old Military Road was established, the first settler, Daniel Varvel of Kentucky, came to the mouth of Kitty Creek. The hillsides were splashed with crimson and yellow, and westward the fertile prairies extended far into the distance. Varvel built his home here, and for years the cabin was a landmark in Jones County. The wayfaring traveler stopped there for the night; it also served as post office, and as headquarters for the men who laid out the Military Road, begun in 1839. Other cabins and a hotel were built, and the settlement was called Monticello.

ANAMOSA, 42 *m.* (829 alt., 3,579 pop.), seat of Jones County, was first called Dartmouth, later Lexington; still later the name was changed to Anamosa *(white fawn)* for the daughter of a Winnebago chief. It is said that the girl fell in love with a young white engineer, and rather than marry the Indian her father had chosen, ended her life by jumping from a high bluff into the Maquoketa River.

A JONES COUNTY SILO

The STATE REFORMATORY FOR MEN is an institution for first offenders under 30 years of age. A department is maintained for mentally ill inmates. The men are employed in making automobile license plates and on State projects, such as the construction of buildings and highways adjacent to, and in connection with, other State institutions.

1. Left from Anamosa on State 64 3.5 *m.* to the boyhood HOME OF GRANT WOOD, the painter *(see ART)*.

2. Right from Anamosa on an improved road is STONE CITY, 4 *m.* (815 alt.), now a deserted village, in which the Iowa art colony lived during the summers of 1932 and 1933. The colony was under the supervision of Grant Wood, who in 1931 had painted *Stone City,* a picture that drew Nation-wide attention. In the sheltered valley of the Wapsipinicon River, Stone City in the 1880's was a flourishing community. The bluffs above the river furnished fine grade limestone, then in great demand. Citizens and quarry owners erected several imposing buildings of white stone: a combined hotel and opera house that was the envy of neighboring settlements; a mill; church; depot; and many private homes, including a magnificent mansion on a high hill, commanding a view of the whole countryside. The introduction of Portland cement at the turn of the century brought reverses to the community, and the quarries closed. Stone City for years was almost deserted. Then for two summers the sleepy little village awakened to new life with the establishment of an art colony. An ice wagon bearing a scene of pioneer America, painted by Grant Wood, is the sole reminder of the colony today. More than 40 artists attended a six weeks session in 1932, and an eight weeks session in 1933. The colony was sponsored by the Iowa Artists Club, in cooperating with the Cedar Rapids Little Gallery. According to the directors, it was established "because it is our belief that a true art expression must grow up from the environment itself. Then an American Art will arrive through fusion of various regional expression based on a thorough analysis of what is significant from these regions." The mansion on the hill became the colony headquarters. The family ice house, with the wooden roof replaced by skylights, served as studio and classroom. Ice wagons were pressed into service when enrollment exceeded the accommodations of the large stone buildings. Some of the wagons were decorated with painted flower boxes, and others were painted with gay designs and resembled circus vehicles. The faculty included Adrian Dornbush, the director, Grant Wood, David McCosh of the Chicago Art Institute, and Florence Sprague.

WAPSIPINICON STATE SCENIC PRESERVE, 42.5 *m.* (L), is a 220-acre area of rocky cliffs, open meadows, and well-timbered hills bordering the Wapsipinicon River. Nine burials of Indian men, women and children, were found around the walls of Horse Thief Cave, a favorite attraction for visitors. There are winding roads, a swimming pool, a golf course, a nursery, nature trails, and a BOY SCOUT camp.

At 42.5 *m.* is the junction with an unimproved dirt road.

Right on this road is RIVERSIDE CEMETERY, 1 *m.,* on a high hill at the confluence of Buffalo Creek and the Wapsipinicon River. Ossian Simonds (1855–1931), landscape artist of Chicago, assisted in planning drives and plantings to preserve the natural features of the area, which has been used for cemetery purposes since 1854. An endowment was created to add more land to the original 15-acre plot for the double purpose of increasing cemetery facilities and conserving the native wildlife abounding in the vicinity.

FAIRVIEW, 45 *m.,* on the crest of a hill, was at one time called Pamaho. Builders of the railroads neglected Fairview, and the village, like others that began hopefully, has not grown as the founders expected. Many houses are deserted, and cornfields overrun some of the former gardens. The post office that was maintained for 64 years was discontinued in 1904. Old buggy wheels are now mounted on posts at street intersections, supporting mail boxes for the convenience of the rural mail carrier.

At 49 *m.* is the junction with an improved road.

Right on this road is VIOLA, 3.5 *m.*, a small village first called Crows Creek for the creek which passes through it. The name was changed by request of the Post Office Department; Viola was selected in honor of the daughter of a pioneer settler. At 6.5 *m.*, is the MATSELL ESTATE. The house, perched atop a wooded cliff along the Wapsipinicon River, was once an outstanding residence in eastern Iowa. Surrounded by 3,000 acres, which extended 4 miles along the river, this house once had butlers and footmen, and peacocks strutted on the green lawns. George W. Matsell (1806–77), New York City's first police superintendent (1845), and a leader in the Tammany organization, purchased the land and brought his family here each summer. He built a small theater for the entertainment of his family and friends. The many hired men on the farm were ordered to address him as "Master". Failure to do so meant immediate dismissal. Today the house is unpainted and generally neglected. The estate has been reduced to 1,058 acres, and is occupied by a tenant.

SPRINGVILLE, 52 *m.* (846 alt., 598 pop.), is on Big Creek. Nathan Brown, a Revolutionary War veteran, and Mrs. Winans, a survivor of the Ft. Dearborn massacre, are buried in the Springville Cemetery.

Right from Springville on an improved road is WAUBEEK, 8.5 *m.*, a village on the Wapsipinicon River, which is the birthplace of Jay G. Sigmund (1885–1937), poet and author. Waubeek was first settled in the spring of 1855. It is rich in traditions of pioneer life, and contains many early homes and private collections of relics. The dulcimer, an ancient musical instrument, is still played by the old settlers. Seamen from the New England coast settled here, and there are relics in many homes associated with a sea-going people. The first school, a stone building constructed in 1859, stands near the south end of the village. The three-story stone general store was built in 1868 by Frederick Braun and Ignatius Beck. Camp Waubeek, a summer camp maintained by the Cedar Rapids Council of Boy Scouts of America, overlooks the river.

At 58 *m.* is the junction with State 13 *(see Tour 2B)*.

MARION, 60 *m.* (848 alt., 4,348 pop.), by Indian Creek, was formerly the seat of Linn County, at present it is known chiefly as a major division point of the C. M. St. P. & P. R. R. The town was named in honor of Gen. Francis Marion, officer in the Revolutionary War. Because of its luxuriant growth of shade trees, it is often called Grove City. The First National Bank here was established in 1863, and has been in continuous existence ever since.

EAST STAR MILL, erected on Indian Creek in 1863, is still in operation at the western edge of town. At the southwestern edge is a park with picnicking facilities and a swimming pool.

CEDAR RAPIDS, 66 *m.* (733 alt., 56,097 pop.) *(see CEDAR RAPIDS)*.

Points of Interest: Municipal Island; Quaker Oats Plant; Coe College.

Cedar Rapids is at the junction with US 30 *(see Tour 13)* and with State 11 *(see Tour 2A)*; US 151 terminates here and the route continues on US 218.

Section b. CEDAR RAPIDS *to* JUNCTION WITH US 61; *108 m.,*
US 218.

Between Cedar Rapids, 0 *m.,* and Iowa City US 218 has more hills and
turns than any other similar length of paved road in the State. The highway passes along the high ridge between the valleys of the Cedar River
(L.) and of the Iowa River (R) for about 12 miles, and skirts the high
bank of the Iowa River for most of the remaining distance. Occasional
plots of well-tilled land are on the slopes of the hills, but for the most
part, trees and undergrowth line the valleys. Much of the land in this
region is still uncultivated, and native wild flowers grow in abundance.

At 6 *m.* is the junction with an unimproved road.

Left on this road is the site of WESTERN COLLEGE, 0.5 *m.,* an abandoned town.
Western College, founded here in 1857 by the United Brethren in Christ, was in
1881 transferred to Toledo, Iowa, where it was known as Leander Clark College; it
was merged with Coe College at Cedar Rapids in 1919.

NORTH LIBERTY, 18 *m.* (801 alt., 161 pop.), a settlement laid out
in 1857, is at the junction with an improved road.

Left on this road to LAKE MACBRIDE STATE PARK, 5 *m.,* on the Iowa River,
a woodland preserve for wildlife and game, containing almost every type of flora
and fauna native to Iowa. A 600-foot dam has been erected just below the confluence of two small creeks, at the west side of the park, creating a lake extending a
mile or more up the valley of each creek. One branch angles northward, the other
extends eastward roughly forming a letter Y. A road, paralleling the lower fork of
the lake, leads to the park entrance. The COTTAGE AREA is on the high ridge between the two forks of the lake; MOOSE LODGE and the bathing beach and bathhouse are on the shore of the upper fork. A drive leads past the CUSTODIAN'S COT-
TAGE to the bridge, where it crosses the lake, leaving the park at the west side. The
park was named for Thomas H. Macbride (1848–1934), an ardent conservationist, and formerly president of the University of Iowa.

IOWA CITY, 24 *m.* (685 alt., 15,340 pop.) *(see IOWA CITY).*

Points of Interest: State University; Old Capitol.

Iowa City is at the junction with US 6 *(see Tour 14).*

South of Iowa City are numerous hills and valleys covered with thick
woods. Southeastern Iowa, between the valleys of the Des Moines and Mississippi Rivers, is a deeply eroded region, and much of the fertile soil has
escaped into the channels of the two rivers. The highway roughly follows
the high lands (R) bordering the Mississippi River valley; to the L. the
country slopes away to the lowlands, broken by occasional bluffs.

At 27.5 *m.,* is the junction with a dirt road.

Left on this road is INDIAN LOOKOUT, 0.5 *m.,* a high bluff commanding a view
of several miles up and down the river. Legend has it that Indian squaws watched
here for the return of their braves from wars with other tribes.

At 50*m.* is the junction with State 2 *(see Tour 15).*

CRAWFORDSVILLE, 56 *m.* (731 alt., 291 pop.), the oldest town in
Washington County, was first named Nealtown, for J. W. Neal and his
brothers who laid out the town site. Later, as a partial inducement to
secure the services of a physician, Dr. Crawford, they changed the name to
Crawfordsville.

At 62 *m.* is the junction with State 78.

Right on this road is WAYLAND, 6 *m.* (738 alt., 625 pop.), a colony of Amish-Mennonites. Their forefathers, for the most part, settled in Pennsylvania after migrating from Germany and Switzerland. There is a much larger settlement of the Amish in southwestern Johnson County at the town of Amish, who retain the old customs of wearing chin whiskers—but no mustaches—and of cutting their hair in a long straight bob, always parted in the middle. Suspenders are strictly prohibited, and all music but hymns is taboo. In the community of Amish are five churches of a semi-liberal type, and two "house churches" the orthodox type; in the latter it is the practice to draw out each word of a hymn to the fullest extent of the breath, taking perhaps 10 minutes to sing 3 or 4 lines in an ordinary song. The group in Henry County, numbering 2,500, are known as Amish-Mennonites and Progressive Mennonites. They are a thrifty people, and accept modern farming methods and the public school system. There are two Progressive Churches, one in Wayland and the other, 4.5 miles to the NE. Outstanding tenets of their religion are pacifism and non-participation in civil government. When they entered the United States the Government acknowledged this principle and classed the Amish, along with Quakers and Dunkards, as noncombatants.

SWEDESBURG, 64 *m.,* a small village bordering the highway (R), was so named because of the large number of Swedish immigrants in the town at the time of its organization.

MOUNT PLEASANT, 74 *m.* (729 alt., 3,743 pop.) *(see Tour 16),* is at the junction with US 34 *(see Tour 16).*

Right from Mt. Pleasant on State 133, graveled, to OAKLAND MILLS STATE PARK, 4 *m.,* lying along both banks of the Skunk River. The old water-mill and dam, for which the park was named, have long since been replaced by a modern hydroelectric plant. The entire area of 111 acres is heavily timbered, and the topography is rugged. There are nature trails, parking and picnic areas.

At 83 *m.* is the junction with State 125, graveled.

Right on this road is SALEM, 3 *m.* (717 alt., 460 pop.), which was settled about 1835 by Quakers from North and South Carolina, and later from Ohio, Illinois, and Indiana. It was the earliest Quaker settlement W. of the Mississippi. Quakers were active in assisting slaves to escape by means of the Underground Railroad. The old LEWELLING HOMESTEAD, an imposing stone house still standing, was one of the refuges for slaves. The ISAAC GIBSON HOUSE was also an underground station. Shaded by cedar trees, it stands on a side street a little distance from the highway at the eastern edge of town. In the cellar, several doors open into separate cells. The doors are strongly made and strongly barred. Formerly there was a passage capable of holding several runaway slaves. It is partly filled with water now, but at one side is a filling where a former tunnel led from the cell to the outside. Iron bars at the window still remain on the building.

The Quakers have a tradition of simple living and plain language. Men once sat on one side of the meeting-house, and women on the other. There was no music used in the religious services, the nearest approach being the chant or rhythm that one who felt deeply gave to his words. Public worship was held twice a week.

Harry C. Pidgeon, born near Salem in 1869, made a 35,000-mile voyage around the world, starting Nov. 18, 1921, returning Oct. 31, 1925, in a boat of his own construction. He christened it the *Islander,* and sailed in a leisurely fashion. He slept with the tiller lashed hard over so that his craft would move only in a circle.

DONNELLSON, 96 *m.* (704 alt., 581 pop.), was first surveyed in the spring of 1881 by H. A. Summers for Esten A. Donnell and others.

Donnellson is at the junction with State 3 *(see Tour 17).*

At 108 *m.* is the junction with US 61 *(see Tour 1),* 12 miles N. of Keokuk.

Tour 2

(Rochester,   Minn.)—Decorah—Dubuque—Bellevue—Sabula—Clinton
—Davenport—(Jacksonville, Ill.); US 52, US 52-67, US 67.
Minnesota Line to Illinois Line, 228 m.

C. M. St. P. & P. R. R. parallels this route between Decorah and Monona, and between Guttenberg and Davenport; C. R. I. & P. R. R., between Decorah and Postville; C. G. W. R. R., between Durango and Dubuque; Cl., Dav. & So. R. R. and
the Dav. R. I. & NW. El. R. R. between Clinton and Davenport.
Jefferson Bus Line and Northland Greyhound Line follow US 52 between Minnesota Line and Dubuque; Burlington Bus Line follows US 67 between Clinton and
Illinois Line.
Roadbed paved, except 55 m., graveled, between Dubuque and Almont.
Accommodations of all kinds available, chiefly in cities.

Section a. MINNESOTA LINE *to* DUBUQUE, *122 m., US 52.*

US 52 crosses the Minnesota Line 53 miles S. of Rochester, Minn., and
for about 45 miles skirts the western edge of a scenic region.

BURR OAK, 3 *m.* (1,212 alt.), on the banks of a small, clear stream,
was first settled in 1850, and grew up in a grove of native burr oak trees
on the old Dubuque-St. Paul trail, which is roughly followed by the route
of the present highway.

At 13.9 *m.* is the junction with an improved dirt road.

Left on this road to the junction with another dirt road, 0.5 *m.*
1. Left here 0.2 *m.* along the bank of a shallow, rapid stream to the end of the
road. From here a pathway leads up the side of a cliff along the rock-strewn bed of
the stream, about 200 feet, to DUNNING SPRINGS. A large cave has been worn by
erosion in the side of a rock bluff, and just outside the cave a spring of unusual
size bursts forth and tumbles down the canyon.
2. Right 1 *m.* to the DECORAH ICE CAVE *(adm. 15¢),* in a high rocky bluff overlooking the Upper Iowa River. The cave is more than 200 feet deep, about 75 feet
of which is open to visitors; it was formed when a stone slab slipped from the face
of the cliff and left a great gap in the rock. Limestone in this region is honey-
combed with fissures, which retain the cold temperatures of winter far into the
summer months. As the moisture-laden air of spring and summer enters the cave,
the moisture is condensed, forming a coating of crystalline, transparent ice, several
inches thick, on the inner walls of the cave. By late fall and early winter usually
enough warm air has entered to melt the ice. Thus within the cavern is the phenomenon of ice in summer followed by warmth in early winter. A path leads from
the cave up the side of the cliff to a rocky promontory, which offers an excellent
view of the city of Decorah and the surrounding valley.

At 14 *m.* is the junction with an improved road.

Right on this road 0.5 *m.* to the TWIN SPRINGS STATE GAME PRESERVE,
where trout, exclusively, are reared for stocking spring-fed streams in northeastern
Iowa. Huge springs from which the park receives its name, supply water for the
fish ponds.

DECORAH, 15 *m.* (875 alt., 4,581 pop.), seat of Winneshiek County,

THE UPPER IOWA

is on the banks of the Upper Iowa River, in the center of a region rich in historic features and geological phenomena. The town was named for Chief Waukon Decorah (Indian, Waa-kaun-see-kaa, *the rattlesnake*), who aided the white men during the Black Hawk War. Waukon was the council chief and orator of his tribe.

The county was named for Winneshiek, chief of the Winnebago Indians, who camped along the valley of the Upper Iowa River. His name is properly Winnishig (*a dirty person who is lying down*). In his own language he was called Wa-ken-ja-goo-gah (*coming thunder*), and was also known as We-lou-shi-ga (*ties them up* or *had them tied up*).

Easterners and English settlers were attracted by the water power available on the Upper Iowa River and, following these, came Norwegian pioneers who made Decorah a center for their people west of the Mississippi. The Decorah *Posten,* a semi-weekly newspaper, has (1938) the largest circulation of any newspaper published in the Norwegian language in the United States.

LUTHER COLLEGE, where students are prepared for the Lutheran ministry, observed the 75th anniversary of its founding in 1936. The DECORAH COLLEGE FOR WOMEN was organized in 1932.

Maintained by Luther College is the NORWEGIAN-AMERICAN HISTORICAL MUSEUM (*adm. 10¢; open 2-5 p.m. Sun. in summer; by appointment in winter*), which was formally opened in June 1933. The people of Norwegian birth and descent in the United States have seriously undertaken the task of creating here an historical museum containing collections clearly illustrating their conditions of life and culture from the time their ancestors first set foot on American soil.

To preserve a true picture of the days of the ox yoke and grain cradles, a group of typical pioneer buildings was built on Luther College campus, along Main Street, as a part of the museum. Among them are several pioneer homes, a log schoolhouse, a parsonage, a drying house of the kind in which grain and malt were dried before grinding, and a hand gristmill; all have typical furnishings.

Among exhibits sent from Norway are wedding costumes, intricately carved chests, collections of wooden ale mugs and drinking bowls, a bridal crown of gold and silver, and a number of ancient fishing boats. In the center of the main floor of the museum is a four-room house of the style popular in Norway in the 1850's, when the first emigrants left that country for America. The house is furnished entirely with articles and materials brought from the old country.

Beyond the cabin group on the campus and adjacent to US 52 is a SWIMMING POOL.

Decorah is at the junction with State 9 (*see Tour 10*). At 24 m. is the junction with State 325, graveled.

Right on this road is SPILLVILLE, 7 *m.* (304 pop.), a small village, where Antonin Dvorak, the Bohemian composer, spent the summer of 1893. Along the banks of the quiet Turkey River at the southeast corner of town, Dvorak is said to have found inspiration for many beautiful melodies he used in his later works. A large monument on the bank of the river has been erected in commemoration of his

RUINS OF BARRACKS, FORT ATKINSON STATE PARK

visit, and the surrounding area has been made a park. The old square, brick and stone, two-story *DVORAK HOUSE* where the composer lived with his family is in the village. Here he worked on some of his great compositions—*String Quartette in F Major, Opus 96,* and the last movement of his *New World Symphony,* an impressionistic interpretation of America. In the center of town is a circular SOLDIERS' MEMORIAL; L., one block from the memorial, is the magnificent ST. WENCESLAUS CHURCH, a reproduction of the cathedral at Kuttenberg, where Dvorak played the organ during his visit here.

Right from Spillville 4 *m.* on a graveled road to the BILY BROTHERS CLOCK FARM *(adm. 10¢).* The Bily (pronounced Bee-ly) brothers, Czechoslovakian natives, have carved a number of huge clocks from different kinds of wood. Several of them are more than nine feet high, and all have musical mechanisms connected with the clock mechanisms. An enthusiastic visitor has termed the brothers "poets in wood", for the extraordinarily elaborate carving on the clocks shows a variety of historic, religious, and other scenes.

CALMAR, 26 *m.* (1,262 alt., 915 pop.), another Czech town, is a shipping center for hay, corn, and flax. Calmar was an important division point on the C. M. St. P. & P. R. R. until the large roundhouse maintained here was abandoned and division points established at Mason City and Marquette. A hotel of unusual size for so small a town was usually filled with railroad employees, but now it is empty most of the time, except for a brief tourist season.

Just E. of Calmar is WHISKEY GROVE, so named because it was a favorite meeting place of soldiers from Fort Atkinson *(see below)* on payday, when a half-breed Indian would dispense a barrel of whiskey he had procured at Fort Crawford, Wis. Officers at Fort Atkinson sought to find the man who sold the liquor, but for a long time they learned nothing. The soldiers refused to betray their half-breed friend.

Calmar is at the junction with State 11 *(see Tour 2A)*.

Right on State 24, graveled, is FORT ATKINSON, 5 *m.* (1,021 alt., 305 pop.), a small village on the Turkey River, inhabited largely by people of Czechoslovakian descent. On a high bluff overlooking the town is OLD FORT ATKINSON within FORT ATKINSON STATE PARK. This fort was built by the Federal Government in 1840, to protect the Winnebago from the Sac and Fox and the Sioux. Part of a two-story barracks, one blockhouse, and one magazine house remain as they were when the fort was occupied. One blockhouse that was torn down has now been completely restored to its original appearance. Southward, below the bluff, the countryside is seen for miles around. On the side of the hill, below one of the blockhouses, part of a quarry remains, from which rock was taken to build the fort. Another building, standing between the restored blockhouse and the old barracks, was formerly an officers' quarters, and then a farmhouse until the site was taken over by the State.

The northern Iowa prairies W. of Fort Crawford, Wis., were the hunting grounds of various Indian tribes, including the Sioux, Sacs, and Foxes. In the interest of peace, and particularly as a protection against the attacks of the Sioux, a strip of land 40 miles wide was designated by the Government as neutral territory to be left unoccupied.

OSSIAN, 33 *m.* (1,271 alt., 740 pop.), was named for the Irish poet, Ossian, and for the town's first settler, John Ossian Porter, a native of Pennsylvania. Ossian *(little deer)* was a hero and pagan poet of the third century, who told in verse the Gaelic legends of Finn and his warrior band.

CASTALIA, 38 *m.* (1,240 alt., 200 pop.), lies on the route of the old Military Trail, between Fort Crawford, Wis. and Fort Atkinson, Iowa. According to an old story, the village was known as "Rattletrap" owing to the loquacity of the wife of the first settler, Hamilton Campbell, who, it is believed, came here in 1848.

At Castalia is a RECEIVING STATION for the Carnation Milk Co. at Waverly, the only one of its kind in the State. The milk is electrically cooled to a temperature of 35° and then transported to Waverly in insulated tanks that maintain the low temperature.

At 43 *m.* is the junction with US 18 *(see Tour 11)*.

POSTVILLE, 44 *m.* (1,192 alt., 1,060 pop.), was named for Joel Post, who built a house here in 1841, when the surrounding country was an unbroken wilderness inhabited by Indians. The house was a log structure on the trail between Fort Atkinson and Fort Crawford, and soldiers occasionally stopped here when they brought the mail from Fort Crawford.

A GRAIN ELEVATOR was built in 1864 by "Diamond Jo" Reynolds, steamboat and railroad financier, when Postville was the northern terminus of the C. M. St. P. & P. R. R. in Iowa.

Two CHEESE FACTORIES here have a combined annual output of over 350,000 pounds. Neighboring creameries convert their cream into butter. The town is one of the chief contributors to the State's cheese production, which is large.

Postville is in the heart of a rugged and picturesque region. Dense forests cling to the sides of valleys, bordering clear, rapid streams that provide excellent trout fishing. Farmers find the rocky surface hampers cultivation of the land, but the abundant water supply maintains fine pasture land for dairy cattle. Dairying is the principal activity in this part of the State, and many large eastern cities buy their entire supply of butter from the area. The region was settled chiefly by German, Dutch, Norwegian, and Czechoslovakian people.

Left from Postville on State 51 is the LLOYD BRUCE FARM, 14 *m.*, of 98 acres, used for raising turkeys of the Mammoth Bronze Type; in 1936 almost 4,000 were raised here, divided into two flocks. Each flock is kept in a fenced area of about one acre, and each week or so it is shifted to an adjoining acre. The "poults" are ordered in early spring from a commercial hatchery, and then handled and fed as nearly as possible under natural conditions until ready for market. At night the turkeys roost on range houses, in the center of the fenced area, lighted by lanterns, and are well guarded at all times. About half of the entire flock is marketed for Thanksgiving, the rest for the Christmas season.

LUANA, 51 *m.* (1,128 alt., 186 pop.), named for Luana Scott, wife of William S. Scott, an early settler, was organized with the advent of the C. M. St. P. & P. R. R. in the early 1850's. The town has a FARMERS' COOPERATIVE CREAMERY established in 1910.

MONONA, 55 *m.* (1,215 alt., 1,163 pop.), largely a community of retired farmers, was named for an Indian girl who, believing her white lover had been slain by her people, jumped from a high rock into the Mississippi River. Although the group of men who named the town discovered the girl's name was Winona, the original name was not changed.

A sign near the highway in Monona points the way to the residence of Gust Pufahl, which contains a remarkable COLLECTION OF WOOD CARVINGS, made by Pufahl. Each exhibit in this collection, which has taken 15 years to complete, is carved from a single block of wood, without the use of pegs or glue. The collection includes a 20 foot chain, complete with hook; scissors as small as 1/32 inch in diameter and 5/16 inch in length, so cleverly made that they open and close as easily as scissors made of metal. A set of furniture, carved from match sticks, is mounted on cardboard, and includes two chairs, a table, a rocking chair, a washstand, a cot, and a cradle containing the figure of a baby.

In Monona and the surrounding community are many families of Scottish descent. It was in this vicinity that 12 Scots established a cooperative colony, Clydesdale, in 1850, now extinct.

At FROELICH, 62 *m.* (1,017 alt., 50 pop.), is an old-time country crossroads store, still doing business after more than 70 years. Froelich, named for a German family who were among the first settlers of the community and on whose land the town was platted, is at the junction with State 13 (*see Tour 2B*) and US 18 (*see Tour 11*).

At 71 *m.* is the junction with an improved road.

Right on this road is the frame MARK B. SHERMAN HOUSE, 4 *m.*, used at present as a garage. The barn, built in 1847, is still in use, and in its basement are cedar posts, 16 inches in diameter, which were used as supports when it was built.

GARNAVILLO, 72 *m.* (1,066 alt., 365 pop.), named Jacksonville in 1844, was given its present name in 1846 by Judge Samuel Murdock, for a town in Ireland. The main street follows closely the Dubuque-St. Paul trail. One of the remaining landmarks is the GOLDEN CALF HOTEL, once a first class hostelry, now a dilapidated shack.

Garnavillo, though its population is small, is a music center for this vicinity; a $12,000 pipe organ is in St. Paul's Church.

PIONEER ROCK CHURCH, 77 *m.* (L), in the ghost village of Ceres, was built by the first members of St. Peter's German United Evangelical Lutheran congregation in 1858; regular services have not been conducted for many years, but occasionally weddings or special services are held here. The interior, with its short-back pews, a pulpit with winding stairs, and an ancient organ, remains unchanged from pioneer times. The vestry has been made a relic room and many treasured objects connected with early Iowa history are kept there.

The highway runs eastward for a few miles, among the Mississippi bluffs, and drops more than 400 feet to the bed of the river.

GUTTENBERG, 83 *m.* (620 alt., 1,918 pop.), was first known as Prairie La Porte. The name was later changed to Guttenberg, for the German inventor of the printing press, Johann Gutenberg. The change in spelling was due to an error in the first plat of the site filed in the county records.

Guttenberg, lying along the west bank of the Mississippi River, is connected with the opposite side of the river by a ferry. The original settlement was made in 1834. In 1845 the Western Settlement Society, of Cincinnati, colonized the town with German immigrants, many of whom were intellectuals who had fled from military service in Europe. For more than half a century the German language prevailed in the community and Old World customs and traditions held sway.

When the Mississippi was a steamboat waterway huge stone warehouses, now empty and silent along the Guttenberg levees, rang with the shouts of roustabouts. One of the dams in the system of 26 dams and locks for the canalization of the upper Mississippi was constructed in 1936–1937 directly opposite Guttenberg.

Right from Guttenberg on a dirt road to OSTERDOCK, 5 *m.* (92 pop.). Two ICE CAVES just outside the village, in the bluffs bordering the Turkey River, are similar to the Decorah Ice Cave *(see above).*

US 52 closely follows the Mississippi River for several miles before turning directly south across the Turkey River and ascending the bluffs.

At 94.5 *m.* is the junction with an unimproved road.

Right on this road to WHITE PINE HOLLOW STATE PARK, 3.5 *m.* The park abounds with unusual rock formations, exquisite wild flowers, and almost every kind of tree native to this locality. Here, too, is the last remaining stand of white pine in Iowa, part of a huge forest that once extended hundreds of miles to the north. Not only have the great forests vanished, but much of the bird life has disappeared including the passenger pigeons, which at one time flew across Iowa in such numbers that they darkened the sky, appearing during the late 1860's to be long clouds moving southward in autumn and northward in the spring. Such flocks contained millions of the gray birds. Settlers killed them in large numbers, apparently causing no reduction in the size of the flocks. In 1871 the pigeons went north, and that spring marked, for some unknown reason, the last flight. The mystery of their disappearance has not been solved. The Wisconsin Indians attributed some-

ENTRANCE, PIONEER ROCK CHURCH, NEAR GUTTENBERG

thing mystical to their passing. A few wild pigeons were seen in Iowa as late as 1876, but when a lone survivor was discovered in the Everglades in Florida a few years ago, no mate could be found for it and the species became extinct. Among other interesting birds was the sandhill crane. Selecting a high hill, a flock of the cranes would post sentries in military manner and proceed to do their "sun-dance" in intricate convolutions. At intervals they would march around the hilltop, several abreast. These strange dances were also engaged in on moonlit nights in spring, the mating season.

A few years ago, a group of men formed the Dubuque County Conservation Society and secured the option on this 80-acre tract, turning it over to the State for park development. Plans have been made to create a nature study camp at this spot.

LUXEMBURG, 96 *m.* (1,180 alt., 105 pop.), a German settlement, was once known as Flea Hill. The HOLY TRINITY CATHOLIC CHURCH here was built in 1876.

Right from Luxemburg on graveled State 188 are the twin villages of NEW VIENNA and ST. PETERSBURG, 5 *m.,* founded by German families about 1844. At New Vienna an abandoned brewery stands beside the Maquoketa River. An ancient stone tower and a Gothic-type church give the hamlet an Old World atmosphere. At St. Petersburg is a gray stone church of unusual beauty, with pointed arches, spires, and stained glass windows.

At Luxemburg US 52 turns again toward the Mississippi River, crossing the north Fork of the Maquoketa River at 97.5 *m.*

HOLY CROSS, 100 *m.* (111 pop.), founded by German and Irish settlers, was originally established as the Pin Oak post office, with John H. Floyd as postmaster. The name was changed Jan. 30, 1899, to commemorate the large wooden cross with which Bishop Loras had marked the site for a future church. Nearby is the SITE OF PIN OAK TAVERN, a favorite stopping place for stagecoaches and travelers years ago.

Approaching the Mississippi, the highway winds past rugged bluffs and down steep cliffs more than 500 feet to the valley of the Little Maquoketa River.

DURANGO, 113 *m.* (644 alt.), a small town on the Little Maquoketa River, was known in pioneer days as "Timber Diggings." Here the notorious outlaw, "Kaintuck" Anderson, was killed in 1837.

Between Durango and Dubuque the route traverses the valley of the Little Maquoketa. Hills and bluffs, several hundred feet high, form impregnable walls on both sides of the narrow valley, and cattle feed in green pastures beside the river.

DUBUQUE, 122 *m.* (698 alt., 41,679 pop.) *(see DUBUQUE).*

Points of Interest: Shot Tower; sash and door factories; University of Dubuque; Columbia Museum; Eagle Point Park; Grave of Julien Dubuque.

Dubuque is at the junction with US 151 *(see Tour 1A),* US 20 *(see Tour 12),* and US 61 *(see Tour 1).*

Section b. DUBUQUE *to* DAVENPORT, *106 m., US 52-67, US 67.*

Between Dubuque and Davenport the highway follows the high bluffs bordering the Mississippi River, occasionally dipping down to the river's edge and passing through one of the river towns. For years these small villages were busy ports for steamers on the upper Mississippi, and attracted a more cosmopolitan population than the inland towns. Since river navigation in this vicinity has become impossible, most of the towns have experienced a serious loss of business activity, and many of them, with idle sawmills, are nearly deserted. When logging on the Mississippi was a boom activity, these mills were among the busiest on the river; later, the installation of dams and locks made it impossible to float timber down the river from the forests of Minnesota and Wisconsin.

In this region the Mississippi has worn a bed hundreds of feet through the layers of rock. High bluffs line both sides of the river and in many places the valley is from 3 to 5 miles wide. The actual width of the river ranges from 0.5 mile to 2 miles, although the main channel, winding among hundreds of islands, is seldom more than 0.5 mile wide.

At 4 *m.* US 52 and US 67 are united and continue as one route with a well-paved roadbed.

At 6 *m.* is the junction with a graveled road.

Left on this road 1 *m.* to CRYSTAL LAKE CAVE, *(adm. 40¢; guides).* A tunnel more than 3,000 feet long passes through the cavern, winding to a small underground lake of crystal clear water. Sparkling stalagmites and stalactites rest on onyx marble foundations. Probably several miles of cavern extend through this hillside, but only a small part of the total length has been cleared and opened for visitors. The cave was discovered years ago when miners were hunting for lead ore. Colored lights add to the beauty of the rock foundations, some of which resemble animal and human figures. Temperatures of 48° to 50° prevail here, offering welcome relief from the heat of a summer afternoon.

ST. DONATUS, 15 *m.* (674 alt.), was founded by a group of settlers from Luxembourg, a province at various times under the rule of Austria, Holland, France, and Belgium. Some of the customs and traditions of these various European countries are still observed in St. Donatus, although only about 50 inhabitants remain in the village today. Many of the houses are decaying, with a rank growth of vegetation about them. They are two-story structures of stone, aged yellow, and designed as are French houses, without eaves or cellars; most of them are oblong in shape, with a barn in the rear; all have shutters, once painted green, and, excepting one, none have porches. The first floors are at street level, close to the road, with tiny front dooryards surrounded by white picket fences. There are no sidewalks. The village well is at the crossroads. Epitaphs in the small graveyard are in German.

St. Donatus, sheltered in the valley of the Tetes des Morts *(heads of the dead)* River, once bore the same name as the river. Father Michael Flamming, who came here in the early 1850's, so disliked the gruesome title that he changed it. Legend attributes the naming of the river to a bloody battle betwen the Indians and traders that left the stream, now flowing through the village, filled with dismembered heads. A second tale relates that a young Winnebago chief fell in love with Nita, daughter of a Fox chief, and, in a fit of rage upon finding her with Hotiti, a member of her own tribe, spat in her face. The Fox tribe, legend says, resenting the insult, invaded the Winnebago camp—scalping some, forcing others to jump from the cliffs into the stream below. A French pioneer, seeing the scalped heads floating to the Mississippi, named the river.

A few blocks behind an old church (L), on the side of a steep hill, is a four-story stone CONVENT. At the top of the bluff stands a reproduction of the Chapel du Bilchen in Luxembourg, reached by a winding path leading past the Stations of the Cross, consisting of brick alcoves sheltering religious pictures. These were built under the direction of Father Wenniger, a traveling priest. From this bluff is a view of three valleys.

About 1 mile S. of town a large, red brick, AMERCIAN LUTHERAN CHURCH, on the side of another rocky hill, is visible for miles up and down the valley.

BELLEVUE, 25 m. (617 alt., 1,717 pop.), along the Mississippi River, was the seat of Jackson County before Maquoketa obtained the privilege. It was first called Bell View in honor of one of the first settlers, named Bell, who built his home on a bluff overlooking the town site.

Here was staged the dramatic episode in early Iowa history known as the Bellevue War. In the late 1830's the town was the rendezvous of an outlaw gang engaged in horse stealing and other acts of lawlessness. After a number of futile attempts to crush the gang, a posse of 40 men formed a vigilance committee with the purpose of capturing the outlaws. There followed a fierce encounter, in which 4 men on each side were killed and 13 bandits were captured. A vote to decide whether to hang the men or to whip and exile them was taken by dropping beans into a box—white beans for hanging, colored beans for whipping. The majority was three colored beans, and the men were whipped and placed on boats on the Mississippi, with three days' rations, and told not to return to the village.

Until 1936 Bellevue was the eastern terminal of a narrow-gauge railroad that extended to Cascade, a distance of 40 miles. Until 1931 a large player piano manufacturing plant was operated here; the buildings are now used by an oil burner company, employing from 60 to 100 persons. Clay in the vicinity of the town furnishes material for one of the few specialized pottery works in the State. Ulysses S. Grant, when a young man, often came to Bellevue in the interest of his father's tanning business.

The old stone houses, mellowed a soft brown and built close to the streets, the warehouses on the water front remodeled into public buildings, the many homes spreading up a side valley, and the one large castlelike structure make this one of the picturesque small towns on the river. The well-kept river front adds to the town's attractiveness.

Right from the south end of Bellevue on State 62; R. at junction with first graveled road into PARADISE VALLEY. This fertile tract of land, extending for almost 10 miles up the creek, was once owned by A. Potter, whose wealth was so great that he is reputed to have brought his gold from Galena, Ill., in barrels, after he had marketed his products. Several fine old gray stone houses stand by the roadside, though their splendor has passed. In the old POTTER HOME, 3 m. (private), now occupied by Potter's grandson, is an excellent collection of records and notes that cover a period of almost 50 years beginning in the late 1830's. Potter called the spot Paradise Valley because, he said, one had to go "through Purgatory to get there", the roads from Bellevue being almost impassable in the early days.

At the southern end of Bellevue (R) is the entrance to the winding cliff road, leading into BELLEVUE STATE PARK (picnic grounds, pavilion, concession stand; custodian). The park is on a rocky promontory with

THRESHING

perpendicular cliffs rising 400 feet above the surface of the river. Trails wind down the east face of the bluff past unusual rock formations and rough, irregular crevices. PULPIT ROCK, a small slab jutting out from the north face of the cliff, affords an excellent view of the town and the river northward. From the top of the bluff is an excellent view of the sluggish Mississippi stretching away in the distance. Opposite the park is a large island used as a proving ground for the Savanna, Ill., arsenal.

South of Bellevue US 52 closely follows the Mississippi for a few miles, turning away into a region of low bluffs and crossing Maquoketa River. Through this region the glacial river tore its way through strata of blue-gray limestone, leaving long lines of precipitous cliffs. Although the cliffs are half overgrown with vines and brush, they frequently stand out bold and bare. Except in a few spots the walls are two and three miles apart, broken when a tributary enters; but everywhere there is beauty and variety. In some places the cliffs look like cathedrals; in different lights there is a dazzling display of color.

SABULA, 46 m. (603 alt., 759 pop.), is a sleepy, old river town. It was named Sabula in 1846 in honor of Mrs. Sabula Wood. Previously it had been called Carrolport, and then Charlestown. The streets are arched over by tall elms. Many of the homes were built in the middle of the last century and are set in the midst of broad lawns.

On a side street is a large FISH POOL, built by one of the citizens, that occupies the space between the paving and the sidewalk. Spring water is piped into the pool, which is divided into several sections, containing many varieties of fish.

Along the river is a STATE FISH RESCUE STATION, the only one in the State. In June, when the river overflows, fish are washed up on the banks, and when the waters recede the Rescue Station employees pick up the fish stranded on the dry banks and throw them back into the river.

At Sabula US 52 turns L., crossing the river on a toll bridge *(car and driver, 25¢, passengers 5¢)* to Savanna, Ill.; US 67 continues south. For a few miles the road is hilly and winding, with a heavy growth of timber on both sides.

HAUNTOWN, 51 *m.* (R), one of Iowa's many ghost towns, was named for William Haun, who had the first mill in Clinton County and later operated a whiskey distillery in connection with it. On the highway (L) is the old mill structure with a millrace that runs several hundred feet from the river. At one time there were more than 115 inhabitants, but when the railroad failed to pass through the village, everyone moved away. Before the Civil War a distillery here produced nine barrels a day of the product called Elk River Whiskey.

Elk River, nearby, received its name because of the number of elk horns that were found along the banks of the stream by the early settlers. After the Civil War the heavily timbered hills in this neighborhood were a haven for horse thieves, several of whom were summarily hanged by Clinton County "vigilantes" during the turbulent years.

ALMONT, 55 *m.* (661 alt., 25 pop.), was formerly known as Elk River; its present name was selected because of a steep hill in the vicinity. Here the graveled road ends and paving begins. Almont is slightly inland, but a few miles farther south the road slopes toward the river again.

At 58 *m.* is the junction with a graveled road.

Right on this road 3.8 *m.* is the DAVID SHADDUCK STONE HOUSE *(private)*, built in 1866.

CLINTON, 65 *m.* (593 alt., 25,726 pop.) *(see CLINTON).*

Points of Interest: River Front Park; Clinton Co. Plant; Old Stone House; Eagle Point Park.

Clinton is at the junction with US 30 *(see Tour 13).*

Right from Clinton on State 136, paved, is GOOSE LAKE, 13 *m.,* a little town in Deep Creek township. The lake for which it is named is several miles away. Deep Creek flows through a wide valley that was once the bed of the Mississippi River; the southern part of the valley widens into a wide savannah, in the center of which is Goose Lake, now but a fraction of its former size. At one time the entire valley was a vast lake or bayou, with the present bluffs of the Mississippi as its shores. Copious springs feed Goose Lake, so that it did not completely vanish when drainage districts were established.

CAMANCHE, 71 *m.* (598 alt., 728 pop.), was designated the first seat of Clinton County, organized in 1840. It is one of the four Iowa towns still existing under special charter. On Sunday, June 3, 1860, a cyclone almost destroyed the town, killing many people.

Along the shore of the Mississippi near the town are a number of picturesque homes of fishermen, with nets drying nearby in the racks; pollution of the river has ruined fishing on the Iowa shore, causing many small fishing boats to lie idle at their moorings.

Between Camanche and the river stands one of the two pecan groves in the State, both of which are Clinton County.

At 77 *m.* US 67 crosses the wide mouth of the Wapsipinicon River. An Indian village once stood on a plateau here, where Marquette and Joliet are said by some to have first landed on Iowa territory. On a large island at the mouth of the river is the second pecan grove *(see above).*

Along the highway for a few miles are unusual rock formations of a porous limestone—a form of coral similar to some of the formations in Florida—indicating that at one time this section of the country was a part of the ocean bed.

LE CLAIRE, 88 *m.* (576 alt., 691 pop.), was formerly two separate villages, Parkersburg and Le Claire. A hamlet called Middletown grew up between the two, and all three were incorporated under the name Le Claire, in honor of Antoine Le Claire, pioneer benefactor of the county and founder of Davenport.

Le Claire was the boyhood home of William F. (Buffalo Bill) Cody. Isaac Cody, father of Buffalo Bill, was a pioneer settler of Scott County. William, one of five children, was born Feb. 26, 1846, on what was then known as the John S. Wilson farm, 1.5 miles NW. of Le Claire. Later the Cody family moved to a village house that was recently purchased by the C. B. & Q. R. R. and shipped to the Cody Memorial Park at Cody, Wyo.

Le Claire was also the home of Capt. James Buchanan Eads, an engineer, who, among other accomplishments, opened the mouth of the Mississippi River to permit vessels to enter, and erected at St. Louis the bridge bearing his name. Capt. Eads' father, Thomas Eads, in 1836, built the first frame house in Le Claire. Having invented a diving bell, he formed a partnership in 1843 for salvaging shipping from the river.

About 150 feet from the highway (L), on the banks of the Mississippi, stands a huge ELM TREE, sometimes called the Green Tree Hotel, 13 feet in circumference, with a spread of 193 feet. Antoine Le Claire had meetings with the Indians and early settlers under it. Roustabouts and lumberjacks who came up and down the river on packet boats and rafts, after spending their earnings in the saloons, often slept off their intoxication under the Green Tree Hotel; and they sometimes spent two or three days here waiting for a boat—and another job—to come along. Later the tree was marked with a monument bearing this inscription:

"Dedicated to Col. Wm. F. Cody
'Buffalo Bill'
By his friend and boyhood
playmate, Joe Barnes
Erected, 1924."

PLEASANT VALLEY, 94 *m.* (582 alt.), originally named Valley City, received its present name from the township. Capt. Harry Hawley, soldier in the War of 1812, bought a land-claim near Pleasant Valley from Buck Spencer, paying $1,400. He was the first man to bring onion seeds to Iowa, and the first to raise onions commercially in the State. Each season he took his crop on a flatboat to St. Louis where he found a ready market. From this small venture has developed the Pleasant Valley Onion Growers Association, with sales and shipments handled through a brokerage company in Chicago. Hundreds of acres are planted in onions every season, producing thousands of bushels for market.

The two-story frame SPENCER HOUSE *(private)* was built in 1856 by Roswell Spencer, one of the early settlers in Pleasant Valley. The early hand-carved furniture, fine china, rugs, and draperies have been preserved, and today the house is furnished as it was in 1856. High shelves of old books, both English and American, are in the library. Above the shelves are framed maps of varying age; the oldest is said to be 340 years old. The most publicized article here is a leaf from the Gutenberg Bible.

BETTENDORF, 103 *m.* (575 alt., 2,769 pop.) *(see Tour 14)*, is at a junction with US 6 *(see Tour 14)*.

DAVENPORT, 106 *m.* (559 alt., 60,751 pop.) *(see DAVENPORT)*.

Points of Interest: the Palmer School of Chiropractic; Antoine Le Claire Park; Credit Island; St. Ambrose College; Iowa Soldiers' Orphans' Home.

Davenport is at the junction with US 6 *(see Tour 14)* and US 61 *(see Tour 1)*.

South of Davenport US 67 crosses the Mississippi River on a free bridge to Rock Island, Ill., 136 miles N. of Jacksonville, Ill.

Tour 2A

Calmar—Oelwein—Independence—Cedar Rapids; State 11.
Calmar to Cedar Rapids, 102 m.

The C. R. I. & P. R. R. parallels this route between West Union and Cedar Rapids; W. C. F. & N. R. R., between Center Point and Cedar Rapids.
The Jefferson and Greyhound Bus Lines follow the highway between West Union and Cedar Rapids; the Interstate, between Cedar Rapids and Calmar.
Roadbed graveled between Calmar and West Union; paved between West Union and Cedar Rapids.
Tourist accommodations of all kinds, mainly at West Union, Oelwein, and Independence.

State 11 branches S. from its junction with US 52 at Calmar, 0 *m.*, *(see Tour 2)*, and winds over hills and through quiet, timbered valleys.

At FESTINA, 5 *m.*, a Bohemian hamlet, is the church of the parish of Our Lady of Seven Dolors, built in 1863. It is one of the few old churches in the State in which regular services are conducted.

Right from Festina, on an improved road, to ST. ANTHONY'S CHAPEL, 2.5 *m*. The outside dimensions of the building are 12 by 16 feet, and within are four pews, seating only two persons each. The road follows the valley of the Turkey River, and the little chapel—standing on a grassy plot (L)—is especially impressive in the light of a bright moon. It was built in 1885 by John Gartner and Frank Huber, on the site of the first log church, Old Mission, of Our Lady of Seven Dolors parish. In a pioneer cemetery back of the chapel is a large bronze marker in memory of Gartner or Johann Gaertner. Near the chapel is the OLD MISSION MILL, on the site of a gristmill operated when Ft. Atkinson *(see Tour 2)* was occupied. Flour ground at the old mill supplied the garrison and also the Indians at the mission.

ELDORADO, 9 *m*. (924 alt.), a hamlet, was so named in the 1860's. Two women, Mrs. Newton and Mrs. Towner, pioneering in women's fashions with bloomer dresses, earned for the little settlement the name "Bloomertown", by which it was known for miles around.

An indication of the limitations of early homes of the settlers is found in the account of the first wedding in the settlement (1849) which took place in a cabin characterized as "not very high posted." When Gabriel Long, of West Union, 6 feet 6 inches tall, performed the ceremony, his head was upstairs, while the bride and groom, Polly Kerr and Eliff Johnson, stood below on the first floor.

At 12.5 *m*. is the crest of a steep hill, from which a panorama of farmsteads, timbered lands, streams, and meadows is visible.

WEST UNION, 17 *m*. (1,107 alt., 2,056 pop.) *(see Tour 11)*, is at the junction with US 18 *(see Tour 11)*.

Small creeks in this vicinity afford good fishing. In the surrounding hills and fields is an abundance of small game such as squirrel, rabbit, and quail. There are many picnic spots, easily accessible and with much natural beauty. The region is noted for its many springs.

FAYETTE, 26 *m*. (1,002 alt., 1,083 pop.), is the seat of UPPER IOWA UNIVERSITY, a non-sectarian Christian college with an enrollment of about 300 students. The 14-acre campus lies in the center of town, along the banks of the Volga River. The school was organized, in January 1857, as Fayette Seminary, after Col. Robert Alexander and Samuel H. Robinson had donated the land and a sum of $50,000. It was formerly sponsored by the Methodist Episcopal Church. In addition to a liberal arts curriculum, there are schools of music and business. In the MUSEUM, third floor of library building, are collections of zoological, geological, ethnological, and historical interest. Many of the specimens were received from the Smithsonian Institution, while others represent the work of the faculty and student body, or friends of the college. There are a series of casts of North American Indian implements; a collection of domestic utensils, fabrics, wearing apparel, musical instruments, and weapons of warfare from the Philippine Islands; and a group of collections from New Mexico.

The METHODIST CHURCH, of Gothic design, is a cruciform structure, completed in 1876. Fifty years after its completion, excavation of rock under the old church was begun, and rooms were added. The entrance room, with plain walls and bench, is a reproduction of the cell where William Tyndale was imprisoned for translating the Bible. An old-style circular top door leads to the Lutherhaus, a model of the Wittenberg room where Luther made his translation 400 years ago. Light streams through a window, with heavily-leaded, hexagon-shaped panes, a duplicate of the one in the Lutherhaus in Wittenberg, Germany. The central room (Broad Room) contains the UPPER IOWA FIREPLACE, built of rocks from every State in the Union and from abroad. This room has a door with long black hinges and a latch string, and is a copy of a Franciscan cell under the Cathedral at Assisi, Italy. In the kindergarten a sunken sandtable lies beneath doors in the floor. The WESLEYAN NICHE is a small museum in the center of the church.

At 31 *m.* is the junction with State 154, graveled.

Left on this road 9 *m.* into BRUSH CREEK CANYON STATE PARK. This area, acquired in the autumn of 1936, is undeveloped, with the exception of a road into the park leading to a parking area. Plans have been made to fence the park and provide facilities.

MAYNARD, 35 *m.* (1,099 alt., 409 pop.), on the Little Volga River, was named in honor of Henry Maynard. The FARMERS' CREAMERY here manufactures Iowa Brand butter. Near Maynard is the DAIRY FARM of P. P. Stewart, whose Holstein cows have long been listed on the honor roll of Holstein herds in the United States.

OELWEIN, 43 *m.* (1,039 alt., 7,794 pop.), was named for a German who gave part of his property for the railroad station and right-of-way. At one time it was known as "The Hub" because it is the central midwestern division point of the C. G. W. R.R., and also because six railroads converge here. There are large railroad shops.

A LOG CABIN, a block west of the business district, was erected by L. M. Burch in 1852.

At 44.5 *m.* is LAKE OELWEIN, formed by a dam that backs up the water of Otter Creek. The park has swimming, boating, and fishing facilities, and a number of summer cottages.

At 46 *m.* is junction with State 190, graveled.

Right on this road is FAIRBANK, 7 *m.*, an Amish-Mennonite settlement established many years ago. The people here have refused to use motor cars, tractors, or other modern conveniences, and, in accordance with their faith, dress as their ancestors did and travel by horse and buggy. Recently 39 Amish-Mennonites from Yoder, Kans., joined them because the expanding oil fields in Kansas threatened their tranquil farm life.

HAZLETON, 48 *m.* (998 alt., 499 pop.), first known as Superior, but renamed in 1863, is on Otter Creek, a clear winding stream. The creek was named because of the numbers of otter found here by early settlers.

INDEPENDENCE, 59 *m.* (921 alt. 3,691 pop.) *(see Tour 12)* is at the junction with US 20 *(see Tour 12)*.

Right from Independence, on a dirt road, is LITTLETON, 11 *m.*, a small settlement of "Hook and Eye Dutch." They are a religious sect, in many ways similar to the Mennonites and Amish, fundamentalists in their doctrine, and strict in compliance with it. They have no church edifice, but hold services in the homes of members. The minister is selected from the congregation, not because of special training, but because of thorough knowledge of the Bible. He serves without salary, but is given a small acreage from which to supply his family's needs. The buildings are seldom painted, and never trimmed. In the homes are no rugs, chairs, or curtains. Bare unfinished benches, tables, beds, and other furniture are fashioned by the farmers themselves. Daily scrubbing keeps everything spotlessly clean. Only in the buying of beautiful dishes do the women indulge in any aesthetic extravagance. Little girls, like their mothers, dress in long, dark blue, or black, dresses with full skirts and deep hems, and wear little white caps. Their hair is combed once a week. The men wear black clothes, the coats having wide neckbands. In winter the topcoats have capes of elbow length. All fastenings are made by means of hooks and eyes, from which comes the name "Hook and Eye Dutch." They use a horse and buggy for traveling, and in summer no top is raised on the buggy because they believe the sun is no harder on them than on the horse. They will neither buy nor sell on Sunday, do not approve of divorce, and marry within their own colony. When a young man wishes to marry he goes to the minister and asks him to see the parents of the girl. The minister then reports to the young man and the necessary arrangements are made. The young man is clean shaven until his marriage, but after that grows a beard. After the marriage a small house is built behind the larger house of the young man's parents. This is called the "Grandpa House", because the parents move into it, giving the larger house to the newly-weds. As the minister assumes the intiative in arranging marriages, supervises the necessary agreements, and performs the ceremony, so he likewise is the court of appeals in time of disputes and disagreements. However, it is very seldom his services are needed in such a capacity. The "Hook and Eye Dutch" do not employ legal services if their difficulties can possibly be settled out of court; they do not take part in politics, do not take oaths of office, and never carry arms or go to war.

WALKER, 77 *m.* (890 alt., 456 pop.), named for W. W. Walker, an official of the C. R. I. & P. R.R., is the center of a large farm and dairy territory.

CENTER POINT, 83 *m.* (819 alt., 812 pop.), was settled in 1839 by Bartimeas McGonigle, and was then known as McGonigle's Point. J. M. Bartleson who came here from Virginia in 1855, was one of the stage drivers on the mail route established by the Government between Cedar Rapids and Waterloo. Center Point was the half-way station between these cities.

Among the many historic and prehistoric specimens in the J. F. WILSON COLLECTION in this town are a tooth of a mastodon, found in a remarkable state of preservation about 3 miles S. of town, 19 feet below the surface of the earth, and an old brass buckle, found while workmen were digging a well near Fairfax. The buckle bears a coat of arms and the date 1776.

A HICKORY GROVE in the village contains one tree more than 100 feet high and 4 feet in diameter. S. W. Snyder, director-at-large of the American Society for Horticultural Science, owns the grove, and follows the practice of preserving the old trees rather than planting new ones. It is his belief that the nuts from naturally propagated trees are far superior to what he terms "nuts from commercialized trees."

ROBINS, 97 *m.* (858 alt., 120 pop.), a suburb of Cedar Rapids, was named for its first postmaster and storekeeper. With its far-flung area, covering 2,570 acres, the town is second in area in the county only to Cedar Rapids, although there are but 45 homes, a post office, and a few stores.

CEDAR RAPIDS, 102 *m.* (733 alt., 56,097 pop.) *(see CEDAR RAPIDS).*

Points of Interest: Municipal Island; Quaker Oats Plant; Coe College.

Cedar Rapids is at the junction with US 218 *(see Tour 1A)* and with US 30 *(see Tour 13).*

Tour 2B

Junction with US 52 (Froelich)—Strawberry Point—Manchester—Junction with US 151 (Marion); State 13.
Junction with US 52 to Junction with US 151, 77 m.

The C. M. St. P. & P. R. R. partly parallels this route; and the I. C. R. R. parallels it between Manchester and Central City.
Roadbed paved except for 5 m. S. of Strawberry Point.
Good tourist accommodations available mainly at Elkader and Manchester.

State 13 branches S. from US 52 *(see Tour 2),* 1 mile S. of Froelich *(see Tour 11),* and winds through the rough, rocky hills and valleys of a scenic region in northeastern Iowa.

At 4 *m.* is the junction with a graveled road.

Right on this road is FARMERSBURG, 2 *m.,* where (1938) one of the five major projects of the United States Soil Conservation Service in Iowa is in progress, with farmers cooperating. This erosion control work consists of planting trees, building check dams in gullies, strip cropping, and liming.

ELKADER, 11 *m.* (761 alt., 1,382 pop.), seat of Clayton County, was in 1845 named for an Algerian chieftain, Abd-el-Kader, who was then making a valiant defense against the inroads of French imperialism in his country. At that time the attention of the whole world was turned toward Algeria.

The first GLASS SCHOOLHOUSE in Iowa was built here in 1936. The walls of this two-story building, which is 173 feet long and 148 feet wide, are composed of hollow glass blocks 8 inches square and 4 inches thick, laid on edge in much the same way as are building bricks in older structures. Corrugation on both sides makes the blocks translucent, admitting a maximum amount of natural light without glare and with proper diffusion. Glass walls shut out noise and provide insulation against extreme heat and cold. The building, costing $148,000, and financed by insurance from the previous building, which burned in 1936, a bond issue, and P.W.A. funds, provides accommodations for 500 pupils classified from the third grade through high school. The cantilever type of floor construction was used, with floors of asphalt tiling and metal lath, plastered and then painted. Desks and tables in classrooms and laboratories are of chemically treated hard rubber.

Oren R. Thomas, the architect, born (July 3, 1896) in St. Joseph, Mo., received his professional education at the Armour Institute of Technology in Chicago, and came to Des Moines, Iowa, in 1918, where he has specialized in the designing of school buildings.

Spanning the Turkey River, in the center of Elkader, is a large STONE ARCH BRIDGE, built of native stone, with two arches 90 feet long.

Opposite the courthouse, on the riverbank, is a STONE MILL; only the tower of the original structure, built in 1849, remains in the rebuilt mill. The place is now used for flour making and grinding grain.

Elisha Boardman and Horace D. Bronson, partners, said to have been the first white men to cross the Mississippi River from Prairie du Chien, Wis., to McGregor (see Tour 11), built the first log cabin here on the site of the present railroad station.

Right from Elkader on an unimproved road, following the Turkey River to BIG SPRINGS, 7 m., tumbling from the rocks on the opposite bank of the river.

At 13.5 m. is the junction with a surfaced dirt road.

Left on this road is COMMUNIA, 3.5 m., a town where remnants of a group of buildings erected in 1847 by nine Germans and a Frenchman, still stand. The colonists were tradesmen with no farming experience. Each contributed all he owned to the general fund, and shared the land and profits. Later the colonists bought 1,400 acres of land. In 1856, for reasons unknown, the inhabitants by agreement dissolved the organization and divided land and money. The post office, established in 1854, was discontinued in 1855; reestablished in 1857, it was finally discontinued in 1903. The OLD COLONY HOUSE—a weather-beaten public hall, now abandoned—and a $50,000 FLOUR MILL, also in disuse, are all that remain of the village. The mill was designed by John Thompson, builder of many stone mills in northeastern Iowa.

LITTLEPORT, 7 m. (203 pop.), on the Volga River, grew up on the site of the former meeting ground of Indians for councils of war and peace conferences. Here they loaded their canoes with pelts before moving down the Volga to the trading post, where they exchanged furs for powder and whiskey. Two graves at the foot of a hill are said to be those of Indian brothers who died in a fight over a girl. The village, which was settled by 1848, is subject to disastrous floods of the river, a comparatively small stream named for the Volga River of Russia.

At 14.5 m. is the junction with a graveled road.

Left on this road is MEDERVILLE, 3 m., a small village on the Volga River, settled in 1868 by Henry Meder, who built a sawmill and flour mill here. The mill burned years ago, leaving only massive stone walls that rise in picturesque beauty near a modern bridge. Nearby are the KRAMER TROUT PONDS (open to visitors), a new venture attracting sportsmen from a wide area. The ponds were formed when water filled old stone quarries.

STRAWBERRY POINT, 26 m. (1,213 alt., 1,128 pop.) has a whole milk CREAMERY handling more than 23,000,000 pounds annually. The town was so named because a few miles distant wild strawberries once grew in abundance.

At 27.5 m. is the junction with State 19, graveled.

MILL NEAR COMMUNIA

Right on this road is BACKBONE STATE PARK *(camp and picnic sites;
bathing, boating, fishing facilities)*, 4 *m.*, first and largest State park in Iowa.
Dedicated May 28, 1920, it now comprises about 1,450 acres within a huge horseshoe bend of the upper Maquoketa River. The DEVIL'S BACKBONE, from which
the park takes its name, is a long narrow ridge of rugged, limestone rocks, in many
places rising precipitously 80 to 100 feet. A second range of rock towers behind
and above the primary ridge, so that the river flows along a gorge often as much
as 200 feet in depth. Fascinating accounts have been written of the many caverns
and crevices, the deep springs, and grassy woodlands in the park. Ferns and wild
flowers are abundant. Many of the rock formations resemble columns, towers,
castles, battlements, and flying buttresses. From the observatory in a tower on top
of the ridge (reached by a well-marked path) the river is seen for 25 to 30 miles.
There are many nature trails, a large auditorium, a deer range, and a trout
hatchery. In the park is an artificial lake about 100 acres in area, recently created
by the erection of a concrete dam across the Maquoketa River. The lake has a
beach of clean, white sand.

At 31 *m.* is the junction with State 10, graveled.

Left on this road to EDGEWOOD, 3 *m.* (1,165 alt., 638 pop.), first known as
Yankee Settlement and renamed in 1875; L. 2 *m.* on a graveled road to BIXBY
STATE SCENIC PRESERVE *(picnicking facilities and nature trails)*, a 69-acre
tract embracing a number of topographical features of particular scientific interest.
In the preserve is the LOG CABIN home of Ransom J. Bixby, for whom the area
was named; he was an early settler in this region. Here are spectacular rocky cliffs
and spring-fed streams, framed in a rugged, heavy woodland where many varieties
of wild flowers grow. On the south terrace of a little stream is the BIXBY ICE CAVE.
Although it is not as large as the Decorah Ice Cave *(see Tour 2)*, the ice is more
abundant. On May 31, 1936, the snow of winter still remained at the entrance to
the cave. Behind the snow the coating of ice extended down a steep incline about
20 feet, increasing in thickness from a few inches near the entrance to more than
2 feet along the floor near the lower end. The cavern is not more than 4 to 6
feet in diameter, and the icy floor makes descent into the cave hazardous. The
limestone walls of the cave absorb the intense cold during the long winter months.
In spring and summer the moisture-laden air entering the cave is frozen by contact with the walls, and many layers of ice pile up by the middle of the summer.
By that time the warm air has gradually heated the rock and begun to melt the ice,
and warm air is found in the cave far into the fall and early winter.

MANCHESTER, 43 *m.* (919 alt. 3,413 pop.) *(see Tour 12)*, is at the
junction with US 20 *(see Tour 12)*.

RYAN, 53 *m.* (1,013 alt., 369 pop.), a small village, was named for
Father Patrick Ryan, first rector of the Catholic Church here.

COGGON, 60 *m.* (916 alt., 503 pop.), first called Green's Mill and
later Nugent, is near the now extinct village of Sodtown, whose buildings
were all made of sod blocks in the early days of settlement.

A dam was completed in 1936 across Buffalo Creek nearby; just above
the dam is a fish-breeding area.

CENTRAL CITY, 65 *m.* (837 alt., 780 pop.), is a trading center for
farmers within a 10-mile radius, most of whom live on modern, well-
stocked farms. It is a terminal for the C. M. St. P. & P. R. R. The EAST
STAR MILL, erected nearby on the bank of the Wapsipinicon River in
1863, is still in use for grinding grain.

At 77 m. is the junction with US 151 *(see Tour 1A)* 9 miles NE. of
Cedar Rapids.

Tour 3

(Rochester, Minn.)—New Hampton—Waterloo—Tama—Oskaloosa—
Ottumwa—Bloomfield—(Kirksville, Mo.); US 63.
Minnesota Line to Missouri Line, 240 m.

C. M. St. P. & P. R. R. parallels this route between Chester and Lime Springs;
W. C. F. & N. between Chester and Lime Springs; W. C. F. & N. El. R. R., be-
tween Denver and Waterloo; C. G. W. R. R., between Waterloo and Traer;
M. & St. L. R. R., between New Sharon and Fremont; C. B. & Q. R. R., between
Oskaloosa and Fremont; C. R. I. & P. R. R., between Oskaloosa and Ottumwa;
Wabash R. R., between Ottumwa and Bloomfield.
Burlington Bus Lines follow the highway between Waterloo and Tama; Interstate
Transit Bus Lines, between Waterloo and Tama and between Oskaloosa and
Ottumwa; Jefferson Bus Lines, between Ottumwa and Missouri Line.
Roadbed paved, except about 8 m., graveled, S. of Montezuma.
Accommodations of all kinds available, chiefly in cities.

Section a. MINNESOTA LINE to TAMA, 120 m.

US 63 crosses the Minnesota Line, 0 m., 53 miles S. of Rochester, Minn.
CHESTER, 0.5 m. (1,230 alt., 238 pop.), formerly known as Eaton-
ville, lies along the banks of the Upper Iowa River, and was once a military outlook post on Military Ridge Trail.

Between Chester and Tama US 63 passes through gently rolling
prairie country.

At 4 m. is the junction with State 157, paved.

Left on this road 1 m. is LIME SPRINGS (1,245 alt., 539 pop.), about three-
fourths of a mile from the Iowa River where a few buildings mark the old town
of Lime Springs. Here is a mill dating back to the early 1850's; the original mill
was burned and rebuilt. In the wall of the miller's house is set a French millstone
formerly used in Governor Larrabee's mill at Clermont and later in the Lime
Springs Mill. Larrabee was the 13th Governor of Iowa (1886–1890).

At 11 m. is the junction with State 9 *(see Tour 10)*.

At 31 m. the highway crosses the East Wapsipinicon River. This part
of Iowa, though mainly level prairie land, is broken by a number of small
streams and rivers, and generally, when within a few miles of a river, the
route becomes marked by hills and curves before winding down into lux-
uriantly green valleys through which the rivers flow.

NEW HAMPTON, 33 m. (1,159 alt., 2,450 pop.), is the seat of
Chickasaw County; first known as Chickasaw Center, it was later renamed
by Osgood Gowen for his old home town in New Hampshire. A controversy arose over the vote in 1856 to decide whether the county seat
should be removed to Forest City (now Williamstown) from New Hampton. A tie vote had thrown the case into court, where Judge Bailey ruled in
favor of Forest City. Refusal of New Hampton to relinquish the records

led to a series of arrests, among them that of the judge. A group of 24 men, led by the constable, forced him into a wagon drawn by a yoke of oxen, but before they had gone far, friends who had secured a writ of habeas corpus from the clerk (acting for the judge in his absence), demanded his release. A pitched battle brought about the judge's release, and those resisting were arrested. Eventually the records were transferred to Forest City, but in 1880, when New Hampton subscribed $5,000 for a new courthouse if built there, the offer was accepted, and New Hampton once more became the county seat.

In Chickasaw County an annual "crow shoot" is held; crows destroy crops, and the nests, eggs, and even the young of the quail, pheasants, robins, and other birds. Two groups are chosen, a captain heading each organization; the contest sometimes begins early in May and continues into June, depending on the number of crows. Often there is a one-day hunt, and the group killing the smaller number of crows is obliged to furnish a big dinner for all the hunters.

In March 1936, The Fisherman-Liar Club was organized here with about 80 members. At the first meeting local members were asked to spin their favorite fishing yarn, tell jokes, sing, or dance the Virginia Reel. Plans were made for other meetings, and the best fishing spots were discussed and trips planned. At each meeting the gold-handled prize cup is passed on the narrator of the best fishing yarn.

Right from New Hampton on a dirt road to a ROCK, 7.5 *m.*, 75 feet in circumference and 50 feet high. The sides are steep and extremely difficult to scale; a ladder on one side enables visitors to reach the top and enjoy the view. There are several local stories about the rock, all discounted. However, it is true that in the early days a promoter from New York came to New Hampton, platted a town around the rock, called it St. Peter, and sold the lots to buyers in the East. The old plat can be seen among county records.

WILLIAMSTOWN, 40 *m.* (204 pop.), first called Forest City, was renamed by William Grant, who applied for the post office.

Williamstown was the scene of a Fox Hunt in January 1936, not for sport, but to stop raids on chicken coops and pigpens of the surrounding farms. A short time before noon more than 50 men, in four groups, each under a captain, started the drive toward a central point where "the kill" of half a dozen foxes took place. The losing group furnished a big feast, using the proceeds of the sale of the pelts to supply it.

Williamstown is at the junction with US 18 *(see Tour 11)*.

At 47 *m.* is the junction with State 334, graveled.

Left on this road is FREDERIKA, 2 *m.* (204 pop.), on the Wapsipinicon River. The town was named for Frederika Bremer (1801–65), a popular Swedish novelist, who visited the United States around 1849 and 1850. At the edge of the village farmers and townsmen constructed a dam on the Wapsipinicon. The lake thus formed was stocked with fish, and space cleared for a bathing beach.

DENVER, 63 *m.* (943 alt., 500 pop.), was called Jefferson City, but, after the Star Mail Route, a service provided persons who carried mail between towns having no Federal service, was established, the town was called Breckenridge. When the mail carrier rode into town blowing his whistle, townspeople came hurrying from all directions, collecting on the main street to receive their mail. In 1863 when a regular post office was established the name was changed to Denver.

Cement blocks are manufactured here.

WATERLOO, 75 m. (856 alt., 46,191 pop.) *(see WATERLOO)*.

Points of Interest: Boulder Church; packing plant; agricultural machinery factories; Dairy Cattle Congress Exposition Buildings.

Waterloo is at the junction with US 20 *(see Tour 12)* and US 218 *(see Tour 3A)*.

HUDSON, 84 m. (888 alt., 474 pop.), lying along Blackhawk Creek, was once an important station on the old wagon thoroughfare between Waterloo and Eldora.

At 89.5 m. is the junction with State 58, paved.

Right on this road is GRUNDY CENTER, 16 m. (976 alt., 1,793 pop.), where the writer, Herbert Quick (1861–1925) first attended school. The SCHOOLHOUSE, now in ORION PARK, is maintained as a memorial to him. Quick, son of Martin and Margaret Quick, was the author of *Vandemark's Folly* and numerous other novels of the days after the log cabin era of Iowa's development. His descriptions of prairies and farm homes, cyclones and blizzards, and the hardships and joys of pioneer life are vivid and accurate in detail. He was born near Steamboat Rock, on a farm in Grundy County, Oct. 23, 1861. His parents, like many other pioneers, came to Iowa in the latter half of the century in wagons drawn by ox teams. From 1877 to 1890 he taught in various schools in the State, after receiving his certificate from Teacher's Institute at Grundy Center. He studied law during this time, was admitted to the bar in 1889, and was mayor of Sioux City from 1890 to 1900; he died while filling a speaking engagement at Columbia, Mo., May 10, 1925.

At 97 m. is the junction with a county road.

Left on this road, is THEODORE F. CLARK STATE SCENIC PRESERVE, 3 m., a picturesque recreational area bordering Wolf Creek *(picnic fireplace and pavilion)*. The 24-acre area is covered with a forest of basswood, slippery elm, American elm, and a variety of other trees.

TRAER, 99 m. (916 alt., 1,417 pop.), was the birthplace (1882) of Margaret Wilson (Mrs. George D. Turner), who won the Harper Prize in 1923 and a Pulitzer Prize in 1924 with her first novel, *The Able McLaughlins*. The scene of the novel is laid in and about Traer, and the characters are the author's Scottish relatives and their friends of the pioneer days of Tama County.

James Wilson (1835–1920), locally called "Tama Jim" Wilson Secretary of Agriculture for 16 years, under Presidents McKinley, Theodore Roosevelt, and Taft, lived on a farm near Traer. He and his parents came from Ayrshire, Scotland, to Connecticut in 1851, and to Iowa in 1855. He began his public service career as a member of the board of supervisors of Tama County; he was professor of agriculture at Iowa State College before entering his Cabinet office.

TOLEDO, 118 m. (856 alt., 1,825 pop.), is the seat of Tama County. The STATE JUVENILE HOME *(open 9:30-10:30 a.m., 3-5 p.m., daily)*, on the old Leander Clark College campus bordering US 63, is an institution for normal homeless, neglected, and destitute children. It has facilities for 335 boys and girls, 4 to 21 years of age, with a modern hospital, a school, and athletic equipment.

Toledo has the only modern Log Church in Iowa, dedicated Nov. 11, 1936. It is 28 feet wide and 50 feet long and seats 250 to 300 persons. The church organization is newly incorporated and adheres to no particular religious creed.

Right from Toledo on a surfaced dirt road is the *SAC AND FOX SANA-TORIUM*, 1 *m. (open daily 9:30-10:30 a.m., 3-5 p.m.)*, built as a boarding school for children from the Tama Indian lands. It was converted into a tuberculosis sanatorim for Indians of all tribes in 1912, when day schools were built for the Indians.

TAMA, 120 *m.* (820 alt., 2,626 pop.) *(see Tour 13)*, is at the junction with US 30 *(see Tour 13)*.

Section b. TAMA *to* MISSOURI LINE, *120 m.*

South of Tama, 0 *m.*, the rolling prairie is broken with hills and valleys.

At 16 *m.* is the junction with US 6 *(see Tour 14)*.

MALCOM, 21 *m.* (892 alt., 381 pop.), is on the bank of Little Bear Creek.

MONTEZUMA, 30 *m.* (958 alt., 1,257 pop.), seat of Poweshiek County, was named in honor of the Aztec emperor of Mexico (1502–1520), whose romantic history caught the fancy of Poweshiek County pioneers.

Shortly after the M. & St. L. R.R. station was built, thirsty thieves crawled beneath it, bored a hole through the floor into each of the largest barrels of beer that had been shipped to Montezuma, and carried off every drop.

Left from Montezuma on State 85, graveled, is DEEP RIVER, 8 *m.* (839 alt., 392 pop.), where Orangeman's Day is held annually on July 12, and a big homecoming celebration staged. This holiday is celebrated by members of the Society of Orangemen, founded in Ireland for maintenance of Protestantism. There was once a large Irish settlement here, and the community is still predominantly Irish.

NEW SHARON, 43 *m.* (859 alt., 1,052 pop.), first called Sharon, later New Sharon to avoid confusion with a town of that name in Warren County, was largely a Quaker settlement in early days.

Right from New Sharon on a surfaced dirt road is the JARARD THOROUGHBRED STOCK FARM, 4 *m.*, particularly known for Clydesdale horses that have frequently won ribbons at important horse shows.

At 48 *m.* is the junction with a surfaced dirt road.

Right on this road is LACEY, 1 *m.* (805 alt.), named for Maj. John F. Lacey, Congressman (1889–1907) from Iowa. Major Lacey donated the land for a railroad, stipulating that the deed should be null and void if the depot was ever closed. When it was burned a box car was moved to the site to serve as a depot. Major Lacey is known for his work on the Public Lands Committee and in forest conservation. He drafted and prepared the law that set aside Yellowstone Park as a national park, and secured enactment of laws to preserve the petrified forests of Arizona, Crater Lake in Oregon, and Yosemite Park in California. He was a pioneer in legislation for protection of bird life. It was through his efforts that the National bison herds were started.

OSKALOOSA, 55 *m.* (843 alt., 10,123 pop.) *(see Tour 15)*, is at the junction with State 2 *(see Tour 15)* and with US 163 *(see Tour 5A)*.

IOWA IN WINTER

FREMONT, 69 *m.* (842 alt., 450 pop.), founded in 1848 and named in honor of Gen. John C. Fremont, the "Great Pathfinder", is on the divide between the Des Moines and Skunk Rivers.

At 72 *m.* is the junction with State 149, paved.

Right on this road is HEDRICK, 5 *m.* (827 alt., 810 pop.). A plot of ground on the southern edge of town was for 43 years the site of the nationally known Hedrick One Mile Race Track, owned by A. Utterback. It was called a kite track because it was shaped like a kite, and for 12 years a week's racing program each August drew as many as 400 horses. One season $18,000 in purses went to winners. Stalls on the grounds accommodated 200 horses, and every barn in Hedrick was pressed into service. Ten to 15,000 people daily packed the amphitheater, which seated approximately 4,000. Breeders of fine horses from all over the United States exhibited their stock for the sake of the advertising. The track was closed in 1902 or 1903.

At 76 *m.* is the junction with a surfaced dirt road.

Right on this road is KIRKVILLE, 8 *m.* (677 alt., 206 pop.). SUNSET INN, on the former Hill and Bayliss farm, is one of the old houses in the community. It was built by William Bayliss and John Hill, two Englishmen who left England in 1840 to seek their fortunes. They were stranded without funds and in 1847, at a cost of a dollar, staked a claim of 240 acres. Until 1866 they lived in a small log cabin, and then built the two-story tavern, which has 13 rooms. Adjoining the house was a large barn, now torn down, that could accommodate thirty horses.

OTTUMWA, 84 *m.* (649 alt., 28,075 pop.) *(see OTTUMWA).*

Points of Interest: Morrell Packing Co. Plant; Central Park; Statue of Chief Wapello; High Point Chapel.

Ottumwa is at the junction with US 34 *(see Tour 16).*

At 97 *m.* is the junction with State 273, graveled.

Right on this road is DRAKESVILLE, 7 *m.* (891 alt., 190 pop.), named for John Adams Drake, original owner of the townsite and a relative of the Englishman, Sir Francis Drake. The old DRAKE HOUSE *(open),* built more than 100 years ago, still stands but some of the fine floors have been ripped up, and have been used to build pigsties. It was here, beside the Old Alexander Trail, main highway of travel west from the Mississippi River to Council Bluffs in pioneer days, that roving Indians, traders, "forty-niners", Mormons, cavalry officers, and agents of the Underground Railroad used to stop. Just across the trail from the Drake House the tepees of a Fox Indian chieftain and his followers were often pitched.

Drakesville was laid out around a rectangular square, similar to the greens in England. The tallest stone in the old Drakesville cemetery marks the grave of the founder of the town. Francis Marion Drake (1830–1903), one of Iowa's governors (1896–1898), was born and grew to manhood here.

LAKE WAPELLO STATE PARK, 13 *m. (picnicking, bathing, camping, boating facilities),* is a rough wooded area of 1,029.5 acres, including an artificial lake covering 250 acres. Large State fish-rearing ponds are maintained here. A few wild turkeys are still found here, and the lake provides fine bass fishing.

BLOOMFIELD, 103 *m.* (845 alt., 2,226 pop.), seat of Davis County, is an important livestock and distributing center in the midst of the most prosperous sheep-growing area in the State. In 1936 approximately 450,000 pounds of wool was marketed from the county.

The name Bloomfield was selected by the county commissioners by drawing a slip of paper from a hat. The other two slips bore the names "Jefferson" and "Davis."

The JAMES B. WEAVER HOMESTEAD is an old-fashioned brick house in a 3-acre wooded area 3 blocks N. of the public square, which is known as Weaver Park. Weaver (1833–1912) was twice candidate for the Presidency of the United States, running on the Greenback ticket in 1880, and the Peoples' Party ticket in 1892.

Near the northern edge of town is a rustic PARK marking the beginning of rows of elm trees forming a green canopy over the road for some distance.

MARK, 113 *m.,* a wayside station, was formerly called Martinsville, but was renamed because of confusion with the town of Martinsburg in Keokuk County.

At 120 *m.* US 63 crosses the Missouri Line 30 miles N. of Kirksville, Mo.

Tour 3A

(Austin, Minn.)—Osage—Waterloo—Junction with US 30; US 218.
Minnesota Line to Junction with US 30, 140 m.

The I. C. R. R. parallels route between Osage and Waterloo; C. R. I. & P. R. R.,
between Cedar Falls and Waterloo; W. C. F. & N. El. R. R., between Cedar Falls
and La Porte City. The Burlington and the Interstate Transit Bus Lines follow
the highway between Waterloo and Cedar Rapids; Jefferson Bus Lines, between
Otranto Station and Waterloo; and Greyhound Bus Lines, between Charles City
and Waterloo.
Roadbed paved throughout.
Tourist accommodations of all kinds available, chiefly in cities.

US 218 crosses the Minnesota Line, 0 *m.*, 12 miles S. of Austin, Minn.,
and runs generally southeastward through predominantly prairie land,
broken by many small streams and several large rivers.

At 4 *m.* is the junction with a surfaced dirt road.

Right on this road is OTRANTO STATION, 3 *m.* (1,172 alt.), a hamlet. Here
is one of the ginseng arbors for which this region is known. Ginseng is a native
plant that will grow wild in rich moist soils, in beech, poplar, maple and other
hardwood forests. It grows about a foot in height, branching into three parts,
each of which divide into five leaflets. The greenish-yellow flowers are borne in
a single cluster, later replaced by bright red berries. The fleshy, wrinkled taproot,
with a sweet taste and aromatic odor, is held in high esteem by the Chinese, who
regard it as a cure for all ills. Roots possessing shapes similar to the human body
are so much in demand that fabulous prices are paid, often as high as 500 times
their weight in silver. One shipment of 500 pounds from this region is said to
have sold for $17,500. Internal strife in China has largely destroyed the principal
market, and consequently most of the arbors in the county have been discontinued.
The plant is grown in lathe houses to provide the necessary shade. An acre requires an initial outlay of about $1,500, and the plants can be harvested only once
in seven years.

ST. ANSGAR, 9 *m.* (1,175 alt., 964 pop.), on the east bank of the
Cedar River, was settled in 1853 by Czechs whose descendants here still
retain many European customs and traditions. Festivals, with native folk
songs, dances, and band music, are frequently held. At the annual fall
festival the entertainment is in the native tongue.

Weddings are the occasion for special festivities. In Czechoslovakia it
was the custom for the bride to give the bridegroom a feather for his hat,
a shirt to wear at the ceremony, and a handkerchief. After the ceremony
each returned home, meeting later at the bride's house for dinner, where
"only the worthy older guests" sat at the table. An adorned wagon carried
the bride's possessions to her new home, which were placed on the wagon
in such a way that everyone could see and admire them.

These customs have been modified by time and distance from the mother-
land, but a few are still observed without change. Every one in town is in-

vited to the wedding celebration, and a chance visitor may find himself caught up in the gaiety and plied with food and drink by the hospitable Czechs. The festivities usually culminate in a dance in which both young and old participate.

The Sokol Societies in St. Ansgar and the surrounding region are the center of folk activities. The society was founded in Bohemia in 1862, as an organization of gymnasts, their programs including instruction in civics, ethics, and matters pertaining to community betterment. "Sokol" means *falcon,* and members of the society wear special dress, with falcon feathers in their caps.

St. Ansgar is the center of a region in which growing and marketing Irish potatoes and onions is the chief industry. During a good harvest year both products are shipped out in trainload lots. Farmers give prizes to any visitor finding weeds in their onion fields.

Along the Cedar River is a picturesque old WATER-MILL, which is still used in grinding feed. Above the river dam there is excellent bass fishing.

At 11 *m.* is a HALL, built by the Czech residents of St. Ansgar to serve as a center for social activities, particularly those of the young people.

OSAGE, 21 *m.* (1,169 alt., 2,964 pop.), seat of Mitchell County, was first settled in 1853 by Hiram Hart, and named Coral in 1854 for the daughter of Dr. A. H. Moore who first platted the town. This plat was never recorded, but on a later plat made by representatives of the banker, Orrin Sage, of Ware, Mass., the town was called Osage (O. Sage) in his honor.

Hamlin Garland (1860–), whose novel *Son of the Middle Border* was autobiographical, resided on a farm near Osage when a boy, and attended the Cedar Valley Seminary, which occupied buildings now used by the high school.

Osage is at the junction with State 9 *(see Tour 10).*

At 22 *m.* is the junction with a dirt road.

Right on this road is SPRING PARK, 1 *m.,* on the banks of the Cedar River. It is a 41-acre area, traversed by many winding graveled roads. A lake formed by damming the river provides a place for swimming, boating, and fishing. There are also picnic facilities and a rifle range.

FLOYD, 36 *m.* (1,099 alt., 350 pop.), on the banks of the Cedar River, was named in honor of William Floyd of Long Island, N. Y., one of the signers of the Declaration of Independence. Rock used for building purposes is quarried along the streams. A good grade of ochre is found in extensive quantities here, as well as clay suitable for manufacture of brick; there are also large beds of sand and gravel.

Southeast of Floyd for 24 miles the highway traverses the hills and valleys along the bank of the Cedar River (L). In Floyd County, where cultivation has not yet deprived the land of native shrubs and trees, there are frequently clumps of wild plum trees—a white mist of blossoms in the spring—on the hills and by the roadside. Wild crab-apple blossoms fill the air with fragrance. Wild grape, gooseberry, black cherry, elderberry, and blackhaw are abundant.

CHARLES CITY, 42 *m.* (1,005 alt., 8,039 pop.), seat of Floyd County, was first known as The Ford; there was once a Winnebago Indian village nearby. The first settlement was made by Joseph Kelly in 1850. The name was changed to Charles City in 1869 in honor of Joseph Kelly's son, Charles.

When Charles W. Hart and his college classmate, Charles H. Parr, began building stationary gasoline engines here in 1896, they also started a series of experiments with machines to be used in farming. Because they built traction motors, their advertising manager, W. H. Williams, coined the new name "tractor." Now the Oliver Farm Equipment Co. Plant is called the HART-PARR WORKS *(open weekdays except Sat. p.m., tours 8, 9, 10, a. m. and 1, 2, 3 p. m.).* The company has distributing agencies in 37 foreign countries, and, at peak production periods, ships trainloads of tractors daily to the agricultural regions of the United States. The Hart-Parr Model 3 tractor is on display in the Museum of Science and Industry in Chicago.

C. A. Fullerton (1861–), known nationally for his pioneer work in the development of music training for school children in rural schools, was born here. Ilza Niemack (1905–), violinist and composer, instructor at Iowa State College at Ames (1936), and at one time soloist for the New York Philharmonic Orchestra, is a native of Charles City. Carrie Lane Chapman Catt (1859–), active in women's suffrage and peace movements, lived when a girl about 4 miles S. of town, and at the peak of her career, lived for a time in the town. J. C. Arthur (1850–), botanist and an authority on rust diseases in plants, was born here and has long been a resident.

An IOWA STATE COLLEGE EXPERIMENTAL STATION is (1938) in operation on the C. C. Patten farm near the southwestern limits of Charles City. It was established to find means of controlling a disease that was destroying the fruit trees. Efforts to save the orchard here, which was one of those most affected, have been so successful that the station will be discontinued before long.

Patten, founder of the Patten Nursery has spent the greater part of his life developing hardy varieties of apples, including Patten Greening. Patten began this work long before any institution in the State had undertaken experiments along this line.

Many of the buildings in the town are of native stone. At the southern edge of town, near US 218, is (L) a PARK, site of a stone quarry where most of the stone for early buildings was quarried. The first old wagon road, leading into town from the south runs through the park.

The SHERMAN NURSERY of 700 acres, at the intersection with State 14 on the southern edge of the city, specializes in growing evergreens. It was founded in 1884 by Erwin Milo Sherman, and for nearly half a century has contributed fine trees, shrubs, and other plants for landscaping purposes in many parts of the United States and of Canada. Six large greenhouses are used for growing roses.

Charles City is at the junction with US 18 *(see Tour 11).*

Left from Charles City on an improved dirt road to a group of 34 INDIAN MOUNDS, 2 *m.* The site was formerly covered by timber, but has been cleared for

40 years. The mounds were originally from 2 to 3 feet above the surrounding ground, but cultivation of the land has cut them down to about 1½ feet. Low and circular or ovate in form, some appear to have been fortifications, others were burial places. From the latter have been taken numerous skeletons that were about 4 feet below the surface in a bowl-shaped excavation. Small pieces of charcoal found in the upper strata, which consisted of soil and ashes, indicate that the soil around the bodies was baked by a fire. Among the skeletons were those of a middle-aged woman, a child, two young adults (one male and one female), and the bones of a six-foot man whose teeth were worn to the jaw. The skull of the woman had primitive development. The mounds vary greatly in size, some being 163 feet long and 30 or 40 feet wide. Handmade pottery, arrow points, drills, hammers, lance points, stone hatchets, and in one instance, a knife, a spear, and a "plum bob" (exceedingly rare in Iowa) were found. Near the southern end of the mound group, on the border of a deep depression, are the remains of extensive earthworks. Around this a fierce battle was once fought, as is shown by the number of arrow and spear points and stone hatchets found here.

In the region surrounding Charles City there is a heavy-bedded, brownish-drab limestone, a fossiliferous stone locally called "Charles City marble." When cut and polished it presents a beautiful marble-like appearance, and is excellent for mosaic or inlaid work. Nuggets of zinc, copper, and iron ores have been uncovered in the drift in various parts of the county.

NASHUA, 53 m. (968 alt., 1,363 pop.), at the confluence of the Cedar and Little Cedar Rivers, was named by E. P. Greeley for his old home town in New Hampshire. The settlement was first called Bridgeport and later Woodbridge.

Left from Nashua on a graveled road is BRADFORD, 2 m., an almost deserted village containing the LITTLE BROWN CHURCH IN THE VALE. This church has become known through the popular hymn, The Little Brown Church in the Vale, written by Dr. W. S. Pitts of Fredericksburg. The building is a weatherbeaten, brown-painted frame structure of severe New England type. The church was built in the 1860's through the cooperative efforts of the congregation. One man donated lots, another logs, and others sawed them into lumber. A "bee" quarried the stone and the village mason laid the foundation. A collection from a Sunday school in Massachusetts was used to purchase the finishing lumber, which was hauled 80 miles by wagon from McGregor, Iowa.

PLAINFIELD, 60 m. (942 alt., 293 pop.), is near the Cedar River. The town was named for Plainfield, Ill., former home of many of the settlers.

WAVERLY, 71 m. (948 alt., 3,652 pop.), was to have been named Harmon for its founder, W. P. Harmon. But the chief speaker at the meeting formally naming the town had spent the morning reading one of the Waverly novels, and in the midst of his address pronounced Waverly instead of Harmon. Harmon raised no objections, and the name was retained.

WARTBURG NORMAL COLLEGE, under the control of the American Lutheran Church, was established here (1935) by merging of schools at Clinton, Iowa, and St. Paul, Minn. It offers a four-year course. The church also maintains an orphans' home here.

The WAVERLY MUSEUM (open), belonging to the college, had its inception in 1894, when Dr. Clarence Albrecht, an explorer connected with the Chicago Museum of Natural History, contributed a large, mounted sea tortoise. American missionaries in New Guinea sent other exhibits, in-

"THE LITTLE BROWN CHURCH IN THE VALE," BRADFORD

cluding war clubs and spears, grass skirts, and cooking utensils of savages. The most valuable object in the large ornithological collection is a South American cockatoo belonging to a now extinct species. Ancient Roman coins, and a pottery lamp found in the Catacombs of Rome are also on view.

The Cedar River flows through the northeast corner of the town.

Right from Waverly on paved State 10, crossing the Shellrock River at 5.5 *m.*; at 12 *m.* is the junction with State 53, paved; R. here to HEERY WOODS STATE PARK, 14 *m.*; a high ridge bordering the beautiful Shellrock River is a feature of this 380-acre wooded area, which is in its natural state.

JANESVILLE, 77 *m.* (891 alt., 331 pop.), on the bank of the Cedar River, named in 1849 by John T. Barrick, first settler, in honor of his wife, was the first town in the county.

CEDAR FALLS, 85 *m.* (854 alt., 7,362 pop.) *(see Tour 12)*, is at the junction with US 20 *(see Tour 12)*. Southeast of Cedar Falls US 218 follows the Cedar River.

WATERLOO, 92 *m.*, (856 alt., 46,119 pop.) *(see WATERLOO)*.

Points of Interest: Boulder Church; packing plant; agricultural machinery factories; Dairy Cattle Congress Exposition Buildings.

Waterloo is at the junction with US 20 *(see Tour 12)* and US 63 *(see Tour 3)*.

Left from Waterloo on a side road to SOUTH WATERLOO CHURCH, 5 *m.*, in the center of a Dunkard settlement in Orange township. Here are 142 fine farms, with a total population of 802. The South Waterloo, or Orange, Church was organized in April 1856, with 12 members, and the present building was erected in 1868 at a cost of $5,000. It is also known as the Tunker Church of Orange, and has a large Sunday School. The plain structure has two entrances and an aisle divides the room into two parts, one of which is occupied by the men, and the other by the women. The Dunkards believe in triple immersion, face downward, and that the Lord's Supper should consist of a full meal, eaten in the evening. Their church has a kitchen for preparing this meal. Repentance of sin, baptism, the Lord's Supper, and foot-washing are doctrinal rites. They do not believe in a paid ministry, do not receive a divorced person into the church unless he or she promises not to marry again during the life of the former partner, and they refuse members belonging to secret societies. They allow no public money to be expended for the poor or helpless of their congregations, providing for them themselves. Anyone who fails in business is aided three times in making new starts. If there is a third failure they accept it as God's will that the unfortunate brother should not succeed. It is the custom, on meeting, to extend the hand and salute with a kiss. They do not vote, take oath of office, or participate in political affairs. They will not bear arms, or study the art of war. During a meal the men sit at one side of the table, women at the other. Their clothes, habits, home furnishings, and religion follow a pattern of stark simplicity. The Tunker love feast is a series of services usually beginning on the forenoon of Saturday and ending with an assembly and sermon Sunday morning. The members are seated around long immaculately white tables, the women wearing white caps—a scene resembling some 15th century painting. Each woman brings food for the feast. Tunker (baptizer) was the original German name for the sect, before it was corrupted to Dunker, and later Dunkard. This sect is somewhat similar to the Hook and Eye Dutch. There is another Dunkard settlement near South English *(see Tour 15)*.

Southeast of Waterloo US 218 runs through a scenic area for 15 miles, among the hills bordering the Cedar River valley.

LA PORTE CITY, 107 *m.* (812 alt., 1,470 pop.), was first called La Porte for the city of that name in Indiana. Because the names were confused in the mails, the word "city" was added. The first iron bridge in Black Hawk County was constructed across Big Creek here in 1867. Big Creek, flowing through the center of the town, is well stocked with bass, catfish, and carp, and furnishes excellent fishing.

VINTON, 126 *m.,* (810 alt., 3,372 pop.), seat of Benton County, was settled in 1839 by Reuben Daskirk and was first known as Northport, later as Fremont; in 1846 the post office in Benton County was established here, and the name changed to Vinton, for Plym Vinton, a Congressman from Ohio, who paid $50 for the honor.

At Vinton is the IOWA STATE SCHOOL FOR THE BLIND. Graduates of the school can enter any Iowa college and continue their education with the aid of a "reader". Modern training methods and facilities enable the students to participate in sports, music, handicraft work, and other activities, despite their handicap. Of the faculty of 66 members, two are totally blind, and many have impaired vision.

WHEELER CORNER, 140 *m.* (1,046 alt.), is at the junction with US 30 *(see Tour 13).*

Tour 4

(Albert Lea, Minn.)—Mason City—Iowa Falls—Ames—Des Moines—Indianola—Lineville—(Chillicothe, Mo.) ; US 65.
Minnesota Line to Missouri Line, 231 m.

C. R. I. & P. R. R. parallels this route between the Minnesota Line and De Moines, and between Summerset and Indianola; C. G. W. R. R., between Manly and Mason City; M. & St. L. R. R., between Nevada and Des Moines; Ft. D., D. M. & So. R. R., between Huxley and Des Moines.
Jefferson Bus Line follows highway between Minnesota Line and Indianola; Interstate Transit Bus Line, between Northwood and Indianola.
Roadbed paved between Minnesota Line and Junction with US 69; elsewhere bituminous surfaced and graveled. Accommodations of all kinds, chiefly in cities.

Section a. MINNESOTA LINE *to* AMES, *124 m.*

For about 7 miles after crossing the Minnesota Line, 11 miles S. of Albert Lea, Minn., US 65 follows low hills bordering the Shellrock River valley. The highway traverses typical prairie country, crossing several rivers, which in this section are comparatively shallow and meandering.

NORTHWOOD, 4 *m.* (1,222 alt., 1,654 pop.), seat of Worth County, is on the banks of the Shellrock River. It was largely settled by Norwegians; the first arrival was Gilbrand Nellum in 1853.

At 15 *m.* is the junction with State 9 *(see Tour 10)*.

At 23 *m.* is the junction with a dirt road.

Right on this road along Lime Creek; the route offers vistas of rolling prairies interspersed with woodland.

MASON CITY, 25 *m.* (1,130 alt., 23,304 pop.) *(see MASON CITY)*.

Points of Interest: Herbert Quick House; clay products plants; Portland Cement Mills.

Mason City is at the junction with US 18 *(see Tour 11)*.

Beets are grown within a radius of 75 miles of Mason City, on contract with the beet sugar refinery there. Farmers contract to plant a given number of acres, the products of which the refinery agrees to buy. Among the 2,000 or so laborers in the beet fields, which are cultivated largely with hand labor, are hundreds of Mexicans. They live in little shacks set far back from the road in corners of the fields. Laboriously bending over the tiny new plants, the laborer—and frequently his wife and children— proceeds slowly along the rows, thinning out the weak plants. Later, as the leaves begin to appear on slender pink stalks, a hoe is used to remove the weeds from around the roots. During the harvest season in early autumn men follow the digging machine, a line of bent figures stooping rhythmically to pick up the plants and cut off the tops, piling the beets on one side and heaping the green leaves on the other, forming long ribbons across the field. The laborers receive on an average of $1.50 a day for their work, which lasts from April till October.

ROCKWELL, 36.5 *m.* (1,130 alt., 750 pop.), on a branch of the Beaver Dam Creek, was named for B. G. Rockwell, at one time owner of the land on which the village stands. It is the home of the Sacred Heart Academy, a Roman Catholic boarding and day school.

SHEFFIELD, 42.5 *m.* (1,076 alt., 1,057 pop.), on the bank of Bailey's Creek, was named for the original owner of the town site. The BAILEY CREEK DAM, on the creek of that name, was constructed of wood, stone, and earth, entirely by volunteer labor under the sponsorship of the Sportsmen's Conservation Club, and was built where an old pioneer bridge formerly spaned the creek in what is now Sheffield City Park. The pool has been stocked with fish common in Iowa streams. A rustic footbridge crosses the stream on the piling that once supported the bridge over which the yoked oxen and prairie schooners trundled on their journey westward.

At 51 *m.* is the junction with a graveled road.

Right on this road to BEED'S LAKE STATE PARK, 3 *m. (fishing, boating, bathing and picnicking facilities)*, containing 267 acres, with a large 130-acre deepwater artificial lake, created by a 170-foot dam; the lake is fed by a creek, whose source, a spring, has never dried up in summer or frozen in winter. The lake was first created in 1857 by F. K. Hansberry for the operation of a flourmill, and was later enlarged to cover 40 acres. The mill ceased operation in 1904. Hampton businessmen sought to buy the property for a park but were unsuccessful in raising funds, and the lake was drained. Through the impetus furnished by the local chapter of the Izaak Walton League of Franklin County the land was purchased and offered to the conservation commission, and development begun. The dike of the original lake is still in its place. A custodian is in charge.

HAMPTON, 53 *m.* (1,145 alt., 3,473 pop.), seat of Franklin County, was founded by Job Garner and George Ryan in 1856. A huge granite boulder marks the site of the Garner cabin. The village was first named Benjamin.

Hampton is the headquarters of the Franklin County Farm Bureau whose activities are typical of those carried on in all counties in the State. Each member family of this voluntary organization pays $10 annual dues. The organization and leadership of boys' and girls' 4-H clubs and of farm projects for men and for women, and the supervision of a service department, an insurance department, and of musical activities, are the principal functions of the organization.

The EARL FERRIS NURSERY, established here in 1881, is unusually large, specializing in evergreen shrubs and trees.

South of Hampton, US 65 traverses level prairie land. In early spring the landscape is delightful, with new willow shoots, pale yellow against late skifts of snow and the older willow groves' gray purple. Every mile has alternating vistas of black plowed ground, fresh-disked fields, and pale green pastures; here and there is the crisscross of cornblades and of fallen stalks in old cornfields.

At 57.5 *m.* is the junction with a side road.

Left on this road is a granite boulder, 5 *m.,* marking the first post office and first town in the county—the now deserted MAYSVILLE. A two-story STONE SCHOOLHOUSE, built in 1856, still stands.

At 66 *m.* is a junction with US 20 *(see Tour 12);* between this point and Iowa Falls the two routes are united.

IOWA FALLS, 72 *m.* (1,107 alt., 4,112 pop.), on the Iowa River, was a village known successively as Rocksylvania and White's Mills before it was incorporated in 1856. The river here flows through a narrow gorge that has limestone walls rising in some places more than 70 feet; back of these are bluffs about 50 feet higher. Scrub cedar and flowering shrubs grow in the crevices of the rocks. In the spring red-orange columbines dot the face of the cliffs. Pigeons nest on the ledges, and cliff-swallows build mud nests in the rocky walls.

At Iowa Falls is ELLSWORTH JUNIOR COLLEGE, a 2-year accredited school with a music department of high standing.

The IOWA FALLS MUSEUM *(open),* erected in 1932 by M. M. Kickels, houses a collection of pioneer relics, including an early bicycle, and the first gasoline buggy and the first telephone brought to the town. There is also a collection of stone relics from Indian mounds, and another of land and water birds. The most important collection, containing nearly a thousand guns, is in glass cases extending from the floor to the ceiling. Among the guns are a tiny muff pistol (miniature cannon), French, Spanish, and American dueling pistols, samples of Chicago gangsters' "rods," and one of the early repeating rifles. The last belonged to P. W. Porter, who invented and made it in 1851; it is the rifle that killed the inventor when he started to show it to Samuel Colt, maker of the Colt's revolver.

At the northwestern edge of town is the IRA NICHOLS BIRD AND FLOWER REFUGE *(visited by permission)*, established by Ira A. Nichols, former editor of the *Hardin County Citizen*. Here are specimens of prairie flora, some now disappearing from the region—shootingstars, bleeding-hearts, gentians, turtlehead, and fawn ladyslippers. A thicket of wild crab-apple forms a long gay wall in the spring.

On the western side of town on the river bluffs are the BAPTIST AS-SEMBLY GROUNDS, where the Iowa Baptist Convention meets each summer for a week and is housed in a small tent city. Lectures and devotional serv-ices fill the program. Tennis courts, boats, bathing beaches, and refresh-ment stands give a resort air to the grounds.

Iowa Falls is at the junction with US 20 *(see Tour 12)*.

Right from Iowa Falls on an improved dirt road to SILOAM SPRINGS, 2 *m.*, a privately owned park containing picnic grounds and a dance pavilion. The spring water is said to have medicinal qualities.

At 83 *m.* is the junction with State 57, paved. Here in 1932, at a tourist park and camp, was held the first big organization meeting of the United Farmers, a group of 6,000 men from six or seven counties. For some time the farmers had been talking of organization and of "taking action" be-cause of the many mortgage foreclosures by insurance and mortgage com-panies. After a day of threshing, they would hold an informal meeting in a county schoolhouse or in some farmer's yard where lanterns were strung up to give light and a hayrack served as a platform. Drawing its main strength from Hardin County, the United Farmers planned a course of ac-tion. When those threatened with eviction and deficiency judgments brought their cases to the United Farmers, pickets were sent out to patrol the farms and warn away would-be renters or purchasers. In one instance, a mortgage company sent 21 prospective renters or purchasers to inspect a homestead whose owner was being dispossessed. Each man was met by the picket-patrol and informed that if he moved there he could not have a telephone (the telephone line is co-operative in that township), his chil-dren could not ride to school on the school bus, his neighbors would not help him thresh or shell corn, and no one would have any social relations with him or his family. The mortgage company finally rented the place to a man who had been living 100 miles away. After a few months of isola-tion the new tenant went to his nearest neighbor to talk to him about the situation, but the neighbor ignored him. The "outcast" finally agreed to leave the farm.

The United Farmers also set up conciliation committees to deal with mortgage companies preparing to foreclose on farms of members. These committees met with company representatives and announced that they would not tolerate evictions and deficiency judgments, that if anyone was to have a chance to buy a farm at a price less than the value of the mort-gage, it must be the original owner. They were usually successful in having the mortgages scaled down and in arranging for the owners to buy back their properties.

TWO GENERATIONS

When in May 1933 the Agricultural Adjustment Administration's program went into effect, the State adopted the idea of conciliation committees, but, without the force of an organized group and no other leverage than persuasive power, it was not very successful in arranging compromises with the mortgage companies. After the introduction of the corn-sealing program and the rise in farm prices, the organization began to lose membership and has (1938) practically disappeared.

Left from the tourist camp on State 57 is ELDORA, 8 *m.*, (1,070 alt., 3,200 pop.), seat of Hardin County. The STATE TRAINING SCHOOL FOR BOYS *(visitors 8-5 except Sat., Sun., holidays)*, is by the highway (R) just outside the city limits. Delinquent boys from 7 to 16 years of age are admitted here, instructed in a trade, and required to finish high school. Twenty-two trades are taught, including tailoring, shoemaking, and scientific dairying. The school was established here in 1868. At first the town was named Eldorado because of a rush for gold here in 1851, but the name was later shortened. John Ellsworth had discovered the glittering particles of gold in the black soil, but no vein was discovered. The city sponsors an annual Whiskers Day when, as a part of the festivities, a kangaroo court imposes heavy fines on all members of the Whiskers Club who have failed to let their whiskers grow for several weeks preceding the affair.

At 9 *m.* is the junction with State 118, which leads (L) through PINE LAKE STATE PARK *(picnicking, bathing and boating facilities)*, covering 533 acres on the east bank of the Iowa River. Small creeks have been dammed here to form two round, mirror-like lakes, covering about 150 acres. High wooded hills along the creek valley form a natural lake basin. A lodge, bathhouse, and columns at the park entrance are built of native sandstone. Four conical Indian mounds, a State fish hatchery and a Y. M. C. A. camp are in the area.

In this park as in almost all parks in the State, in hamlets, villages, towns, and on farms, horseshoe pitching has been a favorite recreation, mainly for older men, since pioneer days. "Barnyard golf" old timers renamed it when golf was becoming popular. Equipment is simple and always at hand in any agricultural community. Courts are usually in a shady place and individual competition is great.

HUBBARD (L), 89 *m.* (1,099 alt., 785 pop.), was a boyhood home of Herbert Hoover, President of the United States 1929–1933. He lived at the home of an uncle near Hubbard, and his grandfather is buried here. A farmers' co-operative creamery is the only business plant in this quiet little village.

ZEARING, 99 *m.* (1,053 alt., 475 pop.), was named Ashhurst in 1882, but Major Zearing, a doctor in Chicago who was visiting in the town, promised to build an Evangelical Church if the town was named for him. The church, built in 1881, was later replaced by a larger building. Coal mining in the vicinity, was at one time a source of local prosperity, but the mines are now inactive.

COLO, 109 *m.* (1,043 alt., 532 pop.) *(see Tour 13)*, is at the junction with US 30 *(see Tour 13)*. For 15 miles US 65 and US 30 run directly west as one route.

NEVADA, 116 *m.* (1,001 alt., 3,133 pop.) *(see Tour 13)*.

AMES, 124 *m.* (926 alt., 10,261 pop.) *(see AMES)*.

Point of Interest: Iowa State College of Agriculture and Mechanic Arts.

Ames is at the junction with US 69 *(see Tour 5)*. Here US 30 *(see Tour 13)* leaves the route.

Section b. AMES *to* MISSOURI LINE, *107 m.*

For 53 miles south of Ames, 0 *m.*, US 65 and US 69 are one route *(see Tour 5, sec. b).*

At 53 *m.*, the routes separate, US 65 turning L. US 69 continues S. *(see Tour 5).*

LUCAS, 74 *m.* (888 alt., 514 pop.)*(see Tour 16),* is at the junction with US 34 *(see Tour 16).*

South of Lucas the countryside has numerous trees, and is hilly.

DERBY, 81 *m.* (1,094 alt., 280 pop.), has held a local Agricultural Fair each September since 1919. Horses, cattle, swine, sheep, poultry, animal pets, agricultural products, fruits, plants, flowers, and culinary products are exhibited in usual fair style, with accompanying bright lights and the noisy confusion of holiday crowds.

HUMESTON, 87 *m.* (1,104 alt., 924 pop.), a dairying and farming trade center established in 1872, was named for Alva Humeston, a railroad official who was active in promoting the extension of the railroad through the town.

At 94 *m.* is the junction with State 3 *(see Tour 17).*

LINEVILLE, 107 *m.* (1,084 alt., 531 pop.), was so named because it lies partly in Iowa and partly in Missouri. In 1851 a pioneer merchant of the town built a store, half in Missouri and half in Iowa. In the Iowa part he sold clothing and groceries, and in the Missouri part he dispensed liquor, operating within the law in both States. The post office is in Iowa. The Missouri-Iowa Line bounds the south side of the town square.

US 65 crosses the Missouri Line 58 miles N. of Chillicothe, Mo.

Tour 5

(Albert Lea, Minn.)—Forest City—Ames—Des Moines—Lamoni—(Kansas City, Mo.) ; US 69, US 65-69.
Minnesota Line to Missouri Line, 227 m.

Minneapolis & St. L. R. R. parallels this route between the Minnesota Line and Forest City, and between Belmond and Indianola; C. R. I. & P. R. R., between Jewell and Des Moines; Ft. D., D. M. & S. R. R., between Huxley and Des Moines; C. B. & Q. R. R., between Delby and Humeston.

The Jefferson Bus Lines follow the highway throughout; Interstate Transit Bus Line, between Blairsburg and Missouri Line; Burlington Bus Line, between Des Moines and Weldon.

Roadbed paved, except 15 m., graveled, between Minnesota Line and junction with State 9.

Tourist accommodations available chiefly in cities.

Section a. MINNESOTA LINE *to* AMES, *110 m., US 69.*

Crossing the Minnesota Line 11 miles S. of Albert Lea, Minn., US 69 passes along the eastern edge of a rich agricultural region. The trees are widely scattered, growing mostly along the valleys of the rivers and small streams. Stretching far into the distance in summer are acres of corn and of yellow oats, with occasional patches of fragrant purple and red clover.

EMMONS, 0 *m.,* on the Minnesota-Iowa Line, is at the junction with a surfaced dirt road.

Left on this road to SILVER LAKE, 7 *m.,* a small body of water about 1 mile long *(boating, fishing, picnic grounds).*

At 5 *m.* are heavily wooded hills *(picnic facilities).*

LAKE MILLS, 7 *m.* (1,266 alt., 1,474 pop.), first known as Slauchville, later as Saylorville, received its present name when a mill was built nearby on the edge of a small lake, now dry.

Left from Lake Mills on a surfaced road 2.5 *m.;* L. here to RICE LAKE STATE LAKE PRESERVE, 3 *m. (picnicking, dancing, baseball, shelter house),* an area of 50 acres bordering Rice Lake. The lake and preserve lie in a large basin covering about 200 acres. Peat bogs are found here; rushes and the tall, grasslike wild rice grow in abundance. Oak and hard maple trees border the south bank. A public golf course is adjacent to the park.

US 69 turns R. at Lake Mills, running directly west for a few miles. At 11 *m.* is the junction with an unimproved dirt road.

Right on this road is SCARVILLE, 4 *m.* (1,246 alt., 163 pop.), named for Ole Scar, who owned much of the land in this vicinity when the town was established. Left from Scarville 4 *m.* is LAKE HARMON, covering about 40 acres; since being drained in 1913, it has become little more than a swamp filled with weeds.

Turning L. here US 69 is an almost straight route for 130 miles. Small lakes, narrow streams, shallow valleys, and groves of trees are variations in the landscape along the road's unswerving course.

LELAND, 18 *m.* (1,217 alt., 164 pop.), was named in 1882 for the town's first postmaster, J. D. Leland. The town sponsors an annual Watermelon Day in August, during which small boys from all parts of the county hitch-hike here to share in the free watermelons served to everyone. The melons are bought by the carload and are served chilled in quarter sections, beginning at noon. Many attend the feast, not only to enjoy the melons, but to witness the youngsters devouring the fruit without fork or spoon. "Who kin eat the most" contests develop quickly, as the red-meated, wedged-shaped cuts are distributed.

FOREST CITY, 22 *m.* (1,226 alt., 2,016 pop.), seat of Winnebago County, is on the banks of Lime Creek. Platted in 1856, it was named by an early settler, Judge Robert Clark, who appreciated the fine timberland near the site. Winnebago County was named for an Indian tribe.

In JASPER THOMPSON PARK stands an ALASKAN TOTEM POLE, procured and erected by Jasper Thompson, for whom the park was named. Thompson was a local banker who collected Indian relics.

WALDORF JUNIOR COLLEGE, operated by the Lutheran Church, has an average annual enrollment of 341 students, the largest (1937) junior college enrollment in Iowa. The building now occupied by the college was formerly a hotel.

Rudolph M. Anderson (1876), Arctic explorer, second in command of the Stefansson Expedition (1908–1912), spent his boyhood here, and Ida Fuller (1868–1922), dancer of the 1890's and sister-in-law of Loie Fuller, was born here.

On May 2, 1890, at 5:15 P.M., a meteor exploded about 11 miles northwest of town. The velocity of the fireball was so great that it passed through the earth's atmosphere in only a few seconds. The course of the meteor, from the spot where it was first seen in the sky until it passed below the horizon, was marked by a ribbon of smoke having straight, sharply defined edges. The phenomenon was visible 300 miles from the spot where it landed, and for many miles around a noise was heard resembling heavy cannonading, accompanied by a "rushing sound" and a noticeable tremor; an area about 4 miles long and 2 miles wide was showered with fragments weighing from one ounce to 81 pounds, some of which are still occasionally found in the vicinity.

In the early 1890's a Flax Palace was built in the town to advertise flax grown in Winnebago County. This crop was favored at the time as the one growing best on virgin soil and preparing the ground for other crops. The palace consisted of a main building, 136 feet in length, with an octagonal one on each side, forming a continuous structure three stories high, with 7,500 feet of floor space. Volunteers—men, women, and children— gathered grain, grasses, wild flowers, vines, and foliage for decoration of the interior. Twelve weaving machines were brought from Chicago to weave flax stems to serve as the covering of the palace; only the seed heads of the grain were visible. At the conclusion of each fair the grain was threshed. After a few years the fair was abandoned. Only one part of the building, one of the octagonal sections, remains. Today sugar beets and sweet corn grow in the fields where flax was formerly planted.

Forest City is at the junction with State 9 *(see Tour 10)*.

At 26 *m.* is junction with surfaced dirt road.

Right on this road to CRYSTAL LAKE, 9 *m.*, a small body of water bordering the town, CRYSTAL LAKE, (1,258 alt., 271 pop.). The lake is 6 to 7 feet in depth *(boating, fishing, bathing facilities)*. Attractive wooded banks are mirrored in the clear waters.

At 33.5 *m.* is the junction with US 18 *(see Tour 11)*.

GARNER, 35 *m.* (1,209 alt., 1,241 pop.), seat of Hancock County, was named for a railroad official, and the county was named in honor of Gen. Winfield Scott Hancock of the U. S. Army. The county seat was transferred from Concord, about a mile distant, when the railroad was built through Garner, missing Concord.

KLEMME, 41 *m.* (1,227 alt., 463 pop.), has a cooperative creamery.

GOODELL, 47 *m.* (1,236 alt., 210 pop.), lies near the west bank of the Iowa River.

Right from Goodell on a surfaced dirt road are the small TWIN LAKES, 6 *m.* *(excellent fishing)*, on each side of the road

BELMOND, 52 *m.* (1,181 alt., 1,733 pop.), the oldest town in Wright County, lies along both banks of the Iowa River. It was named by the young men and women of the settlement in honor of the attractive daughter, Belle, of Mr. and Mrs. Dumond, first settlers here, Belle and Dumond, being combined.

The Belmond *Herald* for many years owned the old Owen Lovejoy printing press, used at Alton, Ill., by Lovejoy whose extreme abolitionist position caused his enemies to throw his press into the Mississippi. The press became the property of the Clear Lake *Observer,* which sold it to the Belmond *Herald* in 1872. The Libby Prison Commission of Chicago bought it later for $100 as an anti-slavery campaign relic.

Belmond has a BEET SUGAR PLANT *(open to visitors),* completed in 1920 at a cost of $1,600,000, with a capacity of 1,500 tons of beets daily. Farmers in the vicinity contract to supply the beets; the yield of beets is sometimes 22 tons an acre, giving 200 to 220 pounds of sugar a ton. The average yield, however, is 9 tons and the return to the farmer about $50 an acre, plus the beet tops returned for use as stock feed.

Right from Belmond on surfaced dirt road to TWIN SISTERS LAKES, 3.5 *m.* *(fishing),* so-named because they are similar in size and close together.

At 53 *m.* is a wooded tract called FRANKLIN GROVE, which includes a 10-acre park.

At 56 *m.* is the junction with a dirt road.

Right on this road to the HARRY BROOKS PONY FARM, 2 *m.,* 20 years ago the largest of its kind in the United States. At that time more than 1,000 ponies grazed in pasture lands along the Iowa River. Ponies are still reared commercially in small numbers.

LITTLE WALL LAKE, 3.5 *m.,* is at CORNELIA, a station on the C. G. W. R. R.; L. here to ELM LAKE, 4.5 *m.* In this vicinity the early settlers often sowed flax as a first crop after breaking the prairie sod. Most attempts to utilize it for making linen failed. The Flax Palace *(see above)* at Forest City was not successful in establishing flax as a northern Iowa crop; however, a number of attempts have been made to raise it for its seed. One such experiment was recently conducted on a tract of virgin prairie covering two sections of land Northeast of Elm Lake. Known locally as the "big pastures," the two sections had been a stopping-place for wild ducks on their migrations; the small ponds were replaced by broad fields of flax that changed to a blue expanse in August merging into the blue of the sky. Threshing machines harvested the seeds, pouring them into two-bushel sacks. Today the land is used for vegetable crops.

SOLBERG, 59 *m.,* named for a Jewish peddler, is a small community with a few houses and a grain elevator.

Right from Solberg on State 10 is CLARION, 5 *m.* (1,170 alt., 2,578 pop.), the only county seat in Iowa that is in the exact center of the county. Incorporated in 1881, the town was named for Clarion, Pa.

In this area, as elsewhere in the world where watermelons are abundant, few farm lads grow up without taking part in a "watermelon steal." A moonlight night is usually chosen so that the melons can easily be found, which also makes it easier for the farmer, with his gun full of rock salt, to see the marauders should his dog give the alarm. Tingling with excitement, the gang steals silently through the cornfield to the secluded spot where the farmer, profiting from experience, has hidden his watermelon patch. Even the rustling of corn leaves makes them halt and peer expectantly toward the farmhouse. Venturing into the patch, trampling on the vines, they yank off the biggest melons, green or ripe. Their arms full, they scurry toward the barbed wire fence to make their escape. Squeezing through the fence, leaving scraps of torn pants hanging on the barbs, scratched and breathless, the boys run frantically toward home, the melons clutched in their arms. In their fright they usually drop and smash the largest and most coveted of the stolen fruit. Plunging across a creek, they manage to soak their shoes with water, and at a slower pace they walk to a sheltered place, perhaps a clump of trees or bushes where they squat and bury their noses into the pieces of melon, broken by being dropped on the ground.

At 69 *m.* is the junction with State 171.

Right on this road to the 12-acre WALL LAKE STATE PARK, 0.5 *m. (picnicking facilities),* along the shore of BIG WALL LAKE, which is a breeding and feeding place for ducks providing excellent hunting. The place was originally named Delkeith in honor of the birthplace in Scotland of Mrs. John R. Stuart whose husband first owned the land. Horace Greeley, in the 1860's, sent a reporter here to write about Wall Lake. He made much of the wall, which was then more in evidence than it is now, implying that it was a wall of masonry constructed by some prehistoric people. Geologists reported, however, that in severe winters, the lake froze to the bottom and the heaving ice brought up the boulders from the lake and deposited them at the waters' receding edge, where they accumulated over a long period of time.

BLAIRSBURG, 79 m. (1,224 alt., 274 pop.), is at the junction with US 20 *(see Tour 12).*

JEWELL, 90 *m.* (1,059 alt., 950 pop.), was named for David T. Jewell, who platted the town in 1880.

Between 92 *m.* and 94 *m.* US 69 curves around the shore of LITTLE WALL LAKE, which formerly extended almost 2 miles, but is now largely swamp and marsh land.

At 99 m. is the junction with State 115, paved.

Left on this road is STORY CITY, 1 *m.* (1,011 alt., 1,434 pop.), on the Skunk River. From 1855, when the town was platted, to the Civil War, the place was a Hoosier settlement known as Fairview. Anticipating the arrival of the railroad, a group of settlers platted Story City adjacent to Fairview in 1878. Later the towns were incorporated as one. At Story City is the only PIONEER SCHOOLHOUSE preserved in the State. It houses a collection of relics and old photographs. The structure, built on the Sheldahl farm in 1860, is surrounded by an old-fashioned rail fence of oak.

Right from Story City 2.5 *m.,* on an unimproved road to the Skunk River, on the bank of which is the DOUBLE TREE. Two elms of different varieties, which started to grow about 10 feet apart, have joined at their tops, and from the point where they are joined, a single sprout has shot upward.

AMES, 110 m. (926 alt., 10,261 pop.) *(see AMES).*

Point of Interest: Iowa State College of Agriculture and Mechanic Arts.

Ames is at the junction with US 30 *(see Tour 13)* and US 65 *(see Tour 4).* For 53 miles S. of Ames US 69 and US 65 are one route.

Section b. AMES to MISSOURI LINE, *117 m., US 65-69, US 69.*

South of Ames, 0 *m.,* is HUXLEY, 9 *m.* (1,035 alt., 362 pop.), platted by a group of Norwegians in 1882. The first settlement in Story County, known as Ballard's Grove, was established on the banks of Ballard Creek just N. of the present Huxley, when Dan. W. and Mormon Ballard, with their families, arrived from Des Moines on Mar. 8, 1848.

At 10 *m.* is the junction with State 210, graveled.

Right on this road is SLATER, 4 *m.* (1,042 alt., 568 pop.). Adjoining Slater on the southwest is SHELDAHL (1,038 alt., 209 pop.), which is in 3 counties and at the intersection point of four townships. A citizen of Sheldahl may send his children to school in Polk County, get his mail in Story County, and go to church in Boone County. If any resident of the town wishes to be governed by a different county administration from that under which he is living, he has only to move across the street. The town was named by and for the Rev. D. Kjaldahl but, because of the difficulty of pronouncing the name and for the sake of euphony, the name was anglicized. Sheldahl has a cooperative elevator and a lumber yard.

Right from Slater on a surfaced dirt road is MADRID, 5 *m.* (1,021 alt., 2,061 pop.), a town platted in 1852 as Swede Point, in honor of many settlers of that nationality. Following a disagreement, when additional land from the estate of Mrs. Anna Dalander was made available to the community, the place was in 1855 renamed for the capital of Spain, eulogized by a Spanish workman locally employed. Two mining companies operate here. The MADRID HISTORICAL ASSOCIATION COLLECTION *(open weekdays, 8-5),* in the high school, has, among other objects, a stone discovered by C. L. Lucas in 1910 on a mound near the Des Moines River, about 3 miles W. of Madrid. Scratched on its surface is the inscription: "Dec. 10, 1845. Found 200 Indians hid on or around this mound. They cried 'No go!' 'No go!' But we took them to Fort D. Lt. R. S. Granger." The message is believed to relate to the evacuation of the Sacs and Foxes according to treaty of Oct. 11, 1842. Many of the Indians were reluctant to go.

Right from Madrid 2.5 *m.* on a dirt road to HIGH BRIDGE, which carries the tracks of the Chicago, Milwaukee & St. Paul Railroad across the Des Moines River. The bridge, built in 1913, is 2,474 feet long and 145 feet high. The river valley at this point is 6,000 feet wide.

At 14 *m.* is the junction with a surfaced dirt road.

Right on this road is ALLEMAN, 0.5 *m.* (1,013 alt., 100 est. pop.), a small farm community having a cooperative oil company and a cooperative elevator.

ANKENY, 19 *m.* (1,001 alt., 632 pop.), was founded in 1895 by Col. J. F. Ankeny as a station on a narrow-gauge railroad, now abandoned.

At SAYLOR STATION, 23 *m.,* is the POLK COUNTRY FARM *(visitors weekdays until 8 p. m.),* with approximately 320 residents, about half of whom are insane incurables. The farm produces dairy products, fruits, and vegetables for use of the institution.

US 69 bypasses the center of Des Moines.

South on E. 14th. to Grand Ave.; (R) on Grand Ave. to River to the center of the city.

DES MOINES, 31 *m.* (800 alt., 142,599 pop.) *(see DES MOINES).*

Points of Interest: Historical Building; State Capitol; Drake University; U. S. Veterans' Hospital; State Fair Grounds.

Des Moines is at the junction with State 7 *(see Tour 14B),* US 6 *(see Tour 14),* and US 163 *(see Tour 5A).*

SCOTCH RIDGE CHURCH, 39 *m.*, owned by a Scotch Presbyterian society, is a white frame structure with arched windows. Pioneers from Ohio settled on this ridge about 1851.

At 43 *m.* is the junction with a surfaced dirt road.

Left on this road is SUMMERSET, 0.5 *m.* (794 alt.), just south of Middle River. A strip coal mine is near the road (L), between the highway and the village.

In this region of heavy growth virgin timber, raccoon hunting is a favorite sport in late fall and early winter. Coon hunting dogs must be intelligent, for they trail a tricky animal at night through water, mud, and weeds. A coon will "mark" a tree—that is, run up a tree for a considerable distance, then jump to the ground and keep running—in order to mislead a dog; but the trained dog knows the trick and circles the tree to see if he can pick up the scent farther on. The animal's craftiness in escaping has become proverbial, and out of this has grown such phrases as "sly as a coon" or "wake as a coon." After running for miles through sloughs, over logs, boulders, through weeds and ditches, the dogs find the track and follow it. When the coon is finally treed, good hunting dogs stay by the tree until their masters arrive, which may be long if the coon and dogs have forded a stream and the hunters have to walk up the river, perhaps several miles, to find a ford. A lantern is used for travel, but a flashlight is better for locating the coon in the tree. One of the men rests the flashlight on the head of the man with a gun, thus throwing the light on the coon, and when it shines in the coon's eyes the gun is fired. If the coon is slightly wounded at the first shot, he will not look at the light again, and it is hard to find him for a second shot.

Sometimes the hunters shake the coon out of the tree and let the dogs dispose of it. Occasionally, it is necessary to cut the tree down to get the coon. Hunters may roast the coon and eat him at once. If the skin is good it is fleshed and sold to furriers.

The raccoon (Ind., arathcone, *the washer*) has a habit of dipping his food back and forth in water, thoroughly soaking it before he eats it. He is carnivorous, eating small birds, eggs, mice, reptiles, frogs and crawfish, occasionally chickens, but will also eat vegetables, especially young corn. He hibernates intermittently.

INDIANOLA, 48 *m.* (969 alt., 3,488 pop.), was selected as county seat when Warren County was organized in 1849. It is said that the surveyors of the town were discussing a suitable name for it while eating lunch. One man had his food wrapped in a newspaper—a rare article in the new country. As the men read the paper before discarding it they noticed an item from a now extinct Texas town called Indianola. The name pleased them and they selected it for the town.

Indianola is often referred to as the "Holy City", because even before prohibition days there were no saloons in the town, and until very recently no cigarettes were sold there.

Men of national repute in the field of education who have lived in Indianola are: Avery Craven (1886–   ), professor of American history at the University of Chicago since 1926; Hugh Jackson (1891–   ), Dean of the Graduate School of Business Administration at Stanford University (1926); Sterling Leonard (1888–1931), professor of English at the University of Wisconsin (1920–31); and Cecil Briggs (1904–   ), associate professor of architecture at Columbia University. Harriet Henderson (1902–   ), an opera singer, also lived in the town.

SIMPSON COLLEGE, established in Indianola in 1860, is a 4-year college of liberal arts, operated under the auspices of the Methodist Episcopal Church. The annual enrollment is about 700. First known as Indianola Seminary, it was named The Indianola Male and Female Seminary in 1861. Six years later the seminary became Simpson Centenary College, the name honoring Bishop Matthew Simpson. Simpson College has been the official designation since 1884. A bronze plaque mounted on a granite boulder marks the site of the first building, a square brick structure 38 feet wide and 48 feet long, which was painted a lead color and was known as Old Bluebird.

Among the ten buildings on the 20-acre campus are the Administration Building, the Library, the Gymnasium, Science Hall, and Barrows Hall, which contains the music school and was named for the late Frank Eliot Barrows (1868–1924), director of the School of Music for many years. Barrows, a pianist who had studied extensively in this country and with Saint-Saens in Paris, built up the school to a position of outstanding merit: the school has a modern pipe organ, as well as many other musical instruments.

BUXTON PARK, with an area of 4 acres, the gift of the late William Buxton, a banker, adjoins the college campus; it has unusually beautiful gardens of perennials—particularly roses—trees and shrubs.

The GRAVE OF ALLERTON, noted Iowa race horse *(see Tour 12, Independence)*, is (L) inside the entrance to the Warren County FAIR GROUNDS. It is enclosed by a fence and bears a marker. He held the stallion record to high wheel sulky, one mile in 2:09¼ at the Independence Kite Track in 1891. The Russian Government purchased Allerton's son, Redlac, to improve the Imperial stock, but the ship on which he was being conveyed to Russia was sunk during the World War by a German U-boat in the North Sea.

Indianola is at the junction with State 2 *(see Tour 15)*.

AHQUABI *(resting place)* STATE PARK, 53 *m.*, is a recreational area of 560 acres, including an artificial lake covering 125 acres. *(Shelter houses, picnic, bathing, and boating facilities; no fishing until 1938 or 1939.)* The area is rough and wooded. The cabins are arranged in clusters, with a central kitchen and dining room for the use of organized groups, such as the Boy Scouts. In the park are a group of white oaks, some of them estimated to be between 400 and 500 years old.

At Ahquabi State Park US 65 *(see Tour 4)* turns L., and US 69 continues S.

OSCEOLA, 77 *m.* (1,132 alt., 2,871 pop.), seat of Clarke County, was named for the Seminole Chief, Osceola, and was first called Osceola City. There is an erroneous local story that the Seminole was buried in an orchard W. of the city. Osceola was settled in 1850 by pioneers from Ohio

and Indiana; Mormons had been living in adjacent territory several years
earlier. It was made the county seat in 1851.

Osceola is at the junction with US 34 *(see Tour 16).*

LEON, 97 *m.* (1,019 alt., 2,000 pop.), seat of Decatur County, when
first surveyed was to be called Independence, but as a settlement of that
name had already been established in Iowa, the town was called South
Independence until the winter of 1854–55;. then the State Legislature
changed the name to Leon in response to a petition submitted by citizens
of the community.

Leon is at the junction with State 3 *(see Tour 17).*

DAVIS CITY, 106 *m.* (914 alt., 548 pop.), on the banks of the Grand
River, is a trading center.

Left from Davis City on a dirt road to the SACRED TREE, 3 *m.,* a squatty old
oak, with wide spreading branches, before a house. There was a legend that it was
sacred to the Indians, but it was probably a burial tree. Indians in this area often
wrapped the bodies of their dead in bark and deposited them in a tree.

South of Davis City the highway passes through New Buda township in
Decatur County. Here was the site of the Hungarian settlement of New
Buda, where Count L. Ujhazy and 20 or more countrymen, later joined
by Francis Varga and several companions, established a colony for refu-
gees from Hungary; they had fled when a rebellion (1848) against Austrian authority was crushed and high penalties for treason were imposed
on the rebels. The settlement did not prove a success. The colonists were
largely statesmen and scholars, unskillful at pioneer farming. They had
believed that the Iowa climate was mild, sufficiently so to raise Turkish tobacco and wine-grapes. Among the 12 Ujhazy estates confiscated by the
Austrian Government was one on which the famous Imperial Tokay wine
was produced; the Austrian emperor reserved this for himself.

Count Ujhazy built a rambling log house, where with his associates he
spent much of his time studying maps and discussing world affairs. When,
in 1853, he became discouraged with prospects in Iowa and moved to San
Antonio, Tex., another Hungarian, George Pomutz, moved into the log
house. He planned to promote a greater New Buda, and had elaborate
maps and blueprints prepared. A few German families bought lots.

Pomutz, who was tall and blond, with wavy hair and full beard and
mustachios, made a striking figure as he rode across the prairie on his
white mare, Highland Mary. It is said that he spoke eight languages.

Pomutz had a brilliant military record in the Civil War. He joined the
15th Iowa Infantry, becoming adjutant and later lieutenant colonel; was
wounded at Shiloh; distinguished himself at Corinth, Vicksburg, Atlanta,
and Savannah; and Mar. 13, 1865, became brevet brigadier general of volunteers. He later wrote the history of his regiment.

In recognition of his military service, Pomutz was appointed United
States consul to Russia, 1866, and consul general in 1874. He died at St.
Petersburg in 1882, leaving a strongbox containing blueprints and papers
relating to New Buda, which gave the impression that he was a very rich
man. He left no actual wealth, however, and was buried at the expense of
charitable Americans. Investigation proved that his papers were worthless.

In fact, the New Buda post office had been transferred to Davis City in 1875. Now all that remains is the name of the colony, perpetuated in the township.

LAMONI, 113 *m.* (1,126 alt., 1,739 pop.), was platted in 1879 as a colony for members of the Reorganized Church of Jesus Christ of Latter-day Saints, who had come to Iowa from Missouri and Nauvoo, Ill. The founding was accomplished by the Order of Enoch, a corporation formed for the purpose of purchasing and developing lands for church settlements. The place was named for a "righteous king" recorded in the Book of Mormon.

In 1881, the *Herald,* official church publication, was moved here from Plano, Ill.

GRACELAND COLLEGE (1895) makes Lamoni an educational center for the denomination, but the church offices have been removed to Independence, Mo. Fourteen college buildings, including several cottages, have been erected around the highest point of a 70-acre campus. A 300-acre tract of farm land, adjacent to the campus, provides employment for students, and supplies the kitchen with poultry and fresh dairy, garden, and orchard products. The institution open also to non-Mormons, became a junior college in 1915; in 1923-24 the third year of instruction was added. Annual events include the presentation of some oratoria by the Graceland Oratorio Society.

Two homes for the aged and a childrens' home were established here by the church, but the former were consolidated and the latter abandoned after legislation made unlawful the transportation of orphans from one State to another.

At 117 *m.* US 69 crosses the Missouri Line, 124 miles N. of Kansas City, Mo.

Tour 5A

Des Moines—Pella—Oskaloosa; US 163.
Des Moines to Oskaloosa, 60 m.

The Keokuk-Des Moines branch of the C.R.I. & P.R.R. parallels the route.
The Interstate Transit Bus Line follows the route between Des Moines and Oskaloosa.
Roadbed paved throughout.
Tourist accommodations of all kinds available, except at Ivy and Otley.

DES MOINES, 0 *m.* (800 alt., 142,559 pop.) *(see DES MOINES).*

Points of Interest: Historical Building; State Capitol; Drake University; U. S. Veterans' Hospital; State Fair Grounds.

Des Moines is at the junction with US 6 *(see Tour 14)*, US 65 and 69 *(see Tours 4 and 5)*, State 7 *(see Tour 14B)*, and State 89 *(see Tour 14C)*.

East from the Des Moines River on Grand Ave., to Frederick Hubbell Blvd.; L. on Hubbell Blvd. to University Ave.; R. on University Ave.

At 11 *m.* is a junction with a dirt road.

Left on this road to the CYRUS HARVEY ORCHARD AND NURSERY, 0.5 *m.*, where many different varieties of fruit and nuts are grown. Each spring the orchard is the setting of a Blossom Time Festival, usually on Sunday. A road winds for a mile and a half through the orchard. Ample space is provided for parking, and the nursery has picnic grounds and facilities. Hundreds of people drive many miles to see the 3,000 trees in bloom. The farmyard is the scene of a program of songs, instrumental music, and speeches by prominent men.

IVY, 11.5 *m.*, is a hamlet on the brow of a long hill overlooking Mud Creek valley.

At 17.5 *m.* is a junction with a dirt road.

Right on this road is VANDALIA, 4.5 *m.*, now almost a ghost town, with a group of old houses and a country crossroads store. The DANIEL PULVER HOME was built in 1854, in Swiss architectural style. Pulver rebuilt it in 1871, leaving the main rooms as they were except for the removal of one fireplace. It is a two-story frame structure with 17 rooms. The basement, with stone walls, 14 inches thick, contained Pulver's workshop, a toy room, a loom room, and a tunnel from the fruit storage room to a rock cave west of the house. His tools, patterns, work-bench, his wife's loom built of red elm, about 1875, and some of her flax and wool work, have been preserved. The loom is still used, principally for rug and carpet weaving. On the first floor are 17 pieces of furniture he made—of walnut, cedar, wild cherry, mulberry, and pine. The floors in the dining room and kitchen are of wild cherry, and those in the other four rooms of oak, sawmarks still showing. The house has 30 hand-made doors, no two alike. In the upper half-story are the East Room and the Dark Room; the former is filled with relics such as spinning wheels, wood dies, warping bars for the loom, copper tools, and pottery. The Dark Room was built for storing coffins, which Pulver made and sold. The coffins —a few still remain here—were constructed of black walnut, roughly shaped to the outline of the human body, padded and lined with white muslin, and finished outside with linseed oil.

PRAIRIE CITY, 21 *m.* (930 alt., 793 pop.), a trading center for farmers and having two elevators, was platted in 1856 by James A. Elliott, whose red brick house, built shortly after the Civil War, is (R) opposite the village water tower. The village is on a beautiful and almost level table-land separating the Des Moines and Skunk rivers.

MONROE, 30 *m.* (922 alt., 936 pop.), was laid out by Adam Tool and recorded under the name of Tool's Point in 1851, but a year later its name was changed to Monroe, for President Monroe; it is known for its beautiful cemeteries. In both this town and Prairie City the population is mainly of Dutch descent; each has a square where band concerts are given on summer evenings; and both towns have an annual Old Settlers' Reunion in August.

Since the decline of Fourth of July celebrations, reunions and homecomings of various groups have become the most outstanding summer holiday events in the small towns in Iowa. On such occasions a small tent city of amusement concessions springs up overnight around the shady square, or in the park; the town band opens a long program of speaking, races, games, and contests. There is also either a vaudeville show by touring professionals, or instrumental and vocal music by local amateurs, and an old fiddlers' contest. Flags hang limply from their poles, or stir faintly in the hot August "corn-wind"; parasols dot the milling crowd which, dressed in its best, lightest, and whitest clothes, congregates around the bandstand or platform, sometimes on temporary plank seats. There is usually so large a crowd in the park that the thick green turf is heeled to dust; to the accompaniment of an old tune from the merry-go-round or modern dance music played by phonographs and amplified, gallons of cold drinks and ice cream are consumed. After supper, when the lights flash on in the late twilight, the band opens a variation of the afternoon program, ending shortly before ten as the platform dance begins; but until midnight the hoarse barkers of the one-day midway exhort those remaining to take one more "chance" or ride. In recent years the Old Settlers' Picnics have become such in name only—a hold-over from the past when buggies, wagons, and horses were tied to hitching racks around the square, now replaced by curbs for the closely parked automobiles. The historic origin of the affair has been lost in a thick commercial coating.

OTLEY, 37 m., (893 alt.), a small trading center and shipping point, was settled in 1867 because of the discovery of a vein of coal in that vicinity; it was named for a railroad official.

PELLA, 43 m. (877 alt., 3,326 pop.), was named by Dutch settlers, more than 700 of whom, headed by Henry Peter Scholte, fled religious intolerance in their native country and came to Iowa in 1847. They adopted for a city seal the motto "In Deo Spes Nostra et Refugium" *(In God is our hope and refuge)*. Pella is sometimes called the cleanest city in Iowa.

In 1853 CENTRAL COLLEGE was opened here, becoming the nucleus of Central University of Iowa; it was a Baptist institution. Dominie Scholte donated a large piece of land when the first building, OLD CENTRAL, was erected. The college, coeducational from the beginning, survived the panic of 1857—when hogs sold at $1.25 a hundred, butter at 5¢ a pound, eggs at 2¢ per dozen, and corn at 10¢ a bushel—and the Civil War, when the entire male student body, 122, enlisted in the Union forces. About 20 years ago control passed to the Dutch Reformed Church of America. Among the buildings are LUDWIG LIBRARY, containing 12,000 volumes, GRAHAM HALL for women, JORDON SCIENCE HALL, and NEW CENTRAL SCIENCE HALL. The average enrollment of the college is 250.

Pella is a city of churches; on Sundays many-toned church bells clamor intermittently from early morning until dusk, and the deserted appearance of the business section is in strong contrast to its Saturday appearance when busy crowds of shoppers and farmers throng the streets. On Saturday evenings in summer the crowd fills the central GARDEN SQUARE, a beautifully landscaped public park, to hear band concerts.

The PELLA HISTORICAL MUSEUM *(open 9-6; adm. 25¢)*, near the square, is a reconstruction of the Wolters house. This structure is painted white with sky-blue shutters, and is furnished like a typical Dutch home. Delft and willow-ware, china, glass, and silver are among the exhibits. One unusual object is a gold medal presented to an early settler by King

William II of Holland as reward for volunteering for action in the Netherlands-Belgium War (1810–1811). The kitchen with its fireplace and furnishings is of particular interest. The museum also contains old documents and relics.

On display at the PELLA NATIONAL BANK is a set of dueling pistols brought by the original colonists, and a cast-iron chest in which all the money and valuables of the colonists, who founded Pella, were stored on the trip from the Netherlands. This was the first strong box used when the bank was started.

Local factories, supplying a Nation-wide market, produce "Pella bologna," cookies, and Venetian blinds. A flour mill, a canning factory, a wagon factory, and an overall factory are also operated here.

Annually during May is held a Dutch Festival, Tulip Time. Thousands of tulip bulbs, imported from Holland, have been planted in gardens and along the curbs in beds of striking design. During the celebration, men, women and children don Dutch costumes, many wearing wooden shoes; the men wear full trousers, and coats having shining brass buttons, and the women, tight-bodiced, full-skirted gowns, white lace caps—the lace points stiffly starched—and snow white aprons. Children are miniatures of their elders, in dress. Each day during the festival week a program is given, including folk dances, folk songs, and Dutch feasts. One of the most notable exhibits is a MINIATURE DUTCH VILLAGE, about 30 feet wide and 60 feet long, containing 50 tiny buildings, canals, roads, vehicles, and figures. Central College students make annual additions to the village.

Many Pella people celebrate a double Christmas, the first on Sint Nicolaas Day—beginning on the eve of December 5—which is the real Christmas as far as the children are concerned, because it is the time for gift distribution. December 25 is then given over strictly to religious services. Sint Nicolaas is usually represented as a tall man wearing a red velvet cloak with a white cross on his breast; on his head is the mitre or bishop's hat, he carries a long gold cane as his scepter and rides a snow white charger loaded with gifts for the good and switches for the bad; his servants, De Zwarte (Black) Piet, do the actual work of distributing gifts. On Sint Nicolaas eve a rap sounds at the door and a large straw man in strange garb is found there leaning against the jamb with the gifts in his pockets or around him. Later the children leave their scrubbed wooden shoes at the door with a few grains of corn, oats, or a carrot for the Saint's white mount; on the following morning these are filled with sugar plums, large spiced cookies, and alphabet letters of pastry. More pastries and cookies than candy are eaten on the holiday.

At 50 *m.* (L) is the large JOHN VORHEES HOUSE built in 1871 to surpass the elegant, 14-room frame JOHN SMITH HOUSE, less than half a mile distant (R), which was built in 1869. Smith's house was the largest and most lavish home in the vicinity, with a walnut staircase—every rung turned by hand—circling up three flights to the square cupola rising above the roof. The cupola, with six windows on each side, was a vantage point from which Smith surveyed his 280-acre farm, watched his melon patch, and kept an eye on his hired men. The house became the talk of travelers through the region, and attracted many visitors.

Vorhees, Smith's neighbor, becoming irked at the prestige Smith's house gave him, decided to surpass him. Until Smith built his house, Vorhees had been the most important man in the community—he subscribed to more newspapers than anyone else, he paid a nickel more a bushel for corn, and $4 a month more than the usual amount to each of the many hired men who tilled his 400-acre farm. Smith's house had two stories—built of wood—so Vorhees, finding clay suitable for brick-making on his farm, set up his own kilns, made his own brick—marketing extra amounts in Pella—and built a three-story brick structure, trimmed with stone. The walnut staircase in Smith's house was imitated, but, to surpass the Smith cupola, Vorhees added a slate roof, with large figures in red slate bearing the date when the house was finished. The cost of the house was nearly $13,000, and placed Vorhees in debt for several years. When the hollow tiles used to support the roof attracted bees, hives were built and the house became known locally as the Bee House. Smith sold his house and farm in 1890, but Vorhees lived in his until he died in 1896.

At 56 *m.* is the KRIZER SEED CORN AND TURKEY FARM, where hundreds of Mammoth Bronze turkeys are raised for market each year, and the Krizer Yellow Dent seed corn, which has won many ribbons at State and National shows, is grown.

OSKALOOSA, 60 *m.* (843 alt., 10,123 pop.) *(see Tour 15),* is at the junction with State 2 *(see Tour 15),* and US 63 *(see Tour 3).*

Tour 6

(Mankato, Minn.)—Algona—Fort Dodge—Adel—Mt. Ayr—(St. Joseph, Mo.) ; US 169.
Minnesota Line to Missouri Line, 239 m.

The C. & N. W. R. R. parallels the highway between the Minnesota Line and Algona; M. & St. L. R. R., between Livermore and Minburn; Ft. D., D. M. & S., between Fort Dodge and Boxholm; C. B. & Q. R. R. (crossing at Afton Junction), between Mt. Ayr and Missouri Line.
Interstate Transit Bus Lines follow highway from Ft. Dodge north to Algona.
Roadbed is intermittently paved and graveled.
Accommodations available chiefly in cities.

South of the Minnesota Line, 0 *m.,* which is crossed 55 m. S. of Mankato, Minn., US 169 for 150 miles traverses an agricultural area widely known for its grain production. Although this section of Iowa is flat prairie land, it is broken by many small streams and large rivers and the highway frequently curves through wooded river valleys.

Trees grow principally along river valleys and around farm houses; on every side are fields used for corn, oats, and other crops.

LEDYARD, 9 m. (1,150 alt., 245 pop.), was platted by the Western Town Lot Co. in 1884. A large part of the town site was at one time owned by William Larrabee, Governor of Iowa (1886–1890), who named the place for his native town in New England.

Asa C. Call, organizer of the Western Town Lot Co. and the leading landholder in the county, donated the right-of-way to the C. & N. W. R. R. in return for its bringing in the line, establishing a stationhouse, and advertising the area. His agents sold the town lots to the incoming settlers at high prices. The railroads often worked hand in hand with land companies and many town sites were initially bought by them at exceedingly low prices.

Ledyard is a farming community, and along the highway in the vicinity are extensive cornfields. Plowing, begun in early spring, is continued until the stalks become too high for the cultivator; the corn is then "laid by" —which is the last plowing. There is a saying that if there is to be a good crop, it must be "knee high by Fourth of July."

At 12 m. is the eastern junction with State 9 (see Tour 10); US 169 turns R., and is united with State 9; at 15 m. US 169 turns L.

BANCROFT, 21 m. (1,189 alt., 854 pop.), was platted in Sept., 1881, by the Western Town Lot Co. (see above and below) and named in honor of the historian, George Bancroft, who acknowledged the honor by presenting the town with 50 books as the nucleus of a library.

An annual Harvest Festival, held here Sept. 1, combined with a Homecoming sponsored by St. John's Parish, draws people from both Iowa and Minnesota. There are various kinds of entertainment, including contests rewarded by prizes, and the day is climaxed by a dance at the Bancroft Pavilion. Proceeds from the festival go into a church fund.

Two large HATCHERIES here ship out large numbers of chicks, but the town is chiefly a trade center for the surrounding farms.

BURT, 28 m. (1,169 alt., 580 pop.), L. of the highway, is a prosperous village, founded in 1881 when the C. & N. W. R. R. was built through northern Iowa. The site was named for Horace G. Burt, chief engineer of the railroad at that time, and, as at Bancroft, the original plat was filed by the Western Town Lot Co. The BURT FARMERS' CREAMERY is the outstanding business concern of the community. In 1932 the Government acquired the entire butter output of the creamery for use in the Navy.

In July harvesting is usually the chief activity in this area, as it is elsewhere in the State. Harvesting is cutting, bundling, and shocking the oats —the main crop—barley, or rye. The pale gold shocks are left standing in orderly rows in the stubble fields under the hot sun, drying before threshing.

Typical of Iowa towns, whether they have 200 or 20,000 inhabitants, is the church supper, often utilized to raise money for paying off church

COVERED BRIDGE, MADISON COUNTY

debts. The older and more conservative members argue that the "House of the Lord" should not be made into a restaurant; nevertheless, all members contribute time and effort, and the products of their gardens and larders. In this town, the Presbyterians serve their suppers in a room opening off the church auditorium but most church basements have been remodeled and equipped as kitchens and dining rooms where large numbers of people can be served. These events are always well-advertised and the townspeople come to have opinions on which group—the Methodists, Baptists, or Lutherans—serve the best food at the lowest prices.

The long, collapsible tables are set up on "horses." The women of the congregation furnish tablecloths but paper napkins are used. If the supper is served at a time near a holiday, such as the Fourth of July, Christmas, or Valentine's Day, the decorations fit the season. The older women work in the kitchen, keeping dishes washed, making coffee, and serving the many kinds of food. The young girls, attractive and willing to smile at customers, act as waitresses. One woman sits by the door, collecting the money, a task that is allotted almost by tradition.

When the first guest arrives, the table is already set with bowls of sugar, pitchers of cream, salt- and peppercellars, and plates of bread. Pickles appear in quantities—thin red beets with brown spices; green dill, sour, and sweet cucumbers; purple and green of olives; and glistening piccalilli, with cucumbers, cauliflower and white onions, all in a mustard sauce. Cole-slaw is also there in huge bowls, apple butter in glass dishes, jellied cranberries, and preserves of watermelon rinds to whet the appetite.

In some places the food, or part of it, is placed on the table in serving dishes, but usually the guest is merely given a plate of mashed potatoes and creamed chicken, the thick blobs of meat and light brown gravy rolling over a crisp brown biscuit. Sometimes the meat course is fried chicken, or Swiss steak. A portion of beans baked in syrup—reddish brown— creamed corn, rutabagas, or even the lowly turnip, fill out the meal. Second helpings are always taken when the bowls of vegetables are left on the table. Ice cream or pie—pumpkin, apple, peach, lemon, custard, or chiffon —is served as dessert.

There is always laughter among the men at the expense of the one who doesn't want to eat his own wife's cooking, while the women joke about the man who drinks five cups of coffee, the one who eats too much, and the rare one who eats too little. They catalog the tastes of every man or woman in the community. Often 200 or 300 people will crowd into the small basement room and the tables will be set and reset four or five times. After the supper is over the tables are folded away, the women count the silverware, the cashier checks the money—often as much as $100 or $200, and the faithful Marthas wash the pots, pans, and other dishes. The church organization realizes a profit in cash, and the townspeople have enjoyed something more than a meal.

ALGONA, 37 m. (1,213 alt., 3,995 pop.), seat of Kossuth County, lies in a wide bend of the East Fork of the Des Moines River. The county, containing 977 square miles, was named for the Hungarian patriot, Louis Kossuth, who had been leading the revolt of the Hungarians against Austria and had met defeat when Russian troops were sent to help subdue him and his followers. He had fled to Turkey where he was in 1851 when the Iowa Legislature created the county. His zeal in the cause of liberty had made him popular with the people in this country. Kossuth came to America shortly thereafter, speaking in many cities on behalf of the cause of Hungary.

The first settlers on this town site were Asa C. and Ambrose A. Call, who arrived in 1854. For some time the community was known as Call's Grove, but at the suggestion of Mrs. Asa Call the present name was adopted—derived from the word Algonquin.

The only forts erected in the county were two built in the spring of 1857 immediately after the Spirit Lake Massacre (see Tour 7), as protection against the Indians. One enclosed the Town Hall, and was called the Algona Stockade. After several baseless Indian scares, the building was torn down, and the material used for plank roads.

In this town were born Gardner Cowles (1861–   ), publisher of the Des Moines *Register* and allied papers, and Harvey Ingham (1858–   ), editor of the same paper. L. J. Dickinson, born at Derby, Iowa, in 1873, and elected by Iowa to the Senate in 1930, has lived here for many years.

Lumber for the first courthouse, built in 1866, was hauled in wagons from the old town of Boonesboro about 90 miles S. The present COURT-HOUSE was built six years later.

The first school at Algona, built during the summer of 1856, was facetiously called Gopher College because it was held in a dugout in the side of a bluff; the hole was walled with logs, and covered with sod. The log walls burned after two years and in time a district schoolhouse was built. In 1867 Father Taylor of the second Iowa band, a group of Congregational and Presbyterian church followers interested in establishing schools, organized Northwestern College here but it had a short existence. Then the Methodists established Algona College, an institution that had one building and a faculty; its president, Orlando Baker, an enthusiastic student of the classics, was teaching them to his boys and girls when this area was still largely undeveloped. Then Prof. J. C. Gilchrist started the normal school that later came within one vote of being made a State institution. The beginnings of Gopher College were recorded in the Algona *Bee,* which was written, not printed; files of this paper are preserved in the State Historical Building in Des Moines.

It is said that feathers were scattered to determine the spots where the trees of HARD MAPLE TREE PARK should be planted; in the park is the municipal TOURIST CAMP.

Algona is at the junction with US 18 *(see Tour 11).*

US 169 turns L. on Main St., R. on Main St. 5 blocks is a junction with a graveled road.

Left on this road, 1.6 *m.,* crossing the East Fork of the Des Moines River to AMBROSE A. CALL STATE SCENIC PRESERVE *(picnicking facilities, nature trails);* R. through a stone gateway on a park road to a large log LODGE, 2 *m.,* on a high bank overlooking the river valley. Here is a marked granite boulder (R), near the site of the first log cabin in Kossuth County, built in July 1854 by Ambrose Call. The park is a wooded area of 134 acres, formerly farm land belonging to the Call family. According to some historians, Inkpadutah and his band of outlaw Sioux camped here before perpetrating the Spirit Lake Massacre *(see Tour 7).*

At 49 *m.* is the junction with State 222, graveled.

Left on this road is LIVERMORE, 2 *m.* (1,134 alt., 66 pop.), a farm trading center on the East Fork of the Des Moines River. An Indian battlefield, where artifacts have been found, is N. of town.

HUMBOLDT, 61 *m.* (1,095 alt., 2,251 pop.), originally called Springvale, was settled by the Rev. S. H. Taft, with a little colony of abolitionists, on the West Fork of the river. It was renamed to honor Baron Alexander von Humboldt, a German scientist (1769–1859), when the C. & N. W. R. R. was built through the town.

In JOHN BROWN PARK, containing 2.5 acres given to the town by the Rev. S. H. Taft, is an ornate FOUNTAIN built by Father Paul M. Dobberstein of West Bend, who directed the construction of the Grotto of the Redemption *(see Tour 11).* The fountain contains a great number of stones sent from all parts of the world, and is topped by a statue of Italian marble, representing Fay Hession, the daughter of Mr. and Mrs. Dennis Hession, prominent local residents. Miss Hession is represented as a bride, in commemoration of a tragic romance. Her fiance, Harry Cook, time-keeper on a construction project, was fatally stabbed before the wedding could take place. Miss Hession's health declined and she died. The fountain was built in 1916.

A boulder in the park, formerly the campus, marks the SITE OF HUMBOLDT COLLEGE, founded in 1869 by the Rev. S. H. Taft and operated until 1926. In 1872 the buildings and endowments were valued at more than $100,000. The first board of trustees included Benjamin F. Gue (1828–1904), historian (see LITERATURE), and J. F. Duncombe (1831–1903), prominent in Iowa history (see FORT DODGE).

RIVERSIDE PARK, now an amusement center, was the training camp of Frank Gotch (1878–1917), winner of the world's wrestling title from George Hackenschmidt (1908). Gotch, a native of Humboldt, is buried in Union Cemetery.

Left from Humboldt on State 10 is DAKOTA CITY, 1 m. (1,125 alt., 448 pop.), seat of Humboldt County, named for the Dakota (Sioux) Indians. Ed McKnight, founder of the village, built a dam across the East Fork of the Des Moines River. It still furnishes water power for operation of the mill there, although, on account of drouths, electric power has been added of late years.

At 68.2 m. the highway crosses the combined forks of the Des Moines River.

FORT DODGE, 79 m. (1,115 alt., 21,895 pop.) (see FORT DODGE).

Points of Interest: Blanden Art Gallery; Public Library; Tobin Packing Plant.

Fort Dodge is at the junction with US 20 (see Tour 12) and State 5 (see Tour 12A).

At 90 m. is the junction with State 50, graveled.

Left on this road is the junction with State 121, 5 m.; L. on State 121, 6 m. into DOLLIVER MEMORIAL PARK, (picnicking and camping facilities), a 538-acre area of rolling woodland bordering the Des Moines River that is a memorial to Jonathan P. Dolliver, U. S. Senator from Iowa (1900–1910). Unusual geological formations, known as copperas beds, are on the banks of Prairie Creek, bordering the west side of the park. A dam across the creek forms a pool, used as a fish nursery. The pool and a memorial shaft here were designed by Lorado Taft. Dolliver was one of six State parks where nature hikes were inaugurated in 1933. Parties were organized under a botanist, an ornithologist, or a geologist, who gave lectures on field exhibits, and directed the placing of markers bearing descriptions of specimens studied. These were left for the guidance of future visitors to the trails.

Adjacent to Dolliver Park is WOODMAN'S HOLLOW, a deep gorge cut into the sandstone by the Des Moines River. The dry slopes on the tops of surrounding hills are covered with a variety of flowers, shrubs, and trees. Near Woodman's Hollow, an attractive dell in the river valley, is a popular picnic ground. Here is WILD CAT CAVE, a series of six or seven shallow chambers in the soft sandstone cliffs. In the summer, moss, ferns, wild flowers, and trees add to the natural beauty of the scene. Streams fed by springs flow through this secluded valley, which is almost entirely enclosed by high, rocky bluffs.

On State 50 is LEHIGH, 7 m. (946 alt., 996 pop.), lying on both sides of the Des Moines River, almost surrounded by precipitous wooded hills heavily veined with coal. Settled early in the 1850's, it was originally known as Slabtown—because of the log slabs with which settlers built shacks along the river. In 1870 this name was abandoned for Tyson's Mill; Oliver Tyson was one of Lehigh's prominent settlers. Still later it was called Vesper, for a town in Pennsylvania, but this was changed to its present name, also in honor of a Pennsylvania town, the former home of a considerable number of the settlers. Other inhabitants in the vicinity came from Michigan. For many years coal mining was the chief industry, but now with the exhaustion of many of the veins agriculture has become more important. Clay digging was begun in the early 1870's, and Lehigh is now one of the largest clay-producing towns in the county. The district has unusual scenic beauty. Several gravel roads follow the river and wind among the hills; hundreds of people drive here to view the great oak-, maple-, and walnut-covered hillsides in their rich autumnal beauty.

Five well-preserved conical mounds lie on a hill overlooking the Des Moines River valley. Twelve linear, and 12 conical mounds are on the Des Moines River bluffs, 4 m. E. of Lehigh.

HARCOURT, 96 m. (1,169 alt., 264 pop.), is a farm community with broad streets, green lawns, and a well-kept business district. In the early 1930's farmers in this vicinity organized a cooperative elevator, which contributes to the town's prosperity.

In the ALBERT YOUNDAL HOME *(visitors welcome)* is a SWEDISH BIBLE that has been handed down to eldest sons for 300 years.

BOXHOLM, 105.5 m. (1,145 alt., 280 pop.), was platted April 22, 1900, and named for the town of Boxholm, Sweden; many of the first residents were natives of Sweden.

Left from Boxholm on State 329, a graveled road, is PILOT MOUND, 5 m. (1,109 alt., 274 pop.). It is near an Indian mound of the same name that was a meeting place for early settlers who lighted bonfires here when they wished to gather recruits. Nearby, in the valley of Upper Bluff Creek, a battle was fought between the Sac and Fox and the Sioux. The Sac and Fox were led by Keokuk, and the Sioux by Wamsapasha; the victory was Keokuk's. Many of the warriors who were slain were buried at the summit of Pilot Mound; some of their bones are occasionally unearthed.

Here the highway roughly parallels the Dragoon Trail of 1835; Col. S. W. Kearny, Capt. E. V. Sumner, Capt. Nathan Boone, son of Daniel Boone, and Lieut. Albert M. Lea passed over this trail with troops. In Iowa the trail crosses the Des Moines River twice *(see Tours 3 and 17)*.

At 116 m. is the junction with US 30 *(see Tour 13)*; US 169 turns L., and is united with US 30 for 4 miles.

OGDEN, 120 m. (1,100 alt., 1,429 pop.) *(see Tour 13)*. At Ogden is the junction with US 30 *(see Tour 13)*. Turning right, US 169 continues southward.

At 133 m. is the junction with State 89 *(see Tour 14C)*.

MINBURN, 139 m. (1,046 alt., 328 pop.), was platted in 1869 by J. B. Hill and D. F. Rogers. A steam-operated saw- and gristmill was the town's first industrial plant; later a planing mill, which is still in operation, was established.

Between Minburn and Adel the highway follows the valley of the North Raccoon River.

At 144 m. is the junction with State 7 *(see Tour 14B)*.

At 146 m. is the DALLAS COUNTY HOME. It has large well-kept buildings, a spacious landscaped lawn, and 536 acres of land. The farm is self-supporting. The board of supervisors of the county oversees the financing of the institution, with one member, appointed each year, holding direct responsibility. One source of income is the breeding and rearing of purebred Belgian horses for market. Each person who can work does his share of maintenance; a few handle teams in the field, others do cleaning and laundry; some do no more than carry milk from the barn to the house, or "slop" to the hogs. The kitchen workers, besides providing balanced meals for 80 or 90 persons and special diets for those who need them, annually can from 3,000 to 4,000 quarts of fruit and vegetables produced on the farm. Each year 35 hogs and several beeves are butchered, made into sausage, cold-pack canned, or put in brine for summer smoking; hundreds of bushels of potatoes, apples, onions, carrots, and about 2,000 cabbages and 100 gallons of sauerkraut are stored. Purebred Holstein cows provide plenty of milk and butter, and about 500 hens supply eggs. The hospital—the first in the State connected with a county farm—has a medical director, two registered nurses, and a dentist.

ADEL, 149 m. (894 alt., 1,669 pop.), seat of Dallas County, is at the confluence of Butler Creek and the Raccoon River. Adel was in 1850 a station on the Dubuque-Council Bluffs stagecoach route. When the town was settled in 1846 it was called Penoach, but the name was changed in 1849 when the place was made the county seat. The county was named for George M. Dallas (1792–1864), Vice President of the United States (1845–49).

Partly because of the numerous waterways, many mills were built in the county in the early days. Most of them are gone now and none are in use, but occasionally their picturesque ruins are visible from the highway. Many small factories were also built because of the waterpower, but modern power methods have supplanted this primitive one.

Workmen digging for clay in an old creek bed here found three ancient axes, possibly prehistoric, buried 23 feet underground; two were made of mica, one of granite; it is thought that they were fashioned by mound builders.

Adel is at the junction with US 6 (see Tour 14).

At 153 m. is the junction with an unimproved road.

Right on this road is the junction with another road, 2 m.; L. to the S. Raccoon River, 2.5 m.; along the banks are a number of MOUNDS (see ARCHEOLOGY).

DE SOTO, 156 m. (890 alt., 319 pop.), L. of the highway, was named for an official of the C. R. I. & P. R. R. when the survey was made in 1868. There is a drain-tile factory here.

At 158 m. is the junction with State 90, a dirt road.

Left on this road to a junction with State 293, 4 m.; L. on this road is VAN METER, 6 m. (874 alt., 400 pop.), the hometown of "Bob" Feller (1918-   ), baseball pitcher.

WINTERSET, 170 m. (1,129 alt., 2,921 pop.), seat of Madison County, was established on a divide between Middle River and Cedar Creek in 1846.

Independence and Summerset were suggested as names for the new town. One of the members of the commission, shivering with cold and slightly under the influence of whiskey,. cried: "Summerset! You'd a damn sight better name it Winterset!"

The CITY PARK *(picnicking facilities; playgrounds)*, on the southern side of town, has much natural beauty. It contains the ANDREW BENNETT LOG CABIN, built in 1864; CLARK'S TOWER, of stone with a winding stairway, built by descendants of the pioneers, Ruth and Caleb Clark; and RENDER LOG CABIN, another relic of pioneer days. A boulder here commemorates the Delicious apple and Jesse Hiatt, the orchardist who produced this popular variety of fruit *(see below)*.

The MADISON COUNTY HISTORICAL SOCIETY MUSEUM *(open 8-6, except Sun. and holidays)* is in the COURTHOUSE, a dignified-appearing oldfashioned building, built of Madison County limestone. One of the museum exhibits is a fine saddle that Mrs. Jane Hornbeck Bennett once refused to trade for the land on which the Kirkwood Hotel in Des Moines now stands. The society has been largely responsible for the preservation of nine covered bridges, of the 13 that were formerly in the county.

Several Indian Camp sites were near Winterset, as indicated by the many arrowheads and flint chips that have been found.

At 177 *m.* is the junction with State 307, a graveled road.

Left on this road to a junction at 3.5 *m.;* L. here to another at 4 *m.;* then R. to the W. B. Landis farm, 4.5 *m.* Here is the original DELICIOUS APPLE TREE, now protected by a woven wire fence, and cared for by a tree expert. In 1872, Jesse Hiatt, a farmer-orchardist living near East Peru, planted seedling apple trees sent from Vermont. When one of the trees failed to bear, Hiatt grafted to it branches of several other varieties. The tree apparently died, but a sprout that grew out of the stump was carefully cultivated and in time brought forth a choice red-striped apple of somewhat unusual shape. Hiatt named it the Hawkeye in honor of his native State. Later, the Stark Bros. Nursery and Orchard Co. of Louisiana, Mo., purchased the right to propagate the Hawkeye. The fruit was slightly changed and improved, and renamed the Delicious.

LORIMOR, 186 *m.* (1,227 alt., 577 pop.), was founded and named by Josiah Lorimor in 1877. Two foundries produce blue-grass stripping machines, power hammers, pressure oil pumps, emery wheels, road drags, and playground equipment.

Between Lorimor and the Missouri Line, US 168 passes through a rough, hilly region.

At 191 *m.* is the junction with an improved county road.

Right on this road to MT. PISGAH MONUMENT, 2 *m.*, a limestone obelisk erected by a commission from the Salt Lake Mormon Tabernacle, in memory of Mormons who died and were buried here. Mormons, fleeing from Nauvoo in June 1846 *(see Tour 1)*, halted at these high bluffs on the Grand River. The valley and timbered groves attracted them and they remained, building log cabins and digging caves on the ridge. They operated a mill, using "niggerheads" (granite boulders) as burrs and horses for power. A spring furnished water, a tabernacle was erected, and a cemetery laid out. Crops were planted on 1,500 acres, plowed with the aid of cows. A post office was opened here in 1850, and the contract for hauling mail from Chariton called for a speed of "one mile an hour"—which was furnished by cows. The leader of the group of Mormons, Bishop Huntingdon, who died here, is believed to have been the first white person buried in Union County. During the first six months of their stay 160 died; several hundred more—800, according to one account—were buried before the survivors departed. After Bishop Huntingdon's death, Coleman Boran, a former New Englander, ruled the colony. When the Mormons moved westward in 1852, Henry Peters bought the land near the mill, and

THE ORIGINAL DELICIOUS APPLE TREE, NEAR WINTERSET

named it Petersville. He made the place a business center for the surrounding country; the first term of county court was held here in 1853.

At 193 *m.* is the junction with US 34 *(see Tour 16),* which unites with US 169 between this point and Afton.

TALMAGE, 194.7 *m.* (1,072 alt.), an almost extinct village (R), had a log tabernacle that was the scene of Mormon debates on polygamy, a subject on which Joseph Smith had received a revelation in 1843. Polygamy was not practiced here.

AFTON, 200 *m.* (1,212 alt., 1,013 pop.), near a large grove of trees on the banks of Twelve Mile Creek, was selected as the seat of Union County in 1855. After the C. B. & Q. R. R. was built through the county in 1869, the seat was moved to Creston, where it has remained.

Mrs. James Baker, an early resident, suggested this name for the village because of her fondness for the Scottish song, *Flow Gently Sweet Afton.*

Near the public square, US 169 crosses the AFTON OVERHEAD CANTILEVER ARCH BRIDGE, one of two winners in the 1931 contest for Class C bridges costing under $250,000, as judged by the American Institute of Steel Construction.

At Afton is a junction with US 34 *(see Tour 16).*

MOUNT AYR, 222 *m.* (1,236 alt., 1,704 pop.) *(see Tour 17)*, is at the junction with State 3 *(see Tour 17)*.

REDDING, 237 *m.* (1,130 alt., 272 pop.), had a post office in 1856; but the town was not founded until 1880 when the C. B. & Q. R. R. was built through the section and the railroad company bought and sold 200 acres of land as town lots. The CONSOLIDATED SCHOOL here cost $36,000.

At 239 *m.* US 169 crosses the Missouri Line, 76 miles N. of St. Joseph, Mo.

Tour 7

(Redwood Falls, Minn.)—Spirit Lake—Carroll—Clarinda—(St. Joseph, Mo.); US 71.
Minnesota Line to Missouri Line, 242 m.

C.R.I & P.R.R. parallels this route between junction with State 9 and Spirit Lake, and between Audubon and Atlantic; C.M. St.P. & P.R.R. between Spirit Lake and Spencer, and Storm Lake and Sac City; M. & St.L. R.R., between Spencer and Storm Lake; C. & N.W. R.R., between Sac City and Audubon; C. B. & Q. R.R., between Villisca and Braddyville.
Interstate Transit Bus Lines run between Minnesota Line and Early; between Audubon and Hamlin; between Clarinda and Braddyville. The Burlington, between Clarinda and Braddyville. Roadbed is intermittently graveled and paved between Minnesota Line and Carroll; paved between Carroll and Missouri Line. Tourist accommodations of all kinds available chiefly in cities.

Section a. MINNESOTA LINE *to* CARROLL, *129 m.*

US 71 crosses the Minnesota Line, 82 miles S. of Redwood Falls, Minn. The flat prairie section of northern Iowa is a treeless country naturally, and for long distances the green fields and brown earth (in winter buried deep under blue-white snow) are bare of any shade or timber, except on the banks of lakes or streams. The highway crosses several large rivers and winds down into fertile valleys, dipping perhaps 100 feet or more below the surrounding prairie.

At 5 *m.* is the junction with State 9 *(see Tour 10)*; US 71 turns R., and is one route with State 9 for 7 miles.

SPIRIT LAKE, 11 *m.* (1,458 alt., 1,778 pop.), seat of Dickinson County, is 1.7 miles south of the lake for which the town was named. This body of water, largest glacier-created lake in the State, covers 5,500 acres and is popular in summer for bathing and water sports; it also provides duck hunting, and bass, pike, and other game fishing. Dickinson

County was named for Daniel S. Dickinson, a former U.S. Senator from New York. Nineteen percent of its area is covered by lakes—19 of them. The lakes, resembling low bowls filled with water and set down in the prairies, are completely encircled by dense borders of trees and forest growth.

Long before white settlers came to this territory in 1856 the lake region had been a rendezvous of the Dakota tribes, which included the powerful Sioux, Omahas, Iowas, and Yanktons. Mini-Wakan *(spirit water)*, corrupted to Minnewaukon by early settlers, is now called Spirit Lake; Okoboozhy (said to be a corruption of a word meaning *place of rest* and also *reeds)* is now East Okoboji Lake; and Mini-Titonka *(big water)*, corrupted to Minnetonka, is now West Okoboji Lake.

French voyageurs may have visited this section by 1700, as one map showing the lake region was made in 1720; and it is thought white trappers of the 18th century knew the place at least by name, since the lakes were vaguely referred to as Lac d'Esprit. In 1838 J. N. Nicollet, who surveyed the territory for the War Department, made a report, setting down the first exact information. He made his observations from a point on Spirit Lake near the present Crandall's Lodge *(see below)*.

A. R. Fulton's *The Red Men of Iowa* (1882) says: "It is related that there was once an island in it (Spirit Lake) which the Indians never ventured upon. They had a tradition that once several of the tribe landed upon the island from a canoe, when they were instantly seized and devoured by demons, and hence the name." There is a legend that when the spirit of the waters, Mini-Wakan, was' angry, the chief decided to appease it with a living sacrifice, a captive called Pale Face Dove. The chief's adopted white son, Star of Day, attempted to rescue her, but a jealous Indian girl had already scuttled the canoe in which the two hoped to escape. When the leaking craft began to sink, pursuers were near but the angry spirit caused a storm to capsize their canoes, drowning them as well as the fugitives.

Rich farm lands flank the lakes, contributing to the town's prosperity, which partly depends on the annual influx of tourists.

The first post office in northwestern Iowa was established in the town of Spirit Lake in 1858. The COURTHOUSE stands on the site of a stockade erected about 1860.

Spirit Lake is at the junction with State 9 *(see Tour 10)*, and with State 276, a paved road.

Right on State 276, at 1.6 *m.,* on the south shore of Spirit Lake, is the junction with State 327; R. on State 327 is ORLEANS, 2.1 *m.* (126 pop.), composed almost entirely of summer cottages and resort hotels. Fire destroyed the Orleans Hotel, one of the largest in the lake region, July 3, 1936. A STATE FISH HATCHERY, where millions of pike fry are hatched each spring for distribution principally to the nearby lakes, is on the north shore of East Okoboji Lake, in ORLEANS STATE PARK.

From Orleans a graveled road leads along the east shore of Spirit Lake. Although the road seldom swerves far from the shore of the lake, the lake view is frequently obscured by the forest. At 7 *m.* is the Minnesota boundary. Left here, along the north shore, to MINI-WAKAN STATE PARK, 7.3 *m.,* a 16-acre tract on a small peninsula extending southward into the lake. Good roads lead into the park. From here is an excellent view southward.

At 9 *m.* is the junction with State 276; L. to CRANDALL'S LODGE (L), on the shore of Spirit Lake. At 10.5 *m.* is HOTTE'S LAKE. At 11 *m.* (R) is another small body of water, MARBLE LAKE, on the shore is the site of the MARBLE CABIN where Indians killed William Marble, taking Mrs. Marble into captivity, in the Indian uprising of 1857 *(see below)*. At 12.3 *m.* is TEMPLAR PARK and the STATE KNIGHTS TEMPLAR HOME.

At 12.8 *m.* (R) is CENTER LAKE, about a mile long and covering 264 acres.

At 13 *m.* is the junction with a graveled road.

Right to the junction with another graveled road, 1.5 *m.,* which leads (L) along the wooded shore of WEST OKOBOJI LAKE with its many deep bays, rocky promontories, and long sandy beaches. West Okoboji, the second largest lake in this region, with an area of 3,788 acres, is a narrow body of water about 6 miles long, varying in depth from a few feet to 135 feet. The water is remarkably clear. Passing HAYWARD'S BAY, OMAHA BEACH, and FORT DODGE POINT, the road rejoins US 71 at 4 *m.,* at the northeastern corner of the town of OKOBOJI *(see below)*.

At 14 *m.* is the junction with another graveled road.

Left along the shore of EAST OKOBOJI LAKE, which is smaller than West Okoboji, with a maximum depth of 24 feet. East Okoboji curves along the eastern side of the town of Spirit Lake to within a short distance of Orleans *(see above)*.

OKOBOJI, 15.3 *m.* (176 pop.), a village on the shore of East Okoboji Lake, was established as a post office in the spring of 1855. Boating and fishing facilities are available here.

Okoboji is at the junction with a road running into the lake country *(see above)*.

ARNOLD'S PARK, 16 *m.* (1,432 alt., 597 pop.), lies just south of the bridge separating West and East Okoboji Lakes. From the lower end of the bridge at sunset the view is particularly impressive, embracing almost the entire length of West Okoboji. The soft light intensifies reflections in the water; the trees stand out black against the brilliant red and gold western sky.

Boating, fishing, and bathing are popular sports here *(steamers, motorboats, sailboats, and rowboats available at wharf)*. A high toboggan slide is well patronized. There is a large pavilion, used for various purposes and seating about 1,000.

Arnold's Park, now chiefly a summer resort, was settled in 1856. Isaac Harriott, W. H. Granger, Carl Granger, and Bertell Snyder, of Red Wing, Minn., and James Mattock of Delaware County, chose the town site between East and West Okoboji Lakes. They planned this as one of a series of towns to be platted by the Red Wing Land Site Co. along a proposed mail route which was to connect St. Paul with some point on the Missouri River. Mr. and Mrs. Rowland Gardner and their four children, including a married daughter and her husband and two infants, arrived from the East and settled a mile from the Mattock and Granger sites. The Gardners were the first victims of the Indian uprising in the spring of 1857.

Although this event is known as the Spirit Lake Massacre—chiefly because the entire chain of lakes was known as Spirit Lake—most of the killings actually took place on the shores of West Okoboji. On March 7, 1857, after the first spring thaw, Inkpadutah *(scarlet point)* and his band of Sioux Indians returned to the lake region after being driven from Smithland by settlers. They found the country in which they had held various religious rites settled by white men: 46 men, women, and children. It had been a severe winter and both Indians and whites had suffered. Game was scarce. The settlers had had no crops the previous year and their food supplies were nearly exhausted. On the day of the attack, Rowland Gardner was preparing to travel to Fort Dodge for provisions. The Indians' resentment and fear of white encroachments because of the destruction of game, their chief food, was fanned by petty insults and disputes at Smithland. The Gardners were at breakfast when an Indian stalked in and, pretending friendship, indicated that he wanted something to eat. A place was prepared for him at the table. Soon other Indians came in, until at last Inkpadutah, a tall middle-aged chief, pitted by smallpox and described as "much like Milton's Satan", and his 14 warriors, with their squaws and papooses, had crowded into the cabin. The dwindling provisions were freely divided until each had been fed.

Then the visitors became sullen. At the demand for ammunition, Gardner handed out some gun-caps. The whole box was snatched from his hand. Another Indian attempted to seize a powder horn from the wall, and Luce, Gardner's son-in-law, forcibly preventing him, was nearly shot in the ensuing scuffle.

About 9 a.m. Dr. Harriott and Bertell Snyder called at the cabin, bringing letters for Gardner to mail at Fort Dodge. Even then, possibly, the massacre could have been prevented—the Indians were roaming about the property and the white people had a chance to confer. Gardner thought the other settlers ought to be warned, and that they should gather in his cabin, the largest and strongest in the colony, and prepare to defend themselves. But the two callers considered the Indians harmless, and returned home without taking any precautions. Later the Indians departed, driving the Gardner cattle before them, shooting the beasts down in front of them, on the trail to the Mattock cabin.

After anxious consultation, two men who had been staying at the Gardner home started out to warn the other settlers. The Gardners, waiting in the cabin, heard several shots. As they feared, the two men were murdered. The afternoon dragged by. Toward sunset, Gardner, unable to remain inactive any longer, went out to reconnoiter. Shortly he returned with the news that nine Indians were coming. His first impulse was to barricade the door and fight until the ammunition was exhausted, but his wife, trusting that a friendly reception would spare their lives, dissuaded him. Gardner greeted the Indians at the door, and at the request for flour, bent over the barrel to scrape what particles he could from the bottom. As he stooped, one of the Indians shot him in the back. Others seized Mrs. Gardner and Mrs. Luce, carried them outdoors and brained them with the butts of rifles.

The Indians then turned their attention to the small Gardner boy and the two Luce children, one a baby, dragging them from the protection of 14-year-old Abigail Gardner, to whom they were clinging, and clubbing them to death with lengths of stove wood. Then the marauders ransacked the house, broke open trunks, ripped up feather beds, and with the bloody scalps of their victims swinging from their belts, proceeded toward the Mattock cabin. There Abigail Gardner, dragged along as a captive, saw more Indians dancing around the flaming building, their war whoops mingling with the screams and groans of the wounded and dying within. Mattock, Carl Granger, Snyder, and Dr. Harriott, rifles still in hand, were among the dead revealed by the glow of the fire. Snyder and Harriott had joined the defense, but too late.

Next morning the warriors smeared their skins with black (the Sioux war color) and for six days continued their activities, killing 40 persons, destroying stock and household goods, and taking several women prisoners. The last of the victims, the Marbles, were murdered March 13, at their home on the shore of Spirit Lake. Unaware of the fate of their neighbors, William Marble readily admitted the Indians, fed them, and agreed, for amusement, to shoot at a target. When his rifle was emptied, Marble was asked to rearrange the target, and as soon as he turned, was shot in the back. His wife tried to run away, but was caught and imprisoned with the other women captives.

A traveler stopped at the Gardner cabin on the night of March 19 and found the bodies of the family. He crept through the underbrush toward the Mattock cabin, narrowly escaped detection when the Indians' dogs started barking, and continued to the Noble and Thatcher cabins, finding the lifeless bodies of his friends. In the morning he went on to Springfield, now Jackson, to report the disaster. Two men carried the news to Fort Dodge, with the result that on March 22 three companies of volunteers started for the lakes. Inkpadutah and his outlaws were never caught and punished. Two Iowans were in 1936 still receiving pensions as widows of men who joined the relief forces on Mar. 23, 1857.

Mrs. Marble and Miss Gardner both lived to reach civilization again. They were purchased by friendly Indians, through missionaries and the State of Minnesota. Abigail Gardner (later Mrs. Sharp) lived until 1921.

At 17 *m.* near the highway, is the SPIRIT LAKE MASSACRE MONUMENT. Now the marble shaft is a stone pyramid over the graves of some of those who were killed. Near the pyramid is a STONE BENCH bearing the inscription, "Abigail Gardner Sharp, Orphaned and Enslaved by the Hostile Sioux, She Lived to Embrace in Christian Benevolence the American Indian and All Mankind."

The nearby GARDNER CABIN *(adm. 25¢)*, where the first victims lived, is protected by a fence. It is now owned by a great-grandson of the Gardners. Relics of the tragic event and several Indian articles are on exhibition there.

Near the Gardner cabin, on a small peninsula jutting out into the lake, is PILLSBURY POINT STATE PARK, a popular picnic ground covering 3 acres.

MILFORD, 20 *m.* (1,441 alt., 1,062 pop.), came into existence with the erection of the Milford flour mills in the summer of 1869. The mill owners platted the town in 1870, but the panic of 1873 and the destruction of crops for four successive years by grasshoppers led to discontinuance of the mills and retarded the growth of Milford soon after its promising beginning. Today it is a trading center for farmers.

FOSTORIA, 27 m. (1,449 alt., 142 pop.), center of a grain-growing and livestock-raising district, is the outgrowth of a pioneer settlement begun in 1869 by Thomas Berry, Peter Nelson, G. W. Clark, Joseph O'Brien, and their families.

At 31 m. is the junction with US 18 (see Tour 11) which unites briefly with this route.

SPENCER, 34 m. (1,315 alt., 5,019 pop.), seat of Clay County, was founded in 1859 and named for former U. S. Senator George E. Spencer (1836–1893). The population includes many Scandinavians as well as people of German, Irish, and English descent.

Spencer's modern appearance is partly owing to a fire July 4, 1931, caused by carelessly handled fireworks, that razed most of the business section, destroying property valued at more than $2,000,000. The citizens immediately made plans for rebuilding, and prohibited the use of fireworks at any time within the town limits.

The SPENCER AIRPORT, enlarged and improved as a W.P.A. Project, covers more than 100 acres, is illuminated, and has four runways.

At the southern end of Spencer is the junction with US 18 (see Tour 11) which branches R. here.

SIOUX RAPIDS, 52 m. (1,308 alt., 958 pop.), was platted in 1858 by Luther H. Barnes, who dreamed of seeing a great city grow here on the banks of the Little Sioux River. The community failed to thrive, and when Barnes left, heart-broken and impoverished, the other residents used his former town stakes for kindling wood. In 1869, when D. C. Thomas and David Evans replatted the town, they named it Sioux Rapids.

REMBRANDT, 58 m. (1,333 alt., 263 pop.), is one of several settlements that grew out of work camps housing employees during the construction of the Minn. and St.L. R.R. from Storm Lake, Iowa, to Winthrop, Minn. First named in honor of Barney Orsland, on whose farm the town was laid out in 1899, it was later renamed for Rembrandt, the Dutch painter.

TRUESDALE (L), 65 m. (1,360 alt., 116 pop.), was named for W. H. Truesdale, a Minn. and St.L. R.R. official. Jacob Long opened the community's first general store in 1901.

STORM LAKE, 72 m. (1,436 alt., 4,157 pop.), seat of Buena Vista County, borders the north shore of Storm Lake.

BUENA VISTA COLLEGE, in the southwestern part of the city, has a faculty of 27, and an enrollment of about 500. The Fort Dodge Presbytery founded the college in April, 1884, at Fort Dodge, but later accepted Storm Lake's offer of 8 acres of land and $25,000 for buildings, dedicating the new school July 8, 1891. It offers courses in the liberal arts, dramatics, speech, and other subjects.

Left from Storm Lake on Lake Shore drive along the northeastern shore of Storm Lake to the junction with a graveled road, 1.5 *m.;* R. here to STORM LAKE STATE PARK, 2.5 *m.,* an 18-acre area bordering the lake. Slippery and American elm grow here.

Storm Lake is at the junction with State 5 *(see Tour 12A).*

EARLY, 88 *m.* (1,331 alt., 632 pop.), on the West Boyer River, was named for D. C. Early, a pioneer, and was settled in the late 1870's, about the time the C. and NW. R.R. was built through northern Sac County.

Early is at the junction with US 20 *(see Tour 12).*

At 98 *m.* is the junction with State 35.

Right on this road to ODEBOLT, 5 *m.* (1,361 alt., 1,388 pop.). In 1911 this community produced $400,000 worth of popcorn. This specialty has brought the town much prosperity. Three nationally known popcorn companies do a large business here. Livestock-growing and diversified farming are other activities in the vicinity. The population here is predomininatly German, Swedish and Scotch.

The ADAMS RANCH, owned more than 35 years by the late W. P. Adams, covers 6,400 acres SW of Odebolt. In the summer nearly 100 men are employed on this farm, which is equipped with its own water and fire hydrant systems, two elevators, a machine shop, a dormitory, and a mess hall for farm hands.

LAKE VIEW, 103 *m.* (1,243 alt., 993 pop.), is a summer resort on the shore of Black Hawk Lake *(cottages for rent; golf, roller-skating, and other amusement facilities.)* The town benefits commercially from the numerous gravel pits in the vicinity. Concrete, surfacing, and ballasting materials, cement blocks, and drainage tile are manufactured here. Another source of revenue is the lake from which about 200 cars of ice are taken each winter. A rich agricultural district surrounds the town, from which is shipped about 2,000 tons of popcorn annually.

The elevation, or wall, around the edge of the lake is similar to that of Wall Lake in Wright County *(see Tour 5).* On the shore, in CRESCENT PARK, stands the BELL CABIN, a log structure built on the hill by the pioneer Bell family in 1871. A concrete and crushed stone STATUE OF CHIEF BLACK HAWK overlooks the lake.

At 105 *m.* is the junction with a graveled road.

Right on this road along the east shore of Black Hawk Lake to BLACK HAWK LAKE STATE PRESERVE *(picnicking facilities),* 1.4 *m.,* a 30-acre recreational and fish and game preserve area. A State wild fowl feeding station is maintained here. Stone wing dams have been built to prevent silt from filling up the bed of ARROW HEAD LAKE, once a gravel pit. On the shore thousands of trees have been planted as a memorial to George Washington. Thirty abandoned gravel pits nearby have been transformed into nursery ponds where fish are reared to fingerling and yearling size.

AUBURN, 116 *m.* (1,240 alt., 359 pop.), was platted by the Western Town Lot Co. and named for Auburn, N. Y. A plant here manufactures a superior type of drain and building tile. Raw materials are taken from beds of clay and carried by cars hung from wire cables for a distance of a quarter of a mile through the Raccoon Valley.

CARROLL, 129 *m.* (1,261 alt., 4,691 pop.) *(see Tour 13),* is at the junction with US 30 *(see Tour 13).*

Section b. CARROLL to MISSOURI LINE, 113 m.

South of Carroll rounded, rolling hills appear like waves on the vast prairie; soft crumbling bluffs line the banks of rivers and streams.

At 14 m. is the junction with State 236, paved, and State 46, paved. At this point US 71 turns L. to continue southward.

1. Right from the junction on State 236 is TEMPLETON, 1 m. (1,431 alt., 428 pop.), known from coast to coast during prohibition days for its bootleg rye whiskey. Many giant stills were operated in the vicinity. During the period when Templeton basked in illegal glory, a small brown jug was suspended across the main street. The town, a shipping point for a prosperous farming area, was platted in 1882 on land owned by William Overmire, and was settled largely by people of German descent.

2. Right from the junction on State 46 is MANNING, 7 m. (1,324 alt., 1,817 pop.), second largest town in Carroll County. Named in honor of O. H. Manning of Carroll, it was platted in 1880 after the southwestern branch of the C. and N.W. R.R. was built. The population, largely German, has often sponsored gay street carnivals, dances, agricultural fairs, and athletic tournaments. In the old days, Manning's Horse-Shoe Bar, 112 feet long, was notable. The property of the Dubuque Brewing and Malting Co., it was set up in a store building in Manning in order to popularize the product, Banquet Beer. The bend in the bar faced the entrance, the two sides extending toward the rear. Often from 10 to 15 bartenders were on duty at one time to serve the patrons.

AUDUBON, 27 m. (1,301 alt., 2,255 pop.), seat of Audubon County, commands an extensive view in all directions from its place on low hills. Named, like the county, for John James Audubon, the naturalist, it is particularly noted for its beautiful trees. The C.R.I. & P. R. R. platted the town in 1878, presenting a town lot to the first child born there.

Farming and canning are the principal occupations in this district. The Audubon canning factory employs approximately 125 people in season.

The CITY PARK, with attractive flower gardens, is in the heart of the business district. In the park is the PUBLIC LIBRARY, facing a garden in which native wild flowers of the county have been transplanted and preserved. Near the library is the WORLD WAR MEMORIAL BUILDING, scene of many community activities. A rock garden beautifies its front lawn.

The first LOG CABIN in the county (adm. free on application to county clerk, next door), built by Nathaniel Hamlin, was removed from its original site S. of the present town of Hamlin, and now stands in the courthouse square. It contains a few old furnishings.

The AUDUBON COUNTY FAIR GROUNDS, where a fair is held annually in September, adjoins the city on the northwest.

South of Audubon, in a fork of the road, are FLOWER GARDENS.

At 28.5 m. is junction with graveled road.

Right on this road .2 m. to 10-acre preserve set aside by Audubon County for protection of wildlife, and wild plants, special attention given to native hardwood trees.

HAMLIN, 31 m. (1,257 alt., 160 pop.), was named for Nathaniel H. Hamlin, first settler in Audubon County (see above), and was at one time considered as a site for the county seat.

Hamlin is at the junction with State 7 (see Tour 14B).

EXIRA, 36 m. (1,227 alt., 937 pop.), founded by Judge D. M. Harris, dates back to 1857, and is the oldest town in the county. The town was named for Exira Eckman of Ohio, who, with her father, Judge John Eckman, was visiting relatives when the town was platted. One of the promoters had intended to call it Viola, for his own daughter; but when Judge Eckman offered to buy a town lot if the place were named for his daughter, the change was made at once.

Exira, on high ground, has an unusual number of trees. Most of the business structures are of brick. An old building, now used as a bakery, was the first county courthouse, before Audubon became the county seat in 1879. A block north of this building is a residence that was the first schoolhouse in the county.

An APIARY, near the City Park, houses 700 colonies of bees that produce 50,000 pounds of honey annually.

Among the five churches in Exira is a small DANISH LUTHERAN CHURCH. Many of the services are conducted in Danish.

At 37 m., R. about 50 feet, is the PLOW TREE. The plow was left standing against a low fork of the tree which is on the Leffingwell farm, in the early 1870's. The tree grew around it and today only a part of the implement is visible.

BRAYTON, 40 m. (1,209 alt., 236 pop.), was named for one of the civil engineers working on the C.R.I. & P. R. R. here in 1878–79. This was one of the first towns in the county to be platted. Near Brayton is a MOLASSES FACTORY producing 700 gallons of sorghum annually. The thick amber syrup is made from sorghum cane, which resembles the kaffir corn and broom corn plants. In September the cane stalks are stripped of their leaves as they stand upright in the field. After the stalks are cut they are hauled to the mill and the juice is pressed out. Molasses-making requires skill and patience; the syrup must be stirred and tested constantly lest it scorch or cook too long. At many mills after the molasses-making has been completed, a big taffy pull is held, the neighbors for miles around gathering for the event.

At 50 m. is the junction with US 6 (see Tour 14).

The highway traverses rolling farm lands, with fields of tall green corn or golden grain and blue-green and brown pastures, interspersed with wooded streams, along the route.

GRANT, 70 m. (242 pop.), on the banks of the Nodaway River, was platted in 1858 under the name of Milford. Later, when it was found that another Milford existed in Iowa, the name was changed to honor Ulysses S. Grant.

Surrounding an old mill on the banks of the river, in the southeastern corner of town, are pleasant PICNIC GROUNDS; the fishing here is excellent. A BEAVER VILLAGE, just above a dam (L), is one of the few remaining in this part of the country. There are a number of beaver in the colony. So common at one time that their pelts were used for money, the beaver has now been almost exterminated. Adult beavers are about 2 feet long from nose to the root of the tail, and weigh 35 pounds or more. The tail is about 10 inches long, and is thick and oval, flattened horizontally for about half its length. It acts as a rudder and an oar in water, and when slapped on the water signals the presence of danger. The substantial homes, made of tree branches and plastered with mud and grasses, are built in the water, or on its edge, and are sometimes three feet high and seven feet across. If the stream is not very deep, the beaver builds a dam to form a pond about the lodge.

Between Grant and the Missouri Line US 71 roughly follows the valley of the Nodaway River.

At 79 *m.* is the junction with US 34 *(see Tour 16)*.

VILLISCA *(pretty place)*, 85 *m.* (1,050 alt., 2,032 pop.), was first known as The Forks, because of its position between Middle and West Nodaway Rivers. The present name is said to be of Indian origin. The predominating racial strains here are Dutch and Irish.

At 99 *m.* is the junction with State 3 *(see Tour 17)*.

CLARINDA, 101 *m.* (1,009 alt., 4,962 pop.) *(see Tour 17)*, is at the junction with State 3 *(see Tour 17)*.

SHAMBAUGH (L), 107 *m.* (973 alt., 278 pop.), is a Mennonite settlement platted by James Shambaugh in 1881.

BRADDYVILLE, 112.8 *m.* (953 alt., 867 pop.), was named for James Braddy, who platted the village in 1878.

At 113 *m.*, on the southern edge of Braddyville, US 71 crosses the Missouri Line, 64 miles N. of St. Joseph, Mo.

Tour 8

(Worthington, Minn.)—Primghar—Denison—Shenandoah—(St. Joseph, Mo.); US 59.
Minnesota Line to Missouri Line, 234 m.

I.C.R.R. parallels the route between Primghar and Cherokee; C. R. I. & P. R. R., between Harlan and Carson; C. B. & Q. R. R., between Carson and Hastings; Wabash R. R., between Solomon and Shenandoah.
Interstate Transit Bus Lines follow this highway between Holstein and Denison, and between Harlan and Avoca.
Roadbed intermittently paved and graveled.
Tourist accommodations of all kinds, chiefly in cities.

Crossing the Minnesota Line 0 *m.*, 10 miles S. of Worthington, Minn., US 59 passes across the comparatively level plains in northern Iowa to the rough hills and valleys in the southern part of the State.

At 5 *m.* is the junction with State 9 *(see Tour 10)*.

SANBORN, 22 *m.* (1,552 alt., 1,213 pop.), is at the junction with US 18 *(see Tour 11)*.

PRIMGHAR, 30 *m.* (1,498 alt., 962 pop.), seat of O'Brien County, is a German settlement. The name combines the first letters of the surnames of eight early settlers.

CALUMET, 44 *m.* (1,430 alt., 240 pop.), a small rural community, like many Iowa towns has an annual Pancake Day, usually in September, sponsored by syrup and pancake flour companies. Farmers and townspeople form in lines and the golden cakes are placed on their extended plates with warm thick syrup poured on generously. It is related that there was once a visitor who had 21 plates of cakes. A fat man's race, a slipper-kicking contest, and various other amusements fill the day and revive appetites. Four bands contribute music for the occasion.

LARRABEE, 52 *m.* (1,366 alt., 189 pop.), was platted and settled about 1887. The town was named for William Larrabee, Governor of Iowa (1886–1890).

This is (1938) the home of one of the two Collister sisters, each of whom in 1923 husked about 100 bushels of corn in a 9-hour day, a record performance.

CHEROKEE, 61 *m.* (1,201 alt., 6,443 pop.), seat of Cherokee County, lies along the wooded banks of the Little Sioux River.

The city schools have a large MUSEUM *(free)* in a classroom of the Wilson Senior High School, containing exhibits of Indian culture of Cherokee County.

The first town of Cherokee was founded in December, 1856, by a colony from Milford, Mass., on a site north of the present city. Blair City, another extinct village, was founded in 1869 SE. of Cherokee.

The new Cherokee was established here in March, 1870, when the railroad was built through the county. After the new town was founded, Blair City was abandoned and its residents moved here.

In February, 1857, the small band of Sioux who perpetrated the Spirit Lake massacre *(see Tour 7)* terrorized the small settlement for three days before going to the Spirit Lake region. When reports of the massacre were received, many settlers deserted the village and it was feared that the town would be abandoned. Later a rude stockade, covering about a quarter of an acre and enclosing a log blockhouse, was erected as a protection against Indians, and the settlers became less fearful.

About 1880 a group of coal prospectors discovered water at a depth of 200 feet in the valley of the Little Sioux, an area that is now part of Cherokee. According to an historian, "The water is the finest and most healthful in the world. It is a semi-soft water and highly magnetic, so much so that a pocket-knife placed in it will become so thoroughly magnetized that it will readily pick up nails, keys or other metallic pieces."

The historian states that neither the source of the water nor the reason for its alleged properties could be determined, but "Wonderful cures, which have baffled medical skill, especially diseases of the bladder, kidneys and liver, have been effected by these waters, even advanced cases of

JUNEBERRY TREE

Bright's disease, diabetes (man's hell on earth), dyspepsia, and all urinary and chronic ailments."

The owner of the land upon which the water was discovered platted an annex to the city called Magnetic Addition, and in 1881 erected a sanatorium known as the Fountain House. Everything to make the premises a place of beauty was accomplished. An artificial lake was excavated which was supplied by the discharge from this beautiful flowing well. The park grounds were elegantly adorned by miniature fountains, drives, walks, flower gardens, and trees. The place was in charge of a Dr. Gee, of Chicago, who for a term of years wrought many cures. This hotel was not only sought by invalids, but as a "place to pass the heated terms of summer in quiet repose." The Fountain House has long since been discontinued, and the remarkable well ceased to flow when the municipal well was sunk five blocks northwest.

West of the town is a plot of virgin prairie, privately owned.

Cherokee is at the junction with State 5 *(see Tour 12A)*.

Right from Cherokee on a graveled road to the STATE HOSPITAL FOR THE INSANE, 2 *m.*, which was opened in August, 1902, to relieve the crowded conditions of other State institutions. The distance around the foundations of the buildings is a little more than a mile. The total investment is about $1,500,000, including the buildings and farm of 1,000 acres. Seven hundred acres are under cultivation.

At 65 *m.* a huge boulder known as PILOT ROCK, visible (R) about a quarter of a mile from the highway. The red Sioux quartzite boulder, was so named because it was a landmark to travelers crossing the prairie. The Indian name was Woven Stone. At the higher end of the rock tons of fragments have broken off and lie scattered about on the ground.

At 82 *m.* is the junction with US 20 *(see Tour 12)*.

IDA GROVE, 93 *m.* (1,225 alt., 2,206 pop.), seat of Ida County, borders the Maple River. It has annual Dutch and Scotch reunions that bring together large groups of old settlers. Old timers say that before the Scotch festival developed into the present day public celebration, "everybody who wasn't Scotch tried to get an invitation to the gay event; Irish, German, English, and Scandinavians said they could trace a great aunt or maybe a 42nd cousin back to the highlands if there was a chance of receiving the coveted invitation."

The highland fling and the sword dance, done by the best Scottish entertainers of the Middle West, are always on the program. The chief event for many years was the piping and dancing of the late Major Cameron, local restaurateur, in his highland regalia; his three granddaughters now carry on in his place.

In earlier days, this was a popular hunting country, with prairie chickens, deer, and an occasional lynx. Today the extensive popcorn fields of the surrounding district furnish a large part of the world supply of this product.

A well-driller in 1902 was employed to dig a well nearby on the Smith and Weston stock farm; at a depth of 30 feet, he struck a barrier that stopped his operations. After some delay, a shovel crew excavated a larger hole and found a pile of boulders, most of them the size of a man's head, arranged as if they had been used as a military breastworks.

Left from Ida Grove on improved dirt road to a junction at 1 *m.;* L. here to an OAK TREE, 1.5 *m.,* one of the few Indian burial trees in Iowa, in a grove on the Judge Moorehead ranch. The branches of the large oak provided positions for the dead, who were placed in a sitting posture. Although there is no record that a body was seen here, the Mooreheads, when they settled on the farm in 1856, found great numbers of brightly colored beads beneath the tree, many embedded several inches in the ground.

SCHLESWIG, 508 *m.* (1,493 alt., 638 pop.), is a shipping center for farm produce. Inhabitants named the town for their home province in Prussia; it had previously been called Morgan, then Hohenzollern. The Schleswig *Leader,* a weekly newspaper established here in 1900, was published in the German language until 1903 when publication in English was begun.

At 115 *m.* is the 120-acre LINCOLN FARM. During his visit to Council Bluffs in 1859, Abraham Lincoln showed an old United States land warrant issued to him for his services as a captain in the Black Hawk War, and voiced his regret that he had never filed it for record, so that his sons, Bob and Tad, might have had tangible proof "that their father was a soldier." A second, signed by President Buchanan, in 1860, was recorded in Crawford County on Dec. 12, 1867. The title for this parcel of land passed from the Lincoln family through a deed signed by Robert T. Lincoln and his wife and dated Mar. 22, 1892. Lincoln had neglected to file the warrant because he felt he was "so poor that I was afraid I could not pay the taxes upon the land if I got it."

DENISON, 121 *m.* (1,170 alt., 3,905 pop.) *(see Tour 13),* is at the junction with US 30 *(see Tour 13).*

At 138 *m.* is the junction with State 268, graveled.

Left on this road is IRWIN, 6 *m.* (1,265 alt., 357 pop.). The second annual Colt Show was held here Sept. 3, 4, 1936, sponsored by local business men.

At 143 *m.* is the junction with an improved road.

Right on this road is WESTPHALIA, 3.5 *m.* (118 pop.). The Rev. Herbert Duren, pastor of St. Boniface Church and the superintendent of the St. Boniface School here, is also a painter. Among his better-known works are *An Iowa Girl* and *October Highways.* Two pictures, *The Westward Movement* and *Deer Land,* hang on the walls of St. Boniface.

HARLAN, 148 *m.* (1,194 alt., 3,145 pop.) *(see Tour 14B),* is at the junction with State 7 *(see Tour 14B).* State 7 and US 59 are united between Harlan and Avoca.

AVOCA, 160 *m.* (1,137 alt., 1,673 pop.) *(see Tour 14B).* Here State 7 *(see Tour 14B)* turns R.

HANCOCK, 167 *m.* (1,113 alt., 312 pop.), was platted in 1880 when the railroad was extended from Avoca, but settlers had arrived here in 1852. An Old Settlers Picnic is an annual event.

OAKLAND, 173 *m.* (1,106 alt., 1,181 pop.) *(see Tour 14),* is at the junction with US 6 *(see Tour 14).*

MACEDONIA, 183 *m.* (1,107 alt., 143 pop.), was founded in 1880. It is on the old Pioneer Trail, now a county road.

At 198 *m.* is the junction with US 34 *(see Tour 16).*

IMOGENE, 211 *m.* (1,044 alt., 303 pop.), on Hunter Branch Creek, was settled by a group of Irishmen in the early 1880's.

The ROMAN CATHOLIC CHURCH, in the Gothic style on an elaborate scale, was erected in 1915. Altars and statuary of Carrara marble, massive gold candlesticks, the Stations of the Cross, and other furnishings were imported from Italy. Stained glass windows depict Bible scenes.

In 1886, August Werner, a local cabinetmaker, planned to demonstrate his "flying machine" at the Fourth of July celebration. People came from miles around to watch. The design of the machine was similar to that later used for the autogiro, having an overhead propeller. When the blades were spun, however, the wooden cogs were sheared off. Werner never recovered from his disappointment, and died in the State Hospital for the Insane at Clarinda.

SHENANDOAH, 221 *m.* (981 alt., 6,502 pop.) *(see Tour 17),* is at the junction with State 3 *(see Tour 17).*

At 234 *m.* US 59 crosses the Missouri Line, 84 miles N. of St. Joseph, Mo.

Tour 9

(Luverne, Minn.)—Rock Rapids—Sioux City—Council Bluffs—Sidney —(St. Joseph, Mo.); US 75, US 275.
Minnesota Line to Missouri Line, 229 m.

I. C. R. R. parallels this route between the Minnesota Line and Rock Rapids, between Le Mars and Sioux City, and between Missouri Valley and Council Bluffs; C. St. P., M. and O. R. R., between the Minnesota Line and Doon, and between Le Mars and Sioux City; G. N. R. R., between Doon and Sioux City; C. & N. W. R. R., between Merrill and Council Bluffs; C. B. & Q. R. R., between Council Bluffs and Hamburg.
The Greyhound Bus Line follows the highway between Missouri Valley and Council Bluffs; Burlington Bus Line between Oakland and Council Bluffs. Between the Minnesota Line and Sioux Center, roadbed intermittently graveled and paved; between Sioux Center and Missouri Line, paved.
Tourist accommodations of all kinds available, chiefly in cities.

Section a. MINNESOTA LINE *to* SIOUX CITY, 75 m.

Crossing the Minnesota Line, 17 miles S. of Luverne, Minn., the route traverses part of the eastern edge of the Great Plains. There is a quiet beauty in this part of northern Iowa, especially in summer, when the pale yellow sheen of wheat fields contrasts with the waving green corn. Herds of blooded livestock graze in the pastures and meadows of alfalfa. Native trees are rare, appearing usually in fringes along streams and rivers; however, farmers have planted trees of all kinds as windbreaks.

ROCK RAPIDS, 6 m. (1,345 alt., 2,221 pop.), seat of Lyon County, takes its name from the rapids in Rock River. It is at the junction with State 9 (see Tour 10).

At 22 m. is the junction with US 18 (see Tour 11).

SIOUX CENTER, 30 m. (1,447 alt., 1,497 pop.), a farming community, has six co-operative societies with interlocking directorates. The largest is the Farmers Mutual Co-operative Creamery which, in 1935, made and sold almost 3,000,000 pounds of butter; the cream is gathered within a radius of 50 miles by 19 trucks. A co-operative burial association here owns a modern funeral home and has a large membership; this is one of the few co-operatives of this kind in the country. Only one member of a family, and no member of the family of an officer, is employed by a co-operative.

Right from Sioux Center on a graveled road to the bank of the Big Sioux River, 14 m.; R. here to the OAK GROVE STATE SCENIC PRESERVE, 16 m., an area of 102 acres; R. from the entrance 0.4 m. on a park road to the PARK LODGE, 0.4 m.; at 0.6 m. is the PICNIC GROUNDS. From a high bluff the lodge overlooks the wooded valley of the Big Sioux River; oak trees and prairie flowers cover the lowlands.

At 36 m. is the junction with State 10, locally called the Million Dollar Corner. It skirts the banks of two sloughs, which in flood periods become the West Fork of the Floyd River. Construction of a bridge over one of the sloughs cost $1,500,000.

Left on State 10 is ORANGE CITY, 4 m. (1,412 alt., 1,727 pop.), a Dutch town founded by Henry Hospers in 1869 and named for Prince William of Orange. Wooden shoes are shipped from a factory here. Tulip Day in this town is a colorful event. The residents have patterned their celebration on that of Holland, Mich., and annually import bulbs from the Netherlands to increase the number of flowers. Dutch costumes—button-covered blouses, wide skirts or pantaloons, and wooden shoes—are worn during the celebration. Dutch bobs show beneath white bonnets and caps. Dutch food weighs down the tables in homes and restaurants. Store windows display family heirlooms from the Netherlands. Thousands of gay tulips decorate business and community floats, bicycles, and autos. The event usually takes place about May 14, but may be postponed for another week if the season is cold.

NORTHWESTERN JUNIOR COLLEGE, founded in 1882, has a 10-acre campus, two main halls, a gymnasium, an athletic field, and a president's home.

MAURICE, 38 m. (1,308 alt., 274 pop.), was named for Count Maurice of Nassau, Prince of Orange and son of William the Silent.

LE MARS, 50 m. (1,224 alt., 4,778 pop.), seat of Plymouth County, was named for the first initials of six young women who visited the settlement in early days—Lucy Underhill, Elizabeth Parsons, Mary Weare, Anna Blair, Rebecca Smith, and Sarah Reynolds.

In 1876 William B. Close of Trinity College, Cambridge, England, acquired a blister while rowing with his team in a regatta at the Philadelphia Centennial. Sitting in the side lines he became acquainted with Daniel Paullin, a banker and landowner of Quincy, Ill. Paullin in glowing terms

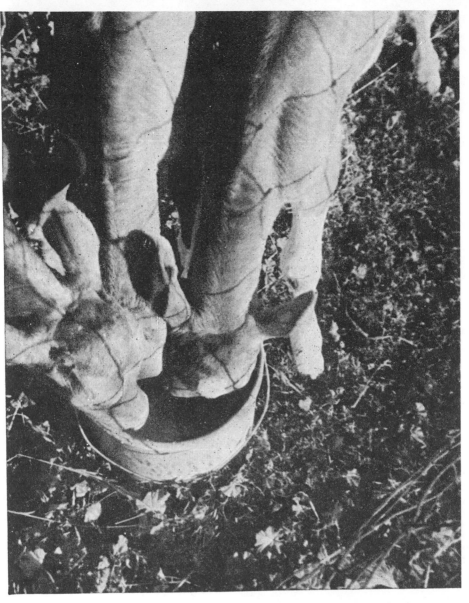

CALVES DRINKING

described the Iowa lands newly opened to settlement by the United States Government, and his enthusiasm inspired Close to visit the area with eastern speculators. Later Close married Paullin's daughter. Close persuaded his brothers in England to come to America and formed a colonization company. They centered operations in Plymouth County, purchasing 30,000 acres at $2.50 per acre; elsewhere they bought tracts of 14,000, 18,000, 19,000, and 25,000 acres. The Iowa Land Co., listed on the London Stock Exchange with a capital stock of $5,500,000, published in England enthusiastic accounts of the opportunities in the new country, offering 40% and 50% profits to investors. Prospective colonists were assured that it would be safe to come to Iowa, for "no one carried revolvers or other firearms, bowie knives and such playthings." By the early 1880's a large group of colonists was on its way from England, and steamship companies specialized in tickets for "New York and Le Mars, Iowa, U. S. A."

The Close brothers aided English farmers in bringing their flocks of sheep, their fat cattle, and their families to the rolling hills of the new country. Younger sons of the aristocracy and remittance men also arrived, wearing fashionable London clothes—top hats and cutaway coats. Heavy gold watch chains dangled across smartly cut vests. Some of these pioneers carried walking sticks, to the wonder of the American settlers.

To assist the enthusiastic but inexperienced settlers, Capt. Reynolds Moreton, a retired British naval officer, started a 1,000-acre training farm a short distance NW. of Le Mars. An English correspondent who visited this place wrote: "Admission to the Captain's establishment is not an easy matter to procure. His boys do all the work of the farm. Lord Hobart, when I was there, was mowing, assisted by two of Lord St. Vincent's sons, and the Hon. Captain was feeding a threshing machine. It was hot, but every one looked happy, even young Moreton, who was firing and driving the steam engine." They imported horses and dogs, constructed a race track, and had a polo team that played against teams in St. Louis and Chicago. They also rode to hounds and went steeple chasing, and on one occasion, in good old western fashion, they galloped into town and, without dismounting, up to the bar of the saloon. Their favorite tavern was nicknamed "House of Lords."

British customs were observed. All the colonists punctiliously dressed for dinner. Here, as in other English settlements, the sun never rose or set on an unshaven British chin. Fashionable dinners and dances were held at the Albion House. The names of some present day lords are found on the records of the St. George Episcopal Church, established in 1882 at Le Mars.

Captain Moreton imported sheep from Sussex—descendants of which command topmost prices now at the Sioux City market—and also bred horses, cattle, swine, dogs, and poultry. His smoked hams are still remembered by those local residents who were fortunate enough to taste them. In his stock pavilion he held sales of the blooded cattle he reared. The stock pavilion remains, like the house and polo barns, battered by storms and neglected. Hundreds of elms, spruce, evergreen, walnut, and fruit trees planted by the captain still flourish.

The drought, grasshopper sieges, bitter winters, and high expenses of the later 1880's and early 1890's caused many of the colonists to lose their enthusiasm. Fuel was scarce, too. Captain Moreton made an attempt at coal mining—a venture causing such rumors and speculations that mineral rights in the vicinity were leased at prices soaring from $100 to $300 an acre and companies were formed to exploit possible strikes. The operations, however, proved so costly that when an extensive boring revealed only lignite, the owners abandoned the project. Captain Moreton, himself a heavy loser, endeavored to justify himself, and the fact that so much money had been expended locally, causing a temporary boom, went far to mitigate the biterness and discontent that might otherwise have resulted.

Eventually the colony disintegrated. William B. Close returned to England, and many others followed. Some went up to Pipestone, Minn., others to Canada. The gay young men, preferring to remain unmarried and irresponsible, developed no local ties; others fled from the severe winters or grew homesick.

People of German and other nationalities bought nearby land and the British atmosphere of the settlement changed. Choice houses and herds were sold, and polo and cricket fields were neglected.

WESTERN UNION COLLEGE, at the southern edge of the city, was founded in 1900 and is under control of the Evangelical Church; it offers courses in music and the liberal arts, has a faculty of 18, and a student body of 300. Seven buildings are grouped on the 15-acre campus; literary and scientific exhibits and a number of relics are shown in the MUSEUM *(free)* on the fourth floor of the Administration Building.

There is a municipally owned PARK *(bathing, dancing, golfing)*, a 50-acre area with two small lakes, in the northeastern part of the town.

Le Mars is at the junction with State 5 *(see Tour 12A)*.

MERRILL, 57 *m.* (1,177 alt., 605 pop.), on the bank of the Floyd River, was platted in 1872 by the Sioux City and Iowa Falls R. R., which was built through the region in 1869. Before the days of the grain elevators, the local grocer, William Frost, often received washtubs full of wheat in payment for his commodities.

A milk concentration plant here ships milk and cream from the surrounding dairy farms to Sioux City.

The municipal SWIMMING POOL is the only artificial one in Plymouth County.

Agricultural Day, featuring a fair and a colt show, is held each year in September.

SIOUX CITY, 75 *m.* (1,135 alt., 79,183 pop.) *(see SIOUX CITY)*.

Points of Interest: Woodbury Co. Courthouse; stockyards; Prospect Hill; Floyd Monument; Morningside College.

Sioux City is at the junction with US 20 *(see Tour 12)*.

Right from Sioux City on State 12 to junction with improved road, 5.7 *m.;* L. to STONE STATE PARK, 6.8 *m.,* an 801-acre area on the Big Sioux River *(picnic and campgrounds, water and sanitary facilities)*. Right on the park drive to the ZOO, 7.8 *m.,* which has brown bears, monkeys, raccoons, and squirrels. Several winding drives lead to high observation points overlooking the plains of South Dakota across the river.

Section b. SIOUX CITY to COUNCIL BLUFFS, 99 m.

Between Sioux City, 0 m., and the Missouri border, US 75 follows the Missouri River (R), which meanders through a wide valley bordered by brown crumbling bluffs; the distance to the opposite shore varies from 3 to 15 miles. The highway winds through the bluffs to the flat river bottom.

SERGEANT BLUFF, 8 m. (1,095 alt., 569 pop.), oldest town in Woodbury County, was platted July 14, 1857. First known as Floyd's Bluff, it was later named Sergeant Bluff, both names honoring Sergeant Charles Floyd, the new member of the Lewis and Clark expedition who died on the journey; he was buried by his companions on the bluff overlooking the river.

Two streams, Big and Little Whiskey Creeks, flowing through the Missouri Valley, gained their names in the early days. Settlers of Sergeant Bluff and of a neighboring village agreed to meet on an appointed day and bridge the creeks for wagon travel. Joe Otten, a saloon keeper, who was unable to join them when the day arrived, sent instead two jugs of whiskey, a small one and a large one. When the workers first met they drank from the large jug to "clear their heads." That day they completed the bridging of the larger stream, and camped for the night on the high ground above. To take their minds off their weariness and the annoyance of mosquitoes, they resorted to the smaller container of whiskey. When the second bridge was completed, the jugs, referred to as "Big Whiskey" and "Little Whiskey," inspired the volunteers to name the two streams accordingly.

SALIX, 14 m. (1,084 alt., 374 pop.), bears the scientific name of the willow that is abundant in the vicinity. The town was platted by the Missouri Land Co. in 1875 and many of its early settlers were Danish or French-Canadian.

Right from Salix on a graveled road to BROWN'S LAKE, 1.5 m., a crescent-shaped body of water (swimming, fishing, boating). A dance pavilion is open during the summer.

SLOAN, 20 m. (1,096 alt., 636 pop.), is at the junction (R) with an improved road.

Right on this road to the bank of the Missouri River, 4 m.; not far from shore is FLOWER'S ISLAND, a 1,100-acre area. Years ago this land was formed at a point on the western shore where the Missouri River gradually swung out in a great curve toward the Iowa shore. An ice jam in 1914 caused the river to cut back through this peninsula, forming an island from land that had formerly been a part of the Winnebago Indian reservation in Nebraska. The Federal Government, which had given each Indian 80 acres, began litigation to establish a legal definition of the land's status when the "present accretion to the Grosvenor tract," purchased from the Indians, was later lost by the buyer in a delinquent tax sale. Wilbur Flower and other squatters who, in the meantime, had moved there, put up shanties, and tilled the soil, claimed they had established a legal right to the land. Many of these 20 families have modern farm machinery, horses and cattle. One squatter, disputing

Flower's leadership, defends with rifle and shotgun a 70-acre tract that he uses. The Federal Government, acting for the Indians, has brought suit to eject the squatters, a suit complicated by the claim of the Grosvenor interests. No educational facilities were available to the children of the colonists until the Works Progress Administration built a log schoolhouse and furnished instructors.

ONAWA (Ind., *awake*), 36 *m.* (1,052 alt., 2,538 pop.), is the seat of Monona County. Monona means *beautiful valley*. Onawa was platted in 1857 by the Monona County Land Co., which also established a ferry at the river, a convenience still in operation. This town is notable for its tree-lined streets, 150 feet wide.

In Onawa, as in other communities in Iowa, old-time dancing is still a favorite recreation that had its heyday in early Iowa. Formerly Saturday afternoons were devoted to washing the buggy, polishing the harness, and fastening rosettes into the mane of the driving mare, preparatory to an evening's dancing of waltzes, square dances, quadrilles, and schottishes. If the dance was held in a barn, lanterns were hung in an empty oat bin. The fiddlers sat in the loft, their music drifting above the heads of the dancers, young and old, as the rhythmic beat was stamped out on the wide board floor.

Right from Onawa on Iowa Avenue, which becomes graveled State 165, and passes BLUE LAKE, 3.5 *m.* (R); along the shore of the lake is LEWIS AND CLARK STATE PARK, 4.8 *m. (beach house, bathing beach, scenic walks)*, a newly developed area in the Missouri River bottomland. The lake, stocked with fish, is one of hundreds formed when the Missouri River made its changes in course. Within the park area are more than 2 miles of paved roads. In 1930, 7,000 trees were planted here as a memorial to Stephen Mather, U. S. Park Commissioner. Opposite the park is a spot where the Lewis and Clark expedition camped on its way to the Northwest.

BLENCOE, 43 *m.* (1,043 alt., 333 pop.), platted in 1881, is served by a ferry operating across the Missouri River from sunrise to sunset, except when the water is icebound. Nebraska farmers convey thousands of bushels of grain on this ferry to Blencoe annually, and do much of their trading there.

RIVER SIOUX, 52.5 *m.* (1,040 alt.), was platted to help establish a line of the Sioux City and Pacific R. R. through the region, but failed to attract business. Thereupon another town, Malta, was laid out on the east side of the river. Neither town prospered—Malta faded into oblivion, and River Sioux is a hamlet beside the bluffs of the Missouri River.

Although today only an occasional fishing boat is seen in many miles on the Missouri River, hundreds of thousands of dollars worth of furs were once carried down its course. Giant cottonwoods and great clumps of willows that grew along the banks of the river furnished the wood from which the canoes of the traders were generally made; the log was scooped out to a thin shell about 2 inches thick at the bottom, leaving it strong, light, and easily managed. The bullboat of the fur traders was made from the skins of buffalo bulls. The mackinaw, a sharp-ended bateau made of timber, was used only in downstream navigation. Since it required little labor to handle them, the men found time for song and, every hour or so, would take advantage of a good stretch of river to rest their oars and talk and smoke. When they reached St. Louis they usually sold the mackinaw boats for $4 or $5 apiece. Keelboats, 60 to 70 feet long with the keel running from bow to stern, were used for military and exploring expeditions. The first large boat to go up the river was probably that of the Lewis and Clark expedition.

The 1850's and 1860's were the golden era of steamboating on the Missouri. The steamboat *Independence* ascended the Missouri 200 miles in 1819, but there was no regular traffic until 1830. The Missouri boats, though not as large as those on the Mississippi, were equipped with state-rooms and bar-rooms, and often carried an orchestra or other entertainers; the decks, surmounted by the texas containing the pilot-house and officers' quarters, were painted a shining white, giving the boats an air of luxury in contrast with the rough cabins on the banks. They aided in the settlement of western Iowa by carrying supplies to the pioneers—lumber and furniture. Usually the boats were greeted at each landing by all the population of a newly settled town. After the railroads arrived, steamboating on the Missouri gradually dwindled.

MONDAMIN (Ind., *corn or in the place where corn grows*), 59.5 *m.* (1,025 alt., 534 pop.), was platted as a railroad town in 1867–68. Fruit growing is the chief industry in the vicinity, and the hills S. and E. of town, covered with orchards, are a beautiful sight in spring. People drive for miles every year to see the blossoms and later to watch the picking and the packing. Thousands of bushels of apples are shipped out annually. Other fruits grown here are grapes, cherries, peaches, and pears.

At 62.5 *m.* is the junction with State 183, a graveled road. Left on State 183 along the Soldier River, through the Missouri Valley bluff lands, to PREPARA-TION CANYON STATE PARK, 19 *m.*, a 160-acre area on the site of the now extinct village of Preparation. All kinds of trees native to Iowa grow here. Many small streams and springs make the park well suited for picknicking and camping. The only remains of the town of Preparation are two houses. The town was founded under the leadership of Charles B. Thompson, a Mormon who settled on Soldier Creek in 1853. The following year a band of Mormons arrived from Nauvoo, and Thompson laid out a village on his claim for them. He called the place by its unusual name to provide a constant reminder that the residents were expected to discipline themselves in readiness to enter the after-life. Thompson alienated his followers when he tried to obtain control of all the land in the colony. The Iowa Supreme Court decided in favor of the colonists. The land was divided among them, but many sold their shares and moved away.

CALHOUN, 66 *m.*, usually called Old Calhoun, was the first village platted in Harrison County; Daniel Brown, who built a log cabin on the site in 1847, laid out and recorded the town Aug. 19, 1853. The name was chosen, old settlers believe, to honor John C. Calhoun, orator and statesman.

MISSOURI VALLEY, 75 *m.*, (1,006 alt., 4,230 pop.), lies by the Willow River just below a rim of high bluffs. Along St. John's Creek, near the town, remains of an Indian village have been found and Indian relics and human skeletons have been unearthed nearby.

The first settler in Missouri Valley was H. B. Henricks, who arrived in 1854. In 1856 the McIntosh brothers came, and the place was first named McIntosh Point, and later St. Johns. When the C. & N. W. R. R. was built through the area the name was changed to Missouri Valley Junction.

The town is a trading and shipping point for farm produce, and a large number of hogs are sold here, many of them having been trucked in from Nebraska.

Missouri Valley is at the junction with US 30 *(see Tour 13)*.

LOVELAND, 80 *m.* (1,007 alt.), a village named for E. Loveland, who settled there in 1856 and built a sawmill, is believed to have the oldest Baptist congregation in the State west of the Des Moines River. Services were first held in 1856.

HONEY CREEK, 85 *m.* (1,008 alt.), named for the nearby stream, was settled by a group of Mormons who were members of the group driven out of Nauvoo, Ill., in 1846. They built a gristmill and established a school that was taught by James Cox in a cabin north of the town. Hirman Bostwick built the first house here on the spot where the railroad station now stands. The Mormons' stay was temporary, but it marked the beginning of settlement in this area. Today Honey Creek is only a hamlet with one store and an elevator.

CRESCENT, 91 *m.* (995 alt., 260 pop.), was formerly known as Crescent City, a name suggested by the shape of the bluffs rising above the town site. First settled by Mormons, Crescent was laid out in 1856. A prosperous future was anticipated, especially if a bridge should be constructed across the Missouri River at that point. The panic of 1857 put an end to this plan, and when some of the business men removed to Council Bluffs, the town ceased to grow.

COUNCIL BLUFFS, 99 *m.* (984 alt., 42,048 pop.) *(see COUNCIL BLUFFS)*.

Points of Interest: State School for the Deaf; General Dodge's Home; Anne Dodge Memorial; Lincoln Memorial; Lewis and Clark Monument.

Council Bluffs is at the junction with US 6 *(see Tour 14)* and State 7 *(see Tour 14B)*; US 75 becomes US 275 at this point.

Right from Council Bluffs on State 192 is LAKE MANAWA STATE LAKE PRESERVE, 4 *m.* The lake was formed about 60 years ago when the Missouri River changed its course, and was restored by the State Conservation Commission in 1933 after it had almost disappeared. The park is being developed (1938) and will have boathouses, a bathhouse, a bathing beach, and other facilities. The lake will be stocked with fish, and the surrounding area landscaped.

Section c. COUNCIL BLUFFS *to* MISSOURI LINE, *55 m.*

South of Council Bluffs, 0 *m.*, at 5 *m.*, is the IOWA SCHOOL FOR THE DEAF *(visitors daily except Sat., Sun.)*, a large State institution notable for its educational work. It was moved from Iowa City to this place in 1870. It has seven buildings on a terrace at the base of the bluffs, overlooking the Missouri River and Omaha, Nebr. A farm of 210 acres surrounds the school. Elementary and secondary education, under the direction of 50 teachers, includes vocational training for the more than 350 pupils.

GLENWOOD, 18 *m.* (1,037 alt., 4,269 pop.) *(see Tour 16)*, is at the junction with US 34 *(see Tour 16)*.

TABOR, 31 *m.* (1,240 alt., 1,017 pop.), was the scene of some of John Brown's anti-slavery activities of 1858–59. In the southeast corner of CITY PARK a bronze marker indicates the campground of John Brown and his followers.

On Center St. is the JOHN BROWN HOME *(private)*, recently renovated. On Park St., facing the park, is the JOHN TODD HOME *(open by request)*, formerly used as a station on John Brown's Underground Railway. High under the eaves are two small oval windows, about 10 inches in diameter, opening into a small room where runaway slaves were hidden. Beneath the house is a long tunnel, connected with the cellar, that provided a place for concealment.

TABOR COLLEGE, incorporated in 1866, was operated by the Congregational Church until 1926, and reopened Sept. 14, 1936, as a private enterprise. There are opportunities here for the students to do part-time work. A 55-acre farm adjoining the campus is run with students' aid to supply the college. Only 20 boys and 20 girls from 1,000 applicants were selected to earn their board and room through the year 1936–37. The students helped to renovate GASTON HALL, the administration building.

SIDNEY, 44 *m.* (1,049 alt., 1,074 pop.), seat of Fremont County since 1851, was named for Sidney, Ohio, where Milton Richard, who platted the town, once lived.

An annual meeting, that became important in the area, was first held in 1889 by men who called their organization the Fremont County Union Veterans' and Sons' of Veterans Association. Whole families drove to town in spring wagons for the holiday, which in later years became a four-day celebration. In 1923, the American Legion took over the management of the event and in the following year added a rodeo to the program; unbroken horses were furnished by farmers in the vicinity.

Now Iowa's annual Championship Rodeo *(min. adm. 50¢)* is held here, lasting four days in the third week in August, under the sponsorship of the Williams-Jobe-Gibson Post. In 1935, more than 82,000 people arrived to witness or take part in the fancy and trick riding contests, bulldogging, calf-roping, dances, and Indian ceremonials. Rodeo clowns, marching bands, and a midway add to the carnival atmosphere. Carloads of western horses are bought and exhibited, then shipped to Nebraska to run on the open range. All buildings, improvements, saddles, livestock, and equipment belong to the Legion and have been paid for with profits derived from the show; the hourly cost to the management has grown from $50 to $2,500. The contests are conducted under rigid Rodeo Association rules; at night floodlights illuminate the arena, making it as light as at midday, and amplifiers carry announcements to the farthest corner of the field.

After expenses have been paid, gate receipts from the rodeos are sometimes used to promote free health clinics for children and for other charities.

At Sidney is the junction with State 3 *(see Tour 17)*.

HAMBURG, 53 *m.* (913 alt., 2,103 pop.), lies below the Missouri Valley bluffs along the bank of the Nishnabotna River. The town was named by a settler for his native city, Hamburg, Germany. A favorite story, lingering from frontier days, concerns a trader named Hitchcock, who built a cabin directly on the Iowa-Missouri Line, 2 miles to the south, and lived there for several years with a collection of wives. Whenever officers from Iowa visited him to ask for an explanation, he retreated to the Missouri end of his house and when the Missouri officers sought to question him, he took refuge in the Iowa end. It was several years before the officers of the two States joined forces and finally brought him to justice.

At 55 *m.* US 275 crosses the Missouri Line, 95 miles N. of St. Joseph, Mo.

Tour 10

Mississippi River—Lansing—Waukon—Forest City—Rock Rapids—(Sioux Falls, S. Dak.); State 9.
Mississippi River to South Dakota Line, 305 *m.*

C. M. & St. P. R.R. parallels the route between Ridgeway and Cresco; C.R. I. & P., between Forest City and Larchwood. The Greyhound Line follows the highway between Cresco and Waukon, Armstrong and Spirit Lake; the Interstate Transit Bus Line, between Armstrong and Spirit Lake; the Jefferson Bus Line, between Decorah and Waukon, Forest City and Leland.
Roadbed intermittently graveled and paved, but more than 50 percent paved.
Accommodations chiefly in cities.

Section a. MISSISSIPPI RIVER *to* FOREST CITY, *143 m.*

State 9 connecting with State 35 in Wisconsin crosses the Mississippi River, the Wisconsin Line, on the BLACK HAWK BRIDGE *(car and driver, 50¢; passengers, 10¢; trucks, 50¢ up)*, 9 miles W. of Ferryville, Wis.

LANSING is at 1 *m.* (630 alt., 1,321 pop.). The first claim on the town site was staked in 1848 by H. H. Houghton who, with John Haney, Sr., laid out the town, in 1851, at the base of MOUNT HOSMER, a sheer rugged bluff rising abruptly from the river to a height of 400 feet. The Winneshiek Trail winds to the top, where a 55-acre picnic grounds has been dedicated to "the Soldiers of All Wars"; in the park is a round burial mound. Three stone crags are named for three Lansing youths who lost their lives in the World War. From the summit is a view embracing parts of Iowa, Minnesota, and Wisconsin, the Mississippi, with its numerous channels and hundreds of small islands, and the Wisconsin bluffs on the opposite side of the river receding in the distance; to the southeast, the

STREAM IN FORT DEFIANCE STATE PARK

abruptly rising Iowa bluffs obscure the view. On the south is the usual LOVERS LEAP, a high precipice overlooking the river, with a story that departs from the usual pattern: an Indian girl had promised her hand in marriage to the braver of two suitors; one of them, to prove his courage, threw himself headlong over the cliff and the other, not to be outdone, hurled himself into the river.

During the season, clam boats drift on the Mississippi, gathering shells for the pearl BUTTON FACTORY here. Early in the 20th century pearl fishing brought good returns.

The WINNESHIEK BOTTOMS of the Mississippi River, opposite the town, are a maze of small green islands and shady sloughs frequented by fishermen; here the little-mouthed bass and wall-eyed pike are particularly gamy. *(Fishing tackle, boats, and guides are available at Lansing wharf.)*

A large FISH POOL, on South Front Street near the river, built about 15 years ago, in spring contains about 250,000 fish. The pool, 500 feet long, 90 feet wide, and 16 feet deep, is supplied by water from an artesian well. The fish, bought from fishermen who seine them from the Mississippi, are held here before being shipped in carload lots to eastern markets. Six pounds of shelled corn are fed daily to each 1,000 pounds of fish.

At the southern end of the town, its front lawn now divided into residential lots, is the OLD COURTHOUSE, a finely proportioned two-story structure in pure Doric style (distyle in antis); it is now in poor condition. It is built of limestone with a severely plain frame cornice and pediment. The recessed two-story porch occupying about a third of the façade has a frame back wall and two round slender columns. There is a pair of plain stone pilasters on each anta (the wall on each side of the porch), the space between the pair unbroken by windows.

1. Left from Lansing on a graded and surfaced road that runs through the most mountainous area in Iowa. WEXFORD, 7 *m.*, a small rural community, has a large ROMAN CATHOLIC CHURCH built in 1848 of rock quarried from the surrounding hills. HARPERS FERRY, 12 *m.* (645 alt., 289 pop.), named in 1860 for David Harper, was an important river landing in the early days of river traffic. The old bar, once patronized by river men, is still in use in the old hotel. This was a community of pearl-fishermen in earlier days. By 1892 a total of 900 conical, linear, and effigy mounds had been found on the terrace occupied by the village.

WAUKON JUNCTION, 16 *m.,* (629 alt., 60 est. pop.), a railroad junction, is by the river. One-half mile N. of the railroad station is PAINT ROCK, formerly bearing a number of Indian paintings that are now dim. A narrow shelf runs along the face of the rocks about 40 feet above the base of the bluff. Above the shelf are outlines of two horned animals, probably buffaloes, drawn in mineral paint, patches of which are smeared for a stretch of several rods along the bluff. It is said that almost every summer Indians come to the bluff and crawl along the nearly inaccessible shelf below the painted figures in order to view these pictographs. At 19 *m.,* on a high plateau, is the junction with State 13 *(see Tour 2B).*

2. Right from Lansing on State 182 to the State-owned FISH FARM INDIAN MOUND GROUP, 8 *m.* (L). This group of about 30 is perhaps the most easily accessible group of round burial mounds in the State. The road passes at the foot of the terrace in which the mounds rise. The terrace is a flat field, but behind it rise high unbroken bluffs; the sloughs, lakes, and wooded islands of the river flood plain spread out below. The mounds have not yet been opened.

At 10 *m.* near where State 182 crosses the Upper Iowa River, is (L) the BROOKMAN LOG CABIN, built in 1852. BLACK HAWK BLUFF rises abruptly behind the cabin several hundred feet above the highway. Tradition has it that after his defeat at Battle Island on the Wisconsin side of the Mississippi, Black Hawk, chief of the Sacs and Foxes, escaped across the river with some of his warriors and their women and children, and hid in a cave in the side of this bluff for several days; the cave is now inaccessible because of the wearing away of the less resistant rock ledges by which it was approached. One pioneer is said to have found seven bear skulls and an old two-edged French sword in the cave. The gigantic face of the cliff is cut with the gashes of many other caves, several of which are accessible. In one, bones of bears, left perhaps from an ancient feast, were found with an Indian arrowhead and charcoal from fires so far below the present floor of the cave as to indicate an age of at least several hundred years.

NEW ALBIN, 12 *m.* (646 alt., 556 pop.), is adjacent to the Minnesota Line; marking the line at the edge of town is an IRON POST, tangible evidence of a boundary dispute. In the winter of 1851–52 the post was brought to Victory, Wis., by steamboat and hauled on a long sled, drawn by oxen, to the place where it now stands. Advocates of a greater Iowa at one time suggested that the boundary be extended as far north as the Minnesota River. At another time Minnesota citizens urged the adoption of the 42d parallel of latitude as the boundary, in which case Dubuque, Iowa, would have been in Minnesota.

Left from New Albin 8 *m.* on a dirt road to the LANE FARM TERRACE GROUP, one of the State's important collections of earth mounds, now nearly obliterated by cultivation. There are 100 or more conical and oval elevations, in 6 parallel lines, and an earthen enclosure 250 feet in diameter.

West of Lansing State 9 winds and twists over rugged and picturesque hills that Iowans like to call "Little Switzerland." Towering bluffs, dripping with long mosses and topped by pines, rise above the road. At each turn and twist conical hills, like monstrous fingers are seen pointing to the sky; or pleasant farmsteads in green valleys; or, in remote places, many-windowed Norwegian farmhouses. Along the route, impressive churches are seen, sometimes in the small towns and sometimes miles away from any village.

German, Dutch, Norwegian, and Bohemian people have settled in this region. Herds of cattle graze in the valleys and on the hillsides, for pasture land is good even though the rock is too near the surface for intensive farming. This area is the most important source of the State's hundred-million-dollar dairying business. Eighty percent of the milk produced in 1935 was used to manufacture butter. In 1936, from 15 to 20 percent of the farm income in Iowa was derived from dairying, and Iowa ranks fourth in milk production among the States. Many farmers have the dual-purpose breeds, using some animals to produce milk and selling others to slaughter-houses. When the pioneers came to Iowa, each family brought at least one cow; cows were used as draft animals, as well as for food, and later the sale of milk sometimes helped to pay off the mortgage, or finance the erection of a frame house or barn. It was not until 1880, however, that the first purebred dairy cattle were brought in.

At 3 *m.* is GETHSEMANE SHRINE, a rural church built of native stone at the foot of a high cliff; it is surrounded by a little cemetery.

CHURCH, 7 *m.* (50 est. pop.), is the center of a small farming community. The CREAMERY here, one of seven in the county, draws the farmers from the nearby communities on weekdays, and the COMMUNITY CHURCH attracts them on Sundays.

The highest hill in the county, IRON HILL, 17 *m.*, forms the divide between the Upper Iowa River and Village Creek. Before the World War, an iron ore strip mine was operated in this hill, 200 feet above the streams; a million and a quarter dollars had been spent in developing the mine. Entrances to the abandoned mines now form great black holes on the hillsides. In the spring of 1937 when the equipment was salvaged by a Cedar Rapids dealer, the 100-ton steam shovels and cranes, the miles of steel rails, the motors and the machines were trucked to Waukon for shipping East as scrap.

In the hilly country surrounding Waukon rattlesnakes are so common that in the summer of 1936 a bounty of 50¢ was offered for three inches of tail with rattles brought to the county officers.

WAUKON, 19 m. (1,216 alt., 2,526 pop.), seat of Allamakee County, was named for a Winnebago chief, known to the settlers as John Wawkon. In Winnebago, Wawkon means *thunder*, but in Sioux it signifies *spirit*.

Seven never-failing springs attracted G. C. Shattuck, the first settler, to the site in the fall of 1849. Later Shattuck deeded 40 acres on condition that the town be made the county seat.

During the second week in October each year, about 10,000 people usually gather here for Corn Day, over which a Corn Queen presides. All the schools in the county are closed, the children marching in a parade or riding on floats. Younger children participate in a doll and buggy parade. Some active young men try to climb a greased pole while the excited crowd shouts encouragement. There is also a hog-calling contest for which farm boys practice all the year. Hog-calling is not so necessary in these days when farms are fenced and swine cannot stray, but in pioneer days there had to be a hog-caller on every farm; every farmer had his own call, and presumably each hog knew his master's voice. Some hogs, however, occasionally wandered as far as the next county, so each farmer cropped the ears of his hogs or branded them with some other distinguishing mark. The homesteaders became expert in recognizing these marks identifying the property of neighbors.

In and around Waukon are streams providing unusually good trout fishing.

DECORAH, 39 m. (875 alt., 4,581 pop.) *(see Tour 2)*, is at the junction with US 52 *(see Tour 2)*.

RIDGWAY, 50 m. (1,209 alt., 348 pop.), has a COMMUNITY CENTER, used for dances, pot-luck dinners, and movies. In the center of an area having many Norwegians, the town has two Norwegian Lutheran churches. Local amusements are typical of those in all small Iowa towns; baseball in a cow pasture draws as enthusiastic a crowd as does a league game in the cities; there is usually a home-run hero, and the crowd bets on whether he'll knock the ball over the first or second pasture fence. Pot-luck dinners held in churches as well as in the community center, always attract many people; the young men have a chance to judge the pies and cakes that the young ladies bake, and everyone rushes to get some of Mrs. Jones' famous chicken pie, or Mrs. Brown's prize baked beans.

At 56 m. is the junction with State 139.

Right on this road to a crossroad at 9 *m.;* L. to NIAGARA CAVERN, 11 *m.* *(open until 10 p.m. throughout year; small entrance fee).* Among the attractions of the many caverns are a 60-foot waterfall 200 feet underground, a "lost" river, a wedding chapel with "united hearts" hanging from the ceiling, a hall of shadows, a devil's bridge, and a wishing well. Picnic grounds and other recreational facilities are in the vicinity.

CRESCO, 59 *m.* (1,300 alt., 3,069 pop.), seat of Howard County, was named by its founder, Augustus Beadle; it is a small town with pleasant homes, streets, and gardens. It is typical of other small towns of the State that are being industrialized. Two leading creameries here in 1935 paid half a million dollars to the farmers; in the same year were shipped more than 400 cars of livestock, 100 cars of eggs, 75 cars of butter, and 50 cars of live and dressed poultry. The County Fair is held here in late summer.

W. B. Berry, a farmer living near Cresco, has successfully experimented with putting more "pops" in popcorn, developing ears with more kernels, and with growing ears of various colors.

At 68 *m.* is the junction with US 63 *(see Tour 3).*

SARATOGA, 74 *m.,* is on the site of an old Indian campground by Crane Creek. The town was named for Saratoga Springs, N. Y., by settlers from the East.

RICEVILLE, 82 *m.* (1,229 alt., 807 pop.), by the Wapsipinicon River, was named for the pioneer Rice family. The main street follows the line between Howard and Mitchell Counties.

On the east bank of the river is the little WILLIS MUSEUM *(adm. 10¢),* the owner of which is a taxidermist. It contains stuffed birds and animals, old guns, and pioneer and Indian relics. The surrounding garden has miniature fish ponds in which water wheels are driven by running water.

At 88 *m.* is the junction with a dirt road.

Right on this road is BROWNVILLE, 1 *m.,* on the bank of the Cedar River. Around Brownville are numerous quarries that furnish stone for house and barn foundations, and crushed rock for county roads. By the dam on the river is a STATE GAME REFUGE AREA. In pioneer days a mill here was owned by Alphonso Brown, for whom the town was named. The dam, at the foot of a hill, is surrounded by underbrush and trees; the steady drip of water over the dam, made of rock, logs, and timbers, is audible from the road.

At 96 *m.* is the junction with US 218 *(see Tour 3A).*

OSAGE, 100 *m.* (1,169 alt., 2,964 pop.) *(see Tour 3A),* is at the junction with US 218 *(see Tour 3A).*

West of Osage the level prairies are often broken by green, wooded valleys that relieve the monotony of long, straight stretches of road. Most of the trees have been planted, forming small groves along the banks of streams. Sometimes at twilight the widely scattered clusters of trees give the illusion of being a forest mass against the successively deepening shades of emerald, violet-green, and brown of the evening sky.

At 120 *m.* is the junction with US 65 *(see Tour 4).*

HANLONTOWN, 129 *m.* (1,202 alt., 190 pop.), has a peat bog on its western edge from which many carloads of the product are shipped each year.

FERTILE, 132 *m.* (238 pop.), was founded in 1869 by William

Rhodes, whose cabin still stands. RIVERSIDE PARK is on an island in the Winnebago River, which flows through the town. Near the park is the old RHODES WATERMILL, which continues to grind its daily grist of whole-wheat flour. The town is in the center of an onion-growing section. The onions thrive in the peat soil.

Right from Fertile on a surfaced road to the SCUNGKAHDAH BATTLEGROUND, 1 m., on the farm of John Kirk. Here the Sioux and Winnebago fought. More than 600 implements of warfare, including clubs and arrows, have been found. JOICE, 8 m. (325 pop.). The Joice Shipping Association shipped 1,238,160 pounds of hogs, 1,141,145 pounds of cattle, and 53,987 pounds of sheep in 1935. Near Joice, at GOOSE LAKE, are peat beds.

At 139 m. is the junction with State 332, graveled.

Left on this road is PILOT KNOB STATE PARK, 2 m., a 375-acre area of hills and ridges covered with dense forests and shrubbery, lying along the valley of Lime Creek. The park was named for a hill rising 300 feet above the prairie; here is a stone lookout, 40 feet high, from which a crazyquilt of green corn fields, meadows, woodlands, and farm homes is visible. On a clear day the hills of Minnesota, more than 20 miles to the north are also visible. In DEAD MAN'S LAKE, is a large bed of American lotus. It is said that a solitary Indian remained in this vicinity after his fellow tribesmen had gone, living in a small log cabin beside the lake. Before his death he became known as the Dead Man.

FOREST CITY, 143 m. (1,226 alt., 2,016 pop.) (see Tour 5), is at the junction with US 69 (see Tour 5).

Section b. FOREST CITY to SOUTH DAKOTA LINE, 162 m.

North of Forest City, 0 m., State 9 unites with US 69 for several miles (see Tour 5). At 7 m. is the junction where State 9 swings R., leaving US 69, which continues S.

THOMPSON, 14 m. (1,259 alt., 538 pop.), founded in 1890, supports a COOPERATIVE CREAMERY.

At BUFFALO CENTER, 24 m. (1,183 alt., 768 pop.), in 1896, was organized the first consolidated school in the State. The people were determined to better the educational opportunities of their children and took turns in conveying them to and from the schoolhouse. Now transportation of students in each consolidated district is cared for at public expense.

At 31 m. is the junction with State 250, paved.

Left on State 250 is LAKOTA, 1 m. (1,156 alt., 409 pop.), originally called Germania because of its predominant German population, but renamed during the World War.

At 36 m. is the junction with US 169 (see Tour 6), which unites with this route to 39 m., the western junction with US 169 (see Tour 6); R. here on State 9.

SWEA CITY, 43 m. (1,174 alt., 695 pop.), first called Reynolds, officially adopted its present name in 1893; it is derived from the Swedish word, Svea, the affectionate term for Sweden. Capt. R. E. Jensen, general agent for the American Emigrant Co., which owned thousands of acres in this vicinity, brought a group of Swedish emigrants to this township in 1870. The company had a story-and-a-half-house where the settlers could live until they built their own homes. At one time there were seven families, totaling 40 persons, living in the receiving home. Later the structure was used for religious services, public meetings, and briefly for a school.

The town was platted by R. M. Richmond, and the first depot was a discarded boxcar.

ARMSTRONG, 52 *m.* (1,237 alt., 767 pop.), named for an explorer and early settler, sprang into existence during the construction of the Albert Lea-Estherville branch of the C.R.I. & P.R.R. The town lies on the East Fork of the Des Moines River.

Before 1900 part of northwestern Iowa was a region of swamps and sloughs. Then a vast network of drainage ditches was dug through the lowlands, reclaiming many acres of swamp land. Gangs contracted to do the jobs, and during the summer months tent villages sprang up in the fields far from town. Some families migrated with the workers and lived with them.

At 59 *m.* is the junction with a graveled road.

Right on this road is DOLLIVER, 4.5 *m.* (1,287 alt., 158 pop.), named for Jonathan P. Dolliver, U. S. Senator from Iowa, 1900–1910. At 6 *m.* is TUTTLE LAKE, source of the East Fork of the Des Moines River; the lake covers 981 acres adjacent to the Minnesota Line. Right along the shore of Tuttle Lake to OKA-MANPEDAN STATE LAKE PRESERVE, 8 *m.* Okamanpedan *(nesting place of the herons)*, the name given the lake by Sioux Indians, was recorded by Jean Nicollet, a Government surveyor who visited this region in 1838. Formerly numerous blue herons made their nests in the tall trees surrounding the lake. The lake was renamed for Calvin Tuttle, who settled on its shores in 1856.

GRUVER, 63.5 *m.* (1,300 alt., 126 pop.), formerly called Luzon, was platted and settled by John and Anna R. Dows in the summer of 1899. The town is near the center of Emmet County, where about 63 percent of the farms are operated by tenants.

Left from Gruver on a graveled road 2 *m.* is the junction with another graveled road; R. 1.5 *m.* is RYAN LAKE, and L. 3.2 *m.* is SWAN LAKE, both controlled by the State Conservation Commission as game and cover refuges. For the last two decades many of the State-owned dry lake beds and marshes, the title to which rested with the old Conservation Board, were leased to farmers. The areas were not fenced, and adjoining landowners grazed them heavily and made a practice of burning the slough grass each year. Game production was seriously handicapped. Under the new Conservation Commission management the land has been turned over to the Game Division for development, lessening possibility of repetition of the event that took place in 1933 at Jemmerson's slough, near Spirit Lake; there, when the grass was burned off, 1,500 pheasants were roasted alive. Some of these areas are now being fenced, and roads, with parking areas, built through them. Many of the State-owned dry lakes and marshes are now planted with trees and shrubs for game cover and food. The State has lost much of its natural lake area in an attempt to reclaim the land for farming. In 1899 there were 109 lakes with 61,000 acres of open water. Now there are 65 natural lakes with about 42,000 acres of open water. Only a few of the lake beds proved valuable for cultivation and the areas were not sold. Under the present system, the farmers leasing such land leave part of the State's share of the crop standing to provide winter feed for game. Throughout the winter of 1935–36 the deep snow and ice in this area made it impossible for pheasant and other game to get food. Thousands would have starved had not a radio appeal brought large gifts of grain for this purpose.

ESTHERVILLE, 70 *m.* (1,298 alt., 4,940 pop.), was named for Mrs. Esther Ridley, the wife of one of the men who assisted in platting the

BLOCK HOUSE, FORT DEFIANCE STATE PARK

town. It was settled in the summer of 1857, following the Spirit Lake Massacre at West Okoboji Lake *(see Tour 7)*. The town, seat of Emmet County, which was named for the Irish patriot, Robert Emmet, is in the valley of the West Fork of the Des Moines River. Most of the business district is around the courthouse square. To the west, immediately across the river, rises a steep, tree-covered ridge.

Estherville is a shipping and trade town for an agricultural area. A beef packing plant employs approximately 100 persons.

At the entrance to the city's rock garden, on the west bank of the river, stands an OLD MILL WHEEL, that belonged to a mill built in 1860 by Adolphus and B. J. Jenkins. It is believed that much of the lumber used in the construction of Fort Defiance *(see below)* was run through this mill.

There has long been an erroneous tradition that the old English word "blizzard" originated in Estherville. Some stories gave credit to a local editor, others to a pioneer, for coining the word. "This is a regular blizzard!" exclaimed Lightning Ellis (according to one version), as he entered an Estherville store during a stormy evening in the early 1870's, and shook the snow from his coat. The editor of the *Vindicator* heard Ellis's remark, and used it in writing a description of the storm. Neighboring editors adopted the revived word frequently during the severe winter of 1880–81. Soon it was common in the national vocabulary. Previously "blizzard" had been employed in the West to describe a sudden sharp blow, a shot from a gun, or a verbal scolding.

Several families here treasure fragments of a meteorite that fell on the Sever Lee farm, 2 miles N. of town, on May 10, 1879, exploding with three deafening detonations; the mass was broken into three large pieces, now in museums in widely separated cities. The largest piece, weighing several hundred pounds, is in the British Museum at London; another is in Vienna, Austria; and the third is in the possession of the University of Minnesota at Minneapolis.

In Estherville State 9 crosses the West Fork of the Des Moines River. At the western end of the bridge is the junction with an improved road.

Left on this road to the ESTHERVILLE CITY PARK and SWIMMING POOL. The FORT DEFIANCE STATE HISTORICAL PRESERVE is at 1.2 *m.* A modern log-cabin SHELTER, 2.5 *m.,* stands on a high hill near the site of the old fort. Within the cabin, which is equipped for meetings of various kinds, is an old picture of Fort Defiance, which was built in 1862–63. The 186-acre preserve is heavily forested. There are scattered picnic areas and many miles of nature trails.

At 72 *m.* is the junction with State 245, graveled.

Left on State 245 is Fort Defiance State Historical Preserve, 2 *m. (see above).*

At 78 *m.* is the junction with US 71 *(see Tour 7).*

SPIRIT LAKE, 84 *m.* (1,458 alt., 1,778 pop.) *(see Tour 7),* is at the junction with State 276, paved.

Right on State 276 is a scenic route encircling SPIRIT LAKE *(see Tour 7).*

At 85.5 *m.* is the junction with an improved road.

Left on this road at 1.3 *m.* is the junction with a dirt road; L. here 0.5 *m.* to PIKES POINT STATE PARK *(swimming, fishing),* a small wooded area along

West Okoboji Lake. At 3.1 *m.* on the improved road is the NORTHWEST IOWA METHODIST CONFERENCE CAMP, on the shore of the lake (L). The road rejoins State 9 at 4.1 *m.*

At 88 *m.* is the junction with State 32, graveled.

Left on State 32 along the irregular west shore of WEST OKOBOJI LAKE *(see Tour 7);* TRIBOJI BEACH is at 1.5 *m.;* LAKESIDE LABORATORY, 3.4 *m.,* started in 1909 by Dr. Thomas Huston Macbride, of the University of Iowa, is on the shore of MILLER'S BAY. At the laboratory, which stands on a tract of 100 acres, the preservation of West Okoboji is being studied. Lecture courses and field studies on the natural history of the lake region are conducted each summer. At 3.9 *m.* is the junction with an improved road that leads to GULL POINT STATE PARK, 5.9 *m. (picnicking facilities),* comprising 71 acres of fine oaks. Overlooking West Okoboji Lake is a boulder-and-log shelter house, constructed by the Civ'lian Conservation Corps. Nature trails wind through the woods and along the lake. CAMP OKOBOJI, 6.9 *m.,* is a regional camp of the national Y.W.C.A. Passing between huge stone gate posts, the road rejoins State 32 at 7.9 *m.* WEST OKOBOJI, INC., 8.9 *m.,* is another resort area. At 10.1 *m.* is the entrance (L) to TERRACE PARK, summer cottage and amusement center. At 11.3 *m.* is the junction with US 71 *(see Tour 7).*

At 95 *m.* is the junction with State 219, paved.

Right on State 219 is LAKE PARK, 1 *m.* (1,469 alt., 978 pop.), by SILVER LAKE. The town was so named because the lake is encircled by a narrow, park-like, timbered strip, composed chiefly of oak. Overlooking the lake is the well-preserved KNOX HOUSE, a log cabin built by C. B. Knox in 1868.

At 105 *m.* a marker beside the road points to RUSH LAKE, which is surrounded by a border of trees and solidly covered with so many rushes that scarcely any water is visible.

At 106 *m.* is the junction with State 237, paved.

Left on State 237 is OCHEYEDAN (pronounced O-chee-dan), 1 *m.* (1,551 alt., 627 pop.). It is reported that the early settlers here suffered extreme hardship during the severe winter of 1871–72. The only houses were sod huts or shacks, small and cold. Many people were lost during blizzards, and some froze to death.

Left from Ocheyedan 1.5 *m.* on improved road is OCHEYEDAN MOUND (1,670 alt.), rising steeply 170 feet above the plain; the length of the mound is about a third of a mile, and its summit is only a few yards in width in some places; on its surface are boulders of granite, Sioux quartzite, and limestone. The name Ocheyedan (Ind., *spot where they weep*) is a memorial to the Indian custom of seeking elevations on which to mourn for their dead.

At 111 *m.* is the junction with US 59 *(see Tour 8).*

SIBLEY, 118 *m.* (1,516 alt., 1,870 pop.), seat of Osceola County, was named in 1872 in honor of Gen. G. H. Sibley of Minnesota.

Cooperatives are predominant here in almost every line of business— coal, oil, grain, poultry, and dairy products. Some of the strongest and largest cooperatives in the States are here and they are frequently used as models by other Iowa groups. One of the largest is the OSCEOLA COUNTY CREAMERY, organized in February 1923. Haulers regularly pick up the cream for delivery to the creamery. If a member of the association sells his cream elsewhere, he has to pay 2¢ per pound to the association for the cream thus sold. The cream, which must test high, is used for butter that has a quality reputation. The Osceola Creamery Cooperative has an annual festival, sometimes attended by 2,000 farmers and their families; dairy exhibits, hot coffee, amusements, and a free movie attract crowds.

Sibley was the home of William L. Harding (1877–1934), Governor of Iowa 1917–1921.

West of Sibley State 9 crosses the eastern edge of the great plains region, an area almost barren of trees except for the few around the occasional farmhouses. Blinding dust storms are not infrequent in this area, the dust being carried from regions farther west.

ROCK RAPIDS, 142 *m.* (1,345 alt., 2,221 pop.), is at the junction with US 75 *(see Tour 9).*

LARCHWOOD, 157 *m.* (1,465 alt., 382 pop.), was so named because of the many larches planted in the vicinity by J. W. Fell, who founded the community in 1870 and planted more than 100,000 fruit and forest trees on land adjoining the town plat. Many of the present trees of the State were planted by early settlers. The law gave exemption then as now from a certain amount of taxation if groves and orchards were planted. The groves made valuable windbreaks, and added beauty to the home sites.

At 160 *m.* is the junction with a dirt road.

Left on this road which crosses Blood Run Creek, 1 *m.,* to BLOOD RUN VILLAGE and MOUND SITES, on a terrace overlooking the Big Sioux River. This is the most extensive Indian village site in the State, covering nearly 100 acres. Formerly there were 143 mounds and an enclosure of 15 acres; one of the mounds covered an extended burial place, which was well below the base line; within the mound were found ear ornaments of fine copper wire wound spirally and on a skull was a quantity of red powder.

At 161.9 *m.* is the junction with a graveled road.

Right on this road, which closely parallels the South Dakota Line, is the entrance to GITCHIE MANITOU STATE PARK *(picnicking facilities),* 5 *m.,* a 48-acre area bordering the Big Sioux River. A road leads through the center of the park. Gitchie Manitou was purchased by the State as a stone quarry to be worked by prison labor. Here outcrops the hardest rock in Iowa, the Sioux quartzite strata, often called Sioux Falls granite. Rare varieties of moss grow in this region, and the area is an excellent place to study grasses, rocks, and woodland flowers. The JASPER POOL, so-named because of its deep color, is one of the most beautiful spots in the park.

At 162 *m.* State 9 crosses the South Dakota Line 17 miles SE. of Sioux Falls, S. D.

Tour 11

(Prairie du Chien, Wis.)—Marquette—McGregor—Mason City—Spencer—(Canton, S. Dak.); US 18.
Wisconsin Line to South Dakota Line, 316 m.

C. M. St. P. & P. R. R. parallels this route between McGregor and Postville, and between New Hampton and Inwood; C. R. I. & P. R. R. between Postville and West Union; C. G. W. R. R., between Fredericksburg and New Hampton; Illinois Central R. R. between Charles City and Floyd; Mason City & Clear Lake El. R. R., between Mason City and Clear Lake; M. & St. L. R. R., between Britt and Algona. Jefferson Bus Lines follow this highway between Spencer and Nashua; Northland Greyhound Bus Lines between Dubuque and Spencer.
Roadbed paved except for a few stretches of gravel between West Union and Charles City, and between Sheldon and S. Dakota Line.
Accommodations of all kinds available, chiefly in cities.

Section a. WISCONSIN LINE to MASON CITY, 127 m.

US 18 crosses the Mississippi River on the MARQUETTE TOLL BRIDGE (cars 75¢, passengers 20¢ each), 2 miles W. of Prairie du Chien, Wis.

MARQUETTE, 1 m. (629 alt., 814 pop.), was first known as North McGregor and later renamed for Father Marquette. He and Louis Joliet were the first to see Iowa territory, viewing it from the mouth of the Wisconsin River in 1673. It is locally asserted that a Frenchman, Giard (see below), settled here in 1779.

Bloody Run Creek, which flows through the town, furnishes excellent trout fishing.

Marquette is a division point for the C. M. St. P. & P. R. R., which provides employment for most of the townspeople. A large pontoon bridge carries the line across the Mississippi here.

South of Marquette for 2 miles US 18 closely follows the Mississippi River, overshadowed by high bluffs (R).

McGREGOR, 3 m. (627 alt., 1,299 pop.), in a ravine with bluffs rising on both sides to a height of about 400 feet was named Coulee des Sioux by early French traders. In 1836 when Alexander McGregor established a ferry from Prairie du Chien, Wis., to the village, it became known as McGregor's Landing. Overlooking the business section is a towering bluff called McGREGOR HEIGHTS; here the American School of Wild Life Protection holds annual sessions in August. This unusual organization has on its faculty naturalists and scientists from many parts of the United States. On McGregor Heights is an OBSERVATION TOWER, affording an excellent view of the river.

Within a radius of 15 miles from the town are hundreds of effigy mounds, fortifications and earthworks. Some of the mounds are 300 feet long; they were built in the shapes of birds, bears, wolves, and serpents. A number of Indian village sites and cave shelters have also been found here.

Ringling Brothers Circus can be said to have originated in McGregor— the five Ringling brothers, who lived here during their childhood, held penny circuses in their back yard.

Left from McGregor on a graveled road to PIKE'S PEAK, 2 m. (1,120 alt.), an excellent observation point. Zebulon Pike, in 1805, was so impressed by the magnificent promontory jutting out into the river that he suggested a fort be built there. In PICTURED ROCK CANYON, below the peak, colored sands have formed fantastic shapes and designs. Nature trails wind from picnic grounds atop the peak down into the canyon.

At GIARD, 4 m., a small village, is the BASIL GIARD MONUMENT. Giard, for whom the town was named, on Oct. 15, 1800, petitioned Gov. Charles Delassus of Upper Louisiana for a grant of 5,760 acres of land along the Mississippi River, including the site of McGregor, and became the legal owner Nov. 20, 1800.

FROELICH, 11 m. (1,017 alt.), is at the junction with US 52 (see Tour 2) and State 13 (see Tour 2B); between Froelich and Postville US 18 and US 52 are one route.

POSTVILLE, 29 m. (1,192 alt., 1,060 pop.) (see Tour 2), is at a junction with US 52 (see Tour 2).

CLERMONT, 36 m. (859 alt., 631 pop.), was originally known as Norway; the first settler, a man named Delaplaine, arrived in 1848. In 1857 William Larrabee, who became the 13th Governor of Iowa, (1886–1890), purchased an interest in the Clermont mills and eventually became sole owner of the property. His former home is on the outskirts of the town.

WEST UNION, 45 m. (1,107 alt., 2,056 pop.), first called Knob Prairie, became known by its present name in 1849. The Fayette County Fair is held here annually during the last week in August.

At the northeastern edge of town is the Blunt home, containing a COL-LECTION OF BELLS (viewed by appointment), among them a Japanese prayer bell, camel bells, one of Della Robbia pottery, and a 16 pound copper cowbell from Switzerland.

West Union is at the junction with State 11 (see Tour 2A).

1. Right from West Union on an unimproved dirt road to DUTTON'S CAVE, 4 m., in a rocky gorge near a small stream; the area has been a popular picnic spot since its discovery in 1849. It consists of a series of rooms and a small chamber that has been named Steeple Cavern.

2. Left from West Union on State 56, graveled, is the junction with an improved dirt road, 1 m.; L. on this road to ECHO VALLEY STATE PARK (shelter house; picnicking facilities), 2 m., a tract of 74 acres purchased by West Union residents who turned it over to the State. In the park are Glover Creek, considered one of the best trout streams in Iowa, and Otter Creek, which has been dammed to form an 8-acre crescent-shaped lake. High bluffs and palisaded rock cliffs surrounding the lake are called ECHO BLUFFS because of a triple echo of even minor sounds.

West of West Union the highway runs through gently rolling land.

FREDERICKSBURG, 65 m. (1,076 alt., 567 pop.), on the Wapsipinicon River, was platted in 1856 and named for Frederick Padden, the founder. This was the home of Dr. W. S. Pitts, a physician who wrote the song Little Brown Church in the Vale. Pitts and his wife are buried here. The Little Brown Church is at Nashua (see Tour 3A).

WILLIAMSTOWN, 71 m., is at the junction with US 63 (see Tour 3). Between this point and NEW HAMPTON, 78 m. (1,159 alt., 2,458 pop.) (see Tour 3), US 18 and US 63 are one route. L. at New Hampton on US 18.

BASSETT, 88 m. (1,029 alt., 149 pop.), is a flag station on the C. M. St. P. & P. R. R. for a German community on the banks of the Cedar River; it was named for a merchant who bought wheat extensively along the route.

CHARLES CITY, 96 *m.* (1,005 alt., 8,039 pop.) *(see Tour 3A),* is at the junction with US 218 *(see Tour 3A),* which unites briefly with US 18 and closely follows the banks of the Cedar River.

FLOYD, 102 *m.* (1,099 alt., 350 pop.) *(see Tour 3A),* is at the junction with US 218 *(see Tour 3A).*

At RUDD, 110 *m.* (1,117 alt., 429 pop.), is the large ARROW HEAD MUSEUM *(open),* owned by Charles P. Ell. It contains a large collection of fossils, rocks, minerals, and Indian arrows, spear and axe heads, and tomahawks.

Rudd was platted as Danville by James Swartwood in 1869, but was renamed for a man who promised to contribute $1,000 for a church if the town were named for him. According to the story, he forgot his promise after the renaming.

NORA SPRINGS, 116 *m.* (1,063 alt., 1,070 pop.), on the Shell Rock River, was formerly known as Woodstock, but acquired its present name because of the many springs feeding the river.

MASON CITY, 127 *m.* (1,130 alt., 23,304 pop.) *(see MASON CITY).*

Points of Interest: Herbert Quick House; clay products plants; Portland Cement Mills.

Mason City is at the junction with US 65 *(see Tour 4).*

Section b. MASON CITY *to* SOUTH DAKOTA LINE, *189 m.*

West of Mason City, 0 *m.,* for about 100 miles, US 18 crosses typical prairie; there are few trees and, stretching far on both sides of the highway, are fields used for growing corn, oats, and other prairie crops.

CLEAR LAKE, 10 *m.* (1,240 alt., 3,066 pop.), named for the six-mile lake on whose shore the town has been built, is a resort popular with Iowans. This area was formerly a hunting and fishing ground of the Winnebago and Sioux, and the settlers had many difficulties with them in the early days.

Clear Lake has thousands of visitors each summer, in part attracted by the nationally known dance orchestras that play here. A park containing two acres of timber, is maintained.

Left from Clear Lake on State 106, closely following the shore of the lake, to CLEAR LAKE STATE LAKE PRESERVE, 3 *m.,* one of the most popular summer resorts and recreational areas in Iowa, with sloping sandy beaches and picnic areas; wading, swimming, and fishing are popular recreations here. Summer cottages are scattered among the trees around the lake, which covers an area of 3,643 acres. The METHODIST CAMP, where Signor Mario Capelli annually produces operas, is on the shore.

Between Mason City and Ventura US 18 closely follows the wooded north shore of Clear Lake.

VENTURA, 15 *m.* (1,263 alt.), at the head of Clear Lake, is known throughout the State by fishermen who buy a "catch" at the *FISH MARKET* here, to show the folks at home. The market also sells many barrels of dill pickles.

GARNER, 23 *m.* (1,209 alt., 1,241 pop.) *(see Tour 5)*, is at the junction with US 69 *(see Tour 5)*.

At 30 *m.* is the junction with a graveled road.

Right on this road to EAGLE LAKE STATE PARK, 2 *m.*, a 27-acre tract of wooded land bordering Eagle Lake. In the spring the park is fragrant with wild crab and wild plum blossoms.

BRITT, 33 *m.* (1,234 alt., 1,593 pop.). An editor, "Bailey of Britt," in 1900 announced that a national Hobo Convention would be held in the town that summer; he followed up the story with imaginative accounts of the wanderers. On the appointed day reporters flocked into the little place from many parts of the country only to discover that they had been hoaxed; however, they entered into the spirit of the occasion, outdoing each other in inventing stories about hoboes who never existed. The publicity actually brought hundreds of hoboes to the town in succeeding summers to elect a "Hobo King." The attendance has dwindled now, but the custom continues.

Britt was the home of John Hammill (1875–1936), Lieutenant Governor of Iowa (1921–25) and Governor for three terms (1925–1931).

Right from Britt on graveled State 111 to the town of CRYSTAL LAKE, 9 *m.* (1,258 alt., 271 pop.), bordering the lake of the same name *(see Tour 5)*.

WESLEY, 44 *m.* (1,257 alt., 462 pop.), was named in 1871 for one of the builders of the railroad section house and station, the first two buildings erected on the town site. The town is a farm trade center.

ALGONA, 57 *m.* (1,213 alt., 3,985 pop.) *(see Tour 6)*, is at the junction with US 169 *(see Tour 6)*.

At 67 *m.* is the junction with State 44, graveled.

Right on State 44 is WHITTEMORE, 1 *m.* (1,206 alt., 604 pop.), platted in 1878 by W. H. Ingham and L. H. Smith. WEST BEND, 9 *m.* (1,197 alt., 634 pop.), was so named because of its proximity to a large bend in the West Fork of the Des Moines River. Although the town was not established until 1880, the first settlers of Palo Alto County, William Carter and Jeremiah Evans, came to this region 25 years earlier. At West Bend is the GROTTO OF THE REDEMPTION, an imposing religious structure whose construction was begun by Father Paul M. Dobberstein in 1928. The grotto stands near SS. PETER AND PAUL CHURCH, 2 blocks from the highway (R), and ST. PAUL'S PARK, a landscaped area containing a small artificial lake. Since Roman times, grottoes (Ital: *grotta, cave*) have been associated with religion and religious symbolism. Medieval shepherds, both men and women, attending their flocks on the mountain sides, were wont to frequent such recesses for prayer when they could not attend public worship. Occasionally the bishop of a district would send a priest up into the mountains; the priest would conduct services, using a cave as a chapel.

In the artificial Grotto of the Redemption, the story of man's fall and redemption is portrayed. Father Dobberstein secured rocks from every State in the Union; shells and coral from the waters bordering America, and thousands of precious and semi-precious stones, ores, fossils, and bits of petrified wood to incorporate in the structure. From the smallest crucifix to the largest statue, the grotto is ablaze with their brilliance. The materials were broken into small pieces and cemented into designs prepared by Father Dobberstein. The central part of the structure consists of three alcoves merging in a dome—symbolizing the unity of the Father, Son, and Holy Ghost. On one side is the Garden of Eden, surrounded by an ornate stone wall. Within the garden, the allegorical story of man's creation is symbolized by a huge stone Tree of Life; Adam and Eve are shown being driven out of Paradise by the angel with the flaming sword. Other grotto structures set forth symbolically the story of the events in the life of Christ.

In SS. Peter and Paul Church is a Christmas Chapel with a creche. Glowing in the center of the group is an immense Brazilian amethyst. Each of the 14 Stations of the Cross has a brilliantly colored scene in mosaic.

CYLINDER, 73 *m.* (1,194 alt., 157 pop.), takes its name from nearby Cylinder Creek, which was so dubbed because, when pioneers were trying to carry a heavy machine across the creek, a cylinder from it became detached and was lost in the water. Cylinder traces its beginning to the erection of a large hay barn here in 1885.

EMMETSBURG, 81 *m.* (1,234 alt., 2,865 pop.), seat of Palo Alto County, lies in the delightful valley of the Des Moines River. An Irish colony of seven families and two unmarried men founded the settlement in 1856. Areas in and around the town that were once dumping grounds have been transformed into parks, playgrounds, and recreation centers, through the efforts of the City Planning Commission, formed in 1914.

MEDIUM LAKE, a narrow body of water about 4 miles long, extends N. from the edge of town.

At 90 *m.* is the junction with State 314, graveled.

Left on State 314 is AYRSHIRE, 6 *m.* (1,293 alt., 343 pop.), a village established in 1881 on fertile farm land. Straight ahead from Ayrshire on an improved dirt road to RUSH LAKE STATE LAKE PRESERVE *(picnicking facilities)*, 12 *m.*, a 62-acre area of rolling woodland on the shore of Rush Lake.

RUTHVEN, 93 *m.* (1,434 alt., 739 pop.), was named for three Ruthven brothers who were settlers. One of them, Alex Ruthven, was several times elected mayor of the village.

Right from Ruthven on a graveled road to LOST ISLAND STATE PARK, *(complete picnicking facilities, bath house)*, 3 *m.*, a 28-acre area bordering LOST ISLAND LAKE. Both the lake and the park are named for an island presumably submerged in the center of the lake. Lost Island Lake is fringed by dense woodland harboring birds and wild flowers of many kinds. Adjacent are Mud, Trumbull, and Round lakes.

At 106 *m.* is the junction with US 71 *(see Tour 7)*; US. 18 turns R., uniting with US 71 for 3 miles.

SPENCER, 107 *m.* (1,315 alt., 5,019 pop.) *(see Tour 7)*.

At 109 *m.* is the junction with US 71 *(see Tour 7)*.

HARTLEY, 127 *m.* (1,462 alt., 1,272 pop.), was named for one of the railroad surveyors who was connected with the construction of the railroad through the county. It is a small trade center.

At 134 *m.* is the junction with US 59 *(see Tour 8)*.

SANBORN (R), 135 *m.* (1,552 alt., 1,213 pop.), was founded in 1878 as a terminal for the C. M. St. P. & P. R. R., and was platted in the same year by J. A. Stocum and John Lawler. It was named for George W. Sanborn, first superintendent of the Iowa and Dakota division of the railroad, and promoter of railroad building in this part of the State. In August the town has an annual celebration, called Play Days, sponsored by business men. The Farmers Cooperative Creamery is a center for the sale of local farm produce.

SHELDON, 146 *m.* (1,421 alt., 3,320 pop.), on the Floyd River, was named for Israel Sheldon, superintendent of the land department of the Sioux City and St. Paul R. R., which later became the Chicago, St. Paul, Minneapolis & Omaha R. R. In 1847 the Board of Supervisors offered a reward of $1,000 to anyone who discovered coal in the county, and later in the same year, offered $25 a ton for the first 100 tons mined. While the reward has never been claimed, the offer has never been rescinded.

During boom times, immediately after the World War, the vicinity experienced inflated prices and land values increased to sums that would have been fabulous to the homesteader here in the 1870's, who during the grasshopper ravages signed this note for a loan:—

". . . . after date, for value received . . . . promise to pay . . . . or order . . . . dollars. Without relief from appraisement, stay or exemption laws, and in case suit is instituted for its collection, anything and everything can be levied upon including the last suit of clothes, the school books and the food of the children, with the coffin or coffins any of the family may be buried in; and in case every article is sold and there remains anything due on the note, I agree that the services of myself and family shall be sold until the demands of the note are satisfied. And I further agree, that in case suit is instituted for its collection, to pay reasonable attorney's fees, together with board bills, hack hire, saloon bills, and miscellaneous expenses of himself and family and near relatives while suit is pending. And I further agree to live on corn bread and sorghum molasses from date until the demands of the note are satisfied, with interest at the rate of 10% payable annually."

BOYDEN, 154 m. (1,424 alt., 446 pop.), was originally a C. M. St. P. & P. station known as Sheridan in 1878, but was renamed in 1889.

HULL, 161 m. (1,435 alt., 905 pop.), first called Pattersonville, adopted its present name in 1882 when it was organized. This is a Dutch community and was the site of two schools, the Hull Institute and the Western Academy, which existed late in the 1890's and during the first part of the 20th century. The WESTERN CHRISTIAN HIGH SCHOOL, a small academy, was organized in 1913. The school in 1937 had an enrollment of 250 students.

Dr. Alexander Ruthven, a zoologist, born at Hull in 1882, became president of the University of Michigan in 1929.

At 163 m. is the junction with US 75 *(see Tour 9)*.

ROCK VALLEY, 170 m. (1,255 alt., 1,204 pop.), on the banks of the Rock River, has a population predominantly Dutch. There are five churches —Dutch Reformed, Reformed, Reformed Church in America, Roman Catholic, and Methodist—and a DUTCH CHRISTIAN REFORMED PAROCHIAL SCHOOL, besides the public school.

Good grade sand and gravel, found along the Rock River valley, are shipped in large quantities for construction purposes.

INWOOD, 184 m. (1,473 alt., 670 pop.), known as Warren when settled in 1883, was later called Pennington. When Jacob Rogers and his wife platted the town in 1891 they called it by its present name.

At 189 m. US 18 crosses the Big Sioux River, which is the Iowa-South Dakota Line, on a free bridge, 4 miles E. of Canton, S. D.

⋘⋘⋘⋘⋘⋘⋘⋘⋘⋘⋘⋘⋘⋘⋘⋘⋘⋘⋘⋘⋘☼⋙⋙⋙⋙⋙⋙⋙⋙⋙⋙⋙⋙⋙⋙⋙⋙⋙⋙⋙⋙

Tour 12

(Rockford, Ill.)—Dubuque—Waterloo—Fort Dodge—Sioux City—(Randolph, Nebr.); US 20.
Illinois Line to Nebraska Line, 328 m.

Ill. Cent. R. R. parallels this route between Dubuque and Rockwell City; C. G. W. R. R., between Dubuque and Dyersville; W. C. F. & N. R. R., between Waterloo and Cedar Falls; F. D. D. M. & S. R. R., between Webster City and Fort Dodge; C. M. St. P. & P. R. R., between Rockwell City and Sac City; C. & N. W. R. R., between Sac City and Sioux City.
Northland Greyhound Bus Line and Jefferson Bus Line follow the highway between Dubuque and Cedar Falls; Interstate Transit Bus Line, between Waterloo and Cedar Falls, Ft. Dodge and Blairsburg, Holstein and Sioux City.
Roadbed paved except between Rockwell City and Sac City, and between Early and Holstein.
Tourist accommodations of all kinds available, chiefly in cities.

Section a. ILLINOIS LINE to WATERLOO, 91 m.

US 20 crosses the Mississippi River, the Illinois-Iowa Line, on the DuBUQUE BRIDGE *(car and driver, 25¢; passengers, 5¢; trucks, 25¢-$1.25 up)*, 94 miles W. of Rockford, Ill.

DUBUQUE, 1 m. (698 alt., 41,679 pop.) *(see DUBUQUE)*.

Points of Interest: Shot Tower; University of Dubuque; Columbia Museum; Eagle Point Park; Grave of Julien Dubuque.

Dubuque is at the junction with US 61 *(see Tour 1)*, US 52-67 *(see Tour 2)*, and US 161 *(see Tour 1A)*.

West of Dubuque US 20 skirts the extreme southern edge of a rugged, picturesque region. High rocky bluffs and deep, narrow gorges, clear cold trout streams, and dense forests create one of the most beautiful areas in Iowa. This part of the State was settled by German, Dutch, Norwegian, and Czechoslovakian people. The rocky ground makes farming somewhat difficult, but an abundant water supply from numerous small streams provides pastures for dairy cattle in the narrow valleys.

US 20, between Dubuque and Fort Dodge, was formerly the RIDGE ROAD. Herbert Quick has written about the route in his novel *Vandemark's Folly:* ". . . but I had to follow the Old Ridge Road west through Dubuque, Buchanan and Blackhawk counties, and westward. It was called the Ridge Road because it followed the knolls and hogbacks, and thus as far as might be, kept out of the slews. The last bit of it so far as I know was plowed up in 1877 in the northeastern part of Grundy County. I saw this last mile of the old road on a trip I made to Waterloo and remember it. . . . The Old Ridge Road went through Dyersville, Manchester, Independence, Waterloo and on to Fort Dodge."

Emigrant bands from the East passed over this route driving livestock. Ox-, horse-, and mule-drawn covered wagons, laden with families and household goods, wore deep ruts in the prairie.

In spring a pageant of many colors passes across the sun-flooded floor of the oak and hickory forests along the route. Scarcely has the snow melted when the flowers of snow-trillium appear like a swarm of flickering white butterflies poised above the brown leaves. Later, masses of scarlet columbines blaze from the rocky hillsides and bushy meadowrue shakes its tasseled clusters near gauzy lavender cranesbill in the open spaces. Deeper in color are the clumps of jack-in-the-pulpit, and the occasional yellow or pink moccasin flower, or showy orchid.

CENTRALIA, 10 *m.*, a hamlet settled in 1837, was platted in 1850 under the name of Dakotah. The inhabitants go to Dubuque for their larger business transactions.

At 11 *m.* is the junction with a graveled road.

Left on this road is PEOSTA, 1 *m.* (1,036 alt.), a small village named for the Indian squaw who is said to have reported the discovery of lead in the vicinity to Julien Dubuque *(see DUBUQUE)*. The ROMAN CATHOLIC CHURCH built in 1924 is unusually large. Father J. Fred Kriebs used unusual methods in obtaining money to pay the enormous debt incurred in building it. One method was to ask each farm-member of the congregation to donate a shoat to the parish; when the animal reached marketable size it was sold, the proceeds of the sale being applied to the debt.

EPWORTH, 16 *m.* (1,034 alt., 464 pop.), was named for Epworth, England, birthplace of John Wesley. ST. PAUL'S MISSION HOUSE was opened here in 1857 under the name of Epworth Seminary. In the course of years, ownership of the seminary has changed several times; in 1932 the place was purchased and renamed by the Society of the Divine Word. On the grounds is an underground GROTTO *(free; offering expected)* of native rock sheltering groups of carved figures depicting scenes in the life of Christ; the entrance to the grotto is dark, but passageways lead to caverns illuminated by a pale, diffused light.

FARLEY, 20 *m.* (1,064 alt., 657 pop.), was named in honor of Jesse P. Farley of Dubuque, who was connected with the building of the I. C. R. R. in 1856–57. The FARMERS' CREAMERY here was awarded a silver medal at the Dairyman's Fair in London, England, in 1878, the year it was organized.

DYERSVILLE, 27 *m.* (944 alt., 2,046 pop.), on the North Fork of the Maquoketa River, was settled in 1837–38 by English families, and in 1848 was named for James Dyer, Jr.

The town has a compact group of stores and staid old houses that huddle together under the shadow of the unusually large ST. FRANCIS XAVIER CHURCH, the two spires of which thrusting upward 200 feet, are visible for miles around. The church was built at a cost of $100,000 and dedicated in 1888.

A WHITE PEACOCK FARM *(private)* is at 1122 E. Victoria St. The first pair of white peacocks here was imported from Amsterdam.

EARLVILLE, 34 *m.* (994 alt., 615 pop.), a village first called Nottingham, was renamed for George M. Earl, an early resident in the vicinity. Ruth Suckow *(see LITERATURE)* maintained an apiary here during the 1920's.

At 38 *m.* is the junction with State 113, graveled.

1. Right here to GREELEY, 7 *m.* (1,139 alt., 343 pop.), first called Plum Spring but renamed in 1863 in honor of Horace Greeley, the journalist. The HOLBERT HORSE FARM, at the north edge of town, covering 250 acres, was established in 1877, and is known by horse breeders throughout the world. Holbert horses have won many high awards at the annual International Livestock Exposition and the National Belgian Horse Show in Waterloo, Iowa.

2. Left on State 113 to DELHI, 5 *m.* (998 alt., 399 pop.), county seat for 40 years. J. L. McCreery, a journalist living here in the 1850's, is credited with having written the poem, *There is No Death,* which has since been set to music. Adjoining Delhi on the north is SILVER LAKE STATE LAKE PRESERVE *(picnic ground),* a 15-acre area bordering SILVER LAKE, which has a clean sandy shore, and is stocked with fish. Footpaths wind through the woods and hills along the river terraces. Among the trees, the small bushes, and deep in the tall grasses, thousands of birds, both migrant and resident, are found. Meadow larks, bobolinks, and red-winged blackbirds are often seen in the open meadows; perhaps the most musical singers are the white-throated sparrows and horned larks.

Right from Delhi 1.5 *m.* on an improved road to a large DAM that has backed up the waters of the Maquoketa River, forming an artificial lake extending several miles upstream. Bass are abundant, and fishing-boats are rented at the dam.

At 40.5 *m.* is the junction with State 116, graveled.

Left on State 116 is a UNITED STATES FISH HATCHERY, 2 *m.* *(picnic grounds).* Along the meandering small creek are the outdoor ponds, in which are trout and other game fish in all stages of development from the egg to full growth at 3 or 4 pounds. During the trout season fishing is permitted above and below the hatchery grounds.

MANCHESTER, 44 *m.* (919 alt., 3,413 pop.), seat of Delaware County, lies along the South Fork of the Maquoketa River. Steiner Eiverson, a Norwegian, in the spring of 1850 built the first cabin here. The town was first known as Burrington, but this name was discarded in 1856 because of its similarity to Burlington. According to one story, the town name was created by twisting Chesterman, the name of an early settler, but it is more probable that the town was named for Manchester, England, whence came many of the early residents of the community. In the early days it was nearly independent of the outside world. There was a wagon factory, several cooperative establishments, a brick kiln, harness makers, and several blacksmith shops. The town is a dairying center. The Dairy City Creamery Co. obtained a Government contract for butter for the Navy about 1907.

Back in the 1890's Saturday was the principal trading day for Delaware County farmers. With the advent of the automobile, business has been more evenly distributed over other days, but Saturday night is still the busiest time in the week for local merchants.

TIRRILL PARK *(picnic facilities, bathing beach),* a level, wooded, 10-acre tract, was donated to the town by R. W. Tirrill.

Manchester is at the junction with State 13 *(see Tour 2B).*

West of Manchester the landscape is gently rolling, and in summer cattle browse in meadows of deep clover. In late summer, the fields of oats and barley are golden with ripe grain. The noise and speed of traffic often drives the singing birds from the highways to wooded spaces along the streams, but there are many on the telephone wires and barbed wire fences, dotted here and there like notes on a music scale. Often heard is the song of the meadow lark, the scream of the bluejay, the dirge-like cry of the mourning dove.

At 60 *m.* is the junction with State 282, graveled.

Left here to QUASQUETON, 5 *m.* (342 pop.), settled in 1842; the site, on the banks of the Wapsipinicon River at a junction of Indian trails in this part of the State, was formerly called Quasquetuck *(swift running water)*. Wapsipinicon *(white potatoes)* River was so named, it is said, because of the white artichokes that grew along its banks. Some romantics account for the origin of the river's name by this legend: Wapsi *(White)*, an Indian girl, and Pinicon, son of a chief of a neighboring tribe, were paddling on the river on the evening of their wedding. One of the girl's former suitors, Fleet Foot, watching them and seeing Wapsi put her hands to Pinicon's lips in a caress, became angered. He drove an arrow into Pinicon's heart, and Wapsi, springing to his aid, overturned the canoe. They sank together. CEDAR ROCK, a large boulder about 1 mile up-stream from Quasqueton, is pointed out as the scene of their death.

INDEPENDENCE, 67 *m.* (921 alt., 3,691 pop.), seat of Buchanan County, is on the high, oak-covered bank of the Wapsipinicon. The town owes its founding to Rufus B. Clark, a trapper, who saw the possibilities of utilizing water power from the river. The name of the town was determined by the fact that its organization was completed about July 4, 1847 (Independence Day); the county was named in 1837 for James Buchanan, then a U. S. Senator, who in 1857 became President.

The STATE HOSPITAL FOR THE INSANE *(visiting hours 2-4 p. m., except Sun. and holidays)*, was opened to patients in 1873. The average number under care is 1,200.

Independence is at the junction with State 11 *(see Tour 2A)*.

Just W. of Independence is a lone, time-worn building, a reminder of the boom days of the town, 1889–1892. On this spot Charles W. Williams operated the "first and fastest kite-shaped race track in the world." The field, which was known as Rush Park, is now used as a pasture. Here for three years the fastest horses in America shattered one record after another. Two outstanding stallions were Axtell and Allerton, both bred by Williams in the same year. Allerton is buried in the Fair Grounds at Indianola *(see Tour 5)*.

Williams built his track on low, swampy ground over a foundation of peat. A layer of black spongy soil was spread five or six inches deep and large embankments were raised on both sides. Following the panic of the 1890's and the resultant decline of interest in horse racing, the popularity of Rush Park collapsed as suddenly as it had begun. Fine horses, however, are still bred in the surrounding territory.

JESUP, 76 *m.* (980 alt., 736 pop.), settled in 1858 and named for a railroad official, lies between the Wapsipinicon and Cedar Rivers. In May the surrounding prairies are colored with pink and white shooting stars and yellow ragwort; often on the higher knolls are the long-plumed purple avens, known as "prairie smoke." Between the knolls are ponds, encircled with marsh marigolds and joined by small streams.

Before the tall prairie grass was turned under by the plow, Iowa settlers were watchful day and night for prairie fires; one of the most memorable in Black Hawk County occurred in 1866. One morning what had been a faint glow against the eastern sky on the previous evening had become a whirling maelstrom of flames, rolling towards the village, soaring forward and upward, and threatening destruction to everything in a mile-wide path.

The land was covered with a dense growth of grass, short on the hilltops, but in the low grounds and along the hillside growing three to six feet tall. Killed by the frost, parched and dried by the sun and wind of autumn, it was highly inflammable. There was a wide area of dry grass between the fire and the homes of the settlers, but a vigorous gale was blowing the flames ahead in a 50-foot wall, and over the flames rose smoke in a great black canopy. The settlers, instead of fleeing, started backfires, so that as the great fire advanced it would meet only long strips of burned grass and would die out from lack of fuel. The backfires, burning against the wind, moved slowly outward; birds and small animals fled frantically before the major fire only to be caught by the backfires. The backfire gradually burned off an area across which the onrushing wall of flame could not leap. The settlers, with smoke-blackened faces and reddened eyes, watched the great flames waver and sink.

WATERLOO, 91 m. (856 alt., 46,191 pop.) (see WATERLOO).

Points of Interest: Boulder Church; packing plant; Agricultural Machinery Factories; Dairy Cattle Congress Exposition buildings.

Waterloo is at the junction with US 63 (see Tour 3) and US 218 (see Tour 3A).

Section b. WATERLOO to FORT DODGE, 109 m.

Between Waterloo and Cedar Falls US 20 closely follows the Cedar River, third largest river in the State.

CEDAR FALLS is at 8 m. (854 alt., 7,362 pop.).

Swimming. Island Park, N. edge city, E. side of Cedar River; municipal pool, adjoining Spring Park on W.

Cedar Falls is a city of wide, tree-bordered streets, parks, attractive lawns, and beautiful homes. The first settlers here were William Sturgis and his family, who built a cabin on the west side of the Cedar River in the spring of 1845, choosing this site because of the water power available. In 1851 the town was laid out and in the next 40 years developed into one of the State's important milling centers. When Black Hawk County was organized (1853) Cedar Falls, then the principal town, was made the county seat. Two years later, however, an election moved the seat to Waterloo, which was nearer the center of the county.

In 1861 a railroad (now the Illinois Central) was completed as far west as Cedar Falls but, owing to lack of funds and the outbreak of the Civil War, it went no farther until 1869. Farmers from a wide area brought stock and grain here for shipment to eastern markets and the streets were crowded and the business houses so busy that they kept open until late at night. When construction of the railroad was resumed, it was found necessary to shut off the millrace in order to build the piers, but the owners of the gristmills and sawmills that had been running day and night charged the railroad company $300 a day damages. This so enraged the railroad officials that they made Waterloo the division point and later built shops there, even though land for that purpose had been given to them at Cedar Falls. Local milling began to decline toward the end of the 19th century and, in the early 1900's, was supplanted by the manufacture of rotary pumps, elevator equipment, seed-corn sorting machines, automobile trunks, brooms, and concrete mixers.

Bess Streeter Aldrich, author of *A Lantern in Her Hand* and *A White Bird Flying,* was born here on February 17, 1881, and attended the local college. In one of her novels, *Miss Bishop,* the locale was the town and the college. Ruth Suckow *(see LITERATURE)* makes her home here. Charles E. Hearst, national president of the American Farm Bureau Federation, was a resident until his death in 1936.

The IOWA STATE TEACHERS' COLLEGE, College St. between 23rd St. and 27th St., is a group of 21 buildings, closely assembled on a 127-acre campus shaded by tall trees. In general the buildings are grouped around an inner and an outer square with a tall campanile in the center. The older buildings, tall, red brick structures, front on College Street. The institution was first housed in a former home for Civil War soldiers' orphans, situated on an almost treeless eminence, surrounded by fields of waving corn. The old building was equipped with stoves burning wood, with kerosene lamps and water buckets, and had crude sanitation. The first session was opened on September 6, 1876, when the president, James C. Gilchrist, then called "the principal," read from the Scriptures and offered prayer. In 1909 the name of the institution was changed from Iowa State Normal School to Iowa State Teachers' College. Homer H. Seerley, appointed president in 1886, was an outstanding educator through the many years of his service.

One-, two-, and four-year courses are provided for the preparation of teachers. In 1936 more than 2,000 students registered in courses offering training in the teaching of commercial subjects, home economics, industrial arts, and other subjects. The four-year course for high school graduates leads to a degree of Bachelor of Arts in education.

Facing College Street is the LIBRARY *(open weekdays 9-9),* a three-story building in the Classic style. On the walls of the general reading room are murals painted by William DeLeftwich Dodge; they illustrate the different phases of civilization—agriculture, education, art, and invention. On the third floor of the building is the MUSEUM *(open school hours)* with collections of special value for the study of the natural sciences. The collection contains a mastodon tusk found in Iowa. BARTLETT HALL, of Georgian Colonial design, accommodating 500 women, and the COMMONS, built in 1933, with cafeteria, lounge, and recreation rooms, extend back of the front line of buildings. The CAMPANILE was erected in 1926 as a memorial to the founders and builders of the college. The tower, 100 feet high, is topped with a belfry, Italian Renaissance in style, where chimes are played at regular intervals during the day. Other buildings on the campus are the men's gymnasium, with a seating capacity in the auditorium of 3,000; George T. Baker Hall for Men (1936) of very modern design; the Vocational Building with laboratories for work in industrial arts, home economics, and natural science; and the Campus School, where students of the college practice teaching under supervision.

The CEDAR FALLS WOOLEN MILL *(visited by permission)*, 107 S. Main St., uses wool from Iowa and elsewhere to manufacture all-wool and part-wool blankets; it also does cleaning and recarding on special orders for private clients.

The VIKING PUMP PLANT *(visited by permission)*, 406 State St., is a large modern factory manufacturing a special type of rotary pump. Established on a small scale in 1911, the company has grown steadily in size.

The CLAY EQUIPMENT PLANT *(open 8-5)*, N. Main St. across the river, is one of the city's oldest factories. Barn equipment, ventilating systems, gates, fences, and steel supplies for stores and business houses are manufactured.

RIVERVIEW PARK, NW. city limits, end of Elizabeth St., contains the EVANGELICAL CAMPGROUNDS, which were purchased in 1916 by the Evangelical Church. The landscaped grounds occupy a site high on the west bank of the Cedar River. The Tabernacle, Missionary Hall, Fairfield Chapel, administration building, two dormitories, a dining hall, and a caretaker's cottage comprise the buildings. Religious conferences and assemblies are held here annually in August, the most notable of which is the Interdenominational Bible Conference, attended by thousands.

Cedar Falls is at the junction with US 218 *(see Tour 3A)*.

NEW HARTFORD, 19 *m.* (895 alt., 500 pop.), on the banks of Beaver Creek, was settled in 1854 and named for Hartford, Conn., whence came many of the town's first residents.

At 25 *m.* (R) is BEAVER MEADOW STATE SCENIC PRESERVE, an undeveloped area of 80 acres.

PARKERSBURG, 27 *m.* (951 alt., 1,046 pop.), in Beaver Valley, was built on a site formerly so covered with heavy brush that pioneers called the place the "brush bed of the beaver." J. T. Parker, hotel keeper and first postmaster, named the town for Nathan H. Parker of Davenport, a well-known writer in the State during the 1850's and 1860's.

APLINGTON, 32 *m.* (958 alt., 622 pop.), was named for Zenas Aplington, the town's first storekeeper.

The surrounding territory was once a wheat-growing region, but now dairying is predominant. Saturday night on the main street here is still, as in pioneer days, the gala time for the farmer and his family, and the rural people prepare for it with enthusiasm and regularity. Somewhat incongruous in the otherwise rural scene is a TILE FACTORY *(open to visitors)*, one of many new industrial developments in the farming area.

AUSTINVILLE, 36 *m.* (1,006 alt., 80 est. pop.), named for the original owner of the site, boasts (1938) that the local bank had on deposit nearly half a million dollars; the stockholders are mostly farmers.

THE DUCK HUNTER

ACKLEY, 43 *m.* (1,092 alt., 1,524 pop.), is known throughout Iowa for its observance of an annual Sauerkraut Day. Free sauerkraut, sausages, and entertainment are provided.

Because Ackley is near the point where the boundaries of Grundy, Butler, Franklin, and Hardin counties meet, the counties unite in conducting a Four-County Fair here each year. It is held without concessions or buildings of its own; exhibits are housed in various public and private structures.

Here, as elsewhere in Iowa, the old-time "swappings" and "tradings" have been replaced by the auction. At the SALES PAVILION almost everything—even purebred stallions—can be purchased. Both farmers and townspeople bring their goods here for disposal; goods can be disposed of by exchange, as well as for cash, and the seller need pay only a small fee for the services of the auctioneer. Rural auctions have long been associated with mortgage foreclosures and sheriff's sales, but in recent years the auction in Iowa has become a new and different type of business activity.

At 51 *m.* is the junction (R) with US 65 *(see Tour 4)* which unites briefly with US 20.

IOWA FALLS, 57 *m.* (1,107 alt., 4,112 pop.) *(see Tour 4)*, is at the junction with US 65 *(see Tour 4)*. US 20 swings R., US 65 L.

West of Iowa Falls US 20 traverses flat prairie land. Extending into the distance in the spring a checkerboard is seen—black squares of deeply plowed fields ready for corn, and the many shaded-blocks of green containing freshly sprouted alfalfa, hay, oats, and new grass. Bordering the creeks the greening pussywillows push forth their claw-like seed pods, and beyond the meadows the larger willows turn with the wind. Along flood plains, in colonies or alone on the prairie, the cottonwoods stand, waving the tassels that burden the winds with floating white shreds.

Both in the spring and fall countless small birds pass through the region —prairie birds, woodland birds, shore birds, and swamp birds, winging along on the annual migrations.

ALDEN, 63 m. (1,116 alt., 793 pop.), on the banks of the Iowa River, though a hamlet, has a CARNEGIE LIBRARY.

Opposite an illuminated dam on the river is RIVERSIDE PARK *(boating and bathing facilities)*.

WILLIAMS, 73 m. (1,212 alt., 500 pop.), is an Irish community; settled by Peter Laforge in 1868, it was named for Major William Williams of Fort Dodge, who commanded a detachment of soldiers sent to aid the settlers following the Spirit Lake Massacre *(see Tour 7)*. In the 1880's the town was destroyed by a cyclone.

The number of wolves in Iowa in recent years has been unusually large; it has been necessary to organize several wolf hunts to rid the hills and river bottoms of this menace to livestock. As many as 200 men have taken part in such hunts. Most counties have never rescinded their offers of bounties for wolves; the wolf pups, dug out in the spring from wooded hillsides, are accepted as well as their parents.

Pheasant hunting is much more common than the search for wolves. About 1900 the ring-necked pheasant was introduced into Iowa, and within a few years had increased in such numbers as to become, in the opinion of many farmers, a pest. Some assert that protection given by the pheasant against destructive bugs is more than offset by its habit of pulling up and eating young corn and other kinds of grain. This, however, is a minor point to hunters who swarm through the central counties during the few days of open season in autumn. Cornfields, swamps, and weed-patches are peopled from dawn until dusk with men seeking the burnished gold bodies with the crimson splashes of color at the throats, which zoom upward in startled flight. Marksmen, expert in quail and clay-pigeon shooting, find that it takes a well-directed shot to kill a pheasant. Because of this, at least half of the birds are merely wounded and hide in clumps of weeds until they die. Severe winters, such as that of 1935–36, take a heavy toll of the birds, their nostrils freezing shut at 30° below zero. Sleet and ice storms also cause their death. Whereas early settlers brought home bags of quail, prairie chickens, and wild ducks, the present-day Iowan is content with a brace of pheasant cocks.

BLAIRSBURG, 79 m. (1,224 alt., 274 pop.), is at the junction with US 69 *(see Tour 5)*.

WEBSTER CITY, 88 m. (1,047 alt., 7,024 pop.), seat of Hamilton County, was settled in 1850 by Wilson C. Brewer, and named in 1856 for the owner of a stage line that extended between Belmond and Fort Dodge. On the banks of the Boone River is KENDALL YOUNG PARK, a 70-acre tract of rolling woodland *(picnic facilities)*, named for the founder of the first Webster City library.

A bronze tablet in the COURTHOUSE commemorates the pioneers who joined the relief expedition sent to aid the settlers in northern Iowa in March 1857, following the Spirit Lake Massacre *(see Tour 7)*.

Abastenia St. Leger Eberle (1878–   ), a sculptor who was born here, has given to the KENDALL YOUNG LIBRARY a collection of 21 small autographed figures in plaster. The Van Ness collection of Indian relics and curios was presented by Capt. W. H. Van Ness.

In the WILSON BREWER MEMORIAL PARK, in the southeast part of town, is the PIONEER BONEBRIGHT MUSEUM *(free 9-5)*, housed in two adjoining log cabins on the old Wilson Brewer place. The first cabin was erected in 1850; the second, built in 1856, was brought here from another site. On display are tools, field implements, cooking utensils, home furnishings, and primitive manufacturing machinery that belonged to Hamilton County pioneers. The attendants explain and demonstrate the uses of the old implements. It was the wish of Frank Bonebright (1868–1934) to "enlighten the future generations and thereby inspire them with keen appreciation of the indomitable courage and persistent accomplishments of the pioneer progenitors."

DUNCOMBE, 97 *m.* (1,108 alt., 354 pop.). The Catholic Church here on August 15 of each year celebrates the Assumption, the ascension of the Virgin Mary into heaven. The celebration opens with a mass; a dinner is served at noon, and the remainder of the day is given over to entertainment, with a dance in the evening.

At 104 *m.* is the junction with a dirt road.

Left on this road 3 *m.* is the CARDIFF GYPSUM CO. PLANT *(for adm. apply to main office)*, named for the Cardiff Giant *(see FORT DODGE)*. According to a State Geological Report, ". . . . There is very little doubt that Iowa contains gypsum enough to supply the Missisippi Valley for centuries to come." Gypsum is formed by the rapid evaporation of inland bodies of water; debris accumulated by the destruction of rocks is carried in mechanical suspension by moving water, either in waves or streams, and dropped when the velocity of the water is no longer sufficient to carry it. The gypsum deposits near Fort Dodge were thus formed. The shaft of the Cardiff Company is 60 feet deep, and the vein of gypsum here is 10 feet thick. The mine is worked by the room-and-pillar system; hand augers are used for drilling, and dynamite for blasting, or "shooting." A considerable amount of water is encountered, necessitating the continuous operation of seven pumps delivering two 4-inch streams to the surface. Sixty tons of rock each 8-hour day is the usual quota of production.

Right 2 *m.* from the Cardiff plant on a dirt road to the CERTAINTEED PRODUCTS CO. PLANT *(for adm. apply to main office)*. Two hundred-fifty tons of rock are crushed daily here and electrically conveyed to the mill to be processed. Gypsum is used in making plaster of paris, cement, fireproof building blocks, porcelain, and glass. The white, crumbling rock also ranks high as a fertilizer. The value of ground gypsum for this purpose was discovered separately in Germany and in France about 1760, and from these countries use of the product spread to England and America.

Right 1 *m.* on a graveled road from the Certainteed Plant are the UNITED STATES GYPSUM CO. MILLS *(adm. by perm. only)*. The mines are electrically lighted and have electric motors for bringing the rock to the cages and electric drills for making holes for explosives. The rock coming from the mines is crushed and reduced to a size that will pass through a 2-inch ring for use in making cement. After passing through driers, some of the material goes to the grinders for reduction to fertilizer. Fine gypsum is heated in huge kettles to a temperature of 325° F. for use in the manufacture of plaster.

During the appearance of Halley's Comet May 4, 1910, a high hill near Fort Dodge was the scene of a strange gathering. For months word had been sent along the roads of America from one gypsy family to another that they should meet at that spot and await the end of the world. This belief that life would end as the earth passed through the gases of the comet was widespread. The gypsies had given away what few possessions they owned, except their personal jewelry. Their colored wagons stood in circles about campfires, with the horses tied to rear wheels. Smaller children were asleep in the wagons, but the children old enough to sense their elders' fears, huddled together in silence. The gypsies waited until noon before realizing that the appearance of the comet had not destroyed them or their appetites.

FORT DODGE, 109 *m.* (1,115 alt., 21,895 pop.) *(see FORT. DODGE).*

Points of Interest: Blanden Art Gallery; Public Library; Tobin Packing Plant.

Fort Dodge is at the junction with US 169 *(see Tour 6)* and State 5 *(see Tour 12A).*

Section c. FORT DODGE *to* NEBRASKA LINE, *128 m.*

Between Fort Dodge, 0 *m.,* and Sioux City US 20 roughly follows the "furrow trail," plowed in 1856 by Alex McCready and his son; it was known to the pioneers as the Great Road. In the early 1850's it was not uncommon for travelers crossing the Iowa prairie to lose their courage, or to start wandering in a circle. McCready, a civil engineer, and his son set out from Sioux City with oxen and plow to mark the trail to Fort Dodge; a parallel furrow, four to six rods from the first, was plowed on the return trip. The ridges thus made served to indicate both to day and night drivers when their teams left the trail. The Great Road, winding to avoid the hills and rough places, was many miles longer than the present highway between the two cities.

MOORLAND, 8 *m.* (1,152 alt., 179 pop.), lies in a region formerly almost covered by ponds or sloughs. In the first decade of the 20th century, the arable acreage in the counties of Kossuth, Humboldt, Buena Vista, Wright, Hamilton, Emmett and Palo Alto, scarcely exceeded that covered by these sloughs and bogs, but with the introduction of modern drainage systems the agricultural picture was changed. In many places lowlands that were drained became fertile fields.

These lands are among the most prolific floral areas in the State. In July the gauzy white-flowered spikes of the arrowhead, above sharp-pointed leaves, are mingled with the small-flowered panicles of water plantain. Flags unfurl until the marsh is blue, and patches of rose-flowered smartweed cast a glow on the waters.

In marshy regions the killdeer is perhaps the best known of the shore and wading birds, but rails, sandpipers, and plovers are also seen. Here in winter the goldfinch feeds on the seed of dandelions and thistles, and jack rabbits and cottontails nest in the tall grasses and brush. Pheasants, dashing along through the roadside weeds, have occasionally rushed against the windshields of passing cars.

ROCKWELL CITY, 26 m. (1,230 alt., 2,108 pop.), seat of Calhoun County, was named for J. M. Rockwell, an early settler; the county was named for John C. Calhoun of South Carolina, statesman and orator during the first half of the 19th century. The town has been called "the golden buckle on the Corn Belt" because it is in the center of the Iowa corn region.

The STATE REFORMATORY FOR WOMEN, established here in 1918, has accommodations for more than 100. Prior to 1918 it was at Anamosa, as a department separate from that for the men. The administration building and three cottages, set in the center of the 219-acre farm, have stucco walls and red tile roofs. The women live in rooms, not cells, each of which has sanitary facilities. There is a library with 1,500 volumes, mostly fiction. Educational work is planned to give practical experience, especially in the cannery, laundry, poultry plant, and kitchen. There are classes in art, stenography, typewriting, and domestic science.

In Calhoun County, as elsewhere in Iowa, cornhusking contests are conducted annually in the fall, whenever the corn is best for husking. At the report of the starting gun the wagons and huskers are off. The contestants often work bareheaded, bare-handed, and bare-trunked. The winner is the one who can husk the most corn in a stated length of time. At the end of the period the corn is weighed and deductions are made for "dirty shucking"—too many husks left on the ears. County winners compete in a State contest, which is usually started by a gun fired by the Governor; large crowds of onlookers follow the wagons and huskers down the long rows of corn.

SAC CITY, 46 m. (1,278 alt., 2,854 pop.), seat of Sac County, lies along the timbered banks of the Raccoon River. The town and county were named for an Indian tribe (Sac or Sauk, *yellow earth*). A county fair is held here every year in August. TULIP BEDS at the W. J. Findley home, 10th and Early Sts., attract hundreds of people every year. A CANNING FACTORY *(visitors welcome)* in 1935 shipped out 82,000 cases of corn.

At 54 m. is the junction with US 71 *(see Tour 7).*

EARLY, 57 m. (1,331 alt., 632 pop.) *(see Tour 7),* is at the junction with US 71 *(see Tour 7).*

Along both sides of the highway are typical Iowa farmhouses, set well back from the road. They are not alike, yet there is a certain similarity because they follow a pattern set by the advertisements in popular farm magazines. Almost every one of the newer houses—large, square, white frame structures, set on concrete blocks—is characterized by an enclosed porch across the front, large windows, a ground-level door to the kitchen, and large chimneys. A neatly fenced garden and a lawn separate the house from the barnyards. A long lane running from the main road to the house is bordered with trees. A hip-roofed building with a large hayloft shelters the cattle and horses. A tall silo towers beside the largest barn, and scattered about are smaller sheds for chickens, hogs, machinery, and grain. The relationship of the buildings and yards is always the same. The inevitable metal ventilators on the roofs of barns and the sharp-pointed lightning rods are symbols of the commercialized standardization of Iowa farm buildings. Every farm has its strawstack, placed usually in a feed lot close to the barns, but occasionally far out in the middle of the fields. Straw piles are round and peaked, or shaped in a long, thin crescent. In the late summer, when threshing begins, last year's stack is only a low hump of trampled manure, but it is soon replaced by a new pile of gleaming yellow straw from the threshed oats.

Straw is used as bedding in the horse and cattle stalls, and frequently as winter forage for the cattle. Hogs make a circular runway around the base of the stack, and cattle, seeking shelter, eat and burrow their way into the moist, warm pile until it looks like a gigantic mushroom or the hut of an African savage. When city cousins spend the day with the farm children, the huge, smooth hillocks become gigantic slides with a never-failing cushion at the bottom.

Many of the farmhouses are new, freshly painted, clean, orderly, and prosperous-looking, but there are also neglected shacks, in grassless yards surrounded by rickety fences. Often the condition of the house and farmyard is a clue to whether a place is occupied by the owners. On some of the rented farms there is often old useless machinery rusting in the rain; chickens peck and flop in puddles of water thrown from the kitchen door; and the hogs are sometimes seen wandering about the front yard. If the farm-owner is an insurance company that wants to rid itself of the property, there is again noticeable standardization. Fence posts painted a distinctive color often indicate to what insurance company the place belongs, though frequently holding companies remove the fences entirely, in order to plow up the last bordering inch.

Spring is the moving season; farm leases date from March 1. With the competition among renters to procure a place, and the constant restless search by renters for better farms, hundreds move every year. Some tenants make all they can out of a "rent farm" but many of them are forced on. Along the roads are trucks loaded with household furniture, grain, children, and even a prized horse or hog. Like gypsy caravans the renters move across the prairies, driving their cattle and horses, dragging farm machinery after them.

SCHALLER, 67 m. (1,393 alt., 724 pop.), is one of the important shipping centers in the popcorn-producing area of northwestern Iowa. Popcorn is widely grown in the home patches but its commercial production centers in Ida and Sac counties, where 20,000 to 25,000 acres are planted annually.

This section of the State lies along the eastern edge of one of the large "dust bowls" most severely affected by the droughts of 1934 and 1936, when dust storms of great intensity were not uncommon. When drought comes the fields are gray with dust under the burning sun.

In early spring, however, the wind-fanned, red-brown grassland, brings forth the pasque flower, and the knolls are almost solid blue as the flowers open wide. The blue fades to gray as the flowers drop their sepals and thrust forth hairy, long-tailed seed pods. In late summer a sea of golden coreopsis tops the upland grasses, and on gravelly hilltops yellow toad flax grows with crepe-petaled primrose and low, spiked mesquite grass. As summer passes, golden-rod appears, wave upon wave; asters—blue, white and purple—bloom in the curling brown grass, and finally the blue gentian brings the floral procession to a close under frosty, autumn skies.

At 79 *m.* is the junction with US 59 *(see Tour 8)*.

At 80 *m.* is the junction with State 131, graveled.

Right on State 131 is HOLSTEIN, 1 *m.* (1,443 alt., 1,300 pop.), founded in 1882 when a branch of the C. & N. W. R. R. was constructed through northern Ida County. The town was named for the area in Prussia, where many of the town's first residents lived before migrating to America. One of the most active chapters of the many Turner Societies, or *turn vereins,* in Iowa conducts physical training classes on regularly scheduled evenings in TURNER HALL, built in 1899. Here small children are trained in accordance with the teachings of Friedrich Ludwig Jahn, a Berlin school teacher, born in 1778. He was a strong advocate of physical training and the movement he started has spread all over the world.

CORRECTIONVILLE, 95 *m.* (1,129 alt., 1,058 pop.), on the Little Sioux River, was so named by surveyors because the town lies on a "correction line" established for verification and correction of land surveying. The town is in the center of a stock-raising district.

MOVILLE, 110 *m.* (1,147 alt., 911 pop.), was named for Moville, Ireland, home town of the first postmaster here. The following dispatch was received by a sub-contractor at Moville, Apr. 28, 1890, from the U. S. Post Office Department.

"Sir: Complaint has reached the Department that the mail carrier on route No. 27637, from Moville to Sioux City, Iowa frequently stops on lower Fourth Street for a glass of beer and a game of billiards, which causes him to fail to connect with the train at Moville. You will please see that this is corrected at once, and that the mails on this route are hereafter carried on schedule time."

In 1932 Moville was one of the centers of Farm Holiday Association activity, which drew wide attention to the economic problems of the farmer. Many of the association meetings were held here during the farm strike that shut off Sioux City's food supply.

During July and August, Band Concert Night *(Wednesday and Saturday)* is a big event for farm families in northwestern Iowa. An atmosphere of excitement and hurry is felt all day. The children start doing the chores without urging; the farmer hastens to do the milking. The mother and daughters spend the afternoon pressing clothes. Supper is hurried through and dishes are washed; chickens are shooed into coops so they can be locked up before the family leaves. Just at dusk the family turns down the dusty country road toward the highway and town. If they are late there will be no parking places near the band—a minor tragedy, for with good luck the family can sit comfortably in the car, munching popcorn, listening to the band, and watching the crowds stroll past. There is real competition for parking places; townspeople, to the dismay of rural folk, often park their cars in the late afternoon, and walk home to supper and back again in the evening for the sake of an advantageous spot.

The band is often a heterogeneous group, made up of older people who have played in it for years, school teachers who have just come to town and are earnestly endeavoring to take an active part in the life of the community, high school students, and even grade school children. When the crowd approves of the music, all the cars set up a great honking of applause; sometimes every piece is followed by a chorus of raucous sirens.

At 116 *m.* is the junction with an improved county road.

Left on this road is LAWTON, 0.5 *m.* (1,170 alt., 259 pop.), named for John Law, on whose farm the town was founded. On the walls of a vacant DUTCH RE-FORMED CHURCH are a number of stenciled designs of an unusual pattern symbolizing the Holy Trinity. In early days a settlement of Winebenarians, a religious sect that observes foot-washing as a ceremony, was established near this town.

In a newspaper dated Aug. 25, 1874, an editor asserted that in the vicinity of Sioux City "we have never seen so much universal prosperity." He had forgotten, apparently, that on July 18, 1874, his paper had announced: "There is, at a moderate estimate, 230 bankrupt farmers within a radius of 20 miles of Sioux City, who have brought about their own wreck by the indiscriminate purchase of agricultural machinery. If they are not skinned out of house and home before another year we will deem ourselves worthy of being dubbed a 'false prophet.' "

At about 125 *m.* is a hill, now locally called Bunker Hill, that was the site of a camp of farm pickets during the Farm Holiday strike in 1932 *(see SIOUX CITY)* when the Sioux City market was virtually closed to truckers for more than a month. Several fights with county deputies took place here.

SIOUX CITY, 128 *m.* (1,135 alt., 79,183 pop.) *(see SIOUX CITY).*

Points of Interest: Woodbury County Courthouse; stockyards; Prospect Hill; Floyd Monument; Morningside College.

Sioux City is at the junction with US 75 *(see Tour 9).*

At Sioux City US 20 crosses the Missouri River, the Iowa-Nebraska Line, on a TOLL BRIDGE *(car and driver, 20¢; passengers, 5¢ each; trucks 25¢)* 55 miles E. of Randolph, Nebr.

Tour 12A

Fort Dodge—Cherokee—Le Mars—Akron; State 5.
Fort Dodge to Akron, 140 m.

Illinois Central R. R. parallels this route throughout.
Graveled roadbed between Barnum and Alta, Aurelia and Cleghorn, Le Mars and

South Dakota Line; remainder paved.
Tourist accommodations of all kinds available.

This east-west route was part of a cross-State road known as the Hawk-eye Highway in the early days of automobile travel.

FORT DODGE, 0 *m.* (1,115 alt., 21,895 pop.) *(see FORT DODGE).*

Points of Interest: Blanden Art Gallery; Public Library; Tobin Packing Plant.

Fort Dodge is at the junction with US 169 *(see Tour 6)* and US 20 *(see Tour 12).*

BARNUM, 10 *m.* (1,174 alt., 148 pop.), was settled at the time of the construction of the Iowa Falls-Sioux City. R. R. through this region. The town's outstanding structure is the COOPERATIVE GRAIN ELEVATOR.

MANSON, 19 *m.* (1,232 alt., 1,382 pop.), was established in 1872 by the Sioux City and Iowa Town Lot and Land Co. Soon afterward, the town was made a relay station on the old Fort Dodge and Sioux City stage line, displacing Yatesville.

At 25 *m.* is the junction with State 17, graveled, which unites with State 5 for 6 miles.

Left on State 17 is the junction with State 124, graveled, 4 *m.;* L. to TWIN LAKES STATE PARK, 4.5 *m.,* a 15-acre recreational area on the shore of NORTH TWIN LAKE *(picnic, bathing, and fishing facilities).* SOUTH TWIN LAKE is separated from North Twin by a strip of land from 500 to 1,000 feet wide, across which passes State 17.

POMEROY, 28 *m.* (1,241 alt., 826 pop.), lying in Iowa's so-called "storm belt," was struck by a terrific cyclone on July 6, 1893; the storm destroyed every building on five nearby farms, then struck the town with full force, sweeping it of buildings. It was reported that "but 21 families were left with no dead or wounded of their own to take care of." In response to Gov. Horace Boies' appeal for assistance, liberal donations came from all parts of the State—about $70,000 in cash, in addition to carloads of lumber, flour, clothing, groceries, and other necessities.

In recent years danger from storms has been lessened by the planting of large groves of trees that often serve to impede the progress of cyclones.

At 31 *m.* is the junction with State 17.

Right on this road is POCAHONTAS, 10 *m.* (1,222 alt., 1,308 pop.), seat of Pocahontas County, named in honor of the daughter of the Indian chief, Powhatan. Lizard Creek weaves through a park of 13 acres.

FONDA, 40 *m.* (1,234 alt., 1,027 pop.), was first named Marvin in honor of Marvin Hewitt, a railroad official, but the post office was called Cedarville because of nearby Cedar Creek. The resulting confusion prompted the citizens to abandon both names and substitute Fonda, a name chosen because it was found in the United States post office directory only once. The Pocahontas County Fair is held here each year in August.

At 43 *m.* is the junction with a dirt road.

Right on this road to SUNK GROVE, 1.5 *m.* *(boating, fishing, and camping facilities),* an 80-acre island in a lake. Many kinds of wild flowers and shrubs grow in the area, which has 27 varieties of trees. This grove, which furnished fuel and lumber in the days before the I.C. R. R. was built, attracted the first settlers to Cedar township in 1868. The water surrounding the grove protected the oak, hackberry, basswood, cottonwood, and other trees from the prairie fires that swept across the country. It early received its name of Sunk Grove because many of the large oak trees growing around its outer edge stood in water from one to two feet deep most of the year, which seemed to indicate that the ground on which they stood had sunk after they began to grow. The lake drains eastward into the Cedar River.

NEWELL, 49 *m.* (869 alt., 812 pop.), situated in a shallow basin between two small creeks where the natural drainage is poor, suffered from high waters until drainage canals were constructed. At times of flood the town was surrounded by water and almost completely shut off from outside communication. The mosquitoes were almost intolerable. A group of business men promoted the building of a large open ditch canal, 9.5 miles in length, with 4 miles of branch canals, draining into Storm Lake. Removal of the surface water has left the mosquitoes without breeding places.

Buena Vista County (1936) has a total of 89.9 miles of open and 518.9 miles of tile drainage ditches. Some rich, tillable soil here, as in other swampy areas of the State, has been made available to farmers by this means. Artificial drainage, however, has created another problem in some parts of the State—that of conservation of water resources *(see NATURAL SETTING).*

At 85 *m.* is the junction with US 71 *(see Tour 7).*

STORM LAKE, 62 *m.* (1,436 alt., 4,157 pop.) *(see Tour 7),* a summer resort, is at the junction with US 71 *(see Tour 7).*

In ALTA, 68 *m.* (1,513 alt., 1,297 pop.), the main street is on the crest of the divide between the Mississippi and Missouri Rivers. This town was named for Altai Blair, daughter of John Blair, an early settler. George Alfred Carlson (1876–1926), elected Governor of Colorado in 1914, was born in Alta.

A MUNICIPAL HOSPITAL was established here in 1912.

David E. Hadden of Alta in 1934 received a grant from the Carnegie Foundation to accumulate and classify data for use in long range weather observation. His theory of weather forecasting by cycles is receiving much attention. Hadden has his own well-equipped OBSERVATORY *(open on request).*

The Buena Vista County Fair is held here. When threshing is done the Iowa farmer is ready to enjoy the fairs held in almost every county. In the early dawn of the fair day, many farmyards show the gleam of a lantern as some 4-H boy or girl anxiously examines a pig, or a calf, or a sheep, to see if more grooming is necessary before the carefully tended animal is loaded into a truck and taken to the fair.

At the fairgrounds friendly crowds mill through the dusty acres; the men gather in groups to talk about the way the corn is filling out and the prospects of a good second crop of hay; the women wander through the exhibition buildings—they lift the cut slices of chocolate cake, having icing half an inch thick, to see if the texture is fine, and watch the light shine through the clear jellies—speculating on whose pies and cakes will win. The young folks take part in the 4-H demonstrations, then rush through the exhibits to see if anyone they know has received a blue ribbon. By sundown the youngest and oldest members of the family are ready to

AUTUMN

go home, but many remain to enjoy the brightly lighted midway and the fireworks.

AURELIA, 75 *m.* (1,387 alt., 723 pop.), a small village, was named for Aurelia Blair, another daughter of John Blair. The town supports a CEMENT BLOCK AND TILE WORKS *(open to visitors)*.

CHEROKEE, 83 *m.* (1,201 alt., 6,443 pop.) *(see Tour 8)*, is at the junction with US 59 *(see Tour 8)*.

In 1937 Iowans participated in the 30th Pilot Rock Plowing Contest, held each year during the second week of September on some farm in Cherokee County. The name refers to the landmark, Pilot Rock *(see Tour 8)*. In plowing contests speed is not the most important factor. The straightness of the furrows, the evenness of the turned-over dirt, and the angle of the turn—all count in the score. In the Pilot Rock Contest different kinds of plows are used—gang plows, sulky plows, tractors—with awards in each class, and a sweepstakes prize. The prize money was at first raised by subscription among the farmers and business men of Cherokee County, but since the incorporation of the Pilot Rock Plowing Match Association in 1923, there is State aid for the prizes. Many farmers decide on the types of plows and tractors they will buy after watching the annual contest. Although the plowing match is the featured event, there is, in addition, a livestock show, exhibitions of women's products, industrial, poultry, and flower shows, baseball games, foot races, acrobatic acts, and pony races.

MERIDEN, 89 *m.* (1,402 alt., 188 pop.), was named Hazzard in honor of a relative of John Blair *(see above)*. The townspeople, however, it is said, "had no love for Mr. Blair" and requested the Post Office Department to change the name.

The QUAKER OATS CO. GRAIN ELEVATOR here buys grain directly from the farmers.

CLEGHORN, 94 *m.* (1,458 alt., 238 pop.), incorporated in 1901, owes its name to a Dr. Cleghorn, who gave or sold all his property to the town on the condition that it was to revert to his estate if "alcoholic liquors are sold or used on the land, other than for medical purposes."

REMSEN, 107 *m.* (1,324 alt., 1,181 pop.), named for Remsen Smith, Sioux City landowner, on July 4, 1936, suffered from a fire, with damages estimated at $400,000. A new depot, grain elevator, two lumberyards, two poultry houses, two hardware warehouses, a food store, a café, a jewelry store, a theater, and four new homes were rebuilt before a year had passed. In the spring of 1937 the State legislature passed a law that prohibits the use and sale of all fireworks, except sparklers and those used in municipal demonstrations, after Jan. 1, 1938. The Fourth of July fires in Remsen and Spencer in recent years were partly responsible for the bill.

Remsen is a flourishing small town; white houses predominate along its many well-paved streets, lined with tall, old trees. One of the beautiful homes is ST. MARY'S CATHOLIC RECTORY. The SISTERS OF ST. FRANCIS CONVENT, where 16 nuns live, is an attractive four-story building.

At 112 *m.* is the junction with a surfaced dirt road.

Left on this road is the PLYMOUTH COUNTY FARM, 1 *m.*, which has four box-car homes for its poor. Boxcar slums, a new type for Iowa, have developed in some instances from good intentions of Iowa counties to assist the poor. Discarded railroad boxcars were purchased and remodeled for use as dwellings; some of them were placed on three county farms. At one time there were families with 31 children living in boxcars here. A problem developed when they attended the nearby country schools; children from well-to-do rural families immediately put the stigma of "poor farm kids" on them.

LE MARS, 118 *m.* (1,224 alt., 4,788 pop.) *(see Tour 9),* is at the junction with US 75 *(see Tour 9).*

BRUNSVILLE, 124 *m.* (1,263 alt., 134 pop.), laid out in 1910 as a railroad station on the C. & N. W. R. R., is a small trading center for the farmers of the vicinity.

AKRON, 140 *m.* (1,147 alt., 1,304 pop.), was platted in 1871 by W. Sargeant, father of F. R. Sargeant who became president of the C. & N. W. R. R. The town's name was first Portlandville but was changed in the belief that it was going to grow to the size of Akron, Ohio. The Big Sioux River furnishes power for the flourmill here that has been in operation since 1871.

Akron is on the Big Sioux River, which at this point is the South Dakota Line.

Tour 13

(Sterling, Ill.)—Clinton—Cedar Rapids—Ames—Denison—Missouri Valley—(Fremont, Nebr.); US 30.
Illinois Line to Nebraska Line, 352 *m.*

C. & N. W. R. R. parallels this route throughout; I. C. R. R., between Denison and Missouri Valley.
Interstate Transit Bus lines follow the highway between Clinton and Missouri Valley; Burlington Bus Lines, between Tama and Ames; Jefferson Bus Lines, between Colo and Ames; Northland Greyhound Bus Lines between Denison and Missouri Valley.
Roadbed paved.
Tourist accommodations chiefly in cities.

Section a. ILLINOIS LINE *to* AMES, *202 m.*

US 30 crosses the Mississippi River, the Illinois-Iowa Line, on the LYONS-FULTON TOLL BRIDGE *(car and driver 20¢; passengers 5¢),* 33 miles W. of Sterling, Ill.

WINDMILL, LINN COUNTY

In the early days of automobile travel this road was a segment of the Official Transcontinental Route.

LYONS, 1 *m.* (598 alt., 5,000 pop.), founded in 1855, is now a suburb of Clinton.

CLINTON, 3 *m.* (593 alt., 25,726 pop.) *(see CLINTON)*.

Points of Interest: River Front Park; Old Stone House; Eagle Point **Park.**

Clinton is at the junction with US 67 *(see Tour 2)*.

Steamboating on the Mississippi near Clinton and other river towns during pioneer days involved much financial risk. Sometimes a single trip up or down the river would net the operators a large profit; perhaps the succeeding trip would be a total loss.

From the early 1830's into the early 1900's lografts on the Mississippi were numerous. Some were 100 feet wide and 300 to 400 feet long, carrying between 20 and 30 men; each raft had a cook shack and shelter house.

High river bluffs and rocky hills line the highway in the immediate vicinity of Clinton, but a few miles farther west the hills flatten out into gently rolling prairies. The country between Clinton and Marshalltown is noted for its fine dairy cattle. Trees grow more thickly here than in other parts of the State, and a few stands of timber are occasionally seen along the river valleys. Hickory trees with hard, light gray nuts are plentiful; when the nuts begin to ripen, they are easily knocked from the trees. A farmer sometimes gathers from 50 to 200 bushels of nuts in his own grove. They are often shipped to the South, where oil is extracted from them for commercial use.

At 13 *m.* is the junction with State 291, graveled.

Left on this road is LOW MOOR, 1 *m.* (643 alt., 271 pop.). The trade name "Low Moor" stamped on rails imported from England for use in railroad construction provided inspiration for the name. The town was one of the many Underground Railroad stations established to aid slaves on their way north.

DEWITT, 22 *m.* (710 alt., 2,041 pop.), named for DeWitt Clinton, Governor of New York in 1817–1822, was first called Vanderburg. The town was formerly the seat of Clinton County; the former county jail is now (1938) used as an ice station. The old courthouse bell hangs in the belfry of the Grace Evangelical Lutheran Church.

DeWitt is at the junction with US 61 *(see Tour 1).*

At 24 *m.* is the junction with an improved dirt road.

Left on this road to CRYSTAL LAKE, *(recreational facilities),* 2 *m.,* a small body of water.

GRAND MOUND, 28 *m.* (721 alt., 438 pop.), was so named because of a nearby glacial terminal moraine known as Sand Mound, eroded now until hardly discernible.

CALAMUS, 34 *m.* (706 alt., 374 pop.), received its name from a wild marsh plant that formerly grew in abundance around the town pump. The plant has a three-petaled flower resembling a miniature iris, and long thin blades of olive green.

WHEATLAND, 38 *m.* (671 alt., 539 pop.), was named by John L. Bennett, who platted the town in 1858, for the home of President James Buchanan near Lancaster, Pa. All the women of the village have gardens, many of them on the bank of the creek that meanders through the town. They take much pride in their phlox, petunias, Rose of Sharon trees, and other plants.

CLARENCE, 51 *m.* (825 alt., 659 pop.), named for Clarence, N. Y., was first called Onion Grove because of the formerly abundant growth of wild onions in the timber along the banks of nearby Mill Creek. The wild onion resembles an ordinary onion but has a stronger flavor and its bulb is never larger than a small marble. It grows best in the loam of the virgin prairie.

At 55 *m.* is the junction with State 38, paved.

Left on this road is TIPTON, 8 *m.* (807 alt., 2,145 pop.), the center of the "Cow War" of 1931 that developed with enforcement of a State law making it mandatory that all cattle producing milk sold for public consumption be tested for bovine tuberculosis. If an animal was found to be diseased, it was purchased from the farmer, at a price set by the State, and destroyed. Opposition to the law centered in Cedar County. Farmers for miles around came to Tipton for mass meetings, where leaders spoke against the bill, alleging that the tests were a political ruse to provide jobs for faithful retainers; many farmers and farm organizations asserted that the tests injured and even killed the cattle, that they caused cattle that did not react to the injections to abort their calves, and that they destroyed the quality of the milk. In March, 1,500 farmers marched to the State House, demanding that the legislature modify the bill.

Despite petitions and protests from delegations of farmers, State veterinarians were sent to Tipton to administer the tests. The farmers posted lookouts at the crossroads and whenever the veterinarians were sighted the lookouts hastened to call together the objectors, who hurried to the farm and prevented the making of the tests. If the veterinarians were able to make the tests, before the objectors arrived, the farmers were usually successful in preventing reading of the results. The rebellion came to a crisis when an injunction was issued by the State restraining 41 farmers from obstructing the work of the testers; veterinarians were ordered to proceed to one farm, accompanied by a force of 60 men, including the Cedar County sheriff. They were met by the farmers. When told to step aside, the farmers answered with a barrage of sticks, stones, clubs, and mud. The sheriff telegraphed Governor Turner that the situation was beyond his control and asked for aid.

On Sept. 22, 1931, Governor Turner issued a proclamation declaring Cedar County under military rule and dispatched State troops to the area. Two thousand men were encamped on the Tipton Fairgrounds. State veterinarians proceeded with the tests under military escort. Several prominent farmers were arrested; whereupon their neighbors stormed the jail and released them. Farmers arrived from other counties to add their protests but the hopelessness of resistance to troops armed with machine guns was obvious. Entire sections were blocked off by soldiers and the veterinarians systematically completed their inspections. Two of the farmer-objectors were later tried and sentenced to Anamosa Reformatory, where each served several years.

STANWOOD, 56 *m.* (531 alt., 847 pop.), was named for an official of the C. & N. W. R. R.

MECHANICSVILLE, 62 *m.* (899 alt., 781 pop.), was so named because the first four settlers of the town were mechanics.

LISBON, 69 *m.* (873 alt., 795 pop.), was colonized in the spring of 1847 by 61 people from Pennsylvania—Christian Hershey, with his sons and grandsons, and their families.

Lisbon is known throughout Iowa for its annual Sauerkraut Day, usually held in September and instituted by the first settlers. Several barrels of kraut and hundreds of pounds of frankfurters are dumped into huge vats, steamed, and served to the large crowd.

MOUNT VERNON, 70 *m.* (847 alt., 1,441 pop.), was named by Elder George Bowman, a Methodist circuit rider. It is said that in 1851 he stopped his horse on the crest of a long hill, and, inspired by the beauty of the scene, knelt to consecrate the spot to Christian education.

Soon after the founding of Mount Vernon, prohibition of the sale of intoxicating liquors became a civic cornerstone; no person could purchase a lot at any price to build a whiskey shop, and if liquor was dispensed on lots already purchased, they reverted to the estate. Timber was once purchased to build a saloon, but when townspeople declared that it would be torn down as soon as it was completed, it was not built. There have been two billiard halls in the town, but when the proprietors permitted gambling and the sale of beer, one of them was forced to leave town, and the other moved his equipment to a farm outside the city limits. Mount Vernon was settled largely by Bohemians.

CORNELL COLLEGE is the center of community life. The school was opened Nov. 14, 1853, as the Iowa Conference Male and Female Seminary, but was renamed in 1855. It had an enrollment of 490 in 1936.

The college has a CARNEGIE ART TEACHING COLLECTION, consisting of 200 volumes, 50 original wood cuts, engravings, etchings, and lithographs, 200 photographs, and color reproductions of paintings and sculpture.

Winifred Van Etten, author of *I Am The Fox,* the Atlantic Monthly prize novel for 1936, was formerly a student and instructor here. Charles R. Keyes, Cornell faculty member and State Archeologist, is responsible for much research work among the Indian mounds of Iowa.

The annual Shakespearean play, produced in March, and the annual May Music Festival, first held in 1899, are outstanding events of the school year. The Chicago Symphony Orchestra, under the direction of Dr. Frederick Stock, presented its 35th annual concert at the Music Festival in May, 1937. At festival time the campus is trim and green, and in the rear the hillside is blue with violets; blossoming apple trees drop white petals on the grass. One of the favorite spots of strolling Cornellians, and one of the first places to which the Chicago musicians go after arriving in town is the NORTON TULIP GARDEN, three blocks from the campus on a terraced slope; around the outer edges are lilacs and blossoming shrubs; slabs of stone form paths that lead to a bench beneath an apple tree at the foot of the garden. Here is a memorable view—tulips of many colors planted in clumps and in irregular groupings and a wide range of colors— pure deep purple, scarlet red-violet, lavender, rose, and pure white.

Left 4.5 *m.* from Mount Vernon on surfaced dirt road to Cedar River; L. here to PALISADES-KEPLER STATE PARK, 6.5 *m. (hotel, fishing, boating, camping, and bathing facilities).* The area has been increased from the initial 100 acres, given by a member of the pioneer Kepler family, to more than 500. A tea-room and dance-pavilion were recently constructed of native limestone and timber. Summer cottages line the banks of the Cedar River that flows between high bluffs known as the Upper and Lower Palisades. Five miles of scenic trails wind through the heavily wooded park, in which are many ancient white oak trees, as well as wild flowers, ferns, and birds.

CEDAR RAPIDS, 87 *m.* (733 alt., 56,097 pop.) *(see CEDAR RAPIDS).*

Points of Interest: Municipal Island; Quaker Oats Plant; Coe College.

Cedar Rapids is at the junction with US 151 and US 218 *(see Tour 1A)* and State 11 *(see Tour 2A).*

WHEELER CORNER, 106 *m.,* is at the junction with US 218 *(see Tour 3A).*

At 109 *m.* is the junction with State 82, graveled.

Left on this road is BLAIRSTOWN, 4 *m.* (839 alt., 488 pop.), where the Hickory Grove Debating Society was organized in the winter of 1858. Two of the questions discussed were: "Resolved that slavery is constitutional," and "Resolved that timber-stealing is morally right." Speaking in the affirmative on the second question, a well-known citizen said he had no confidence in a man who would *not* steal timber; he had improved two farms and had stolen every stick of timber he had used. When asked if he could prove it, he answered that he could—"by every man in the house."

At 115 *m.* is the junction with State 200, graveled.

Right on this road is KEYSTONE, 3 *m.* (875 alt., 499 pop.), settled by Pennsylvania Dutch whose descendants comprise the majority of the population. Keystone has retained its German atmosphere to a large extent. Although the town has no churches, it is said to be a "model of order and propriety."

BELLE PLAINE, 123 *m.* (828 alt., 3,239 pop.), was known as Gwinsville until 1862, when the post office was established. Here are a number of fine artesian wells, many of which have been in operation since the early days of settlement. Belle Plaine is a division point for the C. & N. W. R. R., and a roundhouse, with room for 30 engines, is maintained here.

In July 1894 a very destructive fire swept away nearly two blocks of buildings in the heart of town. Eighty business firms lost their stocks; property valued at half a million dollars, of which only two-fifths was insured, was destroyed.

TAMA, 141 m. (820 alt., 2,626 pop.), named in memory of the Fox Indian Chief, Taimah, was called Iuka when it was platted in 1862. The Iowa River, flowing through the southern part of the town, has a fall here of 25 feet. A power dam has been constructed, creating a great lake (swimming, fishing, boating, skating and hockey facilities).

Tama is at the junction with US 63 (see Tour 3).

The SAC AND FOX INDIAN LANDS, 144 m. (R), is a tract of about 3,300 acres on the banks of the Iowa River, where about 400 Indians make their homes. Though referred to as the Tama Reservation, it is not a reservation, since the land was not reserved to the Indians by the Government, but was purchased by them. It is held in common, with farming areas assigned to individuals for life use.

The Sac, or Sauk, and Fox, or Mesquakie, are closely allied Algonkian tribes; the ancestors of the people living here were driven into Kansas early in the 19th century but after 1845 small groups began to move back into Iowa to rejoin the few members that had remained. In 1856 the Iowa Legislature passed a law permitting them to stay, and urged the Federal Government to pay the Indians the annuities promised to them; this the Government refused to do until 1867, when the group had been joined by tribesmen from Kansas who had saved money from annuities they had received, enabling them to purchase land. In July 1857 the Indians secured a tract of 80 acres, and since then their holdings have increased to approximately 3,300 acres, including farm land and low timberland.

The Indian here is primarily a truck farmer, raising such vegetables as corn, beans, pumpkins, potatoes, and melons on small plots. A resident farmer appointed by the Government teaches modern farming methods. Some of the Indians raise beans that they sell to a canning factory in nearby Marshalltown. Others obtain cash by working as section hands on the railroads, or as laborers in neighboring towns. Some of the men are good carpenters and metal workers, and the women are skillful at beadwork. April is the season of sugar-making here. Spigots are driven into three-inch holes in the maple trees, sometimes four to a tree. With the aid of a yoke across his shoulders the Indian carries buckets of sap to the sugar wickiup where it is boiled down into syrup. These wickiups are round-domed structures, with walls of matted rushes and a potato-sacking roof. A hole in the sacking permits smoke to escape. The sugar is used in ceremonies and as a trading medium. The Indians here use about 100 pounds of maple sugar a year for ceremonial purposes.

Almost all the families have two- or three-room houses, each usually furnished with a stove, a table, one or two beds, and a couple of chairs. Many of the Indians still make wickiups for summer use. Their dress is like that of the average American though it is often very bright in color.

About 10 percent of these Indians have become United Presbyterians, but the rest continue to adhere to the religious beliefs of their ancestors. There are six clans, or religious divisions, each with its own emblems and designs, that practice ancient rituals and have secret feasts and ceremonials. According to their legend, Gitchi Manitou *(the Great Spirit)* made the earth, the sky, the sun, the moon, the trees. One day, however, he became lonesome. The earth was beautiful, but there was no one to enjoy it. So he took up a handful of yellow clay and blew his breath on it four times, bringing to life the first Sac. The Fox Indian was made of red earth.

Some marriages are still performed by tribal rites, but many are made according to State procedure because the Government often withholds annuities from those who do not conform to the State laws. The season of courtship and weddings follows the planting of the corn. The flute, used to accompany the love songs, is made of red cedar and has a range of five or six notes. In their ceremonies the Indians use a drum made of skins of wild animals stretched on a frame-work, and a gourd rattle filled with seeds.

There is no longer a chief here. Just before his death, the last chief appointed a council of five to carry on his work; it conducts the business affairs of the group, divides profits made from the powwows, makes land allotments, and arranges for the building of houses. When a member of the council resigns or dies the remaining members choose another to take his place.

A native policeman maintains order; when disputes arise between members of the tribe they are settled by the tribal council or superintendent of the reservation.

A plot of ground is set aside for ceremonies and dances. Here in the middle of August is held an annual four-day powwow *(open)* that resembles a county fair. There are agricultural exhibitions, and beadwork, baskets, and Indian jewelry are sold. Women and children appear in their brightest dresses and the men bedeck themselves with feathers and paint. During the celebration, the dance of friendship, the war dance, the green corn dance, the buffalo head dance, and the snake dance are presented.

Some of the Christian Indians belong to the peyote cult, and celebrate Easter, beginning at midnight Saturday with rites that are interrupted only for brief intervals of peyote-chewing. The peyote is a bean having a stimulating effect; it "lifts us up, shows us the truth and brings us nearer to Christ and God," the leaders explain. The users of the drug see "images of beautiful colors and forms." The chewing of peyote is prohibited in Iowa by a State law, but the Federally supervised area is exempt from the restriction. The Indians obtain their peyote from Texas. At the beginning of the Easter peyote rites a ceremonial fire is built in the center of a large tepee and the worshippers pray and chant until noon of Sunday. They then file across a mile of rough lowland, through the brush to the river, where those who desire baptism are thrown into the muddy waters.

MONTOUR, 149 *m.* (370 pop.), dates back to 1855, when the settlements of Indian Town and Oxford were combined. In the vicinity of Montour are deposits of "Iowa marble" (limestone).

LEGRAND, 155 *m.* (938 alt., 382 pop.), settled by Quakers, was named for LeGrand Byington, an Iowa City politician. Stone from the LeGrand limestone quarries has been used in the construction of a number of large Iowa buildings, including the State Historical Building at Des Moines. Fossils have been taken from these quarries by B. H. Beane, whose COLLECTION *(see by appointment)* is large. On one small slab of stone, 3 feet wide and 5 feet long, the fossilized remains of 183 starfish, 12 sea urchins, and 2 trilobites were found. The collection includes a large number of blastoids, cystoids, cephalopods, gastropods, shark spines, and shark teeth; among the crinoids (stone lilies) and starfish are some unusually well-preserved specimens.

Le Grand is at the junction with an improved dirt road known as the Lincoln Highway Cut-off.

Right on this road to a huge STONE HILL that figures in local legends as the Devil's Anvil. In early days a regular throbbing or pounding sound from the interior of the elevation gave rise to the story that an immortal blacksmith was working within, and that articles left at evening by the spring would be mended during the night and at dawn could be claimed by the owners. The pounding sound is thought to have been caused by subterranean waters. The Indian story of the hill, told by Horace Poweshiek of Tama, great grandson of the chief, Poweshiek, is that the temper of Wee-twee-ah, the Indian blacksmith spirit, was easily ruffled, and if curious visitors to the spring annoyed him he would send down a flood of water to drown them. The white man's work of "destruction" in the quarries drove Wee-twee-ah away from his smithy, never to return.

MARSHALLTOWN, 164 *m.* (883 alt., 17,373 pop.) *(see MARSHALL-TOWN).*

Points of Interest: Evangelical Deaconess Home; Iowa Soldiers' Home.

Right from Marshalltown on a graveled road to ALBION, 7 *m.* (929 alt., 436 pop.), a town platted in 1852 as Lafayette. Left from Albion 3 *m.* across the Iowa River to MORMON RIDGE, site of a Mormon encampment in the winter of 1844–45. A group known as the Emmett party started west from Nauvoo, Ill., in August 1844, under the leadership of James Emmett. Originally there were about 90 in the company; others joined along the way, which led through Iowa City, following the Iowa River valley northwest into Marshall County. They camped for the winter on a wooded hill, suffering much hardship from cold, exposure, and lack of provisions. Some died and were buried on the ridge. A few graves are still visible in an unmarked plot not far from the road. After wandering in western Iowa and South Dakota, most of the Emmett party returned to Nauvoo, later to travel west in the exodus of 1846. Other groups of Mormons are said to have crossed the county and to have stopped at Mormon Ridge, in similar circumstances of privation, during that year and the next.

STATE CENTER, 179 *m.* (1,077 alt., 1,012 pop.), was laid out by the John Blair Co. in 1865, when the railroad reached this point. The name was suggested by the geographical position of the tract in the State.

COLO, 187 *m.* (1,043 alt., 532 pop.), was the first railroad station in Story County, established when construction on the railroad was halted for the winter at this point. John Blair, a railroad official, named the town for his dog, Colo, which had been crushed near here by a construction train.

At Colo is the junction with US 65 *(see Tour 4)*.

NEVADA, 194 *m.* (1,001 alt., 3,133 pop.), seat of Story County, established in 1853, lies along the banks of West Indian Creek. Thrift, a settler, named the village for his daughter, Sierra Nevada, who had been named for the California mountain range. Much poultry is shipped from here.

On a high hill S. of town is the Iowa SANITARIUM AND HOSPITAL with 40 beds, established in 1899. It is operated under the auspices of the Seventh Day Adventists.

At 198.5 *m.* is the BILLY SUNDAY BIRTHPLACE, now the Guy Dodd farm; here the future baseball player and evangelist was born (1863) in a log cabin, now used as a smokehouse. When Billy, whose father died when he was a baby, was nine years old, he was sent to a soldiers' orphans' home where he stayed for a time, returning later to live with his grandfather near Nevada. "Pop" Anson, captain of the Chicago White Stockings, saw his unusual base running while on a local team, and in 1884, at the age of 22, Sunday became center fielder on the Chicago team. He was the first man in baseball to circle the diamond in 14 seconds, and he asserted that he invented the bunt—then an entirely new method of batting. In 1887, a street mission group caught his attention; he went to church, became converted, and four years later stopped playing baseball to become secretary of the Chicago Y. M. C. A. at $1,000 a year. He was assistant for a time to J. Wilbur Chapman, an evangelist of the 1890's. Billy's first revival meeting was conducted at Garner, Iowa. From that day Bill and "Ma," his wife, were in constant demand for revivals. At his revivals in the cities people waited for hours to get seats in frame tabernacles having pine plank seats and sawdust on the floor. "Hittin' the sawdust trail" was added to the American vernacular by these meetings. The dishpans that were passed from hand to hand, one pan for every row, sometimes brought in more than $5,000 in less than five minutes. The evangelist died from a heart attack in Chicago, Dec. 8, 1935.

AMES, 202 *m.* (926 alt., 10,261 pop.) *(see AMES)*.

Point of Interest: Iowa State College of Agriculture and Mechanic Arts.

Ames is at the junction with US 69 *(see Tour 5)*, and US 65 *(see Tour 4)*.

Section b. AMES *to* NEBRASKA LINE, *150 m.*

US 30 proceeds west from Ames, 0 *m.*

BOONE, 14 *m.* (1,138 alt., 11,886 pop.)

Swimming. McHose Park, end of S. Greene St., publicly owned.

Boone covers the crest of an expansive prairie, east and south of a scenic part of the valley of the Des Moines River. A mining, railroad, and industrial center, it is the seat of Boone County, but does not follow the pattern of many courthouse towns where the square occupies the center of the community. The city consists of the original settlement toward the west, where the courthouse stands, and a newer and formerly rival community, now grown together and identified by Division Street, once the boundary line. Building materials, paving brick, reinforced concrete pipe, machinery and iron implements, brooms and brushes, hosiery thread, and flour are manufactured here. Nearby deposits of bituminous coal, clay, and gravel support six companies. Toward evening the miners drift in from the outskirts to relax in beer halls, attend the movies, and mingle with friends among the railroad and other industrial workers.

In October 1937, Boone was cited by the Bureau of Home Economics, United States Department of Agriculture, as the traditional American Midwest town where "father makes the money in the family." A survey of 494 families showed that only nine percent had more than one breadwinner; the average family was composed of four persons; the annual income was $1,307; and slightly more than half the families rented their homes, none paying more than $40 a month.

Boone County, of which Boonesboro was the first county seat, was named and its boundaries were defined in 1847. By 1851 enough people had arrived to necessitate the building of a courthouse. The site for it was decided on, a stake was driven into the ground, and the town was laid out. The first steam mill was built in the spring of 1854 on Polecat Slough, a west branch of Honey Creek which runs through Boonesboro. In 1865 the first railroad (now part of the Chicago & North Western) was extended into the county. Holders of land here pictured an important future for the county seat town when a committee was asked to meet representatives of the Cedar Rapids and Missouri Railroad Company. The county was asked to give all of its available swamp lands and swamp land funds, and the people of Boonesboro were asked to donate 20 acres of depot grounds, right-of-way through the county, and $10,000 in money.

After the track had been laid, the railroad company expressed some dissatisfaction because the people of Boonesboro had not raised the entire sum promised. The company's representative consulted with the committee but, while awaiting its decision, he inspected a wild tract of land nearby— 1,320 acres owned by a resident of Des Moines, who was willing to sell at $15 an acre. When the committee had done nothing after three days, the representative bought the acre, then known as "Plugtown," which included only one or two shacks. Here, a mile and a half east of Boonesboro, the railroad laid out a new town. This settlement was first known as Boone Station, later as Montana, and then Boone. When the railroad was completed, in August 1865, the road was leased to the Chicago and North Western.

Considerable bitterness resulted between the inhabitants of the rival communities but Boonesboro remained the county seat until 1887, when it was annexed to the city of Boone. It is said that many of the old settlers of Boonesboro would never "set foot" in the city that had supplanted their town as an industrial center.

The ERICSON PUBLIC LIBRARY *(open weekdays 10-9)*, NW. corner 7th and Greene Sts., is named in honor of former Senator C. J. A. Ericson, donor of the original gift of $10,000 that made the building possible. The two-story structure, built in 1900 and enlarged in 1922, is Italian Renaissance in style. The stone coping, arched windows, and a small central balcony form the chief exterior decorative motifs. The library has 35,000 volumes. Carl Fritz Henning's collection of mounted birds is on display.

The CHICAGO & NORTH WESTERN RAILROAD SHOPS *(open to public)*, Delaware St. between 5th and 7th Sts., together with the division offices of the company, employ many of the city's residents.

The BOONE BIBLICAL COLLEGE, 924 W. 2nd St., and its associated institutions, including an undenominational church, radio station KFGO (1370 kc), an old people's home, a boys' and girls' home, was founded in 1891 by the Rev. J. C. Crawford, a Congregational minister. He gradually built up the institution, which comprised old houses that he renovated. There is a laundry, a bakery, a cannery, and a printing-shop. A farm of 160 acres outside the city supplies many necessities for the 250 students and workers. The old people's department was designed particularly to give a place to elderly Christians who desire to continue their religious work. The workers in the institution contribute their services.

The BOONE COAL COMPANY MINE *(open by permission)*, S. Division St. near city limits, is one of the largest mines in the county, employing 92 men. It is of the longwall type: workmen undermine coal veins and depend upon gravity to break the coal in chunks. Coal here belongs to the Cherokee stage of the Des Moines deposits.

In the Sacred Heart Cemetery, SW. city limits, is the GRAVE OF KATE SHELLEY *(see below)*.

Boone is at the junction with State 164, graveled.

Left from Boone on State 164 to LEDGES STATE PARK *(camping and picnicking facilities)*, 4 *m.*, a picturesque area of 684 acres bordering the Des Moines River. Huge ledges rising above Pease Creek, which flows through the park, have given the site its name. Growths of reindeer lichen cover these ledges, and wild flowers bloom profusely along the hillsides and in the wooded ravines. The area is one of the best birding spots in the State; here also live coyotes, foxes, raccoons, a herd of deer, and numerous other native animals. A small Zoo and an OUTDOOR MUSEUM exhibit local flora, fauna, and geological specimens. Here and there hiking trails cross the creek on rustic bridges.

At 16 *m.* the highway crosses the Des Moines River; on the west bank is the junction with a dirt road.

Left on this road to COAL VALLEY, 2 *m.*, and the junction with a dirt road, 2.5 *m.;* L. here to the small village of MOINGONA, 3 *m.*, birthplace of Kate Shelley (1866–1912); nearby is the KATE SHELLEY RAILROAD BRIDGE, spanning the Des Moines River. On the night of July 6, 1881, a storm washed out the bridge over Honey Creek after an engine carrying a section crew had plunged into the swollen stream. Kate Shelley, then only 15 years old, crawled across the river bridge on her hands and knees to warn the Moingona station operator. He flagged the midnight express from the west, saving many persons from a disastrous wreck. Kate Shelley became a heroine. A Chicago newspaper raised a fund to clear the mortgage on the home of her family and Frances Willard, the temperance leader, arranged to send the girl to college. Kate Shelley was station agent at the time of her death in 1912. The present bridge, named for her, was built in 1901.

OGDEN, 22 *m.* (1,100 alt., 1,429 pop.), was named for the capitalist, W. B. Ogden. In the privately owned SICKLER MUSEUM *(adm. on re-*

OPEN CORN CRIBS

quest), assembled by Dr. Daniel Sickler (1850–1936), is a large collection of Indian relics, some of them prehistoric, including pendants, rings, spears, pipes, arrowheads, stone axes, and several ceremonial stones carved to represent birds and butterflies.

Ogden is at the junction with US 169 *(see Tour 6).*

GRAND JUNCTION, 32 *m.* (1,041 alt., 1,025 pop.), was so named because of the junction here of the C. & N. W. and M. & St. L. R. R. In 1870 a local newspaper, the *Headlight,* was responsible for bringing many immigrants here to settle.

The landscape along the main route in this area has little variation, but that along most of the narrow side roads belongs to a different world. Such roads are often slightly bumpy; dust swirls behind the car. Chickens, ducks, geese, sometimes pigs, wander along the roadside, or scuttle out of the way ahead of the car; trees are not cut away as they are along the highway, and cast a pattern of shade offering relief on hot summer days. Nearly every farmyard has a windmill, often vine-covered, and travelers, stopping perhaps to ask for a drink, find hospitality and friendliness. Along these country roads corn is the major crop. In early spring hundreds of acres of plowed land, furrow-striped, stretch far into the distance. Planting season follows. After the first week in July most of the corn is "laid by." When corn is in the milk stage, it is called "roasting ears"; many bushels are canned for winter use; sometimes it is dried instead of canned. In the fall is the husking season. In some parts of the country mechanical cornpickers have been introduced, but the old hand-picking method is still generally used. Before dawn farmers start for the fields, and soon the rhythmic tattoo of corn on the bangboards is heard.

JEFFERSON, 40 *m.* (1,057 alt., 3,431 pop.), seat of Greene County and a market town, was established after a group of settlers came to Des Moines about 1854 and borrowed $200 to purchase the town site. Named in honor of President Thomas Jefferson, it was at first called New Jefferson. Near here there was formerly a large lake, 7 or 8 miles long, called Goose Lake. It was used for fishing, skating, and boating. West of Goose Lake was another lake covering about 20 acres, and beyond a hill nearby, a third lake, a mile long and half a mile wide. All of these have dried up or have been drained.

COUNCIL OAK, possibly more than 100 years old, now stands on the lawn of L. R. Wilcox's home, 702 S. Chestnut St.; it is so called because Indians and whites met here to hold council before the town was platted. It was then the only tree in the vicinity.

There is a municipal SWIMMING POOL at 716 S. Maple St.

SCRANTON, 50 *m.* (1,177 alt., 1,058 pop.). Elk and deer were found in great abundance near here in the early days. The snows of the winter of 1855–56 were so deep that it was impossible for them to escape from men and dogs, and there was wholesale slaughter. Since that time very few deer have been seen in the county. According to an early historian, "their rapid and sudden disappearance astonished everyone."

Scranton is a market town for farmers of the neighborhood who usually come to town on Saturday night, as well as on Wednesday, when there is an evening band concert. There are public TENNIS COURTS *(free)*, lighted at night.

RALSTON, 56 *m.* (1,123 alt., 184 pop.), on the C. & N. W. R. R. was known for many years as Slater Siding. In 1891 when a station was built, the name was changed to honor an officer of the American Express Company.

At GLIDDEN, 61 *m.* (1,226 alt., 854 pop.), in WESTLAWN CEMETERY is the MERLE HAY MONUMENT, of Carolina granite, erected to the memory of the first Iowan to fall in the World War.

SWAN LAKE STATE PRESERVE *(swimming, fishing and picnicking facilities)*, 66 *m.* (L), is a 250-acre park and wild-game refuge, bordering a small artificial lake. Numerous human skulls have been found nearby, probably relics of an Indian battle.

CARROLL, 68 *m.* (1,261 alt., 4,691 pop.), seat of Carroll County, on the banks of the Middle Raccoon River, was named for Charles Carroll, one of the signers of the Declaration of Independence. In the PUBLIC

LIBRARY are a Bible printed in 1665, and the *Works of Josephus* printed in 1556, in Germany.

ST. ANGELA'S ACADEMY, a Catholic high school for girls, is surrounded by high brick walls. At a corner of the campus is the GROTTO OF THE IMMACULATE CONCEPTION, an ornate stone structure built by Father Paul M. Dobberstein *(see Tour 11)*. Stones for the grotto were gathered in many parts of the world. A statue of Carrara marble in the grotto stands against a background of rose-colored quartzite brought from the Black Hills of South Dakota.

The Florencourt House, now the SACRED HEART CONVENT, on the corner of East and Bluff Sts., has high windows and doors and spacious porches with stone pillars; it is surrounded by fine old trees and gardens.

ST. ANTHONY'S HOSPITAL, containing 108 beds, 22 bassinets, is owned and operated by the Franciscan Sisters of LaCrosse, Wis. The first floor contains the chapel, with handmade tiles and a grillwork of brass. Mosaics are laid about the altar. The hospital corporation owns 80 acres of land, including a large orchard and a 20-acre garden.

On the eastern side of town is the $30,000 AMERICAN LEGION SWIMMING POOL *(open)*, constructed in 1932.

The Heider Manufacturing Co. at Carroll produces farm machinery, specializing in the evener, or equalizer, a device used with horse-drawn plows, listers, cultivators, and harrows.

WESTSIDE, 80 *m.* (1,326 alt., 341 pop.), was so named by railroad officials because the town lies west of a long, steep incline in the roadbed. At first the settlement was principally a community of railroad workers, most of whom were veterans of the Civil War. At that time the railroad bought land on both sides of the route to prevent settlement, because of its plan to promote the town of Vail.

VAIL, 86 *m.* (1,260 alt., 622 pop.), had its beginning when a section gang of the C. & N. W. R. R. camped here. The name, that of a railroad official, was selected by Thomas Ryan from Tipperary, Ireland. Vail and its neighborhood has a large Irish population.

In this area there are many signs of Indian occupancy prior to the advent of white settlers. North of town many spearheads and fragments of Indian pottery have been found on the site of an Indian village. The horns and bones of elk and buffalo have been found in Flee Grove on Deer Creek, a spot known to have been a popular hunting ground of western Iowa tribes. An Indian trail formerly ran through the town site.

DENISON, 95 *m.* (1,170 alt., 3,905 pop.), seat of Crawford County, was named for its founder, J. W. Denison, a Baptist minister who came here in 1855 as an agent of the Providence Western Land Co.

In the latter part of the 19th century the Denison *Bulletin* wrote: "The Denison Electric Light Co. turned on steam Monday for the first time, and at eight o'clock the streets were brilliantly lighted. It was a novel sight for many of the young people who had never seen anything like it, and it encouraged the older ones to a new faith in Denison and her future. The lamps burned very steadily and the light afforded was ample to enable pedestrians to find their way home without difficulty unless the jag was already too big." Later the paper commented: "Engineer Rissler of the power station of the electric light company has perfected a steam whistle beside which the proverbial 'Fog Horn' isn't a circumstance. Its bellowing can be heard easily to Vail and beyond and is enough to strike terror to the wicked. You don't have to listen for it; it impresses itself on you with all the weight of a green cucumber nightmare, and is enough to make the glass in the windows of the Rookery Building in Chicago rattle like castanets. Friend Rissler is a genius."

Governor Clyde Herring declared martial law in Crawford County Apr. 28, 1933, after 800 farmers had rioted during a foreclosure sale at the John Shields farm near Denison. Several deputy sheriffs were injured. Next day the sale was concluded under military guard, but adjustments were made in favor of Shields. There were 64 arrests, but no persons were convicted in the ensuing investigation.

In WASHINGTON PARK is a log cabin containing many relics of pioneer days, including a land grant bearing the signature of Abraham Lincoln, dated Mar. 3, 1855. The cabin was built by Sandlandes Bell in 1857, one mile and a half north of Dow City. It was moved to this place in 1926.

The FERGUSON BUILDING, near the courthouse, has a white terra-cotta façade and a red tile roof.

On Broadway St., not far from the courthouse square on a grassy knoll, is a granite block marking the SITE OF FORT PURDY, built by the settlers at the time of the Indian scare in May 1856 *(see Tour 8)*. It is possible that this "fort" was merely the solidly built home of John Purdy, strengthened to withstand possible attack.

In OAKLAND CEMETERY is the large SHAW MAUSOLEUM. Leslie M. Shaw (1848–1932) was Governor of Iowa (1898–1902) and Secretary of the Treasury (1902–1907) under Theodore Roosevelt.

Denison was the home of Clarence Chamberlain (1893–   ), trans-Atlantic aviator.

Denison is at the junction with US 59 *(see Tour 8)* and with State 141, paved.

Right from Denison on State 141 which is united with US 59 *(see Tour 8)* for 3 miles. CHARTER OAK, 14 *m.* (1,232 alt., 688 pop.), named for the Charter Oak of Connecticut. UTE, 20 *m.* (1,205 alt., 616 pop.), by Soldier River, was named for a branch of the Shoshone Indian tribe. MAPLETON, 31 *m.* (1,113 alt., 1,622 pop.), was named by the town's first settler, William H. Wilsey, because of a grove of soft maple trees along the nearby Maple River. SMITHLAND, 40 *m.* (1,090 alt., 389 pop.), first known as White's Settlement, was the scene of a conflict between a group of white men and the followers of the renegade, Inkpadutah, immediately prior to the Spirit Lake Massacre *(see Tour 7)*.

ARION, 102 *m.* (1,140 alt., 269 pop.), was named by N. Richards, a hotel proprietor. It has been almost abandoned since fire destroyed the business section in 1909.

DOW CITY, 104 *m.* (1,142 alt., 588 pop.), near the site of an old Indian village, was named for S. E. Dow, an early settler.

DUNLAP, 112 *m.* (1,097 alt., 1,522 pop.), was named for George L. Dunlap, a railroad official; the site attracted settlers because the view was unobstructed for 10 miles up and down the valley of the Boyer River. The second building erected in the town was a saloon called The Respectable Place. The former OPERA HOUSE, where many well-known actors appeared, was known throughout the State; it is now a garage.

WOODBINE, 122 *m.* (1,058 alt., 1,348 pop.), was named by Mrs. Ann Butler, an Englishwoman, around whose home woodbine grew in profusion. The town lies on a level plain around a huge earth mound covering an area of about four blocks and sloping symmetrically; whether it was built by Indians or is a natural formation has not been determined. On the mound is the city water tower.

In 1887 the WOODBINE NORMAL SCHOOL, with seven departments, was established; it occupies a large brick building.

Near Woodbine are three large apple orchards that produce 2,000 bushels of apples a year, chiefly Jonathan, red and golden Delicious, and Grimes Golden.

LOGAN, 131 *m.* (1,033 alt., 1,654 pop.), was formerly known as Boyer Falls because of its proximity to the falls on the river. The name was changed in 1864 to honor Gen. John A. Logan, an officer in the Civil War. Henry Reel, one of the first settlers, who came here from Indiana, built a dam and a sawmill without the aid of any tools except an axe and a jackknife. The machinery was fashioned from hardwood and most of the gear-wheels were hand-hewn. The mill was later burned and the dam dynamited.

MILLMAN PARK has a playground, a picnic area, tennis courts, and bathing pool.

At 145 *m.* is the junction with State 300, graveled.

Right on State 300 is CALIFORNIA, 1 *m.* (76 pop.), first named Yazoo, for the Yazoo boat-landing on the Missouri River a few miles distant. The name was changed by John I. Blair, who expected that passengers going and coming from California would change cars at the railroad junction at this station.

MISSOURI VALLEY, 139 *m.* (1,006 alt., 4,230 pop.) *(see Tour 9)*, is at the junction with US 75 *(see Tour 9)*.

At 150 *m.* US 30 crosses the Missouri River, the Iowa-Nebraska Line, on the ABRAHAM LINCOLN MEMORIAL BRIDGE *(car and driver, 50¢; passengers, 5¢ each)*, 26 miles E. of Fremont, Nebr.

Tour 14

(Chicago, Ill.)—Davenport—Iowa City—Des Moines—Council Bluffs—(Omaha, Nebr.); US 6.
Illinois Line to Nebraska Line, 314 m.

Route paralleled throughout by the C. R. I. & P. R. R., and between Colfax and Des Moines, by the D. M. & C. I. El. R. R.
Interstate Transit Bus Lines and Burlington Bus Lines follow the highway throughout.
Roadbed is paved throughout.
Accommodations of all kinds available at short intervals.

US 6 bears the heaviest traffic of any highway in Iowa, being used by transcontinental busses and trucks as well as private cars. In the early days of automobile travel, the highway between Davenport and Des Moines was part of a cross-State route known as the River to River Road; between Des Moines and Council Bluffs it was called The Great White Way.

Section a. ILLINOIS LINE *to* DES MOINES, 177 m.

US 6 crosses the Mississippi River, the Illinois-Iowa Line, on the Iowa-Illinois Memorial Bridge *(car and passengers 15¢)* 181 miles W. of Chicago, Ill. This suspension bridge is 5,552 feet long and cost $1,450,000. The toll charge is the lowest on any bridge over the Mississippi River between Minneapolis and New Orleans.

BETTENDORF, 1 *m.* (575 alt., 2,768 pop.), an industrial suburb of Davenport, was a little group of market gardeners' shacks known as Gilbert Town, until 1902, when the Bettendorf Co., manufacturing railroad equipment, moved its plant here. The town was renamed to honor the company's president, W. P. Bettendorf (1857–1910). Most of the town's inhabitants work in factories; these have a wide variety of products, among them bread slicers, automatic oil burners, grain shockers, steel, oxygen gas, and vinegar. The district in which a small number of Mexicans live is known as the "Holy City" a name given it by a former city marshal.

An Artesian Well here, 2,122 feet deep, has a flow of 500 gallons a minute.

Bettendorf is at the junction with US 67 *(see Tour 2)*.

DAVENPORT, 3 *m.* (559 alt., 60,751 pop.) *(see DAVENPORT)*.

Points of Interest: the Palmer School of Chiropractic; Antoine LeClaire Park; Credit Island; St. Ambrose College; Iowa Soldiers' Orphans' Home.

Davenport is at the junction with US 61 *(see Tour 1)* and US 67 *(see Tour 2)*.

The Old Pike skirts the western banks of the Mississippi between the northern and southern boundaries of the State and crosses this route at the site of the present city of Davenport. The first railroad in the State, built in 1855, was the Mississippi and Missouri, which ran between Davenport and Iowa City; US 6 follows its route. Between Des Moines and Council Bluffs this highway is roughly parallel to the route followed by the Des Moines Valley railroad, which was completed about 1867.

At 13 *m.* is the junction with State 228, paved.

Left on this road is WALCOTT, 1 *m.* (730 alt., 398 pop.), a German village, without either a church or a crime record until 1936, when the post office was robbed of $200 in stamps. Before that time the most serious infraction of law in the town limits had been occasional reckless driving. The community has changed little since it was established in 1853.

One block from the town's only bank is THE CASTLE, a two-story structure whose designer attempted to copy an old Norman stronghold. A grayish metal imitation of stone covers the frame building, and a slender tower rises from one corner; beneath the tower is a basement dungeon, once the subject of much speculation in Walcott. The first floor is now a beer parlor, and the second floor rooms are used for club meetings, but when the house was erected in 1905 by Dr. Henry Schumacher, the upper story was his home, and the lower, the village pharmacy. The doctor and his castle are still subjects of local gossip. In the dungeon the doctor had placed two long poles impaling skeletons made of plaster of paris and outlined with phosphorescent paint to awe visitors. Schumacher was an amateur astronomer, and near the castle he erected an observatory in which he placed a fine telescope. The observatory and castle represented an outlay of thousands of dollars, which the neighbors considered an incredibly foolish expenditure. When the doctor died in 1934 some of the contents of the castle were claimed by heirs, but most were sold at public auction. Rare guns, swords used in wars in various countries, rare coins, Confederate currency, spinning wheels, and other relics were found in the rooms. A collection of old newspapers disappeared in a huge bonfire.

Today the air of mystery that long hung about the place is somewhat dispelled by the chatter of bridge-playing women in the upper rooms, and the sounds of masculine talk and of clinking glasses in the beer parlor below.

STOCKTON, 17 m. (720 alt., 110 pop.), was named Fulton in 1855, but later, when a shipment of goods went by mistake to another Iowa town of that name, the name was changed.

DURANT, 20 m. (717 alt., 733 pop.), was named for Thomas C. Durant, a member of the board of directors of the Mississippi and Missouri R.R. and president of the Union Pacific. Two Davenport bankers, Cook and Sargent, who owned large amounts of railroad stock, planned to make the town an important commercial point on the branch line from Muscatine, but serious quarrels between the officials of Durant and of Wilton Junction, the rival village on the line, had unfavorable results for Durant, which was soon outgrown by its rival.

WILTON JUNCTION, 26 m. (683 alt., 1,104 pop.), was ignored by the railroad as a result of conflict with Cook and Sargent. Upon orders from the stockholders the brakemen were forbidden to call "Wilton" when the train reached the town, and for a long time they referred to Wilton as "Muscatine Junction."

A conflict had arisen at the time of the naming of the village, when one group of early settlers insisted that it be named Cedar Junction and another desired that it be given some Indian name. Franklin Butterfield suggested the name of Wilton, that of his native town in Maine, but it was agreed that he should present six names, one of which would be chosen. Wilton and Glendale were among the six, and the latter was decided on at that time. For almost a year the town was known as Glendale, but before the plat was recorded, the present name was selected. The town is a typical railroad junction, with hotels and eating establishments grouped around the station and roundhouse. It is also a small farm trade center, with a creamery that specializes in making cheese.

ATALISSA, 36 m. (658 alt., 187 pop.), stands on what was in 1847 an 80-acre farm owned by William Lundy, who named the village in honor of an Indian woman. A free lot was given to Atalissa Davis, the first white girl born in the town.

WEST LIBERTY, 41 *m.* (673 alt., 1,679 pop.), the trade center of a purebred-stock region, lies near Wapsinonoc (Ind., *smooth surfaced*) Creek, and was first called the Wapsinonoc Settlement. Joseph Smith, the Mormon leader, in 1836 considered this place for the site of the Mormon colony.

West Liberty is supplied with water from an 1,800-foot well. There are many dairy farms in the vicinity, and the Iowa Condensed Milk Co. here has an annual business of about $60,000. The West Liberty MUNICIPAL SWIMMING POOL attracts many people from surrounding towns.

At 41.8 *m.*, on the outskirts of West Liberty, is a junction with a graded road.

Right on this road to the junction with State 1, 7 *m.*

1. Right about 1.5 *m.* on this graveled route to the junction with a dirt road; L. on this route 1.3 *m.* to the WILLIAM MAXON HOUSE, a crumbling stone structure that was at one time a station on the Underground Railroad. Here in 1857–1858 John Brown trained 11 men for the raid on Harpers Ferry, Va.

On State 1 at 3 *m.* is ROCHESTER, where according to firm local belief, Sarah Bernhardt (1845–1923), the actress, was born. According to the story, she was born Sarah King. Her mother died when she was 5, and she ran away from her stepmother's home, joined a troupe of traveling players in Muscatine, Iowa, and later entered a French convent in St. Paul, Minn. Eventually she went to Paris, France, and made theater history. Local legend says that in 1905 a heavily veiled, richly dressed woman, carrying a long, ribbon-bound, pasteboard box, alighted from a train at West Branch (*see below*), the nearest station to Rochester. She hired a livery rig and driver from a local stable and was driven to the Rochester cemetery gate. Her driver returned in a half hour, as she had requested, and drove her back to the station. Curiosity prompted him to return to the cemetery where he found a huge bouquet of roses on the grave of Mrs. King. According to the story, Madame Bernhardt, on a tour of the United States, had appeared at an Iowa City theater the previous night. However, there is no record of such an appearance.

2. Left on State 1 1 *m.* is SPRINGDALE (1,117 alt.), a Quaker settlement where the Conservative Friends' Yearly Meeting is held. Into this quiet village in 1856 rode John Brown, a fervid-eyed man astride a tired mule. "Welcome, Friend," he was greeted according to Quaker custom. The Negro slaves in his company, with scars on their backs from the whippings they had received during servitude, were exhibited. There was a strong antislavery sentiment among the Quakers and they felt justified in aiding the slaves to escape and in offering hospitality to John Brown. Brown went on to Chicago, but his personality and hatred of slavery left a deep impression on the Friends here. In spite of their strict belief in non-violence, after Brown's departure they gathered in the small white meeting house and prayed for his success. The first protest by any religious society against slavery had been made in 1688 at the Friends' Yearly Meeting at Philadelphia; by 1800 most of the Friends had freed their own slaves.

The last time Brown entered Springdale was in the winter of 1858, after he had taken a dozen slaves from their owners in a raid and escaped with them through Nebraska. Here the Negroes were cared for before being sent on to Canada.

WEST BRANCH, 4 *m.* (718 alt., 652 pop.), a small farming center bordering the north bank of the Wapsinonoc Creek, is the birthplace of Herbert Hoover (1874–   ), President of the United States (1929–1933). On the west side of Downey St., is the HOOVER BIRTHPLACE (*open*); by it is a small boulder bearing a bronze plaque. The structure formerly contained only two rooms, but in recent years a second story and attic have been added; it was purchased in 1935 by Allan Hoover, son of the former President, and in June 1937, plans for its preservation were formulated by Herbert Hoover, who came here for the purpose.

BIRTHPLACE OF HERBERT HOOVER, WEST BRANCH

IOWA CITY, 58 *m.* (685 alt., 15,340 pop.) *(see IOWA CITY)*.

Points of Interest: State University; Old Capitol.

Iowa City is at the junction with US 218 *(see Tour 1A)*.

CORALVILLE, 61 *m.* (663 alt., 254 pop.), a suburb of Iowa City, was named in 1866 when excavators, employed on water works, found formations of coral that have since interested scientists.

At 61.7 *m.* (L) is a marker pointing to the site of a CAMP OF THE 1856 MORMON HAND-CART EXPEDITION. Here 1,300 European converts to Mormonism, who had come by train to Iowa City *(see IOWA CITY)*, camped while they constructed hand carts and prepared for the trip overland to Salt Lake City.

At 62.5 *m.* is the junction with State 153, graveled.

Right on this road, at OAKDALE, 1.5 *m.* (782 alt.), is the STATE SANATORIUM FOR THE TREATMENT OF TUBERCULOSIS *(visiting hours, 11 a.m.-1 p.m. and 4-7 p.m.)* containing 480 beds (1937). The sanatorium has its own dairy barns, greenhouse, water works, electric light plant, and talking-picture equipment.

TIFFIN, 66 *m.* (687 alt., 206 pop.), on the banks of Clear Creek, was once part of the farm of Rolla Johnson, who named the place for his former home town, Tiffin, Ohio. At the time of Tiffin's settlement, furniture, even of the most common kind, was very rare west of the Mississippi. The settlers brought with them, in their lumbering, creaking oxcarts, only the barest necessities; tables were made of boards attached to the cabin walls by leather hinges, and were lowered against the wall when not in use, to make more room; three-legged stools and rough benches made of slabs served as seats; bedsteads were bunks with strips of leather for springs; mattresses were small boughs of trees. The furniture shortage was not relieved until William Spicer and Howard Sprague bought a turning lathe for the community.

HOMESTEAD, 79 *m.* (864 alt.) *(see Tour 14A)*, one of the Amana villages, is at the junction with State 149 *(see Tour 14A)*.

LOWER SOUTH AMANA, 84 *m.* (882 alt.) *(see Tour 14A)*, another of the Amana villages, is at the junction with State 220 *(see Tour 14A)*.

MARENGO, 90 *m.* (738 alt., 2,112 pop.), on a level plain along the Iowa River, was named for the plain of Marengo, near Alessandria, Italy, where the Austrians were defeated by Napoleon in June 1800. Mineral wells supply the town with excellent water. Clarence Eugene Whitehill, former Metropolitan Opera baritone, was born here in Nov. 1871.

VICTOR, 103 *m.* (805 alt., 794 pop.), a farming and dairying community, was called Greenville when it was settled by groups of immigrants from Ireland, Belgium, and Germany.

BROOKLYN, 111 *m.* (848 alt., 1,345 pop.). On display at the OFFICES OF THE BROOKLYN CHRONICLE, where a weekly newspaper is published, is a collection of old newspapers and documents, including a number of mortgages drawn up on sheets of sheepskin.

At 116 *m.* is the junction with US 63 *(see Tour 3)*.

GRINNELL, 126 *m.* (1,023 alt., 4,949 pop.). In 1853, when Josiah Bushnell Grinnell, a Congregational minister in New York City, went to Horace Greeley for advice, Greeley made his much-quoted statement: "Go West, young man, go West and grow up with the country!" In March 1854, Grinnell, accompanied by Dr. Thomas Holyoke of Scarsport, Me., and the Rev. Homer Hamlin of Hudson, Ohio, came West and founded the settlement that became Grinnell, on the barren treeless prairie between the Iowa and Skunk Rivers. Two important reservations were made —land was to be set aside for a college campus, and no liquor could be sold in the town. The original deeds to town lots carried the liquor clause, and the provision that the lots reverted to the Grinnell estate on any breach of the contract.

GRINNELL COLLEGE, a four-year liberal arts college, was founded here in December 1855. The college is the dominant factor in the life of the town, and is especially noted for its department of music. It is privately endowed, non-sectarian, and coeducational; among its alumni are Dr. Albert Shaw (1857–   ); Major General C. McK. Saltzman (1871–   ); James Norman Hall (1887–   ), co-author of *Mutiny on the Bounty;* Ruth Suckow (1892–   ), author of *The Folks* and other Iowa stories; Gardner Cowles (1861–   ), publisher of the Des Moines *Register* and allied papers; Harry Hopkins (1890–   ), Works Progress Administration Administrator; Hallie Flanagan (1890–   ), Director of the Federal Theater Project of W. P. A.; and the screen actor, Gary Cooper (1901–   ).

In 1859 Iowa College of Davenport was merged with the Grinnell school; in 1882 the college and part of the town were destroyed by a cyclone, but the college was completely rebuilt through gifts, mostly from people living in the East. The average enrollment for 1935-36-37 was 800.

On the campus of 63 acres grow large numbers of trees, both native and foreign to the State. The college has a SWIMMING POOL *(open to the public in summer)* and other recreational facilities.

There are three public parks—CENTRAL, BAILEY, and MOYLE.

At 1019 Broad St. a bronze tablet on a large boulder marks the SITE OF THE LONG HOME, a rude log structure built by Grinnell and his companions. Grinnell was an ardent abolitionist who assisted in the maintenance of the Underground Railroad, and several times, with Jesse Bowen and William Penn Clarke, he aided John Brown.

Billy Robinson, the "Bird Man," one of the aviators who pioneered in non-stop flights, formerly lived in Grinnell; he was killed while making an altitude flight in March, 1916.

At 137 *m.* is a junction with State 224, graveled.

Right on this road is KELLOGG, 1 *m.* (844 alt., 580 pop.), on the bank of the North Skunk River, a busy community that relies for income chiefly on the MIDWEST METAL STAMPING FACTORY. At the base of the hills near the town, along the North Skunk River valley is the site of a large Indian village. The ground is strewn with flint flakes. At a high point near the old river channel are two elliptical earth mounds about 50 feet long. A number of years ago a trench was sunk in one mound, passing through successive strata of charcoal down to the normal level of the hill. The theory was advanced that the mound had been built up as one floor of a long Indian dwelling.

NEWTON, 145 *m.* (944 alt., 11,560 pop.).

Swimming. Fred Maytag Park, entrance end W. 3rd St. S., June 1 to Sept. 7; Y. M. C. A., corner N. 3rd Ave. and E. 2nd St. N.
Band Concerts. Fred Maytag Park, Wed. during summer.

Newton is the seat of Jasper County. This growing city typifies the development of manufacturing—beginning early in the 20th century—in a State traditionally and preeminently agricultural. Not far from cornfields and red barns, smokestacks of factories rise above the trees and housetops of the city. The square is dominated by a three-story courthouse and faced on all sides by business buildings. Hundreds of factory workers, going to and from work, morning and evening, and the brisk crowds of farmers milling around the square illustrate the city's dual character. The majority of the structures here, built near the end of the 19th century, belong to the city's early period of development.

The first known settlers in the territory that is now Jasper County were Adam Tool, William Highland, John Frost, and John Vance, who came from Jefferson County in 1846. A commission named by the legislature selected a site for the courthouse, placing a pole to mark the place. The city, incorporated in 1857, was named for a Revolutionary soldier, Sergeant Newton, who served under General Marion with Sergeant Jasper, for whom the county was named.

In the 1860's the Mississippi and Missouri Railroad, predecessor of the Rock Island, came into the county, bringing tools and products from the East in quantities. Two of the most flourishing businesses in the early days were the milling of lumber and the manufacture of farm implements. By the 1880's all the land in the county worth farming was in use, but in the next decade the rural population decreased.

The washing machine industry began here in 1898 when a local incubator firm undertook the manufacture of ratchet-slat washers, which were loaded on a one-horse spring wagon and sold in the countryside for $5.00 each. Fred H. Bergman, owner of the company, secured patent rights on the manufacture of a hand-power washer in 1904, and undertook its manufacture. Although discouraged by his associates, who believed it would be difficult to sell washers at $10 each, Bergman persisted and formed the One Minute Manufacturing Co.

F. L. Maytag, who became the "Washing Machine King," had a quarter interest in the Parsons Band Cutter and Self-Feeder Co.; the manufacture of washing machines was a sideline. In 1907 Maytag introduced a hand-power washer designed by Howard Snyder, inventor and demonstrator for the self-feeder company. Snyder added the electric motor in 1911. The next major Maytag improvement was the cabinet type of cylinder washer, employing the principle of the mill race, developed by Snyder in 1917. Snyder's most successful invention, the gyrafoam washer, was placed on the market in 1922.

By 1925 Newton's industrial boom had begun in earnest; production could not keep up with the demand for washers. Workers poured into the city, rents and real estate skyrocketed, living costs mounted higher and higher. From 1925 to 1929 three million dollars were spent in building homes, most of them cottages.

Many civic improvements have been promoted by the Maytag family. These include a hotel, a golf course, and a park. F. L. Maytag's philanthropies embraced gifts of money for the construction of two churches, a hospital, and the Young Men's Christian Association and the Salvation Army buildings. Shortly after F. L. Maytag's death, in March 1937, the washing machine industry employees, previously unorganized, formed union affiliations. Workers in the three largest washing machine companies united with the unions.

The JASPER COUNTY COURTHOUSE, Courthouse Sq., a massive three-story building, its solidity accentuated by horizontal mass lines of Bedford stone spaced with brick, was erected in 1909-11. The building is of neoclassic design with modified Georgian Colonial detail. It is topped by a tall graceful clock tower, rising above the low dome. On the walls of the interior are four murals, executed by Edgar Cameron of Chicago and depicting incidents in the history of the county.

The PUBLIC LIBRARY *(open weekdays, 10-8 in winter; 8-6 in summer)*, 400 1st Ave. W., a two-story, rectangular building of buff-colored brick, with a Colonial fan doorway, was erected in 1902. A room on the second floor contains the JASPER COUNTY HISTORICAL SOCIETY COLLECTION of pictures, records, and relics of the Grand Army of the Republic; and the complete file of the Newton *Journal* from 1877 to 1912. In addition the collection contains a group of fossils, shells, and ores—all from coal mines in the county.

The EMERSON HOUGH HOUSE *(private)*, 423 E. 7th St. N., a frame structure built in 1855 and recently stuccoed, was the birthplace of the novelist in 1857. Emerson Hough attended the Newton public schools, and the University of Iowa, from which he was graduated. Two of his more popular novels are *The Covered Wagon* and *The Mississippi Bubble.*

The GULIELMA ZOLLINGER HOUSE *(private)*, 724 E. 4th St. N., a small frame house in good condition, was the home of a woman who wrote juvenile fiction but disliked children. Miss Zollinger's best known book is *The Widow O'Callaghan's Boys* (1898).

The MAYTAG FACTORY *(guide, tours 9:30 and 1:30, weekdays)* is at 512 N. 4th Ave. W. The processes of making square cast-aluminum tubs, the grey-iron foundry, and the timed conveyor systems are of special interest. The company has one of the largest aluminum molding foundries in the world. The factory, and a recent office building of striking modern design, have more than 13 acres of floor space.

The AUTOMATIC WASHER PLANT *(tours by permission, guides)*, N. 4th Ave. W. between W. 3rd and W. 4th Sts. N., belongs to a company that asserts it was the first (1907) to manufacture electric washing machines selling for less than $100, to make light-weight all-metal machines, to use a radio network in advertising, and to advertise by airplane.

The ONE MINUTE MANUFACTURING PLANT *(tours by permission, guides)*, 401 W. 4th St. N., was the first to make washing machines here.

FRED MAYTAG PARK *(swimming charge only)*, formerly the Jasper County Fairgrounds, covers 40 acres beautifully landscaped and enclosed by an ornamental fence. It was formally opened Sept. 8, 1935, when a $65,000 swimming pool and bathhouse were dedicated. A LOG HOUSE, one of the first in Palo Alto Township, built by Thomas Reese in 1848, was moved to the park in 1936, where it was repaired and restored for use as a picnic shelter.

Right from Newton on a graveled road, 1.5 *m.* to the MAYTAG DAIRY FARM *(free guides)*, with its group of gleaming white houses and barns with green roofs. The herd's average daily yield (1936) of milk was about 225 gallons. Two of the cows of the herd have produced more than 30,000 pounds of milk in a year; five of the cows have had records of more than 1,000 pounds of butterfat a year. In the farm's barns are many modern devices: individual watering cups, concrete feeding troughs, ventilators with electric fans to force fresh air into the building, thermostatically controlled ceiling fans for box stalls which are constructed of gas pipe; there are screens, windows, awnings, and cork floors. An elevator lowers feed from the mows, carriers transporting it from the elevator and silage from the silos to the feed troughs; litter carriers make the cleaning of concrete gutters easy, manure being carried to a storage shed or dumped directly on wagons for transportation to the fields; all buildings are electrically lighted and equipped with automatic fire extinguishers. Signs give the date of birth, names of sire and dam, and the production and show records of each cow. Maytag cattle are exhibited at State fairs, the Dairy Cattle Congress, the National Dairy Show, and elsewhere, and in three years they have won 5 All-American awards out of a possible 15; in 1936 the record was 5 All-American and 1 Reserve All-American awards. Cattle from the farm have been shipped to Japan, China, Mexico, Canada, and South

America. All the male calves are sold for breeding purposes. The average number of cattle in the herd is 160. Seven employees, besides the manager, do the work on the 360-acre farm.

At 147 *m.* (L), on a wooded knoll, is WESTWOOD PARK *(playground equipment, picnicking facilities).* Nearby are the 9-hole NEWTON MUNICIPAL GOLF COURSE *(50¢ weekdays; 75¢ Sun. and holidays)* and two TENNIS COURTS *(free).*

Between Newton and Colfax the rolling terrain levels out along the South Skunk River. Terraces—some three miles wide—border it, forming the bottom-land. To prevent floods on this second-level plain the river has been dredged and straightened for miles, making available for cultivation thousands of acres of terrace land, the richest soil in Jasper County.

COLFAX, 155 *m.* (791 alt., 2,213 pop.), is the birthplace of James Norman Hall (1887–   ), adventurer, author of *Kitchener's Mob* and co-author of *Mutiny on the Bounty.* It was named in honor of Schuyler Colfax, Vice President of the United States during Grant's administration and passenger on the first train passing through the village.

Half the town is built on steep hills; the business district is below. In 1875, miners prospecting for coal in the vicinity struck a spring of water that flowed up the shaft. Other borings resulted in more wells of mineral water; several inns, sanitariums, and hotels were built, the largest of which was the 150-room Hotel Colfax of Moorish design. By 1878 the "Spring City" had doubled its population. In 1909 about $700,000 was spent in remodeling the Hotel Colfax, and in the following year it was headquarters for many conventions, social gatherings, and tourists. Thousands of gallons of mineral water were shipped from here for medicinal uses, and hundreds came to take "the cure"; horse-drawn street cars clattered up and down the cobblestone streets. Since 1910 there has been a slow decline. Two companies used the mineral water to manufacture soft drinks by the addition of carbonic acid and flavoring extract, but this is now a small scale business. At a municipally owned well and fountain in a small downtown park containers are filled without charge.

Near Hotel Colfax, now closed and fenced against trespassing, and the old Epworth League Camp Ground, is an Indian campsite on which for a time stood an airplane beacon. Enough flint and broken fire rock strew this hillside to indicate that the groups camping here were large.

Extensive coal beds are in the vicinity, providing the main source of income. The town has a factory that makes portable canvas buildings for markets in South America.

THE AMERICAN LEGION SWIMMING POOL *(open to public)* is (L) near the highway, and the Colfax GOLF COURSE *(9 holes, 25¢ weekdays, 50¢ Sun. and holidays)* is 1 mile S. of town.

Right from Colfax on State 117, graveled, to the LAWSON WATT FARM, 5 *m.;* here is a large brown BOULDER, weighing between four and five tons. Crude carving on its broad, flat surface is believed to have been done by the prehistoric mound builders *(see ARCHEOLOGY).* Indian tobacco pipes and arrowheads have been found nearby.

At 156.6 *m.* US 6 crosses Squaw Creek, a small tributary of the South Skunk River.

At 159.5 *m.* is a junction with an improved road.

Left on this road 0.8 *m.* stands the 532-foot steel TOWER OF STATION WHO *(visitors 8 a.m.-8 p.m.; guides),* of the Central Broadcasting Company. A two-story brick building houses the transmitting unit. The tower was erected in 1934; the red light at its top can be seen for many miles at night.

MITCHELLVILLE, 162 *m.* (967 alt., 702 pop.), was named for Thomas Mitchell, a hotel proprietor. The following advertisement appeared in the *Harris Overland Guide* of Jan. 1852: "TOM MITCHELL!!! Dispenses comfort to the weary (!) feeds the hungry (!) and cheers the gloomy (!!!) at his old, well-known stand, thirteen miles east of Fort Des Moines. Don't pass by me."

Mitchell founded a Universalist Church here and also a seminary. The seminary buildings were later acquired by the State for the IOWA STATE TRAINING SCHOOL FOR GIRLS *(visitors, 8-11 a.m. and 1-4 p.m. except Sat., Sun., and holidays).* Approximately 200 girls, committed to the school by the courts and ranging in age from 10 to 21 years, are housed here. The school has a program of academic and industrial education, and the girls make their own uniforms—blue for weekdays, white for Sundays —as a part of their training.

DES MOINES, 177 *m.* (800 alt., 142,559 pop.) *(see DES MOINES).*

Points of Interest: Historical Building; State Capitol; Drake University; U. S. Veterans' Hospital; State Fair Grounds.

Des Moines is at the junction with US 69 *(see Tour 5),* US 163 *(see Tour 5A),* State 7 *(see Tour 14B),* and State 89 *(see Tour 14C).*

Left from Des Moines on State 90 is WEST DES MOINES, 4.5 *m.* (814 alt., 4,200 pop.), a former railroad center named Valley Junction. The name was changed by popular vote to West Des Moines, effective January 1938. For years the Chamber of Commerce has sponsored the slogan, "Next to the Largest City in Iowa!"

COMMERCE, 8 *m.* (836 alt.), is a small village on the bank of the Raccoon River; L., across the river, is the junction with State 155, at the end of the bridge. Left on this road into the WALNUT WOODS STATE SCENIC PRESERVE, 9 *m. (picnicking, fishing facilities, camp sites),* one of the most popular State parks in the State. The preserve of 261 acres lies along a bend in the Raccoon River, and received its name because of the thick growth of walnut trees. Here, too, are large red elm trees. Twenty-seven wing dams have been built along the river within the park area, which was formerly the B. F. Elbert farm.

Section b. DES MOINES to NEBRASKA LINE, 137 m.

In Des Moines, 0 *m.,* US 6 runs west from Grand Ave. River Bridge 1 block to 2nd St.; R. 1 block to Keosauqua Way; L. to intersection with 19th St.; R. on 19th St. 1 block; L. on Forest Ave. to Beaver Ave.; R. to Hickman Blvd.; L. on Hickman Blvd.

At WAUKEE, 14 *m.* (1,039 alt., 455 pop.), are the WRAGG CENTRAL NURSERIES, founded in 1863; they ship consignments to many foreign markets.

ADEL, 21 *m.* (894 alt., 1,669 pop.) *(see Tour 6),* is at the junction with US 169 *(see Tour 6).*

REDFIELD, 31 *m.* (958 alt., 870 pop.), on the bank of the Middle Raccoon River, was named New Ireland when the Cavanaugh brothers platted the town in 1850. The post office, first in the county, was known as McKay. The town was renamed Redfield in honor of Col. James Redfield, who was killed during the Civil War.

1. Right from Redfield on an unimproved road to HANGING ROCK, 0.5 *m.,* a colored limestone wall, 75 to 100 feet high and 800 feet long, on the bank of the Middle Raccoon River. The rock received its name, it is said, when several of the Burrows gang of outlaws were hanged to a nearby tree.
   On the HOPE BLACKBURN FARM, 5 *m.,* in a spacious old work shed, stands a large black walnut cabinet in which are parts of a wireless dynamo. Henry Nelson, who used the dynamo, became interested in wireless as early as 1856 in Galesburg, Ill. Nelson is said to have made miniature electric streetcars before the electric trolley appeared, and an electric gold-washer to replace the hand-panning method.
   2. Left from Redfield on an unimproved road is MARSHALL SPRINGS, 4 *m.;* Iowa pioneers came from miles around to drink the clear, cold water, which was believed to cure many ills.

DEXTER, 37 *m.* (1,148 alt., 748 pop.), founded in 1868 bv the C. R. I. & P. R. R., was named for a race horse.

A threshing-machine tooth invented locally was manufactured here in 1906. The factory of the Excelsior Thresher-Tooth Co., first to manufacture the product, burned in 1907. Later the company moved away.

In this town lived Dr. Nelson Percy (1875–   ), inventor of a blood transfusion device, and (1936) chief of staff at the Augustana Hospital, Chicago; Conger Reynolds (1891–   ), managing editor of the Paris edition of the Chicago *Daily Tribune* after the World War, and later in the U. S. Consular Service; and Edwin H. Conger (1843–1907), State Treasurer 1881–85, Ambassador to China during the Boxer Rebellion, and later Ambassador to Brazil and to Mexico.

Along the highway between 41.5 *m.* and Stuart, is a sodium-vapor lamp demonstration; this stretch of dull orange lights was the first of the kind installed in the State. The illumination causes the head-lights of approaching cars to have a diffused and non-glaring appearance; it is hoped that the device will decrease the number of motor accidents. Stuart supplies electricity for this experiment.

STUART, 42 *m.* (1,216 alt., 1,626 pop.), was founded in 1869 by Capt. Charles Stuart of Vermont, for whom the town was named. The C. R. I. & P. R. R. maintained railroad shops here until 1897. This town was the home of John Herriott, Lieutenant Governor of Iowa (1902–1907). The town has its own waterworks and a CARNEGIE LIBRARY. Annually, during the latter part of August, a stock show or fall festival is held here, with horse-breaking, racing, music and dancing as attractions.

ADAIR, 61 *m.* (1,415 alt., 950 pop.), was named for Gen. John Adair who fought in the War of 1812. In 1873 Jesse James and his gang here derailed a C. R. I. & P. train of five coaches. Estimates of the loot obtained from the dazed passengers ranged from a small amount to $3,000. Afterwards, the James boys said that the engineer's death made this the "only job we regret."

ANITA, 69 m. (1,106 alt., 1,256 pop.), was named for Anita Cowles, niece of the surveyor of the town site, Lewis Beason, who platted it in 1869.

There is a band-shell in CONCERT PARK, which is used for open-air meetings, entertainments, and weekly band concerts, during the summer.

Homecoming Day, an annual holiday here, is usually featured by a street carnival. Almost every small town in Iowa has such a day-and-night celebration, usually in late summer or early fall. The carnival is held on the main street when the town has no central square or park. A ferris wheel, merry-go-round, tilt-a-whirl, and similar amusement devices, are erected overnight; a small tent village, facing the sidewalks, springs up; gay bunting covers the fronts of booths; here and there are the lurid banners advertising girl shows, fortune tellers, games of skill and chance, and wrestling shows. It is a day of soda pop, balloons, and popcorn for children; the band plays, and the elders visit, gossip, greet old friends, and applaud the events. Everyone eats ice cream; sometimes a motorcar and other prizes are given away by a lottery; there are many lively contests for prizes. In late afternoon, from an outlying field, come the cheers of a crowd at the ball game. Sometimes a platform, hall, or pavement dance concludes the festivities. By the following noon only a few dismantled stands and a litter of carnival paper and debris are left to prove that Main Street has been a gay White Way for a day.

At 79 m. is the junction with US 71 (see Tour 7).

ATLANTIC, 83 m. (1,164 alt., 5,585 pop.), was thought to be half-way between the two oceans, and its name was to be either Atlantic or Pacific. A coin was flipped, and Pacific won; but when it was learned that a number of other Middle Western towns already had that name, the decision was reversed.

This was the southern terminus of the Atlantic Northern R. R., one of the few community-owned railroads in the United States. The line running between Atlantic and Kimballtown was completed in 1907 and abandoned in 1936. Funds for the building of the road were raised by popular subscription in Atlantic, Elk Horn, and Kimballtown.

A $25,000 ATLANTIC LEGION MEMORIAL BUILDING, 2nd and Poplar Sts., serves as a community center. In the CITY PARK is a $25,000 column of marble, 50 feet high, surmounted by a 10-foot bronze statue symbolic of Liberty and dedicated to the soldiers and sailors of the United States prior to the World War.

In the Atlantic Cemetery a marble spire, 25 feet high, marks the site of a CORPSELESS GRAVE. Erected at a cost of $10,000, the monument was placed on the spot chosen by John Tiernan to be his burial plot. Tiernan died in Florida and was not brought here for burial.

The SHRAUGER AND JOHNSON CO. PLANT produced nearly $5,000,000 worth of folding stoves and Army cots for the Government during the World War; both Swift and Co. and Armour and Co. maintain packing plants here.

The huge ATLANTIC CANNING CO. PLANT *(visitors welcome during canning season)* cans corn; the average output annually is about 50,000 cases. Since 1925 large quantities of pumpkins have also been canned here.

Native trees and wild flowers grow profusely along the banks of Troublesome Creek and the East Nishnabotna River near Atlantic.

Near Atlantic are large fields of pumpkins, a green mass during summer months—heavy yellow patches against the landscape during early autumn. Unlike the "pumpkins" of James Whitcomb Riley's poem, these do not grow between rows of corn or "lie frosty among pale October corn-shock tepees." They are a variety of sweet pumpkin, the seeds for which are furnished to farmers by the canning company on credit; they are a profitable crop in good seasons, bringing from $5 to $9 a ton. From 10 to 20 tons are produced on an acre. Frost will kill the vines, but the pumpkin is safe in the fields until freezing weather.

Hayracks with specially built sides are used to transport the pumpkins from the fields to the factory, where they are tossed into a chute leading to the washing room. From there they go to the slicing room where large knives cut them into segments. The pumpkin is not peeled until after it has been cooked. Machinery converts the yellow globes into pulp, which is canned. An important by-product is the seed, quantities of which are shipped to China and sold through vending machines.

Right from Atlantic on a graveled road, is the junction with a side road, 5 *m.*, at the FIVE-MILE GROVE SCHOOL; L. to a WILD FLOWER PRESERVE, 6 *m.*, begun 25 years ago by Frank C. Pellett, Atlantic author, naturalist, and traveler. More than 200 species of flowers and shrubs, both native and foreign, grow in profusion in a 10-acre timberland.

At 89 *m.* are the HOPLEY STOCK FARMS *(open to visitors)*, where fine horses and cattle are bred; Hopley stock has won many ribbons at national shows. The farms comprise about 5,000 acres.

At 91 *m.* is the junction with State 2 *(see Tour 15).*

At 107 *m.* is the junction with US 59 *(see Tour 8).*

OAKLAND, 108 *m.* (1,106 alt., 1,181 pop.), on the banks of the West Nishnabotna River, was first known as Big Grove, because of the oak trees that grow in abundance around the site. The first bridge to span the river here was built with material and labor furnished by residents of the community.

COUNCIL BLUFFS, 135 *m.* (984 alt., 42,048 pop.) *(see COUNCIL BLUFFS).*

Points of Interest: General Dodge's Home, Anne Dodge Memorial, Lincoln Memorial, Lewis and Clark Monument.

Council Bluffs is at the junction with US 75-275 *(see Tour 9)* and State 7 *(see Tour 14B).*

At 137 *m.,* on the outskirts of Council Bluffs, US 6 crosses the Missouri River, the Iowa-Nebraska Line, on the DOUGLAS STREET TOLL BRIDGE *(passenger cars 10-15¢, passengers 10¢ each)* into Omaha, Nebr.

Left from Council Bluffs, on US 275 to the new SOUTH OMAHA TOLL BRIDGE, with a 5-mile approach constructed, with PWA assistance, at a cost of $1,739,400.

‹‹‹‹‹‹‹‹‹‹‹‹‹‹‹‹‹‹‹‹ ☿ ››››››››››››››››››››››

Tour 14A

Homestead—Amana—Middle Amana—High Amana—West Amana—
Lower South Amana—Upper South Amana; State 149, State 220.
Homestead to Upper South Amana, 12 m.

Paved roadbed between Homestead and Amana; rest graveled.
Tourist accommodations at Homestead, Amana, Lower South Amana, and Upper
South Amana.

This short route winds through the land and villages owned and occupied by the Amana Society, which, for 90 years, was a flourishing community organization founded on a religious basis. The roots of the
Community of True Inspiration were in the Pietist movement that flourished among Germanic peoples in the latter part of the 17th and first half
of the 18th century as a revolt against the dogmatism and ritualism of the
official church, the Lutheran. The province of Hesse, which had the most
liberal government in Germany at the time, became the refuge of the
early congregations of True Inspiration. Even there, however, they suffered
at intervals, and in 1843 a band under the leadership of Christian Metz
(1794–1867), a man remarkable for his combination of great piety and
hard common sense, decided to migrate to America. Within 10 years
about 800 had reached the 8,000 acre tract of land near Buffalo, N. Y.,
which they called Ebenezer *(Hitherto hath the Lord helped us)*. Buffalo
was, however, growing rapidly and the colonists soon found the city influences upsetting to the tranquillity of their haven; in addition, their
numbers made it necessary to buy more land. After careful consideration
they determined to move to the rich frontier country of Iowa. The new
migration started in 1855 and within seven years six villages had been
established and the town of Homestead purchased. The new home received the name of Amana.

The society's communistic system resulted from the migration to America
and was not part of the original aim; the members agreed to it as a means
of keeping their unity and beliefs in the new land. Metz led them into the
arrangement with great skill and intelligence, as the long life and prosperity of the society showed. It was not until 1932 that there was any real
change in the organization and even then it was not complete; until that
time all temporal and spiritual affairs had been in the hands of 13 trustees.
As the communities are now governed, spiritual affairs are under control of
the Amana Church Society, a separate board. The Amana Society is a producing and marketing cooperative with 1,400 members.

While the majority of the inhabitants of Ebenezer were farmers and
artisans, there were a few wealthy members, some of whom turned over

THE AMANA BAKERY

considerable property to group control. The success of the undertaking rested, however, on the practical skills of the members. They could quarry stone, hew wood, build houses, farm, and build mills; and each was assigned to the job he did best, sharing in the community profits on equal terms with the least and the most skilled.

State 149 branches north from its junction with US 6 *(see Tour 14)* at HOMESTEAD (764 alt.), one of the seven villages of the Amana Society.

Homestead was a little village south of the society's original tract, but when, in 1861, the Mississippi and Missouri R. R. was extended to Homestead, the group, realizing the advantage of having a railroad station, purchased the village properties.

The one quiet street has an old-fashioned atmosphere, though it lies close to a main highway where motorists speed along at 50 miles an hour. Unaffected by the modern tempo, the men of the village work leisurely about their shops and farms and the women care for the house and cultivate little gardens. Here and there a bonnet is seen bobbing above a hoe, a reminder that until recently all Amana women wore bonnets to conceal their charm and to restrain vanity. The older women still cling to the custom of wearing long, full skirts of dark material. The plain rectangular houses, showing old German architectural influences, are two stories high with gabled roofs. They are constructed of hard wood, of red brick, or of brown sandstone quarried on the society's land. Formerly the absence of paint on the weather-beaten frame structures gave the villages a dull, colorless aspect in winter; now (1938) about half of the houses are painted; as in the past, however, gardens, with old-fashioned phlox, verbenas, and zinnias, give a brightness in summer to the scene, and pear and apple trees soften the austerity of a plain village. The schoolhouse, the church, the store, and the homes are alike in architectural style. If it were not for the signs bearing such words as "Bakery" or "Meat Market", shops would be mistaken for homes. All signs are lettered simply with black paint.

Here, as in the other villages, the GENERAL STORE sells products made by members of the society, such as woolen blankets and German bread. The MEAT MARKET sells hams "smoked in the tower and aged in the garret", and *schwartzenmagen,* or head cheese, seasoned in the German way. Westphalian-type hams and Amana cured sausage and bacon are shipped by parcel post and express to many parts of the United States.

Between Homestead and Amana, State 149 passes through timbered country and crosses the quiet Iowa River that winds through the heart of the Amana farm land. Here the hepatica and marsh marigold have bloomed undisturbed since the days when Indians fished along the river banks and their prehistoric ancestors constructed their fish traps across its course. A dam of huge boulders, built in the shape of a V, is a short distance from the bridge over the Iowa River; it is reached on foot.

AMANA, 3 *m.* (721 alt.), where the first colonists settled when they came to Iowa, is the oldest of the seven villages. Here houses, aged and timeworn, line the wandering streets that in appearance are reminiscent of those in German dorfs; grape and hop vines climb plain trellises on the otherwise bare walls. In summer the petunias, four-o-clocks, marigolds, and hollyhocks around the houses make crazy-quilts of color, flowers never having been counted among the vanities of life. In Amana live some of the oldest members of the society, those who resented seeing the old friendly system changed to meet the demands of the younger members. These old people have a graciousness and charm that is high recommendation for the early Christian system that bred them. Here as in the other villages, they nod to visitors on the street and usually offer a friendly smile. The austerity of taste is particularly noticeable; and there is a pervasive peace and quiet.

The early respect for craftsmanship has not died out. In this village is a simple little two-story FURNITURE SHOP where cabinet makers construct beautiful pieces of furniture by hand, using wood from walnut and cherry trees grown on the society's land, approximately one-fourth of which is in timber. Amana-made furniture includes reproductions of heirlooms brought from Germany. Copies of early American products, which the Amana craftsmen make exceptionally well, have a good market. The first floor of the building is a work shop; on the second floor are displayed the finished pieces, including Amana cradles, Colonial canopy beds, Amana chairs, and Dutch cupboards.

Second to agriculture in importance among activities in the community is the manufacture of woolen goods that have gained a wide reputation. The MILL *(open to public 6-6)* here is perhaps the best one to visit. It is larger than that at Middle Amana, although not as old, and, despite its modern machinery, has an old-time atmosphere. Power is obtained from a seven-mile millrace. A guide takes visitors through the buildings, beginning in the room where the wool is washed, and ending in the weaving room where the blankets and materials are finished. Suiting is manufactured in about 50 styles; the Amana blankets are woven in the off-season of a good year. Many women and girls now work in the mill, though this is a recent innovation.

In the AMANA BAKERY bread is kneaded by hand and baked in a brick oven that has been heated with pieces of wood. After the wood has burned and there is no fire in the oven, the bread is put in. The loaves, about 100 at a time, are removed by means of long-handled wooden paddles, about the length of canoe paddles. Scarcely a visitor leaves the village without taking along a crusty, two-pound loaf of this hearth-baked bread.

In a plain little building in Amana the officials and clerks transact the million dollar business of the corporation. But for the plain sign, MAIN OFFICE, above the door, the building might be a home or a church. Every employee holding a corporation commission, large or small—the baker, the pharmacist, the storekeeper, and the agricultural manager—makes a daily report to this office.

The inhabitants of the Amana community experienced no drastic readjustments with the change to the new order. There is still plenty of good food, an abundance of cheap fuel, and each member, now a stockholder in the new corporation, receives compensation for the kind of labor he likes best to do. And there are luxuries—and leisure. The younger generation, interested in what the outside world has to offer, actually has already had what that world is still seeking—peace and plenty.

1. Right from Amana on State 220 is the small village of EAST AMANA, 2 *m.*, known for its large herds of sheep, the wool of which is used in the mills at Amana and Middle Amana. Hundreds of Shropshires graze beneath the wide elms and oaks on the rolling pasture slopes. In the spring the sheep are herded into pens where they are sheared of their wool before being sent back to the pastures. Much wool, however, is bought in the Chicago markets for the mills, and shipped in from western States. To aid in the manufacturing, many ingenious pieces of machinery have been invented by members of the society.

CARDING WOOL, AMANA VILLAGE

2. Right from Amana on a gravel road to AMANA LAKE, 1 *m.;* during July and August, thousands of American lotus raise buff-colored blossoms above the water. Near the Lake are picnic and camp grounds.

At Amana the route turns left on State 220. At MIDDLE AMANA, 5.1 *m.*, is the WOOLEN MILL *(visitors welcome),* that has been in operation for almost 80 years. Past the mill flows the seven-mile millrace, a canal overhung with willows and grapevines. In summer liquid-voiced meadow larks flit above the fringe of pickerel weed, and gray rain doves send their tremulous calls over the water. A worn wooden bridge crosses the millrace.

At Middle Amana is a small PRINTING SHOP, where most of the corporation's printing is done; it is able to compete in quality and prices with much larger shops in the cities, printing intricate business forms, advertising leaflets in color with half tones, labels and trade marks. Here for generations have been printed the hymn books used in the Amana churches.

As in the other villages, there is an elementary SCHOOL. Lessons are taught in English five days a week, but on Saturdays and during the summer vacations the children are instructed in German. In the schoolyard, with its gay flower beds, old German game songs are chanted. Until recently the children were not sent to high school; only those who showed ability to profit by training to fill future need in the village for doctors, dentists, and the like, were permitted to continue their education at the expense of the society. After their education had been completed they were expected to return to the society to practice their professions. In 1933 a high school was built at Middle Amana, and now all the children of the Amana Society may attend; under the new form of government any youth may attend college, but at his own expense.

In HIGH AMANA, 7.5 *m.*, old-fashioned brown sandstone houses predominate. Barns, houses, gardens, and orchards blend harmoniously. As elsewhere, every family has its own garden; the old community gardens are used by the corporation as "crop gardens" for the growing of cabbages, beans, potatoes, and onions—the last ranking high among the society's leading commercial crops. The garden work has a social aspect for the women, offering an opportunity to meet and discuss the village news.

Almost every Amana home has been visited by the typical American "antique" hunter, trying avidly to buy the old china, pewter, brass candlesticks, and other objects associated with family history and the years when Iowa was a virgin prairie and "tallow dip" and "lard oil" lamps were used. Old Bibles, with wooden covers and huge brass clasps, the texts followed by the forefingers of six generations, are found in most homes; and rare books of the 15th and 16th centuries, copperplate prints of the same periods, community books of the early 18th century, and manuscript letters almost 200 years old, are in many of the homes.

At WEST AMANA, 9 *m.*, is the FLOUR MILL. With its red-brick tower and weather-beaten, hardwood walls, it is truly a relic. The pioneer farmers for many miles around brought their grain and waited while flour, meal, and feed were ground here, for this was one of the early mills erected in Iowa. Although new machinery has been installed, the old millstones are still in use.

The agricultural manager—each village has one—is in charge of the field crops, the corporation gardens, the dairy, and the hog barns. Farming is carried on in much the same way as elsewhere in the State; modern farm methods and efficient farm machinery are used. The quiet of Amana spring mornings that was undisturbed by the early ox teams is now broken by chugging tractors. Corn, wheat, hay, and livestock are raised; fruit is grown and canned. Much of the cooperation typical of the old regime still exists; when extra labor is needed in a village, the members of another lend a helping hand. But, after a hard day in the field, the workers no longer gather in the community kitchens for their evening meal as in former years.

Carl Flick, an artist of West Amana, caught the spirit of the community kitchen when he painted the last supper there, which was "to youth a symbol of hope and opportunity; to age an evidence of shattered ideals and broken faith." This artist, born within the society in 1904, is a salesman who paints in his spare time. In 1932 his painting *Amana Interior* was exhibited at the Philadelphia National Academy of Fine Arts, and other works with an Amana setting have been exhibited in Chicago and Washington. He has recorded the brown sandstone houses and the winding Iowa River—wild ginger, geranium, and trillium along its banks, and clusters of elderberry, gooseberry, and cattails nearby.

IN AN AMANA HOUSEHOLD

Left at West Amana, continuing on State 220.

LOWER SOUTH AMANA, 11 *m.* (748 alt.), has a general store, meat shop, and bakery, but, like the other villages, the interest of visitors here is mainly in the people and houses. The homes usually contain colored, hand-woven carpets and cherry or walnut furniture. Beds with scroll tops and hand-turned posts, their soft, deep feather-beds stuffed with down plucked from Amana geese, offer inducement to rest. Chairs, with gracefully curved legs and hand-caned seats, writing desks that, when closed, have the appearance of a chest, and tables, with hand-turned spool legs, all lend dignity and charm to the interiors.

When an Amana member needs the services of a doctor or dentist, he is cared for at the cost of the society; when he dies he is buried by the society in the Amana cemetery, under a simple marker exactly like those on other graves.

In the beginning celibacy was regarded as indicative of a higher spiritual state, but gradually this attitude changed. Perhaps the forefathers realized that without marriage, the Community of True Inspiration could not long exist; the fact that six generations have married and remained within the society is a reason for its longevity, while other similar ventures, such as that made by the Shakers, are dying out. For a long time two people who desired to marry had to undergo a year's probation, during which they could not live in the same village. If, at the end of the year, they had remained faithful to each other, and above all, if their spiritual zeal was satisfactory, they were permitted to marry.

The Amana churches are plain, with bare floors, worn with much scrubbing, and undecorated white-washed walls, evidence of the belief of the members that with ornamentation spirituality tends to disappear. Members are no longer suspended from church services as a form of punishment for an offense, but are encouraged to believe that to attend church is a matter of grace. And through the church much of the old spirit of the Community of True Inspiration endures. Work stops on Sunday and almost everyone goes to church—grandmothers and granddaughters in their black shawls and bonnets, leading flaxen-haired youngsters. If the youths think of their automobiles parked for the day, they make no show of restlessness.

At Lower South Amana is the junction with US 6 *(see Tour 14)*.

South of the junction with US 6 is UPPER SOUTH AMANA, 12 *m.* (748 alt), the smallest village of the society. The hotel here is known for its hospitality, and the good German-style meals. Typical Amana food— large slices of Amana-smoked ham, brown-crusted, German-baked bread, home-grown vegetables, *kuchen,* or coffee cake, and apple fritters with corn syrup—is served here.

Tour 14B

Des Moines—Harlan—Council Bluffs; State 7.
Des Moines to Council Bluffs, 143 m.

C. M. St. P. & P. R. R. roughly parallels this route between Des Moines and Panora, and between Harlan and Council Bluffs; C.R. I. & P. R. R., between Harlan and Council Bluffs; M. & St. L. R. R., between Des Moines and Waukee.
Interstate Transit Bus Lines follow the highway throughout.
Roadbed is paved throughout.
Accommodations chiefly in cities.

DES MOINES, 0 *m.* (800 alt., 142,559 pop.) *(see DES MOINES).*

Points of Interest: Historical Building; State Capitol; Drake University; U. S. Veterans' Hospital; State Fair Grounds.

Des Moines is at the junction with US 65 *(see Tour 4)*, US 69 *(see Tour 5)*, US 6 *(see Tour 14)*, US 163 *(see Tour 5A)*.

West from W. 2nd St. and Keosauqua Way to 19th St.; R. 1 block to Forest Ave.; L. to the intersection with Beaver Ave.; R. on Beaver Ave. to Douglas Ave.; L. on Douglas to Merle Hay Rd.; R. on Merle Hay Rd.

(State 7). State 7 and State 89 are united between Des Moines and John-son Station, 9 m. (see Tour 14B).

GRIMES, 15 m. (967 alt., 468 pop.), was named for James W. Grimes, Governor of Iowa (1854–58). The first house here was erected in 1881.

There are two industrial plants here, one making cement, the other can-ning corn produced by nearby farmers on contract; during the harvesting season large numbers of wagons overflowing with green-husked sweetcorn pass along the highway near the town.

DALLAS CENTER, 24 m. (1,068 alt., 852 pop.), was so named be-cause early residents hoped that the seat of Dallas County would be estab-lished here. The town is the home of the Brethren in Christ, and several other divisions of the religious sect known as the Old Order of River Brethren, whose members are baptized in the river. An annual love feast, at which occurs the foot-washing ceremony in connection with communion, is held by the Brethren in Christ in the second week in June. One member washes the feet, another dries them, and the ceremony is sealed with the Kiss of Peace. The communion meal consists of unleavened bread and wine, the ceremony closing with the Kiss of Charity. Another group in the country known as Yorkers, does not maintain a church but usually meets in schoolhouses. The men wear dark coats, standing white collars with no ties, black hats, and well-kept beards. Women wear white caps during the services and shawls draped across their shoulders, covering plain dresses. Members of the order have lived in or near Dallas Center since 1877.

At 27 m. is the junction with US 169 (see Tour 6).

Between Dallas Center and Panora the route passes through rich, level farming land. Oats and, less often, wheat are the first crops harvested. As soon as the grain ripens the binder is brought out; the giant reel sweeps the grain into the sickle and the machine ties it in bundles that are dumped at intervals on one side of the wide swath cut around the field. Harvest hands pick up the bundles and set them in shocks, which are later pitched on hayracks and hauled to the threshing machines. Threshing is a coopera-tive activity, occurring usually in August. The farmers who help one an-other form a "ring," hiring or buying a thresher cooperatively; starting at one end of the "run," they proceed from farm to farm, loading the bun-dles and hauling them from the field, stacking the straw, mowing it away in the barn for bedding, and hauling the oats to the bins or to market. The farmer who has unusually large fields hires extra help, sometimes one man, sometimes two.

The farmers' wives and daughters prepare the food for the hungry threshers. Although the work is hard, threshings are gala occasions with laughter, gossiping, and practical jokes. The children race over the farm, raiding the orchards; in the kitchen they beg for pie and cake in return for bringing in cobs and coal, or wood, to stoke the huge range, or for carrying water to the threshers.

Large quantities of meat and potatoes are prepared; there are also red and yellow sliced tomatoes on huge platters, dressing, scalloped corn, baked beans, coleslaw, macaroni, and cheese. All the standard dishes, plus any new ones the women can devise, are served. The men eat in relays.

Tubs of water are set on boxes in the yard under the trees, where, with much splashing and snorting, the dust and sweat accumulated in the fields or in the hot mow are in a measure washed off. Towels are hung near the tubs, and sometimes a tiny mirror and a comb are attached to a tree or to the wall of a nearby building.

PANORA, 45 *m.* (1,058 alt., 1,014 pop.). The town's name is a contraction of "panorama." The story is that pioneers, viewing the site from a hill, exclaimed, "What a beautiful panorama." In early days a straw hat that hung from the rafters of a log cabin served as the "post office." Passing travelers carried the mail.

In 1861–62 James and John Cline built the PANORA WOOLEN MILLS— a frame building on the banks of the Raccoon River; in 1877 it was converted into a flourmill and is still operated by water power.

Panora was twice the county seat before the honor went to Guthrie Center in 1876; the OLD COURTHOUSE in the center of the town square is now the Panora High School. The high school was county-owned and operated until 1931, when the county substituted a district system.

GUTHRIE CENTER, 53 *m.* (1,077 alt., 1,813 pop.), is in a rugged spot in the South Raccoon Valley. The first settlers here were Pennsylvania Dutch, who came about the middle of the 19th century.

Right on State 25, graveled, to SPRINGBROOK STATE PARK, 7 *m.*, an area of several hundred acres, formerly known as King Park. The road used by pioneers of 1848 runs through the park. Gold seekers also used the route later. There is a spring-fed lake, used for swimming, bathing, fishing, and canoeing. Virgin hardwood trees furnish shade for picnic and camping grounds. Vesper services are held here during the summer months at 6:30 Sunday evening.

Much of the hilly area around Guthrie Center is cut-over timberland. Thick undergrowth and second and third growth timber splash the hillsides with color in autumn. Hazelnut bushes once grew in abundance here, and are still found in uncultivated sections of the region. The nuts grow in clusters, and have rough prickly shells that are thin, brittle, and easily broken.

Black walnut trees grow throughout this area. Every fall, following the first frost, nutting parties range the hillsides gathering the nuts. The trees are just beginning to flame with autumn color; the sky is a brilliant blue— a deeper color than in spring when it often seems washed with pale reflections of the last snow. With sticks and a noisy shaking of branches, the heavy green-hulled nuts are knocked to the ground and gathered into baskets or gunny sacks. Sometimes the nuts are pounded loose from the hulls before they are carried home. Otherwise the nuts are taken home and run through a hand cornsheller to loosen the hulls; they are then spread out to dry.

At 61.5 *m.* is the junction with a dirt side road.

Right on this road to a junction at 3 *m.;* R. here to the 400-acre MENEFEE RANCH, 4 *m.*, where the West Guthrie Colt and Horse Show is held annually about March 15; it lasts two days and has the atmosphere of a fair or picnic. There are riding exhibitions, pulling contests between professional horsemen and teamsters, and a night horse show. Prizes and premiums are offered. The event ends with a dance in the spacious ranch garage.

HAMLIN, 74 *m.* (1,257 alt., 160 pop.) *(see Tour 7)*, is at the junction with US 71 *(see Tour 7)*.

KIMBALLTON, 84 *m.* (378 pop.), has a municipally owned light plant, waterworks, and creamery. The population is Danish by birth or descent.

HARLAN, 98 *m.* (1,194 alt., 3,145 pop.), settled in 1858 and named for James Harlan *(see Tour 8)* is at the junction with US 59 *(see Tour 8)*.

This is the home (1938) of Gov. Nelson G. Kraschel.

Between Harlan and Avoca, along the valley of the West Nishnabotna, have been unearthed numerous stone and flint implements, relics of Indians who once camped in this region.

AVOCA, 110 *m.* (1,137 alt., 1,673 pop.), second seat of Pottawattamie County, was named for the Avoca River in Ireland; Thomas Moore, the Irish poet, lauded the "vale of Avoca," in his poem, *The Meeting of the Waters.* The hamlet was first known as Pacific, later as Botna.

Several small villages, including Newton Hill and Wooster, have been platted near Avoca, but all have disappeared. One of the few remaining herds of deer in the State roams through the woods and fields near here; it is part of a herd that escaped from a nearby park. They usually feed in the valley of the West Nishnabotna River during the winter and wander 25 or 30 miles north during the summer.

WESTON, 135 *m.* (1,035 alt.), is a rural village. Jesse James, the bandit, kept his horses here one winter and robbed a train in the vicinity in the following spring.

COUNCIL BLUFFS, 143 *m.* (984 alt., 42,048 pop.) *(see COUNCIL BLUFFS)*.

Points of Interest: State Home for Deaf; General Dodge's Home; Anne Dodge Memorial; Lincoln Memorial; Lewis and Clark Monument.

Council Bluffs is at the junction with US 6 *(see Tour 14)* and US 275 *(see Tour 9)*.

Tour 14C

Des Moines—Woodward—Junction with US 169; State 89.
Des Moines to Junction with US 169, 39 m.

D. M. and C. I. R. R. parallels the route between Granger and Woodward; C. M. St. P. & P. R. R., between Woodward and Perry. The highway is intermittently paved and graveled.
Tourist accommodations available chiefly in cities.

DES MOINES, 0 *m.* (800 alt., 142,559 pop.) *(see DES MOINES).*

Points of Interest: Historical Building; State Capitol; Drake University; U. S. Veterans' Hospital; State Fair Grounds.

Des Moines is at the junction with US 6 *(see Tour 14)*, US 163 *(see Tour 5A)*, US 65 *(see Tour 4)*, US 69 *(see Tour 5)*, US 6 *(see Tour 14)*, and State 7 *(see Tour 14B)*.

State 89 runs west from 2nd St. on Keosauqua Way to W. 19th St.; R. on 19th St. 1 block to Forest Ave.; L. on Forest Ave. to the intersection with Beaver Ave.; R. on Beaver Ave. to Douglas Ave.; L. on Douglas Ave. to Merle Hay Rd.; R. on Merle Hay Rd.

Between Des Moines and JOHNSON STATION, 9 *m.*, State 89 *(see Tour 14B)* and State 7 are united; at Johnson Station, State 7 branches L.

THE HYPERION CLUB *(private)*, 11.2 *m.* (L), has wide porches overlooking the golf course and a swimming pool, both of which are visible from the road.

At 12 *m.* is the CAMP DODGE RIFLE RANGE. In 1932 a group of 20 families, determined not to go on direct relief, obtained a $600 grant from the Federal Government and the use of a tract of land on the rifle range. A canning factory was built near the barn. The men did most of the garden work, but the women and children occasionally helped in planting and gathering the vegetables. The group raised so much the first year that it was necessary to build a long cave in which to store root vegetables they wished to keep without canning; a surplus was marketed and the money used to buy seeds and plants for the following year; the remaining sum, if any, was divided equally among the members. One of the group is manager and treasurer.

CAMP DODGE, 15 *m.*, is now used chiefly for the summer encampment of the Iowa National Guard. The SWIMMING POOL *(open 10 a. m.-10 p. m., adm. 25¢ and 15¢)*, is under the supervision of the Des Moines Playground Association. Permanent buildings recently erected include a memorial hospital, dedicated to the late Lieut. Col. Wilbur S. Conkling, three mess halls, a large machine shop, a garage, and a bathhouse.

Camp Dodge teems with activity in late summer during the 15 days the Iowa National Guard convenes for field training; the valley, dotted with khaki tents, resounds with the rattle of mess kits, bugle calls, and the tramp of feet, as more than 3,000 men from all sections of the State arrive. The gala occasion is Governor's Day, when the Governor of Iowa reviews the troops; on this day sham battles are fought, in which the camp is divided into defense and attack troops. Armored cars and light tanks make the warfare more realistic.

Camp Dodge was first opened as a camp for Iowa National Guard units in 1907. Its name, given in 1910, honored Gen. Grenville M. Dodge of Civil War fame, who later was active in the building of the Union Pacific R. R. During the World War it became a United States regional training camp. The purchase of additional land and the erection of 1,872 buildings to provide accommodations for 40,000 men was accomplished in less than 90 days; the maximum number of men here at one time, however, was

23,000 in Sept., 1917. The 88th Division of the U. S. army was trained here. Maj. Gen. Edward Plummer was its commanding officer. Although the Federal Government retained more than 1,800 acres at the close of the war, much of the land reverted to farm use. In 1922 the State took over about 600 additional acres for the use of its National Guard encampment. The remainder of the area is the RIFLE AND ARTILLERY RANGE (see above).

GRANGER, 21 m. (889 alt., 319 pop.), was laid out in 1879. It was named for Ben Granger, an official of the Des Moines Northern Railway, a narrow-gauge road running between Des Moines and Boone. Farmers living in the neighborhood contributed $1,000 to help bring the railroad to the town.

Left from Granger on an improved road are the GRANGER HOMESTEADS, 0.2 m., a Resettlement Administration project. On Dec. 15, 1935, 50 families moved into these modern dwellings, each of which has four to six rooms. The dormered houses are cream-colored with green, blue, or brown trim, and have basement, furnaces, bathrooms, running water, and automatic pumps. Light-colored interior plyboard walls, copper-screened doors and windows, and linoleum-covered floors contrast greatly with the dinginess of the former homes of the residents. Near each house is a garage or barn and a chicken coop.

Of the 50 householders selected from 200 applicants, 40 were miners, three store clerks, two railroad men, a carpenter, a barber, a garage man, a farmer, and a manager completed the group. The homesteaders have 30 years to pay for their homes, with interest on the cost at three percent. The average monthly payment is $14.75.

Father L. G. Ligutti, a local priest, had dreamed of a more abundant life for his parishioners. When the Government's offer to finance subsistence homesteads was announced, Father Ligutti immediately sent in an application for a homestead project here.

MORAN, 24 m. (926 alt.), once a shipping point, was named for William Moran who lived on a nearby farm. Within recent years an old lime kiln was found, almost intact, on the side of a hill formerly known as the Rosenkrantz Mound, now as the Sullivan Gravel Pit. Legend says that Matt O'Brien, a settler, constructed the lime kiln and fired it to frighten away hostile Indians in the prairie-schooner days. The Indians had heard that lives were in danger when hills and mountains smoked. After holding councils and debates, they attacked the O'Briens and murdered the entire family.

The nucleus of WOODWARD, 32 m. (1,065 alt., 901 pop.), was a trading post known as Xenia, on a knoll, 1.5 miles from the present town. When the railroad company surveyed this section in 1880 it gave the site its present name; the settlers moved down to be near the railroad.

Twenty human skeletons were uncovered in June 1907 on the outskirts of the town by men digging gravel for road construction. They lay in an area perhaps a rod or more square; each had been struck with some instrument that had crashed through the bone. It was considered possible that the Indians may have been killed by Henry Lott who lived in the neighborhood in 1835 (see FORT DODGE). Lott and his elder son who blamed the Indians for the death of his wife and child, were seemingly

HOMESTEADS AT GRANGER

friendly to the Indians. They persuaded 20 or 30 of them to visit them, and when they were drunk on whiskey, murdered the Indians by bashing in their skulls, and immediately buried the bodies.

Right on graveled road, a continuation of Woodward's main street, 0.3 *m.*, to STATE HOSPITAL FOR EPILEPTICS AND SCHOOL FOR FEEBLEMINDED *(visitors 9 a.m.-4 p.m.)*, occupying 1,200 acres adjoining Woodward on the north. The modern fireproof buildings, including the school, are connected by cement walks and graveled roads; many flower beds decorate the grounds. Believing that color and beauty are helpful in training those admitted to the institution, much effort has been expended to provide attractive surroundings and to give instruction that will appeal to limited mentalities. The inmates find much delight in the brilliantly colored flowers in the greenhouses maintained by the institution.

A beauty shop has been established, where patients are taught to improve their appearance. The staff members dress in bright uniforms. There are no uniforms for the patients, the women and girls selecting attractive prints for dresses. They are taught to produce fine crocheted linens and other articles of handiwork that appeal to them.

In the administration building, there is a modern, well-equipped surgery, dental clinic, and a clinical and X-ray laboratory.

The school is modern in every respect. In the classrooms all desks and other furniture are decorated in bright colors. The school has a capacity of 300 children, and is not graded. Primary, junior, intermediate, and senior courses include craft and vocational training. Special attention is paid to instruction in both instrumental and vocal music. A large band, and a choir give weekly concerts. The children also present plays and other entertainments. The assembly hall has a well-equipped stage, and seats 1,000. Movies, dances, and other entertainments are provided.

At 39 *m.* is the junction with US 169 *(see Tour 6).*

Left on US 169 to a junction with State 17, 1 *m.;* R. on State 17 is PERRY,
5 *m.* (961 alt., 5,881 pop.), a brisk manufacturing town in a large agricultural
area. Many of the farm products are canned or packed, and plows, spades, and
other implements are manufactured here. The town is a division point for the
C. M. St. P. & P. R. R., and the railroad shops provide employment for 150.
Within three years after the railroad was built through the town, the population
jumped from 800 to 2,500.

The town was named for Colonel Perry, one of the owners of the old Des
Moines Valley R. R., now the Minneapolis and St. Louis. John Willis, who built
the first bridge across the Raccoon at Adel, in 1887 laid out the original plat of
220 acres for the town.

The early Selby Mill here made use of a steam boiler and whistle taken from a
steamboat that sank in the Mississippi at Vicksburg after the Civil War. The weird
wail of the whistle evoked what the residents call "steamboat blues."

The PERRY NURSERIES, established in 1872, replace all stock that dies during the
first year after planting. PATTEE PARK, comprising about 21 acres, has a swimming
pool.

Left from Perry 1 *m.,* on 1st Ave. to the George Mullen farm; here is the
FISHPOLE THAT BECAME A PRIZE-WINNING TREE, identified by a bronze marker.
In 1862 J. H. Thornburg, bringing home a string of fish, stuck his pole in the
ground, where it took root and grew. The giant cottonwood was rated the finest
tree of its species in the tree contest sponsored by the Iowa Federated Garden Clubs
in 1936. It has a base circumference of 22 feet and 11 inches, and rises to a height
of more than 100 feet.

Tour 15

Junction with US 61—Oskaloosa—Indianola—Junction with US 6;
State 2.
Junction with US 61 to Junction with US 6, 220 m.

The C. R. I. & P. R. R. parallels this route between Columbus Junction and Knox-
ville, and between Martensdale and Winterset; the C. B. & Q. R. R. between Ack-
worth and Indianola, and for 23 m. W. of Greenfield.
Burlington Bus Line follows the highway between Fredonia and Knoxville, Mar-
tensdale and Lewis.
Roadbed paved, except two graveled sections between junction with US 61 and
Columbus Junction, and between Fontanelle and Lewis.
Tourist accommodations of all kinds available chiefly in cities.

Section a. JUNCTION WITH US 61 *to* INDIANOLA, *129 m.*

State 2 branches west from the junction with US 61 *(see Tour 1),* 15
miles south of Muscatine *(see Tour 1).*

FREDONIA, 9 *m.* (602 alt., 165 pop.), was considered as a possible territorial capital of Iowa, Jan. 21, 1839, receiving only three votes less than Iowa City, which was chosen.

COLUMBUS JUNCTION, 10 *m*. (595 alt., 867 pop.), was so named because it is a railroad junction near Columbus City, 2 miles S. LOVERS LEAP BRIDGE, a suspension foot bridge 262 feet long, with a pergola at one end, is suspended across a ravine 80 feet deep, on the edge of town; it was designed by Byron Lambert of Iowa City and built in 1922 at a cost of $2,500. Mrs. E. B. Tucker of Columbus Junction stimulated the villagers to raise funds for the bridge through cake sales, box suppers, "white elephant" sales, and home talent plays. The origin of its name is not known.

Left on a dirt road to PANSY HILL, 1.5 *m.*, covered with wild pansies in summer. The plants do not survive transplanting.

At 19.5 *m*. is the junction with US 218 *(see Tour 1A)*.

WASHINGTON, 27 *m*. (769 alt., 4,814 pop.), is a typical Iowa county seat, with the courthouse square in the center of the town. The COURT-HOUSE, a red brick structure with elaborate stone trim, is typical of the 1890s.

This town has been the home of Smith Wildman Brookhart (1869–   ) since his childhood. Known as a "dirt farmer," he was elected to the U. S. Senate (1922–1925; 1927–1933).

At 38 *m*. is the junction with State 81, graveled.

Right on State 81 is WELLMAN, 9 *m*. (698 alt., 853 pop.). At the MAPLE CREST CO-OPERATIVE TURKEY FARMS on the edge of town, half a million turkeys, valued at about $2,000,000, are raised annually. The birds are grown by 170 farmers in the vicinity, under contract with the cooperative. Begun about 15 years ago on a small scale, the turkey business has developed into an impressive example of community cooperation.

At 10 *m*. is an OLD MILL on the bank of the English River—all that is left of the town of Wassonville, laid out beneath tall trees in 1848. The mill is operated by water power furnished by a dam.

At 45 *m*. is the junction with State 77, graveled.

Right on State 77 is KEOTA, 3 *m*. (800 alt., 955 pop.), a horse-raising and shipping center. Many farmers trade here, bringing in large quantities of cream and eggs for shipment. Here, in 1880, the only flint glass works west of Cincinnati produced glass of very high quality. Prospects were good but when the vein of sand was mined out, the factory was closed. The building is used today for recreational purposes.

The Singmaster Farms, home of purebred draft horses, were once distinguished by a private herd of buffalo and deer. The last 11 of the buffalo, descendants of one bull and two cows procured by C. F. Singmaster from Yellowstone National Park in 1902, were sold for the market price of beef in 1934. The deer could not be kept confined but ran away singly and in pairs, and formed a roving wild colony along the Skunk River south of Keota. Today the State keeps a game warden on duty in the territory to protect the deer.

At 50 *m*. is the junction with State 159, graveled.

Right on State 159, at 1.5 *m.*, is STATION NO. 9 *(visitors welcome)*, of the Natural Gas Pipe Line Co. of America. This is a booster or compression station used to maintain the force of flow in the natural gas pipe line extending across Iowa. The station, having 15 houses, supplies its own electric power.

At 56 *m.* is the junction with State 149, paved.

Right on State 149 is SOUTH ENGLISH, 11 *m.* (840 alt., 296 pop.); R. from here on a graveled road to the ENGLISH RIVER CHURCH OF THE BRETHREN, 2.5 *m.* Like the Amana Society *(see Tour 14A)* the Church of the Brethren grew out of the German Pietist movement; the sect dates from 1708. Revolting against orthodoxy and scholasticism, the members believed in a religion based on the principles of primitive Christianity. To escape persecution, the group fled to Holland, and later came to America. William Penn transferred the ownership of 8,000 acres of land to them. Known in some localities as Tunkers, Dunkers, and Dunkards *(see Tour 3A)*, they are often mistaken for Mennonites. In the spring of 1854, five families belonging to the Church of the Brethren, including a minister, came to Mount Vernon, Iowa, from Ohio.

From Mount Vernon they moved here, where their minister was asked to preach at a union service in the two-room cabin of an early settler. In 1855 co-workers arrived from Virginia and the English River congregation was organized. The following year a large shed was built, its roof and sides made from prairie grass that had been cut as hay. Services were seldom held at night because of the expense of tallow candles and lard-burning lamps, so the fire hazard was slight.

Essentially an agricultural people, they soon acquired large acreages. Bound to severe simplicity of living by their religious belief, they prospered quickly on the rich Iowa soil, producing everything essential for their needs, including material for clothing. The men wore standing collars, but no neckties. Beards were required, but mustaches forbidden. A love-feast became an important annual event. Preceding the Lord's Supper they engaged in the rite of foot-washing, an expression of humility and friendship. More recent generations have modified the original attitude of antagonism toward education and higher learning, and have established schools and colleges. However, many of the older beliefs have been retained. The members refuse to bear arms and to take the civil oath. During the World War they remained non-combatants, but joined in the work of relief and reconstruction. They have always taken a stand against intemperance, and they believe it a religious duty to take care of their poor.

SIGOURNEY, 56 *m.* (958 alt., 2,262 pop.), seat of Keokuk County, was named for Lydia Huntley Sigourney (1791–1865) of Connecticut, author of many books. When she learned of the honor, she presented the town library with 50 volumes, and directed the planting of the outer row of trees around the courthouse square. Most of the residents are of German descent.

Achilles Rogers, the only Revolutionary War soldier buried in the county, is interred in the Pennington Cemetery; he died at the age of 102 during the cholera epidemic of 1864.

During the period of the Civil War opposing factions in Keokuk County clashed in what became known as the Skunk River War or Tally War. It began in a difference of opinion between those who believed the Federal Government was justified in waging war upon the States attempting secession and those who felt that secession was a State right. The leader of the rebels was a young Baptist preacher, Cyphert Tally, who had come to Iowa from Tennessee. He freely expressed his objections to the war upon the slave-owning States, and was in consequence called a Copperhead.

On Aug. 1, 1863, Tally and some friends, who had held a political meeting in a nearby grove, attempted to pass through South English where the residents had armed against him. A shot was fired, afterwards asserted to have been accidental. This incident, however, began a fight during which Tally was shot in the head. On hearing of Tally's death, a group of armed men gathered. Two thousand Tally sympathizers came from Wapello, Mahaska, and Poweshiek Counties, forming the "Skunk River Army." The people of South English and Sigourney sent a request for aid to Gov. Samuel Kirkwood. Ordering 11 companies of militia to move into Keokuk County, the Governor himself hurried there. The town was filled with armed men determined to defy the State government. The Governor ordered the men to disperse and assured them that the entire military resources of Iowa would be at his disposal to effect their arrest if they remained. After some sullen argument and resistance the men dispersed.

At 64 *m.* is the junction with a graveled road.

Right on this road to WHAT CHEER, 4 *m.* (751 alt., 1,310 pop.), a Scotch and German settlement manufacturing pottery of national fame. The town dates back to 1865 when it was an Indian trading post and agricultural trade center. After the discovery of outcroppings of coal along the little stream, which the settlers named Coal Creek, mines were opened Maj. Joseph Andrews, with the memory of early Rhode Island traditions, proposed the name of What Cheer. Neighbors were skeptical. Nobody had heard of a name like that, they argued. The Major told of how Roger Williams crossed the Seesonk River in a canoe, of how the Indians met him and exclaimed, "What cheer, Netop!" What Cheer in time called itself the "Coal City of Iowa," but by 1889 several of the larger coal veins were worked out. The mines began to close, and many of the miners moved on westward. Then prospectors discovered another source of underground wealth—white clay. A company to manufacture products of clay was formed, with a capital of half a million dollars. Tests later showed that the clay was suited to the manufacturing of table and kitchen ware. Today terra-cotta, garden pots, teapots, pitchers, vases, urns, cups, saucers, and fancy pottery of many varieties are made for a wide market.

Hal O'Flaherty (1890–), war correspondent and editor, and later managing editor of the Chicago *Daily News*, was born at What Cheer.

At 8 *m.* is the junction with another graveled road; R. here 2 *m.* to the junction with a dirt road; L. here to the BRUCE GOLDFISH HATCHERY, 2.25 *m.*, a very large goldfish farm *(picnicking)*.

In the 17 ponds fish vary in length from ¼ inch to 1 foot. Goldfish have been sent from these ponds to many parts of the world. Elgin K. Bruce, Sr., founder of the hatchery, started in the goldfish business in Pittsburgh, Pa., in 1842. He came to Iowa with his family in 1877 and established his plant here on a 60-acre tract. After he died the business was carried on by his two sons, George and Elgin. Japanese fantail, telescope, and "red, white, and blue" are among the varieties reared here.

ROSE HILL, 69 *m.* (822 alt., 275 pop.), founded by James Ornabaum in 1875, is a prosperous center of a purebred hog- and cattle-rearing area. One of the outstanding herds, that of John Brown, seldom fails to rank high in large stock shows throughout the country.

At 74 *m.* is the junction with a graveled road.

Left on this road into LAKE KEOMAH STATE PARK *(boating, fishing, and picnicking facilities)*, 1 *m.*, a 352-acre recreational area with a 250-acre artificial lake. Many plants rarely found elsewhere in Iowa grow here in profusion, including bladder fern, maidenhair fern, flowering fern, touch-me-not, and everlasting columbine. The more plentiful trees are butternut, hard maple, honey-locust, almond leaf and black willow, green and white ash, and red haw.

OSKALOOSA, 79 *m.* (843 alt., 10,123 pop.).

Swimming and Tennis: Edmundson Park, 11th Ave. W. between S. F St. and S. M St.

Annual Events: Southern Iowa Fair, early September, Fair Grounds, entrance 701 N. I St.; Society of Friends (Quakers) Yearly Meeting, late August and early September, Friends' Church, 656 N. C St.; Camp Meeting of Free Methodists, August, and National Holiness Camp Meeting, University Park.

Oskaloosa, seat of Mahaska County, is a quiet college town, the home of Quakers, retired farmers, musicians, and music-lovers. The homes and other buildings reflect that dignity, stability, and serenity characteristic of the Quakers who settled here in 1843.

The city is a marketing center; on Saturdays farmers crowd the streets, rolling their cans of cream into the creameries, talking over prices, and discussing the week's happenings. At the sales pavilion west of the square, livestock, hay, grain, fence posts, and farm commodities are sold. The Mahaska Sheep and Wool Growers Association is a marketing cooperative, with a membership in the surrounding country. The Oskaloosa Poultry Producers Cooperative Association operates a concentration plant and there are three poultry packing plants and three creameries marketing local produce. A cannery provides a market for tomatoes, corn, and beans which are contracted for before the crop is planted.

The city was named for Oskaloosa *(Last of the Beautiful),* a wife of Chief Osceola. The site in early days was on a natural route of travel between the Mississippi and Missouri Rivers. Twenty years after the first members of the Society of Friends arrived their community was of sufficient importance to be host to the joint annual meetings of the societies in the area. It is now the scene of one of the nine Friends' yearly meetings held in the United States.

The first coal mines in the State were developed (1870) in Mahaska County; for the most part these were shallow workings of veins from three to six feet in thickness. By 1910, however, most of the large coal companies had removed to adjacent counties. After the closing of the Mahaska mines, the Welsh miners remained in the county to farm or carry on business in Oskaloosa and other towns. In 1930 there were more Welsh in Mahaska than in any other county in the State.

The Welsh brought with them a love for music that had wide local influence, causing the establishment of various music-making groups. Frederic Knight Logan *(see below),* Thurlow Lieurance (1878–   ), composer of *By the Waters of Minnetonka,* and Mason Slade (1881–1935), the organist, were born here. June Adele Skelton (1887–1928), known on the European concert stage as Mme. Salteni-Mochi, attended the public school here from 1898 to 1906. Homer Samuels (1889–   ), husband and accompanist of Mme. Galli-Curci, as well as Charles L. Griffith (1887–   ), the composer, came from the Welsh settlements near the city.

Samuel H. M. Byers, who wrote the words of the song, *Sherman Marched Down To the Sea,* while in a prison camp in South Carolina, was a native. With Byers in prison was a Lieutenant Tower who, when exchanged, carried the song to his home in Ottumwa hidden in the hollow of his wooden leg.

The STATUE OF CHIEF MAHASKA, on the west side of the public square,

SIESTA

is a memorial to William Edmundson, to whom the Territorial government entrusted the organization of Mahaska County. Sherry S. Fry, an Iowan, modeled the statue in Paris. It won for him a medal of honor and a three-year scholarship in Rome. The OSKALOOSA *Daily Herald* PLANT *(open weekdays 9-4)*, 123 N. Market St., is a red brick, gabled structure of old English design with stone trim. The evening paper published here was first issued in 1850 by Hugh McNeely. His first press, previously used in the publication of the Cambridge (Ohio) *Times,* was loaded on a boat, sent down the Ohio River and up the Mississippi to Keokuk; from there hauled overland by wagon. Four times during the Civil War every employee of the office laid down his tools and took up arms in defense of the Union.

The HOME OF FREDERIC KNIGHT LOGAN (1871–1928), 416 B Ave. E. *(private),* is an attractive story-and-a-half house of rough red brick trimmed with stone. Virginia Knight Logan, mother of the composer, wrote the words for his *Missouri Waltz.* Here Logan also wrote *Pale Moon,* an American Indian love-song, and the waltz of his *Valse Chopinesque.* Logan acted as accompanist to Caruso, Schumann-Heink, and Edith Mason. He was musical director of the Belasco Theatre, New York City, and traveled with Maude Adams from coast to coast during her repertoire tour whose program included *L'Aiglon* and *Peter Pan.*

The log MORGAN CABIN *(open in summer; adm. 10¢),* 1221 S. F St., stands in landscaped grounds adjoining and near the east entrance to Edmundson Park. It was built in the 1840's and is furnished in pioneer style. The cabin is of hewed logs, in an excellent state of preservation. From the rafters hang the saddlebags of one of the first pony express riders of this section. The R. P. WEATHERWAX COLLECTION (open daily), housed in the owner's home at 1104 9th Ave. W., contains bullet moulds, 150 old guns, shot pouches, powder horns, and coins (chiefly gold).

HARMONY HEAVEN *(open weekdays 10-4),* 1302-1304 High Ave., W., the home of the Barnhouse Music Publishing Co., was formerly the home of Charles L. Barnhouse, composer of band and orchestra music. In the aged red brick building among the trees Barnhouse composed many of his well-known compositions. The building, which at one time housed the Oskaloosa College, has been remodeled.

The FRIENDS' MEETING HOUSE, 656 N. C St., designed in the Greek Revival style with Indiana stone trim, was dedicated in 1913, during the Semi-Centennial Assembly of the Iowa Yearly Meeting of the Society of Friends. WILLIAM PENN COLLEGE *(open during school hours),* W. side Market St. at the northern city limits, a co-educational institution, operated under the auspices of the Society of Friends, was opened in September 1873. Following the destruction of the first building by fire in May 1916, several new buildings were erected on a 30-acre campus just north of the old college site. Degrees in liberal arts, in science, and in music are granted here; the enrollment is about 200. Near the campus entrance is the SPENCER MEMORIAL CHAPEL, dedicated in February 1923 to H. L. Spencer, one of Oskaloosa's early businessmen. Georgian Colonial in design and commanding an imposing position on a hill, its white columns face the city. The interior is painted an old ivory; pews are of cypress and the seats are finished in mahogany. The pipe organ, built from plans made by Charles L. Barnhouse, is in reality four organs, each of which can be operated separately. WILLIAM PENN HALL, of simple design, has a four-story central unit supporting an observatory. This building houses administrative offices, the science and the liberal arts departments, and the college MUSEUM *(open weekdays 1-5; free)*; the latter contains a large collection of native drums, spears, and other curios from the interior of Africa. The Women's Dormitory is designed as four separate cottages, named for women famous in Quaker history. A group of 21 paintings, the MAJ. S. H. M. BYERS ART COLLECTION, hangs in the large drawing room.

JOHN FLETCHER COLLEGE *(open during school hours)*, in University Park, a small incorporated city that has grown up around the college, adjoins the eastern limits of the town. Having its own corporate government, the college and city work together to maintain moral standards for the students. The college was organized in 1905 as the Central Holiness University, later changing its name to honor John Fletcher, one of the leading proponents of Methodism and a friend of John Wesley. Coeducational, and founded to give religious training, the college centers around a tabernacle in which yearly camp meetings are held. The five brick buildings stand on a naturally wooded campus. In 1935, there were 181 students in attendance. The Bachelor of Arts degree and diplomas in music and oratory are offered.

Oskaloosa is at the junction with US 63 *(see Tour 3)* and with US 163 *(see Tour 5A)*.

1. Left from Oskaloosa on State 137, paved and graveled, is EDDYVILLE (676 alt., 888 pop.), 10 *m.* In 1840 Jabish P. Eddy was given a permit to open a fur trading post at Chief Hard Fish's village on the Des Moines River; the post grew into the present Eddyville. Because of its position on the Des Moines River, the town developed rapidly; within a short period there were four wholesale and retail grocery stores, two saddlery stores, one plow factory, one woolen factory, a packing house, two breweries, and 14 saloons. Eddyville liquor was sent as far west as Denver in those days. In 1858 the first bridge below Des Moines was built at Eddyville, a drawbridge that permitted steamboats from St. Louis to proceed upriver. It was washed out by ice and high water in the spring of 1885, but was replaced by a free bridge in 1887. Conestoga wagons, with their white tops, rumbled over the rough plank flooring of the early bridge, or paused in Eddyville while a steamboat from St. Louis churned its way through the open bridge and tied up at the wharf beyond to unload its cargo of food and supplies. At one time six large steamboats from St. Louis were tied up at the wharves. But the prosperity of Eddyville faded after the railroad was extended to Des Moines.

Coal was discovered near Oskaloosa, and that town attracted the trade from neighboring territory. The railroad lessened steamboat traffic. Mills closed. Eddyville, as gateway to the Far West, became just another town.

2. Left from Oskaloosa on State 309, graveled (Beacon Road), to the WRIGHT PEONY FARM, 1 *m.*, where three acres of peonies make a brilliant display in the latter part of May and early June. Other perennials provide bloom throughout the summer.

BEACON, 2 *m.* (752 alt., 350 pop.), a Welsh coal-mining community established in 1864, was first known as Enterprise. The population was once nearly a thousand. Hundreds of Negroes were brought here from the South, but the English and Welsh would not allow them to live within the town limits. Before the turn of the century the mines were worked out and the population dwindled to the present figure. The strip method of mining is used, but scarcely more than 50 miners are employed (1937).

3. Left from Oskaloosa on an improved road to the junction with a winding road, 6.5 *m.*, just before the Eveland Bridge is reached; R. here 9.5 *m.*, along the Des Moines River, to the SITE OF THE IOWA PHALANX (1843), one of the American Fourierist colonies. This group came from Watertown, N. Y., and established themselves under a written agreement of social cooperation. Here, at a bend in the Des Moines River, they found a mill site and took up 320 acres of land where lived deer and wild turkey. They built one long house, a phalanstery, partitioning off two rooms for each family. When provisions ran low they traveled to Oskaloosa in ox-drawn wagons. Education of the children at the cost of the group, seven meals daily, opera and drama, joy of life—all were on the program. These people had little money, but they lived well and comfortably. Individual ambitions became strong, and neighboring opposition grew. In 1845 the group disbanded. Within a few years only graves and dilapidated buildings marked the spot of the social experiment.

At 91 *m.* is the junction with a graveled road.

Left on this road is TRACY, 1 *m.* (729 alt.), a small village where in 1933, Dr. W. H. Barker unearthed a slab of black limestone of unknown origin bearing the shape of a human profile.

At 95 *m.* is the junction with State 310, graveled.

Right on this road is HARVEY, 2 *m.* (733 alt., 348 pop.), at the mouth of English Creek. Every kind of tree and shrub native to Marion County—black haw, honey locust, basswood, bittersweet, hazel bush, and others—is represented in an ARBORETUM, three blocks east of Main Street. This collection was made by Dr. William Henry Harrison Barker (1840–   ), over a period of 32 years. Dr. Barker, a dentist, professor, author, engineer, inventor, and country doctor in the course of his life established the arboretum in the interest of conservation. At the front gate stands a white sycamore tree called America's Peace Tree, named in 1917 after America went to war. After the World War, Dr. Barker had planted at the gate of every Government cemetery a white sycamore tree as a symbol of peace. Dr. Barker's stone and log cabin stands among the trees.

Spanning English Creek, near Harvey, are two COVERED BRIDGES, built when the community was first founded. The bridges were covered with high wooden roofs to protect the flooring. A number of these covered structures are still in good state of preservation though many uncovered wooden bridges have long since rotted away. Travelers in the early days of Iowa often found shelter beneath these roofs when blizzards or storms caught them far from home. At the same time, the structure of these bridges created dark shadows at night, offering an ambush for highwaymen, and the unwary traveler was often robbed of his valuables as the wind whistled round the timbers, drowning any possible outcry.

KNOXVILLE, 103 *m.* (910 alt., 4,697 pop.), seat of Marion County, was founded in 1845 and named for General Henry Knox, an officer in the Revolutionary War, who later became Secretary of War and the first Secretary of the Navy.

At the edge of town (R) is the VETERANS ADMINISTRATION FACILITY *(open to relatives 9-4, daily)*, a Federal hospital for the treatment of exservice men suffering from mental and nervous disorders. The present (1937) capacity is 1,015.

The Government owns 345 acres here, of which approximately 50 acres is used for lawns and buildings of the cottage type. Much of the land is cultivated by the patients. Particular emphasis is placed on occupational therapy.

At 104 *m*. the highway crosses the RED ROCK LINE, established in 1842–43, in accordance with a treaty between the Indians and the United States Government; all land lying east of the line being open to white settlement after May 1, 1843, that west remaining Indian territory until 1845. When the line of division was to be abolished in 1845, the Government stationed troops at intervals along the line to enforce the order that no settler should cross it until midnight of Oct. 11, 1845. The settlers, however, practiced the pioneer maxim, "Git a-plenty while yer gittin' an' git th' best!" As the time of expiration of the Indian claim approached, several settlers managed to slip over and select their claims but a greater number waited tensely along the line for the moment when they could dash across. Precisely at midnight the firing of guns announced the moment had come. Covered wagons drawn by oxen rattled over the rough frosted ground, urged onward by the shouts of the excited drivers. Men on horseback swept past, their torches flaring in the wind. Small children, frightened by the noise of firearms, clung close to their mothers.

The claims were paced off in the darkness, and were later found by Government surveyors to be fairly accurate; few disputes arose among the settlers regarding boundaries. On the first night camp fires were built, stakes were driven, oxen were unyoked and turned out to graze, and children returned to their interrupted sleep, unaware that a new chapter in Iowa's history was being written.

At 112 *m*. is junction with State 181, bituminous surfaced.

Left on this road 10 *m*. is MELCHER (948 alt., 1,673 pop.), one of the larger coal-mining towns in Iowa. In the Red Rock mine the coal is hauled more than a mile and a half underground by electric cars. This mine, in operation for 20 years, was the first successful one dug in the Melcher Field. There are 33 coal mines in Marion County.

ACKWORTH, 124 *m*. (857 alt., 82 pop.), a hamlet inhabited principally by Quakers, was named for a city in England of the same name. In 1869 a Friends' academy was established here and $1,000 was sent from Ackworth, England, for books. Meetings were held in the assembly room of the school on First Day, and on Fourth Day, men quitting their work in the fields for the latter. Sometimes a wife would take a clean shirt to her husband in the field where he was working and he would tie his team, wash his hands in a stream, don the garment and set off with her to the meeting for an hour of quiet communion.

INDIANOLA, 129 *m*. (969 alt., 3,488 pop.), is at the junction with US 65 *(see Tour 5)*.

Section b. INDIANOLA *to* JUNCTION WITH US 6, *91 m.*

West of Indianola, 0 *m.,* is MARTENSDALE 10 *m*. (824 alt., 139 pop.), which was established at the junction of the C. R. I. & P. and C. G. W. R. R. as a shipping point for the surrounding farms.

WINTERSET, 26 *m.* (1,129 alt., 2,921 pop.), center of a fruit-growing area, is at the junction with US 169 *(see Tour 6).*

At 28 *m.* is the junction with State 162, graveled.

Left on this road to PAMMEL STATE PARK, 3 *m.*, a 291-acre tract on the banks of the Middle River. The park was named for Dr. Louis Pammel of Ames, an early supporter of the conservation movement in Iowa. There are picnic grounds, a shelter house, and miles of nature trails along the side of the DEVIL'S BACKBONE, a limestone ridge extending the length of the park. The ridge rises 100 feet from the valley floor, within a horseshoe bend of the river. A pioneer named Harmon, who settled here in 1856, tunneled through the ridge, changing the course of the river and creating a fall, where he erected a watermill. The highway now passes through the old tunnel, and traces of the mill site are seen in the brush and weeds at the eastern end of the passage.

In the early days in Madison County, men had to wear leather leggings as a protection against rattlesnakes, and frontier women were often terrified by the discovery of the reptiles within their cabins or near their small children playing outside. The few people who were bitten by snakes were treated with whiskey, which was not always effective as a remedy. In the spring of 1848 the settlers planned a campaign to rid the area of these snakes, organizing a contest, each man pledging a certain amount of corn as an entrance fee which would go as a prize to the winner. A special effort was made to kill the snakes before they left their dens along the river cliffs, usually in April and May, because in summer they scattered to the brush when attempts were made to capture them. July 4, 1848, was set for the end of the contest. The hunters and their families gathered at Guye's Grove for a gala day; barbecued ox and other food was served. They presented their trophies, more than 4,000 rattles. Since the big snake hunt the reptiles have not been so common in Madison County.

GREENFIELD, 51 *m.* (1,368 alt., 1,837 pop.), seat of Adair County, is the receiving and distributing center for a stock-raising and agricultural area.

FONTANELLE, 57 *m.* (1,334 alt., 833 pop.), formerly called Summerset, was the first seat of Adair County. A line of the Underground Railway, which helped slaves to escape from the South, passed through the town between 1850 and 1861.

At 64 *m.* is the junction with State 189, graveled.

Left on this road is BRIDGEWATER, 1 *m.* (1,188 alt., 327 pop.), a livestock-shipping center for the surrounding area. Almost all the grain grown in surrounding townships is sent here to feed stock that is to be shipped to market.

At 69 *m.* is the junction with State 254, graveled.

Left on State 254 1 *m.* is MASSENA (1,211 alt., 475 pop.), named for a town in New York from which many of the early settlers came. When the gold fever hit this vicinity in 1859, a number of settlers left for Pike's Peak, Colo., only to return when the gold was not found. A second exodus to Colorado took place in 1860, and a few of the fortune-seekers remained and prospered in the neighborhood of Denver. By far the greater number, however, were disappointed and returned to Cass County.

At 81 *m.* is the junction with US 71 *(see Tour 7).*

LEWIS, 90 *m.* (1,157 alt., 589 pop.), first seat of Cass County, named for Lewis Cass (1782–1866), U. S. Senator from Michigan, who was also honored by the county name, because he had effected 22 treaties with the Indians, thus helping to open much of the Northwest Territory to settlement. The town, on the banks of the East Nishnabotna River, was an active station for the Underground Railway during John Brown's abolition campaign.

Left on a county road to COLD SPRINGS STATE SCENIC PRESERVE, 1 *m.*, a 6o-acre tract bordering the East Nishnabotna River. A spring-fed swimming pool, built more than 40 years ago, has a good sand bottom. The preserve area was formerly known as Crystal Lake Park.

At 91 *m.* is the junction with US 6 *(see Tour 14)*, 44 miles E. of Council Bluffs.

‹‹‹‹‹‹‹‹‹‹‹‹‹‹‹‹‹‹☼››››››››››››››››››››

Tour 16

(Galesburg, Ill.)—Burlington—Ottumwa—Lucas—Osceola—Red Oak—(Lincoln, Nebr.); US 34.
Illinois Line to Nebraska Line, 270 m.

Route paralleled throughout by the C. B. & Q. R. R.; between Fairfield and Ottumwa by the C. R. I. & P. R. R.
Burlington Bus Line operates between Burlington and Glenwood. Roadbed paved, except 6 m., graveled, between Glenwood and the Missouri River.
Accommodations of all kinds available, chiefly in cities.

Section a. ILLINOIS LINE *to* LUCAS, *135 m.*

US 34 crosses the Mississippi River, in which is the Illinois Line 45 miles W. of Galesburg, Ill., on the BURLINGTON TOLL BRIDGE *(car and driver, 25¢; passengers, 5¢ each).*

In the early days of automobile travel in Iowa, the present route of US 34 was known as the Blue Grass Road. The highway, not usually crowded with traffic, runs through comparatively level country, broken by a few hills.

BURLINGTON, 1 *m.* (532 alt., 26,755 pop.) *(see BURLINGTON).*

Points of Interest: Site of Wisconsin Territorial Capitol; Municipal Docks; Charles Wachsmuth Museum.

Burlington is at the junction with US 61 *(see Tour 1).*

WEST BURLINGTON, 4 *m.* (690 alt., 1,333 pop.), is a thriving town. In 1882 Joel West organized the community that had been known as Leffleer's Station by bringing the workers at the locomotive shops in the north part of town into a realty company, enabling them to buy lots on the installment plan. Any religious denomination that wanted to build a church here was given two lots.

At the western edge of town is a small PARK containing OUR LADY OF

GRACE GROTTO *(small donation expected)*, a dome-shaped structure housing a statue of the Virgin Mary and two angels. The floor, walls, and dome
of the grotto are of crystal geodes; the exterior walls contain stones from
almost every country in the world, as well as from every State in the
Union. The grotto is lighted at night. In the garden are 40 kinds of evergreens; symmetrical paths wind around flower beds, ornamental pools,
and fountains; small footbridges span a miniature lagoon. Near the grotto
are two fountains, each with a large shell, one from the Atlantic and the
other from the Pacific Ocean.

Left from West Burlington on a dirt road 2.5 *m.;* L. to a junction at 3 *m.;* R.
here to another at 3.5 *m.;* L. again to a road at 3.8 *m.;* the FRITZ HOUSE, 5.3 *m.*
was built by John H. Fritz, who migrated from Germany in 1849 and settled here
in 1852 when most of the land was covered with timber and brush. He first constructed a two-room frame house having walls lined with brick; about 1870 two
rooms, constructed of limestone from a nearby quarry, were added.

MIDDLETOWN, 10 *m.* (724 alt., 126 pop.), was laid out early in
1839 by Josiah T. Smith, an emigrant from Ohio. The town was first
named Lewis Point, for an early settler, and was in 1847 renamed by John
Sharp of Pennsylvania.

DANVILLE, 14 *m.* (726 alt., 327 pop.), was settled in 1854 by Alan-
son and Harriet Messenger; here is the BRUSH CREEK BAPTIST CHURCH,
dedicated in 1840 with 11 members.

Left from Danville on a graveled road 3 *m.,* L. to a junction at 4 *m.,* R. here
to LAKE PARK PROJECT, 7 *m.* 613-acres with a lake covering 100 acres. A permanent name has not been selected.

At 16 *m.* (L) is a cluster of evergreens, all that is left of the pioneer
hamlet of Jimtown, named for James Duke, who provided accommodations for stagecoach passengers in his log cabin.

NEW LONDON, 20 *m.* (768 alt., 1,336 pop.), first named Dover in
honor of Abraham C. Dover, owner of the site, is the home of Frank
Lundeen, world champion horseshoe pitcher in 1922–23.

Left from New London on the unpaved Lowell Road to a farm 6.5 *m.* where
is a GEODE BED. The main bed, in Mud Creek, is in some places 30 feet thick.
The concretions, usually siliceous and hollow, can be opened by a blow with a
blunt instrument. The cavities are lined with quartz in the form of bright, transparent crystals; some are wax white or gray chalcedony, others clear colorless car-
bonate of calcium.

MOUNT PLEASANT, 29 *m.* (729 alt., 3,743 pop.), is the seat of
Henry County, which had the first courthouse in Iowa, built in the fall of
1839—a two-story building in the center of the square. Presley Saunders,
the founder of the town, chose the town site because of the elevation,
abundant shade, and good water, and further because it was close enough
to Burlington to enjoy the advantages of river commerce, yet far enough
removed to expand.

Construction of three plank roads radiating from Burlington was authorized by the Iowa Legislature in 1849; one of these, running from
Burlington to Mt. Pleasant, was completed in 1851. At that time the average road was hardly more than a trail, with many rocks and ruts making

travel and transportation extremely slow and difficult. Timber was abundant, however, and the new road was laid with good oak plank, 8 feet long and 3 inches thick, on stringers 2 inches thick and 6 inches wide, costing an average of $2,500 a mile for the first 8 miles. The highway was 30 feet wide, set in a 60 foot right-of-way. This was a toll road in which the rate was 2¢ a mile for a horse and wagon; in 1851 it had returned 20 percent on the investment. But in a few years it was paralleled by the C. B. & Q. R. R. and could not survive the competition. Permission had been obtained to extend the road to Ottumwa, but the work was never undertaken.

IOWA WESLEYAN COLLEGE had its beginning here in 1844. The campus almost in the heart of the city, is a park of 25 acres, containing shrubs, flowers, and many fine trees and seven attractive buildings. First named Mount Pleasant Collegiate Institute, it was named Iowa Wesleyan University in 1849, and Iowa Wesleyan College in 1911. The 4-year accredited college is sponsored by the Methodist Church. It has been coeducational from the beginning; part-time employment is arranged for students who desire it.

A monument in memory of Charles B. Shepherd, who fought at Brandywine and Germantown in the Revolutionary War, and died in Henry County, stands in the MOUNT PLEASANT CEMETERY.

At the end of N. Main St. stands the HARLAN HOUSE *(open)*, an imposing old structure with wide verandas and white columns. James Harlan (1820–1899) became president of Iowa Wesleyan in 1853 and two years later entered a contest for election to the U. S. Senate; he was not seated because the election was irregular, but won in 1860. Abraham Lincoln appointed him Secretary of Interior in 1865 but he resigned after Johnson became President. In 1868 Harlan's only daughter, Mary, was married to Robert T. Lincoln, son of the President. In time, the house was given to the college. On a door, still preserved in the house, are the height measurements, names, and ages of the three grandchildren of James Harlan and Abraham Lincoln.

SAUNDERS PARK *(picnicking and bathing facilities; free tourist camp)* is a 40-acre tract, containing rolling hills covered with many trees; approximately 25 acres have been developed, the rest remaining in its natural state. Many paths wind among the great oaks and maples. A speaker's rostrum has foundations and walls of rock, and a roof supported by roughhewn cedar poles. In 1921 a tract of four acres in the park was given by the city for the HENRY COUNTY SOLDIERS' AND SAILORS' MEMORIAL HOSPITAL.

IOWA STATE HOSPITAL FOR THE INSANE, Asylum Ave. and E. Washington St., was opened in 1861 and was by 1865 filled to its capacity of 400 patients; many additions have been made and in 1936 there were 1,500 patients. In 1935 the State's total investment in the institution was nearly $2,000,000; a fire in August, 1936, caused considerable damage. This hospital is one of four institutions of the kind in the State, but to relieve their overcrowding the State has had to place many patients in county homes.

Mount Pleasant is at the junction with US 218 *(see Tour 1A)*.

At 37 *m.* is the junction with State 129, a dirt road.

Left on this road is ROME, 1 *m.* (626 alt., 144 pop.), settled in 1836. Several celebrated chiefs, with their tribes—Kcokuk, Wapello, Black Hawk, Pashepaho, Appanoose, Hardfish and Kishkekosh—at times hunted in Henry County. One of the principal Indian mounds in the country is near Rome.

LOCKRIDGE, 41 *m.* (732 alt., 231 pop.), was settled in 1836 when Col. W. G. Coop erected a cabin on the site as a trading post.

At 46 *m.* is WOODTHRUSH STATE SCENIC PRESERVE *(picnicking facilities)*, an area of 26 acres established primarily for nature study. The tract is also known as the Hiram Heaton Preserve, in memory of a man (1846–1921) who did much for the preservation of wildlife in this part of Iowa.

FAIRFIELD, 52 *m.* (780 alt., 6,619 pop.), was so named by its founders because of the natural beauty of the site.

PARSONS COLLEGE was founded here in 1875 under the Parsons Endowment Fund provided in the will of Lewis P. Parsons (1793–1855), whose name the school bears. It is controlled by the Presbyterian Church, and has an annual enrollment of about 400. The college was first housed in the Bernhart Henn residence, now EWING HALL, and the first class was graduated in 1880. The campus now contains about 65 acres, mostly wooded.

In EVERGREEN CEMETERY is a MONUMENT TO MRS. M. E. WOODS (1813–1891), who traveled among the Iowa troops with a commissary wagon and a soldier escort during the Civil War. "Auntie" Woods, as she was called, received the honorary commission of major from Governor Kirkwood.

In 1854 the first Iowa State Fair was held here on October 10, 11, and 12. It was promoted by the Iowa Agricultural Society, a group of Jefferson County men who organized for "recognition of agricultural rights"; the Fairfield organization was the first of its kind in the State, but soon had numerous followers.

On the day of the first fair the little town was packed; hundreds of visitors arrived the day before the opening, walking, riding horseback, and using all types of vehicles; there were several two-wheeled carts drawn by ponderous oxen, and even covered wagons, in which families planned to camp during the fair. Some frontiersmen wore long pistols in their belts—both for protection and as ornaments. Interest centered on the display of farm implements gaining favor at the time—plows, harrows, corn planters, reapers, threshing machines, fanning mills, and corn crushers. Prison-made goods were also displayed, in addition to miscellaneous floral paintings, snake collections, fur hats, cloth, and wallpaper. Prizes were offered for a team of oxen of not less than three yokes, for grain cradles, and the like. Entertainment included horseback-riding feats by 18 women, horses and riders being bedecked with colored ribbons. The fair, though not a financial success, set a precedent.

The town has several factories, producing washers, malleable iron, gloves, and mittens, wagons, glass, brushes, and electric wood-working machines.

HOWARD PARK and CENTRAL PARK have beautiful old trees, shrubbery, and green lawns. Central Park was designated as the public square in 1839. These two parks, with the WATERWORKS PARK, contain 98 acres. OLD SETTLERS' PARK of 11 acres, where annual Old Settlers' Reunions are held, contains a log house—the Bonifield Cabin built in 1836, in front of which is the grave of the first white settler in the county.

In the PUBLIC LIBRARY MUSEUM *(open Sat. p.m.; other week-days by request)*, second floor, is a collection of stuffed birds and animals, laces, and Indian relics; there is also an archeological collection purchased from S. B. Evans, a cast of the stone Aztec calendar discovered in Mexico, statues from Rome, articles from Siam, the Philippines, and several miniature reproductions of Mexican villages. In the basement is a room containing a collection of miscellaneous articles used by the early settlers.

The JEFFERSON COUNTY HOSPITAL has a well-equipped laboratory, and an accredited training school for nurses, affiliated with the State University Hospital. Dedicated in 1912, the hospital cost $30,000.

Fairfield is (1938) one of the four Iowa cities having a STATE POLICE BROADCASTING STATION.

Near 58.5 *m.* the highway curves up a grade to a concrete overhead bridge, crossing the main line of the C. B. & Q. R. R., not far from a flag station called BERNHARDT. From this bridge the view embraces geometric fields of green corn, glistening brownish shocks of oats in stubble fields, dull green mats of alfalfa, rippling wheat fields of tawny tan, and flat green pastures where purebred cattle graze. The farm homes, barns, and rural schools are well-built, painted, and have a peaceful, prosperous air.

BATAVIA, 63 *m.* (731 alt., 478 pop.), a prosperous farm village, was first called Greaseville, in honor of one of the town's pioneers. The first cabin school, opened in 1849, contained no windows, and for ventilation the taller boys would push aside the loose clapboards on the roof; the door swung from wooden hinges that creaked loudly. At the north edge of Batavia are the WARD KENNELS.

At 67 *m.* is the junction with State 98, paved for 6 miles.

Left on this road is ELDON, 6 *m.* (630 alt., 1,788 pop.), beyond a steep hill that offers a view of the town, the winding Des Moines River, and rolling farm lands. Eldon is a farm trading center. The Wapello County Fairgrounds are at the town limits.

At 11 *m.* is SELMA, (615 alt.), a hamlet by the Des Moines River. Here is the HINKLE LOG CABIN *(open)*, erected in pioneer days by Thomas B. Saylor and sold in 1868 to Capt. Abraham Hinkle of Virginia. The few nails in the modern roof are the only nails in the entire structure, which was pinned together with wooden pegs. Within are early-day relics and furniture—a spinning wheel, and old-fashioned cradle, home-made furniture, and an ancient fireplace of stone.

AGENCY, 71 *m.* (798 alt., 371 pop.), called Agency City until 1883, was established in 1838 as an Indian agency, following the Treaty of 1837, when the Sac and Fox Indians, with the agent, Joseph M. Street, selected the site on which was built an immense council house.

Street moved his family to Iowa from Prairie du Chien, Wis., in 1838 and before his death in 1840 had gained the respect of his charges. When

Chief Wapello died he was buried, as he had requested, beside his friend, Street. The chief's name was later adopted as the name of the county because he had furthered peaceful relations with the white men. Surrounded by a white picket fence, the graves (L) are on the right-of-way of the C. B. & Q. R. R., which maintains them in return for the original gift of this piece of land. An interesting account of the Indians on the reservation and of the early settlers was written by Maj. John Beach, who succeeded Street as agent.

The five-mile stretch of highway between Agency and Ottumwa winds through rolling timberland with clumps of wild crab and cherry trees here and there.

OTTUMWA, 76 m. (649 alt., 28,075 pop.) (see OTTUMWA).

Points of Interest: Morrell Packing Co.; Central Park; Statue of Chief Wapello; High Point Chapel.

Ottumwa is at the junction with US 63 (see Tour 3).

At 90 m. is the junction with State 213, graveled.

Left on this road is BLAKESBURG, 5 m. (912 alt., 397 pop.); Theophilus Blake donated the land as a site in 1852. The town is on the highest elevation in Wapello County, in a region with many bituminous coal deposits. There are many large dairies in the district.

ALBIA, 99 m. (959 alt., 4,425 pop.), seat of Monroe County, was first known as Princeton. Most of the early settlers came from Illinois, Indiana, and Ohio; those who were the foreign-born were chiefly natives of Germany, Scandinavia, and Ireland.

Until after 1861 the residents of the town used wood for fuel, unaware of the rich deposit of coal beneath the surface in the vicinity. The first method of mining here was stripping. The principal vein, however, was from 200 to 300 feet underground, and shafts had to be sunk to reach it. This area was at one time among the chief coal fields of the State. Two strikes, during which eastern firms took over all marketing contracts, played a part in checking activities here. Production has been limited recently (1938) because of adverse market conditions, but a few mines with considerable output are still operated.

Mine labor is strongly organized in Albia, the largest membership being in the United Mine Workers of America; the local unit has a LABOR TEMPLE, on Benton Ave., opposite the Public Library.

COTTONWOOD PARK, SE. of town, has a small lake that is used for swimming.

STACYVILLE (L), 108 m. (1,208 alt., 529 pop.), was settled about 1850. The village has an excellent Roman Catholic choir.

GEORGETOWN, 108.5 m., though a small hamlet, has a large ST. PATRICK'S ROMAN CATHOLIC CHURCH of gray limestone, built in 1860. The material for the structure was hauled here by oxen, and construction required seven years.

At 123 m. there is excellent fishing in the Chariton River (L), stocked by the State Fish and Game Department.

At 125 m. (L) is RED HAW HILL PRESERVE (picnic area), a 425-

acre area, so named because of the many hawthorn trees on its hills among large elms, oaks, and other native trees and shrubs. The area, primarily a preserve protecting quail and small game, was acquired by the State Conservation Commission in 1936. An artificial lake, between two wooded slopes, is stocked with fish. A beautiful road winds over the hills, that are white in spring, green in summer, and red in the fall.

CHARITON, 126 m. (1,042 alt., 5,365 pop.), seat of Lucas County, lies along the banks of the Chariton River. In the description of the Lewis and Clark expedition, the men recorded seeing here "two rivers," named by the French "The Two Charatons," a corruption of the word Thier-aton. Lewis designated the river as Charliton on his map of 1806, and Clark as Charaton in 1814. Pioneers believed the name to be of Indian origin, signifying *a country rich with honey,* but according to another story, a French-Canadian trader in Missouri, Joseph Chartran, sometimes referred to as Charitone, was so closely associated with the river that it was named for him. The town was first called Polk, then Chariton Point, and finally Chariton.

The town owns a $50,000 water-works, and gas, light and power systems. The surrounding area is mainly agricultural in its interests, though considerable coal is mined. The town ships out farm horses and timothy seed. Oak of the vicinity is cut into furniture stock by a stationary mill, but several farmers operate portable mills in winter to cut wood for their own use. A foundry, machine and railroad shops, a broom factory, a dairy, and ice cream, candy, and bottling plants, and concrete works also provide local employment.

At 127 m. is CRYSTAL WEST LAKE *(adm., 10¢; fishing, swimming, picnicking facilities),* one mile in length. It is controlled by the Chariton Gun Club and is open to flat and speed boats; there are contests and exhibitions in summer. The lake and nearby East and Williamson Lakes are stocked by the State with bass, pike, catfish, carp, and perch.

LUCAS, 135 m. (888 alt., 514 pop.), on the banks of the White Breast Creek, is the birthplace (1880) of John L. Lewis, president of the United Mine Workers of America, and (1938) chairman of the Committee for Industrial Organization. His father came to Lucas from Wales where his ancestors had been miners, mining engineers, and farmers.

In 1882 the White Breast Fuel Co. of Lucas made a practice of paying miners only for the coal that would not fall through a screen of a certain size, instead of for all the coal they mined. Lucas miners were in sympathy with Thomas Lewis, father of John L. Lewis, in his opposition to this practice. The mine operators of the county, considering him a disturbing influence, blacklisted Lewis, and he was forced to leave the mines. For a time he worked in Colfax, Iowa, as a night watchman, but at length he reentered the mines near that town. Before long he was once again active in the labor movement, advocating collective bargaining.

In 1889 the Lewis family moved to Des Moines where Thomas became the custodian of the city jail. Eight years of his son John's education were over before his father's name was removed from the blacklist. At once the old Welsh miner took his family back to Lucas, where John, then 16, went to work in the mines with his father. John was known as an alert, dominating young man, with progressive ideas, who was educating himself in his spare time. The young man managed a local theater and later the local baseball team, and engaged in various local commercial enterprises. When he was 27 he was nominated for mayor, but was defeated. After his political defeat in Lucas, Lewis left Iowa and devoted his energies to the labor movement. By 1908 he had become legislative representative of the Mine Workers of Illinois; and by 1911 he had caught the attention of Samuel Gompers. During the next five years, as representative, organizer, and arbitrator for the A. F. of L., he handled various labor situations in many industries throughout the country. In 1917 he became vice-president of his union and when its president became ill, just before the great coal strike of 1919, was made acting president. During this strike he was instrumental in securing large wage increases for the miners. In 1920 he became president of the union. Lewis attracted international interest in 1937 because of his activities as chairman of the Committee for Industrial Organization (C. I. O.), which he organized and which caused a split in the labor movement.

Both the town and the county were named for Robert Lucas, first Territorial Governor (1838–41) of Iowa, appointed by President Martin Van Buren.

At Lucas is the junction with US 65 (see Tour 4).

Section b. LUCAS to NEBRASKA LINE, 135 m.

South of Lucas, 0 m., at 2 m. is the junction with an unimproved road.

Left on this road is CLEVELAND, 1 m. (899 alt.), a small coal-mining village where electric light, the first used in Iowa, was installed in a mine in 1880. William Haven, a mine superintendent, founded the town in 1878.

OSCEOLA, 16 m. (1,132 alt., 2,871 pop.) (see Tour 5), is at the junction with US 69 (see Tour 5).

At 34 m. is the junction with US 169 (see Tour 6), which is united with US 34 for 6 miles.

AFTON, 40 m. (1,212 alt., 1,013 pop.) (see Tour 6), is at the junction with US 169 (see Tour 6).

CRESTON, 49 m. (1,312 alt., 8,615 pop.), seat of Union County, is in the heart of Iowa's bluegrass country; it was designated headquarters of the Blue Grass League of Southwest Iowa in 1889, and a turreted Blue Grass Palace was erected. Eighteen counties cooperated to build this structure and a similar one in 1890—both entirely covered with bluegrass.

Creston was named divisional headquarters of the C. B. & Q. R. R. in 1869, and machine shops, extensive railroad yards, and a large roundhouse make it a busy place.

Since its founding, Creston has had a struggle to maintain an adequate water supply. The first reservoir was built by the railroad in 1872, where Cherry and South Mulberry Sts. now intersect. Later Summit Lake was created by the erection of a dam across the Platte River. This lake, more than 3 miles long, covers several hundred acres of land. In recent years

McKinley Lake, first known as Railroad Lake, was built as an addition to McKinley Park within the city.

The water supply proved sufficient until the drought of 1934, when about April the water level of Lake Summit was perceptibly low. When the drought continued it was necessary to ration the water, and at length trainloads of water were shipped in daily from Council Bluffs. Rates jumped from 35¢ to $1.50 for 1,000 gallons. At the end of the summer, after unsuccessful drilling for water in the vicinity of Creston, both McKinley and Summit Lakes were enlarged to prevent possible recurrence of the shortage. Today the storage capacity of 610,000,000 gallons is sufficient to supply the city for a period of 480 days without rainfall.

On the curb in front of 600 N. Vine St. is a 30-inch statue of a Negro with a flag in his hand, a relic of the first locomotive that was piloted into town. This locomotive, known as the *J. C. Hall,* originally had a small metal statue in front on each side; one was missing, however, when the engine steamed into town in 1869. Dan W. Scullen, the engineer, presented the statue to another engineer, R. C. O'Brien, who carried it with him on trips through the West. Cowboys, galloping alongside the train, found the remaining figure on the engine so good a target that O'Brien finally shipped it back to Creston.

It is said that the approach of the *J. C. Hall* was signalled with a blast from large steamboat-type whistles; Scullen, discovering that two ears of corn would fit into this whistle, used to wedge them in daily, allowing the steam to cook his lunch.

At 68 *m.* is the junction with a dirt road.

Right on this road is the SITE OF THE ICARIAN COMMUNITY, 1.5 *m.,* settled in 1858. Several old wooden buildings still remain but the former central farm is now operated privately. The group was incorporated under the laws of the State as an agricultural society and at one time had 225 members.

Etienne Cabet (1788–1856), founder of the Icarians, was a French cooper's son who began his career as a lawyer and politician. His radical views made him unpopular with the French Government; and when given his choice between imprisonment and exile, he chose exile in England. There he wrote a novel that he republished in 1840 as *Voyage en Icarie,* after encouragement from Robert Owen and from American radicals. The novel described an island, where the inhabitants received State-regulated wages in State-controlled workshops and where public education, a progressive income tax, abolition of the right of inheritance and eugenic supervision of marriage were carried on, and the newspaper was controlled by the government.

The influence of this novel, particularly on the working classes, was strong and Cabet gained a considerable following. When he announced the establishment of a community run on Icarian principles in America applications for membership poured in. Upon the advice of Robert Owen, Cabet signed a contract with an American land company for, he believed, a million acres in the new State of Texas. In February 1848, when 69 selected colonists signed "social contracts" on the Havre pier just before sailing, pledging themselves to his principles, Cabet declared, "In view of men like these in the advance guard, I cannot doubt the regeneration of the human race."

The Texas venture near Sulphur Prairie failed: when the Icarians reached New Orleans in March they found that their land, instead of touching the Red River, was 250 miles inland, in the midst of an untraveled wilderness reached only by muddy roads and by crossing swollen, unbridged streams. They were able to claim only 10,000 acres, sections of which were widely scattered. The courage and industry of the Icarians were great, but they were mostly artisans and professional men who knew little of farming, and still less of pioneering; many fell ill with malaria, the doctor went insane, and several people died. Realizing the hopelessness of attempting to colonize in Texas, they returned to New Orleans; here, early in 1849, Cabet and other immigrants joined them. In the meantime, three weeks after the first group had left France, the Revolution of February 24, 1848, took place, and the Second Republic was established; many Icarians thought an opportunity had arrived to build an Icaria in France, and slowly to change the Republic into the ideal state. The Home Party urged Cabet to devote himself to communism in his native land, and he was proposed, along with Cavaignac and Lamartine, as a possible candidate for the French presidency. But Cabet refused, and the Home Party left the ranks of the Icarians; the second group that sailed for America, which was to have numbered 1,500, diminished to 19.

After several months, scouts brought to the group at New Orleans a favorable report of Nauvoo, Ill., recently abandoned by the Mormons; but because of a dispute, 200 of the 500 members, including women and children, withdrew, taking $5,000 with them—nearly one-third of the community capital.

It was at Nauvoo, after much hardship and suffering, that the Icarian colony grew and to some extent prospered. Repeated differences, however, were caused by conflict between individualistic tendencies engendered by pioneer life and the practical application of Cabet's principles. Utopia, in Cabet's novel, was governed by a president and a parliament; but, as soon as he arrived in America, circumstances and personal influences made him dictatorial. He did not realize the possibilities of either industry or agriculture, and managed the finances of the community on a cautious, limited scale; he prohibited the use of tobacco and whiskey, interferred in the personal lives of members, and encouraged spying. At length he became so much hated that the members gathered at his house to sing the *Marseillaise* outside his windows, and, in an open meeting, they asked defiantly, "Have we traveled three thousand miles not to be free?" The majority drove him out and he died shortly afterwards in St. Louis.

The migration to Iowa was slow. Corning *(see below)* became the trading point for the produce of 3,000 Icarian acres, which were heavily mortgaged. The colonists were dependent on money sent from France, and after the Revolution in 1848— promising national workshops—the funds dwindled. By raising sheep and taking advantage of the high price of wool during the Civil War—in addition to selling more than half their land—the colonists finally managed to free themselves from debt. While the majority farmed, each member had the right to choose his own occupation as long as he served the interests of the colony and did certain assigned duties. Percheron horses were imported, their sale furnishing considerable revenue to the Icarians, who were among the first to take advantage of the demand for imported stock in an agricultural country.

At one time the community property was worth $60,000 to $70,000. The group had a flourmill, a sawmill, a blacksmith shop, and other enterprises; various periodicals were published during the existence of the colony: one—the *Revue Icarienne*—was an exceptionally well-edited journal and for many years had a wide circulation in France.

A large combined dining and assembly hall was erected; it was used for long discussions, meetings, amateur theatricals, and for balls, to which outsiders were invited. Near the assembly hall were the homes; everything in the community was held in common. A board of six directed affairs within the group, policies being decided by majority vote; except on a few questions, women were excluded from voting. Although Cabet's followers had belonged predominantly to the working classes, some of the Icarians in Iowa were educated men of superior intelligence. At Nauvoo there had been many men and women of gentle birth and brilliant talent; several musicians, two painters of wide reputation, a noted engineer, a physician who had been at the head of his profession in Vienna; Dedant, an authority on bee culture; A. Piquenard—afterward architect of the Westminster Church at Keokuk, and of the capitols of both Iowa *(see ARCHITECTURE)* and Illinois; and Vallet, the sociologist. Don Ignatius Montaldo, friend and companion of Garibaldi and Chateaubriand, joined the colony at Nauvoo, but left; after several years he rejoined it in Iowa, where he died. Antoine Von Gauvain, who had been decorated with the cross of the Legion of Honor, and was later the editor of a newspaper in New York, joined the Icarians. In Iowa, for a number of years he engaged in private tutoring in Greek, Latin, German, and French. The community library contained more than 2,000 well-chosen volumes, a remnant of which was given to Tabor College (see Tour 9).

Each Icarian followed his own bent in religious matters. Sunday was a day for rest, but there were no sects. The approach to problems of living was philosophic. Like the Shaker, the Zoar, the Oneida, and the Amana (see Tour 14A) colonies, the Icarian community established its own schools; the members also took part in the political movements of the country, consistently Republican in State and national affiliations. It is said that all male members who were qualified to enlist joined the Union Army in the Civil War. Their common life was strict and plain, yet it was lived graciously and generously; the general rule was: "From each according to his powers; to each according to his needs."

In the early 1870's a revival of the socialist movement of 1848 swept the country, and both young and old men in the comparatively isolated Icarian commune felt the excitement of the Workers' International and the Paris Commune of 1871. They rebelled against their fathers and those who were losing the ideals and aims of Cabet and becoming orthodox American farmers. They urged new rules to restrict individual vanities, demanding that the elders give up all hoarded things to the common treasury—whether of monetary value or worthless to anyone but the owner because of sentimental associations; they criticized the elders for their private gardens and vineyards, saying they caused competition, greed, and lowered morale; they demanded equal political rights for women; and, above all, they petitioned the elders to open the community to new young people—to all who might choose to sign the commune pledge, regardless of their earlier records. The elders protested and refused, but eventually an agreement was made by which the old group took possession of one part of the property, and the younger group occupied the other; the 39 members of the old group deceptively called themselves the New Icarians. Several members of the young Icarian group withdrew; the rest remained with the organization in Iowa until 1883, when they went to Cloverdale, California; there they formed a new society, under the name of Icaria Speranza, that lasted for several years.

The old group, however, was content with the existence it had evolved and made no effort to expand. Music was taken up again, but there were few young voices; study classes were formed but soon abandoned for lack of interest; one by one the younger men left the colony for farms of their own, or drifted to cities. E. F. Bettannier, last president of the Icarians, was appointed receiver, and the settlement in 1898 gave each of 21 members an equitable share in 1,000 acres.

CORNING, 71 m. (1,117 alt., 2,026 pop.), was platted in 1855, by D. M. Smith of Chariton, who named it for a friend, Erastus Corning, of Corning, N. Y. The COURTHOUSE, a two-story brick building on a hill north of the business district, was erected in 1890. In October 1896 fire destroyed 23 buildings, the loss being estimated at $200,000.

Corning was the home of Judge Horace M. Towner (1855–1937) who served the Third Judicial District of Iowa for 20 years, and was Governor of Puerto Rico for 7 years under the Harding and Coolidge Administrations. It is also the home of Dan W. Turner, Governor of Iowa (1930–1932).

SPRING LAKE (picnicking facilities, play grounds, restaurant, dance hall), principal recreation center of the community, is at the southeastern edge of the city. A pool is supplied with water from nearby springs.

At 80 m. is the junction with State 155, graveled.

Left on this road is NODAWAY, 5 m. (1,084 alt., 334 pop.), a village near a

HUSKING CORN

settlement of Dunkards who have a church where monthly meetings are held. There are many good camping spots on shaded knolls in this rich, well-improved farming country; crabapples, plums, raspberries, strawberries, and gooseberries grow wild in the area. Fishing and hunting are popular along the East or Middle Nodaway Rivers.

At 86 *m.* is the junction with US 71 *(see Tour 7).*

At 92 *m.* is the junction with State 120, graveled.

Left on this road is STANTON, 3 *m.* (1,172 alt., 607 pop.), first settled by a Swede and called Holmstad for a town in Sweden; it is a market town.

RED OAK, 99 *m.* (1,077 alt., 5,788 pop.), in the valley of the East Nishnabotna River, was so named because of the many red oak trees growing on the banks of a small creek nearby. It was founded by Alfred Hebard, and was known as Red Oak Junction until 1901. HEBARD'S HOME, with walnut interior trim, is still standing.

The old frame MILL, built in 1873 on the Nishnabotna, is run by water-power aided by an oil engine.

The MURPHY CALENDAR FACTORY manufactures many of the calendars used in Iowa and a large number of those distributed throughout the United States; the company also manufactures Chinese calendars with Chinese characters, and a number of advertising specialties.

EMERSON, 108 *m.* (1,057 alt., 512 pop.), is the home of many retired land owners and farmers. The railroad is the main cause of the town's existence, its history beginning in 1870 when the rails came through.

At 110 *m.* is the junction with US 59 *(see Tour 8).*

At 113 *m.* is the junction with State 166, graveled.

Left on this road is HASTINGS, 1 *m.* (999 alt., 389 pop.), named for a railroad official. The town was owned, platted, and put on sale by the railroad company in 1872; today it is at the junction of two branch lines of the C. B. & Q. R. R.

At 118 *m.* is the junction with State 41, paved.

Left on this road is MALVERN, 2 *m.* (1,047 alt., 1,320 pop.), founded in 1869, after the completion of the Burlington main line between Omaha and Chicago. The railroad company gave the town its name. THE MALVERN COMMUNITY BUILDING— a large yellow brick building erected at a cost of $60,000—is the center of town life. The auditorium, with a stage and gallery, seats more than 1,000 persons; in the basement are a kitchen, a banquet hall, and the Mills Co. Farm Bureau offices. A MUNICIPAL SWIMMING POOL adjoins the grounds of a cold storage plant. The Mills County Fair is held on the grounds S. of town each August. Malvern has a Craft Club, whose members are encouraged in art and craft work, including wood carving, rug making, furniture making, painting, and sculpture. The requirement for membership is a piece of work that is acceptable to the committee; membership is not limited to residents, many from surrounding counties belonging to the club.

At 123 *m.* is the junction with US 275 *(see Tour 9).*

GLENWOOD, 127 *m.* (1,037 alt., 4,269 pop.), seat of Mills County, was formerly a Mormon settlement known as Rushville. When the Mormons left for Utah, the remaining residents called the village Coonsville in honor of Dr. Libeud Coons, the founder and first physician of the community, but when it was selected as the county seat in 1853, the name was again changed. It is in the beautiful Keg Creek Valley, at the foot of high hills, on which is part of the residential section. The long, winding creek— its course now changed by drainage ditches—emptying into the Missouri River, is shown on Lieut. Albert M. Lea's map of 1835 as Barrel River, and is said to have been so named because of the half-barrels of whiskey found buried near its banks when the first company of U. S. Dragoons surveyed this part of Iowa.

In the southeastern part of Glenwood, beyond the Burlington tracks, is the STATE INSTITUTION FOR THE FEEBLE-MINDED *(open daily to visitors),* a large group of fine buildings on a hill overlooking Glenwood and the Missouri River Valley. The institution is considered a model of its kind. In 1873 Dr. W. S. Robertson of Muscatine saw the need for educating and training the feeble-minded children of the State, and interested the State Medical Society and others in obtaining State aid; a bill was passed in 1876 by the Sixteenth General Assembly of Iowa, authorizing the establishment of the institution. The first small brick building was replaced by a group of modern structures in landscaped grounds; orchards and gardens are cared for by the patients who in 1936 numbered 1,814. About one third of the residents are children, who are taught the same subjects offered in public schools, and are given industrial and manual training. Physical culture, music and home economics courses are included in the curriculum.

Glenwood is at the junction with US 275 *(see Tour 9).*

PACIFIC JUNCTION, 131 *m.* (957 alt., 594 pop.), is 3 miles from the site of the long abandoned village of Pacific City, once a favorite stopping place for emigrants bound for the West Coast. Before passing into oblivion, the old town was briefly the center of the nation's interest. On Nov. 18, 1873, residents were aroused from their usual calm by the approach of a special train with five coaches. From it descended a crowd of 500 promoters, sport fans, a prizefighter named Tom Allen, and a challenger, Ben Hogan, of New York and Philadelphia. Ropes were stretched, a ring hastily improvised, and soon a heavyweight championship bout was in progress, with the world title at stake. It began with "beautiful sparring"; but in the second and third rounds frequent cries of "Foul!" excited the spectators, who rushed the ring, swept it level with the ground, and fought with fists, knives, and pistols in a free-for-all battle. Finally, order was restored. All bets were called off, the prizefight was declared a draw, and Allen and Hogan were each awarded $1,000. Promoters and fighters had chosen Pacific City as the scene of the event after they had been banned from Missouri, Kansas, and Omaha. They sojourned overnight in Council Bluffs, but were prevented from staging the bout when at the request of citizens of the town, Gov. Cyrus Carpenter ordered out National Guard troops from Des Moines.

At 135 *m.* US 34 crosses the Missouri River, which is the Iowa-Nebraska boundary, on the PLATTSMOUTH BRIDGE *(car and driver, 50¢; passengers, 5¢ each)*, 56 miles E. of Lincoln, Nebr.

Tour 17

Mississippi River—Fort Madison—Leon—Sidney—(Nebraska City, Nebr.); State 3.
Mississippi River to Nebraska Line, 271 m.

The C. B. & Q. R. R. parallels the route throughout; C. R. I. & P., between Farmington and Centerville; the Wabash R. R., between Bloomfield and West Grove.
Burlington Bus Line follows the highway between Clarinda and Sidney.
Roadbed paved except for 48 m. of gravel between junction with US 65 and junction with State 25.
Tourist accommodations of all kinds available, chiefly in cities.

Section a. MISSISSIPPI RIVER *to* LEON, *145 m.*

State 3 crosses the Mississippi River, 0 *m.*, the Illinois-Iowa Line, 43 miles W. of Bushnell, Ill., on a toll bridge *(car, driver and 1 passenger, 25¢; other passengers, 5¢ each; trucks, 25¢ up)*.

At 3 *m.* is FORT MADISON (522 alt., 13,799 pop.).

Annual Events: Memorial Day Relay Carnival, high school and preparatory school athletic event, High School athletic field; Mexican Fiesta, Mexican Independence Day, September 15 and 16, on Ave. Q between W. 34th and W. 35th Sts.; Southeast Iowa Colored People's Emancipation Day, August 4, Old Settlers Park.

FORT MADISON is built mainly on flatlands near the Mississippi River but is hemmed in by high hills and steep bluffs. Between the town and the river are the Burlington and Santa Fe Railroad tracks. Flanking the tracks is the long, narrow River View Park, behind which is the compact business district. The encompassing residential districts spread over the flats, and climb the adjacent hills. Fort Madison structures are chiefly of brick; in early days a number of brick kilns topped the nearby hills.

Fort Madison was established as a Government trading post in 1808 for the Indian trade but the natives regarded its presence as a treaty violation, and constantly harassed the place. In August 1813, Chief Black Hawk and his allies finally attacked. Unable to beat off the besiegers, those at the post decided to leave. On the night of September 3, with the Indians waiting in the hills, they gathered what remained of provisions and ammunition, and crawled on their hands and knees through a trench to the boats waiting in the river. As the Indians watched, they saw flames shoot up from the block houses. The last man had set fire to the buildings, and the men were safely away before their foes realized what had happened.

The town grew up around the lone chimney left after the post was deserted. In the intervening years, Indians called the site Potowanek *(place of fire)* and traders used the chimney as a landmark. In 1833 John H. Knapp built a cabin at the foot of what is now Broadway and established a trading post. Many trains of prairie schooners were later ferried across the river here, one point in the southern part of the territory free from inundation at all seasons.

In a letter, Albert M. Lea, who made the first survey of the Des Moines rapids, wrote: "He (the man who drew up the bill naming the county), Starr, and I slept in the same room when he drew up that bill and he put my name down for the first county (now known as Lee), in consideration of my having mapped, described, and named the area now known as Iowa and Minnesota." And later: "It is easy to see how the spelling was changed by transcribing clerks, as my mode of spelling with the final 'a' was unusual; and as I disappeared mainly from that theatre and Captain Lee (Robert E.) had come upon it, the name was naturally attributed to him."

The legislature of the Territory of Wisconsin established the city as the seat of Lee County in 1838, but a courthouse was not erected until 1842. The city's industrial growth was determined to a large extent by the demands of the rural communities that grew up in the back country of Lee County. By 1847, S. D. Morrison was making plows by hand for the local trade, beginning the farm-tool industry that still flourishes. Later, flour and lumber mills were erected, the latter attracting Swedish settlers during the lively days when steamboating and lografting added boisterous notes to the life of the town. The town wharf was at that time either piled high with produce from interior Iowa, or jammed with imported goods.

The town had another growing period in 1879 when the Santa Fe established a freight and passenger division point here, at the western end of its railroad and wagon bridge spanning the Mississippi. Paper mills were opened in 1879, and the manufacture of plows was begun on a large scale. In the early 1900's pearl button, fountain pen, and wax-paper bread-wrapper factories began production.

The design of the LEE COUNTY COURTHOUSE, NW. corner 7th Ave. and Ave. F, the oldest in use in the State, is credited to Father Samuel Mazzuchelli, pioneer priest and architect. Immense Tuscan columns distinguish this structure.

The AMERICAN LEGION HOME (open daily by permission), 718 Ave. F, was the home of the daughter, granddaughter, and great-granddaughter of Betsy Ross, maker of the first American flag. The two-family house was erected in 1858 by William and Jacob Albright.

The W. A. SHEAFFER PEN PLANT (open to visitors), 335 Ave. H, occupies six buildings on the site of old Fort Madison. The company, which started business in the back room of a local jewelry store in 1913, now manufactures fountain pens, pencils, and writing accessories for the national market. The Sheaffer pen was one of the first to use the lever and bar filling device that made obsolete the use of a medicine dropper for filling.

LONE CHIMNEY MONUMENT, Ave. H and 4th St., marks the site of the ruins of the old fort for which the city is named.

The HOME OF GRANDMOTHER BROWN (private), NE. corner 7th St. and Ave. E, is a little three-room brick cottage. The history of Fort Madison was shown in the 1929 Atlantic Monthly prize biography, Grandmother Brown's Hundred Years; the book was written by Mrs. Brown's daughter-in-law, Harriet Connor Brown. This structure was Grandmother Brown's home from 1870 to 1929.

The HOME OF REBECCA POLLARD (private), 828 Ave. D, is Georgian Colonial in style. A teacher of many years' experience, Mrs. Pollard evolved original methods of instruction. Her Synthetic Method of Reading and Spelling, introduced in the 1880's, was used nationally for years. Mrs. Pollard, who also wrote several novels under the pseudonym, "Kate Harrington," lived in this house after 1900.

The S. & J. C. ATLEE LUMBER PLANT (visited by permission), Ave. M between 13th and 14th Sts. on the riverfront, covers 30 acres. It had its beginning in 1837 when John C. Atlee began to do carpentry here.

SHOPTOWN (tours arranged at office, foot of 9th St.), Ave. L between 22nd and 27th Sts., is a maintenance plant of the Atchison, Topeka, and Santa Fe Railroad. MEXICAN VILLAGE, Ave. Q between 34th and 35th Sts., S. of Santa Fe tracks, has stores and closely grouped houses. The Mexicans, who first came to Fort Madison during the building of the river dam near here, cling to the customs and traditions of their native country.

The IOWA STATE PENITENTIARY (open weekdays, except holidays, 9-11 and 1-3; adm. 25¢), east end Ave. E, stands out boldly on a narrow sand ridge that terminates at the base of a high cliff. The State's first penal institution was erected in 1839 and designed on the plan of the Auburn, N. Y., penitentiary—a prison within a prison, a cell for each convict. Before the cell blocks were ready, the prisoners were housed in a walled-in cellar dungeon beneath the oak hallway of the warden's home. Each night, with ball and chain dangling from their legs, they were descended into the cellar through a trap door in the middle of the hallway. In spite of precautions, 7 of the first 12 prisoners escaped before the cells were ready.

Among the 28 prison buildings that stand on the 10-acre tract, provided by the city, is a five-story industrial building. Before 1915, when manufacturers contracted for prison labor, there was some exploitation of the convicts here; because of its abuse the system was abolished by the General Assembly. In 1938 there were three types of labor done by the prisoners. The State operates a chair factory, selling the output to one firm; private firms, having the piece-price contracts, employ other prisoners; and the prison itself carries on such activities as tailoring, knitting, brush and broom making, quarrying, and farming, the products being used by State institutions. Health and sanitary conditions are excellent and a broad recreational and educational program is provided.

Prisoners in their blue denim trousers, working in the fields of the prison farms, look like other working men. Their arrival and departure, usually in automobiles, is taken as a matter of course, and the infrequent executions by hanging cause only a slight stir in the town.

Fort Madison is at the junction with US 61 *(see Tour 1)*.

DONNELLSON, 18 *m.* (704 alt., 581 pop.) *(see Tour 1A)*, is at the junction with US 218 *(see Tour 1A)*.

FARMINGTON, 29 *m.* (567 alt., 1,012 pop.), largest town in Van Buren County, is in the fertile Des Moines River Valley; coal mines and stone quarries are in nearby hills.

When the town was platted in 1839, it was designated the seat of Van Buren County. The first jail was a stump to which prisoners were chained; later a "pine-box," 10 feet long and 8 feet wide, was built. It is said that one man imprisoned here escaped by lifting the jail on his shoulders and carrying it away.

In the vicinity of Farmington is produced a special maple syrup that comes from trees at least 30 or 40 years old. On the few days in March when temperatures are freezing at night and warm by day, sap flows and the farmers work quickly. In favorable weather a maple produces a barrel of sugar water, which is chiefly boiled down to syrup, though some is made into maple sugar.

Left from Farmington on a graveled side road 0.5 *m.* is FARMINGTON STATE PARK *(camping, picnicking facilities)*, covering 109 acres, known as Big Duck Marsh until the Conservation Commission took it over and dammed the outlet to Big Duck Lake in 1920. Lotus grows along a narrow outlet into the Des Moines River. This rugged region was involved in the Missouri boundary war of 1839.

At 35 *m.* is the junction with State 79, paved.

Right on this road to BONAPARTE, 2 *m.* (520 alt., 678 pop.), on the bank of the Des Moines River. It was settled in 1837, and named for the French Emperor by William Meek, founder of the town. In 1867 a $20,000 academy was erected by the Bonaparte Academy Association, and in 1878, when the town had a population of 1,200, there were 168 pupils. On Front Street beyond the bridge, is the TOWN PARK *(free tourist camp)*. In 1839 the Territorial legislature of Iowa granted Meek the right to build a dam and dam locks at Bonaparte; they were completed in two years. The locks, 135 feet long, with a passage way 35 feet wide, are still in good condition. Along the lower end is a fish spillway where tons of fish have been removed from the locks. The 164-acre Grey Health Orchard, producing apples and pears, is near Bonaparte; 50,000 bushels of fruit are shipped every year.

At 48 *m.* is the junction with State 1, paved.

Right on State 1 is a junction with an improved road, 3 *m.*

1. Left here 1 *m.* into LACEY-KEOSAUQUA STATE PARK *(bathing, boating, and fishing facilities, picnicking, camp grounds; 9-hole golf course, log lodge)*. Its 1,260 acres lie within a bend of the Des Moines River; most of the area is covered with timber, with glades here and there; wooded hills overlook the river. There is a 30-acre artificial lake. Wild game is abundant, and wild turkey, prairie chicken, ruffed grouse, and deer find refuge here.

2. Right from State 1, 0.25 *m.* on a road directly opposite the park entrance to the UNITED STATES FORESTRY SERVICE NURSERY. Nearly 4,000,000 small trees are planted here; about 16 acres have overhead irrigation.

3. At 4 *m.* on State 1 is KEOSAUQUA (664 alt., 855 pop.), within the horse-shoe bend of the Des Moines River. The Indian name, Keosauqua, means *great bend*. The town was settled in 1836. The ripples in this bend were the first cause of the Missouri-Iowa boundary dispute, the Honey War, of 1839. In 1816 a Government surveyor had marked the northern boundary of Missouri with mounds, stakes, and blazed trees, and the rapids of the Des Moines River were one of the landmarks on the line. In 1837 Missouri began remarking the line. In searching for the rapids in the river the commissioners found the ripples near Keosauqua, and assumed these to be the "Rapids" of the Des Moines River named in the Act of Congress defining the boundary in 1820. In Iowa the ripples had not been thought of as rapids until so called by the Missouri Commissioners. Out of this dispute grew the "Honey War" involving a 12-mile tract of timberland in the bend. In the disputed territory were many "bee trees," and pioneers in both States adjacent to the strip coveted the wild honey, then the only source of "sweetenin' " for household use. When the sheriff of Clark County, Mo., was taken prisoner by Iowa Militia while tax collecting in the disputed territory, Governor Boggs of Missouri called out the State militia. In the same spirit Iowa volunteer soldiers rushed to arms to hold the disputed ground; in all there were about 1,200 Iowa soldiers and 2,250 Missouri militia. But before beginning hostilities a delegation had been sent to Governor Lucas of the Iowa Territory to propose a peaceable adjustment of the controversy. Commissioners examined the various claimed boundary lines, and on Feb. 13, 1849, the U. S. Supreme Court settled the dispute in favor of Iowa.

The COURTHOUSE here, erected in 1842–43, has been in continual service as a public building since that date; timbers are of oak, more than a foot square and remarkably preserved; the solid brick walls of the first story are 22 inches thick, those of the second, 18 inches; the interior is finished in walnut.

BONNEYVIEW, the town's oldest house, built in 1839, overlooks the river. There is a half-acre CITY PARK with a band stand; an athletic field at the 33-acre FAIR-GROUNDS; and a swimming pool in ANDERSON PARK.

It was down the Des Moines River, through this city, that Charles Kelly's army of the unemployed came from Des Moines on its way to Washington, D. C., in the spring of 1894. At Des Moines they had built flatboats to proceed by water but, below Ottumwa, the bad stretch in the river hampered progress. Jack London, who joined the army at Council Bluffs, wrote a running account of the trip down the river: "Thurs., May 17. We started early, but the army had already passed. By the time we passed Keosauqua we had overtaken them, and running the rapids with safety, found half a dozen boats stove in and on the beach getting repaired. The popcorn man lost 500 cigars and swamped his boat with wife, child and entire outfit on board. Received our morning rations, and with a fair wind, soon passed our fleet. They are getting tired, but once in a while some crack crew gives us a spin to their disgust, and our delight. First over the dam at Bonaparte and into camp. Friday, May 18. A miserable day, chilling rain. Camped in the afternoon in Missouri."

CANTRIL, 50 *m.* (773 alt., 370 pop.), was named for L. W. Cantril, the town's first store proprietor.

MILTON, 55 *m.* (803 alt., 771 pop.), named for the poet, John Milton, was settled in 1847. The town is near the Fox and Little Fox Rivers.

PULASKI, 62 *m.* (833 alt., 376 pop.), was named in 1850 by Columbus Hains, the first postmaster, for Count Pulaski, Polish officer who aided the Colonists in the American Revolution.

BLOOMFIELD, 72 *m.* (845 alt., 2,226 pop.) *(see Tour 3)*, is at the junction with US 63 *(see Tour 3)*.

At 87 *m.* is the intersection with State 142, graveled.

Left on this road is MOULTON, 3 *m.* (987 alt., 1,476 pop.), settled in 1867 and platted in 1868 as Elizabethtown. It was afterward named for J. J. Moulton, a railroad surveyor. The CITY PARK has a bandstand and picnic facilities.

At 95 *m.* is the junction with a rock road.

Left on this road is SHARON BLUFFS STATE SCENIC PRESERVE *(picnic facilities)*, 2 *m.*, a rough, wooded tract of 117 acres along the banks of the Chariton River, adjoining the site of a pioneer village. The village was platted in 1856 by W. C. Packard, who named it Sharon of Palestine. As Centerville *(see below)* grew, the village disintegrated. The pioneer cemetery remains; the rural school perpetuates the town name.

CENTERVILLE, 98 *m.* (1,013 alt., 8,147 pop.), incorporated in 1855, is in a coal-producing section, where more than 600,000 tons are mined annually. A 500-foot gypsum bed is also in the vicinity.

In 1846 the village was platted as Chaldea by J. F. Stratton. The residents, however, called the town Sentersville in honor of Governor Senter of Tennessee. When the name was submitted to the General Assembly in January 1847, the legislators changed it to Centerville, believing the original was an error in spelling. Appanoose County, of which Centerville is the seat, was named in honor of Chief Appanoose *(a chief when a child)*. The first courthouse, built of logs, was replaced by one of stone, having a large outside clock, a gift of an early citizen. Centerville was formerly an important ferry point for boats plying the Chariton River.

The junior college, organized in 1930, gives normal training and courses in the liberal arts; a lighted football stadium, seating 3,000, adjoins the high school.

The CITY PARK of 25 acres, near the center of the city, has recreational facilities including a swimming pool.

BELLE WOODEN PARK was named for Miss Belle Wooden of Centerville, who married Nathan E. Kendall (1868–1936), Governor of Iowa (1921–1925). This 74-acre area is in the extreme northwestern part of the city.

At 101 *m.* is the junction with State 138, graveled.

Right on this road is MYSTIC, 3 *m.* (896 alt., 1,953 pop.), established in the 1880's as a mining center, following the discovery of a rich vein of coal. According

CUTTING GRAIN

to one story, Dennis Vandyke named the town for his birthplace, Mystic, Conn., but according to another version, Vandyke thought an "aura of mystery hovered over the locality" when he first came and he wished to perpetuate this impression in the name. Some of the miners here think there will be a fatality if a woman enters a coal mine, and officials may hesitate to admit women during visiting hours. Some believe that if a miner meets a woman on the way to work, he will be killed or injured in the near future; some will not allow members of their families to work in the mine on the day before Christmas (Swedish); a bird or bat flying into the house is a warning of death to come; to place a corpse before a mirror will cause another death in the family; if the mine cage stops or jerks as it takes the miners up or down the shaft, an accident will occur; and a bird singing at night foretells a disaster. If, after starting to work, a miner returns home for a forgotten article, he sits down to make a wish; also, if one twirls a chair on one leg, a death will occur in the family. Rabbits' feet, buckeyes, asafetida, and horseshoes are carried by many.

PLANO, 107 *m.* (1,030 alt., 153 pop.), was named, supposedly, for Plano, Ill., by a group of Seventh Day Adventists from that town.

PROMISE CITY, 113 *m.* (1,065 alt., 226 pop.), received its name from the Mormons who had a camp here. Fishing in the Chariton River, not far away, is a popular pastime.

CORYDON, 122 *m.* (1,083 alt., 1,768 pop.), seat of Wayne County, and formerly called Springfield, is in the timothy seed-producing section of Iowa.

A log cabin in WALDEN PARK houses relics of early days. The park, which has recreational facilities, a picnic pavilion, is part of the six county Chariton River improvement projects. The CITY RESERVOIR has facilities for boating and fishing. The only soldiers' monument in the county is in the center of the square.

LEON, 145 *m.* (1,019 alt., 2,006 pop.), *(see Tour 5)*, is at the junction with US 69 *(see Tour 5)*.

Section b. LEON to NEBRASKA LINE, 126 m.

West of Leon, 0 *m.*, is DECATUR CITY (1,137 alt., 282 pop.), 5 *m.*, one of the old towns in Decatur County and the first county seat. It is a small trading center, with a public square in which band concerts are given.

KELLERTON, 17 *m.* (1,179 alt., 540 pop.), named for Judge Isaac W. Keller of Mount Ayr, is in the center of a prosperous rural area.

MOUNT AYR, 27 *m.* (1,236 alt., 1,704 pop.), seat of Ringgold County, is on a high rolling prairie. The county was named in 1855 for Samuel B. Ringgold, wounded in the Battle of Palo Alto during the Mexican War of 1846–47.

The first courthouse, built of logs in 1856, was replaced three years later by a larger frame structure, but after 60 years of service the second building was razed and construction begun on a modern building. Disagreements delayed the work and for several years the county had no courthouse. Not until the 1920's was the attractive brick and gray stone building completed; it stands in the square shaded by trees planted 80 years ago.

Mount Ayr is at the junction (R) with US 169 *(see Tour 6)* which unites briefly with this road.

At 28 *m.* is the junction (L) with US 169 *(see Tour 6)*.

BEDFORD, 55 *m.* (1,098 alt., 2,100 pop.), seat of Taylor County, sprawls on a high ridge in the loess-covered hills of southwestern Iowa. On the outskirts of town is BIBBINS PARK, named for its donor, Alfred Bibbins; county fairs, now temporarily discontinued, were held here for many years; a wide gravel driveway winds through the wooded area which has an amphitheater, race track, tennis courts, and playground equipment.

Right from Bedford on an improved road is BEDFORD STATE PARK *(picnicking, swimming, boating, and fishing facilities)*, 4 *m.*, a 375-acre tract surrounding the 150-acre Lake of Three Fires. Nature trails wind over rolling hills and through timber. With the support of the Bedford Commercial Club in 1934, $25,-000 was raised by popular subscription to buy the area. The lake was formed by building a 900-foot earthen dam across a small creek. The name of the lake comes from an Indian legend; three tribes camping near the site of the present lake made a treaty to unite for protection, each tribe keeping a signal-fire going night and day to signify "all is well"; discontinuation of the signal indicated they had moved on. The large sand beach, a State fish hatchery, and a custodian's residence were constructed by the C.C.C. and F.E.R.A.

NEW MARKET, 67 *m.* (1,198 alt., 630 pop.), sprang up along the railroad when a large vein of coal was found nearby; by 1910, 29 shafts had been sunk. Today only one mine is open, employing about 60 men.

There are also several fine walnut groves in the surrounding country.

At 73 *m.* is the junction with US 71 *(see Tour 7).*

CLARINDA, 75 *m.* (1,009 alt., 4,962 pop.), seat of Page County, was a stopping place on the Underground Railway in 1861, and 500 Negroes lived here then; now they number about 150.

The town name honors beautiful Clarinda Buck, a girl popular among the early settlers.

In 1856 the first postmaster established his office in a dugout at a place that is now behind the Clarinda Bank.

There is an excellent view of the city and surrounding countryside from the COURTHOUSE TOWER, which is encircled by a railed observation platform.

Clarinda is at the junction with US 71 *(see Tour 7).*

Right from Clarinda on State 194, bituminous surfaced, to the STATE HOSPITAL FOR THE INSANE, 1 *m., (open daily 9-5, except at mealtime),* a $1,500,000 institution with spacious and beautifully landscaped grounds. The hospital, reached by a winding drive, was opened in December 1888; at the end of June 1934, it had a total of 1,055 acres, most of which were under cultivation. The main building consists of a large number of units so arranged that the sun shines into the windows of all rooms. There are six miles of corridors. The patients farm, operate their own electric power plant, and breed fancy stock. Moving pictures and other recreational facilities are provided.

SHENANDOAH, 94 *m.* (981 alt., 6,502 pop.), was named because of the similarity of the Nishnabotna River Valley, in which the town lies, to the Shenandoah Valley in Virginia—where many of the founders of the village fought with Gen. Phillip H. Sheridan. Numbers of the first settlers were Mormons, and most of them came from a small settlement called Manti, or Fisher's Grove. The town was founded in 1870 when the railroad was completed through Page County.

Five nurseries here ship their products to many parts of the United States. Pioneers in this field were D. S. Lake, who opened the SHENANDOAH NURSERY in 1870, and E. S. Welch, who founded the MOUNT ARBOR NURSERY in 1875. The Henry Field Seed Co., founded in 1907, handles a huge mail-order business and annually ships thousands of baby chicks, seeds, and other products. In 1923-24 a three-story brick annex was built, principally to house the studios of radio station KFNF (890 kc). At the company's annual jubilee in the fall, flowers and shrubs are displayed, free meals are furnished to all visitors, and free entertainment is provided in the broadcasting studios. The Earl E. May Co., established in 1925, is a large seed and mail-order house, operating radio station KMA (930 kc).

At the corner of W. Valley and Sycamore Sts., is DNAKER'S MUSEUM *(adm. 20¢),* containing more than 1,000 specimens of birds, snakes, and reptiles.

Shenandoah is at the junction with US 59 *(see Tour 8).*

SIDNEY, 110 *m.* (1,049 alt., 1,074 pop.) *(see Tour 9),* is at the junction with US 275 *(see Tour 9).* South of Sidney, the two highways are united for four miles.

At 114 *m.* US 275 branches (L).

At 116 *m.* is the junction with State 239, bituminous surfaced.

Left on this road into WAUBONSIE STATE PARK *(picnicking facilities),* 2.5 *m.,* a 200-acre area named for a Pottawattamie Indian chief. In an old legal document the name was spelled "Waubochey." A shelter house stands on a high ridge overlooking the broad flood plain of the Missouri River, affording an excellent view of parts of Nebraska, Kansas, and Missouri. Nebraska City, Neb., is visible on the opposite bank of the river. Footpaths lead over the grass-covered, rounded hills, through densely wooded ravines, to the flat valley more than 300 feet below the highest point in the park. Waubonsie is a botanical preserve of wild flowers and native trees, attracting many students here every year. Proof of the existence of ancient Indian villages in this part of the country is afforded by the abundance of artifacts, including several kinds of pottery, found in the vicinity.

At 126 *m.* State 3 crosses the Missouri River, the Iowa-Nebraska Line, on the NEBRASKA CITY-SIDNEY BRIDGE *(car and driver, 50¢; passengers, 5¢ each; trucks, 50¢ to 85¢),* 3 miles E. of Nebraska City, Neb.

PART IV

Appendices

Chronology

1541 Hernando de Soto discovers the Mississippi River.

1671 Sieur Saint-Lusson takes possession of whole unexplored northwest for France.

1673 Louis Joliet and Father Jacques Marquette are the first white men to set foot on Iowa soil.

1679 Daniel de Greysolon Sieur du Lhut (Du Luth) takes possession of Upper Mississippi region for France.

1680 Michel Accault, with Antoine Auguel and Father Louis Hennepin, travels along the Iowa shore of the Mississippi.

1682 Robert Cavalier, Sieur de la Salle, takes possession of the entire Mississippi Valley for France and names it Louisiana.

1689 Nicholas Perrot takes possession of the Upper Mississippi region for France.

1735 French soldiers under Des Noyelles fight battle with Sac and Fox Indians near the present Des Moines.

1762 France cedes to Spain part of Louisiana west of the Mississippi, later known as the Louisiana Purchase.

1766 Jonathan Carver, trader, arrives in Iowa country.

1781 Wife of Peosta, a Fox warrior, reports the discovery of lead deposits in the Iowa country.

1787 July 13. Congress of the Confederation adopts Northwest Ordinance.

1788 Julien Dubuque, fur trader, obtains sanction from Indians to work lead mines. He settles near site of city now bearing his name.

1796 Julien Dubuque receives grant of land, including lead mines, from the Spanish Governor of Louisiana.

1799 Louis Honore Tesson receives from Spanish Governor grant of some 6,000 acres in the present Lee County; plants first apple orchard in Iowa.

1800 Spain agrees to retrocede Louisiana to France.
Basil Giard is given a grant by Spanish Governor of 5,760 (or 5,680) acres in the present Clayton County.

1801 Spain retrocedes Louisiana to France.

1803 United States purchases Louisiana, including the present Iowa, from France for $15,000,000 with cancellation of certain debts.

1804 At St. Louis Capt. Amos Stoddard, on behalf of the United States, receives Upper Louisiana from France.

Captains Meriwether Lewis and William Clark ascend the Missouri River along what is now western Iowa. Sgt. Charles Floyd of the expedition dies near present Sioux City, first white man known to be buried in Iowa.

District of Louisiana is established and placed under jurisdiction of Governor and Judges of Indiana Territory.

United States makes treaty at St. Louis with five representatives of Sac and Fox tribes for the cession of lands in Illinois.

1805 Territory of Louisiana, including Iowa country, is established.
Lieut. Zebulon M. Pike poles his keelboats up the Mississippi and passes Iowa shore.

1808 Fort Madison, first in Iowa country, is built.

1809 Annual fur trade in the Iowa country valued at $60,000.

1810 Julien Dubuque dies and his settlement disbands.

1812 Territory of Missouri is established, including Iowa area.

1813 Fort Madison is abandoned and burned.

1814 American troops under Zachary Taylor are defeated at Credit Island.

1816 Fort Armstrong established on Rock Island.
Treaty signed by Indians, including Black Hawk, ratifying treaty of 1804.

1819 *Western Engineer* (steamboat) reaches Fort Lisa on Missouri River opposite Iowa Country.

1820 Missouri Compromise makes Iowa region free territory.
Col. Stephen W. Kearny writes account of expedition across Iowa country.
Dr. Samuel C. Muir builds home within limits of present Keokuk.
Western Engineer arrives at foot of Des Moines Rapids in the Mississippi.

1821 Missouri's admission as a State leaves Iowa country without civil government.

1824 Half-Breed Tract established in present Lee County.
Trader Hart sets up trading post near site of present Council Bluffs.

1825 Neutral line established between Sioux, and Sac and Fox Indians.

1829 November 22. Margaret Stillwell born at present Keokuk, first white child born in Iowa.

1830 First school in Iowa is established by Dr. Isaac Galland and taught by Berryman Jennings.
Neutral Ground is established between Sioux, and Sac and Fox Indians.
Miners' Compact, drawn up by miners at Dubuque, is first instrument of government formulated in Iowa country.

1832 Black Hawk War terminates in cession of strip of Indian lands west of Mississippi River known as Black Hawk Purchase.
Winnebago Indians are given part of Neutral Ground.

1833 Indian title to Black Hawk Purchase is transferred to United States

Government and settlers are permitted to remain.

Dubuque, Burlington, Fort Madison, Peru, and Bellevue are founded.

Ottawa, Pottawattamie, and Chippewa Indians are given lands in what is now southwestern Iowa.

1834 Patrick O'Connor commits murder at Dubuque and the first trial and execution in Iowa (both extralegal) take place.

Iowa country is made part of Territory of Michigan.

Half-breeds given fee simple title to Half-Breed Tract by act of Congress.

Fort Des Moines (No. 1) established on west bank of the Mississippi at head of Des Moines Rapids.

First church building in Iowa, a log cabin, is constructed at Dubuque by Methodists.

Michigan Territorial legislature establishes Du Buque and Demoine Counties.

1835 First court under act of Michigan Territorial legislature held in log house at Burlington.

Col. Stephen W. Kearny and three companies of first United States Dragoons march up Des Moines Valley to present site of Boone, thence northeastward to the Mississippi.

Roman Catholics erect church at Dubuque.

1836 First post offices in Iowa established at Gibson's Ferry (later Augusta) and at Iowa (later Montpelier).

Territory of Wisconsin established, including Iowa country.

The *Du Buque Visitor,* first Iowa newspaper, is started at Dubuque.

Congress authorizes laying out of towns of Fort Madison, Burlington, Belleview, Du Buque, and Peru.

Albert M. Lea publishes guide book, *Notes on the Wisconsin Territory,* publicizing the name Iowa for that part of Territory west of the Mississippi.

Sac and Fox Indians cede Keokuk's Reserve to the United States.

First election of members of Territorial Council and House of Representatives held in Dubuque County.

First session of Wisconsin Territorial legislature held at Belmont.

First bank (Miners' Bank) in Iowa is established at Dubuque.

Population of Iowa country, 10,564.

1837 Second newspaper in Iowa, *The Western Adventurer,* is published at Montrose.

Oldest post office in Iowa under same name is established at Wapello.

Sac and Fox Indians cede to the United States 1,250,000 acres of land, known as second Black Hawk Purchase.

Convention of delegates meets at Burlington to consider separation of Iowa district from Territory of Wisconsin.

Second session of Wisconsin Territorial legislature meets at Burlington.

Fire destroys first Capitol at Burlington.

1838 Bellevue and Peru are authorized to incorporate.

Burlington and Fort Madison are granted special charters by legislature of the Territory of Wisconsin, the first incorporated municipalities in Iowa.

James G. Edwards suggests nickname "Hawk-eyes" for residents of Iowa.

July 4. Territory of Iowa is established, including approximately all land between Missouri and Mississippi Rivers north of State of Missouri. Robert Lucas is appointed first Governor of the Territory.

September 10. First election held.

November 12. First Legislative Assembly convenes at Burlington.

Land offices are established at Dubuque and Burlington, and first sales of public lands made.

First temperance society in Iowa organized at Fort Madison.

Camp Kearny is established near site of present Council Bluffs.

October 3, Black Hawk dies at his home near the Des Moines River in Davis County.

Iowa Territorial legislature enacts law providing for incorporation of agricultural societies.

Population of Territory of Iowa, 22,859.

1839 Iowa Territorial legislature enacts first law, setting up system of common schools.

Territorial seal is authorized by act of Territorial legislature.

Iowa City is made capital of Territory of Iowa. Congress gives the territory a section of land for capital site.

Dispute, popularly known as the "Honey War", begins between State of Missouri and Territory of Iowa over boundary.

Penitentiary is established by law at Fort Madison.

Territorial legislature authorizes laying out of road from Dubuque through Iowa City to Missouri boundary. Lyman Dillon plows furrow marking this road from Dubuque to Iowa City.

Johnson County Claim Association adopts constitution.

Supreme Court of Territory of Iowa decides, in the case of Ralph, that slavery is not recognized under Iowa law.

1840 July 4. Cornerstone of Territorial capitol building laid at Iowa City.

Fort Atkinson is founded.

Proposal for statehood is defeated in referendum vote.

Population (U. S. census), 43,112.

1841 Office of superintendent of public instruction is created by law.

John Chambers is appointed Governor of Iowa Territory.

Legislative Assembly convenes for first time in Butler's Capitol at Iowa City.

1842 Referendum on statehood is held and proposition defeated.

Office of superintendent of public instruction is discontinued.

Sac and Fox Indians cede all remaining lands in Iowa.

Legislative Assembly meets in Capitol Building (now Old Capitol) for first time.

1843 Land office moved from Dubuque to Marion.

May 1. Sac and Fox Indians vacate lands east of line passing north and south through the Red Rocks in Marion County.

Fort Des Moines (No. 2) established at mouth of Raccoon River.

"Iowa Band" (Congregational and Presbyterian ministers) begins work in Iowa.

1844 Mount Pleasant Collegiate Institute (now Iowa Wesleyan College) is incorporated.

First constitutional convention held at Iowa City.

Population, 75,152.

1845 Congress passes act for admission of Iowa (and Florida); gives Iowa the 16th section in each township for school purposes.

Constitution of 1844 twice rejected by popular vote.

Col. George Davenport murdered on Rock Island.

Sac and Fox Indians withdraw from Iowa.

James Clarke appointed Governor of Iowa Territory.

Augustus Caesar Dodge sponsors bill in Congress defining boundaries of Iowa.

1846 Second constitutional convention meets at Iowa City.

Constitution of 1846 adopted by popular vote.

Mormons migrate across southern Iowa.

Pottawattamie Indians relinquish lands in western Iowa.

Land office located at Iowa City.

October 26. First election held for State officers.

November 30. First General Assembly of State of Iowa convened at Iowa City.

December 3. Ansel Briggs inaugurated as first State Governor.

December 28. President signs act of Congress admitting Iowa as State.

1847 State University of Iowa established at Iowa City.

Hollanders settle at Pella.

State seal is authorized by act of General Assembly.

Population (State census), 116,454.

1848 First telegraph line laid in Iowa between Bloomington (now Muscatine) and Burlington.

First United States Senators from Iowa chosen by General Assembly.

Removal of Winnebago Indians begins.

Iowa (now Grinnell) College opened at Davenport.

1849 Exodus to California begins, with Council Bluffs as an outfitting point.

Trappist Abbey established near Dubuque.

1850 Population, 192,214.

Hungarians make a settlement at New Buda.

Underground Railroad begins operation in Iowa.

Fort Clarke (Fort Dodge) established.

1851 Sioux Indians cede lands in northern Iowa.

First Iowa daily newspaper established at Dubuque (moved to Burlington 1854; still in existence).

1853 Company incorporated to build Rock Island Railroad bridge.

Iowa State Agricultural Society organized at Fairfield.

Fort Clarke is abandoned.

State asylum for the blind established at Iowa City (moved to Vinton in 1862).

1854 Railroad completed as far as Rock Island (Ill.).

Private school for the deaf opened at Iowa City.

First State Fair is held at Fairfield (at Des Moines since 1885).

1855 State university is opened at Iowa City.

State school for deaf and dumb instituted at Iowa City (moved to Council Bluffs in 1868).

John Brown passes through Iowa.

First prohibition law is enacted.

Amana Colony moves into Iowa.

First railroad in Iowa, Mississippi and Missouri Line, completed from Davenport to Muscatine.

1856 April 14. Train crosses, at Davenport, first bridge completed across Mississippi River.

Mississippi and Missouri Railroad (now Chicago, Rock Island) is completed from Davenport to Iowa City.

Land grants are made to railroads in Iowa.

Mormon hand cart expeditions travel on foot from Iowa City to Salt Lake.

Steamboat *Effie Afton* destroys railroad bridge at Rock Island.

1857 Third constitutional convention convenes at Iowa City.

State Historical Society of Iowa is organized.

August 3. Present State constitution is adopted by popular vote.

Banking corporations, previously prohibited, are authorized.

Legislature creates State bank (closed in 1865).

Spirit Lake Massacre; Sioux Indians attack settlers and kill 30.

Capital moved from Iowa City to Des Moines.

Abraham Lincoln takes part in the Rock Island Bridge Case.

Comprehensive system of free common schools is established by law.

Small band of Sac and Fox Indians return, permitted to buy 80 acres of land in Tama County.

Prohibition law amended to provide license system.

Followers of John Brown's spend winter of 1857–58 near Springdale.

1858 Present educational system outlined by General Assembly.

Law enacted providing for State college of agriculture at Ames.

1860 Population, 674,913.

Barbed wire invented by Iowan.

Icarians start communistic settlement near Corning.

1861 First patients received at hospital for insane at Mount Pleasant.

Civil War. Iowa furnishes nearly 80,000 men during war.

April 15. First regiment of volunteers called out by Governor Kirkwood.

1862 Homestead Act adopted by Congress.

Blockhouses erected in northwestern Iowa for protection against the Sioux.

1863 First national bank under the general banking act of the United States opened at Davenport.

1864 Soldiers' Orphans' Home founded at Farmington (transferred in 1865 to Davenport).
Little Brown Church (near Nashua) dedicated.

1865 Soldiers' Orphans' Home established at Cedar Falls (discontinued 1876).

1866 State begins extensive railroad building; first railroad reaches Des Moines.
Soldiers' Orphans' Home established at Glenwood (discontinued 1875).

1867 First railroad (now Chicago and North Western) completed across State to Missouri River.

1868 First Grange Society in Iowa organized at Newton.
Iowa reform school for boys established at Salem (moved to Eldora in 1873).
First five amendments to Iowa State Constitution ratified. Negro men granted franchise.
Gypsum block for Cardiff Giant purchased at Fort Dodge.

1869 *Western Stock Journal* published at Sigourney.

1870 Population, 1,194,020.
Iowa attains second place among corn-producing States.
Local option (liquor law) adopted.

1871 Cornerstone laid for new State Capitol Building at Des Moines.

1872 First creamery built at Spring Branch, near Manchester.

1873 Men's reformatory at Anamosa established.
Oatmeal mill is established at Cedar Rapids.
Union Pacific bridge across Missouri River at Council Bluffs is completed.

1874 Granger Law passed, regulating railroad rates.
August 10. Herbert Clark Hoover, first President born west of the Mississippi River, born at West Branch.

1875 President U. S. Grant delivers speech at Des Moines.

1876 State institution for feeble-minded children established at Glenwood.
Knights of Labor organized in Iowa.
State Normal School, now State Teachers College, opened at Cedar Falls.

1877 First telephone line built.
William H. Voss and Henry F. Brammer start manufacture of washing machines.
Canal (7.5 miles) opened on the Mississippi River above Keokuk.
English begin settlements in vicinity of Le Mars.

1878 Granger Law repealed.
     Meat packing plant opens at Ottumwa.

1879 Girls' industrial school established at Mitchellville.

1880 Population, 1,624,615.
     Wheat belt begins to pass westward; Iowa turns to production of corn.
     Amendment ratified admitting Negroes to General Assembly.
     James B. Weaver is Greenback Party candidate for President.

1881 Drake University opened in Des Moines.
     Kate Shelley, 15, crosses bridge over flooded Des Moines River on hands
     and knees and saves a train.

1882 Amendment made to State constitution prohibiting sale and manufac-
     ture of intoxicating liquors.

1883 State supreme court declares prohibitory amendment not legally adopted.

1884 Present State Capitol occupied for first time.
     Date of general election changed by constitutional amendment.
     Statutory prohibition is adopted.

1887 Soldiers' home opened at Marshalltown.
     First Corn Palace built at Sioux City (annually until 1891).

1888 Iowa Bureau of Labor Statistics established.

1890 Population, 1,912,297.
     Iowa leads States in production of corn.
     Ottumwa Coal Palace opened, President Benjamin H. Harrison giving
     an address.

1891 Blue Grass Palace built at Creston.
     Baseball World Series held at Sioux City.
     Manufacture of pearl buttons begun at Muscatine.

1892 James B. Weaver is Populist candidate for President.

1893 Cyclone at Pomeroy.
     Iowa Federation of Women's Clubs organized.
     Mulct Law adopted, to permit sale of liquor.
     Iowa branch of American Federation of Labor established.

1894 Severe drought; general depression in business.
     Charles T. Kelly and army of unemployed men march through Iowa.

1896 Beginning of consolidated schools in Iowa.
     Site purchased for Historical, Memorial, and Art Building.
     Battleship *Iowa* launched.

1897 First child labor laws passed.

1898 Spanish-American War, infantry sent to Cuba and the Philippine
     Islands.
     Board of control of State institutions established.
     Icarian Community disbanded.

1899 First automobiles in Iowa displayed at fair in Linn County.

1900 Population, 2,231,853.
     State department of agriculture established.

Washing machine factory is established at Newton.

Good roads movement begins.

1901 Fort Des Moines (No. 3) is established near Des Moines.

Cardiff Giant exhibit at Buffalo results in world-wide publicity for Iowa gypsum beds.

1904 Constitutional amendment adopted changing date and year of State elections.

1908 State sanitarium for treatment of tuberculosis established at Oakdale.

Board of parole established.

1909 State board of education established.

1910 Population, 2,224,771.

1911 Free high school education extended to all qualified pupils.

1912 Beginning of Farm Bureau in Iowa.

State board of arbitration appointed to settle disputes, prevent strikes.

1913 Keokuk Dam is completed.

State highway commission established.

1914 Iowa Art Guild organized.

Farmers' Union organized in State.

William C. Robinson makes non-stop airplane flight to Chicago.

1915 Mulct Law repealed; return to State-wide prohibition.

Provision made for State care of indigent children needing medical or surgical treatment.

1916 Iowa Federation of Music Clubs organized at Davenport.

1917 World War. Camp Dodge built near Des Moines.

Third Iowa National Guard Regiment, the 168th United States Infantry, becomes part of Rainbow Division (42nd), and reaches France in December. During war, Iowa furnished 113,000 men.

Provision made for State parks.

Child Welfare Research Station set up at Iowa City, the first in the United States.

1918 Primary road law passed; Iowa begins to come "out of the mud."

Women's reformatory built at Rockwell City.

1919 State board of conservation created.

Free medical and surgical treatment of indigent adults provided at State university hospital.

Iowa General Assembly ratifies Eighteenth and Nineteenth Amendments to Federal Constitution.

State university radio station (WSUI), said to be first west of the Mississippi, begins to broadcast.

168th Infantry returns to Des Moines.

State juvenile home established at Toledo.

1920 Population, 2,404,021.

Beginning of decline in farm prosperity.

1921 WOC established at Davenport, first commercial radio station in Iowa.

1923 Battleship *Iowa* sunk in target practice.

1924 First regular transcontinental air mail service across Iowa.

1925 State highway commission given charge of primary roads; paving is begun.

1926 Constitutional amendment adopted admitting women to General Assembly.

1927 Iowa Artists Club organized.
Clarence D. Chamberlin, Iowan, makes one of earliest trans-Atlantic flights.

1928 Little Art Gallery opened at Cedar Rapids.

1929 Herbert Hoover, first Iowa-born President, inaugurated.

1930 Population, 2,470,939.

1931 Cattle tuberculin-test "war" at Tipton.

1932 First Reconstruction Finance loan from Federal Government to finance relief operations.
Art colony at Stone City founded.
First Farm Holiday meeting.

1933 Farm Holiday Association meets in Des Moines to demand legislative action from Forty-fifth General Assembly, with farm moratorium legislation resulting.
Iowa convention ratified repeal of Eighteenth Amendment to Federal Constitution.
State enacts liquor law.

1934 Drought year.
State begins to grant old age pensions to indigent persons past 65.
State stores for sale of intoxicating liquors are opened.

1936 Iowa's first law for administration of Social Security Act approved.

1937 New board of social welfare created.

Bibliography

In compiling the following list of books and articles on Iowa, an effort has been made to choose references which are representative, up-to-date, available, and readable. Printed materials concerning Iowa are numerous and comprehensive. The State of Iowa publishes biennially the *Iowa Official Register*. *The Book of Iowa,* which was published by the State in 1932, includes articles on its history, government, resources, and industries.

The State Historical Society, during the past four decades, has issued 88 volumes of historical magazines (including two volumes for 1938), 85 bound volumes, and more than 60 pamphlets (not including reprints), a total of more than 80,000 pages of printed matter on Iowa. The *Iowa Historical Record,* a quarterly published from 1885 to 1902; the *Iowa Journal of History and Politics,* a quarterly begun in 1903 and continuing today; and the *Palimpsest,* a monthly published since 1920, all present historical material.

The first series of the *Annals of Iowa,* a quarterly, was published from 1863 to 1874 by the State Historical Society. The second series, known as *Howe's Annals,* was published by Samuel Storrs Howe from 1882 to 1884. The third series, with 21 volumes up to this date, has been published by the Historical, Memorial, and Art Department of Iowa at Des Moines.

County histories may be found in the Historical, Memorial, and Art Department at Des Moines, in the Library of the State Historical Society of Iowa at Iowa City, or in the local libraries in each county. There are three more or less complete series of county histories: one-volume histories in the late 1870's and early 1880's; one-volume histories, chiefly biographical, in the 1890's; and two-volume histories between 1910 and 1918, of which the first volume is history and the second biography.

The State Historical Society of Iowa has published two bibliographies. Frank L. Mott's *Literature of Pioneer Life in Iowa* (1923) gives a list of guidebooks, county histories, and other publications relating to early Iowa; W. J. Petersen's *Two Hundred Topics in Iowa History* (1932) gives references on various aspects of Iowa history, and is provided with an index.

NATURAL SETTING

Aitchison, Alison E. *Iowa State Geography.* Boston, Ginn & Co., 1921.

Iowa Academy of Science. *Proceedings.* Des Moines, 1887–1934. 41 v.

Iowa. Geological Survey. *Annual Reports.* Des Moines, 1892–1933. 36 v.

Iowa. Weather and Crop Service Bureau. *Annual Reports.* Des Moines, 1890–1935.

Kay, George F., and James H. Lees. *Sketch of the Geology of Iowa.* Des Moines, Iowa Geological Survey, 1926.

Kay, George F., and Marjorie Kay McLaughlin. *Our Home State and Con-*

tinent. Iowa Edition Series edited by Albert P. Brigham and Charles T. McFarlane. New York, American Book Company, 1934.

Lazell, Frederick John. *Some Autumn Days in Iowa; Some Winter Days in Iowa; Some Spring Days in Iowa;* and *Some Summer Days in Iowa.* Cedar Rapids, privately printed, 1906, 1907, 1908, and 1909.

PLANTS AND ANIMALS

Bennett, Henry Arnold. "The Mystery of the Iowa Buffalo." (In the *Iowa Journal of History and Politics,* January 1934, v. 32:60-73.)

Bode, I. T., and G. B. MacDonald. *A Handbook of the Native Trees of Iowa.* Ames, Iowa State College of Agriculture and Mechanic Arts, 1930. (Bulletin of the Extension Service.)

DuMont, Philip A. *A Revised List of the Birds of Iowa.* Iowa City, State University of Iowa, 1934. (University of Iowa Studies.)

Guthrie, J. E. *The Snakes of Iowa.* Ames, Iowa State College of Agriculture and Mechanic Arts, (Bulletin of the Extension Service.)

Osborn, Herbert. *A Partial Catalogue of the Animals of Iowa.* Ames, Iowa State College of Agriculture and Mechanic Arts, 1892.

NATURAL RESOURCES

Crane, Jacob L., Jr., and George W. Olcott. *Report of the Iowa Twenty-five Year Conservation Plan.* Des Moines, 1933. Prepared for the Iowa Board of Conservation and the Iowa Fish and Game Commission.

Iowa. State Planning Board. *A Preliminary Report.* Ames, 1934.

———. *The Second Report.* Ames, 1935.

ARCHEOLOGY AND INDIANS

Black Hawk. *Life of Black Hawk, Ma-ka-tai-me-she-kia-kiak.* Iowa City, State Historical Society of Iowa, 1932. "This edition of the Life of Black Hawk (dictated by himself, turned into English by the Indian interpreter Antoine Le Claire, and committed to paper by J. B. Patterson) is published . . . in commemoration of the treaty of Sept. 21, 1832."

Cole, Cyrenus. *I Am a Man—The Indian Black Hawk.* Iowa City, State Historical Society of Iowa, 1938.

Gallaher, Ruth A. "The Tama Indians." (In the *Palimpsest,* February 1926, v. 7:44-53.)

Keyes, Charles Reuben. "Prehistoric Man in Iowa." (In the *Palimpsest,* June 1927, v. 8:185-229.)

———. "Some Materials for the Study of Iowa Archeology." (In the *Iowa Journal of History and Politics,* July 1920, v. 18:357-370.)

Owen, Mary A. *Folk-Lore of the Musquakie Indians of North America.* London, David Nutt, for the Folk-Lore Society, 1904.

Shetrone, Henry C. *The Mound-Builders.* New York, Appleton, 1930.

Ward, Duren J. H. "The Problem of the Mounds of Iowa." (In the *Iowa Journal of History and Politics,* January 1905, v. 3:20-40.)

HISTORY
General

Aurner, Clarence Ray. *Iowa Stories.* Iowa City, Published by the author, 1917–21. 4 v.

Brigham, Johnson. *Iowa, Its History and Its Foremost Citizens.* Chicago, S. J. Clarke Pub. Co., 1915. 3 volumes, 2 of which are biographical.

Cole, Cyrenus. *A History of the People of Iowa.* Cedar Rapids, Torch Press, 1921.

Gallaher, Ruth A. "The First Hundred Years." (In the *Iowa Journal of History and Politics,* Oct. 1933, v. 31:531-576.)

Gue, Benjamin F. *History of Iowa.* New York, Century History Co., 1903. 4 v.

Harlan, Edgar R. *A Narrative History of the People of Iowa.* Chicago, American Historical Society, 1931. 5 volumes, 3 of which are biographical.

Mahan, Bruce E., and Ruth A. Gallaher. *Stories of Iowa for Boys and Girls.* New York, Macmillan, 1929.

Sabin, Henry, and Edwin L. *The Making of Iowa.* Chicago, A. Flanagan Company, 1916.

Shambaugh, Benj. F. *Documentary Material Relating to the History of Iowa.* Iowa City, State Historical Society of Iowa, 1897–1901. 3 v.

HISTORY
Pioneer Days

Brigham, Johnson. *The Sinclairs of Old Fort Des Moines.* Des Moines, Hertzberg Bindery, 1927.

Lea, Albert M. *Notes on the Wisconsin Territory; Particularly with Reference to the Iowa District, or Black Hawk Purchase.* Philadelphia, H. S. Tanner, 1836. Reprinted in book form in 1936 by the State Historical Society of Iowa under the title, *The Book That Gave Iowa Its Name.*

Macbride, Thomas H. *In Cabins and Sod-houses.* Iowa City, State Historical Society of Iowa, 1928.

Martin, Ethyl E. "The Expedition of Zebulon Montgomery Pike to the Sources of the Mississippi." (In the *Iowa Journal of History and Politics,* July 1911, v. 9:335-358.)

Mott, D. C. "The Lewis and Clark Expedition in Its Relation to Iowa History and Geography." (In the *Annals of Iowa* [Third Series], October 1921, January 1922, v. 13:99-125, 163-192.)

Petersen, William J. "Kearny in Iowa." (In the *Palimpsest,* August 1931, v. 12:289-334.)

POLITICS AND GOVERNMENT

Briggs, John E. "The Removal of the Capital from Iowa City to Des Moines." (In the *Iowa Journal of History and Politics,* January 1916, v. 14:56-95.)

Gallaher, Ruth A. *Legal and Political Status of Women in Iowa.* Iowa City, State Historical Society of Iowa, 1918.

Haynes, Fred E. *History of Third Party Movements since the Civil War, with*

Special Reference to Iowa. Iowa City, State Historical Society of Iowa, 1916.

Shambaugh, Benj. F. *The Constitutions of Iowa.* Iowa City, State Historical Society of Iowa, 1934.

BIOGRAPHIES, AUTOBIOGRAPHIES, AND REMINISCENCES

Biographical volumes published by the State Historical Society of Iowa include:

Briggs, John E. *William Peters Hepburn.* 1919.
Brigham, Johnson. *James Harlan.* 1913.
Clark, Dan E. *Samuel Jordan Kirkwood.* 1917.
Cole, Cyrenus. *I Remember, I Remember.* 1936.
Gregory, Charles Noble. *Samuel Freeman Miller.* 1907.
Haynes, Fred Emory. *James Baird Weaver.* 1919.
Parish, John C. *George Wallace Jones.* 1912.
Parish, John C. *Robert Lucas.* 1907.
Payne, Charles E. *Josiah B. Grinnell.* 1938.
Pelzer, Louis. *Augustus Caesar Dodge.* 1908.

The *Iowa Journal of History and Politics* contains a number of biographical sketches, including:
Gallaher, Ruth A. *Albert Miller Lea.* July 1935, v. 35:195-241.
Gallaher, Ruth A. *Annie Turner Wittenmyer.* October 1931, v. 29:518-569.
Gallaher, Ruth A. *Samuel Ryan Curtis.* July 1927, v. 25:331-358.
Swisher, Jacob A. *Bussey, the Career of Cyrus.* October 1932, v. 30:532-558.

Short biographical sketches are also found in the *Palimpsest;* among them the following:
Gallaher, Ruth A. *J. N. Ding* (J. N. Darling). November 1930, v. 11:499-514.
Gallaher, Ruth A. *S. H. M. Byers.* November 1932, v. 14:429-452.
Gallaher, Ruth A. *Thomas Huston Macbride.* May 1934, v. 15:161-190.
Heizer, E. P., and Fred Davis. *George D. Perkins.* August 1924, v. 5:273-317.
Wagner, Dorothy. *Buffalo Bill, Showman.* December 1930, v. 11:522-540.
Weaver, James B. *James Depew Edmundson.* January 1933, v. 12:1-38.

The following biographies have been issued by various publishers:
Anson, Adrian C. *A Ball Player's Career.* Chicago, Era Publishing Co., 1900.
Bloomer, D. C. *Life and Writings of Amelia Bloomer.* Boston, Arena Publishing Co., 1895.
Burdette, Clara B. *Robert J. Burdette.* Pasadena, California, Clara Vista Press, 1922.
Hoffman, M. M. *Julien Dubuque, His Life and Adventures.* Dubuque, Times Journal, 1933.
Perkins, Jacob R. *Trails, Rails, and War: Life of General G. M. Dodge.* Indianapolis, Bobbs-Merrill, 1929.
Quick, Herbert. *One Man's Life.* Indianapolis, Bobbs-Merrill, 1925.
Thwaites, Reuben Gold. *Father Marquette.* New York, Dodd Mead & Co., 1904.

Wilcox, Earley Vernon, and Flora H. Wilson. *Tama Jim* (James Wilson). Boston, Stratford Co., 1930.

Collected biographies include the following:

Brigham, Johnson. "Glimpses of Iowa Statesmen." (In the *Iowa Journal of History and Politics,* April 1934, v. 32:99-123.)

Clarke, S. J. *Prominent Iowans.* Chicago, S. J. Clarke Pub. Co., 1915.

Gue, B. F. *Progressive Men of Iowa.* Des Moines, Conaway & Shaw Pub. Co., 1899, 2 v.

Swisher, Jacob A., and Carl H. Erbe. *Iowa History as Told in Biography.* Cedar Falls, Holst Printing Co., 1932.

AGRICULTURE

Briggs, John E. "The Grasshopper Plagues in Iowa." (In the *Iowa Journal of History and Politics,* July 1915, v. 13:349-392.)

Hopkins, John A., Jr. "Economic History of the Production of Beef Cattle in Iowa." (In the *Iowa Journal of History and Politics,* January, April, July, 1928, v. 26:65-143, 204-294.)

Iowa. Department of Agriculture. *Iowa Year Book of Agriculture.* Des Moines, 1900–to date.

Iowa State Agricultural Society. *Annual Reports.* Des Moines, 1854–1899, 46 v.

Iowa State College of Agriculture and Mechanic Arts. *Bulletins and Reports.* Ames. (Lists available upon request.)

Roberts, Richard H. "Economic Effects of the Corn-Hog Program in Iowa." (In the *Iowa Journal of History and Politics,* April 1936, v. 34:144-171.)

Ross, Earle D. "The Evolution of the Agricultural Fair in the Northwest." (In the *Iowa Journal of History and Politics,* July 1926, v. 24:445-480.)

Schmidt, Louis B. "The Westward Movement of the Wheat-Growing Industry in the United States." (In the *Iowa Journal of History and Politics,* July 1920, v. 18:396-412.)

Thornton, Harrison John. "Oats in History." (In the *Iowa Journal of History and Politics,* July 1932, v. 30:377-394.)

INDUSTRY, COMMERCE, AND LABOR

Downey, E. H. *History of Labor Legislation in Iowa.* Iowa City, State Historical Society of Iowa, 1910.

Downey, E. H. *History of Work Accident Indemnity in Iowa.* Iowa City, State Historical Society of Iowa, 1912.

Duffield, George C. "Frontier Mills." (In the *Annals of Iowa* [Third Series], July 1904, v. 6:425-436.)

Gallaher, Ruth A. "Money in Pioneer Iowa 1838–1865." (In the *Iowa Journal of History and Politics,* January 1934, v. 32:3-59.)

Preston, Howard H. *History of Banking in Iowa.* Iowa City, State Historical Society of Iowa, 1922.

State University of Iowa. Bureau of Business Research. *Iowa Studies in Business.* Iowa City, 1928 to date, 17 numbers. Include: Labor Attitudes; Industrial Migration; Manufacturing Trends; Chain Stores; Tax Assessments; Motor Vehicles; Meat Packing; and Woodworking.

Thornton, Harrison John. *History of the Quaker Oats Company*. Chicago, University of Chicago Press, 1933.

TRANSPORTATION AND COMMUNICATION

Blair, Walter A. *A Raft Pilot's Log*. Cleveland, Arthur H. Clark Co., 1930.

Hussey, Tacitus. "History of Steamboating on the Des Moines River, from 1837 to 1862." (In the *Annals of Iowa* [Third Series], April 1900, v. 4: 323-382.)

Larrabee, William. *The Railroad Question*. Chicago, Schulte Publishing Co., 1893.

Petersen, William J. *Steamboating on the Upper Mississippi*. Iowa City, State Historical Society of Iowa, 1937.

Powers, Samuel C. E. "The Iowa State Highway Commission." (In the *Iowa Journal of History and Politics*, January 1931, v. 29:42-103.)

RACIAL ELEMENTS AND GROUP SETTLEMENTS

Albertson, Ralph. "A Survey of Mutualistic Communities in America." (In the *Iowa Journal of History and Politics*, October 1936, v. 34:375-444.)

Capek, Thomas. *The Czechs in America*. Cambridge, Mass., Riverside Press Co., 1920.

Faust, Albert B. *The German Element in the United States*. Cambridge, Mass., Riverside Press Co., 1909.

Flom, George T. "The Growth of the Scandinavian Factor in the Population of Iowa." (In the *Iowa Journal of History and Politics*, April 1906, v. 4: 267-285.)

Glazer, Rabbi Simon. *The Jews in Iowa*. Des Moines, Koch Brothers Printing Co., 1904.

Hawley, Charles Arthur. "A Communistic Swedenborgian Colony in Iowa." (In the *Iowa Journal of History and Politics*, January 1935, v. 33: 3-27.)

Shambaugh, Bertha M. H. *Amana That Was and Amana That Is*. Iowa City, State Historical Society of Iowa, 1932.

Shaw, Albert. *Icaria: a Chapter in the History of Communism*. New York, Putnam, 1884.

Van der Zee, Jacob. *The British in Iowa*. Iowa City, State Historical Society of Iowa, 1922.

EDUCATION

Aurner, Clarence R. *History of Education in Iowa*. Iowa City, State Historical Society, 5 v. Vols. 1 and 2, 1914; vol. 3, 1915; vol. 4, 1916; vol. 5, 1920.

Iowa State Teachers Association. *Proceedings*. Des Moines, Published annually, 1869, 1876 to date.

Swisher, Jacob A. "The Iowa Academy of Science." (In the *Iowa Journal of History and Politics*, July 1931, v. 29:315-374.)

RELIGION

Hinkhouse, Rev. J. F. *One Hundred Years of the Iowa Presbyterian Church*. Des Moines, Synod of Iowa, 1932.

Hoffmann, M. M. *The Church Founders of the Northwest.* Milwaukee, Bruce Publishing Co., 1937.

Jones, Louis T. *The Quakers of Iowa.* Iowa City, State Historical Society of Iowa, 1914.

Kempker, Father John F. *History of the Catholic Church in Iowa.* Iowa City, Republican Press, 1887.

Meredith, Mabel M. "Early Iowa Camp-Meetings." (In the *Palimpsest,* May 1927, v. 8:164-168.)

Perkins, W. R. *History of the Trappist Abbey of New Melleray in Dubuque County, Iowa.* Iowa City, State University of Iowa, 1892.

Smith, C. Henry. *The Mennonites.* Berne, Indiana, Mennonite Book Concern, 1920.

Stephenson, George M. *The Religious Aspects of Swedish Immigration.* Minneapolis, University of Minnesota Press, 1932.

Van der Zee, Jacob. "The Mormon Trails in Iowa." (In the *Iowa Journal of History and Politics,* January 1914, v. 12:3-16.)

SOCIAL WELFARE

Briggs, John Ely. *History of Social Legislation in Iowa.* Iowa City, State Historical Society, 1915.

Gillin, John L. *History of Poor Relief Legislation in Iowa.* Iowa City, State Historical Society, 1914.

LITERATURE

Aldrich, Bess Streeter. *Miss Bishop.* New York, Appleton-Century Co., 1933. (See other books by the same author.)

Brown, Harriet Connor. *Grandmother Brown's Hundred Years.* Boston, Little, Brown & Co., 1929.

Dondore, Dorothy Ann. *The Prairie and the Making of Middle America: Four Centuries of Description.* Cedar Rapids, Torch Press, 1926.

French, Alice (Octave Thanet). *Stories of a Western Town.* New York, Scribner, 1893. (See other books by the same author.)

Garland, Hamlin. *Main Travelled Roads.* Boston, Arena Pub. Co., 1891. (See other books by the same author.)

Hughes, Rupert. *In a Little Town.* New York, Harper & Brothers, 1917.

Iowa Authors and Artists. *Prairie Gold.* Chicago, Reilly & Britton Co., 1917.

Kantor, MacKinlay. *Turkey in the Straw* (Poems). New York, Coward-McCann, 1935.

Marple, Alice. *Iowa Authors and Their Works.* Des Moines, Historical Department of Iowa, 1918.

Meigs, Cornelia. *As the Crow Flies.* New York, Macmillan Co., 1927. (See other books by the same author.)

The *Midland.* Iowa City, 1914–33, 20 v.

The *Midland Monthly.* Des Moines, Johnson Brigham, 1893–99, 11 v.

Quick, Herbert. *Vandemark's Folly.* Indianapolis, Bobbs-Merrill, 1922. (See also *The Hawkeye* and *The Invisible Woman,* completing the trilogy on Iowa by the same author.)

Sigmund, Jay G. *Wapsipinicon Tales* (Poems). Cedar Rapids, Prairie Publishing Co., 1927. (See other books by the same author.)

Stewart, Ruth. *Capital City*. New York, Sears Publishing Co., 1933.

Stong, Phil. *State Fair*. New York, Century, 1932.

Suckow, Ruth. *Country People*. New York, Knopf, 1924. (See other books by the same author.)

Wilson, Margaret. *The Able McLaughlins*. New York, Harper, 1923.

THE PRESS

MacMurtrie, Douglas C. "The Beginnings of Printing in Iowa." (In the *Annals of Iowa* [Third Series], July 1933, v. 19:3-22.)

Moffit, Alexander. "A Check list of Iowa Imprints, 1837–1860." (In the *Iowa Journal of History and Politics*, January 1938, v. 36:3-95.)

Mott, David C. "Early Iowa Newspapers." (In the *Annals of Iowa* [Third Series], January 1928, v. 16:161-233.)

SCULPTURE

Vinnie Ream (Mrs. R. L. Hoxie). Washington, D. C., Privately printed, 1908. Folio containing souvenirs of artist's life 1865–78.

ARCHITECTURE

Morrison, Hugh. *Louis Sullivan*. New York, W. W. Norton & Co., 1935.

SPORTS AND RECREATION

Christensen, Thomas P. "The State Parks of Iowa." (In the *Iowa Journal of History and Politics*, July 1928, v. 26:331-414.)

Petersen, William J. "Lexington of the North." (Horse racing at Independence). (In the *Palimpsest*, September 1932, v. 13:333-394.)

Thompson, F. O. "Hunting in Northwestern Iowa." (In the *Iowa Journal of History and Politics*, January 1937, v. 35:73-90.)

Index

The Data Warehouse Lifecycle Toolkit

Advanced Praise for *The Data Warehouse Lifecycle Toolkit*

"*The Data Warehouse Lifecycle Toolkit* represents years of experience and is based in the realities faced by many organizations addressing the complex environment of data warehousing. Ralph and the co-authors represent the knowledge and experience that we all need to be successful. The framework, tasks, templates, and the step-by-step explanations and examples will make this book stand out from the crowd."

—Richard Rist, Vice President, The Data Warehousing Institute

"Ralph Kimball has done it again. The author of the popular *Data Warehouse Toolkit* has produced a comprehensive, thoughtful, and detailed book with will be of inestimable value to harried IT managers who are struggling with the complex details of designing, building, and maintaining an enterprise-wide decision support system. Database designers will appreciate the 'graduate course' on advanced dimensional design, while project managers will benefit from the practical tips gleaned from Ralph's experience designing and deploying hundreds of data warehouses. The book is extremely well written and presents tons of useful information without getting turgid or overwhelming. Highly recommended."

—Robert S. Craig, Vice President, Application Architectures, Hurwitz Group, Inc.